# Engaging Cultural Differences

# Engaging Cultural Differences

## The Multicultural Challenge in Liberal Democracies

Richard A. Shweder, Martha Minow,
and Hazel Rose Markus, Editors

Russell Sage Foundation / New York

**Library of Congress Cataloging-in-Publication Data**

Engaging cultural differences : the multicultural challenge in liberal democracies /
Richard A. Shweder, Martha Minow, Hazel Rose Markus, editors.
    p. cm.
  Includes bibliographical references and index.
  ISBN 0-87154-791-0
    1. Multiculturalism.   2. Multiculturalism—Case studies.   3. Toleration.
  I. Shweder, Richard A.   II. Minow, Martha, 1954–   III. Markus, Hazel.

  MH1271 .E5 2002
  306—dc21                                                                          2001057801

The paper used in this publication meets the minimum requirements of American National Standard for Information Sciences—Permanence of Paper for Printed Library Materials. ANSI Z39.48–1992.

Text design by Suzanne Nichols

RUSSELL SAGE FOUNDATION
112 East 64th Street, New York, New York 10021
10 9 8 7 6 5 4 3 2 1

# Contents

Contents

# Acknowledgments

T he editors and authors owe large debts to people whose care and attention made this work possible. We are most grateful to Frank Kessel, program director for the Social Science Research Council's working group on Ethnic Customs, Assimilation and American Law; a creative scholar, psychologist, and administrator, he has helped structure and develop a series of activities at SSRC informally known as the pluralism project. We also wish to express our deepest thanks to Molly Brunson, Julie Lake, and Tina Harris, program assistants for the working group, for their help in the meticulous and timely production of the manuscript. Thanks also to Laurie Corzett at the Harvard Law School for her help with the final stages of the book. We are grateful to Suzanne Nichols, Emily Chang, and David Haproff at the Russell Sage Foundation for their high professional standards and the care and efficiency with which this book has been produced and published.

This project would not have been possible without the support and vision of Eric Wanner, president of the Russell Sage Foundation. Under his leadership the foundation has become a leading center for research on the lives and well-being of immigrant and nonimmigrant minority groups in the United States and a forum for serious debate about public policy issues.

Most of the preparation of the manuscript took place while Richard Shweder was a Fellow at the *Wissenschaftskolleg Zu Berlin* (The Institute for Advanced Study in Berlin, also known as WIKO). Special thanks to Wolf Lepenies, Jürgen Kocka, Joachim Nettelbeck, and the staff of WIKO for creating and sustaining one of the greatest of the intellectual centers in the world for scholarship in the social sciences and the humanities.

A selection of essays from this collection appeared in the fall 2000 issue of *Daedalus: Journal of the American Academy of Arts and Sciences* 129(4) under the title, *The End of Tolerance: Engaging Cultural Differences*. Stephen Graubard brought his learning, wisdom, and probing questions to several meetings of the working group and to the essays that emerged. We would like to express our gratitude to him and special appreciation that this work could begin before his remarkable tenure as editor of *Daedalus* came to an end.

# Contributors

RICHARD A. SHWEDER is an anthropologist and professor of human development at the University of Chicago.

MARTHA MINOW is professor of law at Harvard Law School.

HAZEL ROSE MARKUS is the Davis-Brack Professor in the Behavioral Sciences at Stanford University and codirector of the Research Center for Comparative Studies in Race and Ethnicity.

CAROLINE BLEDSOE is professor of anthropology at Northwestern University.

DAVID L. CHAMBERS is the Wade H. McCree Collegiate Professor of Law at the University of Michigan Law School.

JANE MASLOW COHEN is professor of law at the University of Texas School of Law.

JOANNA DAVIDSON is doctoral student in anthropology at Emory University.

ARTHUR N. EISENBERG is the legal director of the New York Civil Liberties Union and an adjunct professor of law at the University of Minnesota Law School.

KAREN ENGLE is professor of law at the University of Utah.

KATHERINE PRATT EWING is associate professor of cultural anthropology and religion and codirector of the Center for South Asia Studies at Duke University.

HEEJUNG S. KIM is assistant professor of psychology at Harvey Mudd College.

CORINNE A. KRATZ is associate professor of African studies and anthropology and codirector of the Center for the Study of Public Scholarship at Emory University.

MAIVÂN CLECH LÂM is visiting associate professor of law at the Washington College of Law, American University.

## Contributors

**USHA MENON** is assistant professor of anthropology in the Department of Culture and Communication at Drexel University.

**VICTORIA C. PLAUT** is doctoral candidate in social psychology at Stanford University.

**ALISON DUNDES RENTELN** is associate professor of political science at the University of Southern California.

**LLOYD I. RUDOLPH** is professor of political science at the University of Chicago.

**SUSANNE HOEBER RUDOLPH** is professor of political science at the University of Chicago.

**LAWRENCE G. SAGER** is the Robert B. McKay Professor of Law at New York University School of Law, and visiting professor of law at the University of Texas at Austin.

**AUSTIN SARAT** is the William Nelson Cromwell Professor of Jurisprudence and Political Science at Amherst College.

**CLAUDE M. STEELE** is the Lucie Stern Professor in the Social Sciences and codirector of the Research Center for Comparative Studies in Race and Ethnicity.

**DOROTHY M. STEELE** is associate director of the Research Center for Comparative Studies in Race and Ethnicity and an early childhood educator.

**NOMI STOLZENBERG** is professor of law and codirector of the Center for Law, History and Culture at the University of Southern California.

**MARCELO M. SUÁREZ-OROZCO** is the Victor S. Thomas Professor of Education at Harvard University and codirector of the Harvard Immigration Projects.

**UNNI WIKAN** is professor in the Department of Social Anthropology at the University of Oslo, Norway.

# Introduction

## Engaging Cultural Differences

### Richard A. Shweder, Martha Minow, and Hazel Rose Markus

> We are not an assimilative, homogeneous society, but a fa-
> cilitative, pluralistic one, in which we must be willing to
> abide someone else's unfamiliar or even repellent practice
> because the same tolerant impulse protects our own idio-
> syncrasies.
> —William J. Brennan, U.S. Supreme Court, in *Michael H.
> v. Gerald D.*, U.S. 110, 141 (1987) (dissenting opinion)

*Tolerance* often appears in discussions of difference. Yet what does tolerance mean in liberal democracies such as the United States, Germany, France, India, Norway, and South Africa, where an increasingly wide range of diverse cultural groups hold contradictory beliefs about appropriate social and family life practices? How wide should be the scope of social and legal tolerance? Many emigrating women and men from African countries (notably, Sierra Leone, Somalia, Mali, Egypt, Ethiopia, the Sudan, and the Gambia), for example, take pride in the ritual practices of both female and male circumcision. Yet majority community sentiment and legal regulation in the United States and most European countries permit genital surgeries for boys but treat genital alterations of girls as unacceptable and even grounds for criminal action. Does this unequal treatment of male and female circumcision demonstrate hypocrisy, ethnocentrism, or unjustifiable limits to the tolerance granted ethnic minority groups in the United States and European nations? Does such treatment reflect an important, transcultural difference in the nature of the genital alterations involved or perhaps a misunderstanding of unfamiliar practices? Or does the protection of girls represent the proper elevation of universal commitments to individual rights and justifiable public protections for the vulnerable? If so, should that protection then extend to boys, too, despite Jewish and Muslim practices extending for three thousand years? How should competing beliefs and values that in turn color understandings of practices and facts be evaluated, and by whom?

The essays in this collection explore how liberal democracies do and should respond legally to differences in the cultural and religious practices of minority group residents. Since the terrorist attacks of September 11, 2001, the levels of fear and suspicion in the United States and the "West" about "others" have understandably heightened, while the jeopardy to civil rights and civil liberties has grown. Questions about how to balance commitments to liberty and equal regard with the goals of security, patriotism, and community have taken on a new urgency. But the answers must grow from deeper and more enduring normative analyses of how liberal democracies should respond to the range of differences in the values, religions, and practices of their residents, who are increasingly migrants from around the world. Democratic societies are those in which the authority of those who govern is derived from the will of the people (typically determined by some form of vote). These societies are liberal to the extent that they are organized to guarantee basic liberties (such as freedom of association, expression, and religious practice) as well as various protections (for example, against discrimination, coercion, and abuse) to all society members in pursuit of a good life. Liberal democratic societies, however, are not identical in their legal and moral dimensions or in the extent to which the role of those who govern is kept limited. They differ in the extent to which the meaning of a good life is left up to individuals or families to define privately. They differ in the balance struck between two often contradictory liberal impulses: the impulse to leave individuals free to live their lives by their own personal, cultural, or religious lights and the equally liberal impulse to protect those who are vulnerable from exploitation and to promote social justice. These differences among liberal democracies produce different experiences for immigrant minority groups when public conflicts arise over cultural practices that offend the sensibilities of mainstream or dominant groups.

The authors in this book explore several interrelated questions: Which aspects of American (or Norwegian or German or South African or Indian) law impact on the customs of ethnic minority groups? To what extent does the law presuppose, codify, and hence inculcate the substantive beliefs and values of a cultural mainstream? How much cultural diversity in family life practices ought to be permissible within the moral and constitutional framework of a liberal pluralistic democratic society? How strong are the implications of citizenship for how people in countries such as the United States, Norway, Germany, India, or South Africa marry, arrange a family, discipline and raise their children, conceptualize gender identity, and so on? What does it mean for an ethnic custom or practice to be judged, for example, un-American or un-Norwegian or un-German? How do ethnic minority communities react to official attempts to force compliance with cultural and legal norms of, for example, American or Norwegian or German middle-class life? Finally, how do understandings and misunderstandings of family lives, international and domestic human rights frameworks, and studies of culture contribute to the struggles over accommodation, control, and resistance around issues of cultural difference?

Contested practices under discussion include genital alteration, parent-child relationships, conventions regarding selection of marital partners and other features of marriage and divorce, religiously based clothing requirements for women and girls, religion and schooling, self-segregation by minority groups, and cultural defenses to criminal charges. The authors address how liberal democracies go about accommodating differences or expecting assimilation to a common norm. The chapters explore resources from legal and political theories, ethnography, history, comparative law, and international law as well as domestic doctrinal legal analysis.

The authors include legal scholars, anthropologists, psychologists, and political theorists. The authors met several times as an interdisciplinary working group on Ethnic Customs, Assimilation, and American Law, supported by the Russell Sage Foundation and organized by the Social Science Research Council (see *www.ssrc.org*). Some of the resulting chapters focus on the United States. Some focus on other nations (in particular, France, Germany, Norway, India, and South Africa), where coming to terms with ethnic diversity and cultural differences is a major public policy concern. Some chapters consider the legal and moral grounds supporting tolerance for a given cultural practice, such as polygamy, wearing a head scarf to work, or presenting a photo exhibit in public schools depicting the lives of gay and lesbian families. Other chapters consider the circumstances under which a democratic and liberal order should treat certain practices—such as forced marriage and murderous defense of personal or family honor—as intolerable violations of human rights. Certain chapters examine the changes required if mainstream practices in schools, health care settings, and the criminal justice system in various liberal democracies are to accommodate or accept the diversity of peoples and cultures affected by them. Other chapters examine why some people reach beyond their own communities and embrace the language of universal human rights while for others, the rhetoric of universal human rights does not resonate, even when outsiders believe it should. Reflecting ongoing debate among the authors and the complexity of circumstances examined, some chapters are reluctant to broaden the scope of toleration, while others suggest that mere tolerance is itself potentially confining and demeaning and that appreciation of difference should be the aspiration.

This volume thus is concerned with the aims of tolerance and its proper limits. Taken as a whole the chapters examine definitions of and negotiations over tolerance in practical encounters between state officials and immigrants, members of long-standing minority groups and majority groups, local agents of authority and parents, parents and children, and neighbors and coworkers. The collection examines these issues from multiple perspectives, including those of judges, law enforcement officials, school administrators and teachers; minority group members, new immigrants, and subordinated people (often women and children) within minority groups; activists and academics who want to advance either universal rights or cultural appreciation or some combination of each; people committed to their own group (defined in ethnic, religious, gender, or national terms); and people—whether immigrants or academics—engaged in moving across, and therefore comparing, different societies and legal orders. The chapters do not pursue still further perspectives—such as how economic or political pressures affect responses to immigrants and other "different" groups—although the discussions may prompt inquiries in those directions.

The book thus examines the challenge of multiculturalism in contemporary liberal democracies. Part I describes processes that produce diversity, such as globalization and increasing migration across borders. By considering a range of national contexts in which cultures collide, new questions are raised about how liberal democracies around the world respond to people perceived as different. This section provides many examples of contested practices that often trigger debates over whether or how a liberal democracy should treat people as members of groups for purposes of their legal status and rights—and thereby use state power to enhance group practices and identities. Part II considers forms of cultural accommodation other than group status or rights. This section asks how well the tools of legal analysis and political theory connect liberal values with accommodation for cultural practices that challenge settled assumptions or conventional practice. When tensions arise, what should give? Part III explores how minority groups position themselves vis-à-vis universal human rights claims, transcending national legal systems. Part IV concludes by examining contrasting conceptions of group differences as they affect institutional and legal practices. What gets understood as a difference to be dealt with, and why? The following overview explores these organizing themes with insights drawn from the chapters.

## ONE NATION, MANY CULTURES

In a rapidly globalizing world, peoples from Asia, Mexico, Latin America, and parts of Africa migrate because of better labor market opportunities abroad or political turmoil at home. Some leave because they wish to become cosmopolitan; others seek a safer space to preserve their traditions. Given global economic developments and emerging cultural and political trends, liberal democracies face not only burgeoning numbers of immigrants, but also their own hidden assumptions about the scope and limits of tolerance for cultural diversity.

The particular history (or lack of history) of prior struggles over racial and religious diversity within each nation set the legal and political framework for responses to current immigrants. A nation organized to permit two or more linguistic and religious groups to coexist will greet newcomers with the prior framework for coexistence as the starting point. A nation founded on slavery and still struggling with its legacy will respond similarly, even to new group differences, with a template shaped by racism, slavery, and the political and legal responses to them. Responses to current immigrants in turn shed light on and even raise for reconsideration prior understandings of tolerance and assimilation. In the United States, for example, constitutional doctrines redressing racial discrimination and implementing free exercise of religion—doctrines that adopt some notions of equality and tolerance but also limit them to dimensions of race and religion—set the legal standards when new immigrants engage in practices that teachers, police, employers, and social workers find problematic.

In the United States and elsewhere, recent immigrants may engage in practices or express ideas concerning gender, discipline, authority, sex, marriage, reproduction, intimate violence, and work that clash with the views of other residents from more dominant groups, who are powerful enough to have their views embraced by prevailing institutions. Many immigrants retain strong links to their places of origin and to others in their diasporic communities; many travel back and forth with some frequency. Some emphatically hang on to valued traditions of their ethnic community; some, in contrast, consciously embrace dominant liberal practices. Others are repelled by what they perceive to be highly commercial, violent, degrading, or insufficiently protective practices in the capitalist liberal societies they have entered. They may try to reinforce norms and customs they consider far more ethical and moral than traditions of the cultural majority, and become more insistent about practices that mark them and their families as different from those they encounter in the new land. These immigrants may view the environment of the broader liberal society as sinful, jeopardizing the character and future life prospects of their children. They may feel perplexed and even under siege as intergenerational conflicts emerge within their own families and cultural groups. An immigrant Islamic community in Norway, for example, responded with dismay and horror as Nadia, an eighteen-year-old of Moroccan descent born in Norway, accused her parents of abduction (with the aim of forcing her to marry) and testified against them in court. Unni Wikan examines this incident in detail in chapter 6. For members of the immigrating generation, cultural assimilation may be viewed as a mixed blessing or even a problem, rather than a cure (see Stolzenberg 1993). A South Asian father living in Chicago may decide to forbid his teenage daughter from dating boys in order to protect her chastity and family honor. Resisting assimilation may even serve to protect some immigrants and their children from patterns of criminal behavior and low school performance they find among their neighbors in poor communities where they are able to find a home.

Some immigrants confront prejudice against newcomers, or against people with dark skin, or against people with minority religious beliefs and practices. They may confront restrictive legislation or bureaucratic interventions into the most intimate aspects of their family life. They may find the efforts by child protection agencies offensive and interfering and experience such state interventions as forms of political persecution. "Cultural differences are beautiful," comments Marceline Walter, who directs community education in the New York State Administration for Children's Services, "but they have nothing to do with the law. We can't possibly have a set of laws for Americans, a set of laws for immigrants, and a set of laws for tourists" (Ojito 1997, 3). Should immigrants from Asia, Africa, and Latin America then be given detailed instruction in the norms governing parent-child relations in the United States? What makes such norms valid for everyone in the first place? Are they indeed valid for everyone? When might our

based system would not be countenanced in the United States; it is difficult even to imagine where there would be sources of support for a system structured by the state to enact separate legal regimes for Christians, Jews, Muslims, and other religious groups. Racial, ethnic, and religious profiling by law enforcement and anti-terrorist efforts begin to push in the direction of separate legal treatment, based on group membership. Yet even with these tendencies, the United States would preserve individual rights and one common body of law applied to all, not separate rules or decision-makers. Yet the United States has permitted a somewhat analogous regime in the special context of adoption and child welfare within American Indian communities. South Africa historically pursued a strategy of group-based legal treatment for family law matters, although it deployed the notion of customary law, enforceable within the public regime. With the adoption of the new South African Constitution after the fall of apartheid, the country stands poised to negotiate new relationships between individual and group identities. The new constitution recognizes individual rights to gender equality and children's rights but also recognizes rights to culture, religion, and family. Some advocates have pressed for one universal public law, ensuring the same rights for all regardless of their membership in ethnic or tribal communities traditionally bound by customary law. They have encountered many sources of resistance. As David Chambers explores in chapter 4, the clash over individual and group rights could occasion unprecedented legal innovation; it will not produce an easy or simple answer.

In contemporary Germany and France, claims by Muslims to be treated the same as Christians and Jews could be understood as efforts to embrace the dominant structures of individual rights. Yet historic accommodations for Christians and Jews within the public realm of the state may suggest that the Muslims simply want to be treated as a group, as others have treated them in the past. Katherine Ewing's chapter on the disputes over Muslim claims in France and Germany (chapter 3) thus affords a window on how new groups may challenge prior assumptions about treating rights for individuals and groups.

As these examples indicate, nations—including liberal democratic ones—differ considerably in their constitutional conceptions of the proper relationship between state and religion. In Germany, the state approves of public schools teaching and promoting Christianity; the United States—at least up until the present—has interpreted its Constitution to call for a sharp separation between public schools and religious instruction. These differences can affect not only how the individual nations respond to emerging cultural differences, but also how members of minority groups position and advocate for themselves. Given the German practice of public school religious instruction, Islamic Turks residing in Berlin now ask, why shouldn't Islamic instruction also be available—as an elective—in public schools? The closest analogous argument available for Islamic residents in the United States is that public school facilities should be no less open to an after-school student-organized Islamic group than they are to an after-school Christian group—though both have had to struggle for use of public school facilities.

Freedom of religion can be interpreted as a right of individuals, with no additional protection for groups, yet it can also lead to recognition, support, and preservation of religious groups. As liberal democracies work with their own constitutional frameworks and respond to claims and controversies around religious differences, they press closer toward or further away from group-based protections. Either approach can generate friction with those perceived as different from the dominant group or unable to fit within settled practices.

Communitarian and liberal individualist approaches to cultural diversity bear contrasting implications, especially about whether people should have distinct legal status based on their membership in particular groups. In general, liberal individualists tend to seek a certain type of state neutrality toward the ultimate ends of individuals and toward the good life. For liberal individualists, the state's purpose—and therefore the justifiable limits on its power—stem from a vision of liberty ensuring individuals freedom to act, affiliate with subcommunities if they wish (but also exit from them as they desire), associate with others voluntarily, and express themselves as individuals through choices about religion, culture, and family life. Accordingly, many liberal individualists reject not only pride of place for groups but even using groups as significant categories. Any affiliation with a religious or ethnic group, in this view, is simply a voluntary choice by an individual; it deserves no greater respect than an individual's choice to join a club or give a speech. No exemption or accommodation should be granted due to religious or ethnic group membership unless the same exemption or accommodation arises for individuals who have athletic, political, or artistic affiliations. Procedural justice and nondiscrimination become vital guides for this constitutional vision and the measure of free exercise of religion and, by extension, free exercise of culture. Yet the liberal tradition is complex and variegated enough to permit some to argue that a transcendental or spiritual side to the human nature of individuals in matters of conscience is entitled to special protection from the dictates of majoritarian government rules (McConnell 1990).

Communitarians, in contrast, identify an inherent value in the existence and perpetuation of cultural traditions and the communities sustained by them. They doubt that law can ever be purely neutral or procedural. They evaluate a given constitutional framework as either corrosive or protective of cultural traditions. Communitarians disagree among themselves over whether to identify the community with the entire polity—and thus the state—or instead to view the communities that matter as necessarily smaller and often in tension with the state. Nonetheless, communitarians share the view that society is composed of not only distinct individuals but also social and ethnic groups and cultures. Communitarians reject most the idea of the unencumbered or unbounded self, and see people formed and inevitably embedded in relationships with others. This makes the liberal assumption of the individual as the fundamental unit of analysis seem mistaken or even cruel. Communitarians and liberal individualists may converge or diverge, however, when evaluating how acceptable they find a given ethnic minority practice. These differences may stem from competing theories of the good.

The long-standing debate between liberal individualists and communitarians receives a healthy challenge in arguments by John Rawls, who has called for a kind of political liberalism that respects even worldviews inconsistent with features of a tolerant liberalism. Rawls (1993) argues that in a politically liberal society, "it is unreasonable for us to use political power, should we possess it, or share it with others, to repress comprehensive doctrines that are not unreasonable." Comprehensive doctrines include conceptions of the world and ideas about the good life, including family life, elaborated from standpoints that may include religious and cultural traditions. Taken seriously, this commitment to political liberalism carries with it an injunction to do more than tolerate those who are different and, instead, to scrutinize dominant beliefs and practices to guard against ill-considered restrictions or unjustifiable distinctions in both who can be accommodated and how.

Yet what works well in theory may be far from illuminating in practice and can produce ironic results. Existing institutions governing child protection and schooling may disrupt moral and effective practices held dear by some subcommunities. Moreover, other liberal institutions, such as private property, may empower deeply illiberal communities, whose very empowerment may provoke illiberal reactions in dominant groups and trigger attempts at regulation or eradication.

Even liberal theorists recognize one group that deserves distinctive treatment: the family. Especially challenging for a liberal society committed to the freedom of each individual is to determine how much latitude parents or elders should have to inculcate certain values and not others, offer some experiences and prevent others, and govern children's bodies and bodily movements; for the precise measure of freedom of the parent is restraint on the child. Yet until a certain age (itself a subject of dispute), children simply cannot make decisions for themselves. Especially during this period of massive immigration, predictable points of conflict arise between immigrant parents and children. Such potential conflicts bring into view the limits of liberal democratic deference to self-determination. How much can or should government agents intervene, and on whose side? Should the parent be permitted to exercise control over children in the name of the parent's own self-determination, or should the state step in to protect the child—or assist the child in voicing a preference, preserving future options, or becoming self-determining at once? The parent-child relationship is especially likely to generate conflicts around tolerance for cultural variety. This kinship bond also exposes the limits of individualism even for the adult—that is, when the adult sees him- or herself as a member of an ethnic or religious group seeking to reproduce itself. Here, in efforts to pass on cultural traditions, control of marriage and education are key. Should the liberal democratic state simply exemplify its values through state-sponsored options such as public schools and the secular practices of marriage and divorce? Or should the government also use its coercive power to control decisions parents may wish to retain for themselves concerning the education and marriage of their children? In cases interpreting the U. S. Constitution, the U.S. Supreme Court has at times favored toleration for diverse practices by parents, and at other times ordered restraints on parental control over children's access to liberal democratic values.[1] These inconsistent decisions manifest the compelling arguments on either side.

Creating and respecting group-based legal status, giving strong protections for freedom of religion, and according parents much latitude over their children are three devices liberal democratic states may use to allow considerable room for group-based cultural variety—even if the resulting array of practices is viewed negatively by many in the society. These devices do not, however, dictate results in particular controversies; they do frame the methods of analysis and may tilt the results for or against tolerance for difference.

## CULTURAL ACCOMMODATION AND ITS LIMITS

Debates over accommodation are especially pronounced in societies that seek a secular public space and restrict freedom of religion, or question parental prerogatives. When liberal democracies resist creating group rights, and instead embrace the individual as the proper holder of enforceable rights, accommodation of group-based differences must take other forms. One method is to enforce a sharp distinction between public and private, while ensuring large scope to the private sphere. Within a liberal framework, this makes room for cultural differences—as long as they remain in the private sphere. Typically, this means the sphere of the family; it may also include schooling. Nation-states differ in their legal and cultural distinctions between public versus private, in their ideas about whether children ultimately are the responsibility—and object of instruction—of the state or the parent, and in the stance taken toward the public protection of children. France and Norway are more likely to support consistent public protection of children than are the United States and India.

Employment can be characterized as private and thus insulated from public regulation. When employment and workplaces instead are treated as part of the public sphere and subject to public norms, they become sites for governmental scrutiny of differences in religious practices, attire, treatment of women and sexuality, and other potential points of conflict between employees and either their employers or other employees.

Liberal societies that embrace a right to culture, the best interests of the child, a right to fair trial, and equal protection of the laws may offer resources for accommodating different cultural traditions that might not be initially obvious. As Alison Dundes Renteln shows, arguments for recognizing a cultural defense to certain criminal charges thus can draw on values and rights well-embedded within liberal states. Yet these arguments generate counterarguments (see chapter 3 by Jane Cohen and Caroline Bledsoe); there are no trumps in these debates.

Beyond cultural defenses, public and private, parent and child, state and religion, and group rights, additional points of conflict involve the relation between formal laws and customary practices. How much uniformity of enforcement of formal laws is expected and enacted? How much room should be left, officially or unofficially, for the operation of customary practices? Liberal legal systems may share many fundamental commitments and still differ in the precise degree to which they expect and implement universal enforcement or, instead, permit or even provide for plural norms and local variations.

More important than any of these variations is the fact that any liberal constitutional arrangement does inevitably take a position on the relationships between religion and state, public and private, individual and group, thereby setting highly particular stages for enacting conflicts and negotiations of cultural differences. As a result, constitutional and legal frameworks affect the room available for expressing and maintaining cultural differences, while also arranging how conflicts between mainstream and minority groups will be identified, addressed, and resolved. The public and legal responses to immigrants are closely tied to a nation's stance toward multiculturalism, toward neutrality about religion and race, toward gender equality, and toward conceptions of universal individual human rights.

Thus, most fundamentally, legal systems differ in the extent to which they try to curb or, instead, try to intensify the imposition and inculcation of the substantive beliefs and values of a particular cultural group, whether majority or simply dominant. These differences in legal pressures to assimilate profoundly shape the experiences of cultural minorities, and must be taken into account to understand both processes of conformity and the reasons for resistance to mainstream cultural beliefs and practices. Understanding the relation between these stances and the treatment of particular groups and conflicts requires attention to history but also to the dynamic interaction between groups, ideologies, and formal and informal norms.

## THE UNIVERSAL HUMAN RIGHTS DEBATE: MOBILIZATION AND RESISTANCE

More is involved with conflicts over cultural practices than just domestic constitutions and laws. International law and the discourse of international human rights increasingly offer resources for people to mobilize against traditional cultural practices. Others then face decisions about whether to join or resist the importation of international human rights language in assessments of tensions over cultural practices. In the meantime, international human rights offer institutions and sites for action as well as resources for analysis and debate. As Maivân Lâm reports, women within minority groups, members who identify as tribes, First Nations, or indigenous people have found the use of an international forum promising for mobilization and dialogue otherwise unavailable either within their own communities or inside their own national states. The plural settings available for debating the relationships between rights and culture thus can afford avenues for action even for people with relatively little power in their own settings. Yet when multiple legal arenas become available for debating international human rights, different arguments and results will emerge. Corinne Kratz examines how domestic law, asylum law, and human rights law have affected high-profile debates over female genital modification.

The International Convention on the Rights of the Child provides a vivid example of the contests generated over human rights. Adopted by more than one hundred nations, the convention pursues a strong child-centered approach to social decision making. Its use of the legal principle of the best interests of the child and its articulation of rights running to each individual child strike some critics as corrosive of pluralism and counter to the rights of adults to perpetuate their language, culture, and ancestral lineage. Interpreting this convention, and considering its very meaning in the context of diverse cultural traditions, exposes for debate and disagreement basic questions such as:

- Are parents the ultimate guardians of their children or merely temporary state agents, subject to state review and control?

- Should each parent have equal authority in rearing the children or should cultural traditions—elevating the father according to some traditions, the mother in others—receive public deference?

- When should police, school officials, social workers, religious leaders, or judges second-guess and supersede the judgments of parents about their children?

- When and how should the child's age matter? Should there emerge a cross-cultural, universal notion of when a child becomes an adult for purposes of self-determination, or should cultural and national variety persist on this question? Even before a child reaches adulthood, when and how should the child's expressed wishes—concerning which religion to follow, where to live, where to go to school, what to wear, and whom to marry—matter to third-party actors such as teachers and judges?

- Does the state's assessment of a child's best interests include the child's membership in a given culture or does it abstract the child from that membership, as if the child had no such connection and was really a "citizen of the world"? For example, should it count as part of the child's best interests to have her tribal or ethnic community continue to exist and provide a context for her own development and future? Or are the child's interests better assessed in terms of the education, lifestyle, and income aspirations that the mainstream culture heralds for each individual?

Addressing just these sorts of questions proves divisive within communities and among scholars and theorists. People outside particular communities may be surprised by the degree of resistance to individual rights approaches even among imagined beneficiaries, such as women. Usha Menon portrays a world of Hindu women in a temple town in India in which feminist ideas of individual rights are alien and unappealing.

Anthropologists, long associated with efforts to promote tolerance of cultural variety, have struggled for fifty years with the notion and scope of international human rights, as Karen Engle documents in her chapter. Multiple layers of analysis emerge from such struggles. It is one step to unearth the particular cultural assumptions and potential imperialism behind the rhetoric of international human rights; then we have a choice among cultural practices rather than a collision between rights and culture. It is another step to acknowledge the variety and contestability of views about the flexibility of particular notions, such as children's best interests or freedom of choice, within the human rights world—and the variety and contestability of views about any given cultural practice that allegedly conflicts with a human right. Yet until these levels of analysis proceed, the contrast between rights and culture is a caricature, ungrounded in any genuine practice. (On the supposed contrast between rights and culture see Okin 1999; for a sustained critique of the contrast see Volpp 2001.)

## CONCEPTIONS OF DIFFERENCE AND THE DIFFERENCES THEY MAKE

Lying even further underneath arguments about accommodation of cultural differences are the very perceptions and conceptions of difference held by members of various groups. Close study indicates that contrasting and diverging perspectives of diversity affect how people in different groups make sense of one another and how they express themselves. Yet people may hold ideas of difference that prevent them from even recognizing how others experience their mutual encounters. The actual social position of individuals as well as their historical experiences and cultural frameworks can affect how they understand diversity and approach people they view as different, as Austin Sarat and Victoria Plaut explore in their chapters. Similarly, Hazel Markus, Claude Steele, and Dorothy Steele highlight the way that colorblindness, as a progressive worldview developed in the United States after the civil rights movement, can limit people's abilities to see social dynamics and experiences of others.

In this moment in which cultural collisions, large and subtle, are escalating due to the high levels of mobility across national borders, understanding the variety of potential responsive legal frameworks compatible with liberal democracy would expand the tools available for working through conflicts. By sorting through the promise and peril of group rights, a public-private division, respect for parental rights, commitment to the best interests of the child, strong religious freedom protections, customary law, international law, and recognition of the variety of perceptions and cultural models of diversity, this volume aims to enrich understandings and responses to cultural conflicts. Individuals will continue to differ about how to reconcile commitments to individual freedom and to communal traditions and meanings, yet they may do so with greater understanding of the sources of their differences and even the potential points of convergence.

We hope that this volume will raise provocative and useful questions about the ends and aims of tolerance, and about how free the exercise of culture is and how free it ought to be in societies organized as liberal democracies. We hope that the chapters—in raising questions about the scope and limits of tolerance in the lives of all people living in liberal democratic societies—will inform and prove useful to teachers, lawyers, judges, social workers, physicians, social scientists, and all members of multicultural societies who are trying to make sense of cultural diversity and create the right kind of room for cultural differences. The effort is in many ways inspired by Clifford Geertz's (2000) comment,

> Positioning Muslims in France, Whites in South Africa, Arabs in Israel, or Koreans in Japan are not altogether the same sort of thing. But if political theory is going to be of any relevance at all in the splintered world, it will have to have something cogent to say about how, in the face of a drive towards a destructive integrity, such structures can be brought into being, how they can be sustained, and how they can be made to work.

## NOTE

1. See *Pierce v. Society of Sisters*, 268 U.S. 510 (1925); *Prince v. Massachusetts*, 321 U.S. 158 (1944); *Wisconsin v. Yoder*, 406 U.S. 205 (1972). See also *Mozert v. Hawkins Board of Education*, 827 F. 2d 1058 (6th Cir. 1987).

## REFERENCES

Alston, Philip, ed. 1994. *The Best Interests of the Child: Reconciling Culture and Human Rights.* Oxford: Clarendon Press.

Geertz, Clifford. 2000. *Available Light: Anthropological Reflections on Philosophic Topics.* Princeton, N.J.: Princeton University Press.

McConnell, Michael W. 1990. "The Origins and Historical Understanding of Free Exercise of Religion." *Harvard Law Review* 103(7): 1416–1517.

Ojito, Mirta. 1997. "Culture Clash: Foreign Parents, American Child Rearing." *New York Times*, June 26: 3.

Okin, Susan Moller, ed. 1999. *Is Multiculturalism Bad for Women?* Princeton, N.J.: Princeton University Press.

Rawls, John. 1993. *Political Liberalism.* New York: Columbia University Press.

Stolzenberg, Nomi M. 1993. "He Drew a Circle That Shut Me Out: Assimilation, Indoctrination and the Paradox of a Liberal Education." *Harvard Law Review* 106(3): 581–667.

Volpp, Leti. 2001. "Feminism Versus Multiculturalism." *Columbia Law Review* 101(5): 1181–1218.

One Nation, Many Cultures: Contested
Practices and Group Status in
Liberal Democracies

FIGURE 1.1 / Immigrants Admitted to the United States, Fiscal Years 1900 to 1996

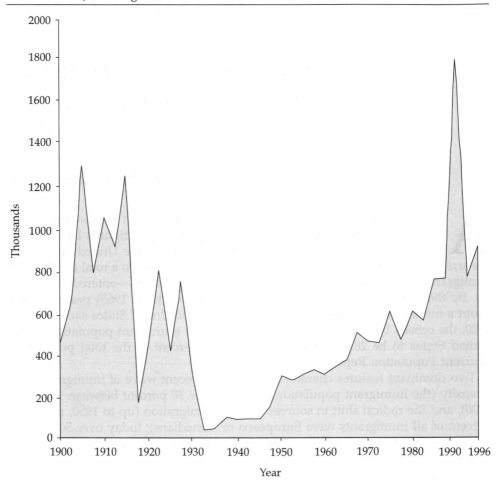

*Source:* Adapted from Immigration and Naturalization Service. 1998. *Statistical Yearbook 1998.* (Washington: U.S. Government Printing Office.)

tion to the world of work are quite limited (see, for example, Suárez-Orozco and Suárez-Orozco 2000). So is the work on the cultural processes of change generated by large-scale immigration. This is in part because labor economists, demographers, and sociologists have set the tone of the current research agenda—while anthropologists, psychologists, legal scholars, and scholars of the health sciences have played a more modest role.

Large-scale immigration is at once the cause and consequence of profound social, economic, and cultural transformations.[1] To analytically differentiate between the two is important. While the claim has been made that there are powerful economic interests in having a large pool of foreign workers (a major cause

FIGURE 1.2 / Immigrants Admitted, Top Countries

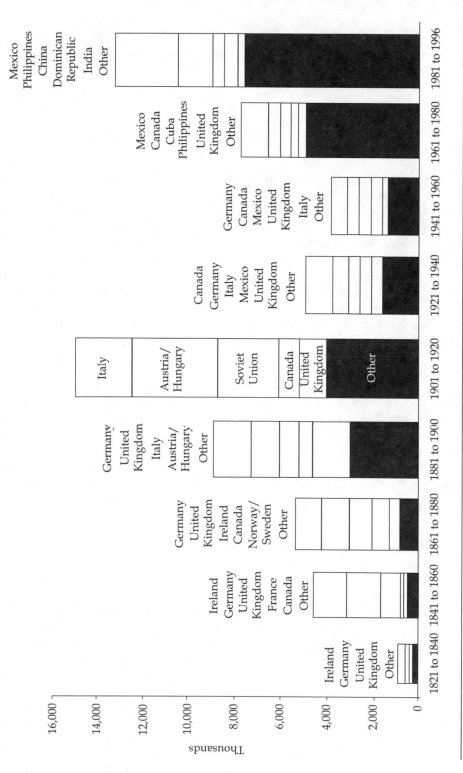

Source: Adapted from Immigration and Naturalization Service. 1998. Statistical Yearbook 1998. (Washington: U.S. Government Printing Office.)

TABLE 1.1 / Foreign Born as Percentage of Total U.S. Population

| | 1880 | 1900 | 1920 | 1950 | 1960 | 1970 | 1980 | 1990 | 2000 |
|---|---|---|---|---|---|---|---|---|---|
| Foreign born | 13.3 | 13.6 | 13.3 | 6.9 | 5.4 | 4.7 | 6.2 | 8.6 | 10.4* |

*2000 foreign born population = 28.4 million.
*Source:* Author's compilation based on Harvard Immigration Projects, 2000.

of large-scale immigration), immigration nevertheless generates anxieties and at times even fans the fires of xenophobia (a major consequence of large-scale immigration). Two broad concerns have set the parameters of debate over immigration scholarship and policy in the United States and Europe: the economic and sociocultural consequences of large-scale immigration.

Recent economic arguments have largely focused on three areas: the impact of large-scale immigration on the wages of native workers (do immigrants depress the wages of native, especially minority, workers?); the fiscal implications of large-scale immigration (do immigrants pay their way taxwise or are they are burden, consuming more in publicly funded services than they contribute?); and the redundancy of immigrants, especially poorly educated and low-skilled workers, in new knowledge-intensive economies that are far less labor intensive than the industrial economies of yesterday.[2]

Reducing the complexities of the new immigration to economic factors can be limiting. An emerging consensus is that the economic implications of large-scale immigration are ambiguous. Research shows that immigrants generate benefits in certain areas (including worker productivity) and costs in others (especially in fiscal terms). Furthermore, we must not lose sight of the fact that the U.S. economy is so large, powerful, and dynamic that immigration will neither make nor break it. The total size of the U.S. economy is $7 trillion; immigrant-related economic activities are a small portion of that total (an estimated domestic gain of $1 billion to $10 billion a year, according to an NRC study) (National Research Council 1997).

That the most recent wave of immigration is made up largely of non-European, non–English speaking "people of color" arriving in unprecedented numbers from Asia, the Caribbean, and Latin America (see table 1.3 and figure 1.3) is at the heart of current arguments over the sociocultural consequences of immigration. While debates over immigration's economic consequences are largely focused on the aforementioned three areas of concern, debate over the sociocultural implications of large-scale immigration is more diffused. Some scholars have focused on language issues, including bilingual education: Are they learning English? Others examine the political consequences of large-scale immigration: Are they becoming American in letter and spirit? Yet others focus on immigrant practices that are unpalatable in terms of the cultural models and social practices of the mainstream population: the eternal issues here are female genital cutting, arranged marriages, and, in Europe especially, the veil.

TABLE 1.2  /  Percentage of Foreign Born by Region of Origin

|  | 1880 | 1920 | 1950 | 1980 | 2000 |
|---|---|---|---|---|---|
| Europeans | 97 | 93.6 | 89.3 | 49.6 | 15 |
| Asians | 1.6 | 1.7 · | 2.65 | 18 | 25 |
| Latin Americans | 1.3 | 4.2 | 6.3 | 31 | 51 |

*Source:* Author's compilation based on Harvard Immigration Projects, 2000.

## RETHINKING ASSIMILATION

Old ideas about immigrant assimilation and acculturation—first articulated to make sense of the experiences of the transatlantic migrants of a century ago—naturally have been dusted off and tried out on new arrivals. In this case, applying the old to the new is not simply a reflex, but rather suggests that thinking about immigration in the United States is always, explicitly or implicitly, a comparative exercise: the here and now of the new immigration versus the mythico-historic record (Suárez-Orozco and Suárez-Orozco 2000). This is a record where equal parts of fact, myth, and fantasy combine to produce a powerful cultural narrative along the following lines: (1) poor but (2) hardworking European peasants (3) pulling themselves up by their bootstraps (4) willingly gave up their counterproductive Old World views, values, and languages (if not their accents!) to (5) become prosperous, proud, and loyal Americans.[3]

Since the United States is arguably the only postindustrial democracy in the world where immigration is at once history and destiny, every new wave of immigration reactivates an eternal question: How do the new immigrants measure up to the old immigrants? This was asked one hundred years ago when the new immigrants were Irish, Italians, and Eastern Europeans and the old immigrants were English (see figure 1.2). The recurring answer is predictable. New immigrants *always* fail the comparative test by falling short of the mythico-historic standards set by earlier immigrants. Hence the most basic rule governing public attitudes about immigration: we love immigrants at a safe historical distance but are much more ambivalent about those joining us in the here and now (Suárez-Orozco and Suárez-Orozco 2000).

Thus the question many are asking today is, are the new immigrants of color recreating the structures of the foundational mythico-historic narrative, the grammar of which was articulated in Irish, Italian, and Eastern European accents in the streets and docks of the Lower East Side of Manhattan one hundred years ago? Or is today's unprecedented racial and cultural diversity—more than one hundred languages now are spoken by immigrant children in New York City schools—generating an entirely new script? Is what we hear today an incomprehensible Babelesque story, not only unlike anything we heard before but

TABLE 1.3 / Region of Birth of Foreign-Born Population

| Year | Total | Region of Birth Reported | | | | |
|------|-------|--------|------|--------|---------|---------------|
| | | Europe | Asia | Africa | Oceania | Latin America |
| 1900 | 10,341,276 | 8,881,548 | 120,248 | 2,538 | 8,820 | 137,458 |
| 1960 | 9,738,091 | 7,256,311 | 490,996 | 35,355 | 34,730 | 908,309 |
| 1970 | 9,619,302 | 5,740,891 | 824,887 | 80,143 | 41,258 | 1,803,970 |
| 1980 | 14,079,906 | 5,149,572 | 2,539,777 | 199,723 | 77,577 | 4,372,487 |
| 1990 | 19,767,316 | 4,350,403 | 4,979,037 | 363,819 | 104,145 | 8,407,837 |

*Source:* Author's compilation based on Harvard Immigration Projects, 2000.

quite likely to contribute to our already polarized race relations and chronic underclass problems? Will today's new arrivals be like our mythical immigrant ancestors and assimilate, becoming loyal and proud Americans? Or, conversely, will they by sheer force of numbers redefine what it is to be an American?

Much of the analytic—as well as *emotional*—framework for approaching the topic of immigration was developed as the young nation was in the process of metabolizing the great transatlantic European immigration wave of a century ago. Ideas about assimilation and acculturation (often used interchangeably) were first introduced in the social sciences to examine the processes of social and cultural change set in motion as immigrants began their second journey: insertion into mainstream American life (see Park and Burgess 1965; Gordon 1964; Alba and Nee 1997). The basic theme in the narratives of assimilation and acculturation theories that came to dominate the social sciences predicted that immigration sets in motion a process of change that is directional—indeed, unilinear—nonreversible, and continuous.

The direction or aim of the process was said to be structural assimilation (typically operationalized in terms of social relations and participation in the opportunity structure) and acculturation (typically operationalized in terms of language, values, and cultural identifications) into what was the prize at immigration's finish line: the middle-class, white, Protestant, European American framework of the dominant society.[4] The process as narrated in the social science literature seemed to neatly follow the van Gennepian structural code: *separation* (from social relations and from participation in the opportunity structure of the country or culture of origin), *marginality* (residential, linguistic, economic, especially during the earlier phases of immigration and acute among the first generation), and finally, a generation or two after immigration, *incorporation* into the social structures and cultural codes of the mainstream.

The process of change was said to be nonreversible in that once an immigrant group achieved the goals of acculturation and structural assimilation, there is, so to speak, no going back. This is in part because scholars of immigrant change conceptualized it as a dual process of gain (new culture, participation in new social structures) and loss (old culture, old social structures). Lastly, the process was said to be continuous because it took place transgenerationally. The immi-

FIGURE 1.3 / Racial-Ethnic Composition of the United States

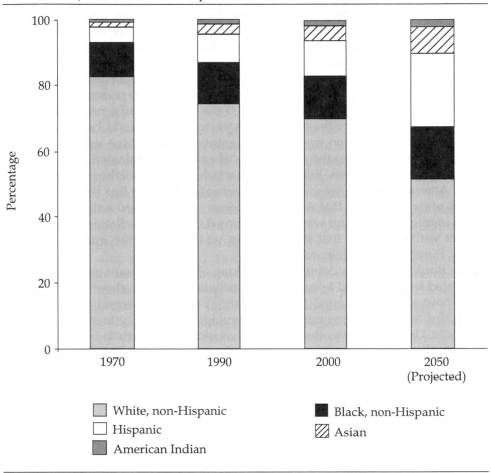

Source: Council of Economic Advisors for the President's Initiative on Race. 1998. *Changing America: Indicators of Social and Economic Well-Being by Race and Hispanic Origin.* (Washington: U.S. Government Printing Office.)

grant generation (outsiders looking for a way in), the second generation (Americanized insiders), the third and fourth generations (the *Roots* generation in search of symbolic ethnicity), and so on, all had their assigned roles in this telling of the immigrant saga.

The dominant narratives of immigrant assimilation were structured by three reasonable assumptions: the *clean break* assumption, the *homogeneity* assumption, and the *progress* assumption. These assumptions need to be reexamined in light of some of the distinct features characterizing the latest wave of immigration.

First, immigration was theorized to take place in clearly delineated waves (versus ongoing flows) between two more or less remote, bounded, geopolitical

characterized the new postindustrial economy in terms of the hourglass metaphor. On one end of the hourglass is a well-remunerated, knowledge-intensive economic sphere that has recently experienced unprecedented growth. On the other end is a service economy where low-skilled and semiskilled workers continue to lose ground in real wages, benefits, and security. Furthermore, the new economy provides virtually no bridges for those in the bottom of the hourglass to move into more desirable sectors. Some scholars argue that unlike the low-skilled industry jobs of yesterday, the kinds of jobs typically available to low-skilled immigrants today do not offer serious prospects of upward mobility (Portes 1996).

Another defining aspect of new immigration is the intense social segregation between immigrants of color and the white middle-class European American population. While immigrants always have concentrated in specific neighborhoods, today we are witnessing an extraordinary concentration of large numbers of immigrants in a handful of states in large urban areas polarized by racial tensions. Some 85 percent of all Mexican immigrants in the United States reside in three states (California, Texas, and Illinois). As a result of an increasing segmentation of the economy and society, large numbers of low-skilled immigrants "have become more, not less, likely to live and work in environments that have grown increasingly segregated from whites" (Waldinger and Bozorgmehr 1996). By and large, these immigrants have no meaningful contact with white middle-class culture; rather, their point of reference is more likely to be conationals, coethnics, or African American culture.

Perhaps the lethal blow to the assumption of homogeneity comes from what I call the culture of multiculturalism. Rather than face a "relatively uniform 'mainstream'" culture (Portes 1996), immigrants today must navigate the complex currents of multiculturalism—that is, models and social practices that shape the experiences, perceptions, and behavioral repertoires of immigrants in ways not seen in previous eras of large-scale immigration. A hundred years ago, certainly no culture of multiculturalism celebrating ethnicity and communities of origin existed. Indeed, the defining ritual at Ellis Island was the renaming ceremony, a cultural baptism of sorts. Some chose to change their names to avoid racism, anti-Semitism, or simply to blend in. Hence, Israel Ehrenberg was reborn as Ashley Montague, Meyer Schkolnick was reborn as Robert Merton, and Issur Danielovitch Demsky was reborn as Kirk Douglas (Friedman 1999).

Immigrants today enter social spaces where racial and ethnic categories are important, often charged gravitational fields with important political and economic implications. The largest wave of immigration into the United States took place after the great struggles of the civil rights movement. In that ethos, racial and ethnic categories became powerful instrumental as well as expressive vectors. Expressive ethnicity refers to the subjective feeling of a common origin and shared destiny with others. These feelings typically are constructed around such phenomena as historic travails and struggles (for example, the Serbian sense of peoplehood emerging from defeat six centuries ago at the hands of the Ottomans in the Battle of Kosovo), a common ancestral language (for example, the Basques), or religion (for example, the Jews in the Diaspora) (Romanucci-Ross and DeVos 1995).

Instrumental ethnicity refers to the tactical use of ethnicity. In recent years, identity politics has become a mode of expressive self-affirmation as well as strategic politics. This is in part because ethnic categories now are a critical tool of the state apparatus. Nation-states create categories of people for various reasons, such as the census, taxation, and apportionment for political representation. Ethnic categories generated by state policy are relevant to a variety of civic and political matters; further, they are appropriated and used by various groups for strategic needs.

Panethnic categories such as Asian American and Hispanic are created by demographers and social scientists for purposes of data development, analysis, and policy. The term *Hispanic*, for example, was introduced by demographers working for the U.S. Bureau of the Census in the 1980s as a way to categorize people who are either historically or culturally connected to the Spanish language. Note that Hispanic, the precursor to the more au courant term *Latino*, is a category with no precise racial or national origins meaning. Indeed, Latinos are white, black, indigenous, and every combination thereof; also, they originate in more than twenty countries as varied as Mexico, Argentina, and the Dominican Republic.[10]

For large numbers of new arrivals today, the point of reference seems to be the cultural sensibilities and social practices of their more established coethnics—that is, Latinos, Asians, Afro-Caribbeans—rather than the standards of increasingly remote white middle-class Protestant European Americans.

## THE PROGRESS ASSUMPTION

The foundational narratives of immigrant assimilation typically depicted an upwardly mobile journey. The story was elegant in its simplicity: the longer immigrants remain in the United States, the better they would do in schooling, health, and income. As Robert Bellah once noted, "The United States was planned for progress" and each wave of immigrants was said to recapitulate this national destiny. This assumption also needs rethinking in light of new evidence. A number of scholars from different disciplines using a variety of methods have identified a disconcerting phenomenon: for many new immigrant groups, length of residency in the United States seems to be associated with *declining* health, school achievement, and aspirations (see Kao and Tienda 1995; National Research Council 1998; Rúmbaut 1995; Steinberg, Bradford, and Dornbusch 1996; Suárez-Orozco and Suárez-Orozco 1995).

A recent large-scale National Research Council study considered a variety of measures of physical health and risk behaviors among children and adolescents from immigrant families, including general health, learning disabilities, obesity,

FIGURE 1.4 / Mean Risk Behavior by Ethnic Group and Immigrant Status

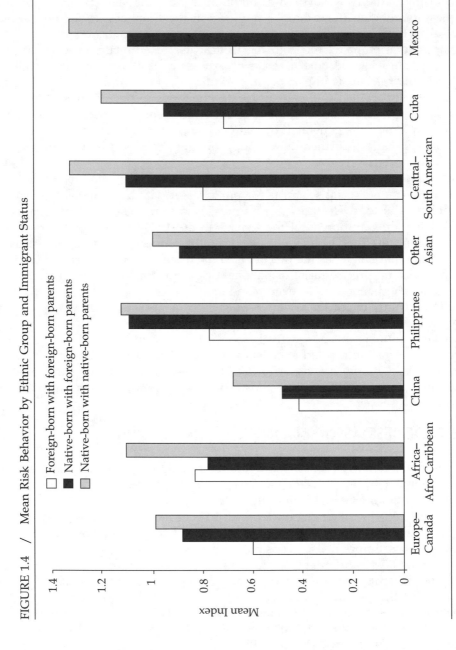

Source: Adapted from National Research Council (1998, 84).

emotional difficulties, and risk behaviors. The NRC researchers found that immigrant youth tend to be healthier than their counterparts from nonimmigrant families. These findings are counterintuitive in light of the racial and ethnic minority status, lower overall socioeconomic status, and higher poverty rates of many immigrant children and families. The NRC study also found that the longer immigrant youth are in the United States, the poorer their overall physical and psychological health. Furthermore, the more Americanized they became, the more likely they were to engage in risky behaviors such as substance abuse, unprotected sex, and delinquency (see figure 1.4). While the NRC data are limited, they nevertheless should be cause for reflection.[11]

In the area of education, the sociologists Rúmbaut and Portes surveyed more than 5,000 high school students in San Diego, California, and Dade County, Florida. Rúmbaut (1995) writes,

> [A]n important finding supporting our earlier reported research, is the *negative* association of length of residence in the United States with both GPA and aspirations. Time in the United States is, as expected, strongly predictive of improved English reading skills; but despite that seeming advantage, longer residence in the US and second generation status [that is, being born in the United States] are connected to declining academic achievement and aspirations, net of other factors. (See also Portes and Rúmbaut 2001.)

In a different voice, Reverend Virgil Elizondo, rector of the San Fernando Cathedral in San Antonio, Texas, articulates this same problem. "I can tell by looking in their eyes how long they've been here. They come sparkling with hope, and the first generation finds hope rewarded. Their children's eyes no longer sparkle" (Suro 1998, 13).

A number of scholars currently are exploring the problem of decline in school performance, health, and social adaptation of immigrant children. Preliminary research suggests several factors. The various forms of capital that immigrant families bring with them—including financial resources, social class and education background, psychological and physical health as well as social supports—have a clear influence on the immigrant experience. Legal status (documented versus undocumented immigrant), race, color, and language also mediate how children and families manage the upheavals of immigration. Economic opportunities and neighborhood characteristics—including the quality of schools where immigrants settle, racial and class segregation, neighborhood decay, and violence—all contribute significantly to immigrants' adaptation. Anti-immigrant sentiment and racism also play a role. These factors combine in ways that seem to lead to very different long-term outcomes. Until better longitudinal data are available, one no longer may assume that immigration inevitably leads to measurable progress.

## UTOPIA

In the United States, two distinct migratory formations are taking place that have different causes and generate divergent outcomes. One migratory formation is made up of highly educated, highly skilled workers drawn by the explosive growth in knowledge-intensive sectors of the economy. Immigrants today are more likely to have advanced degrees than the native-born population (see figure 1.5). These immigrants come to thrive. They are among the best-educated and skilled folk in the United States.

Immigrants with doctorates are overrepresented: half of all entering physics graduate students in 1998 were foreign-born (see "Wanted: American Physicists" 1999).[12] Thirty-two percent of all scientists and engineers working in California's Silicon Valley are immigrants (see Saxenian 1999).[13] Roughly a third of all Nobel Prize winners in the United States have been immigrants. In 1999, all (100 percent!) U.S. winners of the Nobel Prize were immigrants. Perhaps with the exception of the highly educated immigrants and refugees escaping Nazi Europe, immigrants in the past tended to be more uniformly poorly educated and relatively unskilled than they are today (see Borjas 1995).

These immigrants are likely to settle in safe, middle-class suburban neighborhoods—the kind that tend to have better schools. Not surprisingly, their children are outperforming native-born children in grades, prestigious national science competitions, and in the nation's most exclusive colleges—two of the three top Intel Science prizes in March 2000 went to immigrant youth. These highly educated and skilled immigrants are moving rapidly into the more desirable sectors of the U.S. economy, generally bypassing traditional transgenerational modes of immigrant status mobility (see Waldinger and Bozorgmehr 1996). Never in the history of U.S. immigration have so many immigrants done so well so fast. For them, immigration means Utopia realized.

## DYSTOPIA

The other migratory formation is made up of large numbers of poorly educated, poorly skilled or unskilled workers. Nearly 35 percent of all Latin American immigrants in the United States have less than a ninth grade education—compared to nearly 5 percent of the native population (see figure 1.6).

Poorly educated and unskilled immigrants come to survive—some are escaping economies that went belly up during global restructuring, others violence or war. These immigrants tend to settle in areas of deep poverty and racial segregation. Concentrated poverty is associated with the "disappearance of meaningful work opportunities" (Wilson 1997). Youngsters in such neighborhoods are chronically underemployed or unemployed and must search for work elsewhere. In such neighborhoods, with few opportunities in the formal economy, underground or informal activities tend to flourish. These kinds of economies

FIGURE 1.5 / Percentage of Population with a Bachelor's Degree or Higher, by Origin in 2000

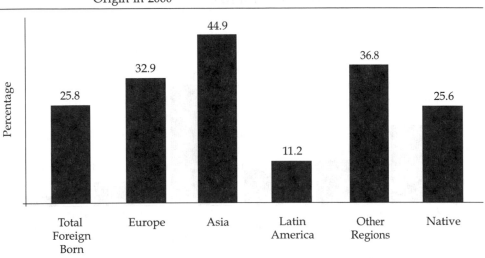

Source: *Profile of the Foreign Born Population in the United States: 2000*. Current Population Reports. (Washington: U.S. Government Printing Office for U.S. Bureau of the Census.)

often involve the trade of illegal substances and are associated with gangs and neighborhood violence. This ethos—not white middle-class Protestant European American culture—is the primary point of reference for many poor immigrant children of color today.

When poverty is combined with racial segregation, the outcomes can be devastating.

> No matter what their personal traits or characteristics, people who grow up and live in environments of concentrated poverty and racial isolation are more likely to become teenage mothers, drop out of school, achieve only low levels of education, and earn lower adult incomes. (Massey and Denton 1993)

Today's global economy is unforgiving of immigrants without skills and credentials. Furthermore, low-skill service jobs not only lead nowhere in status hierarchy but also fail to provide for basic family needs. Indeed, among new immigrants, a pattern of declining returns to education means that with more schooling they will be getting less rewards in the posteducation opportunity structure than ever before in the history of U.S. immigration (see Myers 1998, 188). The high school graduate who bypasses college and enters the workforce with no special skills has only a limited advantage over the high school dropout (see Murnane 1996).

Poor, low-skilled immigrants of color have few options but to send their children to schools in gang-infested drug and prostitution neighborhoods.[14] Too

and alcohol. Yet for many immigrant youth, without robust socioeconomic and cultural safety nets, engaging in such behaviors is a high-stakes proposition where one mistake can have lifelong consequences. Whereas a white middle-class youth caught in possession of drugs is likely to be referred to counseling and rehabilitation, an immigrant youth convicted of the same offense is likely to be deported.

The current wave of immigration involves people from fantastically diverse and heterogeneous cultural backgrounds. Beneath surface differences a common grammar can be identified among groups as culturally distinct from one another as Chinese, Haitian, and Mexican immigrants. The importance of family ties, hard work, and optimism about the future are examples of shared immigrant values.[18]

Consider the case of strong family ties among immigrants. Many come from cultures where the family system is an integral part of their sense of self. Family ties play a critical role in family reunification—an important force driving new immigration. Furthermore, family ties are accentuated once immigrants settle because immigration poses many emotional and practical challenges that force immigrants to turn to one another for support (see Suárez-Orozco and Suárez-Orozco 2000).

Hard work and optimism about the future likewise are central to the immigrant's raison d'être. The immigrant's most fundamental motivation is to find a better life. Immigrants tend to view hard work as essential to this project. That many immigrants do the impossible jobs that native workers refuse to consider is an indication of how hard they are willing to work. Immigrant family ties, work ethic, and optimism about the future are unique assets adding to the total cultural stock of the nation.

Immigration generates change. The immigrants themselves undergo a variety of transformations, and likewise the immigration process inevitably changes the members of the dominant culture. In the United States today, we eat, speak, and dance differently than we did thirty years ago, in part due to large-scale immigration. Yet change is never easy, and changes brought about by new immigration require mutual calibrations and negotiations.

Rather than advocating that immigrant children abandon all elements of their culture as they embark on their uncertain assimilation in a new country, a more promising path is for that country to cultivate and nurture the emergence of hybrid identities and bicultural competencies.[19] These hybrid cultural styles blend elements of old and new culture, unleashing new energies and potentials.[20]

The skills and work habits required to thrive in the new century are essential elements of assimilation. Immigrant children, like all children, must develop this repertoire of instrumental skills. Yet maintaining a sense of belonging and social cohesion with their roots is equally important. When immigrant children lose their expressive culture, social cohesion is weakened, parental authority is undermined, and interpersonal relations suffer. The unthinking call for immigrant children to abandon their culture en masse can only result in loss, anomie, and social disruption.

The model of unilineal assimilation emerged in another era. The young nation then was eager to turn large numbers of European immigrants into loyal citizen workers and consumers. Theirs was a time of nation building and bounded national projects. Even then, accounts of immigrants rushing to trade their own for American culture were greatly exaggerated. German Americans, Italian Americans, and Irish Americans all left deep imprints in American culture. Even among fifth-generation descendants of the previous great wave of immigration, cultural symbols and ethnicity remain an emotional gravitational field (see Glazer and Moynahan 1970).

Beyond the argument that maintaining the expressive elements of culture are symbolically important and strategic from the viewpoint of social cohesion, another argument is worth considering. Globalization changes everything; inter alia, it makes the tenets of unilineal assimilation largely irrelevant. Today being able to operate in multiple cultural codes has clear and unequivocal advantages—as anyone working in a major (and now, not so major) corporation knows. Dual consciousness has instrumental and expressive advantages. Yet public policy in the United States does not make dual consciousness an effortless strategy among immigrants. The highly charged debates over bilingualism—especially bilingual education—are part of a larger environment that treats dual consciousness as a threat to national cohesion rather than an asset in the era of globalization. While many view immigrant cultural skills (including linguistic ones) as a threat, I see them as precious resources to be cultivated.

A renowned historian once said the history of the United States is in fundamental respects the history of immigration (Handlin 1951). Throughout history, U.S. citizens have welcomed newcomers ambivalently. The fear then, as now, focused on whether the immigrants would contribute to the American project. The gift of hindsight demonstrates just how essential immigration has proven to making and remaking the American fabric. With diversity, however, comes conflict and dissent. Working through frictions in the public sphere by reasoned debate and compromise is central to the idea and practice of democracy.

Immigrant children are uniquely poised to play a significant role in the remaking of American democracy. In the era of multiculturalism and transnationalism, their bicultural experiences and skills prepare them well to be the cultural brokers able to find common ground.

## NOTES

1. Theorists of immigration have argued that transnationalized labor recruiting networks, family reunification, and changing cultural models and expectations about, for example, what is an acceptable standard of living, are all powerfully implicated in generating and sustaining new migratory flows. Wars nearly always generate large-

scale immigration: World War II gave birth to the Mexican bracero program that started the largest wave of immigration to the United States in history. Without the cold war, today there would not be over a million Cuban Americans in the United States. The Southeast Asian diaspora is the product of the war in Indochina. The million or so Central Americans that now make the United States their home arrived following the intensification of U.S.-backed counterinsurgency campaigns in El Salvador, Guatemala, and Nicaragua in the 1980s.

2. A great deal of energy has gone into assessing the economic consequences of immigration. Research findings on the economic consequences of immigration are somewhat ambiguous. Often they are contradictory—some economists claim that new immigrants are a burden to taxpayers and an overall negative influence on the U.S. economy, and others suggest that they continue to be an important asset.

    A recent study on the economic, demographic, and fiscal effects of immigration by the National Research Council (NRC) concludes, "immigration produces net economic gains for domestic residents." Not only do immigrants "increase the supply of labor and help produce new goods and services" but their presence also "allows domestic workers to be used more productively, specializing in producing goods at which they are relatively more efficient. Specialization in consumption also yields a gain." The NRC estimates that the immigration-related "domestic gain may run on the order of $1 billion to $10 billion a year." On the other hand, in fiscal terms the NRC data suggest, "immigrants receive more in services than they pay in taxes." Although there are important differences by state—California, for example, is more negatively impacted than other states—the panel calculates that "if the net fiscal impact of all U.S. immigrant-headed households were averaged across all native households in the U.S., the burden would be . . . on the order of $166 to $226 per native household." The NRC study further suggests that while immigration is a plus in overall economic terms, low-skilled new immigrants have contributed to a modest drop in the minimum wage of low-skilled workers—a 5 percent drop in wages since 1980 among high school dropouts can be attributed to the new immigrants. No evidence, however, suggests that new immigration has hurt the economic condition of African Americans (National Research Council 1997, 3–5, 7). For another overview of immigrants and the economy see Borjas 1999.

3. For a recent exquisite treatment of this narrative see Prell 1999.

4. The process of change was said to be unilinear in that all new arrivals would be expected to undergo roughly the same process of change.

5. Borrowing the delicious words of Luís Rafael Sanchez, many new immigrants today live neither here nor there but rather in "la guagua aérea"—the air bus.

6. Since 1990, while the Hispanic population in the United States grew by more than 30 percent, its buying power has grown by more than 65 percent, to about $350 billion in 1997. This is changing the way business is conducted in many parts of the country.

7. Cornelius (1998) argues that over time Mexican immigrants in the United States are less likely to invest in capital improvements in their sending communities. In fact, he argues, a new feature of the Mexican experience in the United States is that as Mexican immigrants become increasingly rooted in the U.S. side of "the line," they mainly go back to their sending communities for rest and relaxation.

8. Culturally, immigrants not only significantly reshape the ethos of their new communities but also are responsible for significant social transformations back home. Levitt (2001) has argued that Dominican "social remittances" affect the values, cultural models, and social practices of those left behind.

9. I concur with Alejandro Portes when he argues that we can no longer assume that new immigrants will assimilate into a coherent mainstream. Portes (1996, 6) articulates a critical question that is now in the minds of many observers of immigration:

> The question today is to what sector of American society will a particular immigrant group assimilate? Instead of a relatively uniform "mainstream" whose mores and prejudices dictate a common path of integration, we observe today several distinct forms of adaptation. One of them replicates the time-honored portrayal of growing acculturation and parallel integration into the white middle class. A second leads straight in the opposite direction to permanent poverty and assimilation to the underclass. Still a third associates rapid economic advancement with deliberate preservation of the immigrant community's values and tight solidarity.

10. Nor do such categories address the sensibilities rooted in history and generation in the United States. A Latina can be a descendant of the original settlers in what is now New Mexico. Her ancestors spoke Spanish, well before English was ever heard in this continent. Her family has resided in this land before the United States appropriated the Southwest territories, yet she is considered just as much a Latina as a Mayan-speaking new arrival from Guatemala who crossed the border last week.

     So too the term *Asian* brings together people of highly diverse cultural, linguistic, and religious backgrounds. A Chinese Buddhist and a Filipino Catholic both are considered Asian American, though they may have little in common in terms of language, cultural identity, and sense of self.

11. The data reported are largely cross-sectional panel data, some of it self-reported. Better quality longitudinal data are needed to develop a clearer sense of the factors leading to these worrisome trends (see National Research Council 1998).

12. Of course not all of these foreign-born physics graduate students are immigrants—some indeed will return to their countries of birth while others surely will go on to have productive scientific careers in the United States.

13. I am thankful to Professor Michael Jones-Correa of the Department of Government at Harvard University for alerting me to this important new study.

14. In one such site, one of our research assistants found that boys sneak out of school at noon to watch pornographic films at a shop across the street. Many of these schools are dilapidated and unkempt. Violence is pervasive. In an elementary school, a young girl was found raped and murdered on school premises. In another, an irate parent stabbed a teacher in front of her students. Tremendous ethnic tension exists in many schools. In one of our sites, students regularly play a game called Rice and Beans (Asian versus Latino students) that frequently deteriorates into violence. In many sites, immigrant students report living in constant fear; they dread lunch and classroom changes, as hallways are sites of confrontation and intimidation, including sexual violence.

15. An ethnographic study of a number of immigrant schools in Miami found three factors consistently present in schools with so-called cultures of violence. First, school

officials tended to deny that the school had problems with violence or drugs. Second, many of the school staff members exhibited "non-caring" behaviors toward the students. Lastly, the schools took lax security measures (Collier 1998).

16. These schools affect the opportunities and experiences of immigrant children in immediate ways. They tend to have limited resources. Classrooms typically are overcrowded. Textbooks and curriculum are outdated. Computers are few and obsolete. Many of the teachers may not have credentials in the subjects they teach. Clearly defined tracks sentence students to noncollege destinations. Lacking English skills, many immigrant students often are enrolled in the least demanding and competitive classes that eventually exclude them from courses needed for college. These schools generally offer few (if any) Advanced Placement courses critical for entry in many of the more competitive colleges. The guidance counselor–student ratio is impossibly high. Since the settings are so undesirable, teachers and principals routinely transfer to better assignments elsewhere. The result is many schools with little continuity or sense of community. Children and teachers in these schools are preoccupied with ever-present violence, and morale is very low.

17. For a superb but pessimistic study of how "persistent, blatant racial discrimination," along with inferior schools in high-crime neighborhoods is implicated in the transgenerational decline of West Indian immigrants in New York City, see Waters 1999.

18. For an overview of recent research on immigration and family ties see Rúmbaut 1996; Suárez-Orozco and Suárez-Orozco 1995; Falicov 1998. For an overview of immigrant optimism and achievement orientation see Kao and Tienda 1995, 1–19.

19. I concur with LaFromboise and her colleagues (1998) on the need to reconceptualize what they call the linear model of cultural acquisition.

20. Margaret Gibson (1988) articulates a theoretical argument on immigrant transculturation and a calculated strategy of "accommodation without assimilation" in her study of highly successful Sikh immigrants in California. For a theoretical statement on the psychology of ethnic identity and cultural pluralism see Phinney 1998.

# REFERENCES

Ainslie, Ricardo. 1998. "Cultural Mourning, Immigration, and Engagement: Vignettes from the Mexican Experience." In *Crossings: Mexican Immigration in Interdisciplinary Perspectives*, edited by Marcelo M. Suárez-Orozco. Cambridge, Mass.: David Rockefeller Center for Latin American Studies and Harvard University Press.

Alba, Richard, and V. Nee. 1997. "Rethinking Assimilation Theory for a New Era of Immigration." *International Migration Review* 31: 826–74.

Basch, L., N. G. Schiller, and C. S. Blanc. 1995. *Nations Unbound: Transnational Projects, Postcolonial Predicaments and Deterritorialized Nation-States*. Basel, Switzerland: Gordon and Breach Science Publishers.

Binational Study. 1998. *Migration Between Mexico and the United States*. Washington: U.S. Commission on Immigration Reform.

Borjas, George. 1999. *Heaven's Door: Immigration Policy and the American Economy*. Princeton, N.J.: Princeton University Press.

———. 1995. "Assimilation in Cohort Quality Revisited: What Happened to Immigrant Earnings in the 1980s?" *Journal of Labor Economics* 13: 463–89.

Collier, Michael. 1998. "Cultures of Violence in Miami-Dade Public Schools." Working Paper of the Immigration and Ethnicity Institute, Florida International University.

"Commentary." 1998. In *Crossings: Mexican Immigration in Interdisciplinary Perspectives*, edited by Marcelo M. Suárez-Orozco. Cambridge, Mass.: David Rockefeller Center for Latin American Studies and Harvard University Press.

Cornelius, Wayne. 1998. "The Structural Embeddedness of Demand for Mexican Immigrant Labor." In *Crossings: Mexican Immigration in Interdisciplinary Perspectives*, edited by Marcelo M. Suárez-Orozco. Cambridge, Mass.: David Rockefeller Center for Latin American Studies and Harvard University Press.

Current Population Reports. 1999. *Profile of the Foreign-Born Population in the United States: 1997*. Washington: U.S. Government Printing Office for U.S. Bureau of the Census.

Durand, Jorge. 1999. "Migration and Integration." In *Crossings: Mexican Immigration in Interdisciplinary Perspectives*, edited by Marcelo M. Suárez-Orozco. Cambridge, Mass.: David Rockefeller Center for Latin American Studies and Harvard University Press.

Eckholm, Erik. 1999. "For China's Rural Migrants, an Education Wall." *New York Times*, December 12: A6.

Falicov, Celia. 1998. *Latino Families in Therapy: A Guide to Multicultural Practice*. New York: Guilford.

Friedman, Lawrence J. 1999. *Identity's Architect: A Biography of Erik H. Erikson*. New York: Scribner.

Gibson, Margaret. 1988. *Accommodation Without Assimilation: Sikh Immigrants in an American High School*. Ithaca, N.Y.: Cornell University Press.

Glazer, Nathan, and Daniel Patrick Moynahan. 1970. *Beyond the Melting Pot*. Cambridge, Mass.: MIT Press.

"Global Acts: Immigrant Children, Education and the Post-National." Forthcoming. *Harvard Educational Review*.

Gordon, Milton M. 1964. *Assimilation in American Life: The Role of Race, Religion, and National Origins*. New York: Oxford University Press.

Gutierrez, David G. 1998. "Ethnic Mexicans and the Transformation of 'American' Social Space: Reflections on Recent History." In *Crossings: Mexican Immigration in Interdisciplinary Perspectives*, edited by Marcelo M. Suárez-Orozco. Cambridge, Mass.: David Rockefeller Center for Latin American Studies and Harvard University Press.

Handlin, Oscar. 1951. *The Uprooted*. Boston: Little, Brown.

Higham, John. 1975. *Send These to Me: Jews and Other Immigrants in Urban America*. New York: Atheneum.

Kao, Grace, and M. Tienda. 1995. "Optimism and Achievement: The Educational Performance of Immigrant Youth." *Social Science Quarterly* 76: 1–19.

LaFromboise, Teresa, Hardin Coleman, and Jennifer Gerton. 1998. "Psychological Impact of Biculturalism: Evidence and Theory." In *Readings in Ethnic Psychology*, edited by P. B. Organista, K. Chun, and G. Martin. New York: Routledge.

Levitt, Peggy. 2001. *The Transnational Villagers*. Berkeley and London: University of California Press.

Massey, Douglas, and Nancy Denton. 1993. *American Apartheid*. Cambridge, Mass.: Harvard University Press.

Moya, Joya C. 1998. *Cousins and Strangers: Spanish Immigrants in Buenos Aires, 1850–1930*. Berkeley: University of California Press.

Murnane, Richard. 1996. *Teaching the New Basic Skills: Principles for Educating Children to Thrive in a Changing Economy*. New York: Martin Kessler Books, Free Press.

Myers, Dowell. 1998. "Dimensions of Economic Adaptation by Mexican-Origin Men." In

Universalism and particularism assume a double face in Indian politics. Universalism assumes either a liberal or nationalist form: the liberal universalism, for example, of the Nehruvian era that accented equality and social rights; and the more recent nationalist universalism of the Bharatiya Janata Party (BJP)'s Hindutva (Hinduness) ideology, which argues that a common Hindu identity transcends and subsumes all social differences. Pluralism too has spawned two faces: protective discrimination on behalf of disadvantaged and discriminated-against groups to promote equality of opportunity; and a more recent striving for group representation, to distribute benefits proportionally among all social groups.

Indian law and politics have vacillated between universalism and particularism, and both feature in the constitution. The Supreme Court in a landmark case, *Balaji v. State of Mysore* (1963), tried to quantify the proportionate weight that should be accorded to each. The case involved group rights in the form of quotas in university admissions and government jobs for Dalits (ex-untouchables) and for OBCs. On one hand, Article 16(1) of the constitution guarantees "equality of opportunity in matters of public employment," and Article 16(2) protects against discrimination in public employment on the ground of "religion, race, caste, sex, descent, place of birth, residence. . . ." On the other hand, Article 16(4) provides that "nothing in this article shall prevent the State from making any provision for the reservation of appointments or posts in favour of any backward class of citizens which, in the opinion of the State, is not adequately represented in the services under the State." The court split the difference; it limited permissible reservations to 49 percent. Beyond 49 percent, the court held, would be a *fraud on the constitution* because it would impinge on the constitutional mandates providing for equality before the law (Article 14) and prohibiting discrimination (Article 15). In other words, *Balaji* in 1963 weighted legal pluralism in the form of group rights at 49 percent and legal universalism in the form of equal citizenship at 51 percent.[1]

This issue is not new in Indian history. The institutional progenitors and philosophical lineages of legal pluralism and legal universalism were differentially mobilized and reinforced by East India Company, colonial, nationalist, and postcolonial political actors. The rise of Hindu nationalism and the articulation of a Hindutva ideology in the 1980s and 1990s lent new meanings and urgency to the tension between pluralism and universalism. The BJP's turn in the late 1990s from the nationalist variant of universalism to a variant of particularism presaged a fundamental change. The move began to transform the theory and practice of particularism from protective discrimination (for example, reservations for backward castes) toward proportionate representation of all castes. This new version of pluralism advanced a conception of the Indian political community composed of diverse groups rather than equal citizens, a conception inimical to maintaining the 50–50 balance. In a multicultural society and state that tries to accommodate the contrasting imperatives of equality and diversity, the tension is likely to continue.

## THE COMPANY DISCOVERS AND LEGITIMIZES DIFFERENCE: CULTURAL FEDERALISM AND LEGAL PLURALISM

*Cultural federalism* is a term we have coined to suggest that India has dealt with diversity in ways that recognize legal identities on the basis of cultural as well as territorial boundaries. The Ottoman millet system—under which leaders of Greek Orthodox and Christian, Armenian, Jewish, and other communities were given civil as well as religious authority over their respective flocks—represents a significant historical example of cultural federalism. As we shall see, early East India Company doctrine and practice followed similar principles. In independent India, cultural federalism is given expression in Article 29 of the constitution (what might be called the multicultural clause), which protects the interests of minorities by granting them the right to "conserve" their "language, script and culture," and Article 30, which gives minorities the "right to establish and administer educational institutions."[2] These provisions are in tension with the universalist proposals of Article 44—a nonjusticiable Directive Principles of State Policy that enjoins the state to "endeavor to secure for the citizens a uniform civil code throughout the territory of India."

So why did Warren Hastings, who in 1774 became the East India Company's first governor-general, Sir William Jones, a company judge in Bengal and one of the first Englishmen to master Sanskrit (Kejariwal 1988, 32–33), and the stellar scholars, also servants of the East India Company, who comprised the founding generations of the Asiatic Society of Bengal, adopt a policy of cultural federalism and legal pluralism? Why did they decide to apply "the laws of the Koran with respect to Mohammedans and that of the Shaster with respect to Hindus"? Why did Jones construct a world composed of Hindus and Muslims? Why and how did he construct the categories *Hindu* and *Muslim*—categories that, in different guises and with changing meanings and consequences, are present at the beginning of the twenty-first century?

A postcolonial perspective leads to reading nineteenth- and twentieth-century categories and outcomes into the mentalities and intentions of eighteenth-century actors. The motive becomes imperial power, and the tactic, religious division. Power becomes as unnuanced a determinant of thought as control of the means of production.

We read the ideas and actions of Hastings and his Asiatic society colleagues—including their construction of Hindu and Mohammedan—as shaped by two concerns: the sources and meaning of civilization as understood by eighteenth-century Europeans; and, for Hastings in particular, a powerful sense of being a *local* ruler. Hastings, Jones, and their Asiatic society colleagues, all trained in European classical traditions, developed a civilizational eye. Legal pluralism was seen in terms of large, coherent cultural wholes defined by great languages and their classic texts. In their cultural imaginations, Hastings and Jones treated Sanskritic and Persian civilizations as equivalent to those of Greece and Rome. Their sense of being local rulers led them to do what they thought local rulers did—rely on the laws of the peoples under their authority to administer justice. Anachronistic efforts to read divide-and-rule communal politics into company policy need to be modified by attention to the civilizational perspective and self-understanding of company servants as local rulers.

English eighteenth-century representatives of the East India Company acted as agents of the Mughal emperor. At least nominally, they understood themselves as agents, not principals. At this stage of the British relationship to India, these agents' mentality, as Mehta (1999) might have put it, was more Burkean than Lockean, more attuned to pluralist multiculturalism than to liberal universalism.[3] Hence, company representatives recognized and accepted the existence and value of different civilizations on the Indian subcontinent. A Burkean consciousness accounts for what we characterize as Hastings's policy of cultural federalism that made each group subject to its own laws. In a much-quoted memorandum, Hastings ordered that in all suits regarding inheritance, marriage, caste, and other religious usages and institutions, "the laws of the Koran with respect to the Mahomedans [*sic*] and those of the shastra with respect to the Gentoos [Hindus] shall be invariably adhered to; on all such occasions the Moulvies or Brahmins shall respectively attend to expound the law, and they shall sign the report and assist in passing the decree" (Majumdar 1952, 8, 361).[4]

## AN INDIAN THEORY OF SELF-REGULATING GROUPS

Henry Thomas Colebrooke, leader of the second generation of Asiatic Society of Bengal Orientalists, distinguished Sanskritist, author of *The Hindu Law of Inheritance* (1883 [1798]), and founder of the Royal Asiatic Society, joined other scholars in the belief that in India, the laws of groups preexisted the state. Colebrooke (1830, 174, 177) cites an injunction from Bhrigu, a mythical lawgiver, that calls on each category of person to litigate controversies according to its own law:

> The frequenters of forests should cause their differences to be determined by one of their own order; members of a society, by persons belonging to that society; people appertaining to an army, by such as belong to the army . . . husbandmen, mechanics, artists . . . robbers or irregular soldiers, should adjust their controversies according to their own particular laws.

Sanskrit law texts held that the king should oversee the self-regulating society rather than create laws for society. The *Manusmriti*, initially translated from Sanskrit into English by Sir William Jones, holds that "the king [was] created as the protector of the classes and the stages of life, that are appointed each to its own particular duty, in proper order" (Doniger 1991, 131). Nor were such injunctions found solely in the Hindu texts favored by early British Orientalists such as Jones and Colebrooke. Richard Eaton (1993) shows us numerous exemplars of legal understandings in sixteenth-century, Mughal-ruled Bengal, where Muslim administrators enforced laws particular to specific communities. Such an understanding of Indian society supported the view that Indian society was constituted by groups.

## LEGAL UNIFORMITY AND INDIVIDUAL RIGHTS ENTER THE CONTEST

Group concepts flourished under company rule as long as Jones and his Orientalist brethren held sway. Their view of the value of Indian civilizations and social formations and practices was challenged and largely overturned in 1828 with the arrival of Lord William Bentinck, the first of a series of liberal and utilitarian governors-general. Liberal individualist themes now competed with earlier Orientalist constructions of India as a society constituted of groups. Liberal utilitarians in the era of Bentinck and Thomas Babington Macaulay strove to liberate Indians from domination by groups, to unravel individuals from the grip of family, caste, and religious community, to strengthen individual choice against collective decision. Until Queen Victoria's 1858 proclamation reversed its course, the Benthamite thrust posited that individualism and universalism were a requirement for progress and civilized living.

Individualism and legal universalism gained a formidable ally when in 1835 Thomas Macaulay joined Bentinck's government as law member of the council. Macaulay, who unashamedly admitted having "no knowledge of either Sanskrit or Arabic," alleged in a rightly notorious passage, "that all the historical information which has been collected from all the books written in the Sanskrit language is less valuable than what may be found in the most paltry abridgements used at preparatory schools in England" (Wolpert 1982, 215). Macaulay wrote a minute on education that convinced a majority of Bentinck's council to overturn the Orientalist support for Indian learning and languages. Macaulay's vision was to make a universal out of a particular, to assimilate all mankind into the higher civilization of the educated Victorian. His goal was to form "a class of persons, Indian in blood and colour, but English in taste, in opinions, in morals, and in intellect" (Wolpert 1982, 215).[5] In 1835, Bentinck's council agreed to allocate its educational funds to teaching western learning to young Indians in the English language. By 1885, English higher education had produced a national Indian elite who had "studied the classics of English literature and . . . followed . . . the course of politics in Europe [including] the rise of nationalism" (Coupland 1944, 23). The national elite were on the road to liberal universalism. In 1885, seventy-two of them met in Bombay to form the Indian National Congress. They imagined (or most did) that India would be a nation, constituted by individuals acting on majoritarian principles.

## REACTION AGAINST LIBERAL UNIVERSALISM

A new discourse began after the 1857 revolt by Indian troops against their British officers and against British rule more generally. The revolt destroyed British confidence; loss of control—not only military but also cultural—was unexpected and sudden. "Henceforth, the British in India would always walk in fear . . . now the British stepped back permanently into their neat little compound, fenced and right-angled, of facts and rules" (Fowler 1988, 150).[6]

Queen Victoria's 1858 proclamation repudiated and reversed the utilitarian- and evangelical-inspired liberal universalism of company policy that extended from Bentinck and Macaulay in the 1830s through Dalhousie in the 1850s. Yet the retreat functioned to moderate rather than eliminate the processes of rationalization and universalization already set in motion.

Nonintervention was thought an appropriate remedy for the causes believed to have led to the 1857 revolt—utilitarian and evangelical inspired "reforms" and "annexations" under the doctrine of "lapse" (Stokes 1959).[7] The queen, who in 1877 was made Queen-Empress of the British empire in India, pledged to respect and protect India's alien diversity, including its religious practices. The proclamation declared

> it to be our royal will and pleasure that none be in anywise favoured, none molested or disquieted, by reason of their religious faith or observances, but that all shall alike enjoy the equal and impartial protection of the law; and we do strictly charge and enjoin all those who may be in authority under us that they abstain from all interference with religious belief or worship of any of our subjects on pain of our highest displeasure. (Wolpert 1982, 240–41)

Victoria's retreat from the utilitarians' efforts to rationalize Indian administration and to codify Indian law left Indian society with a viable group life, but stood in tension with an incompatible universalizing discourse.

## GROUP RIGHTS AS DEFENSE AGAINST MAJORITARIANISM

Legal pluralism and legal universalism provide different types of protection. Legal pluralism defends group rights against majoritarianism. For this reason Sir Sayyid Ahmad Khan, the preeminent Muslim modernist reformer, contributed mightily to the British resurrection of a corporate theory of Indian society. Sir Sayyid found the formal creation of Indian nationalism in 1885 by anglicized liberal universalists a threat and a challenge. From his perspective, Muslims had much to fear from claims that an Indian nation existed. Few Muslims had responded to Macaulay's call to become "English in taste, in opinions, in morals, and in intellect," or to Sir Charles Wood's call to be educated in English language learning. Sir Sayyid typified the ambivalence of his time. On one hand, he encouraged Muslims to join Anglo-Victorian universalism, founding the Muhammedan Anglo-Oriental College at Aligarh to create an alternative anglicized elite among Muslims (Gilbert 1973, 171–206). On the other hand, he created a protective arena for Muslim group rights.

Sir Sayyid found it difficult to accept Congress's one nation theory. For him India was "inhabited by different nationalities"; India's institutions had to take that fact into account. In 1883, in a debate in the Governor-General's Council on the Central Provinces (now Madhya Pradesh) Local Self Government Bill, he warned the council that

> in borrowing from England the system of representative institutions, it is of the greatest importance to remember the socio-political matters in which India is distinguishable from England. . . . India . . . is inhabited by vast populations of different races and creeds. . . . The community of race and creed makes the people one and the same nation. . . . [T]he whole of England forms but one community. . . . [I]n India . . . there is no fusion of the various races . . . the system of election, pure and simple [that is, majority rule], cannot be adopted. (Quoted in Coupland 1944, 156)

Without a homogeneous nation—and in Sir Sayyid's view, India for the foreseeable future could not be a homogeneous nation—safeguards such as reserved seats, separate electorates, weightage (extra seats for minorities), and nominated members were necessary to insure "due and just balance in the representation of the various sections of the Indian population" (Coupland 1944, 155–56).

Muhammad Ali Jinnah, the father of Pakistan and its Qaid-i-Azam (great leader), was a figurative son of Aligarh—that is, the kind of anglicized modern Muslim that Sir Sayyid sought to create. Jinnah too, fearing a Hindu majority, searched for mechanisms that would allow a Muslim community to have its fair share of seats in the chambers of government. Sir Sayyid had spoken of "many nations"; in 1937, Jinnah began speaking of two, Pakistan and India. With partition into two successor states in 1947, 10 percent (35 million then, 110 million now) of India's population were Muslims. How, without rajlike safeguards, was the new state to recognize and legitimate difference and protect minority rights in a parliamentary democracy with universal suffrage and majority rule?

## COMMUNAL RESERVATIONS AS GROUP ENTITLEMENT

In preindependence India, the answer to Sir Sayyid's challenge—how to reconcile minority rights with majority rule—was communal reservations. Until the second half of the nineteenth century, the colonial government's policy had expressed the group principle mainly through legal practice in the arena of personal law. As representation of Indians was timidly and haltingly introduced into local and provincial governments in the 1880s, the principle took on politi-

minorities to stop thinking in terms of subnational minority groups. "I have all along held," he said, "that India is one nation." His resolution carried "with nearly everyone present agreeing or saying they did" (Austin 1966, 154).

Partition had taught not one but two lessons: that minority safeguards, particularly reservations, can harden cleavages that lead to secession; and that Muslims in partitioned India would continue to feel endangered by what many perceived as a Hindu majority. Muslims needed reassurance that their corporate identity was recognized and that their corporate life was secure.

## GROUP RIGHTS FOR LOWER CASTES

If religious categories prior to independence dominated the debates about legal pluralism, since independence and increasingly at the dawn of the millennium other social categories, notably caste and women, have moved into the foreground.

As we have seen, reservations of legislative seats for scheduled castes (SCs) and tribes (STs) survived in Articles 330 and 332 of the constitution when those for religious groups were eliminated. The provisions for SCs and STs had their forerunners in the British privileging of so-called backward castes, expressed in their protection, via "communal awards," of non-Brahman castes in the south beginning in the 1910s (Irshick 1969). Positive or protective discrimination on behalf of depressed or backward classes in public employment (but not in legislatures), already commonplace in the south, was extended nationally in the 1990s by wide-ranging reservations on behalf of other backward classes (OBCs)—an administrative euphemism for the lower castes traditionally ranked above the ex-untouchables (Galanter 1984; Rudolph and Rudolph 1983 [1967]). Such new expressions of legal pluralism were generated by the horizontal mobilization of lower castes in the countryside, where 75 percent of India's voting population lives. Their high levels of participation in national and state electoral politics has radically transformed the sociological profile of India's national parliament, state assemblies, and their cabinets. The rise of the OBCs in first state and then national politics has tended to marginalize the upper-caste, upper-class elites who dominated Congress party politics in the Nehru-Gandhi dynasty era.

A second backward classes commission (Government of India, Backward Classes Commission 1980) chaired by B. P. Mandal was established to try to implement what the constitution seemed to promise, reservations for other backward classes.[12] Reporting in 1980, the Mandal Commission presented the country with an anthropological index organized by states specifying 3,743 backward castes. These were the castes said to qualify as beneficiaries under the constitutional clauses urging special care for "backward" citizens.[13] The commission estimated that backward castes listed in its report constituted 52 percent of the population; it recommended, however, that only 27 percent reservations be set aside for the OBCs listed. Reservations totaling 52 percent when added to the 22.5 percent already reserved for SCs and STs would violate the Supreme

Court's standard in *Balaji* that reservations totaling more than 50 percent would be a fraud on the constitution, in part because exceeding 50 percent would unduly encroach on the equal rights clauses of the constitution.

Even before the Mandal Commission made its recommendations, many Indian states already had enacted legislation providing reservations in educational institutions and government jobs for backward castes. When Prime Minister V. P. Singh's government began to implement the Mandal Commission recommendations in 1990, the BJP, protecting its upper-caste and bazaar merchant constituency, withdrew its support from his coalition government and soon after launched a rath-yatra, or national pilgrimage, on behalf of Hindutva. After riots and self-immolations mainly by disgruntled upper-caste, upper-class students, the government fell and a midterm election followed. In 1991, a Congress government under Prime Minister Narasimha Rao took office. It too began cautiously to implement the Mandal Commission's recommendations. By 2000, the BJP had executed a 180-degree turn on Mandal, fully embracing and even expanding reservations. Today, OBC politics and reservations have been, if not fully normalized, at least accepted as part of the rules of the game. Legal pluralism in the form of reservations for particular lower castes seems well established at the start of the twenty-first century.

## MINORITY RIGHTS FOR RELIGIOUS COMMUNITIES OR A UNIFORM CIVIL CODE?

After independence in 1947, religious collectivities continued to claim exemption from universal rules. Having wiped out reservations of legislative seats on the basis of religion, the constituent assembly proceeded to write Article 29, which guarantees the right to maintain distinct cultures. "Any section of the citizens of India . . . having a distinct language, script [Gurmukhi was a script used by Sikhs; Urdu by Muslims] or culture [a euphemism for religion] shall have the right to preserve the same." Article 30 guarantees the right of religious minorities to establish educational institutions and bars the state, which supports private educational institutions—including religious ones—from discriminating against them.[14] Both articles raise the question of whether it is constitutionally permissible to have different laws for different groups defined according to religion. Not really, the constituent assembly wanted to say; it almost said as much. The constituent assembly almost asserted that a uniform civil code supersedes the varieties of personal law—but at the last minute, it held its hand.

At the urging of liberals such as Minoo Masani, Amrit Kaur, and Hansa Mehta, the constituent assembly considered including a uniform civil code in the justiciable provisions of the constitution (Dhagamwar 1993, 218–21). Abolishing the differences in personal law would "get rid of these watertight compartments," said Masani, "which keep the nation divided" (Austin 1966, 80).

The provision died in committee but eventually was included in the Directive Principles of State Policy, nonjusticiable articles (36 through 51) included in Part

IV of the constitution. The directive principles articulate the imagined social revolution of the Nehruvian nationalist generation; they express purposes and goals but create no justiciable rights. The hesitancy to include an actionable uniform civil code in the constitution reflected the other face of the Nehruvian secular nationalists: their concern for the sensibilities and needs of India's religious minorities. They were to be not only citizens with equal rights but also members of religious communities whose different cultures and identities would be secure and honored through the continued existence and viability of their personal law.

## FROM PROTECTIVE DISCRIMINATION TO POPULIST PLURALISM

In the 1990s, universal principles came to be espoused by strange bedfellows. In the constituent assembly of 1950, advocates of a uniform civil code (UCC) were enlightenment liberals and secularists. In the 1990s, the most forceful advocates of the UCC became the anti-Muslim Hindu nationalist Bharatiya Janata Party. Embracing universalism in the form of a uniform civil code enabled the BJP to combine Hindu majority nationalism with ending so-called privileges for minorities—particularly the Muslim minority. Support for a UCC placed the BJP on the same side as equal rights activists, notably feminists who deplored what they regarded as the subjection and oppression of women under Islamic law and practice. At the same time, a uniform civil code provided a respectable way to end the "pampering" of Muslims by denying them "special privileges," such as males being allowed to have multiple wives and unilaterally divorce them. For the BJP and its allies in the sangh pariwar (family of Hindu associations) the legal universalism of the UCC became a respectable way to be anti-Muslim. As a result, some liberal pluralists and feminists developed second thoughts about mandating a UCC. By the late 1990s, however, the BJP reversed itself, adapting to its political circumstances; it came to recognize that accepting group claims and minority rights had become a condition of success in the complex task of coalition making. Further, the BJP moved beyond protective discrimination of the disadvantaged to a populist pluralism designed to mobilize advantaged groups.

The BJP had begun its rise to fame and fortune in the 1990s as a party of integral nationalism, of a Hindutva ideology and rath-yatras (chariot pilgrimages) that crisscrossed Bharat's sacred spaces featuring a symbolically caged, martial Lord Ram. Millions en route came to see him, and to endorse this image of a semitized Hinduism of one God, Lord Rama, one book, the Ramayana, and one people. Identities based on caste, community, class, religion, region, or language were to be subordinated to a Hindu identity and subsumed by a Hindu nation. Minorities no longer were to be privileged and pampered. Muslims and Christians were stereotyped as suspect persons: said to be the progeny of foreign conquest and alien creeds, their loyalty doubted, they were sometimes made victims of a theory and practice of cultural racism.[15]

The rath-yatras led to intense mobilization of Hindu extremism that crested on

December 6, 1992, in the nationally televised destruction of the Babri Masjid (Babar's Mosque).[16] This mobilization was not simply an act of fanatics; it reflected the BJP's effort to establish Hindu nationalist uniformity to counter caste-based legal particularism. The media summarized the struggle as Mandir (Hindu temple) versus Mandal—that is, Hindu unity versus caste reservations. In 1990, as mentioned earlier, in a move that surprised not only the country at large but also supporters of the government—including at that time the BJP—Prime Minister V. P. Singh moved to implement the long-quiescent Mandal Commission report recommending that reservations in central government jobs and educational institutions up to 27 percent be made available to OBCs. V.P. Singh's rivals read him as going for a midterm election in which he would lead a national coalition of parties catering to the disadvantaged minorities—the OBCs, the SCs and STs making up 49 percent of the population, and the Muslims whose 11 percent would ensure victory to Mandal particularism. The BJP's response was Mandir universalism. When V.P. Singh launched Mandal reservations, the BJP began to play the Hindu card that it had spent decades preparing: regardless of caste and creed, region or language, all Indians were children of a Hindu civilization.

For a moment in the early 1990s, the BJP appeared to some to be the wave of the future, a new dominant party to replace the Congress. In the post-rath-yatra, post-Hindutva tenth national election in 1991, the BJP more or less doubled its vote share, up from 11.5 percent in 1989 to 20 percent, and increased its seat share by almost 50 percent, jumping to 120 (of 545) parliamentary seats from 86 in 1989. Yet by the eleventh national election in 1996, the wave seemed to have crested. The party's vote share remained more or less constant at 20.3 percent, but its yield of seats increased to 161 from 120 as it picked up seats from the Congress in multicornered contests.

The party's postelection experience proved sobering. The eleventh national election, like the ninth and tenth, had yielded another hung parliament in which the BJP was the single largest party. Following convention, President R. Venkataraman gave Atal Behari Vajpayee, the BJP's parliamentary leader, two weeks to try to form a government. Despite skilled wooing and generous incentives, no party was prepared to cross the aisle to join the BJP as the head of a coalition government. The BJP found itself treated as a pariah, an outcast. Its hand in the violence and lawlessness that destroyed the Babri Masjid, its "communalist" minority threatening Hindutva ideology, and its three Hindutva policy planks—the demand for a uniform civil code, removing Article 370 (the constitutional provision giving Muslim-majority Kashmir autonomous status), and building a temple for Lord Rama at the site of the Babri Masjid—proved to be anathema to possible partners.

The BJP entered the subsequent 1998 and 1999 parliamentary elections as a centrist rather than an extremist party. The party put its Hindutva ideology on a back burner, dropped its three Hindutva policy planks, and moved skillfully to create a preelection coalition (principally with regional parties) based on a common minimum program. Since regional parties were willing to join with a BJP that presented itself as architect of a moderate centrist coalition, the 1998 and

1999 elections resulted in BJP-led National Democratic Alliance (NDA) governments. In 1998, although its vote increased to 25.6 percent from 20 percent and its seats to 181 from 161, the party again did not make the hoped-for breakthrough to majority status. The BJP could not, it seems, realize its aspiration to replace Congress as India's dominant party. The 1999 election results seemed to confirm that the BJP had reached a plateau in its efforts to garner votes and seats. The BJP's vote share dropped to 23.8 percent and its seats remained steady at 182. The party's success in forming the 1999 BJP-led NDA coalition government, with regional parties playing leading roles, depended on its abandoning Hindutva extremism for centrist moderation. The old party system of one dominant centrist party—the Congress—producing majority governments had ended with the ninth national election in 1989. A centrist BJP by 1999 had learned to master the new multiparty coalition government party system.

After the trauma of 1996, the moderate BJP leadership executed a U-turn in its relationship to universalism and particularism in the face of objections from the sangh parivar. The smoke and mirrors of Hindutva ideology, the universalism of India as a Hindu nation, obscured the fact that the BJP had only a limited support base. Hindutva proved to be the ideology of northern India's urban upper (twice born) castes and higher-income, better-educated classes, particularly of the party's long-standing core supporters, upper-caste Hindu bazaar merchants. In its effort to broaden its base and appeal, the party began to embrace the very Mandal strategy it had sought to counter with Mandir: it began cultivating support from the OBCs and negotiating alliances with regional parties.

Of the 296 members of parliament supporting the BJP-led NDA coalition government after the 1999 election, 114 were members of regional parties. These BJP allies were supported more by lower than upper castes, the poor more than the rich, and the secular than the Hindutva-minded. Quite apart from the alliance's common minimum program and Prime Minister Vajpayee's positioning as a moderate in his own party, the BJP-led government was constrained by the ideologies, policy preferences, and support bases of its regional party allies to be centrist and moderate.

The BJP's reversal in relation to Mandal Commission reservations involved particular policies for wooing of state parties such as the AIA-DMK (All India Anna Dravida Munnetra Kazhagam) and the DMK in the southern state of Tamilnadu (formerly Madras). Tamilnadu had a long history dating back to the 1920s of anti-Brahmanism, a movement closely associated with establishing reservations for backward castes (Rudolph and Rudolph 1983 [1967], 33–87). The castes involved often were backward in ritual rank when compared to Brahmans but politically and economically dominant and thus forward in the countryside, where most Tamilnadu's voters live. As a consequence, Tamilnadu's reservations for backward castes and SCs taken together have for some years exceeded the Supreme Court–mandated 50 percent. The BJP moved to please its southern coalition partners, sheltering state-level reservations that exceeded 50 percent by placing them in the constitution's ninth schedule, where they are immune from court challenge.[17]

The BJP also succeeded for a time in augmenting its OBC base in the north.

Kalyan Singh, an OBC leader and a Hindu nationalist for some time, served twice as BJP chief minister of Uttar Pradesh. In consequence, the BJP was able to rule India's most populous state with substantial support from OBC voters. With Kalyan Singh's de facto defection during the 1999 parliamentary election, the BJP experienced disastrous losses in Uttar Pradesh, dropping from 57 to 30 of Uttar Pradesh's 85 seats. Sensing trouble in Uttar Pradesh, the BJP scrambled to consolidate its position elsewhere in the north. Late in the campaign it promised to categorize as OBCs the Jats of Rajasthan. Although in ritual rank terms Jats counted as shudras, in contemporary Indian society they were perceived by most bureaucratic and academic observers as a relatively prosperous and educated middle caste. Historically, Jats were reputed for their prowess as agriculturalists (in Punjab, Haryana, and western Uttar Pradesh), as politicians (Charan Singh had served as prime minister and Devi Lal as deputy prime minister), and for supplying ruling lineages for two of Rajasthan's twenty-two erstwhile princely states.[18] Immediately after the election, the BJP delivered on its campaign promise by declaring Rajasthan's Jats (and 125 other castes) eligible for OBC reservations (see *Times of India*, November 21, 1999).

It was a fateful choice, suggesting that advantaged as well as backward castes could be read as OBCs. The immediate fruit of the campaign promise was to balance the Uttar Pradesh losses with significant gains for BJP in Rajasthan. Its seats jumped from 5 (of 25) in 1998 to 16 in 1999, a gain of 11 seats while Congress slumped from 18 to 9. Rajasthan's Congress chief minister had opposed the listing as an attempt by an advantaged middle caste to muscle in on scarce reservations. The reservations for Rajasthan Jats immediately led to demands to extend reservations to Jats in other north Indian states.

Jat reservations read in tandem with BJP efforts to allow reservations in the south to exceed 50 percent suggest that India's perspective on pluralism was on the verge of a fundamental transformation—turning from reservations for the disadvantaged to proportionate representation for all castes. In early April 2000, a decision of the NDA cabinet further threatened the 50–50 formula enunciated in *Balaji*: it shepherded through parliament the Eighty-first Amendment Act. The act countered the 1993 Supreme Court's reiteration in *Indra Sawhney v. Union of India* that not more than half of all government jobs could be subject to reservations. The Eighty-first Amendment authorizes government to exempt the backlog of unfilled reserved seats in government jobs carried over from the previous year from the overall 50 percent ceiling on reservations (Basu 2001, 160). *India Today* spoke for a good deal of editorial opinion when it strongly objected, "The 50 percent limit was an eminently sensible one that reconciled social justice with meritocracy" (*India Today*, April 10, 2000).

## CAN SPLITTING THE DIFFERENCE HOLD?

Reservations for backward castes have helped to promote equality of opportunity in a society noted for a debilitating caste hierarchy. In this sense, OBC reservations have deepened and strengthened democracy in India. Much has been written and said about how fair distribution of the benefits and costs of economic development can strengthen democracy. In similar fashion, OBC reservations can strengthen democracy by promoting a more fair distribution of status. The politics of OBC reservations have fueled identity politics, a symbolic politics of self and social definition. OBC reservations are an aspect of a social revolution that has changed the balance of political power in favor of lower castes as well as expanding group esteem. Despite the fact that OBC reservations reach relatively few and despite the fact that they threaten standards in government performance and education, they have helped to give low-status castes a stake in the social and political order. According to Yogendra Yadav, reservations, combined with lower-caste political mobilization and participation in democratic voting, "did bring about something of a revolution. . . . The role of ritual Hindu hierarchy as a predictor of secular power has diminished dramatically over the last fifty years" (Yadav 1999, 35). The imperatives of democratic politics in a pluralist society have had curiously contradictory effects. On one hand, political prudence has led the BJP to shelve a nationalist universalism threatening to the cultural identity of minorities. An exclusivist party found that greater inclusivity pays political dividends. Again, the same imperatives have led the BJP, an upper-caste party, to a pluralism formally respectful of lower-caste claims. These can be counted as gains. On the other hand, a democratic propensity to expand as well as contest support bases is moving India from a policy of protective discrimination for disadvantaged castes toward a policy of proportionate representation of many castes. India is moving from protective discrimination to populist pluralism. The result has been to challenge the 50–50 balance designed by the Supreme Court to split the difference between liberal universalism and multicultural pluralism.

The 50–50 balance forged by the Supreme Court in *Balaji* between the universalist equal citizenship clauses of the constitution and the pluralist clauses that protect cultural minorities and benefit disadvantaged-status groups have served India well. The balance splits the difference between contradictory criteria: treating all citizens equally on one hand and protecting group rights and claims on the other. The Supreme Court has found ways over the years to hold these contradictory principles in dynamic tension. Whether the court will be able to protect equal citizenship and merit along with minority rights in the face of powerful political pressures for reservations for advantaged as well as disadvantaged castes and a common Hindu nationalist identity remains for the future to reveal.

## NOTES

1. The Supreme Court in *Balaji v. State of Mysore* stated,

   There can be no doubt that the Constitution-makers assumed . . . that while making adequate reservation under article 16(4) [which permits reservations in government employment or government-funded institutions, such as universities, for "any backward class of citizens"] care would be taken not to provide for unreasonable, excessive or extravagant reservation . . . therefore . . . reservations made under article 16(4) beyond the permissible and legitimate limits would be liable to be challenged *as a fraud on the Constitution.* (Basu 1994a, 93)

For constitutional provisions and detailed commentary on them based on case law, including a discussion of percentages, see Basu's humorously named 2,000-page *Shorter Constitution of India* (1994b, 81).

*Balaji* was confirmed in the monumental decision on reservations of 1993, *Indra Sawhney v. Union of India*:

Clause (4) [of Article 16] should be strictly construed and in a manner that does not render the guarantee in Clause (1) altogether nugatory or illusory. . . . Thus in the interests of the backward class of citizens the State cannot reserve all the appointments under the State or even a majority of them.

Summary in Basu (2001, 152).

2.  Article 29 provides that "any section of the citizens of India . . . having a distinct language, script [such as Gurmukhi for Sikhs and Urdu for many Muslims] or culture [the identity and way of life—the ethnicity—inter alia of Muslims, Sikhs, Christians] shall have the right to conserve the same." According to Basu, Article 29 protects "the cultural, linguistic and similar rights of any section of the community who might constitute a 'minority' from the . . . democratic machine . . . being used as an engine of oppression by the numerical majority" (Basu 1994a, 367). Article 25 guarantees individual citizens the right to "profess, practice and propagate" their religious beliefs, and Article 256 guarantees to "any denomination and any section thereof" the right to "manage its own affairs in matters of religion."

3.  Mehta (1999, 154–55) develops the following distinction with respect to India.

Burke reflected on and wrote about various major sites of the empire—Ireland, America, and India. . . . [He saw that] the British empire was neither predominately Protestant nor Anglophone . . . [and] the exercise of power and authority was implicated with considerations of cultural and racial diversity, contrasting civilizational unities, the absence of . . . consensual government, and alternative norms of political identity and legitimacy.

If for Burke, difference was all—that is, if persons were always and inevitably marked—for Locke, sameness was all. Human nature was the same everywhere and always. For Mehta, Locke's ideas in *Two Treatises on Government* capture "liberal universalism," a world of "transhistorical, transcultural, and most certainly transracial" principles and persons. "Institutions such as laws, representation, contract all have their justification in a characterization of human beings that eschews names, social status, ethnic background, gender, and race. . . . [T]he universal claims can be made because they derive from certain characteristics that are common to all human beings" (Mehta 1999, 51–52).

4.  From *Proceedings of the Committee of Circuit at Kasimbazaar*, 15 August 1772, quoted in Majumdar (1952). For a longer discussion of Warren Hastings's role in the initial defining of difference see Rudolph and Rudolph 1997, 219–51.

5.  The high point of the Bentinck era's liberal universalism was probably Article 47 of the East India Charter Act of 1833, which was more honored in the breach than in the

observance. The article proclaimed, "No Native of said Territories . . . shall, by reason of only of his religion, place of birth, descent, colour, or any of them be disabled from holding any Place, Office, or Employment under the said Company" (Wolpert 1982, 213). Some thought that Nirad Chaudhry, who died at 101 at Oxford on July 31, 1999, epitomized what Macaulay had in mind; he was the world's "last Englishman." See Ian Jack in the obituary in *Front Line*, August 27, 1999.

6. Fowler's romantic pen contrasts Lord Auckland's (George Eden, governor-general from 1836 to 1842) sister, Emily Eden's, easy familiarity and admiration for Indians and things Indian with Charlotte Canning's (wife of Lord Canning, governor-general before and during the 1857 revolt and viceroy from 1858 until 1862) alienation from and fear of India. After 1857, such "easy conviviality between Indian ruler and English was . . . gone forever. . . . They sensed that the Indians hated them; and so they ruled with an iron hand, but one which trembled a little" (Fowler 1988, 150).

7. "Lapse" was a doctrine practiced particularly by Governor-General Dalhousie (1848–1856) barring succession in princely states of adopted heirs. For a comprehensive and insightful account of the motives and consequences of annexation see Fisher 1993.

8. For a critical perspective on reservations by a scholar sympathetic to the Muslim role in preindependence politics see Hardy 1972.

9. The fast was seen by Dr. B. R. Ambedkar, leader of the untouchables and subsequently the law minister who guided the drafting of free India's constitution, as an attempt by conservative Hinduism to deny autonomy to untouchables. The fast was the opening drama for Gandhi's extended campaign throughout the 1930s against the practice of untouchability—a campaign seen by today's radical Dalits as paternalistic and demeaning, but which led to the special provisions on behalf of scheduled castes (ex-untouchables) in the constitution. For some aspects of the debate see Rudolph and Rudolph 1983 [1967].

10. See Articles 330 and 332 reserving seats in national and state legislatures for scheduled tribes and scheduled castes. Unless renewed and extended, the reservations were to expire in ten years after the coming into force of the constitution, in 1950. (Reservations have been renewed by amendment in each ten-year period since 1950.)

11. See Austin 1966, 151–54, for a discussion of the ambivalent quality of some of this support.

12. The first backward classes commission was chaired in 1955 by Kaka Kalelkar, who concluded that "backwardness could be tackled on the basis or a number of bases other than that of caste" (Transmittal letter, Government of India, Backward Classes Commission 1955, vol. 1, n.p.).

13. The constitution evades using the term *caste* and refers rather to "backward classes," evidence of the founders' interest in privileging criteria other than caste. Special provisions for "socially and educationally backward classes" are exempted from the prohibition, under Article 15, of discrimination on grounds of religion, race, caste, sex, and place of birth. Article 340 provides for the appointment of a commission to investigate the conditions of the backwards and recommend remedies (Government of India, Backward Classes Commission 1980, 63, 92). The Supreme Court declared the Mandal reservations valid in *Indra Sawhney v. Union of India* (1993).

14. The high bar, sometimes referred to as "a wall of separation," between the state and religious institutions, including educational institutions, that characterizes U.S. practice does not govern Indian law and practice, nor did it British, where state grants in aid to religious institutions are common practice subject to certain standards.

15. For the background, context, and character of BJP ideology and politics see Andersen and Damle 1987; Jaffrelot 1996; Hansen and Jaffrelot 1998; Hansen 1999.

16. See Hansen 1999, 182–85, for a detailed account of the background, execution, and immediate consequences of the destruction.

17. It is possible that the placing of this legislation in the ninth schedule could be challenged as violating the "basic structure" doctrine enunciated in *Keshavananda Bharati v. Union of India*.

18. "Just before the last Lok Sabha elections, the Jat Mahasabha in Rajasthan called upon the community not to vote for the Congress for its failure to secure for them this reservation. The BJP promptly stepped in to champion the cause of reservation for Jats" (Behera 1999).

# REFERENCES

Andersen, Walter, and Shridar Damle. 1987. *Brotherhood in Saffron*. Boulder, Colo.: Westview Press.

Austin, Granville. 1966. *The Indian Constitution*. New York: Oxford University Press.

Basu, Durga Das. 1994a. *Introduction to the Constitution of India*. 16th ed. New Delhi: Prentice Hall of India.

———. 1994b. *Shorter Constitution of India*. 11th ed. New Delhi: Prentice Hall of India.

———. 2001. *Shorter Constitution of India*. 13th ed. Nagpur: Wadhwa.

Behera, Ashok K. 1999. "BJP Runs into OBC Reality." *The Statesman*, November 19, 1999.

Cannon, Garland. 1970. *Letters of Sir William Jones*. 2 vols. London: Oxford University Press.

Colebrooke, Henry Thomas. 1883 [1798]. *Two Treatieses on the Hindu Law of Inheritance*. Calcutta: B. Bannerjee.

———. 1830. "On Hindu Courts of Justice." *Transactions of the Royal Asiatic Society of Great Britain and Ireland*. London: Parbury, Allen.

Coupland, Reginald. 1944. *The Indian Problem: Report on the Constitutional Problem in India*. Vol. 1. New York: Oxford University Press.

Dhagamwar, Vasuda. 1993. "Women, Children and the Constitution." In *Religion and Law in Independent India*, edited by Robert D. Baird. New Delhi: Manohar.

Doniger, Wendy K., trans. 1991. *The Laws of Manu*. New Delhi and London: Penguin Books.

Eaton, Richard. 1993. *The Rise of Islam and the Bengal Frontier, 1214–1760*. Berkeley: University of California Press.

Fisher, Michael H., ed. 1993. *The Politics of the British Annexation of India, 1757–1857*. New Delhi: Oxford University Press.

Fowler, Marian. 1988. *Below the Peacock Fan: First Ladies of the Raj*. London and New Delhi: Penguin Books.

Galanter, Marc. 1984. *Competing Inequalities: Law and the Backward Classes in India*. New Delhi: Oxford University Press.

Gilbert, Irene. 1973. "Autonomy and Consensus Under the Raj: Presidency (Calcutta); Muir (Allahabad); M.A.O. (Aligarh)." In *Education and Politics in India*, edited by Lloyd I. Rudolph and Susanne Hoeber Rudolph (171–206). Cambridge, Mass.: Harvard University Press.

Government of India. Backward Classes Commission. 1955. *Report of the Backward Classes Commission* (*Kalelkar Report*). New Delhi: Manager of Publications.

———. 1980. *Report of the Backward Classes Commission* (Mandal Report). New Delhi: Manager of Publications.

Government of India. Supreme Court. 1963. *Balaji v. State of Mysore*, All India Reporter, Sup. Ct. 647: 664 (1963).

———. 1993. *Indra Sawhney v. Union of India*. All India Reporter, Sup. Ct. 477 (1993).

Hansen, Thomas Blom, and Christophe Jaffrelot, eds. 1998. *The BJP and the Compulsions of Politics in India*. New Delhi: Oxford University Press.

Hansen, Thomas Blom. 1999. *The Saffron Wave: Democracy and Hindu Nationalism in Modern India*. New Delhi: Oxford University Press.

Hardy, Peter. 1972. *The Muslims of British India*. Cambridge: Cambridge University Press.

Hirschman, Albert. 1970. *Exit, Voice and Loyalty*. Cambridge, Mass.: Harvard University Press.

Irshick, Eugene. 1969. *Politics and Social Conflict in South India: The Non-Brahman Movement and Tamil Separatism*. New Delhi: Oxford University Press.

Jaffrelot, Christophe. 1996. *The Hindu Nationalist Movement in Indian Politics*. New York: Columbia University Press.

Kejariwal, O. P. 1988. *Asiatic Society of Bengal and the Discovery of India's Past*. New Delhi: Oxford University Press.

Majumdar, R. C., ed. 1952. *History and Culture of the Indian People*. Vol. 8. London: Allen & Unwin.

Mehta, Uday Singh. 1999. *Liberalism and Empire: A Study in Nineteenth-Century British Liberal Thought*. Chicago: University of Chicago Press.

Rudolph, Lloyd I., and Susanne Hoeber Rudolph. 1997. "Occidentalism and Orientalism: Perspectives on Legal Pluralism." In *Cultures of Scholarship*, edited by Sally Humphreys. Ann Arbor: University of Michigan Press.

———. 1973. *Education and Politics in India*. Cambridge, Mass.: Harvard University Press.

———. 1983 [1967]. *The Modernity of Tradition*. Chicago: University of Chicago Press.

Stokes, Eric. 1959. *The English Utilitarians in India*. Oxford: Clarendon Press.

Wolpert, Stanley. 1982. *A New History of India*. New York: Oxford University Press.

Yadav, Yogendra. 1999. "Politics." In *India Briefing: A Transformative Fifty Years*, edited by Marshall Bouton and Philip Oldenburg. Armonk, N.Y.: M. E. Sharpe.

# Chapter 3

## Legislating Religious Freedom: Muslim Challenges to the Relationship Between Church and State in Germany and France

### Katherine Pratt Ewing

For many Americans and other inhabitants of the modern world, the ideal of living under a democratic government includes the enjoyment of religious freedom. Americans tend to presume that religious freedom can only be ensured by the principle of the separation of church and state, as articulated in two clauses of the First Amendment to the U.S. Constitution: "Congress shall make no law respecting the establishment of religion, or prohibiting the free exercise thereof. . . ." The intent of this separation is to make religion a private matter, so that individuals may freely choose whether and how to practice a religion. An absolute separation between church and state, however, is by no means simple to maintain. Religion is invariably a social phenomenon (as Emile Durkheim demonstrated in his classic *Elementary Forms of the Religious Life*), and the state inevitably finds itself dealing with religious communities and institutions that transcend the individuals involved. Though the metaphor of a wall is the most pervasive trope used to conceptualize the church-state relationship in the United States, in practice the wall is quite porous; indeed, the government and religious practice are intertwined in many ways.[1]

In the United States, issues surrounding infringement of religious freedom and questions about whether certain practices represent government establishment or support of religion have been subject to scholarly scrutiny and increasing litigation only since the 1940s. One reason for the increasing contestation over how to implement this provision of the Bill of Rights is the changing relationship between minority practices and those of the mainstream, which until recently had been unself-consciously Christian Protestant. There has been a tremendous expansion of cases claiming that an individual's or group's right to the free exercise of religion has been infringed by the provisions of universally applicable laws.[2] In response to such cases, Congress enacted the Religious Freedom Restoration Act in 1993 that in turn was struck down in 1997.[3] On the other side, invocations of the establishment clause of the First Amendment have challenged aspects of public practices previously taken for granted as generically spiritual that are now objected to as Christian. While Americans have become more self-conscious about church-and-state issues and about the rights of minorities more generally, increasing secularization of public spaces is not an inevitable trend. Recently, a shift away from making public spaces as secular as possible and toward religious pluralism can be seen in a Supreme Court ruling allowing display of religious symbols as a free-speech issue and recent efforts to bring study of religion and the Bible into the classroom.[4]

As in the United States, where minorities have challenged previously taken for granted government and other public practices tinged with Christian symbolism, many European countries where Muslims are a relatively recent but rapidly growing minority are being forced to reconsider their existing solutions to conflicts over religious freedom. Responses to these Muslim challenges—often colored in the political arena by popular perceptions of radical Islam and its presumed threat to democracy—have brought issues of the relationship between religion and state into politics, courtrooms, and newspapers as Muslims (both as individuals and groups) object to what they see as unequal treatment of their own religious practices under existing laws. In the process, these challenges highlight the fact that in recent history, European countries have handled issues of religious freedom and secularism and their implementation in public policy and the law in different ways. In consequence, efforts to manage and accommodate Muslim challenges have given rise to different discourses and solutions surrounding the idea of religion in its relation to the state.

Several distinct issues often are conflated: religious freedom, secularism, relations between church and state, and individual versus group rights. A reconsideration of the relationships among these issues is particularly timely. The principle of church-state separation and privatization of religion as a matter of individual rights in the second half of the twentieth century have been taken as the paradigmatic solution of the problem of religious difference and diversity. Furthermore, this principle of individual rights has been expanded as a model for handling cultural and ethnic difference more broadly, often with less than satisfactory results.

Yet now, confronted by ethnic conflicts that have erupted in one nation-state after another, scholars and policy makers have sought new solutions that go beyond the idea of individual rights. The philosopher Will Kymlicka, for instance, is among those who have advocated reconsidering minority rights in terms of group rights. Kymlicka has been active in offering suggestions to governments all over the world about how best to handle their minority populations, and he has gone so far as to promote some version of "separate but equal" in his writings and advice to governments (Zachary 2000). Kymlicka has argued that before World War II, many governments treated ethnic minorities as groups rather than as individuals with respect to the law and public policy. Following the Holocaust, however, was a perception that such group-focused policies had contributed to Germany's justification of expansionism, in the name of protecting ethnic Germans in other countries. Thus, after the war there was a shift away from protecting minority groups and toward emphasizing the human rights of the individual. It was assumed that if the rights of the individual were strictly protected, no further rights needed to be attributed to specific minority groups. Based on this understanding, the United Nations "deleted all references to the rights of ethnic and national minorities in its Universal Declaration of Human Rights" (Kymlicka 1995, 3).

This shift from minority rights to universal human rights was seen in postwar liberal thought as a natural extension of how religious minorities had been protected for centuries (Kymlicka 1995, 3). Postwar liberals may have thought that religious tolerance based on the separation of church and state and individual rights provided a good model for dealing with ethnocultural differences—a kind of "benign neglect" (Glazer 1975, 25). But this liberal notion of the church-state relationship in a modern democracy is an abstraction that does not accurately reflect the range of accommodations between church and state that continue to characterize European governments and the vicissitudes of actual practice in the United States. Now that the adequacy of the hands-off approach to ethnic and cultural diversity—the privatization of ethnicity—has been seriously challenged in a global environment where minority unrest is one of the main political concerns of our time, the search for new solutions must include a reexamination of the relationship between church and state as it actually has been played out in specific countries characterized by the presence of large religious minorities.

The classification of church-state systems in Western Europe traditionally has been based on a tripartition into *separation*, *concordatarian*, and *national church* systems. It has been argued recently that this classification focuses only on formal aspects and pays insufficient attention to the actual legal powers given to churches and protections afforded to individuals (Ferrari 1995). How the system actually works can best be seen in situations where the status quo has been challenged, since such challenges expose implicit understandings and accommodations that may not even be consistent with explicit doctrines and ideologies concerning the church-state relationship. Conflicts over the status quo are precisely what many countries in Europe are experiencing in recent decades, as they struggle to accommodate and assimilate large numbers of Muslims who were encouraged to come to these countries as unskilled labor in the 1960s, when economies were thriving and labor was in short supply.

The following discussion focuses on challenges that Muslim communities have raised to existing practices and law in Germany and France. Germany has a large Turkish immigrant population (2.4 percent of the population), and France has a large number of Muslims, primarily from the former colonies of Algeria and Morocco (1 percent of the population).[5] This chapter addresses the question of what these Muslim challenges and the array of responses to these challenges reveal of German and French discursive practices concerning the idea of religious freedom, the issue of individual versus group rights, and efforts to rethink the relationship between religion and state in a modern democracy.

however, did not abate until the twentieth century, and the French government has had many dealings with and given formal recognition to the various religious communities of Catholics, Protestants, and Jews, basing their interactions on the Catholic model of hierarchical authority and territorial organization (Torfs 1996, 958). Official neutrality through separation of church and state in many respects has given way to plurality.

We can see this in French efforts to create a satisfactory relationship with its Muslim population, who now constitute 1 percent of those who claim religious affiliation in France (in comparison with 15 percent church-attending Catholics, 2 percent Protestants, and 1 percent Jews; see Torfs 1996, 950). The French government has had difficulty responding to the needs of various Muslim communities because Muslims lack the single hierarchical structure characteristic of the other religious groups. France's interior minister in the mid–1990s, Charles Pasqua, who bore much of the responsibility for managing the highly visible and controversial expressions of political violence involving specific radical groups of Muslims at that time, felt that the lack of structure in the Muslim community was dangerous (Viorst 1996, 95). Expressing similar sentiments, members of the French government have articulated the wish that the Grand Mosque of Paris function as a "Muslim Vatican" (Viorst 1996, 80). The French government often uses the Imam of this mosque, who represents what the government sees as a moderate Islam, as a spokesperson for the Muslim "community." Yet when controversies arise involving Koran classes or the visible expression of Islam through the wearing of a head scarf, the principle of strict secularism in government spaces returns to center stage.

Germany too is accustomed to dealing with a central, hierarchically organized church administration, even among its large numbers of Protestants, and rights are accorded to religious groups rather than individuals. In contrast to France's laicism, churches in Germany are public-law corporations and can be subsumed under the category of concordatarian systems, in which agreement exists between the state and various established religious communities (Ferrari 1995). Germany's Basic Law calls for a "church tax" levied on all individuals who claim religious affiliation with one of the established churches. The German government in turn allocates funds for church-sponsored schools and hospitals, training teachers for religious instruction in public schools, and other social services provided by the churches.

The current system in Germany is the outcome of an intense struggle during the nineteenth century between Catholics and Protestants. As in France, Catholicism was associated with traditionalism and backwardness; but in Germany, Protestantism was a powerful force, rhetorically associated with rationality (as in Weber's classic essay, *The Protestant Ethic and the Spirit of Capitalism*) and with the "true" German national character. In the late nineteenth century, nationalist intellectuals saw the state and its power as an important vehicle for modernizing the population and containing the Catholic clerical system. Policy makers believed that compulsory education in secular, confessionally mixed schools would be the best means by which to integrate the two religions while "recasting an ignorant and apathetic population into a respectable, responsible citizenry" (Smith 1995, 39).[6]

Under Otto von Bismarck, efforts to contain the Catholic Church resulted in escalating conflict between Catholics and Protestants, played out in schoolrooms and churches. One outcome of this Catholic resistance was the emergence of a wide range of Catholic organizations with an effective overall organizational structure (Smith 1995, 50). Protestant efforts to resist Catholicism also stimulated an overarching organizational structure, the Protestant League. In a foreshadowing of church ideology under Nazism, this group depicted the Catholic spirit as alien to German character. By a similar logic, Judaism eventually became the prime target, the quintessential Other in this process of consolidating German nationalism. Today, of course, Judaism has been recast as an important element of the German nation and has a prominent place in church-state institutional arrangements. Yet echoes of nationalism and guilt over the Holocaust still resonate loudly in Germany today, and fear is considerable—coming from Muslims and liberal Germans alike—that the Muslim has supplanted the Jew as the threatening Other within. These fears can be seen in debates surrounding establishment of new policies toward Muslim groups and practices. In these institutional and legal settings, Muslim challenges and demands for public recognition, space, and support have occurred.

## FREEDOM TO WEAR A HEAD SCARF

One of the most pervasive and visible signs of difference among Muslim minorities in Europe is the head scarf worn by many practicing Muslim women. The head scarf has been the focus of intense public controversy in both France and Germany, and in each case courts have ruled against women who sought to wear a head scarf in a public school. These rulings were based ostensibly on arguments about the need to safeguard secular education in schools, but public opinion against the head scarf is shaped strongly by an impulse articulated by many feminists: the need to protect the basic human rights of Muslim women, whose oppression is presumed to be manifest in the religious requirement that they wear a head scarf.[7] The political significance of the head scarf in public debate and polarization of positions around it have been shaped in large measure by a discourse that developed within the context of the European colonial project: colonial policy makers appropriated the language of early feminism to justify their own colonial domination in the name of freeing women from oppression (Ahmed 1992). Ahmed has argued convincingly that colonial administrators, intent on showing evidence for the inferiority of non-European societies, established the association of the veil with oppression, claiming that the Muslim practice of secluding women stood in contrast to a more enlightened European practice. Ahmed also highlighted the self-contradictory aspects of this argument: the men who preached feminist concerns within the context of Muslim societies often were the same men who fought against feminist demands for the vote and equal opportunity at home. For the past century, then, gender, in the form of the dress and position of women, has been a vehicle of political debate concerning the organization of civil society and its relationship to modernity and the West. In this context, the covering of women is regarded as antithetical to the development of a modern population.

For many modern secularists and feminists, the head scarf continues to be a symbol of the oppression of Muslim women. For politically active Islamists, the head scarf as an element of a pan-Islamic ideology signifies rejection of western domination and secularism and the return to a properly ordered Muslim society. Furthermore, many Muslim women who wear head scarves are highly educated and aware of their human and civil rights. These women also argue that they are equal to men in Islam, and that in many situations the head scarf liberates women by enabling them to enter public spaces that would otherwise be difficult for them due to continuing harassment by illiberal and patriarchal men. Its contemporary meaning thus has been constituted in part out of the politics surrounding Islamization and the threat that many secularists and secularist governments feel as Islamization becomes increasingly visible as a social and political force. As Islamists move into positions of power in many Muslim-majority countries, the significance of the head scarf increasingly is linked to the nature of religious freedom and state authority wherever imposition of Islamic law includes mandatory covering of women.

Yet laicism as a state policy may impose similar constraints on religious freedom.[8] Both Turkey and France are officially laicist, and in each case the authority of the state to control women's dress has been controversial, just as under Islamist regimes. In these cases, however, the women who insist on wearing a head scarf are the ones subject to the controlling authority of the state. In Turkey, the imposition of laicism on what was characterized as a backward, superstitiously religious population was one of many top-down efforts at social transformation. Since the establishment of the Republic of Turkey as a laicist state in the 1920s, women have not been permitted to enter state-controlled schools or practice professions such as medicine or law with a head covering in place. Controversy surrounding this prohibition became visible in the 1980s and continues as growing numbers of women explicitly challenge state authority by refusing to remove their head scarves when they attend school, doing so in the name of democracy and religious freedom.

In France, laicism involves similar constraints on the freedom of religious practice. As in Turkey, state institutions such as public schools are to be rigorously secular. With respect to Muslims, the French government has endorsed the principle that absolute separation of church and state means that individuals and groups are forbidden to manifest their religious practices and beliefs in government settings such as public schools. The result is controversy over the permissibility of head scarves for Muslim girls while in school. In a well-publicized dispute that began in 1989, three teenage Muslim girls living in a town north of Paris challenged what they defined as an infringement of their religious freedom when they were expelled from their high school because they refused to remove their head scarves (the Arabic hijab). The argument used by French authorities to justify their position draws on an Enlightenment-based perception of the public schools' mission: to neutralize religious differences while imbuing students with French civilization (Viorst 1996, 85). In 1994, in response to continuing controversy over the issue, the French education minister issued a directive that head scarves would not be permitted in state educational institutions. This caused consternation not only for Muslims but also for Jews, who up until that point had been permitted to wear yarmulkes in state schools without question (Doering 1995). The rule, however, seems to have left room for wearing a yarmulke or a crucifix, while barring the head scarf for being "outrageous, ostentatious, or meant to proselytize" (Viorst 1996, 86). The Ministry of the Interior viewed the head scarf as a threatening assertion of Islamist fundamentalism, because it was seen as a symbol of fanaticism and the submission of women (Viorst 1996, 86). Muslim leaders responded by taking the issue to court. In France as well as in Turkey, this controversy highlights a key difference between the principles of laicism and religious freedom. In this case, the government used the principle of laicism with respect to groups it perceived as threatening, while allowing individuals in other, more dominant groups (Jews and Christians) freedom of religious practice in the same setting.

Although Turkish-German Muslim women frequently describe Germany as a place where Muslims are freer to practice Islam than in laicist Turkey, similar controversies have arisen in Germany. There, strict separation of church and state in the French sense does not exist, and state emphasis is on religious freedom and tolerance and the right to a religious education. Thus far, most specific legal cases addressing this issue in Germany have involved Muslim girls being forced to participate in compulsory gym and swimming classes in which wearing a head scarf would be impossible, and these generally have been resolved by rulings that exempt covered Muslim girls from such compulsory activities. Yet the courts have been uncertain about how to respond. One court, for instance, ruled that Muslim immigrants should be pressured to adapt, while another court emphasized the need for these women to protect their identities.

Although Muslim girls and women in Germany have not been prevented from wearing head scarves in the classroom as they have in France and Turkey, recently there have been cases of Muslim women who lost their jobs as public school teachers because they insisted on wearing a head scarf in the classroom. In a 1998 case that has received considerable attention, a young Afghan refugee, Fereshta Ludin, was denied a position as a public school teacher because she refused to remove her head scarf (Hilbk 1998).[9] When during her teacher training Ludin first was assigned an internship in an elementary school and parents objected to her head scarf in the classroom, the culture minister of Stuttgart decided that since the state has a monopoly on teaching positions, it could not refuse to place her (Barbieri 1999, 922).[10] The issue came up again when Ludin applied for a regular teaching position, and after considerable debate, the culture minister in the state of Baden-Württemberg decided against her on the grounds that wearing a head scarf is not a religious duty for Muslim women, and that its contested nature within Islam makes it a political symbol that the state should not endorse. Several reasons have been put forward to justify the state's refusal to allow Ludin to teach: as a civil servant, she would have a constitutional duty to act as a neutral and objective representative of the state. Parents entrust their children to the state in sending them to school, and since children are especially vulnerable in the classroom, being exposed to a teacher wearing a head scarf would violate the children's religious freedom. Further, since the practice of wearing a head scarf is a controversial and politicized issue among Muslims themselves, a policy tolerating it in the German civil service would send a political message that the state had taken sides, "supporting a side linked in the public mind with cultural exclusivism, the repression of women, and intolerance" (Barbieri 1999, 922). Many groups welcomed the decision, because "it would promote the integration of Islamic young people into our society" (Lüders 1998, my translation).

On the other side, some have argued that disqualifying a woman for a teaching position because of her head scarf would violate her right not to be discriminated against on religious grounds and the right not to be subjected to a religious test for a government position (Barbieri 1999, 920). Some also challenged the notion that the school system is religiously neutral, since the state sponsors courses in religious instruction and allows wearing crucifixes in the classroom (Barbieri 1999, 922).

Writing in the German weekly *Die Zeit*, Dieter Grimm, a former justice of the federal constitutional court, pointed out that Germany's Basic Law is based on the rights of the individual to freedom and self-determination, and that these rights can be interpreted to protect the autonomy of different social subsystems and all aspects of their political, economic, and cultural ways of life (Grimm 2000). In this statement, Grimm has translated the principle of individual rights to one of group rights. From his perspective, the experiences of national socialism have made Germans even more sensitive to these rights. According to Grimm, however, the compulsion to adapt to a German way of life and the principles of fundamentalism are two parallel extremes, both of which must be avoided—because fundamentalism is the opposite of tolerance, it must be banned from the classroom.

In making this point, Grimm downplays the issue of Muslims' individual rights, focusing more on the threat posed by fundamentalists as a group. Although he does not extend his discussion specifically to the permissibility of the head scarf in the classroom, from this position, the issue comes down to whether wearing a head scarf is a manifestation of unconstitutional group activity or merely an expression of the individual's personal religious observance. By focusing on fundamentalism as the practice of a cultural minority, one may reason from Grimm's position against its permissibility the argument that the head scarf must be banned in public schools. France's Ministry of the Interior argued that the head scarf is a symbol of fundamentalism. In the German case of Fereshta Ludin, the argument similarly was made that since the scarf does serve as a political symbol, its signaling effect—rather than the wearer's personal convictions—must be the deciding factor (Hilbk 1998). Grimm has expressed the opinion that this issue can only be resolved at the level of constitutional law and has pointed out that the German Basic Law was not written with modern "multiculturalism" in mind (Grimm 2000). The Muslim presence thus clearly poses a constitutional challenge for Germany.

## MUSLIMS AND RELIGIOUS EDUCATION IN PUBLIC SCHOOLS

Despite the principle of strict separation of church and state in France, some effort has been made to bring Muslim activities within the purview of the government. For example, the Paris mosque was granted a lucrative government contract for butchering meat according to Muslim law. This step was taken chiefly because the mosque is moderate in orientation; the government would like its leader to be able to act as a spokesperson for the Muslim community at large, thereby displacing Muslim groups that it regards as radical or fundamentalist. Yet other Muslim groups protested that the government was showing favoritism to one group, forcing withdrawal of the contract (Viorst 1996, 93). The French government also supplies Muslim chaplains for the prisons and the military. Like the United States, however, France does not sponsor religious education within public schools. Thus, the idea of delivering such education to Muslim children has not taken shape as an issue for Muslims in France.

Since Germany does offer such religious instruction, the issue is one of central concern for Germany's Muslims and has had a profound influence on the politics of competing Muslim organizations as well as on the everyday lives of Muslims. According to Eckard Nordhofen, head of central development in the German Bishops' Conference,

> The constitutional law of the Federal Republic addresses religious freedom. Religious freedom is a human right. No compulsion [to practice religion] may be imposed, which is a negative religious freedom. But there is also positive religious freedom. Religion classes are a result of a positive religious freedom. (Nordhofen 1998, my translation)

Within the framework of German law, groups have been pushed to fulfill specific criteria in order to qualify as religious organizations. Complaints are common within Muslim communities that the government has not honored existing laws and regulations when it comes to giving official status to Muslim organizations. For example, the director of a Muslim preschool that recently had received local government funding complained that her organization had been ignored for years before being able to force the government into granting the school the official status that would entitle it to government funding.[11] This example is just one of many instances of politicians and officials either stalling or finding a technical rationale for keeping at bay what many feel is a threatening possibility: that Muslim religious education will promote radical fundamentalism.

Despite behind-the-scenes political maneuvering that has slowed government support of Muslim schools and the integration of Islam into the school curriculum, many people feel that to integrate Muslim organizations into the system is important. While in Berlin, I spoke informally with German professionals and academics, several of whom expressed the view that to have Islamic education in the schools, where it is visible, is better than to have it happen in "some garage" where fanatics could influence young Muslims in dangerous ways. For these people, government support entails government oversight.

The key question for politicians, the courts, and the various Muslim organizations is which group should be authorized to set up an Islamic curriculum and train teachers. In a case decided by the Berlin Administrative Court, the Islamic Federation of Berlin was the plaintiff in a suit brought against Berlin's School Senate Administration in which the federation demanded permission to conduct religious education in the public schools (Verwaltungsgeericht Berlin 1997). The federation claimed that it had been a registered organization (Verein) since 1980, functioning as an umbrella organization for twenty-five member organizations.

As stated in the judgment, the Islamic Federation had first applied for permission to conduct religious instruction in 1980. The application was denied by the School Senate on the grounds that the plaintiff acted not as a religious community (Gemeinschaft) but only as a religiously oriented association (Verein). Over the course of the following twenty years, the federation repeatedly rewrote its charter, reapplied, and was denied, the process culminating in appeals to the administrative court in 1987, 1993, 1997, and again in 2000. The grounds for the negative decisions through 1997 were made on the argument that the plaintiff was not a religious community.

It was argued that Islam is characterized by different organizational structures, different legal schools based on different legal collections (fatawa) and strong sociocultural forms. The groups of the Islamic Federation had only the Koran and Sunna as a common basis. It therefore did not have a structure analogous to a Christian denomination with sufficient commonalities among groups within the organization (Verwaltungsgeericht Berlin 1997, my translation).

The ruling also included the following points, which articulated German misgivings about an organization that many viewed as fundamentalist:

- One of the participating member organizations was not a religious community and, therefore, the Islamic Federation constituted a secular interest group.

- The participating organizations' 1,127 members were only a minority of Berlin's 140,000 Muslims, according to the 1987 census.

- Religious differences between the member organizations and other believing Islamic orientations, and thus the distinctiveness of this organization, has not been made clear.

In response, the federation argued that it did meet the definition of religious community as specified in the school laws (Schulgesetzes). Furthermore, it asserted, to the extent that Islam is not a homogeneous religion, the same situation holds for Christian religious communities, which also are not homogeneous. Finally, the federation pointed out that its teachers are experienced in religious instruction, had demonstrable theological degrees, and were required to be tolerant in their instruction of Islam.

What are the issues embedded in this ruling? A highly charged question is whether the goals of the Islamic Federation are really political and not just religious. This ruling includes a reference to one of the member organizations of the Islamic Federation not being religious. According to a German lawyer who was working on the most recent appeal when I spoke with him in November 1999, the offending member was actually a political group.[12] The literature on Islam in Europe frequently depicts Islamist groups operating freely on German soil, having left Turkey because of political repression, and portrays some of these groups as having political aspirations to replace Turkey's secularist government and to propagate Islamic fundamentalism. This fear is further reinforced by the idea that Islam is presumed to make no separation between church and state, in contrast to post–Enlightenment Christianity. In an interview for *Die Zeit*, a so-called representative of the Turks (Vertreter der Türken), Kenan Kolat, said,

> Islam today is still of a more political nature than is Christianity, which is strongly secularized. Islam much more strongly shapes everyday life. If an organization misuses Islam for its Islamist political goals, we are against its being able to give religious instruction in the schools. For us, the Islamic Federation is such an organization. (Mehr 1998, my translation)

An important element of this case is the wrangling between rival umbrella organizations of Muslims. These rival organizations received no direct mention in the ruling, but they played a significant role in how the contest has developed over the years. A rival organization to the Islamic Federation in Berlin of comparable size (in terms of the number of mosques under its control) is DITIB, which has direct and overt ties to the Turkish government through Turkey's Directorate of Religious Affairs (Diyanet) and controls all mosques and religious schools in laicist Turkey. The Islamic Federation, in contrast, has close ties to Milli Görüş, which is characterized by Turkish officials as well as by German media as a fundamentalist organization, originally closely linked to Turkey's Islamist Welfare Party. The Welfare Party (renamed the Virtue Party after being banned in January 1998) controlled the Turkish government for a short time and worked to replace laicism with a policy more supportive of Islam. Ali Kılınç, the director of DITIB in Berlin and thus a Turkish government employee, felt strongly that his organization, representing a moderate, progressive Islam, should be given authorization to teach Islam in Berlin's schools instead of the Islamic Federation.[13]

In January 2000, the 1997 decision against the Islamic Federation of Berlin was overturned. The federation was given the status of a religious organization (Religiongemeinschaft), and the Berlin School Senate was ordered to authorize the federation to offer religious instruction in Islam to Muslim schoolchildren. According to news reports on the decision, the German government apparently still is concerned about the lack of integration of the Muslim community, split as it is into a number of competing umbrella organizations. At least one journalist, however, has suggested that the government has focused excessively on this issue as a pretext for doing nothing about Islamic education (Spiewak 2000).

The decision, though targeted specifically at Islamic religious instruction, has broader implications for the issue of religious instruction in public schools. It came in the midst of a hot debate in the press and in the Berlin government about the future direction of religious instruction. In Berlin, religious instruction in one of the officially recognized religions—Catholicism, Lutheran Protestantism, and Judaism—was voluntary for elementary school children, the alternative being a study hall. During winter 1999 and 2000, Berlin's new senator for education (a member of the center-right Christian Democratic Union) announced that he planned to push for compulsory religious instruction—an announcement that generated controversy and stimulated a powerful response from a disparate array of individuals and organizations that formed an alliance to resist this move.

Many people took the opportunity to argue that religious instruction should be replaced with some form of ethics course, a proposal that had been debated on and off for many years and was influenced in part by the feeling, particularly strong among many former East Germans, that state sponsorship of religion is inappropriate. An article in *Die Zeit* shortly after the court ruling about the Islamic Federation pointed out,

> It forces the Senate to act indirectly against the prevailing spirit of the times: while many local school politicians and the Pedagogical Front argue against the supposedly dated influence of the churches in school instruction and seek to replace their influence with a non-confessional ethics class, the Berlin Senate must now go in the opposite direction. It must introduce religion classes of all confessions as a regular school subject with grades and trained teachers. (Spiewak 2000, my translation)

In contrast to Germany's other states, where religion is a proper instructional subject, the organization of instruction in Berlin until this point had been entirely under the control of the official religious organizations. Throughout fall 1999, the two issues—ethics versus religious instruction in the schools, and which organization should represent Islam to Muslim schoolchildren—had been brewing as discrete controversies with their own distinct histories. The first involved the merging of East and West Berlin and a rising proportion of the German population that lacked any church commitment. The second involved the rising discontent among the ever-growing Turkish community about unequal treatment in the schools. The presence of increasingly vocal Muslims thus has changed the terms of the ethics debate.

# CONCLUSION: MUSLIM CHALLENGES TO THE STATUS QUO

In using the example of religious difference to cast the United Nations Universal Declaration of Human Rights solely in terms of individual rights—based on the premise that group affiliations are a private matter outside of state purview—its authors clearly were mistaken in their understanding of how religious communities have interacted with the state in Europe. Consideration of actual practices in Germany and even in France (which has had the most sharply articulated rhetoric of separation since 1905) indicates that these governments have dealt with religious communities—including even Protestants—as corporate groups. Muslims have threatened the status quo, not because they have group expectations (as an American observer who regards religion as an individual, private matter might expect), but because no single, clear organizational structure subsumes all Muslims. The German setup encourages umbrella organizations to vie for official status and recognition. Interestingly, the German difficulty in handling Muslim education in school apparently has not stimulated the question of why a single organization must control all religious education curricula and teacher training in the schools. An alternative solution might be to give parents a choice of school, so that if they do not agree with the orientation of a religious teacher in one school, they could request a transfer to another school.

The case of France suggests that this or some other solution has not emerged in Germany because equal treatment of each sect or organization is not the critical concern of those who obstruct implementation of an Islamic curriculum. Though France lacks the program of religious education in public schools that Germany has, the French government also is frustrated by the lack of a single official head of a Muslim church. Both governments are afraid of Muslim extremists and are seeking modes of surveillance of all Muslims that do not infringe too blatantly on the rights of individuals.

Some Germans accuse the Milli Görüş (with which the Islamic Federation is affiliated) of practicing dissimulation, as certain communities of Shi'a Muslims have done at various points in their history—indicating a fear of what this organization is truly up to. Much of the controversy centers around women's dress. Struggles over the head scarf in France and Germany are couched in somewhat different rhetorics, but in debates in both countries can be heard views valorizing assimilation that echo German and French nationalism and an equation of progress and rationality with northern European cultural practices. In discourses going back to the nineteenth century, the head scarf has been seen as a sign of the traditional Muslim oppression of women. This was linked closely with the idea that traditional Muslim leaders strive to control their communities autocratically through their interpretation of Islamic law, in which separation of the political, the social, and the religious does not exist. If the state were to recognize such a community, it would create a direct conflict between individual human rights and the right of the group to control its members. Such symbolic associations do not hold for most Muslim communities, however, even for those whose women wear head scarves. Covered women active in Milli Görüş in fact argue for their rights in terms of freedom of choice and the principles of democracy. This cannot be just dissimulation, since they enact these principles in their own lives, becoming well-educated and publicly active, in contrast to stereotypes of the covered woman as oppressed victim.

The presence of large Muslim populations challenges church-state arrangements, not because Muslim goals are so different from those of other religious communities, but because European governments do not trust that Muslims respect individual rights and the principle of religious freedom. Muslims may reject laicism without rejecting either the individual rights of their own community members or the group rights of other communities. Their presence in European societies should help us disentangle concepts about religious freedom, individual rights, and the relationship between church and state that often are confused in popular discourse.

---

Support for this project was funded in part by the American Academy of Berlin, where I held a Berlin Prize Fellowship during the fall of 1999 in order to conduct ethnographic research among Turkish Muslims. Funding also was provided by the Trent Foundation, Duke University's Center for European Studies, Duke's Arts and Sciences Research Council, and the Provost's International Fund at Duke. I would like to thank Emine Öztürk and Bedra Sorgec for their invaluable research assistance.

## NOTES

1. Though the idea of the separation of church and state can be traced back to Roger Williams in the 1630s (Williams 1652), the concrete image of a wall to characterize this separation was articulated by Thomas Jefferson in 1802 and has continued to be elaborated throughout the twentieth century (see Voth 1998). On the idea of porousness see Kilpatrick 1984, 5.

2. Examples include *Employment Division of Oregon v. Smith*, 494 U.S. 872 (1990), which challenged a law prohibiting the use of certain drugs that are part of a group's religious practice.

3. See *City of Boerne v. Flores*, 117 Sup. Ct., 2157, 138 L. Ed 2d 624 (1997). Among the grounds for the decision were the determination that the act went beyond the supposed intent of "restoring" religious freedom and appeared to attempt to change the substance of constitutional protections, thereby exceeding the power of Congress. The act also imposed a heavy litigation burden on the states and curtailed their power to impose general regulations. While the act was in effect, it had been argued that it "forces every level of government to give special consideration to the ritualistic minutiae of every sect and belief, except where there is a compelling state interest" (Tamm 1999, 12).

4. The ruling on displaying religious symbols followed a 1995 Supreme Court ruling that upheld the right of the Ohio chapter of the Ku Klux Klan to erect a cross during the Christmas season in a public area of Columbus. (*Capitol Square Review and Advisory Board et al., Petitioners v. Vincent J. Pinette, Donnie A. Carr, and Knights of the Ku Klux Klan* 515 U.S. 753, 1995; see McMorris 1995). On religious education in schools see, for example, Peterson 2000.

5. Figures are from the CIA's *World Factbook* website, at *www.odci.gov/cia/publications/factbook*. Muslims account for 1.7 percent of Germany's population, while a large number of Germans, 26.3 percent, are unaffiliated or "other." In contrast to the CIA, it is striking that Germany's Federal Statistics Office does not list Muslims as a separate category on its website, *www.statistik-bund.de*, though the number of Jews, which is smaller than the number of Muslims, is listed.

6. Much of the following summary is based on Smith 1995.

7. Susan Moller Okin (1999, 39) defines feminism as the conviction that women should be fully equal to men, with the opportunity to live lives as freely chosen and fulfilling as men can, and argues that the call for multiculturalism in the form of group rights threatens women's rights.

8. Jean Bauberot (1994) has articulated a useful distinction between *secularization* and *laicization*. Laicization can be characterized as a reduction of the legal position of religion and its subordination to nonreligious functionaries, while secularization is a reduction in the social importance of religion.

9. The Hilbk article (1998) is based in part on an interview with Fereshta Ludin.

10. Barbieri insightfully has presented and analyzed this controversy from the perspective of group rights.

11. A director of Islamischer Frauverein, interview with author, Berlin, November 23, 1999.

12. Ralph Poscher, conversation with author, Berlin, December 9, 1999.

13. Ali Kılınç, interview with author, Berlin, September 23, 1999.

# REFERENCES

Ahmed, Leila. 1992. *Women and Gender in Islam: Historical Roots of a Modern Debate*. New Haven: Yale University Press.

Barbieri, William. 1999. "Group Rights and the Muslim Diaspora." *Human Rights Quarterly* 21(4): 907–26.

Bauberot, Jean. 1994. "Laicite, Laicization, Secularisation." In *Pluralisme Religieux et Laicites dans l'Union Europeenne*, edited by Alain Dierkens (9–17). Bruxelles: Editions de l'Université de Bruxelles.

Dawson, Philip. 1984a. "Constitution of 1791." In *Historical Dictionary of the French Revolution, 1789–1799*, edited by Samuel F. Scott and Barry Rothaus (236–38). Westport, Conn.: Greenwood Press.

———. 1984b. "Declaration of the Rights of Man and of the Citizen." In *Historical Dictionary of the French Revolution, 1789–1799*, edited by Samuel F. Scott and Barry Rothaus (301–3). Westport, Conn.: Greenwood Press.

Doering, Martina. 1995. "Franzosen streiten um das Kopftuch." *Berliner Zeitung*, January 17, 1995.

Durkheim, Emile. 1995 [1912]. *The Elementary Forms of Religious Life*. Translated by Karen E. Fields. New York: Free Press.

Ferrari, Silvio. 1995. "The Emerging Pattern of Church and State in Western Europe: The Italian Model." *Brigham Young University Law Review* 1995: 421–37.

Glazer, Nathan. 1975. *Affirmative Discrimination: Ethnic Inequality and Public Policy*. New York: Basic Books.

Grimm, Dieter. 2000. "Das Andere darf anders bleiben: Wie viel Toleranz gegenüber fremder Lebensart verlangt das Grundgesetz?" *Die Zeit*, February 17, 2000. Available at: *www.archiv.zeit.de/daten/pages/200008.toleranz_.html*.

Hilbk, Merle. 1998. "Im Glauben eine Heimat finden." *Die Zeit*, no. 31. Available at: *www.archiv.zeit.de/daten/pages/199831.ludin_html* (accessed February 2000).

Kilpatrick, James. 1984. "A Porous Wall of Separation." *Nation's Business* 72: 5.

Kymlicka, Will. 1995. *Multicultural Citizenship*. Oxford: Oxford University Press.

Lüders, Michael. 1998. "Ich bin doch kein Alien." *Die Zeit*, no. 31. Available at: *www. archiv.zeit.de/daten/pages/199831.kopftuch1_.html* (accessed February 2000).

Mandel, Ruth. 1996. "A Place of Their Own: Contesting Spaces and Defining Places in Berlin's Migrant Community." In *Making Muslim Space in North America and Europe*, edited by Barbara Metcalf (147–66). Berkeley: University of California Press.

McMorris, Frances A. 1995. "Legal Beat: Local Governments Relax Ban on Religion in Holiday Displays." *Wall Street Journal*, December 26, 1995: B3.

Mehr, Max Thomas. 1998. "Schulfrei für all Götter?" *Die Zeit*, November 19, 1998. Available at: *www.archiv.zeit.de/daten/pages/199848.streitgespraech_.html*.

Nordhofen, Eckard. 1998. "Bei uns bleibt Er tot." *Die Zeit*, December 22, 1998. Available at: *www.archiv.zeit.de/daten/pages/199853.t_religion_.html*.

Okin, Susan Moller. 1999. *Is Multiculturalism Bad for Women?* Princeton, N.J.: Princeton University Press.

Peterson, Samantha. 2000. "School Board Hopeful Wants Bible Course." *Herald-Sun* (Durham, N.C.), April 7, 2000: C1.

Smith, Helmut Walser. 1995. *German Nationalism and Religious Conflict: Culture, Ideology, Politics, 1870–1914*. Princeton, N.J.: Princeton University Press.

Spiewak, Martin. 2000. "Das Recht auf Unterricht." *Die Zeit*, March 2, 2000, no. 10/2000.

Tamm, Rudra. 1999. "Religion Sans Ultimate: A Re-examination of Church-State Law." *Journal of Church and State* 41(2): 253–84.

Torfs, Rik. 1996. "Church and State in France, Belgium, and the Netherlands: Unexpected Similarities and Hidden Differences." *Brigham Young University Law Review* 1996: 945–71.

Verwaltungsgericht Berlin. 1997. *Islamischer Föderation gegen das Land Berlin*, VG3 A 2196.93, December 19.

Viorst, Milton. 1996. "The Muslims of France." *Foreign Affairs* 75(5): 78–96.

Voth, Ben. 1998. "A Case Study in Metaphor as Argument: A Longitudinal Analysis of the Wall Separating Church and State." *Argumentation and Advocacy* 34(3): 127–39.

Weber, Max. 1976 [1904]. *The Protestant Ethic and the Spirit of Capitalism*. Translated by Talcott Parsons. London: Allen & Unwin.

Williams, Roger. 1867. *A Bloudy Tenant of Persecution for Cause of Conscience*. Vol. 3. Rhode Island: Narragansett Club.

Zachary, G. Pascal. 2000. "A Philosopher in Red Sneakers Gains Influence as a Global Guru." *Wall Street Journal*, March 28, 2000: B1, 4.

# Chapter 4

# Civilizing the Natives: Customary Marriage in Post-Apartheid South Africa

David L. Chambers

For several hundred years whites ruled South Africa, systematically manip-
ulating black people to the whites' advantage. For the most part, however,
colonial and settler governments tolerated the continuation within black
communities of traditional marriage practices that the white Christians considered uncivilized. In 1994, South Africa changed governments. A black majority
Parliament came to power, adopting a constitution dedicated to equality and
human dignity. Four years later, the Parliament adopted a new marriage law
that, though permitting some of the external trappings of the traditional marriage system to continue, eliminated by law much of the core of its male-centered rules.

From the point of view of legislators who voted for it, the new law was required in order to promote gender equality under the new constitution. From
the point of view of traditional leaders and some other rural dwellers, the new
law was unjustifiable because it failed to honor black people's own traditions in
a new black South Africa. This chapter is about points of view—the multiple
points of view of South Africans, and the point of view of one admiring American, trying to understand.

## CUSTOMARY RULES AND PRACTICES

About 78 percent of South Africa's population is black. About 12 percent is
white, the rest primarily Indian or mixed race, called *coloured*. Nearly half of all
black Africans still live in rural areas, the great majority in traditional groups
headed by hereditary kings or chiefs and by headmen and subchiefs. The largest
of these groups are the Zulu, the Xhosa, the Pedi, the Sotho, the Tswana, the
Tsonga, and the Swazi. All are hierarchically organized and, in nearly all, only
men can be chiefs or senior counselors. Nelson Mandela himself was of a royal
Xhosa family, picked by the chief (a male) to be the principal adviser to the
chief's son, who was in line to become the next chief.

Each of these cultural groups has its own customs and rules—rituals and

meaning of lobolo) that the husband's family, through payment of lobolo, has acquired the woman's reproductive capacity.

Do women who live in rural customary groups today lead lives of subordination and degradation? This is a difficult question to answer—and not just because of the difficulty of deciding what should count as a degrading life. Many studies have been written about the experiences of black South African women, but few are recent or methodologically rigorous (Reyher 1948; Mathabane 1994; Romero 1988, 7–47; Romero 1998; Bozzoli 1991).[3] Stories abound of twentieth-century women who were forced by their fathers to marry an older man they did not know, who experienced intercourse with their husband as a physical violation, and who were treated much like a servant (Reyher 1948). At the same time, most accounts of married women's lives are mixed but more positive. H. J. Simons, one of the most thoughtful white South African observers of customary practices, believed that in circumstances in which rural husbands and wives lived in an extended family of the husband's relatives, most women, while not equals, were at least "junior partners in a joint family enterprise" (Simons 1968, 15, 64). The system of rules sought to ensure that no woman was without a male responsible for her well-being. Moreover, during the marriage—especially after bearing children—women typically exercised considerable authority in the operation of their households. The beleaguered new wife became the powerful mother-in-law a generation later. To be sure, customary unions continued to be potentially polygamous, but fewer and fewer men could afford second wives.

By the mid–twentieth century, large numbers of black Africans no longer lived in rural settings or in extended family arrangements, and the practice of male control of wealth no longer matched many urban or rural women's experiences or needs. Many married black women lived in cities where they were employed primarily as domestic workers; they were paid directly by their employers and controlled the income they earned. Large numbers of rural men worked in the cities or mines and provided neither support nor protection for their wives who remained in the country. Polygamy had become a parody of itself: frequently, a man married in the country, then moved to the city, leaving his wife and children behind, and married again.

By moving to the cities, many women (and young men) largely evaded the old practices, but many rural women still suffered from their effects. Some stayed in marriages they wanted to leave owing to pressure from their fathers, who sided with the husbands and did not want to return lobolo. Others were left without resources on the death of their husband, when a male relative of the husband claimed the family assets but failed to provide for the widow's care. The tradition of male dominance, coupled with the decline of extended family living arrangements, probably also has contributed to the extremely high levels of physical abuse to which African men subject their wives (Kaganas and Murray 1994).

Among white South Africans married under civil law, it is equally debatable whether wives experience the equality in their relationships that official rules now proclaim. In South Africa as elsewhere, white men earn more than white women, and neither British nor Afrikaner South African men are known for egalitarian attitudes toward marriage. Still, by the 1990s, married women were formal equals under common-law rules but not under customary practices.

## DOMINANCE AND TOLERANCE

The story of the positions that South African colonial governments' settlers took toward customary rules and practices during the nineteenth and twentieth centuries is too complex to relate in a few paragraphs (see, for example, Schapera 1955; Comaroff and Roberts 1981; Simons 1968; Bennett 1985). British and Afrikaner settlers for the most part regarded black African marital practices as barbaric: at worst, lobolo as a transaction in which men sold their daughters into slavery, and polygamy as uncurbed lust. Yet colonial and settler governments generally tolerated these practices. In a context in which blacks greatly outnumber whites, tolerance proved consistent with efficient administration (Simons 1968, 19–26). The British secured the reluctant loyalty of the chiefs by protecting the chiefs' authority. The chiefs in turn applied the customary rules to their peoples, who provided an inexpensive source of labor to white farmers and households. As stated by Theophilis Shepstone, architect of the British policy in Natal, "The main object of keeping natives under their own law is to ensure control of them. You cannot control savages by civilized law" (Simons 1968, 28).

As part of its system of control, the British government created special native courts to apply customary law in disputes among black South Africans. In some parts of the country, customary rules were codified by British lawmakers, who learned the rules from chiefs and other male headsmen and rendered them into English legal language that was often inaccurate in translation and more male-centered than actual practice (Robinson 1995, 457, 460). Courts routinely applied these codified customary rules, but even so, the degree to which courts were willing to give such rules legal effect was limited. In each of the ordinances and statutes that authorized courts to apply customary laws in suits between blacks, a proviso always directed the court not to do so when it found a particular custom "repugnant to the general principles of humanity recognized throughout the whole civilized world" (Royal Instruction of March 8, 1848) or "opposed to the principles of public policy or natural justice" (Government of South Africa 1937, *The Black Administration Act of 1927*, sec. 11). In addition, the same courts refused to treat women within customary unions as a wife for purposes of certain common-law and statutory benefits. Thus, unlike a wife in a civil marriage, a customary spouse could not collect from certain statutory insurance funds on the death of her husband in a motor vehicle accident (*Suid-Africaanse Nasionale Trust en Assuransie Maatskappy Bpk v. Fondo*, 1960 [2] SA 467 [A]).

By the late twentieth century, courts rarely invoked the repugnancy clauses and Parliament had extended some statutory benefits of civil marriage to spouses in customary unions. The unions of rural black people were accepted as marriages by all the people who counted to them, and for most, the state recognized their relationship in the few contexts in which it made any difference. Unlike the United States government in its campaign against the Mormon church in the late nineteenth century, the whites in South Africa—however brutal their policies—never declared polygamy a crime for people living in customary unions, never prosecuted and imprisoned thousands of polygamists or drove thousands of others into hiding, and never sought to remove the children of polygamous parents on the ground that polygamous practices were inherently harmful (Larsen 1971, 99–100, 181–83, 213–16; Bradley 1993).[4]

## THE NEW CONSTITUTIONAL ORDER

After World War II, the Afrikaner-led National Party won control of South Africa's government and, over time, imposed its apartheid policy of rigid segregation. Blacks ceased to be citizens of South Africa. Those needed by whites for labor were forced to live as migrants at the mines or in all-black townships outside the cities. Those not needed were relegated to so-called homelands ruled by black leaders who were in large part puppets of the South African government. In 1994, after years of internal struggle and international condemnation, the National Party agreed to relinquish control to the black majority. Parliament adopted a new constitution called the Interim Constitution, hammered out between the National Party and the African National Congress (ANC) with the participation of other smaller parties, and the homelands were reabsorbed into South Africa. The promulgation of the constitution led directly to the elections in 1994 in which black South Africans, voting for the first time, brought a black-controlled government into power. Two years later, in 1996, a Final Constitution was adopted, drafted by a committee of Parliament dominated by the ANC.

The Interim and Final Constitutions sound many themes—individual freedom, human dignity, universal suffrage, a parliamentary system of government—but no theme is sounded more forcefully than that of equality. This is hardly a surprise, given the nation's sordid history. Somewhat surprising to many, however, is that the new constitutions emphasized equality based on sex as strongly as equality based on race. The prominent place of sex equality grew out of the ANC's adoption in the 1960s of Western human rights ideology as well as the participation of South African women and women's groups in the anti-apartheid liberation efforts and in negotiations over the constitutions (Murray and O'Regan 1991, 33, 36–41; Albertyn 1997, 39; Andrews 1997, 307, 324).

As completed, the Interim Constitution opens with these words:

In humble submission to Almighty God,
We, the people of South Africa declare that—
WHEREAS there is a need to create a new order in which all South Africans will be entitled to a common South African citizenship in a sovereign and democratic constitutional state in which there is equality between men

and women and people of all races so that all citizens shall be able to enjoy and exercise their fundamental rights and freedoms.

Similarly, the first substantive section of the Bill of Rights in the Final Constitution provides that "everyone is equal before the law and has the right to equal protection and benefit of the law," and continues by declaring that neither the state nor any person may

> unfairly discriminate directly or indirectly against anyone on one or more grounds, including race, gender, sex, pregnancy, marital status, ethnic or social origin, colour, sexual orientation, age, disability, religion, conscience, belief, culture, language and birth. (*Constitution for the Republic of South Africa* 1996, sec. 9 [1], 9 [3])

The constitutions' drafters were well aware of the potential impact of the equality clauses on gender-based family rules of customary groups; so too were traditional leaders. In deliberations, these leaders advocated that customary rules—particularly customary family rules—be treated as a separate system of laws exempt from the constitution (Currie 1996, 36). The chiefs and other traditional leaders argued that traditional ways, tolerated but demeaned during apartheid, deserved to be embraced in a new black nation.

As eventually adopted, however, the Interim and Final Constitutions took a quite different approach to customary leaders and customary rules. The drafters—though many considered themselves members of customary groups—held less positive views than did chiefs about customary rules and about the chiefs themselves. Like the chiefs, the drafters deplored mistreatment of customary groups during apartheid. They remembered that as recently as the 1970s, whole customary villages had been bulldozed, the members pushed off to homelands or scattered to townships such as Soweto near the big cities, and their land confiscated for use by whites. At the same time, many drafters and other new black members of Parliament viewed themselves as fortunate to be city dwellers today, free of the day-to-day control of the male elders. Many who were women dismissed the traditional leaders' call for a revival of African identity and customs as a ruse to justify continued repression of black women (Hassim 1993).[5] Moreover, many black ANC members had spent the previous three decades condemning appeals to ethnic affiliations, because the white apartheid government exploited such appeals to divide black South Africans.

In the eyes of the ANC, many customary leaders themselves stood in a morally ambiguous position. They were viewed as old men selfishly protecting their own power and as social conservatives out of step with progressive ideas. The version of customary law that they defended was, in the views of many, inauthentic—distorted and frozen in the last century by the interaction of patriarchal black male elders and patriarchal white male colonial judges and administrators. Worse, many traditional leaders before and during apartheid had entered into a Faustian bargain with the white government, under which they were permitted to retain control over members of their groups only so long as they refrained from supporting ANC efforts to overturn the existing regime. A few traditional leaders in the new Parliament were celebrated opponents of apartheid, but others, many of whom were members of the Zulu-dominated Inkatha Freedom Party, were seen by the ANC as collaborators with the white rulers.

Thus, in the end, the Final Constitution, adopted by a Parliament in which a majority of members were black, reflects a mixed view of blacks' own traditional cultures. On the affirmative side, the Final Constitution declares that the country's official languages, formerly Afrikaans and English, are now to be "Sepedi, Sesotho, Setswana, siSwati, Tshivenda, Xitsonga, Afrikaans, English, isiNdebele, isiXhosa, and isiZulu" (1996, sec. 6[1]). The constitution (sec. 30) further guarantees to all the right "to participate in the cultural life of their choice" and directs courts to "apply customary law when that law is applicable" (sec. 211); it even provides that "the institution, status, and role of traditional leadership, according to customary law, are recognized" (sec. 211 [1]). Yet the constitution simultaneously makes customary rules and traditional leaders subordinate to Parliament and the Bill of Rights. Yes, all citizens have the right to participate in the cultural life of their choice; "but," continues the same provision, "no one exercising these rights may do so in a manner inconsistent with any provision of the Bill of Rights," and traditional leaders may continue to hold their offices but "subject to the Constitution." And yes, courts are to apply customary law but are to do so "subject to the Constitution and any applicable legislation that specifically deals with customary law." In other words, customary law may be changed by Parliament as freely as it can change judge-made common law or its own prior legislation.

Given these constitutional provisions, it may appear that the old gender-based customary family rules must be rejected today as unconstitutional, inconsistent with the equality clause of the Bill of Rights—and perhaps the new Constitutional Court will someday so hold. Remember, however, that the constitution does not prohibit all discrimination but only discrimination that is "unfair."[6] Furthermore, even "unfair discrimination," an elusive notion under the court's early jurisprudence (*President of the Republic of South Africa v. Hugo* 1997),[7] will be tolerated if the state can demonstrate that a discriminatory regulation comes within the terms of a general limitations clause in the constitution (sec. 36) that permits restricting any of the rights in the Bill of Rights "to the extent that the limitation is reasonable and justifiable in an open and democratic society based on human dignity, equality, and freedom."

## THE RECOGNITION OF CUSTOMARY MARRIAGES ACT OF 1998

In November 1998, four years after coming to power, Parliament adopted a new law regarding customary marriage. The legislation was developed for Parliament by the South Africa Law Commission, a government agency long in existence but reconstituted under the new government. The commission appointed a project committee and retained as the committee's principal drafter T. W. Bennett, an expert on customary law and human rights law at the University of Capetown's law school. When the committee began its work, members readily agreed that customary unions entered into in the past would be relabeled as marriages. No more separate and unequal. Regarding customary marriages entered into in the future, however, the committee was less certain how to proceed and received many suggestions from academics and groups.

At the extremes, two quite different models were available. As a first approach, the committee might have recommended that Parliament adopt a single national law of marriage that prescribed for all South Africans the requirements and consequences of marriage, just as nearly all states in the United States have a single statutory form of marriage. Couples would be free to conduct their marriage ceremonies any way they wished—the delivery of cattle, an exchange of vows in church, a feast of goat, a five-tiered cake, whatever—but the requirements of a legally valid marriage, the registration system, and the legal effects of marriage would be the same for all. As the new uniform law, Parliament might have cast into statutory language the rules of one of the customary groups or some amalgam of customary rules. Or Parliament might have adopted for everyone the existing civil law under which whites and Christian blacks typically married.

Such an approach was conceivable, but the committee never seriously considered it. No one set of rules could be acceptable to all groups. Each customary group was proud of its practices and would not have given them up lightly for some other customary group's rules. Zulu practices could not be privileged over Xhosa or vice versa. By the same token, South African Christians would have found unacceptable any system in which a husband could have more than one wife.

The second model for Parliament was simply to declare that all unions and marriages henceforth were considered marriages and, for the future, leave to each couple to choose the marital regime under which it wished to be united. All systems would be recognized as equal, and the state would enforce the rules of the marital system chosen by the couple or empower the group's tribunals to enforce those rules. This is more or less the approach that has been taken in Israel regarding Islamic and Christian marriages.

This approach had much more appeal to the committee; it also was the approach that chiefs and other traditional leaders of customary groups wanted. In its purest form, however, such an approach was unacceptable to many liberals and feminists, both black and white, because in their view many of the customary rules bearing on married women were intolerable and unconstitutional. In fact, some women had fought for the gender equality language in the constitution as much to secure equal rights at home as to secure equal rights in the public sphere (Murray and O'Regan 1991, 39–40).

In the end, after receiving written comments from a large number of individuals and groups, the committee and commission recommended a middle course (South Africa Law Commission 1997), and Parliament in turn accepted the commission's recommendations. As adopted, the first substantive section of the Recognition of Customary Marriages Act of 1998 declares that all customary unions entered into in the past are to be relabeled marriages and for the future, all customary marriages that comply with the provisions of the act are valid. The rest of the act regulates the content of customary marriage. Three themes dominate. The first is to insure that each partner truly chooses to marry: marriage must be with consent. The second is to declare women and men formal equals within the marriage relationship. In the absence of an antenuptial contract, husbands and wives in customary marriages will be treated as holding property equally as community property. Married women are given the power to acquire and dispose of assets, to enter into contracts, and to litigate in their own name. The final theme is to inject the state bureaucracy into the regulation of customary marriages, first by requiring that all marriages be registered with government officers and second by permitting divorce only when it is granted by a family court. The family court judge divides the couple's property, awards alimony, and decides which parent is the more appropriate custodian for the children.

Within this structure, the new act permitted some important aspects of customary marriage to continue. Most significantly, customary groups are free to retain lobolo as a condition of a valid marriage. In addition, child marriage still may occur if a group's rules permit it and, in the particular case, the child consents and both parents concur. Levirate marriage—a widow's marrying her late husband's brother—still may occur so long as the widow consents. Even polygyny is permitted to continue, so long as the interests of the first wife are protected. A man may enter a valid second marriage during the course of a first marriage so long as he enters into a written contract with his first wife fairly dividing the property accrued to that point and persuades a magistrate's court, after a hearing, that the contract is equitable to everyone concerned.

How much of customary marriage remains? If lobolo is the heart of customary marriage, customary marriage still has its heart. If polygyny is of symbolic importance even in decline, it too survives. From another perspective, however, the new act maintains the trappings of customary marriage but empties it of most of its content. The act replaces patriarchal marriage with partnership marriage. Even the polygamy provision is structured to make sure that the first wife (or wives) get their full share of the partnership out of the marriage up to that point. Moreover, although customary courts may perform mediation, they cease to have any formal authority to order a resolution of disputes.

## DEMOCRACY AND RECOGNITION OF MINORITY CULTURES

Two different views might be taken of the process that produced this revolutionary legislation and of the substance of the act itself.

The first is to regard the act simply as a healthy example of democracy in action. Writing thirty years ago, H. J. Simons believed that in the face of changes wrought by a market economy, both polygamy and lobolo had outlived their original protective and communal functions and ought to be reformed or abolished. Yet he also believed that "Africans themselves, and not an all-white legislature, should bring about the change" (Simons 1968, 84, 96).[8] The new marriage act is, to use Simons's term, genuinely a work of "Africans themselves" (see also Bronstein 1998, 388, 402–5).[9] The majority of the new Parliament's members are black. For those who are married, lobolo almost certainly was negotiated. The act thus can be seen as law reform from the inside, by a legislature elected by all the people, including the rural black people most affected by it. Indeed, some black South Africans regard Mandela, Mbeki, and the other black Parliament members as democratically elected successors to the hereditary chiefs.

The content of the act also can be defended substantively as paying just the right level of tribute to tradition. Most black South Africans, both women and men, accept the ceremonies and financial transactions associated with becoming married that are preserved by the new legislation (Prinsloo, van Niekerk, and Vorster 1998, 86–89). The social meanings of these transactions are changing with time and are less oppressive today to women than in the past. At the same time, in this view, the act appropriately repudiated the old limitations on a married woman's capacities to contract, inherit, hold land in her own name, and appear in court. These rules not only constricted women's position within the home and family but also curtailed women's dealings with third parties not part of their group. These also were rules whose historic authenticity had been most discredited and whose boundaries today are most contested in the daily lives of members of the groups. The new law thus enables black urban and rural women to enter into marriage through the familiar lobolo rituals they accept, while empowering them as legal equals in the private and public sphere. Lobolo, like the engagement ring in Western cultures, may be transformed into a symbol simply of affection, respect, and commitment.

A second, opposing view of the new legislation is to regard the act as suppressing minority cultures. Customary groups are now a nonurban minority who did not genuinely exert a voice in the legislation. As a formal matter, the Parliament of South Africa, like the Parliament of some other democracies, is not elected by districts. Each party creates a nationwide list of candidates, voters cast one vote for their party of choice, and each party gets a number of seats in Parliament roughly equal to the percentage it receives of the total vote. A considerable majority of the ANC members of Parliament are urban dwellers.

Urban Parliament members might have sought the views of rural people and adopted legislation that served their wishes, but in adopting this legislation, Parliament largely relied on the Law Commission, and the commission in turn had little systematic information about the opinions of rural dwellers. Many rural residents will welcome the legislation as adopted, but others will not. It is not only male elders alone who believe in traditional ways; in much of Africa, rural women are the community's most rigorous enforcers of customs that appear to outsiders to subjugate women (Romero 1998). From the viewpoint of some practitioners of customary rules, the passage of the Recognition of Cus-

tomary Marriages Act must contain a bitter irony: for 200 years, white governments oppressed black people, but at least permitted them to practice their old
family ways; no sooner did a black-controlled government take over than it gut-
ted their own people's traditions—"recognition" by evisceration. Patikile Holomisa is a member of Parliament, traditional chief, controversial politician, and
President of the Congress of Traditional Leaders. In 1997, after the adoption of
the Final Constitution, he lamented, "Such is the tragedy of post-colonial Africa
that, after attainment of freedom, its political leaders find it easy, convenient and
acceptable to adopt the political system of their erstwhile oppressors and yet
find it difficult and problematic to restore indigenous forms of rule."[10] In Holomisa's view, the black ANC members of Parliament had swallowed feminist and
liberal ideologies foreign to Africa and inimical to its way of life. To him,
the Parliament members were much like the British judges of a century before,
who had rejected some customary marriage practices as repugnant to civilized
society.

As Holomisa's critique suggests, the new legislation dishonors customary
groups in a more fundamental way than simply changing the substantive rules
of marriage. The act also changes the decision maker about the rules. The system
of customary rules rested on living practice, with traditional leaders influencing
its shape through their role as resolvers of disputes; they were lawgivers. The
new legislation takes the decision about the rules' content out of the fluid process of living practice and takes the job of judging out of the hands of traditional
leaders.

Which view of the legislation is more nearly accurate, that it was the sound
product of a sound process, or that whatever the end result, the process inappropriately slighted the autonomy of traditional groups? The slight, if it occurred at all, surely did not exceed the reach of Parliament's powers under the
new constitution. The constitution explicitly makes customary law subject to
change by Parliament. Yet Parliament might have chosen to accord customary
groups and their leaders more deference than it did; after all, the constitution
explicitly recognizes the "status and role of traditional leadership," directs courts
to apply "customary law," and proclaims the freedom of individuals to participate in the cultural life of their choice. One might reasonably infer from these
sections that the drafters had something more in mind than simply preserving
old forms while draining them of content.

The remainder of this chapter will explore the attractions and drawbacks of
the deferential approach that Parliament decided not to take. What if Parliament had adopted a recognition act that actually recognized customary rules in
their totality and left it up to the groups themselves to make changes from
within, over time? What if customary courts, not magistrates, had been
entrusted with the initial responsibility for protecting married women from
"unjust discrimination" under the constitution?[11] Might this approach have
eventually produced an egalitarian version of marriage consistent with the
new constitutional regime, but also more consistent with honoring traditional

groups and practices? While I am not at all certain, the following are some reasons for having given it a try.

Thandabuntu Nhlapo, a member of the South Africa Law Commission who served as liaison between the commission and Parliament on the customary marriage legislation, wrote an article a few years before the act's passage that suggests a basis for concern about the approach his own commission and Parliament took. In the article, Nhlapo strongly criticizes the operation of existing customary rules as they applied to women, but worried that "abandonment of these [traditional] values may pose an even greater threat to social cohesion by creating a cultural vacuum in circumstances in which there are no ready substitutes" (Nhlapo 1991, 111, 116). He worries about treating women as independent when they are not yet independent in fact. Consider, for example, the widow who asserts her newly created property rights on the death of her husband but in so doing, offends the husband's family. She may gain a short-term benefit from the community property at the price of a long-term loss of links to the husband's clan.[12]

Yet another ground for preferring reform from within is provided by Justice Albie Sachs of South Africa's new Constitutional Court, a person who has written and thought a great deal about customary law (Welsh, Dagnino, and Sachs 1987). Sachs gave a speech recently in which he expressed confidence in the capacity of customary law to evolve to address new social problems. He spoke of what he considered the core notions of customary law that deserve to survive.

> The deep principles of social respect, coupled with the all-embracing processes involving listening and hearing, . . . of reintegration of defaulters and delinquents into the community, of attempting always to restore equilibrium. . . . At the heart of traditional African legal concern is a sense of human solidarity, of regard for all. No one is cast out or left by the wayside.[13]

Sachs believed that many surviving customary rules "formalized and frozen by magistrates, missionaries and patriarchal male elders in the colonial and apartheid era" were unfit for the current circumstances of African women and particularly African widows, but called not for substantive remedial legislation but rather a revitalization of customary law that would return it to its roots. "It is important," he said, "that democracy not be regarded as a blunt instrument that clubs customary law on the head." Sachs reported on his observations during eleven years of exile in Mozambique (he was an ANC partisan whose arm was mangled by a bomb planted by the South African police in an assassination attempt). There, Sachs recalled, a newly democratic government created "community courts" made up of "people of standing" in the locality. The judges sat in panels of three or more, at least one of whom was a woman. The panels dealt with family issues with informed wisdom, reaching "fair and practical" results. Sachs did not recommend exactly the same approach for South Africa, but sought the help of his audience in designing new institutional arrangements with comparable promise.

If Sachs is correct, traditional leaders in South Africa might have been nudged to include women in decision making and respond in new ways to women's and children's needs for new forms of economic protection in an era in which men are not always nearby to provide support. These leaders might have learned that new rules are needed to make certain that women and children are not "cast out or left by the wayside." Barbara Oomen (1999), a Dutch anthropologist who has been studying rural black life in the village of Hoepakranz in the Northern Province over the last few years, recently related the story of Rosa Diphofa, a single mother who wanted land of her own to build a home (Oomen 1999). Diphofa "had read in the papers" that she was now entitled to land on the same basis as men. Though unable to speak for herself at the chief's court, an uncle spoke on her behalf. The chief, Rosa reported, was "most surprised" by her claim, but after a "big discussion" with his advisers, he granted her request. Rosa spoke with pride of her achievement.

> His decision went through the village like a bushfire. . . . The women, especially the single ones, were very happy for me and helped me with the money from the Credit Club—1100 rands—to buy corrugated iron sheets. . . . They have helped me with the construction. People were very surprised that I knew how to build a mud wall but I just sat down, thought about it, and started. All the time I felt this strength. Now there are other women who will also ask for land.

Even without an altered perception of women's entitlements, the chiefs might have had a pragmatic incentive to foster change in order to encourage women to choose to stay in the countryside and marry under customary rules rather than to hold out for a civil marriage. In urban areas, customary practices already have begun to change. A recent empirical study of black Africans living in urban townships near Pretoria found that today at the dissolution of a marriage lobolo rarely is returned to the husband, even when the woman is "at fault," and children typically remain with their mothers (Prinsloo, van Niekerk, and Vorster 1998).

As an outsider, I find an intuitive appeal in leaving the process of change to customary groups to negotiate from within. The old rules protect the status of men, but men were expected to bear significant responsibilities for their families—for their wives, their children, and their brother's children. Might not internally generated changes to provide for women and children command more respect and adherence from those to whom they apply, and leave the rural women who press for them with more real power in their communities? Moreover, might not internally generated changes reflect more understanding of local needs than bureaucratic courts applying fixed rules of community property? In some ways, the claims for leaving changes up to the groups are little different from arguments made in the United States for leaving family law rules up to states rather than the federal government—the arguments for government closer to the governed.

Having said this, I thoroughly distrust my intuitions. I have a liberal American's preference for protecting diversity without an adequate appreciation of the circumstances of those stuck with living diverse lives (Walzer 1997). My version of internal change may well be romantic and implausible. The Recognition of Customary Marriages Act probably rests on a realistic assessment by the ANC that men who are customary leaders are simply unlikely to be willing to share power with women or transform and revitalize customary rules in the ways that Justice Sachs expects. Few chiefs will respond like the chief in Hoepakranz. Moreover, internal reform inevitably would stretch over many years. A virtue of the act as adopted is that it gives property rights and other protections to women who marry now and who, especially in rural areas, cannot yet realistically demand to marry under civil law. These women have been subordinated by whites and by black men for many centuries and have waited too long for equality before the law.

Whether these rights that are due to them now under the act actually will accrue to the women for whom they are intended is a different question. The experience in America suggests that statutory reform in family law rarely produces immediate change in behavior within homes. That experience is particularly likely to be repeated in South Africa, where Parliament, which has passed much forward-looking legislation in the last few years, often has been unable, in a faltering economy, to provide the financial resources and infrastructure necessary to make new programs come to life.[14] The Recognition of Customary Marriages Act was adopted more than three years ago, in 1998. Only in November 2000 was a registration system put into place. Magistrates' courts have heard very few cases involving divorces of customary marriages. Indeed, in many rural areas, no accessible magistrates' courts exist.

When I asked people who had been involved in the legislative process whether they thought men and women would comply with the legislation, few thought they would. Most thought that rural couples would fail to register their customary marriages (indeed, recognizing this probability, the act provides that failure to register shall not affect the validity of a customary marriage). Only one person interviewed believed there to be any likelihood that the sorts of men who currently enter polygynous marriages would comply with the requirement of coming to a magistrate's court for approval before taking another wife. Few thought that most women or men married under customary law would petition a magistrate's court for a divorce, even if a court were nearby. For most black Africans in rural areas, life will go on pretty much as it always has, at least in the near future. Changes in practices will occur over time not because of statutes or courts, but because of the pressures of the market economy and images of an outside world that rural people increasingly see. If this is so, customary groups may obtain the opportunity that Parliament thought they had rejected to do the task of reforming themselves.

I am grateful for the advice of many friends in South Africa while working on this chapter, particularly for the critical comments of Thomas Bennett and Matthew Chaskalson.

## NOTES

1. The Matrimonial Property Act of 1984.

2. Thus, for example, a person in a customary union could invalidate the union by entering into a civil marriage with someone else, but not vice versa.

3. Extremely interesting work has been conducted recently in three villages in South Africa's Northwest Province by the Dutch anthropologist Barbara Oomen. See Oomen 1999.

4. See also *In re Black*, 283 P. 2d 887 (Utah 1955).

5. Speech of Nozi Routledge-Madlala, at the Symposium on Customary Law and Gender, Johannesburg, November 3, 1997. Ms. Routledge-Madlala was a member of Parliament and chair of the ANC Women's Caucus.

6. The Constitutional Court has decided no cases challenging the constitutionality of customary rules. The one significant lower court decision in which a challenge was made to customary family laws held that the customary rule that permits only men to inherit was "discriminatory," but not "unfair" to a widow, because the inheriting male had an obligation to provide for the widow. See *Mtembu v. Letsala*, (2) SA 936 (1997); see also Currie 1994.

7. In the context of sex discrimination, see the opinions in *President of the Republic of South Africa v. Hugo*, (6) BCLR 708 (1997) (opinions of Justices Goldstone, Kriegler, Mokgoro, and O'Regan).

8. As to lobolo, Simons (1968, 96) wrote, "But no change will be effective, nor should any be attempted, without the support of African opinion and that will be obtained only when Africans are able to manage their own affairs."

9. This is the position taken by Victoria Bronstein in "Reconceptualizing the Customary Law Debate in South Africa," 1998, *South Africa Journal of Human Rights* 2: 388, 402–5.

10. Speech to the Northern Province Council of Churches, May 23, 1997.

11. If taken, this approach would have been much like that in the United States in a somewhat different context: the application of the U.S. Constitution's Bill of Rights on Indian reservations. A federal statute creates a bill of rights for reservation Indians, but, as interpreted by the U.S. Supreme Court, leaves the enforcement of these rights up to the tribal courts. See *Martinez v. Santa Clara Pueblo*, 436 US 49 (1978).

12. This example comes from a conversation with Likhapa Mbhata, a senior researcher with the Gender Project at the Centre for Applied Legal Studies, Johannesburg, October 1999.

13. Justice Albie Sachs, address to the Southern African Society of Legal Historians, January 13, 1999, 12.

14. For example, the government has had difficulty implementing new legislation regarding land redistribution and legislation authorizing compensation for those who were victims of crimes of the white government during apartheid.

# REFERENCES

Albertyn, Catherine. 1997. "Women in the Transition to Democracy in South Africa." In *Gender and the New South Africa Legal Order*, edited by Christine Murray. Kenwyn, South Africa: Juta.

Andrews, Penelope E. 1997. "Striking the Rock: Confronting Gender Equality in the New South Africa." *Michigan Journal of Race and Law* 3(2).

Bennett, Thomas W. 1985. *Application of Customary Law in Southern Africa*. Cape Town, South Africa: Juta.

———. 1995. *Human Rights and African Customary Law*. Cape Town, South Africa: Juta.

Bozzoli, Belinda. 1991. *Women of Phokeng: Consciousness, Life Strategy, and Migrancy in South Africa, 1900–1983*. Portsmouth, N.H.: Heinemann Educational Books.

Bradley, Martha Sontag. 1993. *Kidnapped from That Land: The Government Raids on the Short Creek Polygamists*. Salt Lake City: University of Utah Press.

Bronstein, Victoria. 1998. "Reconceptualizing the Customary Law Debate in South Africa." *South Africa Journal of Human Rights* (3): 402–5.

Comaroff, John, and Simon Roberts. 1981. *Rules and Processes: The Cultural Logic of Dispute in an African Context*. Chicago: University of Chicago Press.

Costa, Anthony. 1998. "The Myth of Customary Law." *South Africa Journal of Human Rights* 4: 525.

Currie, Iain. 1994. "The future of customary law: lessons from the lobolo debate." In *Gender and the New South African Legal Order*. Kenwyn, South Africa: Juta & Co.

———. 1996. "Indigenous Law." In *Constitutional Law of South Africa*, edited by Matthew Chaskalson et al. Kenwyn, South Africa: Juta.

Hassim, S. 1993. "Family, Motherhood, and Zulu Nationalism: The Politics of the Inkatha Women's Brigade." *Feminist Review* 43: 1.

Kaganas, Felicity, and Christina Murray. 1994. "Law and Women's Rights in South Africa: An Overview." In *Gender and the New South Africa Legal Order*, edited by Christina Murray. Kenwyn, South Africa: Juta.

Larsen, Gustave O. 1971. *The "Americanization" of Utah for Statehood*. San Marino, Calif.: Huntington Library.

Mathabane, Mark. 1994. *African Women: Three Generations*. New York: HarperCollins.

Murray, Christina, and Catherine O'Regan. 1991. "Putting Women into the Constitution." In *Putting Women on the Agenda*, edited by Susan Bazilli. Johannesburg: Raven Press.

Nhlapo, Thandabuntu. 1991. "Women's Rights and the Family in Traditional and Customary Law." In *Putting Women on the Agenda*, edited by Susan Bazilli. Johannesburg: Raven Press.

Oomen, Barbara. 1999. "'We Want to Secure Our Hope': Women and Land Rights in South Africa." In *Women Challenging Society: Stories of Women's Empowerment in Southern Africa*, edited by Madelein Maurick and Bram Posthumus. Amsterdam: Netherlands Institute for Southern Africa.

Prinsloo, M. W., G. J. van Niekerk, and L. P. Vorster. 1998. "Perceptions of the Law Regarding, and Attitudes Towards, Lobolo in Mamelodi and Atteridgeville." *De Jure* 31(1): 86–89.

Reyher, Rebecca Hourwich. 1948. *Zulu Woman: The Life Story of Christina Sibiya.* New York: Columbia University Press.

Robinson, K. L. 1995. "The Minority and Subordinate Status of African Women Under Customary Law." *South Africa Journal of Human Rights* 11: 457.

Romero, Patricia. 1988. "The Autobiography of Nongenile Masithathu Zenani." In *Life Histories of African Women,* edited by Patricia Romero. London: Ashfield Press.

———. 1998. *Profiles in Diversity: Women in the New South Africa.* East Lansing: Michigan State University Press.

Schapera, Isaac. 1955. *A Handbook of Tswana Law and Custom.* 2d ed. London: Oxford University Press.

Simons, Harold Jack. 1968. *African Women: Their Legal Status in South Africa.* Evanston, Ill.: Northwestern University Press.

South Africa Law Commission. 1997. *Harmonisation of the Common Law and the Indigenous Law.* Pretoria: South Africa Law Commission.

Walzer, Michael. 1997. *On Toleration.* New Haven: Yale University Press.

Welsh, G., F. Dagnino, and Albie Sachs. 1987. "Transforming Family Law: New Directions in Mozambique." In *Women and Law in Southern Africa,* edited by Alice Armstrong. Harare: Zimbabwe Publishing House.

# Chapter 5

# Immigrants, Agency, and Allegiance: Some Notes from Anthropology and from Law

### Jane Maslow Cohen and Caroline Bledsoe

Within the past decade, more than ten million people have legally immigrated to the United States, a number greater than ever before, within a similar span. Unlike prior immigrant waves, most of these recent arrivals are non-European and appreciably "foreign." For one thing, many within this cohort do not speak any English. Their manifold languages derive from a vast array of linguistic families—entire language groups, in many instances, that have no etymological relationship to English at all. In the aggregate, these immigrants claim allegiance to an inestimable number of ethnic and other groups, many of which lay claim to a unique cultural status on the basis of various amalgams of precept, practice, history, and tradition. Individuals within this immigrant wave may even consider themselves to belong to more than one such affiliative group—and with cause, as we will see.

On entry, those who hail from this myriad of origins set out, bundled in their myriad allegiances, for any place in any state they choose. Unlike the forced migrations and the stringent ghettoizations that scarred nineteenth- and early twentieth-century immigration into the United States, new arrivals are free of formal constraints on where they may go. Recent immigrants thus have formed a wide variety of settlement patterns throughout the states.

By most comparative diachronic or contemporary measures, this combination of extraordinary immigrant diversity, coupled with untrammeled geographic diffusion, represents a remarkable event. What is more, these comings and remainings have electrified surprisingly few fault lines of day-to-day popular opposition—a situation that seems particularly striking in view of the hostility toward individuals of Middle Eastern descent or Islamic religious practice that the calamitous terrorist attacks on the U.S. on September 11, 2001, could have unleashed.

These emerging features—mounting cultural diversity and apparent intergroup tranquility—should whet both theoretical and empirical interests, especially among liberal scholars. And yet they may. But during the period of the large immigration swell that we have mentioned, a different tendency played out—one that found liberal scholars from a variety of disciplines intent on delineating a range of criticisms of the various democracies and their institutional substrates for what have been taken to be deficiencies in their so-called accommodation—the most capacious rubric of critique—of minority affiliative groups. These criticisms left little room for attention to the quiet successes of intergroup relations that we observe.

The general critical position of these liberal academic commentators faced off against a different cadre of critics of government policy—the reactionary right which, during this same period, sought to direct national attention to two issues that were intended to stoke mainstream fears: the considerable flow of illegal immigrants and the much rarer phenomenon of law-breaking, in the conventional, non-terroristic sense, by legal as well as illegal members of immigrant groups. Both issues were, of course, designed to provoke a Congressional response.

This certainly happened, although the response was interestingly contained. Congress began to pump vast amounts of money into the Immigration and Naturalization Service, which soon acquired the largest budget of any civilian agency, directing that the monies be aimed at improved border and crime control. At the same time, Congress turned a deaf ear to charges that the agency's treatment of detainees, including political asylum claimants, ranged from callousness to the commission of human rights abuses. But neither then nor even now, in the wake of September 11, did Congress authorize a national sweep of illegal immigrants, as occurred in one or another measure in response to both of the twentieth century's World Wars. Nor did Congress alter the terms of basic immigration policy in regard to legal entry. As of this writing, the numbers of legal immigrants have been allowed to continue to grow.

Rather than debating the wisdom of these positions, the most energized branch of liberal scholarship pursued a more robust mission, invigorating its institutional critique through the advocacy of diversity by means of a heightened regard for group-based norms and practices. The resultant effort to theorize the virtues of otherness feeds (and is fed) on the construct that there are essential distinctions between the identities of individuals who belong to affiliative groups and those whose identities have been formed out of other stuff. The liberal principle of equal regard thus becomes a call for special regard, as the central claim on liberal theory and institutional design becomes the obligation to treat with appropriate care these distinctions between *them* and *us*.

In their mutual reliance on such a dichotomy, critics of liberal policy from without and critics of liberalism from within have become odd bedfellows, strangely married to the same theoretical construct. The existence of this right-left conceptual consortium is more than a little awkward for the purposes of political address. Invoking strict conceptions of otherness and difference, however, does far more than to etiolate the terms of political debate. It helps to reify, from two otherwise distinct segments of the political spectrum, the categorical assumptions that undergird the creation and preservation of what one anthropologist pointedly has termed "our natives" (Shore 1996, 55).

One consequence of assuming such categorical differences, whether to heroize or demonize otherness, may be that opportunities for scholarly inquiry go begging. Consider our social tranquility hypothesis. Our working assumption is that the apparent achievement of relatively unperturbed immigrant absorption is likely to represent a manifestation of two interrelated phenomena. One is that the ideal of equality of regard has become so incorporated into everyday behavior within communities in the United States that it facilitates tolerance among people. The second phenomenon is less neatly described. It implicates a collection of behaviors, not necessarily self-conscious, through which individuals modulate their earlier group attachments and interweave them in new and perhaps experimental adaptations to settled mainstream groups. Only the tandem workings of these elements—relatively tolerant social norms in the new homeland and an openness to adaptive social behaviors on the part of newcomers across a wide range of encounters—can account for what we find so deserving of notice: the attractive sequela of our generous contemporary immigration policies, in contrast to the inflammatory issues of illegal entry and criminal violence that partisans of harsh deportation measures and restrictive quotas have pressed, in service of their demand.

Ours is a hypothesis that invites empirical pursuit. Only through rigorous observation and the study of ground-level situations that involve newcomers and their affiliative groups can we expect to learn about the actual workings of geopolitical transitions and host-community response. The empirical move that we invite depends on a willingness to conceive of group-influenced behaviors as mutant social variables that may be recombinant in the flux of circumstance. Indeed, this is how liberal theory regards even the highly freighted matter of religious identity and choice. How else to explain the interdenominational fluidity of the Protestant conscience in America?

Our conception of the socially adaptive capacities of individuals is prefigured within an interdisciplinary literature that stands apart from that which undergirds most accommodationist political advocacy. Here we refer to powerful reformulations of earlier social science notions about the nature and workings of groups, individual allegiance to groups, and matters of personal agency. This literature is replete with framing and interpretive devices that help to explain the second of the two social phenomena we have described: the capacities of large numbers of immigrants to negotiate creative and practical options on the ground. This work resists characterizations that emphasize distinctions between *them* and *us*, speaking instead to commonalities of human conduct and concern. Spearheaded by anthropologists and sociologists alike, these moves have transformed the theoretical apparatus through which groups, agency, and allegiance are understood.

This work encourages a fundamental shift in understanding group allegiance and individual agency. Like most revisionist efforts, its strongest claims may prove to be overstated. Yet the tilt in this literature toward multigroup allegiance and the importance of individual agency provides a much-needed correction to cultural theory as it has been applied to questions of immigrants and the law. This tilt helps to explain the surprisingly tranquil and flexible interaction of new immigrants and those who preceded them to the United States, many of whom are themselves within a few generations of immigrant status. This successful interaction in turn stands as data in support of this literature.

This same turn toward a heightened recognition of the importance of individual agency must guide the employment of whatever institutional vehicles are used to bring members of terrorist organizations to justice, not only in the United States and under the aegis of its sovereign authority, but by means of the authority of any of the now-threatened countries in the world. Without a strong conception of individual moral agency, only leaders of terrorist organizations could be held accountable for the perpetration of atrocious acts. Domestic advocates of accommodation have made arguments that reach in that direction in regard to the application of the conventional criminal law, although these arguments at present are contained within a literature which has sought to address matters involving the criminal justice system before the events of September 11. Thus, it is not yet clear how accommodationist arguments might address terrorist acts—whether, for example, they might attempt to exclude acts carried out in the name of holy war from other sites of analysis.

An accommodative stance might still be pressed in ordinary criminal courts hearing conventional criminal cases, on the ground that anything short of culturally accommodative reforms is likely to serve as an ongoing irritant between the dominant majority and cultural minority groups—a notion that is at the core of the accommodationist claim. Convinced as we are that accommodationism's theoretical—as well as practical—shortcomings are most clearly visible in the case that has been raised against the criminal justice system, it is that case that we proceed to examine below.

Advocates of cultural accommodation within the United States have proposed a variety of devices intended to liberalize the effective use of what has been called *cultural evidence* in defense of members of immigrant and other subgroups charged with committing domestic crimes. The source of many of these crimes is theorized as a license or mandate authorized to a given defendant by his or her culture[1] to engage in conduct prohibited by American law because it is regarded as both a harm and a wrong. In starkest terms, the accommodationist position treats such normative differences between the dominant legal culture and immigrant and other ethnic subgroups as a sufficient warrant for differences in judgment regarding criminal culpability and punishment, especially in cases involving the direst of punishment. The friction that characterizes the resultant debate stems from the fact that many of the cases that achieve media prominence, even notoriety, involve the commission of serious and even deadly crimes against women or children.[2]

In such instances, the notion that deep and wrongful injury has taken place to which the law must respond has not been a matter of settled and long-standing consensus. Rather, one main goal of the feminist theory movement has been to eliminate from the criminal law the patriarchal excuses for the injury of women or children that have riddled and embarrassed it, and to press, on both the domestic and international human rights fronts, for a unifying, equality-driven conception of justice. Not surprisingly, therefore, the feminist response toward a more plural criminal law—one that would privilege the status of culture by denigrating the equal status of victims—has been overwhelmingly hostile. Yet when the cultural evidence cases involve female defendants (an inventory on which we will draw in what follows), feminist theorists fight bitterly over the correct normative approach, thereby defeating a feminist-theoretical opportunity to generate a coherent response.[3] This division is hardly surprising. Gender biases within Anglo-American criminal law have been uniformly patriarchal, whereas female-biased customs occasionally receive sympathetic treatment within other systems of law. For some feminists to repudiate the incorporation of such sympathies into the U.S. criminal justice system is understandably difficult—the more so because of feminist advocacy, on behalf of female criminal defendants, for doctrinal accommodation outside the terms of the pluralist debate.

For the purpose of confronting accommodationism, therefore, the best arguments against any formal installation of cultural pluralism within the criminal law must draw on a fuller store of both normative and pragmatic intuitions than feminism per se can supply. In what follows, we draw on three sources of insight that the present debate over accommodationism does not sufficiently reference. One source is the recent social science literature on individual agency, group allegiance, and identity that already has been sketched. The second collects some practical questions about the potential handicaps of a pluralist approach in the face of multiplying diversities, such as are present in the United States. The third draws on the liberal normative tradition of the criminal justice system to invoke, in force, its governing ideal of equal justice under law.

The accommodationist call for structural criminal law reform cannot survive the challenge of these approaches, each of which helps to root the perspectives with which we began: overall intergroup tranquility in the presence of rapid and diverse immigrant absorption suggests the plausibility of theories that treat individual attachments to culture as complex, evolutionary, and permeable. The accommodationist movement is grounded in assumptions about culture that take these attachments to be stable, unyielding, and considerably impermeable. Intergroup tranquility suggests that practical adaptations based on a congeries of factors—not least, the influence of equal regard—are at work. Accommodationist advocacy sets aside these factors by insisting on the supervening urgency of special regard. While it is implausible that the extraordinary cultural diversity being fostered by U.S. immigration policy could enforce or reinforce ethnic bounds, accommodationism seeks to promote a criminal justice system formally restructured to reinforce cultural bounds. Our position is that a tolerant nation of evolving diversities should resist the impulses toward change that criminal law accommodationism seeks.

Our efforts are intended to cast doubt on any holistic drive toward cultural accommodation, especially any that would target the criminal law. The theme of mutual adaptation, together with the concerted rejection of criminal law reform, is presented in order to refine the current debate—especially the debate internal to liberalism—over the ways in which liberal political, social, and theoretical norms and evolving cultural precepts and practices should converge.

# THE PRESS OF ACCOMMODATIONISM TOWARD CRIMINAL LAW REFORM: SOME EXAMPLES

During the past two decades, the period that includes the most recent immigration wave, a practical turn has gained currency within the strategies of criminal law defense work. This involves the use of so-called cultural evidence in order to blunt the force of the state's case.[4] Underlying the strategy is the proposition that "persons socialized in a minority or foreign culture, who regularly conduct themselves in accordance with their own culture's norms, should not be held fully accountable for conduct that violates official law, if their conduct conforms to the prescriptions of their own culture" (Magnarella 1991).[5]

The criminal law process provides a wide spate of opportunities for such evidence's receipt. This helps to account for the successes that the criminal defense bar has had in deploying cultural evidence on its clients' behalf. Yet the case law of this period also suggests some resistance or reluctance on the part of justice system personnel to accept such evidence as credible or probative on the terms offered. These are the terms that accommodationist scholars have identified as the sites of needed reform.

To gain a sense of what is at stake, we begin with some examples from the recent criminal case law, much as accommodationist advocates do. The examples that follow track the literature: they are among the cases most standardly treated as rallying points.[6] As in much of the scholarship, they are presented in capsule form.

## Case 1. Chen

In a New York case, a Chinese man killed his wife by smashing her skull with a hammer after she admitted having committed adultery. The couple had immigrated to the United States a year earlier. The trial judge allowed a defense based on diminished capacity, one of the traditional criminal law excuses that mitigate full culpability for the commission of murder. The basis of the plea was that, according to traditional Chinese values, a wife's adultery proves a husband's weakness. In the court's judgment, this belief caused the husband to "crack" under the pressure of his wife's confession, leading him to kill her straightaway. Bolstered by the expert testimony of an anthropologist, defense counsel persuaded the presiding judge not to convict the husband, Dong Lu Chen, of premeditated murder but rather to find him guilty of the lesser offense of second-degree manslaughter. The maximum sentence for the crime in question was imprisonment for fifteen years. The judge sentenced Chen to probation—no jail or prison time—and released him (see *People v. Chen* 1989; Jetter 1989).

The Chen case generated instant notoriety and what one reporter described as "a long, cold shadow over New York's Chinatown" (Jetter 1989). Two years after the event, according to this account, battered Chinese women remained afraid to report their husband's acts. "If a wife-killer gets only probation," one of them reasoned, "what if you only get hit or beaten?" (Jetter 1989).[7]

## Case 2. Kong Moua

In a California case, a member of the large Hmong Laotian refugee community was charged with rape and kidnapping by the parents of a young woman from the same community after he attempted to marry her through the practice of zij poj niam, or bride capture. According to this custom, the defendant claimed, the would-be husband proceeds, after an initial flirtation that is considered mutual, to carry the woman off to his parents' home where he is expected, in order to evidence his virility, to overcome her protests by having intercourse and thus consummate the marriage. Within this practice, it is understood that a woman's failure to protest signifies that she is unchaste.

According to reports that followed, the would-be husband, Kong Moua, was surprised by his arrest, having apprehended his intended at the university where she worked, driven her to his parents' home, engaged in sexual intercourse over her protests, then claimed to have effectuated their marriage. On the basis of anthropological evidence submitted to the prosecutor and presiding judge prior to trial, and after conferences were held with clan elders, the court found Moua to have been sincere in his belief that the woman's protests were merely ritualistic rather than based on an Americanized lack of consent. Accordingly, a plea bargain was struck: Moua was allowed to plead guilty to the relatively minor offense of false imprisonment, for which he served a short jail sentence and paid a modest fine (see *People v. Kong Moua* 1985).

## Case 3. Kimura

In another California case, a Japanese woman who had resided in this country for more than a decade drowned her two young children and then tried to commit suicide (see *People v. Kimura* 1985; "The Cultural and Legal Dimensions of Infanticide" 1990, 1–90). The woman, Fumiko Kimura, reportedly had become despondent after learning of her husband's adultery. The commission of oya-ko shinju—parent-child suicide—understood to be a customary response to such a humiliation, is currently criminalized but punished relatively lightly in Japan, in the case of suicides that fail.

Four thousand Japanese residents of the Los Angeles area petitioned the district attorney, seeking to have the case treated in accordance with "modern Japanese law," such that the indictable offense would have been not premeditated murder, but a charge significantly less grave. This request formally was refused, but having charged Kimura with premeditated murder, the prosecutor then accepted her plea bargain to the lesser charge of voluntary manslaughter on the ground of temporary insanity. Kimura had been examined by several forensic psychiatrists, all of whom concurred in the diagnosis that at the time of the crime she was seriously depressed. Having served a year in jail awaiting trial, Kimura was sentenced to probation, psychiatric treatment, and jail time equal to the time already served. She therefore left the courtroom at liberty—a sentence at least as lenient as that which she was likely to have received in Japan.

## Case 4. Wu

In yet another California case, a Chinese woman, Helen Wu, was convicted by a jury of second-degree murder, for which she was sentenced to a prison term of fifteen years to life (see *People v. Wu* 1991). She killed her eleven-year-old son by strangling him, then attempted to take her own life. At trial, the prosecution pressed the theory that she intended the boy's death as revenge against his father, who had rejected her many times over several years.

Seeking to excuse Wu's act, the defense placed the defendant's state of mind at issue in several ways. All of these depended on expert testimony, received at trial, of Wu's culturally based sense of shame and humiliation at her husband's hands, her fear for the boy's welfare, and her conviction that she could best protect him in the afterlife. The trial judge refused to instruct the jury as Wu's lawyer proposed. On appeal, however, the decision was reversed, so that on retrial a jury could be instructed on Wu's entitlement to the American excuse of unconsciousness—and therefore, lack of requisite intent—at the time of the act, based on evidence of her culturally influenced state of mind. At her second trial, Wu was convicted of voluntary manslaughter, a lesser crime than any charge of murder. She was sentenced to a prison term of eleven years (see Kataoka 1992, B1).

## "Reforms" Reconsidered

When accommodationist arguments take aim at the criminal law, their consensus view is that cultural norms merit the law's special regard. At a general level, as has been noted, their positions converge. As the discussion that follows illustrates, however, the issues of how and where to ground a cultural defense—not its justice or necessity—create divisions among those who have entered the field.

The most commonly advanced of the accommodationist positions would locate the excusing force of cultural evidence within the body of traditional criminal law defenses, so as to make no new conceptual waves. In criminal law terms, however, the idea that underlies this view is unorthodox in that the states of mind that ordinarily satisfy the necessary conditions of excuse doctrine involve individuals whose debilitated mental states render them not culpable—that is, not blameworthy as a matter of criminal responsibility—for their conduct. As their general formulations suggest, at least some accommodationists would al-

low adherence to minority group norms to function in the place of highly individuated pleas such as mental illness, thereby inverting the shape of the underlying basis for excuse from narrow and individualized to broad and group-specific. The claim, then, is: "my culture made me do it." The use of excuse
doctrine, which now functions to provide only highly restrictive pleas for the
significantly aberrant, thus could become a broad-scale challenge to notions of
criminal culpability, as individuals claiming merely to have engaged in the sanctioned behaviors of an unlimited number of groups seek refuge from punishment here.[8]

Not surprisingly, criminal defense lawyers are reluctant to mount claims that
are so bluntly antagonistic to the primary norms of the criminal law. Instead,
they tend to avoid confrontational strategies by selecting narrow and conventional evidentiary frames, pressing the available evidence into them. The *Kimura*
case illustrates this point. In *Kimura*, the state of California set out to prove that,
since Ms. Kimura willfully engaged in a prohibited act—that of drowning her
two young children—and intended to commit it at the time (as by all accounts
she did), she should be prosecuted for their premeditated murder. The defense
aimed not to exculpate her but to mitigate her responsibility for the crime. Her
lawyers could have tried to convince the court that, as a humiliated Japanese
wife, she behaved in accordance with custom in killing her children. Yet they
shrank the terms of her defense from "my culture authorized these murders" to
a plea of temporary insanity—a far more conservative choice.

Accommodationist advocates are far from uniformly comfortable, however,
with this sort of conventional strategizing. Some have argued that the insanity
defense in *Kimura* amounts to a cultural insult. Because the practice of oya-ko
shinju has been rationalized as a means to secure the otherworldly welfare of
children, some say that it should be treated as a justified rather than an excused
act—one that should not be a punishable wrong. Only a defense that would
allow evidence of the act's cultural ground to be admitted on its own uncom-
promised terms could provide a person of Japanese ancestry—adhering to the
traditional norm in a case of oya-ko shinju—an opportunity to be understood in
authentic terms. That the custom in question is now banned in its country of
origin might be thought to compromise this position. In instances such as this,
adherents of the authenticity approach sometimes conclude that American law
should apply whatever treatment of a cultural act applies in the homeland as of
the time of the act's commission—in the case of oya-ko shinju, then, a light
punishment.

The defense of *provocation*—where the force of impulse is recognized as a
factor that mitigates culpability—functions as a second example of an approach
that seeks to rely on available doctrinal resources, in this instance, one that satis-
fies the adherents of authenticity more easily than does the insanity defense.[9] In
the *Chen* case, for example, the anthropologist who testified for the defense
opined that the defendant behaved reasonably for a man "from mainland
China" (Coleman 1996, 1124).[10] Asked to compare Chen's reaction to his wife's
adultery to that of a "reasonable" American husband, the anthropologist an-

swered, "In general terms, I think that one could expect a Chinese to react in a much more volatile, violent way to those circumstances than someone from our own society" (Volpp 1996).[11] Indeed, some accommodationists argue that the excuse of provocation, as deployed in *Chen*, is the ideal American home for a culture-based defense (see Sing 1999).

The accommodationist use of provocation as a cultural lever in the criminal law nods toward two of its other claims, one more constrained than the provocation defense, the other, a good deal more robust. The constrained variation is like provocation in that it focuses on the defendant's state of mind. Where provocation recognizes that a partially forgivable impulse may cloud the volitional element that constitutes part of the definition of murder, however, some accommodationists narrow their claims to instances where the actor's cultural background can be used to show that he or she lacked the requisite malevolent impulse that a specific crime definitionally requires. They point to cases where the actus reus (the physical act prohibited by law) has undeniably been committed, but the mens rea (the mental state of the accused) required to label the act a crime is lacking. This is the route by which the *Kong Moua* case enters the accommodationist argument, offered as an instance of cultural injustice: a Hmong suitor such as Moua would believe himself to be engaged in a traditional courting practice shrouded in ritualized consent understood to be the formality of female protest, not in the commission of a rape.[12] The case of Helen Wu represents another instance in which a cultural variable was brought forward to negate the mens rea element of the crime.

The claim that we take to be more robust than provocation involves moving from the concept of *excuse* in criminal law to that of *justification*. Excuses typically involve reasons why an act, albeit wrongful, may be considered less than fully blameworthy on account of the involuntarily constricted moral judgment of the actor. Justifications go further. They accept the act as one that, under the circumstances, is not itself a wrong; rather, the otherwise blameworthy act becomes, on account of context, one that is condoned. The classic justification is self-defense, a powerful register of the moral judgment that not every killing is a wrong.

Excuses, because they tend to single out circumstances distinct to the individual actor, may be quite amenable to cultural information that may be offered in defense of the conduct without any theoretical effort being made to cover group-wide norms. The indexing of justifications to culture is more extreme. Justifications typically pertain to standards of behavior appropriate to the reasonable person. The underlying theory is that a reasonable member of the community in which the act took place would have behaved similarly to the defendant at the time and in the context of what actually happened. Thus, nothing is peculiar or exceptional about the actor's conduct: quite the reverse. The reasons that justify the act must be external to the actor: it is not her mental state but, rather, events outside of herself that prompt its occurrence. If these causes are deemed sufficient, the act is judged to have been justified and the actor is fully exonerated.

The reasonable person standard that is treated as the template in the adjudication of justified criminal acts was challenged, beginning a couple of decades ago, as discriminatorily gender-biased and therefore unjust. Until then, the invariant Anglo-American standard had been that of the "reasonable man." In cases involving female victims, rape being the paradigm, the standard's gender bias effectively was shown to discredit unjustly some appropriate types of response. Only in some jurisdictions is a gender-sensitive standard (when the crime itself is gender-sensitive) now in use. Thus far, the standard for justification has been resistant to virtually all other attempts at inflection, including race and class.

The accommodationist position argues that the reasonable person standard should be rendered culturally sensitive as well as gender-sensitive, though not race- or class-sensitive. On this account, crimes such as Kimura's deserve to be treated as justified if a contemporary Japanese wife, shamed by her husband's adultery, would consider oya-ko shinju a reasonable and rational set of acts, as the custom encodes. This accommodationist move would redistribute the criteria for judgment about the reasonableness of action from the political community responsible for promulgating the law to the multitude of affiliative groups who are to receive it.[13] Indeed, such a move is seismic in significance, as it fractures the political foundation of the criminal law, according to which a jurisdiction is constitutive of a single juridical community, one whose members are fully and equally responsible to each other under the sovereign's law.

Some accommodationists have pressed past the existing resources of the criminal law—excuse and justification included—to argue for more stable, freestanding forms of cultural defense. Their most stringent hope is for a formal defense that could be pleaded separately whenever minority-group cultural norms and the dominant culture's legal norms conflict.[14] Such a defense would not need to be classified as *either* a justification or an excuse; it would constitute a category independent of both.

A modest instance of this sort of claim concerns ignorance of the law, which is rarely accepted as a legal excuse, though prosecutors and sentencing judges may treat a defendant's innocence of knowledge of the law's applicability as an ameliorating factor in the charging or sentencing process. Some accommodationists argue that the circumstances of the newly arrived immigrant—his or her foreignness—ought to make us especially sympathetic and lead the criminal law to recognize a formal defense based on ignorance of the law as such. In this spirit, some argue that immigrants should be exempt from the general requirement of criminal law knowledge for a specified period after their arrival. Suggested intervals have ranged from one year to as many as ten. (The idea of a fixed period for special accommodation might appeal to some who believe that cultural norms may be compelling. The idea of a time-sensitive excuse treats the force of those norms to weaken, expectably, with time.)

A third proposal for the formal annexation of cultural norms we already have seen in the accommodationist claim that a successfully pleaded cultural defense should give rise to culturally congruent sanctions: those (for example, in *Kimura*) that would be levied had the case been prosecuted in the defendant's culture of origin. This sort of cultural congruence in sentencing, of course, is a harbinger of a full-blown cultural defense, one that indexes criminal liability, rather than mere culpability—as in the other suggestions—to the cultural label one is understood to wear.

The United States clearly is becoming a more ethnically diverse society. Criminal law accommodationism would have it that, as the population becomes less well-represented by its Anglo-European origins (and more greatly represented by persons with different ethnic roots), a unified system of justice shaped around the dominant culture's mores becomes manifestly unfair. In its place, a more plural system of criminal justice is required. Given that this idea has no existing home within the traditional aims of the criminal law, accommodationism has sought to institutionalize its agenda by drawing heavily on a long-established purpose: the *individualized* search for just outcomes that is a central and incontestible inspiration of this branch of law.

The claim that a defendant's sources of normative understanding and justification may be important to the search for individualized justice is what prosecutors, in their exercise of authority over the charging function, and sentencing judges, with their wide discretion to act both mercifully and justly, are granted the authority to probe every day. This is no more or less the case in regard to immigrants or persons who claim ethnic distinctiveness than in regard to anyone else. As a concerted prompt to the justice system to change its ways, we find that the general position as well as the specific mandates that accommodationism seeks are both incomplete and flawed. These conclusions are discussed in the following section.

## CULTURE, ETHNICITY, AND RULES

In the conception that dominates accommodationism, groups are regarded as isolates: islands of social formation distinct from one another, entities whose customs are fixed. Until recent decades, this understanding was shared by many anthropologists. Indeed, anthropologists were the chief disciplinary authors of these ideas. While it was well-recognized that groups were not homogeneous internally, ethnicity was treated as a stable category as late as the 1960s, while ethnic groups were treated as islands of isolation. In his description of anthropological history, Bradd Shore notes that theories of culture in the 1960s and even into the 1970s were dominated by disembodied systems, structures, and programs that implied

> knowledge without any particular knower in mind and structures of thought that lacked any flesh-and-blood thinkers. . . . People appeared more as the passive sites of cultural programming than as purposeful agents, strategists, and meaning makers. . . . [Thus,] the culture concept gained in clarity at the expense of its concrete agents. We came to know more about cultural systems in general than we did about people in particular. (Shore 1996, 54–55)

The last several decades, however, have seen a sea change in anthropology and sociology. Many group definitions formerly taken for granted now are seen as having been arbitrarily imposed, whether as artifacts of colonial conquest or as temporary conglomerates. Even more important has been a shift in the overall orientation toward social life. Labeled by various terms—*social strategies, interactionism, social constructionism, managing meaning,* and *practice theory,* among others (see Giddens 1977; Carrithers 1992; Maines 1997; McDermott and Roth 1978; Comaroff and Roberts 1981; Hanks 1996)—such approaches have sought to supplant the perception that tradition guides behavior and maintains stasis. These newer works hold that individuals, acting within their various roles and identities, exercise agency. They size up situations, evaluate alternative courses of action, and carry out actions with intent.[15] Instead of assuming the fixed truth or validity of a claim, the social order is recognized to contain a multiplicity of normative as well as strictly coercive elements. In an arena of contestation over meaning, subordinate groups attempt to reshape the intentions and forms of imposed institutions through the ways in which claims are laid, documented, and pressed. Tension arises between agency and constraint, and coercion inevitably becomes involved. Yet norms and rules can be resources for social and self-definition: they do not operate only as constraints. Indeed, in the field as a whole, as Shore (1996, 55) describes,

[T]he agents of culture are no longer hypothetical or average natives but look like real individuals with specific histories, particular interests, and concrete strategies. Rather than as members of homogeneous cultures, we now are more likely to conceive of our natives as enmeshed in complex power relations.

Applied to the interpretation of ethnicity and ethnic group relations, such formulations interpret identity as a continuing process of boundary creation, maintenance, and reconstruction. Rather than assuming that any cultural characteristics immutably separate groups, the field now grants attention to the situational quality of ethnicity, to the fluidity with which groups blend and divide. Similar conceptions guide notions of individual identity. In particular, Fredrik Barth (1969), who observed that people use ethnic labels to define themselves in interaction with others, opened up the realization that people can have multiple ethnic identities and loyalties.[16] Indeed, a range of ethnic labels is typically available and in many contexts a person can *choose* to be categorized by any of a selection of ethnic labels. Rather than defining behavior, ethnic labels may be used to explain it after the fact. As Ronald Cohen (1978) has concluded, the division into an exclusive grouping is always done in relation to significant others whose exclusion at any particular level of scale creates the we-they dichotomy. What does this mean for the dynamics of ethnic relations in new settings? As Cohen (1978, 384) observes, "[T]he study of contemporary peoples in a complex world has now clearly shifted from ethnic isolates to one in which the interrelations between such groups in rural, urban, and industrial settings within and between nation-states is a key, possibly *the key* element in their lives."

Having abandoned the assumption that any set of characteristics immutably separates groups, anthropologists have come alive to the idea that ethnic labels may be applied situationally, purposefully, and creatively. New-origin myths can be fictionalized in order to rationalize legitimacy, create links between previously disparate groups, or generate the impression of past greatness. In short, the melting pot precipitates as often as it melts. To be sure, the idea of ethnicity serves as an integrative function of our psychic modalities. Together with other attributes of personal identity, ethnicity is capable of inviting mental gyrations through time and space. To assume otherwise—as models of tradition-bound behaviors implicitly do—is to set ethnic persons apart from the adaptive, psychically mobilized balance of humanity. It is to lock them out of evolving perceptions of cognition that have inspired psychology and psychiatry since Freud.

To the extent that these recent perceptions of agency, allegiance, and culture trigger concerns about the accuracy of social description and the dynamics of individual agency, they must apply to legal as well as all other codes of behavior by persons who claim membership in groups, some of which operate on the basis of mutually contradictory, internally contested, or otherwise unstable norms. This more complex and plausible understanding of groups and group membership poses significant challenges for claims that regimes of law should bend to culture. It suggests that, upon arrival in the United States (or any new and normatively unfamiliar social setting), immigrants will draw on a large repertoire of creative resources to find ways to respond. It also suggests that the variant states of traditional norms are unlikely to dictate their responses.

Across the fluid and wide-ranging span of intercultural negotiations that will ensue, most adaptations will be uneventful, especially in regard to the law. In some instances, however, adaptations will result in behaviors that are defined as violations, including, occasionally, serious violations of the criminal law. The fact that violations of extant codes are bound to occur within the ambit of individual reactions to the normatively unfamiliar is a fact beyond debate. The pungent question that accommodationism puts is what ought justly to happen, as an institutional matter, by way of response.

## Cultural Vagaries and Group Variations

Accommodationist claims on the criminal law's resources are vigorous. They reflect the courage to lead a charge against the authorized processes—even the normative legitimacy—of the justice system. Nor is it less than admirable that the enterprise is funded by liberal principle—the toleration principle, most of all. What is surprising is to encounter, nearly everywhere within the argument, the marriage of passionate conviction regarding the need for cultural tolerance to languid conception regarding the meaning of culture itself.

As noted earlier, the new social anthropology of agency is grounded in insights that cause severe damage to the accommodationist stance. At a bare minimum, it requires the accommodationist position either to reject the liberal concept of agency as irrelevant to all or most new immigrants, or to interpolate some powerful theory that is capable of justifying the unique treatment of culture as a matter of justice apart from—indeed, superior to—gender, race, and class.

The literature of accommodationist advocacy ignores these challenges. Relying instead on a politics of virtually unbounded inclusion, accommodationism leaves the concept of culture without observable bounds. Indeed, the use of "culture" sometimes codes for ethnicity; other times for foreignness or recent immigrant heritage; still elsewhere, for the group allegiances of minority or indigenous peoples; then again, for certain complexities in relation to individual agency that "enculturation" or other aspects of socialization are claimed to bring about.

The lack of conceptual consistency that pervades the use of culture sweeps before it a host of lesser-included terms. Sometimes culture is understood to refer to a society: groups and the structures by which they are organized or the behaviors their members perform. Thus, multiple references allude to the force of *traditions, practices, beliefs, norms, precepts, standards, values, influences, commands, moral demands,* and more. In less developed countries, for example, culture is commonly understood as the force of tradition that guides behavior before the modernity conferred by income, schooling, and development erases it. In these instances, culture is a barrier to modernity, for better or worse. Within the frame of this conceptual blur, no inquiry attaches to the crucial question: What, if any, is the different normative weight that might attach to a *rule* or a *command* versus a *prerogative* versus a *practice* or a *norm*? Is an act based on any of these entitled to the same presumptive weight as any or all of the others for the purpose of establishing a defense of criminal conduct under law?

At stake is an element deeper than the clarity of nomenclature or conceptual cohesion. The vague ascriptions of culture and its constitutive elements mask the need for a clearer theory of the link between belief and behavior than accommodationist advocacy provides. If the motivating cause of a cultural defense is the need to take the normative obligations of others seriously when their conduct violates our laws, then it is surely necessary to understand the meaning that underlies their behavior. That a criminal defendant claims allegiance to a culture different from that in which he or she is being tried provides an insufficient understanding of the causal relationship between the cultural predicate, the agent, and the act.

This is precisely the issue that gets signaled, but not thereafter parsed, in the most general and convergent of the accommodationist views described earlier. There, it becomes evident that, for accommodationism, cultural conditioning may be so powerful that individuals cannot discard it. "Enculturation" is "exceedingly difficult" to supplant (Renteln 1987–1988); persons from other cultures "will be likely to feel morally obligated to follow [foreign] norms" ("Cultural Defense" 1986, 1300). Indeed, the conformity of individual behavior to "foreign cultural values" because it is "sanctioned" or "promoted" in the homeland should give onto its excuse as a matter of "logic" here (Maguigan 1995, 39–40). As a matter of motivating cause, these claims are different from one another. The idea that ignorance of the law should be excusable is different from the idea that an inability to conform one's conduct to the law should be excusable, or the further idea that an act based on a preferred cultural prerogative should be excusable. These represent separate behavioral kinds.

Not surprisingly, these separate behavioral kinds give rise to differing normative concerns. So does the lack of description of any limiting conditions that might attach to the advocacy for accommodationism, given the kinds of practical issues such claims must invite. Questions of design and feasibility are conspicuously absent, as lacking in presence as any interrogation of the concepts of groups, agency, and allegiance or the concept of culture itself. The following section illustrates the kinds of practical concerns that are absent from notice in these texts.

## PLURALISM AND CRIMINAL LAW

The problems entailed in the revision of the criminal law, were it to take systematic account of culture, are magnified substantially by the increasing diversity of the population United States law is intended to rule. Indeed, the very expanse of U.S. immigration policy confounds, in the most practical terms, the moves that accommodationism would make. The following analytic elements should demonstrate our point.

### Scale and Internal Variation

The sheer number of ethnic groups whose customs, norms, and practices might qualify for accommodation, on present argumentative terms, is staggering. As earlier described, the diversity of countries that send immigrants to the United States has escalated sharply since 1965, when the United States removed national origin quotas from immigration law. New York City alone has taken in immigrants from over one hundred countries. More to the point, *countries* serve as the standard measure of immigrant diversity, while accommodationism would service *groups*. Regions from which many of our recent immigrants hail help to illustrate the difference. Sub-Saharan Africa has hundreds, if not well over a thousand, ethnic groups. Nigeria alone is estimated to have between two and three hundred. If we consider as well that ethnic groups often have subgroups, the permutations escalate even more rapidly. Divided into more than fifty kingdoms, the Yoruba of Nigeria comprise a salient case. As an anthropologist who has studied them has observed, "[I]mmigrant groups and conquerors from without and interkingdom wars all contributed to produce a kaleidoscopic pattern of culture and structure that seems to defy classification. One could, I think, write a textbook on comparative political systems drawing almost all one's examples from the Yoruba!" (Lloyd 1967, 547–82).

In themselves, these observations about quantity and variation are neither here nor there. It is the possibility of accommodation in the form of one or another kind of special systemic accord that generates concern for the fair administration of the law. How could the police, prosecutors, judges, and juries be expected to evaluate the substantive force, with respect to individual behavior, of a multiplicity of social, legal, and moral codes? In exercising their arrest and charging functions, respectively, neither police nor prosecutors have the benefit of expert witnesses, as a matter of institutional design. Should they rely on the participants in acts of wrongdoing to decode the relevant norms? Within the trial system, expert witnesses do get employed. There, perhaps, anthropologists should be called to testify, for both the prosecution and the defense, to explicate the source, meaning, and significance of the allegedly responsible norm. But this is likely to be an unobtainable ideal. It is implausible to assume that there are enough anthropologists, let alone a pool of willing anthropologists, with sufficiently accurate and detailed knowledge of the normative permutations of some vast array of groups.[17] What might emerge from such testimony, moreover, is unlikely to resemble straightforward fact. Instead, the repeated invocation of a forensic of anthropology is more likely to crush the very idea of fact under the weight of conflicting interpretations, the plausibility of which may be difficult to judge according to any consistent or otherwise reliable standard of account.[18]

## Group Eligibility and Cultural Ephemerality

Another form of difficulty that attaches to the possible grant of special excuse on the basis of ethnicity or other group affiliation is the question of who should be eligible to receive a cultural defense. For first-generation immigrants qualifications might include evidence of long-standing residence in the country of origin; but again, multiple complications arise. What about political refugees who have spent little or no time in the country they consider their own? And how could prior residence be certified among immigrants from countries with poor civil registration systems? Moreover, many of those who engage in ethnic or other traditional practices are not themselves immigrants; instead, they are members of diluted generations. What of immigrants who, even after lengthy periods of residence in the United States, have not gained awareness of American cultural norms? Ms. Kimura's heavily documented cultural insularity over a decade of residence in the United States is a powerful case in point. Should self-chosen cultural insularity yield an entitlement to special regard? And what about the American ideal of *equal* regard? Should Kimura's attempt to practice a custom that is culturally deprivileged, as a matter of Japanese law, be entitled to the same quality of regard as, for example, the prerogative of Mr. Chen, on the arguable (at best) assumption that Chinese communism would have sanctioned it? Then what of Ms. Wu, from the Chinese-ruled island of Macau, and her claimed belief in the safety of an afterlife for her son? Should the integrity of her cultural defense be measured against that of Kimura and Chen? What then is to become of Kong Moua and the integrity of his beliefs? And what of the parents of Kong Moua's intended bride, who, although they shared his ethnicity, sought his prosecution, not his cultural protection from the law?

Our tiny case inventory references first-generation immigrants only. But let us pursue for a moment the possibility of accommodation in the case of diluted generations. Persons who declare themselves to be of Asian or Hispanic ancestry comprised 68 percent of the "foreign" population noted in the 1990 census. Estimates show that while 13 percent of foreign-born Asians marry outside their racial-ethnic group, 34 percent of second-generation marriages and 54 percent of third-generation marriages occur with people outside their groups. Out-marriage differences among the generations are even sharper among Hispanics, who marry non-Hispanics 8 percent of the time in the first generation, 32 percent in the second, and 57 percent in the third (see Smith and Edmonston 1997, 132).[19] That so many immigrants marry outsiders, and that their children marry yet more often afield, raises the question of whether living arrangements within the United States that foster group insularity should give rise to a normative shield. How many generations or instances of out-marriage could be claimed to bear a sufficient imprint of an ethnicity's customary norms to allow for the mitigation of rules that constrain other subjects of the laws of the United States?

Since the accommodationist emphasis on culture ascribes no necessary ontology as the basis for an actual claim, should a person's psychological attachments to a culture require a physical or an ancestral base at all? What if just any member of American society were to adopt a set of cultural mores, then claim for a legally aberrant act the benefit of an accommodative stance? In short, should ethnic self-identification foster the delamination of legal norms?

One way to cut through the dilemmas posed by questions of ethnic identity for legal purposes would be simply to allow self-declaration: if you say you are Mende (a Sierra Leonean group), then you are Mende. Self-declaration is the usual strategy adopted, without adversion or comment, in demographic surveys (including the census) that elicit an individual's name, gender, race, marital status, and relationship to the household head. Of course, people might well designate themselves by more than one ethnicity: for example, American and Mende.[20] Indeed, the 2000 census allowed analogous possibilities in its queries on race. With reference to each household member, question 6 of the Long Form asked, "What is this person's race? Mark one or more races to indicate what this person considers himself/herself to be." A total of fourteen race possibilities were offered, and even then the respondents could report more than one or fill in one not listed.

Individuals also identify themselves, as a matter of unopposed convention, according to the context in which a particular issue arises (see E. E. Evans-Pritchard 1940; Barth 1969). A woman who considers herself simultaneously American, African, Sierra Leonean, and Mende may describe herself in Africa as an American and in the United States as an African. When she is among other Africans, however, she may speak of herself as Sierra Leonean and, when among other Sierra Leoneans, as Mende. In sum, "The division into an exclusive grouping is always done in relation to significant others whose exclusion at any particular level of scale creates the we/they dichotomy" (Cohen 1978, 387).

If self-identification were to be allowed for purposes of legal excuse, then at least as a matter of presumption, the relevant practices that each group are said to follow should be allowed into the proceedings as well. Complications would quickly mount. Immigrants, no less than nonimmigrants, move easily within multiple worlds with contradictory sets of norms, and they selectively draw on certain cultural items and not on others (Portes and Rumbaut 1996, 241). That, according to the social theory on which we have drawn, is an unexceptional form of adaptive behavior. Yet the most interesting complications would arise from strategic code-switching: an individual might situationally choose to specify one affiliation rather than another, with highly pragmatic intent. So might her lawyer, for the after-the-fact purposes of the defense.

## Group Affiliation and Group Integrity

This brings us to the broadest of the issues that relate to culture and its translocation. Even more vexing than the complications posed by the identificatory choices that individuals tend to make is the integrity of the concept of an ethnic group and, hence, of the practices it would appear to sanction. Anthropologists of an earlier generation saw ethnicity in terms of homogeneous groups with primordial ties stemming from commonalties of blood, religion, language, residence, and long-standing custom (Geertz 1973, 277). Most contemporary anthropological work argues that ethnicity emerges only in interaction: struggles for recognition and resources lead groups to reconfigure their boundaries, to intensify their differences through cultural symbols that previously held little interest, even to invent new cultural symbols altogether (see Barth 1969; Cohen 1974, ix–xxiii).[21] As Barth's signal insights have borne out, ethnicity is not a set of survivals from earlier cultural traditions, but rather a situational and perpetually emergent phenomenon. Since so much of culture is discretionary, the authenticity of specific practices may be less important, in context, than the sense of community they create.

Thus the fluid nature of cultural dynamics, as reflected in the social theory on which we rely, supports a strong basis for concern about the pressures and temptations against reasonable legal conformity that may result from the official, indiscriminate tolerance of group norms. In pointed terms, feminists and other critics of accommodationism fear that such tolerance will help to sustain patriarchal norms at the expense of the women and children who are left vulnerable to them. The desecration of victims' rights to equal justice in service of a demand for more greatly individualized justice would seem an intolerable mistake.[22]

## EQUAL JUSTICE?

By long-standing consensus among scholars of both criminal and constitutional law, the lodestar aim of the criminal justice system is not the individualization of justice; it is equal justice under law. This goal, radically underattended in the accommodationist literature, demands the balance of individualization, not its sacrifice. The normative architecture of the criminal justice system accommodates both goals as a matter of design. Yet, given the forces that have shaped the United States, norms of constitutionalism and political morality have come to place the principle of equality at the fore.

This fact has compelling implications for the question of cultural accommodation. Extraordinary opportunity already exists for the individualization of justice within the criminal law. The very length of the criminal law process (which places the capacity for discretionary judgment in the hands of a series of professional and nonprofessional role players, distributed across a framework of widely separate institutional forms) enhances the cause of individualized inquiry. In addition, police have discretion over arrests; prosecutors have discretion over whether and how to charge; trial judges have discretion over the admission of evidence (including evidence adduced by experts); the jury, once charged by the judge, has discretion over the finding of culpability; trial judges have sentencing discretion; and the process of review within a multitiered judiciary contains independent bases of discretion.

Each criminal case, however, should not represent an arbitrary, individuated affair. The domains of discretion noted above are not only institutionally framed and bounded but normatively bounded as well. It is concerns for the even-handed administration of justice that provide these normative bounds. Wrought into the normative architecture of the law—and the criminal law in particular—is the ideal that like cases should be treated alike. High among the virtues of this insistent feature of criminal justice is the protection it offers against systematic bias.

This protection, however imperfect, is particularly important in a nation such as the United States that has not yet cured itself of the ugly legacy of racism. Within memory, racism was a prominent formal feature of our legal system. As a noted scholar writing recently about race and racism observes, it has been a crime, during intervals of American history "for African Americans to flee slavery, defend themselves or other African Americans from physical violence, learn to read, or disobey segregationist laws" (see Kennedy 1997, 76–77).[23] While racial discrimination, not least within the processes of the criminal justice system, is no longer authorized by statute or constitutional norm, pernicious elements of bias survive: racial profiling by the police, the extreme racial imbalance implicated in death penalty convictions, and the submerged racial components of jury selection endure.

The availability of cultural defenses would have the inevitable consequence of introducing what would amount to highly discretionary play into the joints of

America's criminal justice system. Prosecutors, judges, and juries faced with cultural variables all would have the opportunity to respond with leniency or to insist on the letter and full severity of the law. As things now stand in this society, it is impossible to imagine that African Americans would be the beneficiaries of this play of discretion; that they as a group would be its victims seems a near certainty. The conversion of what is effectively a two-tiered justice system into a three-tiered version—whether the third tier be broad or narrow, and whether intended to mediate justice on the basis of ethnicity or even (ironically) race—can find no home in justice in our time and place. The strand of feminist literature that stands in strong opposition to this form of accommodation was provoked by the legitimate fear that women and children would be the most prevalent victims of the criminal conduct for which culture would be invoked as explanation and apology. But the threat of accommodationism to equal regard reaches further, to the worst of our fault lines: race.

Were it plausible to imagine that three-tiered justice would in practice be only two-tiered after all, because African American criminal defendants would share fairly in its benefits, then this objection to accommodationist claims would be met. The possibility that all criminal defendants would share fairly in the benefits of multitiered justice is beyond contemplation, however, even on the basis of idealized accommodationist argument.[24]

As case law progress becomes clearer, it should be possible to delineate a reliable body of judgment, one that is based on a substrate of theoretically as well as practically inspired insights that stay grounded from case to case. We hope that those insights that come to rest as secure, systemic judgments will include the following:

- Culture is not a carapace that protects its wearer from the legal consequences of social adaptation when people move from place to place.
- The fluid dynamics of personal agency and allegiance include complexities of behavior that are chosen, not only given, and that are subject to strategic manipulation, on the most persuasive theoretical account.
- The individualized parsing of human behavior is a painstaking job, not a casual one, never less than when it becomes enrolled as a project of the coercive, lawgiving state.

For reasons that include the foregoing, culture and its copious transcriptions into the terms of cultural identity cannot provide the basis of exemption or privilege in the law. Nevertheless, there must be manifold instances in which evidence of cultural practice may prove relevant to the aims and methods of the criminal law. Such evidence should then be, just as it now is, admissible. Nothing that we have claimed, in opposition to the accommodationist press for change, has meant to deny this conventional and unchallengeable fact.

Three further concerns for the administration of justice are as follows: First, the core conceptions of moral and legal wrongdoing and the characteristics of mind and action that define our understanding of the criminal law should not function as just another element of the fluid social dynamics of immigrant absorption. Otherwise, the effect would be to substitute for the necessity of a definable public order a set of institutional workings that imitates Zeno's Paradox: as new immigrants set out to learn what adaptive conformity to the criminal law entails, they might discover that the law has surrendered its demand of behavioral conformity so as to adapt its norms to theirs. Immigrants seeking to make well-grounded judgments about their new social responsibilities cannot be expected to adapt successfully to ceaselessly shifting law. To the degree of likelihood that criminal law interdiction actually deters antisocial behavior, the fragmentation of interdiction or punishment (or both) would not likely better deter such behavior. Indeed, given the treacherous relationship between immigration policy and law enforcement, immigrants may have stronger incentives than most nonimmigrant groups to conform to the law.

Second, immigrants are entitled to no less justice than anyone else: all defenses and strategies of defense that are applicable to their condition must be available on their behalf. If the norm of social toleration operates with at least moderate success in the contemporary United States (and there seems good reason to believe that it does), then our country will not demand that immigrant ethnic groups conform their behaviors to an unfairly stringent set of demands.

Third, and closely related to this point, immigrants are not entitled to more justice, a different brand of justice, or a unique quality of justice when they stand at the criminal bar. In a legal system still riddled with racial injustice, our hope is that sustained demands for closely calibrated just outcomes, together with sustained appeals for mercy, would have a generalized ratchet effect, whereby the intentionally general language in the law might facilitate more justice overall.

This is not what the accommodationist vision consists of. It is a claim for special, not general, relief. In our view, the least tolerable of any outcomes that encompass social revision would be a three-tiered justice system: one for African Americans, a second for the ethnically privileged, and a third for everyone else. The mild predictions of improved community relations to which accommodationists look forward would be dwarfed by justified African American despair.

Recent social theory confirms that culture, alive to possibility, changes perpetually. Individuals' allegiances are multiple, and ethnic groups, with their ephemeral boundaries, include members whose worldviews are responsive to new concepts, practices, and ideas. At the same time, the receipt of an unprecedentedly large influx of recent immigrants is but one of many factors that should help to keep the host culture from getting pickled.

The processes that social theory has come to describe suggest that most cultural differences will find appropriate room for negotiation and accommodation. This room should be found, we have argued, outside the criminal law. Indeed, the newly settled and the long-settled may, as neighbors, adopt the stances of part-time anthropologists. As mutual observers, as friends, as possible romantic partners, as traders of goods, services, and influential norms—all may come to walk around problems and approach them from several sides in ways that transcend the boundaries of cultural ephemera.

The authors are indebted to Frank Kessel, Martha Minow, and Rick Shweder for their encouragement, which was warm and yet appropriately critical; to Julie Lake, Program Assistant at the Social Science Research Council, and the members of the SSRC Working Group on Ethnic Customs, Assimilation and the Law for comments on an early draft; to Emily Chang of the Russell Sage Foundation for manuscript assistance; to Larry Sager and Ken Simons for comments on a later draft; to Hillary Russell for research assistance; and to William Kaleva and Julie DeBenedictis for their valiant labors in manuscript preparation. Bledsoe is grateful to Jane Guyer for her insightful thoughts. Cohen is indebted to faculty workshop participants at Vanderbilt Law School and the University of Texas School of Law and to Dean (now President) John Sexton, New York University School of Law, for his gracious hospitality during fall 1999, when the position of Senior Scholar allowed early work on this chapter to take place.

## NOTES

1. In most contemporary anthropological usage, the term *culture* refers to ideational elements: templates or mental schemes by which individuals or groups imbue the world with meaning. See Shore 1996 for trenchant observations on the notion of culture, particularly an exposition of the idea of culture as models or schemes.

2. Issues embedded in family life—mating customs, child discipline, and spousal sexual fidelity, for example—have become sites of significant cultural differences that implicate criminal law. The claims that accommodationist arguments have brought to bear on the relevant case law by their nature are not limited to domestic cases. Still, there has been no press for normative accommodation within most of the nondomestic criminal case law and even less within the vast body of nondomestic civil law.

3. For an example of arguments that divide feminist theorists compare Coleman 1996 with Volpp 1996.

4. Criticisms of the academic debate over accommodationism are not intended to extend to separate issues regarding the strategies and ethics of the criminal defense bar, on which no judgment is passed.

5. Magnarella's position represents a common formulation of accommodationists' general claim. Further examples are as follows.

   The values of individuals who are raised in minority cultures may at times conflict with the values of the majority culture. To the extent that the values of the majority are embodied in the criminal law, these individuals may face the dilemma of having to violate either their cultural values or the criminal law. . . . [P]ersons raised in other cultures, who are subject to influences that inculcated in them a different set of norms, will likely feel morally obligated to follow those norms. Once norms have acquired this moral dimension, conformity with conflicting laws becomes more difficult ("Cultural Defense" 1986, 1293, 1300).

   The point of the cultural defense is to recognize that the power of enculturation makes it exceedingly difficult for someone from another culture to make his conduct conform to standards of the dominant American culture (Renteln 1987–88).

Recognition of a [cultural] defense presents the question whether isolation (or separation, or estrangement) from the dominant culture should excuse a defendant from criminal liability by exempting him or her from the presumption that all know, and are able to conform their behavior to, the law (Maguigan 1995).

The logic behind the cultural defense dictates that a defendant, often a recent immigrant or refugee, should be allowed to introduce evidence of her foreign cultural values in order to mitigate or negate her culpability. In other words, a defendant should not be punished as severely (and in some cases should not be punished at all) for behavior that is sanctioned or even promoted by the culture of her homeland (Sing 1999, 1849).

6. These cases, either singly or as an ensemble, are featured in many of the writings that form the basis for our discussion. These writings include Brelvi 1997; Bryant 1990; Chiu 1994; Choi 1990; Coleman 1996; Renteln 1993; D. Evans-Pritchard and Renteln 1994; Fischer 1998; Gallin 1994; Goldstein 1994; Kim 1997; Lam 1993; Magnarella 1991; Maguigan 1995; Sheybani 1987; Sing 1999; Spatz 1991; Taylor 1997; Terhunes 1997; Tomao 1996; Volpp 1994; Woo 1989.

7. The facts of the *Chen* case have been mirrored in at least one other instance of wife murder by a recent immigrant; see *People v. Toa Moua* 1985. Moua, a member of the Hmong Laotian community, killed his wife after she informed him that she planned to accept employment with another man, an act, the court was informed, "tantamount to infidelity within the Hmong culture." On account of this cultural difference, Moua was permitted to plead guilty to voluntary manslaughter rather than murder, and was given half the maximum sentence for that crime.

8. As Sanford Kadish, the doyen of American substantive criminal law scholarship, has reflected, "To blame a person is to express a moral criticism, and if the person's action does not deserve criticism, blaming him is a kind of falsehood and is, to the extent the person is injured by being blamed, unjust to him. It is this feature of our everyday moral practices that lies behind the law's excuses" (Kadish 1987, 257, 264).

The defense of diminished capacity within extant criminal law involves proof of a mental condition other than insanity (the basis of an independent defense) either to negate the specific intent or mens rea, one of the definitional elements of most serious crimes (in states that allow it, the defense's broader use is here), or to negate the intent element of just one crime—murder. The two uses result in different outcomes. Under the broader theory of use, the prosecution's failure to prove an element of a crime results in exculpation. Under the narrower theory applicable only to the gravest offense, a successful use of the defense results in reducing a murder charge to a lesser felony. States presently restrict the use of the defense differentially in ways that have been criticized as arbitrary. The aforementioned split outcome results in a second level of arbitrariness. The treatment of the expert evidence necessary to the defense represents a third. With substantial reason, one critical observer has termed the present status of the defense "undiminished confusion in diminished capacity" (Morse 1984).

At the level of legislation and judicial application is considerable skittishness about the use of this defense. An authoritative source has commented that the partial responsibility defense "brings formal guilt more closely into line with moral blame-worthiness, but only at the cost of driving a wedge between dangerousness and social control" (American Law Institute, Comment 10, 72).

9. Through the defense of provocation or *heat of passion*, as it was historically termed, the law recognizes one possibility for diminished moral and legal culpability for the crime of murder. The defense contains understandably strict proof requirements, but its restrictions have not lessened the doubts of its critics as to its present-day moral viability. See, for example, Dressler 1982.

10. The testimony presented in *Chen* by the sole anthropologist who testified as an expert has provoked sharp criticism in the literature, regardless of major authorial differences on other points. Compare Coleman 1996, 1138–39; Maguigan 1995, 93–95; Volpp 1996, 1590–92.

11. The presiding judge's acceptance of the provocation defense in *Chen* is a disturbing puzzle that remains unsolved. The defense requires demonstration of an allegedly uncontrollable response to a sudden event or news. Yet the evidence in *Chen* included the fact that the victim either told or suggested to her husband that she was involved with another man weeks before the murder. Unless this evidence was contested (which it was not), it should have deprived Chen of the defense. Moreover, evidence was introduced at trial that Chen had delusional bouts in which he heard the voice of his wife's supposed lover. This is hardly the mental state of a reasonable or typical Chinese man. Leti Volpp is the only commentator to have raised these disturbing themes (Volpp 1994, *nn*25–31 and accompanying text).

12. According to one authority, *rape*, a term that has no precise cognate in the Hmong language, is adopted from the English language when used by the Hmong to refer to two specific kinds of acts: a sexual affair with the wife of another, and a sex act with a girl without her parents' permission (see Hammond 1991, 11, cited in Evans-Pritchard and Renteln 1994, *nn*113–15).

13. Alison Dundes Renteln, for example, has argued that standards of reasonableness are not merely context-specific but also group-specific. In her view, judgments about reasonableness must belong to those within, not outside, the group to which the actor whose conduct is under scrutiny belongs (see Renteln 1993, 496–504).

14. The need for a new and independent cultural defense has been claimed by at least four authors within the literature: Lam 1993; Renteln 1993; Sheybani 1987; and the anonymous author of the early and influential "Cultural Defense in the Criminal Law" 1986.

15. Shweder (1990, 1–43) provides astute descriptions of the interpenetrating relationship between the self and the environment: human intentionality shapes not only immediately visible outcomes, but also the surrounding world that in turn lends meaning to behavior. For example: "[N]o sociocultural environment exists or has identity independent of the way human beings seize meanings and resources from it, while every human being has her or his subjectivity and mental life altered through the process of seizing meanings and resources from some sociocultural environment and using them."

16. See also Tully 1995, who suggests that because each citizen is a member of more than one cultural group, the need for toleration is essential in the most personal ways.

17. In cases of cultural defense, anthropologists have been called to testify as expert witnesses about the practices of particular groups. In a number of the cases, however, the welfare of the groups under scrutiny arguably has been vulnerable to the idiosyncratic knowledge, apparent biases, and even articulateness of a lone scholarly explicator.

    Intriguingly, Professor Holly Maguigan dismisses the potential utility of an independent cultural defense, seeing it as "misguided" because, among other reasons, a workable legal definition of culture is impossible to develop. Still, Maguigan encourages the vigorous presentation of cultural evidence through other devices, on the explicit assumption that prosecutors, judges, and juries will be able to arrive at reliable causal and factual determinations and otherwise sort out cultural evidence. Her split judgments on the justice system's abilities to come to terms with culture seem motivated by her desire to preserve some uses for the defensive use of cultural evidence to aid in justice for "outsider" defendants.

    Maguigan's treatment of outsider defendants does not differentiate between the needs and interests of African American criminal defendants and ethnic immigrant defendants. The following section addresses concerns about the potential for negative spillover effects that might flow from privileging ethnic but not racial culture claims (compare Maguigan 1995, 45 and 96–99).

18. The recognition that anthropologists often have differing perceptions of the people with whom they work has drawn wide attention within the discipline and beyond. For two examples compare Freeman and Mead 1983 with Mead 1928; and Lewis 1951 with Redfield 1930. For an overview of anthropological restudies see Kloos 1994, 37–56.

19. Indeed, this trend may intensify, since so many immigrants move quickly to the suburbs instead of being confined to urban settings, as were immigrants of the past.

20. In a recent undergraduate class taught by Caroline Bledsoe at Northwestern University, a young woman from Africa reported that she identified strongly with three Sierra Leonean ethnicities whose languages she spoke: Mende (her father), Temne (her mother), and Krio (the elites on the coast, through kinship ties). She also felt close allegiance to the Wolof people in Senegal, where she had spent much of her life (hence, she also spoke Wolof and French). Further, she considers herself an American, by virtue of having immigrated to the United States and because she holds an American passport.

21. Subsequent work has gone further, seeing ethnic designations and the group dynamics they claim to describe as political creations. See, for example, Hobsbawm and Ranger 1983; and Williams 1989, 431. For a recent statement in economic theory that emphasizes group emergence rather than staticism see Arthur 1999, 107.

22. One further equality-based justification for cultural accommodation might exist: a need to remediate systemic abuses of discretion toward cultural groups that accommodationism seeks to promote. Our own review of the recent case law that implicates the use of cultural evidence finds no such systemic discrimination in place.

23. Kennedy's (1997) historical observations usually are offered in dead-on prose uninflected by obvious emotion. In this, his latest book, Kennedy's well-known steeliness reflects both style and prescriptive substance in a manner that has not been uncritically received. For a review that enlists passionate commitment to the cause of her

critique, see Johnson 1998 (review of Kennedy's book). The details used in Johnson's account to justify its strength of purpose are drawn significantly from the ongoing history of racism within the criminal law.

24. For a recent and illuminating discussion of leveling down versus leveling up with the ideal of equality see Simons 2000.

# REFERENCES

American Law Institute. Model Penal Code, Comment 10, §210.3, 72.

Arthur, Brian. 1999. "Complexity and the Economy." *Science* 284.

Barth, Fredrik. 1969. *Ethnic Groups and Boundaries: The Social Organization of Cultural Difference*. London: Allen & Unwin.

Brelvi, Farah Sultana. 1997. "News of the Weird: Specious Normativity and the Problem of the Cultural Defense." *Columbia Human Rights Law Review* 28: 657.

Bryant, Taimie L. 1990. "Oya-Ko Shinju: Death at the Center of the Heart." *UCLA Pacific Basin Law Journal* 8: 1.

Carrithers, Michael. 1992. *Why Humans Have Cultures: Explaining Anthropology and Social History*. Oxford: Oxford University Press.

Chiu, Diana C. 1994. "The Cultural Defense: Beyond Exclusion, Assimilation, and Guilty Liberalism." *California Law Review* 82: 1053.

Choi, Carolyn. 1990. "Application of a Cultural Defense in Criminal Proceedings." *UCLA Pacific Basin Law Journal* 8: 80.

Cohen, Abner. 1974. "The Lesson of Ethnicity." In *Urban Ethnicity*, edited by A. Cohen. London: Tavistock.

Cohen, Ronald. 1978. "Ethnicity: Problem and Focus in Anthropology." *Annual Review of Anthropology* 7: 379–403.

Coleman, Doriane Lambelet. 1996. "Individualizing Justice Through Multiculturalism: The Liberals' Dilemma." *Columbia Law Review* 96: 1093.

Comaroff, John L., and Simon Roberts. 1981. *Rules and Processes: The Cultural Logic of Dispute in an African Context*. Chicago: University of Chicago Press.

"The Cultural Defense in the Criminal Law." 1986. *Harvard Law Review* 99: 1274.

"The Cultural and Legal Dimensions of Infanticide." 1990. *UCLA Pacific Basin Law Journal* 8(spring): 1.

Dressler, Joshua. 1982. "Rethinking Heat of Passion: A Defense in Search of a Rationale." *Journal of Criminal Law & Criminology* 73: 421.

———. 1993. "A Justification of the Cultural Defense as Partial Excuse." *Southern California Review of Law and Women's Studies* 2: 437.

Evans-Pritchard, Deidre, and Alison Dundes Renteln. 1994. "The Interpretation and Distortion of Culture: A Hmong Marriage by Capture Case in Fresno, California." *Southern California Interdisciplinary Law Journal* 4: 1.

Evans-Pritchard, E. E. 1940. *The Nuer: A Description of the Modes of Livelihood and Political Institutions of a Nilotic People*. Oxford: Clarendon Press.

Fischer, Michael. 1998. "The Human Rights Implications of a Cultural Defense." *Southern California Interdisciplinary Law Journal* 9: 663.

Freeman, Derek, and Margaret Mead. 1983. *The Making and Unmaking of an Anthropological Myth*. Cambridge, Mass.: Harvard University Press.

Gallin, Alice J. 1994. "The Cultural Defense: Undermining the Policies Against Domestic Violence." *Boston College Law Review* 35: 723.

Geertz, Clifford. 1973. *The Interpretation of Cultures*. New York: Basic Books.

Giddens, Anthony. 1977. *Central Problems in Social Theory: Action, Structure, and Contradictions in Social Analysis*. Berkeley: University of California Press.

Goldstein, Taryn. 1994. "Cultural Conflicts in Court: Should the American Criminal Justice System Formally Recognize a 'Cultural' Defense?" *Dickinson Law Review* 99: 141.

Hammond, Ruth. 1991. "Call It Rape." *Twin Cities Reader*, March 27, 1991: 11.

Hanks, William F. 1996. *Language and Communicative Practices*. Boulder, Colo.: Westview Press.

Hobsbawm, Eric, and Terence Ranger. 1983. *The Invention of Tradition*. New York: Cambridge University Press.

Jetter, Alexis. 1989. "Fear Is Legacy of Wife Killing in Chinatown: Battered Asians Shocked by Husband's Probation." *New York Newsday*, November 26, 1989: 4.

Johnson, Sheri Lynn. 1998. "Respectability, Race Neutrality, and Truth." *Yale Law Journal* 197: 2619.

Kadish, Sanford H. 1987. "Excusing Crime." *California Legal Review* 75: 257.

Kataoka, Mike. 1992. "Indio Woman Who Strangled Son Sentenced to 11 Years in Prison." *Press-Enterprise* (Riverside, Calif.), October 31, 1992: B1.

Kennedy, Randall. 1997. *Race, Crime, and the Law*. New York: Pantheon Books.

Kim, Nancy S. 1997. "The Cultural Defense and the Problem of Cultural Preemption: A Framework for Analysis." *New Mexico Law Review* 27: 101.

Kloos, Peter. 1994. "Replication, Restudy, and the Nature of Anthropological Fieldwork." In *Reconstructing the Mind: Replicability in Research on Human Development*, edited by René Van der Veer, Marinus van Ljzendoorn, and Jaan Valsiner. Norwood: Ablex.

Lam, T. Anh. 1993. "Culture as a Defense: Preventing Judicial Bias Against Asians and Pacific Islanders." *UCLA Asian American Pacific Islander Law Journal* 1: 49.

Lewis, Oscar. 1951. *Life in a Mexican Village: Tepoztlán Restudied*. Champaign: University of Illinois Press.

Lloyd, P. C. 1967. "The Yoruba of Nigeria." In *Peoples of Africa*, edited by James L. Gibbs, Jr. New York: Holt, Rinehart & Winston.

Magnarella, Paul J. 1991. "Justice in a Culturally Pluralistic Society: The Cultural Defense on Trial." *Journal of Ethnic Studies* 19: 65.

Maguigan, Holly. 1995. "Cultural Defense and Male Violence: Are Feminist and Multicultural Reformers on a Collision Course in Criminal Courts?" *New York University Law Review* 70: 36.

Maines, David R. 1997. "Social Organization and Social Structure in Symbolic Interactionist Thought." *Annual Review of Sociology* 3: 235–59.

McDermott, R. P., and David R. Roth. 1978. "The Social Organization of Behavior: Interactional Approaches." *Annual Review of Anthropology* 7: 321–45.

Mead, Margaret. 1928. *Coming of Age in Samoa*. New York: William Morrow.

Morse, Stephen J. 1984. "Undiminished Confusion in Diminished Capacity." *Journal of Criminal Law & Criminology* 75: 1.

*People v. Chen*. 1989. No. 87–7774. New York Sup. Ct.

*People v. Kimura*. 1985. Los Angeles Sup. Ct. No. A–091133.

*People v. Kong Moua*. 1985. No. 315972–0. Fresno Sup. Ct.

*People v. Toa Moua*. 1985. No. 328106–0. Fresno Sup. Ct.

*People v. Wu*. 1991. 286 California Reporter 868.

Portes, Alejandro, and Rubén G. Rumbaut. 1996. *Immigrant America: A Portrait*. Berkeley: University of California Press.

Redfield, Robert. 1930. *Tepoztlán: A Mexican Village*. Chicago: University of Chicago Press.

Renteln, Alison Dundes. 1987–88. "Culture and Culpability: A Study in Contrasts." *Beverly Hills Bar Association Journal* 22: 17.

Sheybani, Malak-Mithra. 1987. "Cultural Defense: One Person's Culture Is Another's Crime." *Loyola Los Angeles International & Comparative Law Journal* 9: 751.

Shore, Bradd. 1996. *Culture in Mind: Cognition, Culture, and the Problem of Meaning*. Oxford: Oxford University Press.

Shweder, Richard A. 1990. "Cultural Psychology—What Is It?" In *Cultural Psychology: Essays on Comparative Human Development*, edited by Richard Shweder. Chicago: University of Chicago Press.

Simons, Kenneth W. 2000. "The Logic of Egalitarian Norms." *Boston University Law Review* 80: 693.

Sing, James J. 1999. "Culture as Sameness: Toward a Synthetic View of Provocation and Culture in the Criminal Law." *Yale Law Journal* 198: 1845.

Smith, James P., and Barry Edmonston. 1997. *The New Americans: Economic, Demographic, and Fiscal Effects of Immigration*. Washington, D.C.: National Research Council.

Spatz, Melissa. 1991. "A Lesser Crime: A Comparative Study of Legal Defenses for Men Who Kill Their Wives." *Columbia Journal of Law & Social Problems* 24: 597.

Taylor, Todd. 1997. "The Cultural Defense and Its Irrelevancy in Child Protection Law." *Boston College Third World Law Journal* 17: 331.

Terhunes, Cassandra. 1997. "Cultural and Religious Defenses to Child Abuse and Neglect." *Journal of American Academy of Matrimonial Lawyers* 14: 152.

Tomao, Sharon. 1996. "The Cultural Defense: Traditional or Formal?" *Georgetown Immigration Law Journal* 10: 241.

Tully, James. 1995. *Strange Multiplicity: Constitutionalism in an Age of Diversity*. Cambridge: Cambridge University Press.

Volpp, Leti. 1994. "(Mis)identifying Culture: Asian Women and the Cultural Defense." *Harvard Women's Law Journal* 17: 57.

———. 1996. "Talking 'Culture': Gender, Race, Nation, and the Politics of Multiculturalism." *Columbia Law Review* 96: 1573.

Williams, Brackette. 1989. "A Class Act: Anthropology and the Race to Nation Across Ethnic Terrain." *Annual Review of Anthropology* 18: 401–44.

Woo, Deborah. 1989. "The People v. Fumiko Kimura: But Which People?" *International Journal of Sociology of Law* 17: 403.

# Chapter 6

# Citizenship on Trial: Nadia's Case

## Unni Wikan

On October 3, 1997, Norwegians awoke to the news that Nadia, a Norwegian citizen, eighteen year old, had been kidnapped by her parents and brought to Morocco, where she was being held captive. The purpose reportedly was to have her married by force. It was Nadia herself who managed to sound an alarm by way of a phone call to a fellow employee at a store where she worked and had failed to show up on Monday, September 1, giving no notice. She was in a terrible state, telling how she had been drugged, beaten, and forced into a van that had transported her, in handcuffs, with her family to Morocco. Stripped of her passport, she was now being held in her father's house, and she was desperate to be set free.

Her colleague contacted their boss, who went straight to the police; when the police were slow to take action, he contacted the Ministry of Foreign Affairs.[1] They acted expeditiously. The Norwegian ambassador in Morocco was informed and a rescue plan was conceived. The ambassador would try to negotiate with Moroccan local authorities and with Nadia's father for her release.

There was every reason for Norway to engage itself, for not only was Nadia a Norwegian citizen, but so too were her parents. Her father had come to Norway in 1971 at the age of twenty and had held Norwegian citizenship since 1985—as had her mother, who joined him in 1978. Norway does not recognize dual citizenship. Thus, from the point of view of Norway, the judicial statuses of Nadia and her parents were clear. Moreover, the crime, if so it was—and at this point there was much to indicate that a crime had been committed—had been perpetrated on Norwegian soil.[2] Hence there was no question about Norway's right and duty to investigate the case and try to work out a solution.

But there was one big hurdle, and it concerned citizenship. That one state does not recognize dual citizenship matters little as long as another state with which a citizen is affiliated does, and Morocco did. This had serious consequences, especially for Nadia. A Norwegian adult, she was transformed into a Moroccan child—for the legal age in Morocco is twenty, not eighteen, as in Norway. Nadia therefore came under her father's jurisdiction as undisputed legal head of his family. If he found it warranted to keep his daughter locked up, that was his business. All Moroccan authorities could do was to help Norway locate the family, as they did.

A week of tense negotiations conducted by phone between the Norwegian ambassador and Nadia's father ensued. Norwegians meanwhile followed the case with utmost suspense, as Nadia's case—Nadiasaken—had become a national issue, and the outcome was fraught with uncertainty. Three times her father promised to set Nadia free, only to renege on his word—leading the ambassador at one point to call him a liar. A key problem was the father's insistence on a guarantee of safe passage, meaning he would not be prosecuted on his return to Norway. This the ambassador could not and would not extend; it was up to the police to decide what to do after a thorough investigation. But when all hope was deemed to be lost, Nadia suddenly appeared in the Oslo airport, her father having paid for her ticket himself. She was met by her brother, a friend of his, and a social worker who was a family friend. According to the media, Nadia was exhausted but happy to be back in Norway. All she wanted was to rest and be left in peace. A week later, she was reunited with her family when they too returned to Norway.

What was the reason for Nadia's father's sudden change of heart? Probably the interruption of all social welfare benefits to the family. This had been a final and drastic move on Norway's part. Though by no means poor, the family incurred a heavy loss: about 188,000 Norwegian kroner a year (U.S.$21,350 at the time) with the father's disability pension (due to heart disease) and three child allowances. In addition, the family had a comfortable flat at subsidized rent. Stopping these payments was justified on the grounds that the family had left Norway for more than a month without informing the social welfare agencies. This constituted a breach for which it was possible to effectuate sanctions, which Norway did with the desired result. Nadia was set free.

But hardly had Nadia been reunited with her family before her case took a new turn: she recanted her story. According to the media, it had all been fantasy and fabrication. Actually, Nadia had gone to Morocco on her own accord to visit her sick grandmother, but when the family wanted to remain in Morocco longer than she wished, she became desperate. So she pulled off the lie to marshal help. She was deeply sorry about the disturbance she had caused and the pain inflicted on her family. Now all she desired was to be reconciled with them.

It goes without saying that this new development caused quite a stir, and many wondered what was really going on. Some Moroccan and Pakistani youths with whom I spoke complained that Nadia had let them down. She had had a golden opportunity to become a rallying point for other youths threatened with forced marriage and now, she had chickened out for fear of reprisals. What she had done was perfectly understandable, but to stand brave for so long and then give in . . .

There were also debates in the media—some of which I participated in myself—regarding the plight of the second generation, especially in regard to forced marriage (a common problem in Western Europe). Not that these issues had not been discussed before, but Nadia's case had been a catalyst giving them added urgency and a human face.

Following Nadia's admission of lying, her parents were reported to be preparing a lawsuit against two national newspapers and the Ministry of Foreign Affairs for having scandalized their name. A sizable compensation would be claimed; but it was not to be. A year later, Nadia's parents were brought to court by the Norwegian state on a charge of "having forcibly held someone against her will" (frihetsberøvelse). The minimum sentence is one year in prison; the maximum is fifteen years.

Because I was called as a cultural expert for the court, I attended the whole proceedings.[3] I also met with Nadia's parents and her grandfather outside court, in their home, in the company of a leader from the Moroccan community, who served as mediator. The story that follows draws on this engagement.[4]

The trial lasted five days, with an extra day for the verdict. Witnesses for the defense were Nadia's grandfather, brother, brother's friend, a social worker,[5] two Moroccan girls, a leader from the Moroccan community, and a few other family friends. Witnesses for the prosecution were Nadia, the ambassador, police who investigated the case, a psychologist whom Nadia had seen after her return to Norway, and a few of her Norwegian friends. In addition, the prosecution presented as evidence a tape of two telephone conversations between Nadia and her parents that Nadia had helped the police record without her parents' knowledge. The defense attorneys protested vigorously, but after a thorough consideration, the judge decided to allow the tapes.

Half of the trial (two and a half days) was spent on Nadia's parents' testimony, since proceedings were slowed by translation. Nadia's mother said in court that she knew no Norwegian, though I know her to speak quite well, and her husband was not entirely fluent. Yet with so much at stake, it was only natural that they would seek the added assurance translators provide.[6]

The parents' story repeated what Nadia had said on her return to Norway: she had gone to Morocco of her own accord to visit her sick grandmother. Supposedly, she had pleaded with them to let her go, against the warnings of Nadia's mother that she might lose her job were she unable to notify her boss; they had to leave in great haste. Yet so much does Nadia love her grandmother that she did not care.

The parents conceded that there had been problems between Nadia and them at times, but they had never done anything but act in Nadia's best interests. They were trying to save her from herself and her bad Norwegian friends, they said. To that effect, they were willing to go to some lengths, naturally, but never to the point of beating her or kidnapping her or keeping her locked up. Nadia always had been free to do what she wanted. She had been a loved, even a spoiled, child. Moreover, in Morocco Nadia had been free to go where she wanted; there had been no keys, no locked doors, as Nadia admitted in court. But, as she said, where would she go (without her passport, without money, with informers all around)? "The whole country had kidnapped me!"[7]

Faced with the necessity of having to brand their daughter a liar, Nadia's parents turned to an age-old recourse: throwing the blame on others (Wikan 1980, 1996). It was not Nadia's fault that she did what she did; she was under the sway of Norwegian bad influence, from both her schoolmates and some journalists who, the parents claimed, wanted to make money on her. These people had tricked her into inventing lies to sell her story.[8]

But according to Nadia's subsequent testimony, her parents also believed her to be under another kind of influence: supernatural jinns that had taken control over her. To her horror, she had been subjected to various cleansing rituals in Morocco (a description was given as part of the closed trial); but this was not something the parents talked about in court. At no point did they present themselves as anything but modern, educated people—which indeed they were. Nor did the defense attorneys try to mount any kind of cultural defense based on the parents' supernatural beliefs, which they might not even have heard about before Nadia's testimony—although such beliefs are widespread among Moroccans in Norway. On the contrary, the defense tried to capitalize on the parents' good standing as being of a prominent and cosmopolitan Moroccan family. The court was shown photos of Nadia's grandfather's palace in Morocco, and of her parents' stylish house.[9] Bringing jinns into the picture only could have complicated this image, though in fact it might have helped explain why Nadia was kept so long in Morocco: for cleansing rituals to work, one must not cross the sea for a month.

The crown witness for the prosecution was Nadia. She made her entry from a back door, avoiding the onslaught of gazes that were sure to meet her had she entered from the front, for she was a celebrity already, through no wish of her own. Indeed, she had been in hiding for more than a year. And when she testified in court, two policemen sat guard behind her, just for security.

To bring one's parents to court—especially one's mother—is considered the utmost outrage among Muslims (as among many others). It did not matter that it was not she who had done so (the charge had been brought by the Norwegian police); in the eyes of the community and her family, Nadia was a traitor. She received threats on her life.

Nadia entered the courtroom with a blanket over her face to avoid the gaze of the public—but also to avoid her parents' eyes. She had asked that they not be present in the courtroom, and they were sitting in the translator's cubicle to the back; but the cubicle was only a few steps away, with nothing but a glass wall separating her and her parents.

She had not made it a condition of her testifying that they be absent from the courtroom, but she had pleaded, and her wish had been granted. No one doubted the agony she must have been going through. Nor did anyone doubt the pain of her parents' hard-tested emotions. They had not seen each other for a year, parents and child, not since the day Nadia first decided to tell the truth after all, having first done it in Morocco, and then having repented to cover for her parents on her return to Norway, only to be overcome by fear that they might let her down again—then who would believe her cries for help? She also was concerned about her little sister, whom she adored and who might one day come to share her fate, as well as unknown others in the same shoes. So she retracted her cover-up story, contacted the police (whom she knew to be conducting an investigation of her parents) to tell the truth, and cooperated with them to gather evidence against her parents.

Nadia was a fragile-looking young girl as she entered the courtroom with the black blanket covering her head. Yet as soon as she stood up in the witness stand, blanket removed, she appeared steadfast and strong in her demeanor. She spoke with a clear voice, and answered every question lucidly. At times she broke down. The memory was too much for her. Some time into her testimony, her attorney suggested that she be allowed to sit in front of the witness stand, the box at her back.

That must have been a relief. Standing, Nadia felt the full force of her parents' gaze hitting her from the back. She had made no concession to them in how she appeared. She was dressed in black pants and a black sweater, both tight-fitting, but not immodestly—from a Norwegian perspective. Her parents would have felt differently. Knowing that how she dressed had been a point of contention between Nadia and her parents, I cannot help wondering if she did it on purpose. Yet why should she not appear her own self in court when that was precisely what the battle had been about, her right to be her own person?

I never turned to look at her parents throughout Nadia's testimony, but I know others did; one journalist reported her father shaking his head in exasperation at times as she told the court her story. Her mother reportedly cried a lot. The next day Nadia's father asked to be allowed to speak in court, out of turn. He accused his daughter of being a liar, and refuted all of her testimony. How could any parents do to their daughter what she accused them of doing? Could anyone be so callous? Nadia had brought shame on the whole family and herself, he claimed; that was why she was desperate. She was not a virgin anymore, and in Morocco, a girl who is not a virgin before marriage has no future.

In revealing that Nadia was not a virgin, Nadia's father went public with a secret that need not have been revealed, and thus he may be seen to have triggered the shame that otherwise could have remained undisclosed. Nadia was more discreet. She revealed to the court, as part of a closed hearing, that she had told her mother on the way to Morocco that she had slept with a boy.[10]

Now her father had exposed the disgrace, bringing shame on himself, as it might seem, by making the matter public. Perhaps he felt so disgraced by his daughter's misdemeanors that there were no holds barred and nothing to lose: better to reveal the depth of her fall and be done with it. "Here in court," he said, shaking his head, "you think it is we who have committed a wrong. But Nadia cries because her honor is destroyed. Everything she tells you is just lies and falsehood. Yet I know that she does not mean any of this. It is her accomplices who are making her do it. Nadia has forgotten the nine months in her mother's womb, the care and affection she received, her childhood, her upbringing until she came of age. Now we are repaid for the kindness we as parents have shown," said Nadia's father while her mother cried openly.

According to Nadia, her parents had planned to marry her to a twenty-one-year-old Moroccan (whose picture her mother had shown her) so that he could get a visa to Norway and so that she would "become Moroccan." Indeed, this was what the whole battle had been about: Nadia's wish to be Norwegian versus her parents' insistence that she "become Moroccan" and "become Muslim."

The retraction she had produced on her return to Norway was at her parents' instruction. Recanting her story was their deal for setting Nadia free: she would ensure that they would not be prosecuted by taking the blame herself. Nadia's concern for her younger siblings also contributed to her trying to pull off the lie.

That Nadia and her parents had long been at loggerheads is clear: six months before her abduction, Nadia had contacted the child welfare agency regarding her father's ostensible abuse. Her father, she said, beat her and was furious because she was "too Norwegian": she was not allowed to wear makeup, wear pants, go out to dance, have a (Pakistani) boyfriend. Her father had even gone to a café where she had worked and threatened some of the staff that he would kill them if they did not make Nadia quit. He did not want her to work in such a place (this was confirmed by the people in question).

As a result, Nadia was placed under child welfare custody for three months, living in a youth institution. She moved home only after her eighteenth birthday (when she legally became an adult) and with her father's assurances that he would not beat her. Apparently, the move was voluntary. As Nadia said in court, however, the project (her word) of the child welfare agencies was not her own: they were set on reuniting her with her family against her will.

The problems did not go away; they resumed. Nadia's brother said in court that he did not love her anymore, not after she had said that she did not want to be a Muslim. Her parents said in court that they had nothing against Nadia being "Norwegian." She could do as she liked, even marry a Norwegian; but they did not like her drinking and smoking and staying out late at night. Would any parent, even a Norwegian parent? Two girls who served as witnesses for the defense confirmed this—that Nadia's parents had given her full freedom, even to marry the Pakistani if she wanted—but her parents naturally were upset by Nadia's disgraceful behavior. Had she not been seen drunk in the street on occasion?

Yet Nadia herself told a different story, about being beaten and oppressed to "become" a Muslim and Moroccan: "Did you not tell me I would have to stay in Morocco till I was married and had a baby and only then could I return to Norway?" Nadia asked her mother in a taped telephone conversation presented as evidence in court. "And did you not threaten me that I would have to remain in Morocco till I rotted?"

"You have misunderstood me, my daughter, I was only joking," said the mother.

"That is hardly a joking matter," said Nadia.

A key witness for the defense was Nadia's maternal grandfather, a prominent and wealthy patriarch who wielded considerable influence in his home district in Morocco. A cordial man, he left in disgust. "I thought Norway was a democracy where there was justice before the law. But this is not democracy! The judge chose to believe a young girl over her family; they sided with her. That is injustice." He would go back to Morocco to tell the people so and launch a court case against the ambassador who had vastly overstepped his powers. "He even of-fered to send a car to pick up Nadia—from her own family!" Worst of all were the things the ambassador had said to the media, and now in court. The grand-father wanted his family's honor restored, and he was going to do it by suing the ambassador.·

Had not Nadia gone to Morocco of her own free will to visit her sick grand-mother? Had she not begged her parents to let her go, even though they had been concerned that she would let her employer down by not showing up for work? The grandfather's testimony on these points was in line with that of the parents. They had told the court how the decision to go to Morocco had been made impromptu on a Saturday night. The telegram (from Nadia's mother's brother) telling the family of the grandmother's serious illness and urging them to come had arrived the day before, but no tickets were available for a flight to Morocco until two weeks later. So Nadia's father was thrilled when by sheer good luck on Saturday, he met a man who was driving to Morocco the next day; by chance the man had five seats free in his delivery van—just enough to ac-commodate Nadia's family.[11] Yet this meant that the decision to go was not made until Saturday night. Nadia came home late that night and went to work early the next morning, so it was mid-Sunday before she was informed of the family's decision to travel that night. To her mother's delight she insisted on coming along. "I could not believe my ears when Nadia said she wanted to come," said her mother in court. But so much does Nadia love her grandmother that she was even willing to let her employer down and risk losing her job ("I'll get it back," her mother reported her as saying). Yet the Norwegian state prosecutes the fam-ily for having forced Nadia to go, even kidnapping her! The grandfather was outraged.

When questioned about his wife's illness, however, the grandfather was at a loss: well, she is sick all the time. . . . How is she sick? Well, she has diabetes and she faints and such things. . . . Does she faint often? How could he know, he doesn't sit at home . . . and so on.[12] It was a sad spectacle. Watching Nadia's mother watch her father was heart-rending. Whether his exalted status had for-bidden them out of respect to instruct him in their story, or whether he had forgotten his lines or was just out of place in court, I cannot tell.[13] Anyway, his testimony undermined the parents' story.

Someone who might have corroborated the parents' story—the driver with whom they went to Morocco—could not be brought as a witness because he could not be identified. The parents claimed not to know anything about him save for his first name—which did not sound plausible, given that they had spent five days together. According to Nadia, they also had spent a night in his house in Morocco.

Other witnesses came out for the parents, among them the social worker. She said she could not imagine that the family would do anything bad to Nadia; she knew them to be kind and caring people. She also painted a rather dreary pic-ture of Nadia, as did two Moroccan girls—Nadia's friends, they said—along with her brother and a friend of his. They all declared or implied that Nadia was a rather "loose" girl, fond of drinking, smoking, and staying out late at night; but this was not Nadia's own fault, they said. Her schoolmates in high school were such a bad influence on her. Time and again this point was stressed by witnesses for the defense. Not Nadia herself but rather her schoolmates caused her to fall.

A crown witness for the prosecution was the ambassador. Space prohibits a lengthy discussion of his testimony, but it made a strong impression on the court. He painted a most unflattering picture of Nadia's parents. Her father, he said, had threatened to beat Nadia if Norway did not grant him "free passage." Her mother had called all Norwegian women whores.[14] Nadia had been close to a breakdown and had been cajoled and threatened by her parents in the worst possible ways—as all the staff at the Norwegian embassy in Morocco could confirm, for they had listened in on telephone negotiations. The ambassador's testimony was entirely in line with Nadia's.

Another strong witness for the prosecution was the psychologist whom Nadia had been seeing for a year since she came back from Morocco, and who gave vivid testimonies of the traumas she had suffered.

In the end, the Norwegian state chose not to include a charge of forced marriage against Nadia's parents. Although Nadia clearly was convinced they had a marriage in mind for her, there was no firm evidence of this. The charge was that of forcibly holding someone against her will, with a stipulation that the offense had exceeded one month, as it had in Nadia's case.

The jury took only three days to reach a verdict. Both parents were found guilty. Nadia's father was sentenced to one year and three months on suspension, her mother to one year. Her father also was sentenced to pay a fine of 15,000 kroner (about $1,700) and "court proceedings costs" (saksomkostninger) of 60,000 NOK (about $6,800) connected with bringing witnesses from abroad, the defense lawyer's journey to Morocco, and the like.

Nadia's parents thus received a sentence lighter than the legal minimum for the crime of which they were convicted. My role may have had some significance here; the published verdict indicates as much. As a witness I was asked to answer truthfully every question but also to bring up any matter that I judged to be of significance to the case. I did, speaking at some length on what I judged would be the cost to Nadia and her family should her parents, and especially her mother, be thrown in jail.

I was alarmed, I said, to find that whereas Nadia had had a lot of support among youths in the Moroccan community before the trial, she had lost it now. Instead, she was harshly criticized by nearly everyone; the reason I heard was that she was "throwing her parents in jail." People do not care that it is the Norwegian state that charged the parents. To them Nadia is guilty, and of the most horrible deed: of throwing her mother in jail. Elaborating on the mother's position in Islam, I tried to make it comprehensible that the reactions would be as they were. I also gave some objective reasons why the mother should be treated more leniently. As a wife in Islam she is subject to the law of obedience, being duty-bound to obey her husband. Hence, the benefit of the doubt should be the mother's in particular. In its published verdict, the court also noted that as there was no evidence that the mother had beaten Nadia, she should receive a milder sentence than the father.

The court granted that for the sake of the whole family, the parents must not be jailed. Yet to establish a firm precedent and underscore the seriousness of the crime also was necessary. The final sentence was in accordance with the prosecutor's procedure. He had pleaded forcefully for Nadia's case, asking the court to sentence her parents while keeping the options for family reconciliation open.

In its verdict the jury noted that there had been attempts by several witnesses to present Nadia in a disreputable light. The court, however, had a positive impression of Nadia as a clear-headed (ryddig) and bright girl. In the view of the court, Nadia deserved respect for the way she managed to carry through with her testimony. The court could not see that evidence had been presented to indicate that her demeanor was any different from that of other Norwegian girls her age.

In this, the court followed the recommendation of the prosecutor, who had advocated that Nadia receive some form of redress (oppreisning) for the injustice she had suffered from the massive attempts by some witnesses to blacken her reputation and portray her as a liar.

In the end, Nadia stood in willful independence, a solitary figure bereft of expressed support within the Muslim community, where she was perceived by many as a traitor. Her parents' attempts, corroborated by others, to make Nadia appear the dupe of bad Norwegian friends were totally against her own wish: to be perceived as a person in her own right. In time Nadia has become a role model for others, both female and male, who gained strength and felt support from her case—without her ever trying to capitalize on her name. The only pictures that appeared of Nadia in the media were a snapshot published while she was in Morocco, and one of her under the black blanket on her way to court. Nor has she ever agreed to be interviewed.[15] She lives quietly at a secret address, but I know that she has helped others who have sought her out. And by her example she has come to lend courage to others, none of whom lent her support during the trial, but who in the aftermath stand on her shoulders. To understand how that came to be, let us look at the premises and implications of the verdict.

It was the matter of citizenship that decided Nadia's fate in more than one way. Obviously, had she not been a Norwegian citizen, the Norwegian government could not have interceded on her behalf. Yet it was important that her parents also were Norwegian citizens. This is clear from the writ of the verdict, which states:

> The defense attorneys have argued for acquittal on the grounds that Nadia, according to Moroccan law, becomes legally an adult (myndig) only at twenty years of age. Moroccan citizens are not freed from their citizenship if they acquire another. Nadia had, therefore, dual citizenship. Her parents

must therefore have assumed that she was a child and/or minor in Morocco, and that they were in their full right to keep her there against her will.

The court does not agree. When the parents have taken the step of applying for Norwegian citizenship for themselves and their children, this implies both rights and duties. An application for citizenship means that one has decided for oneself which state one wants to be most closely connected with, if not emotionally, at least judicially. That also means that one has to submit to (innordne seg) the rules applying in this state. The parents were well aware of what the legal age in Norway is. For a Norwegian citizen resident in Norway one cannot assume that Moroccan law should apply during short-term visits in that country, and especially not when [Nadia] has been brought there against her will. The criminal offense (det straffbare forholdet) was initiated in Norway. . . . Forcibly holding Nadia against her will was therefore in violation of the law.

Ignorance of the law (rettsvillfaring), which also has been claimed as grounds for acquittal, is likewise not applicable, according to the court. Forcibly holding a person against her will is illegal in most states, if not in all. As residents of Norway, and as Norwegian citizens, [Nadia's parents] must know the rules at least in this country.

Both the subjective and objective conditions for sentencing (domfelling) are present, and the accused are sentenced according to the charge.

The verdict further states:

The case arises from culture conflicts. But it is the parents who have chosen to live in Norway. After many years of residence here, they are fully aware of how Norwegian society functions, for good and bad. That they wish to maintain the customs of their country of birth is unobjectionable, so long as these customs do not come into conflict with Norwegian law. Children can develop in ways that are different from what the parents hope for. But that is the risk in having children, and—not least—in letting them grow up in a different culture. The parents have made a choice as to which country their children will be molded by. That circumstance may have such consequences as resulting in the case currently before the court. Using violence and forceful deprivation of the freedom of movement as an answer is unacceptable.

The court also notes that the family continues to live in Norway and that they have two children below school age who will grow up here. Therefore, there must be aspects of Norwegian society that they, in sum, perceive as more positive than the negative ones. (Judgment in court case no. 98–3021 M 77, 8–10)

The verdict was a clear statement of what the Norwegian state demands of its citizens according to the law, and it was historic. For the first time, a Norwegian court declared—in blunt language—what citizenship entails. Reactions varied accordingly: outrage from many members of the Muslim community and others who sympathized with Nadia's parents, and satisfaction from still others, some Muslims included.

Mohammed Bouras, chairman of the Islamic Council, declared, "This is an insult to all Muslims. It implies that we are bushmen who do not follow Norwegian laws and rules!" The issue of citizenship and the judge's emphasis on the duties entailed in taking Norwegian citizenship provoked his wrath. He also was quoted as saying, "The charges and the verdict are an offense against the family and us Muslims. The judge is requiring us to respect Norwegian laws, but does not show us any respect" (*Dagbladet*, November 11, 1998). Mr. Bouras had been a witness for the defense. Others were quoted as saying, "This is directed against us Muslims! The Norwegian state does not care about Nadia. They are just using her against us" (*Aftenposten*, November 11, 1998).

Clearly, the verdict added insult to injury. "Justismord!—Miscarriage of justice!" cried an editor and friend of Nadia's family (*Dagbladet*, November 11, 1998). "A declaration of war!" announced a prominent journalist (Waage 1998). His concern was that by not making any concession to Nadia's parents, the judge and jury had not only done injustice to them but antagonized the Muslim community—and reactions were bound to come. There was nothing wrong with the sentence, as he saw it; rather, the premises of the verdict were unacceptable. "[Saying that] the parents ought to know how Norwegian society functions and that it is they themselves who have chosen to live here—[is] a form of paternalism (besserwissen) that can only be like salt in open wounds," he wrote (Waage 1998).

Nadia's parents appealed the verdict on the spot: their attorneys recommended it, their honor demanded it, and the monetary fine seemed an insult. I believe they would have been happy not to have to go through the whole ordeal again, but such a recourse seemed precluded in the setting.[16] Also, there were some members of the Moroccan community who wished Nadia's parents would accept defeat on the grounds that their case seemed too weak and the evidence against them too strong. But in the end, their efforts to appeal came to no effect.

Nadia's father died of heart disease six months after the trial. The Norwegian state subsequently withdrew its charge against Nadia's mother. Nadia's brother, who wanted to proceed with the case, tried to appeal to a rarely applied section of the law to appear in his father's stead, but he was refused, to the mother's relief. So far, an open reconciliation between Nadia and her mother and younger siblings has not been possible, due to her brother's rage.[17] Nadia is living by herself and managing relatively well—though suffering greatly from her father's death. There are those who say that Nadia caused his death, but it may be well to remember that according to Islam, the time of one's death is written at birth; it is foreordained and cannot be changed.

Nadia's case poses a number of basic questions: What are the limits of cultural tolerance? How do we balance respect for human rights with respect for cultural difference? What of the rights of the child versus the rights of parents? How do we enforce the law in the case of violations committed with the best of intentions, such as to protect one's child from harm? Religion also is an issue:

Should not Muslims, for example, be granted respect and the right to bring up their daughters in accordance with their religion?

These and other issues came to the fore in Nadia's case, and though the court attempted to reach a solution, as it had to, I think no one who witnessed the trial felt there were any winners. Nadia was reported by her attorney to have said that she was glad the court believed her. Beyond that, she made no statement. Her case split a family and caused irreparable suffering. I, for one, said in court that it might have been better had it not been tried. Mediation might have been better. In retrospect, however, I have my doubts, having come to realize how hard the issues were. Moreover, as the jury said in its verdict, the graveness of the crime demanded that it be tried.

The power of Nadia's case lies in the resonance of its story through time and place. One need not be Norwegian or Muslim or Moroccan to be drawn in. The issues are universal, the resolution particular, but anyone can take the various elements and move them around—play with them—if you wish. In real life, something must be done. If not, that too has consequences. Real consequences.

"Citizenship in Western liberal democracies is the modern equivalent of feudal privilege—an inherited status that greatly enhances one's life chances," wrote Joseph Carens (1987). Let me end with a story that complements Nadia's case and throws it into relief. It highlights some of what remains to be done if the thrust of Carens's dictum is to be borne out, and pertains to the plight of the child.

In 1994, three-plus years before Nadia, another Norwegian girl, fourteen years old, was brought out of the country to Morocco, her parents' original homeland. They too were longtime Norwegian citizens. I shall call the girl Aisha.

Like Nadia, Aisha had appealed to the child welfare agencies for help due to her father's violence. Unlike Nadia, Aisha came from a family well known for its malfunctioning. Aisha's urgent appeals and those of her teachers on her behalf failed to impress the child authorities. After a brief respite with a foster family, Aisha was reunited with her family by force. Two weeks later she was taken out of the country and not heard from again until four years later, when she reappeared in Oslo. Meanwhile, Aisha had been married by force and had her schooling interrupted, so she is left without even an elementary school certificate. Aisha also is a Norwegian citizen, but all attempts on her school's and my part to make Norwegian authorities intervene for her failed.[18] As one significant document states, "Because she has gone with her family to her homeland [sic!], Norwegian jurisdiction does not for the time apply to the family."[19]

With the hindsight of Nadia's case, we can see why that would be. Aisha was only a child. Nadia was, after all, an adult—according to Norwegian law. For Norway to intervene on Aisha's behalf between Aisha and her parents therefore would be much more difficult. Also, Nadia struck an alarm: she managed to get to a telephone. Aisha never reached that point. There are other relevant contrasts, too. But the main point has been made: despite differences in each case, clearly it takes more for a child to be heard and have her or his rights as a Norwegian citizen protected than for an adult. Therefore, the rights of the child must be strengthened, especially when dual citizenship is involved, and particularly for females.

Because Norway failed to stand by this citizen, she has been subjected to forced marriage—something Nadia was spared. Now when she is back in Norway at all, it is only because she is being used as merchandise (*vare*), as she says—to bring in a husband who would not get a visa but for her. This is called *family reunification*.

Aisha defeated her family: she ran away. To her surprise, her father—who had threatened to kill her—gave up her passport and marriage certificate to the police when they came to his door requesting them. She now wonders if he has taken a lesson from the Nadia case. Is he afraid they will cancel his social welfare benefits too?

Family reunification is a double-edged sword. On the one hand, it exposes children of immigrants in Europe, not just Norway, to immense pressure to comply with arranged marriages, and in many cases to real force. In Pakistan, for instance, marriageable girls in Norway are called *visuni*—visas; and Norwegian-Moroccan girls are spoken of as gold-edged papers. On the other hand, family reunification is a salvation for girls such as Aisha and many others who return to Norway thanks only to their quality as visas. If not for that, many more girls might have become missing persons.

Nadia's case has a moral lesson. Human rights must take precedence over what may be termed *cultural rights*. Human rights are based in moral individualism: they are entitlements of the individual as against the state, the family, the church, or other controlling powers—and they apply across the board in liberal democracies. No distinction can be made on the basis of ethnicity, religion, or other factors. Equality applies, as does the right of exit from the group, as Nadia and Aisha have chosen. The policy implications are that a pluralistic society requires a social contract to protect the rights of all members. A strong state, not a weak state, is the best guarantee of human rights, as Michael Ignatieff (1999), among others, has argued. I see the verdict in Nadia's case as an attempt by the Norwegian state to make a case for citizenship—a dissipated notion that needs to be reinvented in our times. Nadia's and Aisha's cases show clearly what is at stake.

Dual citizenship often is presented by academics as an asset, a resource—and so it is for the likes of them. I hope to have made a case for the perils of dual citizenship. In this, as in many matters, the crucial question is, for whom is dual citizenship an advantage? Who stands to lose and who to gain? Children, I have argued, may be the main losers, and girls most of all. Would that policy makers and other interested parties heed the implications of Nadia's and Aisha's stories and thus reconceptualize citizenship and realize what is in jeopardy.

Telling Aisha's story to a friend in Oman recently, and dwelling on the injustices of the Norwegian state, I was struck by her comment, "She was lucky. She at least had a place to go!" My friend was right. A citizen of a European welfare state, Aisha now can call on help—after having lost four years of her life. Sacrificed at fourteen on the altar of culture, Aisha is now ready, and will be helped, to get her life in order and have her human rights protected. She cannot fully appreciate how, but a girl named Nadia helped lay the foundation by changing Norwegian history.

## NOTES

1. This contact was made on September 10, two days after Nadia's call. This means that efforts by the authorities to keep the matter secret from media exposure were successful for about twenty days; the news did not break until October 3.

2. In fact, an international arrest order had been issued against Nadia's father in case he should leave Morocco.

3. I had been called as a witness for the defense, but when I realized that this meant that I could only be present during my own testimony (as applies to all witnesses), I asked for a redefinition of my status, and it was granted.

4. I know more than I am able to tell, since I was also present during a part of the proceedings that was closed to the public during Nadia's testimony. In addition, I withhold information given me in trust by Nadia's mother. Also not included are telephone conversations with the father's defense attorney and private conversations with the Moroccan leader and others. My account is public, based on what was revealed in the court and media. All translations into English of the testimony given in court, as well as any translations of quotes from other sources, are my own.

5. The social worker was a friend of Nadia's brother, having been assigned by the child welfare agencies to help him get his life in order.

6. Two interpreters were present, one in Berber for Nadia's mother, one in Arabic for her father. Since I know Arabic, I could follow much of what was said by the father (not all, owing to dialect differences between his Moroccan and my Egyptian), and even a part of her mother's speech, for Berber contains a host of Arabic words and expressions. Having translators clearly provided the defendants with a degree of flexibility, as misunderstandings and inconsistencies could be attributed to the translators, who also in some cases helped the defendants in their answers.

7. This point surfaces time and again in stories of girls kidnapped and taken to the Middle East or South Asia by their parents: they have nowhere to go and cannot possibly escape, even though their feet are not tied and the doors are not locked. The dangers of even attempting escape are so dreadful that the risk cannot be run, and the chances of succeeding are minuscule. These girls live under the threat of death and are observed in all and everything they do. Among forty-odd Norwegian second-generation immigrant girls abducted and married by force by their parents (or threatened to be married), I know of only three cases in which the girl managed to escape (see Karim 1996; Storhaug 1996, 1999; Wikan 2002).

8. Nadia's father also argued in court that Norwegian authorities and police had pressured Nadia into keeping to her original story of falsehoods.

9. Nadia's parents owned a house valued at about $120,000 (U.S.) in Morocco that they used as a holiday residence.

10. I cannot help but wonder why she did it, and guess it might be to dissuade her parents from trying to marry her by force. Now her mother would know that the virginity test on her wedding night would scandalize the whole family.

11. This part of the parents' story rings less than true. From what I know (and I have many friends within the Moroccan-Norwegian community), people traveling to Morocco overland usually have their cars loaded, for there is a constant stream of waiting passengers, and recruiting them is a way of sharing costs and company. Thus, finding a driver who is about to go with a near-empty van would take more than sheer good luck.

12. Nadia's grandmother's illness was a key issue during the trial. As proof of their case, the parents presented a telegram they had received from Nadia's mother's brother, saying, "Your mother is ill. Come urgently." Yet Nadia's mother said she did not phone her family in Morocco during the seven days it took for them to reach home; Nadia's father said he phoned the day the telegram arrived but not after. By the time they arrived in Morocco, the grandmother was quite well. The jury found the story less than plausible. As stated in the premises of the verdict: when a close family member is gravely ill, one usually uses a phone to convey the message. The telegram appeared to be part of a cover-up operation. Moreover, if the grandmother had been so ill, one would have expected the parents to make contact during the seven days.

13. As Nadia told the story in court, she had been forbidden to tell the family in Morocco that she had been forced to come. The appearance was to be given that she did it voluntarily.

14. This caused quite a stir when it became known through the media. Several prominent Norwegian women, among others, were appalled to be so designated and voiced their complaints in no uncertain language. Their critique was directed not just at Nadia's mother but at other immigrants who enjoy the fruits of the Norwegian welfare society while deprecating its basic values of equality and freedom. Nadia's mother was devastated by the reaction she had triggered, and I tried to cushion the blow by explaining to the court and media that to call someone *whore* in the Middle East is no big deal: it is a common swearword devoid of the connotations it carries in the West. This does not deny the fact (as I did not say) that Nadia's mother may well have meant that Norwegian women are whores.

15. After this went to press, Nadia has reappeared in the public. The precipitating event was a tragic honor killing in Sweden, on January 21, 2002 (the murder of Fadime Sahindal), that triggered intense debates also in Norway, regarding forced marriage and the prospects for freedom for youth of immigrant background. Nadia decided she had a part to play in enlightening the public and politicians, and in working for human rights. She had been in hiding for more than three years.

16. I base this judgment on four sources: talks I had with the mother the evening before and her public statements that all that mattered to her was to be reconciled with Nadia; Nadia's testimony in court that her father actually wanted to release her in Morocco once the ambassador intervened but her mother's family was wholly against it; the father's heart disease; and reports from a close friend and trusted person in the Norwegian-Moroccan community that the father came to him shortly before his death and expressed his regret that he was forced to continue with the appeal. Whether he wanted to or not, the father had little choice but to proceed with the appeal for the

sake of the family's honor. The fact that he had married into a family far above his own family's standing complicated matters further. His marriage to Nadia's mother appears to have been a love marriage conducted against her family's wishes (which might have been why they went to Norway in the first place). To jeopardize her family's honor further by refraining from launching the appeal would have been out of the question, as I understand it.

17. After this went to press, a reconciliation took place between Nadia and her family, her brother included. But it was broken when Nadia went public in February 2002, advocating the right of girls of immigrant background to freedom and equality. Her brother reportedly threatens her life now.

18. I was contacted by the school and asked to help after Aisha disappeared. For further descriptions of the case see Wikan, 2002, *Generous Betrayal*.

19. Because the case was confidential, I cannot reveal the source of this quotation, but it stems from a superior official body (not a court) to which the case was appealed.

# REFERENCES

Carens, Joseph H. 1987. "Aliens and Citizens: The Case for Open Borders." *Review of Politics* 49(3): 251–73.

Ignatieff, Michael. 1999. "Whose Universal Values? The Crisis in Human Rights." *Praemium Erasmianum Essay*. The Hague: Foundation Horizon.

Karim, Nasim. 1996. *Izzat—For ærens skyld*. Oslo: Cappelen.

Storhaug, Hege. 1996. *Mashallah*. Oslo: Aschehoug.

———. 1999. *Hellig tvang*. Oslo: Aschehoug.

Waage, Peter Normann. 1998. "En Krigserklæring." *Dagbladet*, November 11.

Wikan, Unni. 1980. *Life Among the Poor in Cairo*. London: Tavistock.

———. 1996. *Tomorrow, God Willing: Self-Made Destinies in Cairo*. Chicago: University of Chicago Press.

———. 2002. *Generous Betrayal: Politics of Culture in the New Europe*. Chicago: University of Chicago Press.

# Part II

# Cultural Accommodation and Its Limits

# Chapter 7

# Accommodation and Coherence: In Search of a General Theory for Adjudicating Claims of Faith, Conscience, and Culture

Arthur N. Eisenberg

The promise of American life, at least in its idealized form, embraces a commitment to pluralism. Yet the precise contours of this commitment remain unresolved and in some instances, deeply contested. We celebrate our history as a nation of immigrants. We extol the remarkable richness and diversity provided by a broad array of individuals and groups with divergent religious beliefs and practices and with varied cultural and ethnic backgrounds and customs. Yet the social and political response to such diversity has been decidedly mixed.

Unconditional acceptance of diversity has been tempered in part by an assimilationist conception of America as a melting pot that surfaced as early as the 1780s in the observations of Crévecoeur's *Letters from an American Farmer*. This idea acquired common currency at the beginning of the twentieth century and resurfaced episodically at century's end in the form of initiatives such as the English Only movement of the 1990s. Broad acceptance of diversity also has been thwarted by spasmodic outbursts of nativism and isolationism and by more persistent attitudes of racial bigotry that course through the national experience. Such acceptance has been blunted as well by a more generalized social impulse toward conformity described by Tocqueville as a "tyranny of public opinion."

Unconditional accommodation of diversity also has come into conflict with the demands of democratic governance. Such demands generally require adherence to majoritarian decision making and to normative standards of behavior as reflected in laws of general applicability. Whether and under what circumstances individuals can claim an exemption from laws of general applicability to pursue religiously motivated or conscientiously inspired or even culturally driven practices remains a constitutional question of considerable controversy. This chapter seeks to explore that question.

Consideration begins with the free exercise clause of the First Amendment, a textual provision that at first blush would seem to offer some promise for protecting religiously inspired conduct from the proscriptive reach of laws of general applicability. Yet in *Employment Division, Department of Human Resources of Oregon v. Smith* (1990), a deeply divided Supreme Court narrowed significantly the reach of that textual provision. In *Smith*, the Court held that, in the ordinary course, the free exercise clause provides no exemption from laws of general applicability for individuals whose religiously motivated behavior places them in conflict with such laws.

In the *Smith* case, four justices argued that religiously based claims for exemptions from laws of general applicability were entitled to special judicial consideration, and that laws burdening the free exercise of religion should be subjected to the most exacting form of judicial scrutiny known to constitutional adjudication. A majority of the Court, however, rejected the suggestion that free exercise claims require courts to engage in a skeptical evaluation of laws that intrude on religious conduct. They concluded that, except for laws directed exclusively or discriminatorily at religious beliefs and practices, free exercise claims deserve no serious judicial consideration at all.

Congress responded to the Court's decision in *Smith* by enacting the Religious Freedom Restoration Act (RFRA) in 1993. The enactment attempted to offer a regime of statutory protection for the free exercise of religion that Congress concluded had been erroneously withdrawn by the Supreme Court's ungenerous interpretation of the free exercise clause in the *Smith* case. The enactment did so by adopting the adjudicative standard urged by the four justices who did not join the majority in *Smith*.[1] The statute required that laws significantly burdening the free exercise of religion could be applied only if such application were narrowly tailored in the pursuit of compelling interests.

The RFRA statute and the position urged by the dissenting and concurring opinions in *Smith* have been criticized on three basic grounds. First, the statute and position of the minority in *Smith* inappropriately and unjustifiably would privilege religiously inspired conduct without according similar solicitude to comparable behavior resting on strongly held beliefs not rooted in religion. Second, the exacting standard for adjudicating free exercise claims, as urged by the *Smith* minority opinions and as provided for in RFRA, would invite spurious claims and, as Justice Scalia warned, allow widespread nullification of laws of general applicability, where every person "would become a law unto himself" (*Employment Division, Department of Human Resources of Oregon v. Smith* 1990, 885). Third, the judicial attempt to enforce and evaluate seriously the *authenticity* of free exercise claims and *centrality* of behavior to a claimant's belief system would require courts to intrude inappropriately and beyond their competence into the religious beliefs and practices of individuals.

These are serious criticisms. The critics properly argue that in privileging only religiously motivated conduct, RFRA was too narrow in its protective reach. The solution to this problem of underinclusiveness, however, need not require a regime of unyielding uniformity in which no serious judicial protection is provided to individuals who act out of deeply held convictions or long-standing religious or cultural traditions. Instead, the solicitude offered to religiously motivated conduct could be extended—under a properly crafted statute or fully conceived constitutional principle—to behavior that rests on other deeply held grounds, such as conscientiously based or culturally driven conduct.

Such expansion of categories of behavior entitled to special protection, however, would reinforce concerns about opening the floodgates to widespread nullification of obligations imposed by majoritarian decision making. Moreover, these concerns would prove formidable—indeed, fatal to this conceptual enterprise—if in addition to expanding the categories of protected behavior one were to adopt the exacting standard of judicial review urged by the minority in *Smith* and adopted by Congress in RFRA.

The conflict between the majority and minority in *Smith* offered a choice between two extreme adjudicative standards for resolving free exercise claims. But these are not the only available standards for resolving constitutional controversies. Indeed, the Supreme Court has identified a middle ground and has done so precisely in a controversy involving a conflict between a law of general applicability and expressive conduct rooted in ideological conviction. In *United States v. O'Brien*, a 1968 case involving the burning of a draft card as a form of symbolic speech, the Supreme Court articulated an adjudicative standard that, on its face, is not so rigorous as to allow individual claims to nullify general obligations on a routine basis; and yet the Court's standard in that case does not invite unrestrained deference to majoritarian judgments. The Court offers a standard that should be explored as a basis for evaluating the sorts of claims that are likely to surface when individuals seek exemptions from laws of general applicability on grounds of religious compulsion, or even upon grounds of cultural tradition or claims of individual conscience.

Such an exploration requires consideration as to whether it is appropriate for courts to inquire into the *authenticity* of individual claims, and whether courts are competent to conduct such an inquiry. The answer to these questions can be informed by judicial experience in applying statutes that permit individuals to seek exemptions from laws requiring compulsory military service and exemptions from laws that require vaccinations as conditions for entry into public schools. This judicial experience suggests that courts are capable of fairly evaluating such claims.

Before addressing these matters, it is appropriate to consider more fully the current constitutional impasse that serves as the starting point for this discussion.

## THE *SMITH* CASE AND CONGRESS'S RESPONSE

*Employment Division, Department of Human Resources of Oregon v. Smith* (1990, 872) involved the most recent and most significant examination by the Supreme Court of the reach of the free exercise clause of the First Amendment. In this case, the Court not only resolved the specific application of the free exercise clause to the particular controversy before it but also addressed the general standard of judicial analysis that, according to the Court, should pertain whenever an individual engaged in religiously motivated conduct seeks an exemption for such conduct from a law of general applicability.

At issue in the *Smith* case was "whether the Free Exercise Clause of the First Amendment permits the State of Oregon to include religiously inspired peyote use within the reach of its general criminal prohibition [directed at the] use of that drug, and [therefore] permits the State to deny unemployment benefits to persons dismissed from their jobs because of such religiously inspired use" (*Smith* 1990, 874). The case arose when two individuals, Alfred Smith and Galen Black, were terminated from their employment as counselors at a drug reha-bilitation clinic because they had used peyote as part of a sacramental ceremony of the Native American Church. Upon termination, the employees applied to the State of Oregon for unemployment compensation and were denied benefits on the ground that "they had been discharged for work-related 'misconduct'" (*Smith* 1990, 874). The Oregon Supreme Court held that the state could not, con-sistent with the free exercise clause, deny unemployment benefits to individuals who lost their jobs for having engaged in a religious practice. Yet by a narrow six to three vote, the United States Supreme Court reversed. The Court con-cluded that under the circumstances of the case, the denial of unemployment benefits did not violate the First Amendment.

In support of this conclusion, Justice Scalia, writing for the Court, offered an argument that initially purported to address the text of the free exercise clause. The text of the provision states simply that "Congress shall make no law . . . prohibiting the free exercise [of religion]." Nevertheless, Justice Scalia managed to read into the text a distinction between laws that intrude upon beliefs and laws that limit conduct. Unsurprisingly, he gave primacy to the protection of belief. "The free exercise of religion means, first and foremost," he wrote, "the right to believe and profess whatever religious doctrine one desires" (*Smith* 1990, 877).

In drawing this distinction, however, Justice Scalia acknowledged that even conduct or behavior would be protected by the free exercise clause in circum-stances where a state law targets a particular religious practice or where an enactment seeks to prohibit behavior only when such behavior was undertaken for religious purposes. By way of example, Justice Scalia observed that "[i]t would doubtless be unconstitutional . . . to ban the casting of statues that are to be used for worship purposes or to prohibit bowing down before a golden calf" (*Smith* 1990, 877–78). Yet he balked at what he regarded as the attempted exten-sion of the free exercise clause to circumstances where a law of general appli-cability comes into conflict with a religious practice. He further concluded that "the right of free exercise does not relieve an individual of the obligation to comply with a valid and neutral law of general applicability on the ground that the law proscribes (or prescribes) conduct that his religion prescribes (or pro-scribes)" (*Smith* 1990, 879).

The distinctions fashioned by Justice Scalia can be found nowhere in the text of the free exercise clause. Indeed, the textual reference to "free exercise" might well suggest that the provision was intended to protect at least some forms of physical behavior or conduct as well as belief (McConnell 1990).² Consequently, to support his conclusions, Justice Scalia looked to judicial precedent. To do so, he was required to contend with a particularly unruly set of cases.

In two cases, for example, the Court previously had reviewed the denial of unemployment benefits to individuals who refused to work on Saturdays for religious reasons and were discharged for failing to work. The Court had concluded that the denial of benefits in these circumstances violated the free exercise clause. In a third case, the Court had reviewed the denial of unemployment insurance to an individual who, on the basis of religious objections, quit his job at a factory that produced military weapons. The denial of unemployment insurance rested in part on the state's conclusion that refusal to work for religious reasons was not "good cause." In that case, as well, the Supreme Court held that the denial of unemployment compensation constituted a violation of the free exercise clause.

In an attempt to avoid the precedential force of these unemployment insurance cases, Justice Scalia explained that these "cases stand for the proposition that where the State has in place a system of individual exemptions, it may not refuse to extend that system to cases of 'religious hardship' without [a] compelling reason" (Smith 1990, 884). Yet unlike Smith, none of the earlier unemployment insurance cases involved the termination of an employee for violating the state's criminal laws. Accordingly, Justice Scalia attempted to distinguish these earlier cases as having "nothing to do with an across-the-board criminal prohibition on a particular form of conduct"—as was the case in Smith (1990, 884).

Moreover, beyond the unemployment insurance cases, Justice Scalia was required to contend with other judicial precedent upholding free exercise claims in the face of laws of general applicability that had been invoked to prohibit religiously inspired conduct. In one case, the Court invalidated a Connecticut statute employed to prevent members of the Jehovah's Witnesses from soliciting contributions in New Haven (Cantwell v. Connecticut 1940). The statute, at issue, allowed solicitation by religious and charitable organizations in circumstances where the representatives of these organizations secured permits to engage in such activity. The statute also conferred standardless discretion on a municipal agency to grant or deny the permits. For this reason, the statute could have been invalidated under general First Amendment principles requiring precision of regulation where expressive activities are at stake. Nevertheless, the Court's decision holding the statute unconstitutional rested on the free exercise clause. In a second case (Murdock v. Pennsylvania 1943), the Court held unconstitutional a Pennsylvania ordinance that had imposed a licensing scheme on persons engaged in door-to-door solicitation where such a licensing system was employed to prevent Jehovah's Witnesses from distributing their religious material and seeking contributions. Again the decision rested on the free exercise clause. Justice Scalia distinguished these two cases on the ground that they involved laws that restricted not only the free exercise of religion but also burdened more general forms of free expression.

In similar respects, Justice Scalia attempted to distinguish two other cases. In

*Pierce v. Society of Sisters* (1925) the Court had reviewed an Oregon statute that required all children between the ages of eight and sixteen years to attend public schools. In response to claims by parents who wanted to send their children to private religious schools, the Court found that the application of the statute to these parents and children violated the free exercise clause. Similarly, in *Wisconsin v. Yoder* (1972), the Court held unconstitutional, under the free exercise clause, the application of Wisconsin's compulsory school attendance law where Amish parents objected to a statutory requirement that children attend school until the age of sixteen. In *Smith*, Justice Scalia concluded that both the *Pierce* and *Yoder* decisions turned on the fact that, in addition to burdening the free exercise of religion, the statutes at issue also intruded on rights of parental decision making. In this regard, Justice Scalia repeated the observation in *Yoder* (1972, 882) that "when the interests of parenthood are combined with a free exercise claim . . . more than merely a 'reasonable relation to some purpose within the competency of the State' is required to sustain the validity of the State's requirement under the First Amendment."

Finding no similar combination of interests in *Smith*, Justice Scalia concluded that neither Smith nor his colleague raised any claim under the free exercise clause worthy of serious constitutional consideration. In this regard, he specifically rejected the form of heightened judicial scrutiny previously employed by the Court in the unemployment insurance case of *Sherbert v. Verner* (1963). Under the *Sherbert* analysis, governmental actions that substantially burden a religious practice must be justified by a compelling governmental interest. Justice Scalia rejected the *Sherbert* standard of review and concluded that the standard was unwarranted in light of the Court's precedent.

Justice Scalia reinforced this conclusion with several policy arguments. First, he expressed concern about the potency of the *compelling interest* standard of judicial analysis and of the capacity of that standard to impede the government's ability to enforce general prohibitions directed at socially harmful conduct. He observed that the "compelling state interest" standard of judicial review would render "presumptively invalid, as applied to the religious objector, every regulation of conduct that does not protect an interest of the highest order" (*Smith* 1990, 888). He wrote,

> To make an individual's obligation to obey . . . a law contingent upon the law's coincidence with his religious beliefs, except where the State's interest is "compelling"—permitting him, by virtue of his beliefs "to become a law unto himself" . . . contradicts constitutional tradition and common sense. (*Smith* 1990, 885)

On this matter, Justice Scalia further suggested that it would be possible to limit the strong burden of justification imposed by the compelling interest formulation by applying this formulation "only when the conduct prohibited is 'central' to the individual's religion" (*Smith* 1990, 886–87). Yet he abjured inquiry into the *centrality* of beliefs on grounds of propriety as well as judicial competence. He suggested that it is improper for courts to inquire into and evaluate the importance of a particular practice to one's religious faith. Further, he asked, "What principle of law or logic can be brought to bear to contradict a believer's assertion that a particular act is 'central' to his personal faith?" (*Smith* 1990, 888).

At bottom, Justice Scalia therefore concluded that religiously motivated practices cannot be exempted from the proscriptive or prescriptive reach of normative legal requirements except where such laws are targeted at specific religious practices or are motivated by hostility to such practices. In the absence of those circumstances, Justice Scalia, writing for the Court in *Smith*, held that a religious objector to a law of general applicability can assert no claim whatever under the free exercise clause. Indeed, under Justice Scalia's analysis, a religious objector's claim of exemption from a law of general applicability should be dismissed without any judicial examination whatever of the countervailing justifications for the enactment and without any inquiry as to the necessity of the application of the enactment to the religious practices.

This conclusion drew criticism from four members of the Court. Justice O'Connor agreed with Justice Scalia that Smith's free exercise claim should have been rejected—but only after a balancing inquiry that involved an assessment of the burdens imposed by the statute at issue and the importance of the state's interest in enforcing the statute. In this regard, Justice O'Connor expressed the view that for the state to prevail its interest must be "compelling." She wrote,

> The compelling interest test effectuates the First Amendment's command that religious liberty is an independent liberty, that it occupies a preferred position and that the Court will not permit encroachments upon this liberty, whether direct or indirect, unless required by clear and compelling governmental interests of the highest order. (*Smith* 1990, 895)

For this reason, Justice O'Connor criticized the abandonment of the "compelling state interest" formulation by Justice Scalia, and she urged a case-by-case evaluation of the competing interests (*Smith* 1990, 889). Applying that case-by-case approach, Justice O'Connor arrived at the conclusion that the state's overriding interest in preventing drug abuse outweighed any free exercise claim asserted by *Smith*.

A different conclusion was reached by three dissenting justices. Justices Blackmun, Brennan, and Marshall criticized Justice Scalia's abandonment of the compelling interest formula just as Justice O'Connor had done. Unlike Justice O'Connor, however, the three dissenting justices would have balanced the competing interests differently and would have concluded that "Oregon's interest in enforcing its drug law against religious use of peyote [was] not sufficiently compelling to outweigh [Smith's] right to the free exercise of . . . religion" (*Smith* 1990, 921).

Justice Scalia's opinion in *Smith* also drew fire from Congress. In response to the decision of the Court in *Smith*, Congress enacted the Religious Freedom Restoration Act of 1993. By its terms, the statute provided that "[g]overnment shall not substantially burden a person's exercise of religion" unless it first demonstrates that "application of the burden to the person" is the "least restrictive means" to further "a compelling governmental interest" (RFRA 1993, § 2000bb–1[a]–[b]). RFRA was designed to provide, through statutory protection, what the Supreme Court in *Smith* had rejected as a matter of constitutional principle. The enactment sought to require that courts evaluate religiously based claims for exemptions from laws of general applicability against the requirements of the compelling state interest test.

The statute clearly privileged religiously motivated behavior over other conscientiously driven conduct not rooted in religion—and this privileging of religion properly was criticized in a series of articles by Professors Eisgruber and Sager (Eisgruber and Sager 1994a, 1994b, 1996; *City of Boerne v. Flores* 1997).[3] At the heart of this criticism was the observation that "religious conscience is just one of many very strong motivations in human life and there is no particular reason to suppose that it is likely to matter more in the run of religious lives generally than will other very powerful forces in the lives of both the non-religious and the religious" (Eisgruber and Sager 1994a, 1263).

This criticism seems plainly correct; and yet the Court's decision in *Smith* also seems unsatisfactory. It offers no legal recourse whatever for individuals who seek the most modest exemption from laws of general applicability. Suppose, for example, a public school were to adopt a dress code that prohibits students from wearing any cap or head covering while inside the schoolhouse, and suppose a young man whose faith and upbringing were consonant with Orthodox Judaism were to seek relief from this policy in order to wear a skullcap during the school day. Under the standards announced by Justice Scalia, writing for the Court in *Smith*, the student's request for an exemption from the general requirements of the school's dress code would be rejected. Similarly, a Sikh who wished to carry a ceremonial dagger on his person might run afoul of a law prohibiting the carrying of concealed weapons. Again, under *Smith*, the Sikh's request for an exemption from the general prohibition would be rejected even if the ceremonial dagger were welded into a protective sheath and therefore posed virtually no threat as a potential weapon. Under the decision in *Smith*, both requests for exemptions would be rejected without any balancing whatever of the justification for imposing the laws of general applicability. Indeed, under *Smith*, the requests for the exemptions would provoke no constitutional conversation at all.

This blanket denial of accommodation, under any and all circumstances, seems neither appropriate nor necessary. Eisgruber and Sager are correct in their observation that individuals hold a broad variety of beliefs and traditions that are not simply religious, and that in many circumstances behavior may be motivated by deeply held views that are not necessarily religious. But the solution to the underinclusiveness of the approach urged by Justice O'Connor in *Smith* and by those who drafted RFRA need not be a regime where no protection is ever extended to religiously motivated practices. Indeed, the solution to the underinclusiveness properly criticized by Eisgruber and Sager could involve an expansion rather than a contraction of constitutional or statutory protections.

A fully conceived constitutional principle—or a properly crafted statute—could privilege not only religiously motivated conduct but could extend its protective reach to all behavior grounded in deeply held convictions or long-standing traditions. That the tradition that animates the behavior is more appropriately described as cultural rather than religious should not matter. Likewise, that the belief system that inspires the conduct rests on a rational construct rather than one founded on religious compulsion also should not matter. These conclusions turn in large measure on the recognition that individuals often seem to practice some but not all of the rituals within their religious traditions. And, the choice of which rituals to follow seems to turn on customary practices of a cultural nature as much as on religious mandate. Thus, the line between cultural and religious tradition is not especially clear; nor, for these purposes, is the distinction between rational choice and religious compulsion.

Accordingly, a decision to provide special constitutional or, if necessary, statutory protection to a broad range of conscientiously, religiously, or even culturally driven conduct might be said to rest on several grounds. First, such a decision would rest on our collective recognition of the special importance of religious experience and practices to a great many individuals. Moreover, the decision would rest on the recognition that custom and culture often influence an individual's choice as to which religious rituals are to be practiced. The decision also would rest on an understanding that many individuals act out of deeply held views that are not necessarily rooted in religion. Cultural tradition occupies the place for some individuals that, for others, is occupied by religious tradition. Further, the decision would rest on the recognition that the line between belief and ritual or between conscience and conduct is not always clear. Finally, the decision would rest on a respect for individual conscience and on the virtue of allowing individuals to think as they wish and, to the degree possible, to act as they think.

So understood, what ultimately unites our solicitude of such behavior is a respect for the sovereignty of individuals. We can honor that sovereignty by recognizing a basic right of autonomy that embraces freedom of belief as well as expressive manifestations of deeply rooted belief. Under principles of democratic governance, this right of autonomy cannot be unlimited. As properly conceived, however, such a right might hold that when individuals act out of deeply held beliefs or traditions, the state must accommodate such behavior unless it has strong reasons not to do so.

## SYMBOLIC EXPRESSION AND THE *O'BRIEN* CASE

Recognition of a right of autonomy of the sort described in the foregoing discussion undoubtedly would reinforce concerns expressed by Justice Scalia in *Smith* that each person "would become a law unto himself [or herself]" (*Smith* 1990, 879). One may, however, recognize a right of autonomy without at the same time insisting that, in every circumstance, encroachment on such a right is presumptively unconstitutional and must be found invalid unless narrowly tailored in pursuit of compelling interests. The Supreme Court's symbolic speech cases are instructive in this regard.

In *United States v. O'Brien* (1968), the Supreme Court reviewed the conviction of David Paul O'Brien for having burned his draft card in violation of a provision of the Universal Military Training and Service Act, which made it a crime to destroy knowingly a certificate issued by the Selective Service System. O'Brien claimed that in burning his draft card he had been engaged in a form of symbolic speech to express his opposition to the military engagement in Southeast Asia. O'Brien argued, therefore, that the application of the federal statute to his ideologically motivated conduct burdened his right of political expression, and that to survive constitutional scrutiny the government was obligated to demonstrate that the application of the statute was "narrowly tailored" in the pursuit of "compelling interests."

In exploring O'Brien's claim, Chief Justice Warren, writing for the Court, expressed concern about the potentially open-ended nature of claims of symbolic speech. "We cannot accept the view that an apparently limitless variety of conduct can be labeled 'speech' whenever the person engaging in the conduct intends thereby to express an idea" (*United States v. O'Brien* 1968, 376). Nevertheless, without defining the sort of conduct that would be entitled to First Amendment protection as symbolic speech, Chief Justice Warren implicitly acknowledged that at least in some circumstances, symbolic expression deserves First Amendment protection. Yet in *O'Brien*, the Warren Court declined to apply the compelling interest standard of adjudication in circumstances where a statute curtailing symbolic expression was not clearly directed at the suppression of ideas. Instead, the Court announced,

> government regulation is sufficiently justified if it is within the constitutional power of the Government; if it furthers an important or substantial government interest; if the governmental interest is unrelated to the suppression of free expression; and if the incidental restriction on alleged First Amendment freedom is no greater than is essential to the furtherance of that interest. (*O'Brien* 1968, 377)

Applying this standard, the Supreme Court upheld the application of the federal statute to O'Brien's act of symbolic speech.

In the flag desecration cases, the Court revisited and reinforced its symbolic speech doctrine. In *Texas v. Johnson* (1989), for example, the Court reviewed the conviction of an individual who participated in a demonstration during the 1984 Republican National Convention to protest the policies of President Ronald Reagan and who burned an American flag as part of the demonstration. Johnson was convicted of violating a Texas law prohibiting the desecration of the American flag. The Court found the conviction inconsistent with the First Amendment.

In reaching this conclusion, the Court again addressed the concern that, in recognizing a constitutional right to engage in symbolic speech, it might be opening the door for all sorts of claims by individuals who engage in illegal conduct and then seek to secure constitutional protection for such conduct by asserting that the conduct conveys an idea. On this matter, the Court noted,

> in deciding whether particular conduct possesses sufficient communicative elements to bring the First Amendment into play, we have asked whether "[a]n intent to convey a particularized message was present, and [whether] the likelihood was great that the message would be understood by those who viewed it." (*Texas v. Johnson* 1989, 404)

Having concluded that Johnson's conduct in burning the flag clearly was intended to convey a message and was so understood, the Court went on to consider the legal standards that should pertain under the First Amendment in symbolic speech cases. In this regard, the Court articulated two distinctions. First, the Court distinguished between direct communication in the form of speech and writing and expression that is conveyed symbolically through various forms of conduct. Second, the Court distinguished between laws that are expressly directed at the communicative nature of conduct and laws of general application that only incidentally burden expressive conduct. On the basis of these distinctions, the Court in *Johnson* fashioned a two-tiered analysis of First Amendment cases. The Court recognized that "[t]he government generally has a freer hand in restricting expressive conduct than it has in restricting the written or spoken word" (*Johnson* 1989, 446); and that where a law of general applicability incidentally burdens expressive conduct, the adjudicative standards from *United States v. O'Brien* will be applied. The Court also noted, however, that "a law directed at the communicative nature of conduct must, like a law directed at speech itself, be justified by the substantial showing of need that the First Amendment requires" (*Johnson* 1989, 406).

Under the facts of the *Johnson* case, the Court found that the flag desecration statute under which Johnson was prosecuted was aimed at the suppression of speech, and that the prosecution therefore could not be sustained when measured against the exacting standard of adjudication appropriate to such circumstances. In reaching this result, however, the Court reconfirmed in *Johnson* that the somewhat more relaxed *O'Brien* standard should be applied to those cases where a statute of general applicability incidentally burdens conduct designed to express an idea.

The *O'Brien* test offers an appropriate adjudicative standard for resolving controversies involving laws of general applicability that incidentally burden conduct rooted in conscience, religion, or custom. This is so for at least two reasons.

First and foremost, in its basic structure, the *O'Brien* test provides an appropriate balance between competing interests. The standard is not so exacting as to allow individual claims to nullify routinely obligations imposed by majoritarian decision making. Yet on its face, the standard does not invite unrestrained deference to majoritarian lawmaking.

Second, the *O'Brien* standard was developed precisely to resolve a conflict between a law of general applicability and conduct rooted in ideological conviction. This circumstance is closely analogous—and in some instances, identical—to the conflict between laws of general applicability and conduct rooted in religion or custom or conscience. Thus, the *O'Brien* test is tethered to and emerges from a textual provision—the free speech clause of the First Amendment—that on its surface protects free expression but that, at bottom, has been found to protect ideological conviction and conscience by protecting the behavioral manifestation of belief in the form of symbolic speech.[4] So understood, if we must find any textual source for the constitutional right of autonomy asserted here, that source may well be the First Amendment provision upon which the *O'Brien* case rests.[5]

Some may well remain skeptical with respect to the capacity of the *O'Brien* standard to provide meaningful protection for individuals who seek exemptions from laws of general applicability. Although in theory the *O'Brien* standard offers the promise of an analytical approach that strikes a fair balance between the demands of majoritarian decision making and the claims of individuals asserting constitutionally based exemptions from such demands, in reality the Supreme Court's application of the *O'Brien* test has not been especially accommodating of the constitutional claims advanced by individuals. As noted earlier, in the *O'Brien* case itself, the Court upheld the prosecution of an individual for engaging in symbolic speech by burning a draft card. The Court ruled in favor of the government's position, even though the administrative interest in prohibiting selective service registrants from defacing or mutilating their own draft cards did not seem particularly compelling.

Similarly, in a recent application of the *O'Brien* test, the Supreme Court upheld an Erie, Pennsylvania, ordinance banning public nudity and found that the ordinance could be applied, consistent with the First Amendment, to prohibit nude dancing at local establishments (*City of Erie v. Paps* 2000). Again, the Court applied the *O'Brien* standard in a manner that favored majoritarian decision making and disfavored the assertion of constitutionally protected expression. Moreover, it did so despite an absence of evidentiary support for the claim that, in prohibiting nude dancing while permitting erotic dancers to perform wearing minimal costumes, the municipality had developed a legislative scheme that would reduce in any serious way the harmful effects perceived to be caused by the existence of erotic dancing establishments.

Despite these examples of the Supreme Court's skewed application of the *O'Brien* test in symbolic speech cases, such imbalance is neither inevitable nor necessary. Indeed, in a parallel First Amendment context, a legal standard similar to the *O'Brien* test does operate effectively to provide an appropriate balance of competing interests. In addition to the symbolic speech cases, an *O'Brien*-like test also is applied to evaluate the constitutionality of government decisions that limit the "time, place and manner" of First Amendment events such as demonstrations, parades, and rallies. In these circumstances, lower federal courts have applied this test in a fact-intensive manner to strike a reasonable balance between the claims of individuals seeking to engage in expressive activity and the justification offered by government seeking to restrict such expression (*Million Youth March v. Safir* 1998; *Housing Works v. Safir* 1998; *United Yellow Cab Drivers Association v. Safir* 1998).

Moreover, in the *Paps* case, Justice Souter argued that the proper application of the *O'Brien* test requires courts to engage in a serious factual inquiry in order to evaluate the nature of the expressive interests at stake and to determine the government's justification for restricting expressive conduct and the connection between that justification and the regulation at issue (*City of Erie v. Paps* 2000). If the sort of fact-intensive inquiry urged by Justice Souter were to be adopted, the *O'Brien* test could be fashioned as an appropriate analytical tool for evaluating the claims advanced by individuals who, on grounds of religion or culture or conscience, seek an exemption from laws of general applicability. A fact-intensive inquiry under the *O'Brien* test would allow courts to give serious consideration to claims of conscience, culture, and faith and would require governmental entities to provide good reasons for seeking to override these claims.

In many instances, the government will have good reasons to override individual claims. Thus, for example, civil rights statutes that prohibit discrimination on grounds of race or gender within public institutions or within the commercial marketplace likely would be found to rest on interests that are sufficiently compelling so that individuals seeking exemptions from such laws on grounds of religion, culture, or conscience would and should find such requests rejected (*Bob Jones University v. United States* 1983; *Newman Piggie Park Enters* 1966–1968). However, a request for an exemption generally should be granted where the exemption would impose no significant burden on third parties. The student that seeks an exemption on religious grounds from a school rule prohibiting wearing hats in the classroom would and should secure such an exemption.

At bottom, an invigorated *O'Brien* test calling for serious factual inquiry into competing interests and claims at the least would provide individuals seeking religious, cultural, or conscientious-based exemptions from laws of general applicability with a judicial opportunity to assert such claims. This is an opportunity that individuals do not, at present, enjoy under the current state of constitutional doctrine respecting the free exercise clause.

## EVALUATING THE AUTHENTICITY OF CLAIMS

Under a fact-intensive *O'Brien* inquiry, however, courts would need to evaluate the authenticity of claims of conscience or custom or religion. In *Smith*, Justice Scalia expressed deep reservations about such an inquiry. His reservations seemed to rest on two grounds. First, he appeared to suggest that having courts inquire into the sincerity of one's beliefs or the centrality to one's belief system of the practices at issue is inappropriately invasive.[6] Second, he seemed to suggest that such inquiries are beyond the competence of a court to resolve.

The answer to the first objection has been provided by Professor Laurence

Tribe, who noted that privacy concerns of the sort suggested by Justice Scalia are less persuasive when an individual voluntarily seeks a special exemption from the state and where the price of such an exemption is the requirement that the individual explain the nature of one's beliefs (Tribe 1988, 1245). The answer to the second objection is provided by the body of judicial experience that has developed as courts have been called on to entertain claims for exemptions made by individuals who, on grounds of conscientious objection, seek relief from combatant service in the military or who, on grounds of religious objection, seek an exception from the general requirement that children must be vaccinated in order to attend public schools.

Congress has provided that individuals may seek an exemption from combatant service in the military if such individuals "by reason of [their] religious training and belief [in "a Supreme Being" are] conscientiously opposed to participation in war in any form" (*United States v. Seeger* 1965). In *United States v. Seeger*, the Supreme Court interpreted and applied this statutory provision in circumstances where individuals seeking conscientious objector status were somewhat hesitant when it came to asserting that their objection rested on a belief in a Supreme Being. In *Seeger*, the Court held that a belief in a Supreme Being was not necessary so long as "the beliefs professed by [an applicant] are sincerely held and . . . are, in [the applicant's] own scheme of things, religious" (*Seeger* 1965, 185). In *Welsh v. United States* (1970), the Court extended the principles of *Seeger* on behalf of an individual whose belief system might not have been regarded as traditionally religious but whose "sincere and meaningful belief . . . occupie[d] in the life of [the claimant] a place parallel to that filled by the God of those admittedly qualifying for the exemption" (*Welsh* 1970, 339).

Courts have been reasonably successful at applying these standards and in conducting the essential inquiry into the sincerity of beliefs. As District Judge Charles Wyzanski noted in reviewing a conscientious objector claim in 1969,

> the suggestion that courts cannot tell a sincere from an insincere conscientious objector under-estimates what the judicial process performs every day. Ever since in *Eddington v. Fitzmaurice* (1882) [citation omitted], Bowen, L. J., quipped that [the] "state of a man's mind is as much a fact as the state of his digestion," each day courts have applied laws, criminal and civil, which make sincerity the test of liability. (*United States v. Sisson* 1969, 909–10)

Further support for the capacity of courts to inquire into the sincerity of beliefs is provided by the judicial experience vis-à-vis requests for exemptions from laws that require children to be vaccinated before they attend public schools. New York and a number of other states have determined that "subjecting individuals to compulsory vaccination without exception fails to pay sufficient heed to the fact that inoculations offend certain individuals' religious beliefs" (*Sherr v. Northport-East Northport Union Free School District* 1987). Accordingly, New York law allows parents of schoolage children to seek an exemption from the compulsory vaccination laws if they are "bona fide members of a recognized religious organization whose teachings are contrary" to the requirements of the compulsory vaccination statute (New York Public Health Law 2002 § 2164). In applying this statute, state courts "appear uniformly to have found that the exemption cannot be limited to members of recognized religious groups" (*Sherr* 1987, 86). Consequently, courts are ultimately required to assess the sincerity of the individual applicant on a case-by-case basis.

As interpreted by the New York courts, an individual who is not a member of a religious community that maintains a religious objection to vaccinations nonetheless may apply for and secure an exemption. As a practical matter, however, those individuals who are not members of a like-minded religious community will have a more difficult time sustaining their request for relief from the general requirements of the law. As one court noted, "Undoubtedly, membership in an organized religious denomination . . . would simplify the problem of identifying sincerely held religious beliefs, but we reject the notion that to claim protection [under the statute] one must be responding to the commands of a particular religious organization" (*Lewis v. Sobol* 1989, 506, 513). That same court observed that "a person need not rigidly adhere to each and every tenet of his faith in order to qualify as a sincere believer. Religion, as most things, are practiced in degrees of adherence . . . [and individuals] must be free to follow those religious principles they deem most important and no inference of insincerity may be found to flow from their failure to follow the whole gamut of their religious tenets" (*Lewis* 1989, 515). Individualized inquiries are inescapable. Yet experience with the application of the religious exemption set forth in the New York Public Health Law suggests that courts are competent to undertake such inquires.

This experience can be imported from the narrow confines of the public health law and extended more broadly to inquiries into a full range of claims for religious, cultural, or conscientious exemptions from laws of general applicability. This is not to say that such inquiries into the authenticity of claims will be a simple undertaking; it is to say, however, that such inquiries are not beyond the competence of courts.

In sum, it is possible to fashion a fact-based adjudicative approach that strikes an appropriate balance between the demands of democratic governance and the claims of individuals who seek exemptions from laws of general applicability in order to pursue religiously motivated or conscientiously inspired or even culturally driven practices. Such an adjudicative approach will necessarily involve case-by-case determinations. In arriving at such determinations, courts can utilize the *O'Brien* standard to provide broad guidelines and provoke a serious evaluation of competing claims. *O'Brien* will not, however, provide a prescription that will dictate the outcome of particular controversies. Specific controversies will be resolved through a traditional common-law approach under which courts will balance conflicting claims and weigh evidence as well as policy considerations within the broad framework of the *O'Brien* doctrine. Under this common-law approach toward constitutional adjudication (Strauss 1996), precedent

*City of Boerne v. Flores.* 1997. 521 U.S.

*City of Erie v. Paps.* 2000. 529 U.S.

de Crévecoeur, Hector St. John. 1997 [1782]. *Letters from an American Farmer,* edited by Susan Manning. Oxford: Oxford University Press.

Eisgruber, Christopher L., and Lawrence G. Sager. 1994a. "The Vulnerability of Conscience: The Constitutional Basis for Protecting Religious Conduct." *University of Chicago Law Review* 61: 1245–87.

———. 1994b. "Why the Religious Freedom Restoration Act Is Unconstitutional." *New York University Law Review* 69: 437–76.

———. 1996. "Unthinking Religious Freedom." *Texas Law Review* 74: 577–614.

Emerson, Thomas. 1970. *The System of Freedom of Expression.* New York: Random House.

*Employment Division, Department of Human Resources of Oregon v. Smith.* 1990. 494 U.S.

*Housing Works v. Safir.* 1998. WL 409701.

*Lewis v. Sobol.* 1989. 710 F. Supp.

*Lyng v. Northwest Indian Cemetery Protective Association.* 1988. 485 U.S.

McConnell, Michael W. 1990. "The Origins and Historical Understanding of Free Exercise of Religion." *Harvard Law Review* 103: 1416–1517.

*Million Youth March v. Safir.* 1998. 155 F. 3d 124.

*Murdock v. Pennsylvania.* 1943. 319 U.S.

*Newman Piggie Park Enters.* 1966–1968. 256 F. Supp. 941, 944–45.

New York Public Health Law. 2002. § 2164 (9).

*Pierce v. Society of Sisters.* 1925. 268 U.S.

Religious Freedom Restoration Act of 1993. 42 U.S.C. §§ 2000bb–2000bb–4.

*Sherbert v. Verner.* 1963. 374 U.S.

*Sherr v. Northport-East Northport Union Free School District.* 1987. 672 F. Supp.

Strauss, David A. 1996. "Common Law Constitutional Interpretation." *University of Chicago Law Review* 63: 877–935.

*Texas v. Johnson.* 1989. 391 U.S.

Tribe, Laurence. 1988. *American Constitutional Law.* 2d ed. Mineola: Foundation Press.

*United Yellow Cab Drivers Association v. Safir.* 1998. WL 274295.

*United States v. O'Brien.* 1968. 391 U.S.

*United States v. Seeger.* 1965. 380 U.S.

*United States v. Sisson.* 1969. 297 F. Supp.

*Welsh v. United States.* 1970. 398 U.S.

*Wisconsin v. Yoder.* 1972. 406 U.S.

# Chapter 8

# The Free Exercise of Culture: Some Doubts and Distinctions

Lawrence G. Sager

The reference is to the free exercise of religion: in the hands of some of its most ardent advocates, the constitutional ideal of *free exercise* means that it is a matter of considerable regret whenever a person is thwarted in the pursuit of that which is required by his or her religious beliefs. On this view, religiously motivated persons have a presumptive right to disobey otherwise valid laws—a right that can be defeated only on a showing that a very important governmental interest requires that they, like other citizens, be required to obey the law in question. Given the surprising prevalence of this general picture of religious liberty, some are tempted to take it as given, and then expand it to include the liberty of persons who are members of special groups within our society, groups that share a common and distinct web of beliefs, practices, and attributions of value and meaning. Persons in the grip of such a cultural web, the suggestion would go, ought to enjoy a presumptive right to act according to the dictates of their culture, notwithstanding the requirements of otherwise valid laws. This may or may not be a claim about what the Constitution itself requires; at the least, the claim is that we would be a more just society were we to recognize such a right and shape our laws accordingly.

In this blunt form, the idea of a free exercise of culture gives rise to serious concerns about the scope and distribution of liberty within our political community. In this chapter, I offer some early thoughts about the nature of these concerns and possible directions for refining the idea of a free exercise of culture.

My doubts about this form of the claim for the free exercise of culture trace in part to the understanding of the free exercise of religion that inspires it. Perhaps that mistaken understanding is the best place to begin.

## FREE EXERCISE OF RELIGION AND FREE EXERCISE OF CULTURE: PARALLEL DOUBTS

The idea that religiously motivated persons are sovereigns among us, possessed of a presumptive right to disobey otherwise valid laws, runs headlong into two substantial, related objections (Eisgruber and Sager 1994, 1997, 2000). The first is that religions are enormously diverse in the conduct that they underwrite. Religious belief can inspire virtue, reflection, and sublime beauty. Religious belief also can inspire bigoted hatred and exploitation. Some of the most ennobling threads of human history belong to religion; the same can be said of the most grotesque and evil. Religiously motivated conduct is far too vast and varied a category of behavior to be a plausible candidate for a presumptive exemption from laws that bind the rest of us.

The second objection to the idea that religiously motivated persons are presumptively immune from laws that constrain them applies even to laudable religious commitments. Consider the following pairs of constitutional claimants:

- Two women who wish to open up soup kitchens in their homes, which are in residence-only zones. Both are deeply committed to relieving the suffering of the poor, but only one considers her commitment to derive from the commands of her religious faith.

- Two sets of parents who wish to home school their children, and face legal obstacles. Both couples are moved by concern for the moral and cognitive development of their children, but only one couple is guided in this respect by the precepts of their religion.

- Two same-sex couples who wish to be married. Both couples are deeply in love and committed to a shared life, but only one couple is constrained by the requirements of their religion to marry someone of the same sex.

The pattern can be extended in many directions. The point is this: at the heart of our constitutional instincts and tradition is the moral spark of what we can call *equal liberty*, the ideal of equal citizenship among a free and diverse people. Nowhere is this general constitutional ideal more vivid than in the domain of religious liberty. For the state to privilege Christians over Jews, or Jews over Muslims, or anyone over anyone else by virtue of their religious beliefs is plainly impermissible. How could this essential proposition of political and constitutional justice license the privileging of what we describe as religious commitments over other deep, laudable, and binding human commitments?

Together, these two objections—one based on the vast and morally variegated scope of religiously motivated conduct, and the other on the indefensibility of privileging such conduct over other deep and laudable human commitments—make implausible the presumptive liberty reading of free exercise of religion. It might seem to follow that the more radical idea of a free exercise of culture is simply a nonstarter. But this need not be so.

To reject the presumptive license of religious believers to disobey applicable law is not to reject the idea of free exercise of religion, merely one understanding of that constitutional stipulation. We can reconceive of free exercise as an instantiation of the broad ideal of equal liberty rather than as a bizarre exception to that ideal. On this account, the Constitution neither privileges nor ignores religion. On this account, the Constitution protects religion in general and minority religious faiths in particular from discrimination bred of the hostility or indifference to which such faiths are notoriously vulnerable. This equal liberty reading of the free exercise of religion makes moral sense of the idea of free exercise, explains much of our somewhat anomalous constitutional past in this area, and charts an attractive course for our constitutional future.

And, once our understanding of the free exercise of religion is rehabilitated, the normative distance between religion and culture may not be so very great. Some of the most appealing claims for free exercise involve circumstances where culture sits just behind and—at least in public perception—dominates religious belief. This is certainly true of *Wisconsin v. Yoder*,[1] for example, where members of the Amish sect won the constitutional right to remove their children from any formal regime of education at the age of fourteen—two years earlier than was permitted by state law. *Yoder* is by a considerable margin the most robust recognition of free exercise rights in our constitutional jurisprudence, and the Supreme Court's opinion placed heavy emphasis on the Amish way of life, noting that "the Amish community has been a highly successful social unit within our society, even if apart from the conventional mainstream."[2] Also, cases in which the Court has rebuffed the free exercise claims of Native American religions have been singularly controversial.[3] Quite possibly, the criticism with which these decisions were met was fueled by the sense that Native American religious groups are the remnants of distinct cultures fighting for survival.

A common form of the claim for a right of free exercise of culture is as follows. There are durable and traditional groups that share a common and distinct web of practices, values, and beliefs. Some of these groups exist within our national borders and thus are vulnerable to our laws. When we—the mainstream we—make judgments about practices within these cultural subgroups, we often do so in ignorance of the reasons behind such practices, because we see them in isolation, out of their rich, complex, and largely alien context. Thus we condemn, regulate, and even punish that which we do not understand or value.

But any embrace of the free exercise of culture must respond to concerns that closely parallel those we encountered with regard to the free exercise of religion. First, were the state to permit cultural groups to create their own legal microenvironments, it might well find itself licensing these groups to inflict substantial and unjust harm on those over whom they claim authority. Second, here too there is a problem of the maldistribution of liberty: Under what circumstances, if any, are we justified in selectively extending liberty to those who act under the goad of deep cultural norms while withholding the same liberty from those who act out of abiding moral, political, familial, or artistic commitment?

At its core, this is an appealing argument, one that invokes the political virtues of intercultural empathy, ethical humility, and epistemic caution. But this argument is easily overread in support of indefensibly broad cultural license. We can both better preserve the core of this claim for the free exercise of culture and inhibit its tendency to overreach if we observe a number of useful distinctions.

## Character and Moral Probity

We can begin with the distinction between character and moral probity. Good people, acting for reasons they perceive to be good reasons, can surely do bad things. Slaveholders in a certain time and place may have genuinely believed that they were doing the best thing for their slaves. Fathers and mothers in a certain time and place may genuinely believe that they are doing the best by their daughters when they facilitate their daughters' lives as maternal domestics for those daughters and do everything possible to block independent, educated, and professional alternatives. These slaveholders and these parents may well be good people. They may worry about others and act on their behalf as they see best; they may even do so under circumstances that require substantial sacrifice. Without more, however, our sympathy or respect addresses the question of character, not the question of what is demanded by justice or morality more broadly. Nothing in this picture should convince us that it is right for persons to be held as slaves or for women to be relegated to something approaching domestic servitude.

What happens when we add the element of cultural separateness to this picture? With cultural separateness comes a substantial increase in the possibility that good persons may commit acts that in our studied judgment are bad, in the strong sense of unjust or immoral. Or perhaps it is better to put the matter in the obverse: with cultural separateness comes a substantial increase in the possibility that persons who commit acts we have reason to regard as bad may nevertheless be good persons. Yet the point remains: we may have reason to think well of persons who are moved by culturally endorsed beliefs or traditions to commit acts that we would otherwise condemn; but it does not follow we should withdraw our condemnation of those acts. Nor is a favorable judgment of character under these circumstances a reason not to try to deter such acts by civil or criminal regulations.

## Ethics and Morality

If character can be redeemed by culture, why not moral probity? Here, a second distinction presents itself. Some matters—for example, certain aspects of child-rearing—connect to things that groups of people understandably value but are not necessarily portable between or among groups. Whether or not children at various ages sleep with their parents, whether or not parents spank their children, whether parents encourage independence and free choice or demand strict obedience and narrow conformity, whether parents are open or closed about nudity, encourage or discourage touching of various body parts, and so on— some or all of these may be matters of what a group is comfortable with and how a group thinks people should live, rather than questions of what is morally required. Yet other matters are not at all like that: slavery, for instance, or the historic treatment of women or the physical and psychological injury of children and radical foreshortening of their life options. The vocabulary with which such a distinction is expressed is surprisingly unstable. I am familiar with a usage that speaks of a group's local set of values about how it thinks its members should behave as its *ethics*, and judgments about right and wrong or good and evil that apply across groups as propositions about what *morality* requires. But what matters here is the distinction, not the labels.

In considering claims in the neighborhood of the free exercise of culture, we should not generalize from the observation that some firmly held precepts of right and wrong upon reflection turn out to be matters of local, conventional value only, to the mistaken conclusion that all principles of right and wrong are similarly local. This is not to suggest that the ethics-morality distinction neatly maps the boundary of the free exercise of culture, with morality-grounded laws binding everyone and ethics-grounded laws binding only members of the dominant group from which the ethical consensus emanates. Matters are more complicated than that. For example, some moral derelicts cannot appropriately be reached by law at all, like the behavior of X, who has enjoyed a long-standing friendship with Y, but in a moment of irritation with Y, fails to tell him of an opportunity that would have been of enormous professional and economic advantage to him. And there are some matters of social ethics that may be enforced against individuals or members of groups who do not share the ethical sensibilities of mainstream culture, like prohibitions against public nudity or public displays of sexual intimacy. The line between ethics and morality may have consequences for some matters, like the propriety of the state intervening in parents' decisions as to how their children should be disciplined. Even here, it is unclear whether cultural separateness enters the picture—it is unclear, that is, whether parents' membership in a cultural subgroup that supports their child-rearing approach adds anything to the claim of parents qua parents to autonomy in a broad range of child-rearing decisions. So the distinction between ethics and morality should not be overread as demarcating the boundary of the state's authority with regard to cultural groups. But the distinction remains important in evaluating free exercise of culture claims—important, that is, as a reason to resist the idea that because some social norms are local to their culture of origin all must be.

## Epistemic and Normative Invocations of Culture

The child-rearing examples suggest a third distinction, that between epistemic and normative claims of cultural license. Deep-seated attitudes toward such practices as spanking and physical intimacy may inspire inaccurate, largely unexamined factual beliefs about what is important to the well-being of children and what is not. Too quick judgments from outside a dense cultural web about events inside that web compound the reasons for epistemic doubt. The ramifications, consequences and, indeed, the meaning of some acts or gestures may be deeply shaped by the cultural context in which they take place. Well settled, broadly pursued practices antithetical to those in the mainstream should encourage mainstream observers—especially, perhaps mainstream lawmakers—to take a hard second look at their factual beliefs and normative judgments before regulating against such culturally endorsed practices. But this is a case for epistemic caution, for being slow to judge. Our initial sense that a particular practice is deeply wrong may well survive a hard second look; and when it does, our reasons for discouraging or prohibiting that practice remain.

We might pause for a moment at the suggestion—sometimes made in epistemic terms on behalf of the free exercise of culture—that the salient circumstances most likely to be overlooked by mainstream decision makers involve life within the minority culture. The claim is not that our moral judgments should defer to those that prevail inside the minority culture. Rather, the point is that if we in the mainstream fully understood the conditions of and prospects for a good life within the minority culture, we would see that our moral commitments are misplaced or deflected with regard to those whose lives are centered in that culture. Thus, for example, parents who choose to limit their daughter's education, insist on her accepting life as a subordinate domestic, or require her to undergo genital modification, might defend their actions as crucial to their daughter's long-term happiness as wife, mother, and respected member of their community. Or thus, the owner of a restaurant might insist that hiring women or persons of a different racial or ethnic background would be utterly defeating of his enterprise and its value to his community, because members of his group could never feel comfortable being served food in a restaurant by anyone other than a man who was one of them.

## Exogenous and Endogenous Groups

Arguments of this sort themselves turn on a distinction, that between *exogenous* and *endogenous* groups. When an anthropologist counsels us in these terms to be slow to judge or condemn the people of a distant culture whose lives she shares with us, the case for tolerance or acceptance might be relatively strong if we imagine a traditional, insular culture, comparatively resistant to outside intercourse. But when the argument is made on behalf of behavior in a group that is settled within our national boundaries, we have reasons to embrace it with care, if at all. Now questions of choice, consent, and exit push to the fore: we do not assume that the daughter will choose to live her life wholly within the confines of the group to which her parents feel allegiance; and we surely do not welcome decisions made on her behalf that substantially constrain her options to do otherwise. The parents' belief as to what is best for their daughter in this example depends on their prior foreshortening of their daughter's range of choices, a foreshortening we have reason to worry the daughter has not chosen for herself. The restaurant example should have unhappy associations for anyone familiar with the history of civil rights legislation regarding public accommodations and equal employment opportunity. To be sure, associational and egalitarian values can conflict in such settings, but we have made a strong commitment to equality, choosing on moral grounds to insist that the eradication of caste is prior to the integrity of group values or associational choice, even in relatively small employment settings. In the restaurant example, the cultural claims of a tightly knit immigrant group do not in any obvious way sound a different note than the claims of whites in Selma, Alabama, circa 1964.

## Protection and Privilege

This last point, about the connection between contemporary calls for the free exercise of culture and the emphatic rejection of comparable claims in other settings, introduces the concern that a right to the free exercise of culture would indefensibly privilege persons motivated by the forces of culture over those in the grip of other powerful life forces. Such persons, for example, might be deeply moral and attached to the plight of the poor and hungry, or abidingly devoted to the welfare of their families, wrapped in the heat of artistic creation or, for that matter, consumed with their own medical infirmities. Why do pressures of cultural membership carry a distinct and privileged charge?

To answer this challenge by referring to the comparable privilege enjoyed by religiously motivated persons will not do. An important ground of our earlier discussion about the need to reshape and rehabilitate the free exercise of religion was the impossibility of justifying the privileging of religious commitments. Constitutional law has come to recognize this problem and has firmly retreated from the privileging view of religious liberty. The problem with privileging culture among other motivational forces becomes clear if we reshape the pairs of cases considered earlier in connection with the free exercise of religion:

- Two women who wish to open soup kitchens in their homes, which are in residence-only zones. Both are deeply committed to relieving the suffering of the poor, but only one considers her commitment to derive from the precepts of her culture.

- Two sets of parents who wish to home school their children, and face legal obstacles. Both couples are moved by concern for the moral and cognitive development of their children, but only one couple is guided in this respect by principles embedded in their culture.

- Two same sex couples who wish to be married. Both couples are deeply in love and committed to a shared life, but only one couple is constrained by their culture to marry someone of the same sex.

The free exercise of culture, like the free exercise of religion, need not claim any such privilege. There are two distinct judgmental stances in our constitutional tradition. In the area of free expression, for example, we view speech as *privileged* to a high degree. A claimant who locates her behavior within the core of protected speech activity acquires the privilege of substantial immunity from the reach of governmental authority, even if her speech increases the likelihood that injuries to the property or persons of others may occur. She may speak in a fashion that is injurious to others. She may even and especially speak in a fashion that is injurious to the public interest as it is presently conceived. In contrast, while African Americans are singled out for special and beneficial constitutional attention, they are not privileged but *protected*. An African American equal protection claimant insists on parity, not advantage: she demands that the state behave in a fashion fully consistent with her status as an equal citizen, as opposed to treating her as a member of a subordinate class who by virtue of that membership does not enjoy the same concern and respect. The difference in these judgmental stances originates in the underlying nature of constitutional concern: privilege flows from the perception of virtue or conceptual precedence; protection flows from the perception of vulnerability to discrimination. The privileging of religion over other important human commitments is normatively indefensible and practically unworkable; so too is the privileging of culture. The free exercise of culture, like the free exercise of religion, can be made normatively appealing and tractable only if understood as calling for protection rather than privilege.

## Inclusion and Exemption

Some sense of the direction that the free exercise of culture will take—if understood as protecting minority cultures from discrimination rather than privileging them—is afforded by considering two possible sorts of claims that a criminal defendant might make based on the cultural predicate of his behavior. Let us imagine a member of an immigrant community who kills someone. He argues that he acted under circumstances that constituted extreme provocation for persons who, like himself, are steeped in the values and traditions of his community. Indeed, he argues, what he did is regarded as justifiable within his community. Now imagine two different sorts of claims that might be thought to flow from this cultural defense. One claim argues that the provocation under which the defendant acted should qualify for mitigation of criminal liability or penalty under extant legal doctrine, notwithstanding the culturally specific nature of the provocation. This is a claim for *inclusion* within available, more general legal categories. The other claim is for a freestanding permission to commit what would otherwise be a serious criminal act absent any available doctrine of excuse or mitigation. This is a claim for *exemption* from otherwise valid general laws. By their nature, claims for inclusion are likely to be epistemic rather than normative in the sense in which we used those terms earlier; and more to the immediate point, they are likely to be offered from the stance of protection rather than privilege. In contrast, claims for exemption are likely to be normative rather than merely epistemic, and likely as well to be offered from the stance of privilege. For just these reasons, claims of inclusion are much to be preferred.

## General and Selective Claims of Liberty

This preference for claims of parity over those of advantage can be extended to embrace one final distinction, that between general and selective claims of liberty. General claims of liberty are claims of constitutional right of the sort with which we are familiar. They are in principle available to all, and they assume the form like "the state may not intrude into the decisions of people with regard to X," or "the state may not regulate speech on grounds of Y." Selective claims of liberty assume the form "persons motivated by Z are entitled . . ." General claims of liberty have the great advantage of offering the benefit of constitutional justice on equal terms, and for just that reason they are to be preferred. While in principle available to all, general claims of liberty serve best the interests of those whose enterprises bring them into conflict with the norms of social majorities. A robust regime of general liberty is thus the best possible environment for religious and cultural minorities. The protection of speech and belief and the rights of parents to choose among regimes of education for their children inevitably will accrue most to the advantage of those whose speech is an irritant, whose beliefs are foreign, and whose ambitions for their children do not conform to prevailing views.

A skeptic might at this point respond that this promise of evenhanded treatment—of the fair extension of general principles of liberty to the circumstance of cultural minorities—is less generous and ought to be less comforting to members of cultural minorities than it appears. Less generous and comforting because ultimately the question of what rights any of us have remains in the hands of those in the cultural mainstream. This could be thought of as a general conceptual objection or as a more gritty, how-things-will-go-in-practice concern. As a general conceptual matter, we should remember that this inquiry began with the question of what political justice requires of us with regard to providing space for the practices of nonconforming cultures. This is a question that, in the end, we can only address ourselves.

The objection has more force if it is understood as a claim that we may have a tendency to short-change claimants from minority cultures, especially when appeal to our own normative commitments comes from unfamiliar and superficially unbecoming quarters. Here two responses are important. First, we have already concluded that we should proceed to normative judgment with particular care when judging members of nonconforming cultures, that a hard second look is in order. Second, we can take some comfort in what we might think of as the democratic virtues of our nonmajoritarian judiciary. It is in the nature of our constitutional processes in particular and of our legalistic, judge-intensive, dispute-resolution processes in general, that individuals are offered formal opportunities to insist that their personal circumstances fall within the beneficial scope of established norms and principles. Our legal system surely has its share of liabilities as well as virtues, but in this regard, at least, it may serve well the interests of persons who respond to nonconforming cultural impulses.

A common thread runs through the choice of epistemic over normative invo-cations of culture, protection over privilege, inclusion over exemption, and gen-eral over selective claims of liberty. The governing idea is the use of settled and generally applicable judgments—from the domains of social consensus, consti-tutional law, statutory enactment, and judicially developed common law—as the baseline against which the rights of cultural minorities are to be assessed. Epis-temic concerns and the principle of equal liberty require that we be slow to judge the unfamiliar, and that we take a hard look at our own factual beliefs and normative judgments before we condemn culturally endorsed practices. So too, they require that extant legal categories of excuse and mitigation be open to the distinct experience of cultural minorities. And finally, of course, they require that our robust tradition of constitutional liberty—including the rights of speech and belief, the right of parents to guide their children's development, and the right of persons to be free from governmental intrusion into decisions that ought to be theirs alone—be available on full and fair terms to cultural minorities. What they do not require is the privileging of pressures and commitments of culture over other abiding human interests, projects, and commitments. In each in-stance, the goal is parity and the implicit metric is that of extant commitments and provisions.

As a regime of liberty premised on protection rather than privilege, the free exercise of culture would enjoy three important advantages. First, the bench-marks of this approach are settled judgments about competing and conflicting claims that beset any effort to delineate the scope of individual and group choice in a modern political community; the risk of licensing immoral or unjust behav-ior in the name of culture is accordingly abated. Second, this approach aims at parity rather than special advantage and avoids the normative objection that cultural impulses are being indefensibly advantaged over other important hu-man concerns. And third, this approach substantially reduces a set of concerns not yet addressed. Increasingly, what has become clear to anthropologists and others is that living within a culture as a discrete condition characterized by irresistible adherence to fixed norms is highly problematic at best, and precar-iously wrong at worst.[4] Certainly, in the case of the groups that concern us most in this context—immigrant groups transplanted from their place of origin and now situated in the midst of a large and diverse political community with pow-erful forces that conduce to some degree of assimilation—a simple view of what it means to live within a culture is likely to be a badly distorted understanding. Immigrants are likely to be members of a number of crosscutting groups, and their allegiance to any one group is likely to be incomplete, complex, and possi-bly evanescent. The privileging view of the free exercise of culture, however, requires a monolithic, binary judgment: if you are in the grip of culture in the right way, you are entitled to respond to its commands, even at the cost of violating laws that would otherwise bind you. If you are not so situated, you are relegated to the status of an ordinary member of our political community and obliged to obey its laws. An approach to the members of cultural groups that offers them special prerogatives only if they fulfill the conditions of an essentially mythic idea of culture is almost certainly doomed to failure on this ground alone. In contrast, an approach that works to see that members of nonconforming minority groups enjoy the benefit of legal perquisites that are in principle available to all is far less dependent on the idea of cultural imperatives. The call for epistemic caution can be applied generously to all cultural groups that underwrite nonconforming practices, notwithstanding the possibility that these practices are to some degree contested within any given group, for example. Eligibility for extant categories of excuse or mitigation can be determined on the basis of the particular implicated event and its connection to cultural traditions—a far more narrow and tractable inquiry. And for these purposes, at least, applying general principles of liberty to cultural minorities is a comparatively unproblematic enterprise.

Once rebuilt as an antidiscrimination principle, as a principle of parity rather than advantage, the free exercise of culture should have powerful appeal for a political community committed to liberty and fairness. So understood, what that principle inspires is a combination of caution, empathy, and evenhandedness. These are political virtues that should require no defense.

## NOTES

1. 406 U.S. 205 (1972).

2. *Yoder* is offered here as evidence of the intuitive force of cultural concerns, not as a laudable instance of the judicial protection of religious liberty. *Yoder* would have been a sound decision only if it was predicated on a more general right of parents to make reasonable choices about the developmental regimes to which their children will be subject, or if Wisconsin were to have offered some parents the sort of choice it was withholding from Amish parents.

3. In *Lyng v. Northwest Indian Cemetery Protective Association*, 485 U.S. 439 (1988), the Bureau of Land Management had decided to build a road through land deemed sacred by a Native American religion, threatening to cripple the religious group's ability to practice their faith. The Supreme Court rejected a free exercise challenge to the bureau's decision; Congress responded by refusing to fund the road until it was relocated. In *Employment Division, Department of Human Resources of Oregon v Smith*, 494 U.S. 872 (1990), the Supreme Court held that members of the Native American Church were not constitutionally entitled to ingest peyote as part of their religion's sacrament. Congress responded with a small blizzard of legislation aimed at protecting the church members' right to ingest peyote.

4. This point was brought home by its forceful presentation in Cohen and Bledsoe, ch. 5 herein.

# REFERENCES

Eisgruber, Christopher L., and Lawrence G. Sager. 1994. "The Vulnerability of Conscience: The Constitutional Basis for Protecting Religious Conduct." *University of Chicago Law Review* 61: 1245–1315.

———. 1997. "Congressional Power and Religious Liberty After *City of Boerne v. Flores*." *Supreme Court Review* 79: 139.

———. 2000. "Equal Regard." In *Law and Religion: A Critical Anthology*, edited by Stephen Feldman. New York: New York University Press.

# Chapter 9

# The Culture of Property

## Nomi Stolzenberg

In the long, strained relationship between liberalism and community, property occupies a curious place. Many people have viewed private property as an agent of cultural disintegration and atomization, and for good reason. Private property seems to epitomize individual rights. At the same time, it bespeaks a basic commitment to capitalism—an economy organized around the principles of the market, made up of contractual exchanges among property owners, and thus characterized by the exercise of the quintessentially individual rights of private ownership and freedom of contract. The oft-noted shift from Gemeinschaft to Gesellschaft has long been associated with the rise of the market economy (Tonnies 1957). Yet, in ways that have yet to be fully appreciated, private property rights also have played a significant role in fortifying small subcommunities, cementing their boundaries, and endowing them with effective forms of collective control over both resources and members. A few scholars have studied the role played by property rights in constituting, shaping, and preserving communities (Ellickson 1993; Alexander 1989; Weisbrod 1980). For the most part, however, the subject has been ignored both by scholars of property and scholars of *communitarianism*, as the concern with preserving communal bonds and cultural traditions has come to be called. Notwithstanding the centrality of private property to liberalism, property rights have largely escaped the attention of contemporary communitarian critics.

The aim of this chapter is to rectify that inattention by pointing out the broad range of effects on communal life and cultural relations that result from establishing a system of private property. These are referred to as *cultural effects* of private property, to distinguish them from strictly economic effects (such as maximizing wealth, promoting competition, or entrenching monopolies and inequalities of wealth and class), and to distinguish them from political effects (such as generating the material preconditions for an effective democracy). Most property scholarship focuses on the economic functions of property law; a smaller body of scholarship addresses the important political functions of property law; still less attention is paid to its cultural functions (Alexander 1997; Michelman 1987). Yet property law has profound consequences for cultural relations. Property law affects the ability of cultural groups to survive, and even to be formed in the first place. It affects the boundary lines drawn between—and within—groups. It affects the shape of power relations within and among different subgroups, and the nature of groups' interactions with one another. On a larger scale, property law affects the extent to which society generally is characterized by the presence of relatively insular, segregated, and autonomous subcultures. It also affects the degree to which cultural differences are correlated with differences in wealth and class—which is to say, more broadly, that property law plays a significant role in determining the extent to which matters of distributive justice are intertwined with cultural relations.

This is not to say that property law is the exclusive, or even the dominant, force in determining the pattern of cultural relations in society. Many factors play a role in determining which cultural groups form, which groups thrive and which decline, how tight-knit and insular as opposed to permeable they are, what their beliefs and practices are, whether they change or remain static, and what their relations with the rest of the world are like. But access to property and territorial control, through the acquisition of real estate, is often of critical importance to all of these dimensions of cultural and communal life. The cultural consequences of the system of private property to which liberalism is dedicated must be investigated before conclusions about the impact of liberalism upon community can be drawn.

## THE COMMUNITARIAN CRITIQUE OF LIBERALISM

Liberalism has long been viewed as the enemy of tradition and community. With its emphasis on the individual as the fundamental unit of society, its dedication to individual rights, and its implicit commitment to a market-based economy, liberalism has seemed to pose three intertwined threats. First, individualism, by definition, seems to be opposed to the communitarian values of cultural autonomy and group rights. Second, the market economy, which fosters the mobility of property as well as social mobility, unleashes dynamics that seem almost guaranteed to erode the traditional ingredients of historically rooted communities, including social fixity, geographic proximity, territorial control, and ultimately, the very sense of attachment to a historic place. The third threat is posed by the basic elevation of rights over alternative conceptions of the good. Individual rights such as freedom of choice can undermine traditional conceptions of social and religious duty, along with the familial and quasi-familial relationships of dependency, authority, and mutual obligation that rest on such conceptions. Consider, for example, how the values of sexual autonomy and reproductive choice have challenged the traditional structure of authority within the family. Newfangled legal claims, such as a child's right to "divorce" her parents, represent the culmination of the ascendance of individual rights over non-rights-based values.

Many objections to rights-centered discourse emanated historically from conservatives, who oppose any form of political ordering that breaks down traditional structures of social and political authority. In their eyes, a system dedicated to protecting individual rights is objectionable precisely because, by elevating the individual over the social unit, it is calculated to undermine the patriarchal forms of authority that traditionally have undergirded family, communal, and political life (Koerner 1985; Herzog 1998). Another tradition of criticism focuses on liberalism's underlying individualism and the consequent devaluation of relationships, experiences, forms of being, and ways of life that cannot be reduced to an aggregate of individual behaviors or choices. Well before political theorists and sociologists writing in the 1980s popularized communitarianism, concerns about the fate of community in a liberal order had been voiced by early proponents of a vision of cultural pluralism, as well as by representatives of particular groups who felt a growing threat to their existence. As the medieval corporatism gave way to new patterns of political order, and the individual replaced the group as the political subject of the modern nation-state, not a few such newly minted individual subjects looked back ruefully to their groups' recent experiences of insularity and ghettoization that, they now realized ironically, had cemented their culture, fortified their faith, and even bestowed on them meaningful forms of collective political power (Sandel 1982; MacIntyre, 1981; Bellah et al. 1985; Kallen 1924; Myers and Rowe 1997).

Notwithstanding that these are separate traditions, criticisms of individualism, the critique of rights, and the defense of tradition, culture, and community always have been interwoven. The critique of rights always has been a basis of radical criticisms of capitalism (Marx 1978). Indeed, the common concern of conservatives and communitarians—that rights rob people of care and social protection while legitimating their oppression—has been articulated nowhere more forcefully than by radical critics of the market. Yet curiously, the relationship between the egalitarian critique of the market and the conservative and communitarian critiques of individualism and individual rights has tended to go only one way. While critics of the market often rely on critiques of individualism and rights, neither conservative nor communitarian critics of liberalism have had much use for egalitarian critiques of the market. The point may be most obvious in the case of conservatism. Conservative critics of liberalism rarely focus their ire on the institutions of the market, saving their wrath for the folly of individual rights instead. Much less frequently noted, but at least as significant, is the neglect of the market by communitarians. Only scant attention is paid to the market economy as opposed to other types of economic orders in contemporary communitarian literature. Absent is any sustained analysis of the consequences of a market-based economy for groups struggling to maintain their traditions, create a distinctive community, or establish a measure of cultural autonomy. Indeed, if one were just to read contemporary communitarian literature, one might well form the impression that cultural groups have no political economy—as if the pattern of cultural relations in society were somehow impervious to the distribution of economic power.

Only a moment's reflection suffices to suggest the implausibility of a total disconnect between the distribution of wealth and the distribution of cultural power. We are all readily reminded that issues of concern to cultural pluralists and communitarians cannot plausibly be divorced from economics in the real world. The fact remains, however, that we lack an adequate understanding of how economic and cultural forces intersect. More basically, we lack any systematic way of thinking about how they interact.

Property—property rights and property law—may provide a way in. Property constitutes the access to material resources and territorial control that is essential to any real community. As soon as this material dimension of community is recognized, the long-standing idea that property and community are an antinomy starts to look implausible. The question remains whether private ownership of property is antithetical to communitarian and cultural pluralist aims. Yet even this version of the antinomy strains credulity, in light of the evident flourishing of small communities and parochial cultures in the midst of liberal societies. Across America, in the suburbs as well as the cities, immigrants and coreligionists are carving out communities in separate neighborhoods where they can establish their own communal institutions, social service agencies, and financial institutions. Moreover, increasing numbers of communities have managed to secede from established local government jurisdictions to form their own local municipalities, composed of members of a single cultural or religious group.

Our question concerns the extent to which these developments are either enabled or thwarted by the liberal regime of private property. If private property rights only inhibit the emergence of community, as legend would have it, then we should just chalk these developments up to the tenacity of communities in the face of adversity. If it turns out that private property rights indeed enable these developments to occur, then a revision of our understanding of the relationship of private property to community—and liberalism to communitarianism—is in order.

## THE CULTURAL EFFECTS OF PRIVATE PROPERTY

Three case studies may serve to illustrate the dramatic range of private property's cultural effects. Our first case, which involves the historic community of the Mashpee Indians in Cape Cod, Massachusetts, bears out the standard communitarian story about liberalism by illustrating private property's atomizing effects. Mashpee provides a vivid example of a shift from communal to individual ownership of property, which directly resulted in the erosion of the community's traditional boundaries. At the same time, the Mashpee story challenges any facile equation between cultural erosion and the utter dissolution of a culture by forcing us to consider the possibility that dramatic cultural change, even pervasive assimilation, might result not so much in cultural annihilation as in *new* forms of cultural identity and community, which are themselves worthy of respect.

Our second case, a religious community in Oregon called Rajneeshpurham, is in some ways less and in other ways more typical of communal experiments in America. Widely regarded as a cult, the Rajneeshees neither fit into our standard categories of minorities nor follow a conventional religious faith. Yet the community successfully availed itself of legal forms of property ownership that were used in the past by well-accepted religious groups to establish separate communities. Only when the community moved beyond its assertion of private ownership to try to establish its own local government did it run into serious legal trouble. The case thus illustrates the significant advantages of private property over more overtly public forms of power, while at the same time demonstrating some of the limits that are placed on the forms of communal ownership and self-rule in a private property regime.

The case of Rajneeshpurham also illustrates the folly of critics who focus exclusively on the relatively rare attempts of communities to establish overtly public forms of power (for example, local governments) while neglecting the much more ubiquitous use of private property and private contracts to establish mechanisms of external exclusion and internal communal control. Whether one comes to celebrate or deplore the creation of effective group autonomy, to ignore mechanisms of private government that depend on the coordinated exercise of individual property and contract rights—and that accomplish the tasks of excluding outsiders and controlling insiders most effectively—seems misguided.

These points are reinforced by our third case study, which involves the community, the town, and the possibly unconstitutional public school district of Kiryas Joel. Kiryas Joel, a village in the suburbs of New York composed exclusively of Satmars (followers of an ultra-orthodox Hasidic Jewish sect), came to notoriety when its inhabitants prevailed on the State of New York to create a public school district within the village's boundaries, thereby enabling them to run a school—in Yiddish—in conformity with their cultural preferences. The school district is avowedly not religious, but nonetheless it was immediately sued for violating the establishment clause of the Constitution, which prohibits the state support of religion. Although a series of state statutes authorizing creation of the district have been held by federal courts to be unconstitutional, the ultimate legal fate of the public school district remains uncertain while the legislature keeps trying to craft an authorizing statute that will pass constitutional muster (*Board of Education of Kiryas Joel v. Grumet* 1994; *Grumet v. Pataki* 1998). Almost completely ignored in this controversy is the private community of Kiryas Joel—the highly insular, tight-knit, culturally distinctive community of coreligionists, organized around a charismatic hereditary religious leader who dictates virtually every aspect of his followers' lives. Regardless of how the issue of the constitutionality of the school district is resolved, this community will continue to exist. That is, the community will continue to exert its considerable powers of internal discipline vis-à-vis dissenting members, as well as its formidable powers of exclusion whereby the homogeneity of the community is maintained. Only the most formalistic—or legalistic—of observers would deny that these powers of internal collective control and external exclusion constitute forms of political power. Yet as a formal, legal matter, these powers flow entirely from the exercise of *private*, individual rights of property and contract. They are therefore not subject to constitutional restraints that limit the exercise of governmental power.

Like Rajneeshpurham, Kiryas Joel serves as a reminder of the role private rights can play in helping subcommunities to escape the strictures of democratic, constitutional principles that are placed on official governments. In their *private* capacity, members of Kiryas Joel have been able to style various conflicts with the surrounding secular culture (for example, objections to female bus drivers and the state's refusal to provide special education services on the site of private religious schools) as assertions of private individual rights (*Board of Education of the Monroe-Woodbury Central School District v. Weider* 1988; *Bollenback v. Monroe-Woodbury Central School District* 1987).

Kiryas Joel also illustrates a successful attempt by a private community to secede from the existing local government and establish a local government of its own. Unlike Rajneeshpurham, Kiryas Joel's incorporation as a separate municipality went unchallenged, and the Village of Kiryas Joel, unlike the school district of Kiryas Joel, appears to be legally secure. The success of the village incorporation in Kiryas Joel once again illustrates the power of private property, in this case the power of property owners to convert their private rights of ownership into political, local governmental power. Despite the well-publicized holdings against the constitutionality of the school district, the judicial reasoning emphasized in the Kiryas Joel litigation actually underscores the ability of private property owners to use their rights to both create and legitimate communal governmental power—so long as they follow certain basic rules of political engagement with the larger community.

Together, Mashpee, Rajneeshpurham, and Kiryas Joel provide a broad picture of private property's complicated cultural effects.

## MASHPEE

Mashpee involves a group of Native Americans who do not fit standard definitions of a tribe. Brought together by a Christian missionary, the original members of Mashpee were survivors of a number of different Indian tribes that had been decimated by diseases spread by English settlers. The founder, who fashioned himself as their savior and benefactor, created a plantation in Cape Cod, Massachusetts, in the model of a trust, presided over by himself. This meant that the land was to be held in trust for the benefit of Mashpee members, in perpetuity. Eventually, management of the trust passed to the Mashpee themselves; but the land long remained subject to collective control, including prohibitions on transferring land to nonmembers. Even when land ownership formally devolved from the trusteeship to individual occupants, it remained subject to this members-only restriction on property acquisition until 1870 (Clifford 1988).

This group-based restriction on the transfer of property rights was linked to political power in two quite different ways. Internally, the members-only restriction solidified, and indeed helped to constitute, collective autonomy and control. Collective restraints prevented property from falling into the hands of outsiders and kept the community together, both physically and culturally. They guaranteed that the Mashpee stayed together as a unit and provided them with a territorial base for self-rule. Externally, the collective restraints on property reflected the stigma attached to members of a supposedly inferior, backwards race. Native Americans were long thought to lack the independence and mental capacity necessary to exercise the rights of private property responsibly—a notion that was taken to justify their exclusion from the franchise as well as their inability to control the transfer of their own property. In the mid-nineteenth century, the state finally agreed to extend the franchise to Mashpee men, but only in exchange for lifting the members-only restriction on property ownership. The members of Mashpee then voted on whether to accept this bargain, which made citizenship and the receipt of individual rights conditional upon the forfeiture of collective rights and privileges. As James Clifford (1988) recounts the story, Mashpee members clearly recognized the trade-off, with "modernists" within the community arguing in favor of accepting the political rights of citizenship and dissolving the group-based restrictions on property transfers. According to the modernists, permitting the Mashpee to become full-fledged private property owners would lead to their economic betterment by enabling them to buy and sell real estate while reflecting their status as political equals. Traditionalists in the community, however, cautioned that economic enfranchisement would be ephemeral and only lead individual property owners to sell off their patrimony, lured by the quick profits promised by unscrupulous land speculators. Ultimately, the traditionalists predicted, short-term economic gains would evaporate, leaving members of the community even worse off, both individually and economically (inasmuch as their homes and land would be lost) and collectively and culturally (in that the community as a whole now would be deprived of its traditional material, territorial, economic, and political base). The modernists nonetheless prevailed. The Mashpee-only restriction on property was dissolved, and eventually the traditionalists' fears were largely borne out. By the 1970s, more than half of the land in Mashpee was owned by people with no Mashpee heritage, and control of local government had fallen out of the hands of the Mashpee as well.

In many ways, the history of Mashpee seems to illustrate the standard story about the corrosive effects of private property rights on traditional cultures and communal bonds. At the same time, it provides a caution against equating the values of cultural tradition and difference with a simple, preservationist strategy of insulating groups from the market and wider political realms. In a telling episode, more than a century after the Mashpee Indians decided to dissolve the collective restraints on property, their descendants attempted to win back the property they had lost by bringing a land reclamation lawsuit. For centuries, federal law had denied Native Americans the right to choose whether to sell or otherwise transfer their land, requiring that the consent of the federal government be obtained prior to any transfer. In the 1970s, Native American legal advocates turned this law to advantage, making it the basis for recovering land that in fact had been transferred without the federal government's consent (Parker 1989; Clinton and Hotopp 1979). The Mashpee suit was nipped in the bud, though, when the court held that the Mashpee did not constitute a tribe and were therefore not eligible to sue for the reclamation of land. Weighing in favor of the court's decision was the fact that Mashpee was originally created as a sort of ersatz tribe out of the remnants of various historic tribes, and the further fact that the Mashpee displayed a high rate of intermarriage and cultural assimilation—developments facilitated by the dissolution of group-based restraints on property. By the time of the lawsuit, many individuals claiming descent from the original Mashpee tribe (they refer to themselves as the Wampanoag) were culturally as well as physically estranged from their heritage; indeed, the desire to *reverse* the process of cultural assimilation and revive a largely dormant culture seems to have accounted for much of the motivation behind the suit.

To the court, these facts simply negated the existence of an authentic Native American "tribe." Commentators on the case widely agree, however, that this judgment rests on a false equation of cultural tradition with cultural stasis (Clifford 1988; Minow 1991).[1] Cultural anthropologists have long pointed out the ethnocentric fallacy of assuming that indigenous cultures are static and insulated from one another (Clifford and Marcus 1986; Marcus and Fischer 1986). Every culture evolves in response to its surrounding environment, including other cultures—a recognition that calls into question the logic of the court. At the same time, this recognition calls into question the basis for criticizing liberalism's so-called atomizing effects. After all, if every culture is dynamic and interactive with other cultures, if cultural boundaries are constantly shifting, and if assimilation does not *negate* cultural difference and identity, then what precisely is wrong with inducing change and assimilation? Moreover, if nothing is inherently wrong with it, then what is wrong with enforcing the logic of the liberal market, which calls for the dissolution of group-based restraints on the transfer of property and simultaneously fosters the mobility of culture and land?

# RAJNEESHPURHAM

The case of Rajneeshpurham provides an illuminating counterpoint to Mashpee. Rajneeshpurham, a religious commune in Oregon, was formed by the leaders of an Eastern-inspired religious group (Fitzgerald 1981). Perhaps unwittingly, the leadership followed a legal model that was already well-established by the nineteenth century when Protestant religious settlements and "bible camps" were at their peak of popularity (Stockwell 1998). Under this model, the religious group formally incorporates a nonprofit or charitable corporation under the laws of the state. As a corporate entity, the religious group is entitled to acquire property; as a nonprofit or charitable entity, it is exempt from strictures that ordinarily apply to property owners, including the traditional common-law requirement to refrain from imposing limits on the transfer of land.

Traditionally, Anglo-American property law regarded restraints on the free transfer of land as being inimical to the institution of private property. Courts customarily voided restraints on the acquisition of land, first, because such restraints were perceived to limit the owner's freedom to choose whether and to whom to convey his land; and second, because they were viewed as impeding the circulation of property in the market. A free and open market in property was regarded as the key to a productive economy. It also was regarded as a democratic, leveling force: the free circulation of property in the market was seen as having the salutary effect of breaking down dynastic fortunes and eroding the concentrations of wealth that give rise to social castes. For all of these reasons, restraints on the free transfer of real estate—or what the law evocatively calls restraints on the *alienation* of property—generally were prohibited as a matter of common law.

But exceptions to this general law were always carved out, for example, for marital property and for people regarded as members of a backwards and inferior race, as we saw in the early history of Mashpee. Another important exception to the common-law rule against restraints on alienation was drawn for charitable trusts and nonprofit corporations. For religious groups to set up the kinds of communities they wanted to would have been extremely difficult had such an exception not been drawn—and there were sharp critics of the policy decision to do so (Alexander 1985, 1189–1266). The exception facilitated the desire of groups to escape the licentiousness of the general society by creating controlled communities with behavioral restrictions on property use (for example, temperance pledges) as well as restrictions limiting occupancy of the property to members approved by the religious group. Applying traditional common-law rules in favor of the free alienation of property would have prevented such strictures from being enforced, and severely interfered with the formation of such highly regulated communities. The legal forms of the nonprofit corporation and the charitable trust—deemed to be exempt from the common-law rule against restraints on alienation—provided a way of circumventing the traditional rules.

Like the earlier bible camps and Christian communist societies, Rajneeshpurham adopted the legal form of a private nonprofit corporation exempt from the rules requiring individual control over the sale and transfer of land. This legal form is particularly well-suited to a community such as Rajneeshpurham—run as a commune and presided over by a strong religious leader. That individual residents lack the rights of private property owners is perfectly compatible with the commune format: that the corporate entity exercises all of the rights of a private property owner comports with devotion to and dependence on a charismatic leader. From a legal standpoint, the nonprofit corporation that owns the land in Rajneeshpurham, and is run by the Rajneesh leader and his close associates, is a single legal actor. Like any individual property owner, the corporation is essentially free to use its property and grant (or deny) entrance to others as it likes. How the managers of the corporation choose to use the property is seen as no more the court's business than an individual private property owner's decision about whom to invite for dinner.

Only when the community attempted to assume the form of a public, local municipal corporation in addition to the form of a private corporation did it run into trouble. Although the Rajneeshees followed the routine democratic procedures prescribed by state law for establishing a new muncipality, the Oregon Supreme Court determined that permitting a local government to be established within the geographic confines of Rajneeshpurham would be tantamount to establishing a "miniature theocracy," in contravention of the constitutional prohibition against state-established religion (*Oregon v. City of Rajneeshpurham* 1984). According to this logic, using the legal form of private corporate ownership to create a homogeneous population ruled by a charismatic leader and devoted to the same religious way of life is fine; but drawing the boundaries of a political jurisdiction to be coterminous with such a population is constitutionally illegitimate.

# KIRYAS JOEL

Kiryas Joel took the logic of this public-private distinction several steps further. The case of Rajneeshpurham demonstrated how collective power can be instituted through the legal form of a private corporation. Yet corporations, like trusts, lodge control over property exclusively in the managers or leaders of the community. Individual members, who may end up occupying property and establishing homes in the community for decades—even generations—are, from a legal point of view, more like guests than owners. They are not merely *restricted* with respect to the right to control the use and transfer of the property they occupy; they have no legal right to the property at all. Legal forms such as nonprofit corporations and trusts thus are well-suited to groups like the Rajneeshees or traditional Mennonites or nineteenth-century utopian communities, which reject the very principles of private ownership and participation in the market economy in favor of a commune-like economic and social structure. The inhabitants of Kiryas Joel, however, do not reject either private property or the market economy. Notwithstanding their general opposition to secular modern life, Satmars show no reluctance to own private property or participate in market exchanges. Moreover, notwithstanding the pervasive role of the rebbe (the religious leader who controls every aspect of Satmar life), a commune was never what the Satmars had in mind. For all their defiance of the dominant cultural conventions, the Satmars in Kiryas Joel are conventional property holders. Like most Americans, they either own or rent their own family home or apartment. In Kiryas Joel, no single corporate entity owns and controls all the land in the community; instead, the ownership of real estate is dispersed among the many individuals and families who make up the community.

This raises the question of how the real estate in Kiryas Joel remains safely— and exclusively—in the hands of Satmars. We have seen already in the case of

Mashpee how freeing individual owners from any legal obligation to keep property within the hands of community members easily can lead to individual owners selling off their piece of the cultural patrimony. Why has this not happened in Kiryas Joel—where the population is reputed to be 100 percent Satmar—and what would keep it from happening in the future?

Roughly speaking, there are two basic ways to prevent property from being transferred to outsiders in the absence of either corporate control or publicly enforced restrictions. The first is to establish formal restraints on the alienation of private property. Formal restraints on the transfer of property to outsiders can be instituted in the form of mutual pledges or *covenants* that, in the quaint terminology of the common law, "run with the land." In other words, private owners (subject to certain legal restrictions) can enter into mutual agreements regarding the use or transfer of their property that bind not only them, but also successive owners of the property in question. Thus, the Satmars could have entered into a series of restrictive covenants covering all of the property in the community and embodying an obligation not to sell to non-Satmars or not to sell without the community's consent. Such a network of restrictive covenants would simulate the sort of collective control over property transfers afforded by the corporate-commune structure without eliminating the other prerogatives of private property ownership.

One problem with restrictive covenants is that their legal validity is questionable. On one hand, restrictive covenants embodying restraints on the sale and rental of property are widely enforced in the context of planned communities and condominiums governed by homeowner associations. For example, consent requirements, which require the approval of other members or of a homeowner association, are now a common and legally approved feature of the contemporary real estate landscape (French 1994, 119).[2] On the other hand, racially restrictive covenants—once a common device used to prohibit the transfer of property to blacks, Jews, and other "non-Caucasians"—were declared unconstitutional by the U.S. Supreme Court more than five decades ago (*Shelley v. Kraemer* 1948). There has never been any authoritative ruling declaring whether religiously restrictive covenants or ethnic or other nonracial group-based restrictions are similarly illegal. Such covenants might well be deemed to violate laws prohibiting discrimination in the real estate market; but that they could be found to be legally valid expressions of the rights to freedom of association and choice is also conceivable. Further complicating matters is the possibility of using consent requirements, which do not overtly distinguish buyers or renters on grounds of religion or group membership, but which easily could be used to filter out nonmembers in ways that might escape legal monitoring.

The possibility of using consent requirements to exclude nonmembers of the Satmar community points to the more general issue of informal choice—the second basic way that exclusion often is achieved. It is commonly said, by way of explaining situations such as Kiryas Joel, that people "just like to live with their own kind." The implication is that the existence of a homogeneous population is a matter of mutual choice: Satmars don't want to mix with non-Satmars, and non-Satmars don't want to mix with them. Buried in this commonplace are both a descriptive and a normative claim. Descriptively, the claim is that the *cause* of such segregation is not compulsion, but rather happily harmonious individual preferences. Normatively, the implication is that nothing is wrong with such a situation if everyone is happy and no one is being coerced. This logic is readily applied to Kiryas Joel, where the Satmars wanted to secede and form their own community and their neighbors were relieved to have them do so. If there are no non-Satmars seeking entry into Kiryas Joel's real estate market, then the answer to the question of how homogeneity is maintained seems to be, simply, personal choice.

Ideally, such choices are reciprocal—the prospective buyers (or renters) whom the homeowner would reject have as little interest in acquiring the property as the homeowner has in them. Yet homeowners have the freedom to reject a particular buyer or renter (or to choose not to sell or rent at all) even when the choice is not reciprocal. In the absence of formal covenants restricting the freedom to transfer property, individual property owners easily can exercise their right to choose in a way that expresses a communal consensus against transferring property to outsiders. Indeed, the stronger the extralegal bonds cementing the community, the less the need to formalize those bonds in legal covenants. In a tight-knit community such as Kiryas Joel, bound by a strong sense of mutual obligation and fealty to a religious leader, an agreement not to convey property to outsiders easily could be instituted as a social practice without being formalized as a legal covenant—and thereby could escape potential legal detection and invalidation.

Yet there are two basic problems with the informal preference model of group formation and preservation. First, even within a community as cohesive as Kiryas Joel, individual preferences inevitably are not quite as harmonious as the choice model suggests. As in Mashpee, there have been defectors from the community consensus in Kiryas Joel, some of whom have been subjected to harsh internal discipline. Such internal dissent challenges the descriptive accuracy of the choice model of group-based exclusion.

The second problem stems from lack of harmony between the preferences of outsiders and insiders. Perhaps no one is seeking entry now, but it is only a matter of time before a non-Satmar will want to settle in Kiryas Joel. At that point, exclusion can no longer be said to be a function purely of *mutual* choice, even if every Satmar remains opposed to admission.

To the extent that we are concerned about the justice of excluding people from property on the basis of their group affiliation, focusing on the constitutionality of a public school district—or a village—with a homogeneous population seems a lot like having the tail wag the dog. After all, countless school districts and local governments in America have had religiously homogeneous populations (usually members of the same Protestant denomination). According to the prevailing legal logic, these situations are unproblematic as long as the boundaries of these governmental jurisdictions are not deliberately drawn to accommodate a particular religious group, but rather "just happen" to contain homogeneous populations. Local populations, of course, never just happen to be homoge-neous. Keeping outsiders out—and suppressing factionalism within—require ef-fective mechanisms of social control. As we have seen, in a liberal society where governmental restraints on who can live where are prohibited, private property rights exercised in a coordinated fashion can do the trick.

## COMMUNITARIANISM FROM THE BOTTOM UP

Cases such as Rajneeshpurham and Kiryas Joel refute the long-standing notion that a liberal regime of individual rights and private property is inimical to com-munal autonomy and the preservation of distinct cultural traditions. In lieu of the sort of top-down approaches to separating groups and endowing them with their own territory and jurisdiction found in nondemocratic societies (such as the former Soviet Union or the Ottoman Empire) or in consociational de-mocracies (such as Switzerland), the coordinated exercise of the rights of private property can serve to separate and endow subgroups from the bottom up. As the Mashpee case illustrates, a liberal regime of property rights also creates cer-tain threats to traditional ways of life that may be avoided in nonliberal regimes. To conclude, however, that liberalism is simply antithetical to communitarian goals and forms of social and political organization would be a gross over-simplification. On the contrary, groupness flourishes in—not despite—liberal re-gimes.

That said, the shape that groupness takes in liberal and nonliberal regimes is not exactly the same. To observe that communitarianism can be fostered from the bottom up as well as from the top down is not to say that the strategies afforded by private property give all groups the same opportunities, nor that any group has precisely the same opportunities as found in top-down regimes. Indeed, both liberal and nonliberal regimes enable and disable the formation and perpetuation of cultural subgroups, in different and distinctive ways.

Perhaps the most obvious way in which bottom-up and top-down regimes differ is in the role played by economic wealth. In theory, top-down regimes can endow groups with separate territories and independent political jurisdictions regardless of their resources. By contrast, the ability of a group to amass private property in quantities sufficient to establish effective forms of community con-trol necessarily depends on access to economic resources. The founders of Kiryas Joel and Rajneeshpurham had to possess substantial amounts of capital to ac-quire large numbers of contiguous lots in suburban New York and a large, open tract of land in Oregon, respectively. The Mashpee never could have obtained such prime real estate without the intervention of their self-styled paternalistic founder. Without such benevolent interventions, many groups simply lack the economic means to establish comparable islands of territorial and cultural auton-omy. In top-down regimes, wealth may influence the disposition of political power to recognize a particular group and endow it with valuable resources, but in principle, the link between economic and cultural power can be broken. By contrast, in bottom-up regimes, the link between economic and cultural power is much tighter—indeed, cultural power appears in many respects to be a mere *effect*, or privilege, of economic power in a private property–based regime.

This is not to deny that communities of poor people are found in liberal societies. On the contrary, the segregation of rich and poor—ghettoization—is positively fostered by the dynamics of the real estate market. Yet this phenomenon itself reflects the tight correlation between the distribution of economic power and that of cultural power, which distinguishes liberal from nonliberal regimes. Of course, the ghetto is hardly unknown to nonliberal societies, but precisely what distinguishes the liberal ghetto from the traditional one is the feature of class segregation. Ghettoized subcommunities in traditional nonliberal regimes— epitomized by the Jewish Ghetto of sixteenth-century Venice, for example—typically exhibit a "full complement of classes," often living side by side (or stacked on top of one another) (Walzer 1997). By contrast, subcommunities in market-based regimes tend to be economically homogeneous.

The salience of wealth in shaping cultural boundaries in a liberal regime raises questions about the justice of the distribution of cultural power in liberal regimes. Questions about the validity of group-based restrictions on private property cannot be resolved without attending to the interaction between economic and cultural power in a private property regime. Consider the recent controversy over community land trusts—that is, nonprofit corporations established to extend the benefits of private property ownership to the poor (Seeger 1989; Abromowitz 1991). Community land trusts sell homes and rent the underlying real estate to eligible applicants at prices set substantially below market value. The trusts maintain the affordability of properties by restricting the ability of the owner-renters to transfer their property and, hence, profit from the real estate market. Owner-renters must either sell their property back to the trust or sell with the consent of the trust at below-market prices. Either way, both the price limitation and restraints on free transfer offend the traditional common-law rule against restraints on alienation. The question posed in lawsuits challenging the validity of these restraints is essentially the same as that posed in cases concerning religious communities, such as the nineteenth-century bible camp and twentieth-century spiritual commune: Should use of trusts and non-profit corporations be permitted to evade common-law rules in favor of the free alienability of property? The earlier cases seemed to pose a basic conflict between the value of communal autonomy on one hand, and the values of the free market on the other. Community land trusts raise a further complication: Do principles of economic justice as well as cultural pluralism justify overriding the mechanisms of the free market? Furthermore, what best serves the cause of economic justice in such a case—enforcing restrictions to maintain affordable housing, or letting the first generation of beneficiaries capture the profits available to them in the open real estate market? The community land trust poses a dilemma similar to that confronted by traditionalists and modernists in Mashpee: opting out of the market in order to insulate a community from corrosive market forces denies community members the economic and political benefits of participating in the market, but allowing individual members to participate in the economic benefits of the market may lead to the dissolution of the community as such.

Such dilemmas reflect the link between issues of distributive justice and cultural pluralism in a liberal market society. Bottom-up communitarianism is distinguished from top-down communitarianism not only by the tightness of this link, but also by the basic tension between the norms of an open market and open society and those of group autonomy and cultural pluralism that inheres in liberalism. The validity of group-based restrictions on private property is always open to challenge in a liberal regime on two legal grounds: laws against discrimination and laws against impeding the free circulation of property. Yet, as we have seen, such laws do not mean that all group-based restrictions on the transfer of property are invalid. Exceptions to antidiscrimination and pro-alienation laws frequently have been carved out for the sake of protecting other liberal values, such as freedom of association. Nonetheless, antidiscrimination law and rules against restraints on the alienation of property together form a significant countervailing force. Although market forces give rise to concentrations of economic and cultural power—that is, wealthy enclaves and poor ghettos—they also foster a degree of economic and social mobility, which tends to break down or at least reshuffle cultural groupings. This, of course, is what gives rise to the customary communitarian lament: the norm of alienable property promotes a degree of cultural integration (or disintegration, from the communitarian point of view) unimaginable in more traditional, top-down societies—as the history of Mashpee bears out.

The fact that both integration and disintegration are taking place reflects the complicated phenomenon of cultural dynamism highlighted in the Mashpee case. That the more cultures are separated and insulated from one another, the better preserved they will be may well be true; but is a culture best preserved by arresting or by permitting its development? The tension between cultural preservation and cultural development is built into the very concept of a cultural tradition. Property law clearly has consequences for how this tension is resolved in any particular case. Inasmuch as property law allows collective restraints on the transfer of property, cultural interactions may be inhibited and cultures may well become, so to speak, pickled.[3] Conversely, if property law discourages collective restraints, exposure to other cultures may be promoted with potentially dynamic—or destructive—results. Laws that allow collective restraints to be imposed on property favor the freedom of group seclusion over the freedom of others to influence the secluded group. Laws that void such collective restraints foster integration and exposure between members of diverse groups, thereby favoring the freedom to influence others over the freedom of seclusion from others. Property law thus affects the balance between the forces of dynamism and stasis within and among different subcultures.

Indeed, property law has consequences for all three of the dimensions of cultural life identified so far: the extent of cultural dynamism (as opposed to stasis); the extent of cultural integration (as opposed to group seclusion); and the extent to which access to wealth shapes the pattern of cultural relations. In comparison to top-down regimes, bottom-up communitarianism tends to promote integration and cultural innovation, even to the point of a particular culture's disintegration. Yet the dynamic of integration is offset significantly by the tendency of inequalities of wealth to become entrenched in the form of economic segregation, which in turn shapes and limits (and, ironically, sometimes projects) the formation of cultural groups. Of course, this is a vastly oversimplified picture of private property's cultural effects; but even an oversimplified picture represents an advance over property scholarship that pays little heed to the cultural dimension of property and communitarian scholarship that neglects the property dimension of culture. The time has come for scholars of property and scholars of community and cultural pluralism to come together and help us to chart out the complex interrelationship between property and culture.

## NOTES

1. The Wampanoags of Mashpee today may be on the brink of receiving offical recognition as a tribe, and its members bear witness to the "development of a strong Wampanoag identity" since the failed litigation (Davis 2000).

2. The common law has been reformed to allow such covenants, which would have been void under the traditional rule against restraints on alienation.

3. The *pickling* formulation comes from Professor Wendy Gordon.

## REFERENCES

Abromowitz, David M. 1991. "An Essay on Community Land Trusts: Towards Permanently Affordable Housing." *Mississippi Law Journal* 61: 663–82.

Alexander, Gregory. 1985. "The Dead Hand and the Law of Trusts in the Nineteenth Century." *Stanford Law Review* 37: 1189–1266.

———. 1989. "Dilemmas of Group Autonomy: Residential Associations and Community." *Cornell Law Review* 75: 1–61.

———. 1997. *Commodity and Propriety*. Chicago: University of Chicago Press.

Bellah, Robert, Richard Madsen, William M. Sullivan, Ann Swindler, and Steven M. Tipton. 1985. *Habits of the Heart: Individualism and Commitment in American Life*. Berkeley: University of California Press.

*Board of Education of Kiryas Joel v. Grumet*. 1994. 114 Sup. Ct.

*Board of Education of the Monroe-Woodbury Central School District v. Weider*. 1988. 531 N.Y.S. 2d.

*Bollenbach v. Monroe-Woodbury Central School District*. 1987. 659 F. Supp.

Clifford, James. 1988. *The Predicament of Culture: Twentieth-Century Ethnography, Literature, and Art*. Cambridge, Mass.: Harvard University Press.

Clifford, James, and George E. Marcus. 1986. *Writing Culture: The Poetics and Politics of Ethnography*. Berkeley: University of California Press.

Clinton, Robert N., and Margaret Tobey Hotopp. 1979. "Judicial Enforcement of the Federal Restraints on Alienation of Indian Land: The Origins of the Eastern Land Claims." *Maine Law Review* 31: 17–90.

Davis, William A. 2000. "Spirit of the Wampanoag Tribal Leader Russell Peters Recalls Battles That Helped Forge Their Identity." *Boston Globe*, March 21: D1.

Ellickson, Robert. 1993. "Property in Land." *Yale Law Journal* 102.

Fitzgerald, Frances. 1981. *Cities on a Hill: A Journey Through Contemporary American Cultures*. New York: Simon & Schuster.

French, Susan. 1994. "Tradition and Innovation in the New Restatement of Servitudes: A Report from Midpoint." *Connecticut Law Review* 27: 119–29.

*Grumet v. Pataki*. 1998. 675 N.Y.S. 2d.

Herzog, Don. 1998. *Poisoning the Minds of the Lower Orders*. Princeton, N.J.: Princeton University Press.

Kallen, Horace. 1924. *Culture and Democracy*. New York: Boni and Liveright.

Koerner, Kirk E. 1985. *Liberalism and Its Critics*. London: Croon Helm.

MacIntyre, Alisdair. 1981. *After Virtue*. London: Duckworth.

Marcus, George E., and Michael M. J. Fischer. 1986. *Anthropology as Cultural Critique: An Experimental Moment in the Human Sciences*. Chicago: University of Chicago Press.

Marx, Karl. 1978. "On the Jewish Question." In *The Marx-Engels Reader*. 2d ed., edited by Robert Tucker. New York: Norton.

Michelman, Frank. 1987. "Possession and Distribution in the Constitutional Idea of Property." *Iowa Law Review* 72: 1319–53.

Minow, Martha. 1991. "Identities." *Yale Journal of Law & the Humanities* 3: 97–130.

Myers, David N., and William V. Rowe. 1997. *From Ghetto to Emancipation: Historical and Contemporary Reconsiderations of the Jewish Community*. Scranton, Penn.: University of Scranton Press.

*Oregon v. City of Rajneeshpurham*. 1984. 598 F. Supp.

Parker, Linda S. 1989. *Native American Estate: The Struggle Over Indian and Hawaiian Lands*. Honolulu: University of Hawaii Press.

Sandel, Michael J. 1982. *Liberalism and the Limits of Justice*. Cambridge: Cambridge University Press.

Seeger, Christopher A. 1989. "The Fixed-Price Preemptive Right in the Communinty Land Trust Lease: A Valid Response to the Housing Crisis or an Invalid Restraint on Alienation?" *Cardozo Law Review* 11: 471–501.

*Shelley v. Kraemer*. 1948. 334 U.S.

Stockwell, Foster. 1998. *Encyclopedia of American Communes, 1663–1963*. Jefferson, N.C.: McFarland.

Tonnies, Ferdinand. 1957. *Community and Society*. East Lansing: Michigan State University Press.

Walzer, Michael. 1997. *On Toleration*. New Haven: Yale University Press.

Weisbrod, Carol. 1980. *The Boundaries of Utopia*. New York: Pantheon.

The key idea that individuals acquire cultural categories in a largely unconscious process is called enculturation (Shimahara 1970). The cultural defense depends on the idea that individuals are socialized to think in a particular way. Anthropologist Ralph Linton (1961, 39) explains enculturation in this way:

> No matter what the method by which the individual receives the elements of culture characteristic of his society, he is sure to internalize most of them. This process is called enculturation. Even the most deliberately unconventional person is unable to escape his culture to any significant degree. . . . Cultural influences are so deep that even the behavior of the insane reflects them strongly.

The precise psychological processes of enculturation have been studied by cultural psychologists and anthropologists (Markus and Lin 1999; Shore 1996; Shweder 1991). Crucial to the argument is the notion that culture strongly influences perception and behavior. Consequently, the law should take account of the manner in which cultural conditioning affects individuals when their actions violate the law.[9]

## THE CULTURAL DEFENSE

A cultural defense is a defense employed by individuals who claim that their culture is so ingrained that it predisposes them to actions—actions which may conflict with the laws of their new homeland. Consequently, they maintain that they ought not be held fully responsible for violating the laws. The extent of the reduction in culpability can vary from complete to none whatsoever. In many cases, it may be most appropriate for the cultural defense to function as a partial excuse (Renteln 1993).

Although such a defense is not officially part of any known legal system,[10] cultural factors have been incorporated in legal systems all over the world for many centuries (Renteln and Dundes 1995). The cultural defense should be interpreted broadly to include decisions concerning all phases of legal process, such as whether to arrest, prosecute, and if so, for what offense. Culture can affect the trial at which guilt or innocence is decided, and it can be considered as a mitigating factor at sentencing.[11] Though many assume the cultural defense is used primarily in criminal proceedings, it also arises in civil cases.[12] After all, the distinction between criminal and civil matters is culturally dependent, and the same set of facts can give rise to both criminal and civil actions (Sellin 1938).

This chapter will be mainly concerned with criminal cases in which the focus is on the defendant's state of mind.[13] Most crimes are defined in such a way that the crucial elements are the intent (mens rea) and the act (actus reus). Simply put, if a person intends to commit an act and does so, he or she is guilty of the offense regardless of motive. A mother who steals a loaf of bread to save her starving children is technically guilty of theft. Because the motive for the action is treated as distinct from intent, and because cultural imperatives usually relate to motive, it has proven difficult to introduce evidence concerning culture in courts of law (Renteln 1993). A defendant's motive may, however, be considered as a mitigating factor at sentencing under most circumstances.

Whether one is prepared to entertain a cultural defense often depends on which of the three main theories of punishment—retribution, deterrence, and rehabilitation—one favors (Renteln 1993). The notion that a person who commits a culturally motivated act is less blameworthy is based on retribution and the corollary principle of proportionality—that is, that a person should be punished only as much as he or she deserves.

Those who think punishment is principally for deterring other crimes may fear allowing cultural traditions because the ethnic minority community might interpret the court's judgment lessening the punishment as giving license to continue a practice. If the law is supposed to promote assimilation of the newly arrived, then it should not permit cultural factors to influence legal proceedings. But the law is often a poor vehicle for altering cultural identity.

A similar problem may exist for rehabilitation. It is unclear what it would mean to rehabilitate a person who follows tradition. If the purpose of the law is to force assimilation, then rehabilitation would require rejecting the cultural defense. If, however, the point is that the culturally motivated act is not one that requires condemnation, then it does not make sense to "rehabilitate" a person who is simply acting in accordance with his or her culture.

The cultural defense, to the extent it is justified in particular cases, is predicated on the retributive idea that a person who commits a culturally motivated act deserves less punishment than another person who commits the act without such a motive. To determine in actual cases whether a defendant is less culpable necessarily requires a case-by-case approach. Sometimes defendants will put forward false claims not based on culture. Others may be able to show that a tradition is an authentic part of the culture but will not be able to demonstrate that that the cultural imperative affected them personally.

There will also be the problem of determining whether the cultural tradition is permitted or required in another culture. Eating a dog may be considered a delicacy in some countries, but its consumption is certainly not required. By contrast, burning deer meat to be consumed by ancestors indeed may be culturally required. For some, a cultural defense seems more legitimate when actions are required rather than optional. Even were there a stronger rationale for taking culture into account for required actions, the cultural defense is still relevant in cases in which individuals' voluntary actions were also motivated by culture.

The cultural defense requires that one accept the theory of cultural relativism, according to which every group has its own set of moral standards (Renteln 1988). To be fair, the law must recognize that individuals have different types of moral reasoning that are derived from their upbringing. Fundamental work in cultural psychology has demonstrated the extent to which psychological processes are strongly influenced by culture. The implication is that there is no single moral code against which all behavior can be judged. Hence, it is crucial that the cultural context of action be considered for justice to be served.

Philosophically, the cultural defense represents another way of trying to achieve the goal of individualized justice, a goal which is well established. To a large extent, many legal systems already accept this approach by tailoring punishment based on the attributes of individuals. The law makes distinctions between adults and children and between the sane and the insane. Having the law adjust punishment in light of cultural characteristics is not a departure from established jurisprudence.

The question to which I now turn is whether existing legal protections concerning the right to culture obligate governments to adopt a formal cultural defense. Since most domestic legal systems lack such an explicit right to culture, I concentrate on international legal standards.

## THE RIGHT TO CULTURE UNDER INTERNATIONAL HUMAN RIGHTS LAW

International law guarantees the right to culture in various provisions.[14] Article 15 of the International Covenant on Economic, Social and Cultural Rights guarantees the right to participate in the cultural life of one's community, but it has been criticized for "a highbrow bias"—that is, for being applied mainly to "high culture" (O'Keefe 1998). The strongest statement of a right to culture is found in Article 27 of the International Covenant on Civil and Political Rights (ICCPR), which provides:

> In those states in which ethnic, religious, or linguistic minorities exist, persons belonging to such minorities shall not be denied the right, in community with the other members of their group, to enjoy their own culture, to profess and practice their own religion, or to use their own language.

Article 27 has been interpreted to require affirmative steps on the part of governments to protect culture (Cholewinski 1988; Akermark 1997, 127–31) and contains no limitations clause.[15] Some object to the negative formulation "persons . . . shall not be denied," and wonder what groups can invoke the right.[16] The main problem is that Article 27 has been applied in a relatively small number of decisions of the Human Rights Committee, the body which enforces the ICCPR, and consequently the scope of its potential application remains unclear (Akermark 1997; McGoldrick 1991; Thornberry 1991; Anaya 1996).[17]

One might have expected that Article 27 would often be invoked in litigation because virtually all nations have ratified the ICCPR. This has not been the case, and the right to culture remains controversial. Although other types of basic rights are self-evident, the right to culture seems to require additional philosophical justification.[18]

With regard to theoretical justifications of the right to culture, there are two separate, parallel literatures on the subject. One is the political theory scholarship revolving around Will Kymlicka's position (Kymlicka 1992, 1995a, 1995b; Kukathas 1992a, 1992b); the other is the international law literature focusing on the interpretation of Article 27 of the ICCPR and the instruments concerned with the protection of cultural heritage (Prott 1988). Neither debate has taken much account of the discussion in the other. Furthermore, there has not been any serious attempt to connect the right to culture to the cultural defense, though it is precisely in cases involving the cultural defense that individuals seek to protect some of their cultural rights.[19] Before turning to the arguments in favor of the cultural defense, I will briefly outline the main issues which have been discussed in the scholarly literature which bear on the question of the cultural defense.

It is remarkable that philosophical discussions of cultural rights are extraordinarily negative, focusing mainly on the threat posed by such rights.[20] Will Kymlicka, who is widely regarded as a champion of cultural rights, does not defend these rights for immigrants but only for minorities who have long been residing in a nation-state. Moreover, Kymlicka would only allow the protection of cultural rights for societies structured along liberal lines—that is, societies that resemble the ideal democratic system. Those who question Kymlicka's theory are not willing to defend a much more generous version of cultural rights. Chandran Kukathas, for example, takes the view that cultural rights should be protected as long as individuals have the right to leave or "opt out." A theory that emphasizes the need to ensure that people can escape from culture has an underlying view of culture that is extremely negative.

The most sophisticated analysis of cultural rights under international law is found in the work of Sebastian Poulter (1987). His theoretical position is as follows: if a cultural tradition violates human rights, it should not be permitted; if disallowing a cultural tradition violates human rights, it should be permitted. There are a few difficulties with his argument, the most important of which is that Poulter relies on international human rights standards as the basis for determining what behavior is reasonable. In fact, many scholars have questioned the philosophical foundations of international human rights law, charging that they are Eurocentric (Renteln 1990; Sinha 1996; Beyerly 1998; Anonymous 1993). Even if one rejects the notion that Poulter's standard is a neocolonial one, he overlooks the complex tensions among rights. For example, when Poulter discusses the Muslim girls whose parents want them to go to single-sex schools to illustrate the situation in which he would allow cultural rights, he ignores the possibility that the girls may wish to attend a coeducational institution, in which case they would regard their parents' victory as a violation of their human rights.[21]

Poulter's analysis highlights the hierarchy problem—the reality that the right to culture must necessarily be limited. If one can show that cultural traditions deserve legal protection, then the question is, what are the limiting principles? Even if the right to culture is a human right, that does not deny that other competing rights must also receive protection. As no analytic framework exists that is capable of solving all rights conflicts, a case-by-case approach is desirable.

Though one might have hoped with Poulter that international human rights law would solve the problem, the system is inadequate to the task, at least at the present time. Even if jurisprudence were more developed, the status of international law in domestic legal systems makes it unlikely that the approach would be followed. Furthermore, the scope of protection of cultural rights under international law is obscure, as the pertinent rights have been restricted to limited contexts, such as disputes over sacred sites and exclusive membership rules.[22] While in principle the right to culture as a human right conceivably could provide the foundation for the cultural defense, it has yet to be applied in this context. More compelling justifications for a cultural defense are afforded by better-established rights. Hence, we now turn to a consideration of how general principles, already part of some legal systems, might facilitate the use of cultural defenses.

## EQUAL PROTECTION

One of the most important principles of justice is equal protection of the law.[23] Failure to allow the consideration of cultural information in a court of law sometimes violates this fundamental idea. In many areas of law there is a fiction of objective reasonableness. The behavior of a criminal defendant is to be evaluated in light of the probable reaction of the so-called objective reasonable person. The fiction becomes problematic when criminal defendants from other cultures are provoked by actions, words, or gestures (Anonymous 1996) that would not provoke the reasonable person (Howard 1961; Saltman 1991; Minow and Rakoff 1998).

*Trujillo-Garcia v. Rowland* (1992–1994) demonstrates the cultural bias in the interpretation of the reasonable person standard. The case involved two Mexican Americans playing poker. After Jose Padilla lost $140 to Eduardo Trujillo-Garcia, he went home, but returned four days later, demanding his money back. When Padilla said, "chinga tu madre," Trujillo-Garcia's reaction to this challenge to his honor was to grab a gun from his waistband and shoot Padilla.[24] One of the main legal arguments was that Trujillo-Garcia had been provoked by the insult, the most offensive possible in Mexican culture (Paz 1961).

The provocation defense requires showing first that the defendant was provoked (known as the subjective version), and second that the "objective reasonable person" would have been provoked.[25] At the trial, Trujillo-Garcia argued that the phrase was so offensive that he was provoked to commit an act of violence. Those who do not speak Spanish have difficulty comprehending the seriousness of this insult: the phrase is considered "fighting words" and conjures up images of violation of the mother (associated with the Virgin Mary); it has an obscene connotation as well as a blasphemous one.[26] Trujillo-Garcia was convicted of second-degree murder and received a sentence of fifteen years to life.

The argument on appeal was that the failure of the trial court to consider the words in their cultural context as part of the analysis of reasonableness consti-

tural defense that would enable parents to explain their motive, the parents have no clear way to explain to the court the cultural context of their actions.

In contrast to standard child abuse cases in which there is no way to ensure the consideration of cultural evidence relating to parents' motive, the legal definition of child sexual abuse does include motive, because the crime is a specific intent crime. This means that not only must the adult intend to touch the child and do so, but in addition the adult must touch the child for the purpose of sexual gratification. Nevertheless, because there is such a preoccupation with this subject, Americans often assume the existence of the specific intent.

In the Krasniqi case, an Albanian immigrant father allegedly touched his four-year-old daughter in the genital area during a martial arts tournament at which his son was competing (Brelvi 1997).[42] Both children were immediately removed from the parents, though the mother was allowed visitation rights. When the mother violated the court order by taking the children to see their father, that led to the termination of the Krasniqi parental rights.[43] The Texas Supreme Court upheld the decision of the family court to terminate the parental rights of the Krasniqis. Though Mr. Krasniqi was subsequently acquitted of criminal charges in the criminal trial a few years later, this had no effect on the family court decision. The parents were unable to see their children again.

Another case that led to the separation of a family was *State of Maine v. Kargar* (1996). Mohammed Kargar, an Afghan refugee, kissed his son's genitals as a sign of love without any sexual connotation (Wanderer and Connors 1999). The father displayed his affection not only in family photographs but in front of American neighbors. Though he maintained that his actions were innocent with written statements from scholars and a religious leader substantiating this claim, Kargar was convicted of two counts of gross sexual assault and was required to live apart from his family for several years during the appeals process. His conviction was reversed on appeal under a de minimis law on the basis of the argument that the legislature could not have envisaged the application of the law to this conduct.[44] Despite the reversal, the expectation was that the practice had to cease.[45]

From the vantage point of the dominant culture, some traditions affecting children seem unacceptable. States generally reserve the right to intervene to protect children from parents who harm them. The question is whether parents who try to maintain the cultural identity of their children actually harm them. In U.S. law, the courts generally sanction intervention if a child has a life-threatening condition and the parents have a religious objection to medical treatment.

According to international law (the Convention on the Rights of the Child), children have both a right to practice their culture under Article 30 as well as a right against traditions prejudicial to their health under Article 24(3). The obvious difficulty is to decide when the parents' right to their exercise of culture outweighs the child's right to protection from the culture. If one can identify those customs that involve irreparable harm to children, that would be a limiting principle for the recognition of parents' right to culture. When, as in most cases, the cultural traditions do not involve any threat of harm, then parents have a right to pass on their traditions to their children. When a tradition requires an irreparable harm or change and the child has moved from one society to another, my view is that the child should not be subject to the tradition until reaching the age of majority. At that point the child can opt to have the ritual scarification, genital cutting, or other permanent bodily change (Renteln 1994).

## SOME CRITICISMS OF THE CULTURAL DEFENSE

One criticism of the cultural defense is that it puts the tradition on trial rather than the individual. This is offensive not merely because it "essentializes" culture (that is, treats a tradition as widely accepted and uncontested) but also because it freezes the tradition, as though there were only one version. There is no question that the ways in which the legal system operates does result in some oversimplifications of customs. Nevertheless, the fact that information has to be presented in a particular manner does not deny the relevance of the information for the responsibility or punishment of the individual. It is crucial to verify the cultural claims asserted in disputes to see whether there is consensus around a tradition or whether it is contested.

Another objection to the cultural defense is that it relies on determinism, sometimes expressed as "my culture made me do it." According to this critique, a person who comes from a particular culture will automatically act in a certain way, given certain conditions. This argument is predicated on a mistaken view of culture. In fact, no culture theorist argues that culture influences behavior to that extent. Culture shapes cognitive processes, so that individuals will be predisposed to act in particular ways, but it does not determine their actions.

One of the strongest criticisms has come from feminists, who equate the argument in favor of the cultural defense with the oppression of women. These critics generally cite only cases in which women have been victims, rather than those in which women are defendants, themselves invoking the cultural defense. In fact, in some of the most significant cultural defense cases, such as *People v. Kimura* and *People v. Wu*, women who attempted parent-child suicide sought to explain their culturally motivated behavior to the court.[46]

A key argument seems to be that allowing cultural defenses would undermine women's rights and children's rights. One scholar argues that taking culture into account results in an equal protection violation for the victims of the culturally motivated offense (Coleman 1996). Her position does not acknowledge that the criminal law is supposed to make punishment proportional for the defendant in light of the mens rea. If there is any validity to the cultural defense argument, then the point is that the act is not as morally culpable if it is motivated by a cultural imperative. Moreover, the law permits the consideration of motive when a crime is influenced by race hatred, even though the act committed by the racist is identical to that committed by a nonracist. Equal protection does not require that sentences be identical.

Where the use of the cultural defense might risk conveying the message that violence against women is acceptable, the jury can reject it. Just because an individual is entitled to raise a defense in no way means the argument should prevail. According to the irreparable harm principle, traditional acts such as honor killings would be unacceptable uses of the cultural defense.

## POLICY ISSUES

If a cultural defense were to be formally adopted, a number of questions would have to be addressed. Would all groups be entitled to raise a cultural defense? Some object to the idea that subcultures would be entitled to use a cultural defense, because they fear that right-wing groups such as the Ku Klux Klan or gangs might invoke it to avoid punishment. Others insist that the defense should be available to all and that it is unfair to limit its use to immigrants. There does not appear to be any reasonable way to limit the groups that could use the cultural defense.

Although it seems ill-advised to try to limit the use of the cultural defense to any predetermined list of groups, those who wish to use the defense should have to meet some requirements. They should have to show: that the practice in question is an "authentic" part of their way of life; and that the conduct of the person raising the defense was influenced by the tradition. Since the cultural defense would require that the courts treat cultural evidence as admissible, the jury would have to make these determinations.

In the case of immigrants and refugees, as opposed to minorities and indigenous peoples, the question is sometimes asked whether they should only be entitled to raise the defense for some limited period of time. It does not seem possible to assume that individuals would become assimilated by any particular point in time. While the question of whether someone is first, second, or third generation might be relevant to deciding to what extent the tradition affected his or her behavior, there is no guaranteed passage of time after which people cease to be influenced by their cultures. Many groups that migrated long ago still follow their traditions, for example, Jewish families who circumcise their sons.

One response to the conundrum of culture conflict might be to have legislatures consider each controversial tradition.[47] When legislatures have considered cultural practices, they almost invariably prohibit them—for example, the consumption of pets, female genital cutting, and charreadas (Mexican-style rodeos).[48] It is, therefore, more likely that the judiciaries will, on occasion, authorize the perpetuation of traditions because courts can invoke their power of judicial review to counter discriminatory acts of the majority.

Some customs should be discouraged. In the new country, some forms of behavior such as touching children in the genital area, folk remedies that leave scars, and marriage practices that do not involve consent by women are socially unacceptable. Those who act in these ways will undoubtedly have encounters with legal authorities. Even if it is important that these acts be limited, the individuals do not necessarily deserve to be imprisoned. There are other methods of informing the newly arrived of the dominant culture's expectations that are far less punitive.

The international community has established the right to culture as a fundamental human right because traditions are crucial for the maintenance of individual and group identities. To date, there has been no move to apply this right to authorize the adoption of the cultural defense in legal systems. This may reflect a belief that those who move between cultures must conform to the standards of the new society.

Even if we accept the proverbial wisdom of "When in Rome . . ." and that a common code of conduct is necessary for the existence of a society, it does not follow that minority cultures deserve no protection. To the extent that a democracy guarantees principles such as equal protection, religious freedom, and the right to a fair trial, these cannot be used only on behalf of the majority. Justice requires the equal enforcement of existing laws to ensure that all individuals are protected.

Culture shapes individual identity in crucial ways. The failure of the law to recognize this has resulted in injustices. Until the right to culture is understood to be a basic human right, individuals will continue to be told that they must become assimilated, that their background is irrelevant, and that there is only one correct way to behave. To avoid depriving these individuals of their basic right to justice, we must allow the cultural defense.

## NOTES

1. The judge did not dispute the defendant's claim that his religion required him to wear the kirpan. Indeed, Mr. Singh would be socially ostracized and subject to divine retribution for failure to comply with religious law.

2. This example reflects the ambivalence many feel about the recognition of other cultural traditions; it also demonstrates how judges commonly uphold the law technically but avoid imposing punishment. Judges often give suspended sentences to achieve this result.

3. Judges often exclude such information as irrelevant, though nothing in the evidence codes requires them to do so.

4. I wish to emphasize at the outset that I am arguing that defendants should have the right to describe their cultural traditions to the court. This does not mean that I think the arguments should necessarily be given much weight. Much depends on the particular circumstances.

5. Though most of the examples are taken from the United States, comparable culture conflicts exist in many other countries.

6. This proverb is attributed to Saint Ambrose. For analogues in other countries see Ojoade 1978–1979, 13–18.

7. It is likely that Mr. Singh would be prosecuted were he to appear before the judge again. Having been given notice that wearing the kirpan is considered a violation of the law, he is expected to make his behavior conform to the law.

8. Many incorrectly assume that the cultural defense is used mainly by Asian defendants. See, for example, Roberts 1999, 85–110; Maeda 2000; Koptiuch 1996, 215–33.

9. That culture strongly influences individuals does not mean that they can never resist their ingrained reactions. Some individuals will depart from culturally prescribed patterns of behavior, while others will follow them. Hence, it is erroneous to equate enculturation with cultural determinism.

10. The formal adoption of an official cultural offense was considered and rejected in Australia and Canada.

11. My view is that culture is properly considered during the guilt and sentencing phases, depending on circumstances.

12. For example, many cases involve religious objections to the performance of autopsies. Some religious minorities believe that the body, if mutilated, will be perpetually in that condition in the afterlife. Usually the family's objection is outweighed by the government's interests in solving a crime or investigating an epidemic. See, for example, *Albareti v. Hirsch* 1993, 21.

13. Lawyers sometimes accept the proposition that culture can disprove one of the elements of a crime.

14. It is beyond the scope of this chapter to determine whether the right to culture is part of customary law or is a fundamental right (ius cogens).

15. Article 18 (the religious freedom provision) contains a limitations provision. Some contend that it was understood that limitations applied to Article 27 as well (see Poulter 1998, 82). Others deny this, noting that the drafters would have included the limitations had they intended there to be any. In the definitive treatise on the ICCPR, Manfred Nowak (1993) rejects the notion that restrictive provisions from other articles apply to Article 27.

16. The negative formulation makes sense if the right to culture will only be invoked when there is interference with the exercise of the right. Historically, there was some question as to whether immigrants, refugees, and those temporarily residing in a country could use this right. Oddly enough, though Article 27 is considered the minorities' rights provision, it has mainly been used in disputes involving indigenous groups (though many do not consider themselves minorities).

17. The Human Rights Committee is only empowered to review complaints against states that have ratified the Optional Protocol to the ICCPR. Only one nation, France, tried to evade responsibility for enforcing Article 27.

18. Most human rights are assumed to be valid. For instance, the right to life, the right against torture, and the right to free and periodic elections are considered self-evident.

19. One philosopher rejects entirely the notion that culture is relevant to culpability; see Moody-Adams 1994.

20. Susan Okin (1999) advances the argument that protecting cultural rights undermines women's rights.

48. Occasionally, legislatures exempt religious minorities from general laws—for example, Jewish and Muslim communities are permitted to engage in the ritual slaughter of animals in accordance with shechita and halal, respectively.

# REFERENCES

Akermark, Athanasia Spiliopoulou. 1997. *Justifications of Minority Protection in International Law*. London: Kluwer.

*Albareti v. Hirsch*. 1993. *New York Law Journal* (July 7): 21.

Alston, Philip. 1994. *The Best Interests of the Child: Reconciling Culture and Human Rights*. Oxford: Clarendon Press.

Anaya, S. James. 1996. *Indigenous Peoples in International Law*. New York: Oxford University Press.

Anh, Nong The. 1976. "Pseudo-Battered Child's Syndrome." *Journal of the American Medical Association* 236(20): 2288.

Anonymous. 1993. "Aspiration and Control: International Legal Rhetoric and the Essentialization of Culture." *Harvard Law Review* 106: 723–40.

Anonymous. 1996. "What's A-O.K. in the U.S.A. Is Lewd and Worthless Beyond." *New York Times*, August 18: E7.

Bartlett, John. 1992. *Familiar Quotations*. 16th ed. Boston: Little, Brown.

Beyerly, Elizabeth. 1998. *Eurocentric International Law: Contemporary Doctrinal Perspectives*. Buffalo: William S. Hein.

Black, J. A. 1986. "Misdiagnosis of Child Abuse in Ethnic Minorities." *Midwife Health Visitor and Community Nurse* 22: 48–53.

Brelvi, Farah Sultana. 1997. "'News of the Weird': Specious Normativity and the Problem of the Cultural Defense." *Columbia Human Rights Law Review* 28: 657–83.

Canadian Commission for UNESCO. 1977. "A Working Definition of 'Culture.'" *Cultures* 4(4): 78–83.

Carberry, Charles M., and Harold K. Gordon. 1996. "Anatomy of an Acquittal: The Cultural Use of Cash." *Money Laundering Law Report* 6(9): 1.

Cholewinski, Ryszard. 1988. "State Duty to Ethnic Minorities: Positive or Negative?" *Human Rights Quarterly* 10: 344–71.

Clinton, Olabisi L. 1990. "Cultural Differences and Sentencing Departures." *Federal Sentencing Reporter* 5: 348–52.

Coleman, Doriane Lambelet. 1996. "Individualizing Justice Through Multiculturalism: The Liberals' Dilemma." *Columbia Law Review* 96: 1093–1167.

Evans-Pritchard, Deirdre, and Alison Dundes Renteln. 1994. "The Interpretation and Distortion of Culture: A Hmong Marriage by Capture Case in Fresno, California." *Southern California Interdisciplinary Law Journal* 4: 1–48.

Feldman, Kenneth W. 1984. "Pseudoabusive Burns in Asian Refugees." *American Journal of Diseases of Children* 138: 768–9.

Gaw, Albert C. 1993. *Culture, Ethnicity, and Mental Illness*. Washington, D.C.: American Psychiatric Press.

Gordon, Milton M. 1964. *Assimilation in American Life: The Role of Race, Religion, and National Origins*. New York: Oxford University Press.

Harris, Harry. 1988. "Ancient Healing Practice or Child Abuse? Southeast Asian Coining Custom Alarms School Officials, Police." *Oakland Tribune*, May 9: A1–A2.

Howard, Colin. 1961. "What Colour Is the 'Reasonable Man'?" *Criminal Law Review*: 41–8.

*Jack and Charlie v. the Queen*. 1985. 2 SCR 332. Canadian Sup. Ct.

Koptiuch, Kristin. 1996. "'Cultural Defense' and Criminological Displacements: Gender, Race, and (Trans)nation in the Legal Surveillance of U.S. Diaspora Asians." In *Displacement, Diaspora, and Geographies of Identity*, edited by Smadar Lavie and Red Swedenburg. Durham, N.C.: Duke University Press.

Kukathas, Chandran. 1992a. "Are There Any Cultural Rights?" *Political Theory* 20: 105–39.

———. 1992b. "Cultural Rights Again: A Rejoinder to Kymlicka." *Political Theory* 20: 674–80.

Kymlicka, Will. 1992. "The Rights of Minority Cultures: Reply to Kukathas." *Political Theory* 20: 140–46.

———. 1995a. *The Rights of Minority Cultures*. Oxford: Oxford University Press.

———. 1995b. *Multicultural Citizenship*. Oxford: Oxford University Press.

Lears, T. J. Jackson. 1985. "The Concept of Cultural Hegemony: Problems and Possibilities." *American Historical Review* 90.

Leusner, Jim, and Susan Jacobson. 1997. "Two Dealers of Reptiles Go to Jail." *Orlando Sentinel*, August 17, 1997.

Li, Jisheng. 1996. "The Nature of the Offense: An Ignored Factor in Determination of the Application of the Cultural Defense." *University of Hawaii Law Review* 18: 765–96.

Linton, Ralph. 1961. *The Tree of Culture*. New York: Alfred A. Knopf.

Lock, Margaret M. 1978. "Scars of Experience: The Art of Moxibustion in Japanese Medicine and Society." *Culture, Medicine, and Psychiatry* 2: 151–75.

Maeda, Donna K. 2000. "The 'Cultural Defense' and Legal Constructions of Race, Culture, Nation." In *Postcolonial America*, edited by Richard King. Urbana: University of Illinois Press.

Maguigan, Holly. 1995. "Cultural Evidence and Male Violence: Are Feminist and Multicultural Reformers on a Collision Course in Criminal Courts?" *New York University Law Review* 70: 36–99.

*Mak v. Blodgett*. 1992. 970 F 2d 614 (9th Cir 1992), 754 F Supp.

Mandell, Louise. 1987. "Native Culture on Trial." In *Equality and Judicial Neutrality*, edited by Sheilah L. Martin and Kathleen E. Mahoney. Toronto: Carswell.

Markus, Hazel Rose, and Leah R. Lin. 1999. "Conflictways: Cultural Diversity in the Meanings and Practices of Conflict." In *Cultural Divides: Understanding and Overcoming Group Conflict*, edited by Deborah A. Prentice and Dale T. Miller. New York: Russell Sage Foundation.

McGoldrick, Dominic. 1991. "Canadian Indians, Cultural Rights, and the Human Rights Committee." *International and Comparative Law Quarterly* 40: 658–69.

Minow, Martha, and Todd Rakoff. 1998. "Is the 'Reasonable Person' a Reasonable Standard in a Multicultural World?" In *Everyday Practices and Trouble Cases*, edited by Austin Sarat et al. Evanston, Ill.: Northwestern University Press.

Moody-Adams, Michele. 1994. "Culture, Responsibility, and Affected Ignorance." *Ethics* 104: 291–309.

Nowak, Manfred. 1993. *The U.N. Covenant on Civil and Political Rights: CCPR Commentary*. Kehl am Rhein: N. P. Engel.

Ojoade, J. O. Olowo. 1978–1979. "When in Rome, Do as the Romans Do." *Midwestern Language and Folklore Newsletter*. Vols. 1 and 2.

O'Keefe, Roger. 1998. "The 'Right to Take Part in Cultural Life' Under Article 15 of the ICESR." *International and Comparative Law Quarterly* 47(4): 904–23.

Okin, Susan Moller. 1999. "Is Multiculturalism Bad for Women?" In *Is Multiculturalism Bad for Women?* edited by Susan M. Okin. Princeton, N.J.: Princeton University Press.

Paz, Octavio. 1961. "The Sons of La Malinche." In *The Labyrinth of Solitude: Life and Thought in Mexico*, edited by Octavio Paz. New York: Grove Press.

*People v. Kimura*. 1985. Los Angeles Sup. Ct. No. A-091133.

*People v. Singh*. 1987. 516 NYS 2d 412 New York City Civ. Ct.

*People v. Trujillo-Garcia*. 1988. Appellant's Supplemental Brief. Court of Appeal, California First Appellate District, Division One, No. A038099.

*People v. Wu*. 1991. Cal. App. 3d 614, 286 California Reporter 868.

*People v. Wu*. 1992. Jan. 23. Order of depublication.

Pomorski, Stanislaw. 1997. "On Multiculturalism, Concepts of Crime, and the 'De Minimis' Defense." *Brigham Young University Law Review*: 51–99.

Poulter, Sebastian. 1987. "Ethnic Minority Customs, English Law and Human Rights." *International and Comparative Law Quarterly* 36: 589–615.

———. 1998. *Ethnicity, Law, and Human Rights: The English Experience*. Oxford: Clarendon Press.

Prott, Lyndel V. 1988. "Cultural Rights as Peoples' Rights in International Law." In *The Rights of Peoples*, edited by James Crawford. Oxford: Clarendon Press.

Renteln, Alison Dundes. 1988. "Relativism and the Search for Human Rights." *American Anthropologist* 90: 56–72.

———. 1990. *International Human Rights: Universalism Versus Relativism*. Newbury Park, Calif.: Sage.

———. 1993. "A Justification of the Cultural Defense as Partial Excuse." *Southern California Review of Law and Women's Studies* 2: 437–526.

———. 1994. "Is the Cultural Defense Detrimental to the Health of Children?" *Law and Anthropology* 7: 27–106.

———. 2000. "Raising Cultural Defenses." In *Cultural Issues in Criminal Defense*, edited by Rene Valladares and James Connell. New York: Juris.

Renteln, Alison Dundes, and Alan Dundes. 1995. *Folk Law: Essays in the Theory and Practice of Lex Non Scripta*. Madison: University of Wisconsin Press.

Roberts, Dorothy. 1999. "Why Culture Matters to Law: The Difference Politics Makes." In *Cultural Pluralism, Identity Politics, and the Law*, edited by Austin Sarat and Thomas R. Kearns. Ann Arbor: University of Michigan Press.

Saltman, Michael. 1991. *The Demise of the "Reasonable Man": A Cross-Cultural Study of a Legal Concept*. New Brunswick and London: Transaction.

Sellin, Thorsten. 1938. *Culture Conflict and Crime*. New York: Social Science Research Council.

Shimahara, Nobuo. 1970. "Enculturation—A Reconsideration." *Current Anthropology* 11.

Shore, Bradd. 1996. *Culture in Mind: Cognition, Culture, and the Problem of Meaning*. New York: Oxford University Press.

Shweder, Richard A. 1991. *Thinking Through Cultures: Expeditions in Cultural Psychology*. Cambridge, Mass.: Harvard University Press.

Shweder, Richard A., and Edmund J. Bourne. 1982. "Does the Concept of the Person Vary Cross-Culturally?" In *Cultural Conceptions of Mental Health and Therapy*, edited by Anthony J. Marsella and Geoffrey M. White. Dordrecht: D. Reidel.

Sinha, Surya Prakash. 1996. *Legal Polycentricity and International Law*. Durham, N.C.: Carolina Academic Press.

*State of Maine v. Kargar*. 1996. 679 A2d 81 at 85n5.

Thornberry, Patrick. 1991. *International Law and the Rights of Minorities*. Oxford: Clarendon Press.

*Trujillo-Garcia v. Rowland*. 1992. U.S. Dist. LEXIS 6199. U.S. District Court, 1993 U.S. A

LEXIS 36122 (Nov. 10, 1993), U.S. Court of the Appeals for the 9th Circuit. 114 SCt 2145 (May 31, 1994, cert. denied). Unpublished disposition.

*Trujillo-Garcia v. Rowland.* 1992. Memorandum and Order by Judge Marilyn Hall Patel. U.S. Dist. LEXIS 6199.

UNESCO. 1970. *Cultural Rights as Human Rights.* Paris: UNESCO.

United States Sentencing Commission. 1995. *Federal Sentencing Guidelines Manual.* St. Paul, Minn.: West.

*United States v. Tomono.* 1997. U.S. District Court, Middle District of Florida, Orlando Division, Order. No. 91-127-CR-ORL-22.

*United States v. Tomono.* 1998. U.S. Court of Appeals for the 11th Circuit, 143 F 3d 1401.

Wanderer, Nancy A., and Catherine R. Connors. 1999. "Culture and Crime: Kargar and the Existing Framework for a Cultural Defense." *Buffalo Law Review* 47: 829–73.

Woo, Deborah. 1989. "The People v. Fumiko Kimura: But Which People?" *International Journal of the Sociology of Law* 17: 403–28.

Yeatman, W., and Viet Van Dang. 1980. "*Cao Gio* (Coin Rubbing): Vietnamese Attitudes Toward Health Care." *Journal of the American Medical Association* 244(24): 2748–49.

Yeo, Stanley M. H. 1990–1991. "Recent Australian Pronouncements on the Ordinary Person Test in Provocation and Automatism." *Criminal Law Quarterly* 33: 96–104.

# Chapter 11

# "What About Female Genital Mutilation?" and Why Understanding Culture Matters in the First Place

Richard A. Shweder

Female genital mutilation (FGM, also known as female circumcision) has been practiced traditionally for centuries in sub-Saharan Africa. Customs, rituals, myths, and taboos have perpetuated the practice even though it has maimed or killed untold numbers of women and girls. . . .

FGM's disastrous health effects, combined with the social injustices it perpetuates, constitute a serious barrier to overall African development.
—Susan Rich and Stephanie Joyce, "Eradicating Female Genital Mutilation" (n.d.)

On the basis of the vast literature on the harmful effects of genital surgeries, one might have anticipated finding a wealth of studies that document considerable increases in mortality and morbidity. This review could find no incontrovertible evidence on mortality, and the rate of medical complications suggest that they are the exception rather than the rule.
—Carla M. Obermeyer, "Female Genital Surgeries" (1999)

Early societies in Africa established strong controls over the sexual behavior of their women and devised the brutal means of circumcision to curb female sexual desire and response.
—Olayinka Koso-Thomas, *Circumcision of Women* (1987)

In fact, studies that systematically investigate the sexual feelings of women and men in societies where genital surgeries are found are rare, and the scant information that is available calls into question the assertion that female genital surgeries are fundamentally antithetical to women's sexuality and incompatible with sexual enjoyment.

—Carla M. Obermeyer, "Female Genital Surgeries"
(1999)

Those who practice some of the most controversial of such customs—clitoridectomy, polygamy, the marriage of children or marriages that are otherwise coerced—sometimes explicitly defend them as necessary for controlling women and openly acknowledge that the customs persist at men's insistence.

—Susan Moller Okin, *Is Multiculturalism Bad for Women?*
(1999)

It is difficult for me—considering the number of ceremonies I have observed, including my own—to accept that what appears to be expressions of joy and ecstatic celebrations of womanhood in actuality disguise hidden experiences of coercion and subjugation. Indeed, I offer that the bulk of Kono women who uphold these rituals do so because they want to—they relish the supernatural powers of their ritual leaders over against men in society, and they embrace the legitimacy of female authority and particularly, the authority of their mothers and grandmothers.

—Fuambai Ahmadu, "Rites and Wrongs" (2000)

On November 18, 1999, Fuambai Ahmadu, a young African scholar who grew up in the United States, delivered a paper at the American Anthropological Association Meetings in Chicago that should be deeply troubling to all liberal free-thinking people who value democratic pluralism and the toleration of differences and who care about the accuracy of cultural representations in our public policy debates.[1]

Ms. Ahmadu (2000, 283) began her paper with these words:

I also share with feminist scholars and activists campaigning against the practice [of female circumcision] a concern for women's physical, psychological and sexual well-being, as well as with the implications of these traditional rituals for women's status and power in society. Coming from an ethnic group [the Kono of Eastern Sierra Leone] in which female (and male) initiation and "circumcision" are institutionalized and a central feature of culture and society and having myself undergone this traditional process of becoming a "woman," I find it increasingly challenging to reconcile my own experiences with prevailing global discourses on female "circumcision."

To me, female genital mutilation is a violation of the physical and spiritual integrity of a person," states Tilman Hasche, a political asylum lawyer (quoted in Egan 1994), summarizing a not uncommon view among public intellectuals in the United States and Europe.

Much of the press in the First World similarly has been swayed. Media coverage that affects American opinion about African customs has been influenced extensively by anti-FGM activists and advocacy groups who represent the African practice of female genital alteration as a scourge or disease that needs to be eradicated, who write books with stirring titles such as *Women, Why Do You Weep?* and who presuppose that any deliberate alteration of that part of the female anatomy is an example of the patriarchal oppression of women and must be viewed as a mutilation. "Here is a dream for Americans, worthy of their country and what they would like it to be," writes A. M. Rosenthal, the distinguished columnist for the *New York Times*. "The dream is that the U.S. could bring about the end of a system of torture that has crippled 100 million people now living upon this earth and every year takes at least two million more into an existence of suffering, deprivation and disease. . . . The torture is female genital mutilation" (Rosenthal 1995, A25). In his op-ed essay Rosenthal then proudly advertises three advocacy groups, including the organization that publishes *The Hosken Report* (Hosken 1993), an anti-FGM document that has been widely distributed to opinion makers in the United States and has impressed many journalists.

Equally noteworthy, however, is that these judgments seem precipitous and fundamentally misinformed to many anthropologists who study gender, initiation, and life stages in Africa. Many anthropologists and other researchers who work on these topics have long been aware of discrepancies between the global discourse on female circumcision (with its images of maiming, murder, sexual dysfunction, mutilation, coercion, and oppression) and their own ethnographic experiences with indigenous discourses and with social and physical realities at their field settings and research sites (for example, Abusharaf 2001; Boddy 1989, 1996; Gruenbaum 1996, 2001; Johnson 2000; Kratz 1994, 1999; Obiora 1997; Parker 1995; Shell-Duncan and Hernlund 2000a; Walley 1997).

Perhaps the first anthropological protest against the global discourse came in 1938 from Jomo Kenyatta, who, prior to becoming the first president of postcolonial Kenya, published a doctoral thesis in anthropology at the London School of Economics and Political Science (Kenyatta 1938). He described both the customary premarital sexual practices of the Gikuyu (lots of fondling and rather liberal attitudes toward adolescent petting and sexual arousal) and the practice of female and male circumcision.

Kenyatta's words have an uncanny contemporary ring and relevance. First he informs us,

> In 1931 a conference on African children was held in Geneva under the
> auspices of the Save the Children Fund. In this conference several European delegates urged that the time was ripe when this "barbarous custom"

should be abolished, and that, like all other "heathen" customs, it should be abolished at once by law. (Kenyatta 1938, 131)

Kenyatta goes on to argue that among the Gikuyu a genital alteration, "like Jewish circumcision," is a bodily sign that is regarded "as the *conditio sine qua non* of the whole teaching of tribal law, religion and morality"; that no proper Gikuyu man or woman would have sex with or marry someone who was not circumcised; that the practice is an essential step into responsible adulthood for many African girls and boys; and that "there is a strong community of educated Gikuyu opinion in defense of this custom" (Kenyatta 1938, 133, 132).

Nearly sixty years later, echoes of Jomo Kenyatta's message can be found in the writings of Corinne Kratz, who has written a detailed account of female initiation among another ethnic group in Kenya, the Okiek. The Okiek, she tells us, do not talk about circumcision in terms of the dampening of sexual pleasure or desire, but rather speak of it "in terms of cleanliness, beauty and adulthood." According to Kratz, Okiek women and men view "genital modification and the bravery and self-control displayed during the operation as constitutive experiences of Okiek personhood" (Kratz 1994, 346).

Many other examples could be cited of discrepancies between the global discourse and the experience of many field researchers in Africa. With regard to the issue of sexual enjoyment, for example, Robert Edgerton (1989, 254n22) remarks that "[G]Kikuyu men and women, like those of several other East African societies that practice female circumcision, assured me in 1961–62 that circumcised women continue to be orgasmic." Similar remarks appear in other field reports (for example, Lightfoot-Klein 1989; Gruenbaum 2001, 139–43).

With regard to the global discourse that represents circumcision as a disfigurement or mutilation, Sandra Lane and Robert Rubinstein (1996, 35) offer the following caution.

An important caveat, however, is that many members of societies that practice traditional female genital surgeries do not view the result as mutilation. Among these groups, in fact, the resulting appearance is considered an improvement over female genitalia in their natural state. Indeed, to call a woman uncircumcised, or to call a man the son of an uncircumcised mother, is a terrible insult and noncircumcised adult female genitalia are often considered disgusting. In interviews we conducted in rural and urban Egypt and in studies conducted by faculty of the High Institute of Nursing, Zagazig University, Egypt, the overwhelming majority of circumcised women planned to have the procedure performed on their daughters. In discussions with some fifty women we found only two who resent and are angry at having been circumcised. Even these women do not think that female circumcision is one of the most critical problems facing Egyptian women and girls. In the rural Egyptian hamlet where we have conducted fieldwork some women were not familiar with groups that did not circumcise their girls. When they learned that the female researcher was not circumcised their response was disgust mixed with joking laughter. They wondered how she could have thus gotten married and questioned how her mother could have neglected such an important part of her preparation for womanhood.

These ethnographic reports are noteworthy because they suggest that instead of assuming that our own perceptions of beauty and disfigurement are universal and must be transcendental, we might want to consider the possibility that a real and astonishing cultural divide exists around the world in moral, emotional, and aesthetic reactions to female genital surgeries. No doubt, of course, our own feelings of disgust, indignation, and anxiety about this topic are powerful and may be aroused easily and manipulated rhetorically with pictures (for example, of Third World surgical implements) or words (for example, labeling the activity *torture* or *mutilation*). If we want to understand the true character of this cultural divide in sensibilities, however, we need to bracket our initial (and automatic) emotional-visceral reactions and save any powerful conclusive feelings for the end of the argument, rather than have them color or short circuit all objective analysis. Perhaps, instead of simply deploring the "savages," we might develop a better understanding of the subject by constructing a synoptic account of the inside point of view, from the perspective of those many African women for whom such practices seem both normal and desirable.

## MORAL PLURALISM AND THE MUTUAL "YUCK" RESPONSE

People recoil at each other's practices and say "yuck" at each other all over the world. When it comes to female genital alterations—or lack thereof—the mutual yuck response among peoples is particularly intense and may even approach outrage or horror. From a purely descriptive point of view, this type of physical modification is routine and normal in many ethnic groups: for example, national prevalence rates of 80 percent to 98 percent have been reported for Egypt, Ethiopia, the Gambia, Mali, Sierra Leone, Somalia, and the Sudan (Shell-Duncan and Hernlund 2000a, 10–12). In African nations where the overall prevalence rate is lower—for example, Kenya (50 percent), Côte d'Ivoire (43 percent), and Ghana (30 percent)—it is typically because some ethnic groups have a tradition of female circumcision while others do not. Thus, for example, within Ghana ethnic groups in the north and east circumcise boys and girls, while ethnic groups in the south have no tradition of female circumcision.

In general, for both sexes the best predictor of circumcision (versus the absence of it) is ethnicity or cultural group affiliation. Circumcision is customary for the Kono of Sierra Leone, for example, but for the Wolof of Senegal it is not. For women within these groups, one key factor—their cultural affiliation as either Kono or Wolof—trumps other predictors of behavior, such as education level or socioeconomic status. Among the Kono, even women with a secondary school or college education (such as Fuambai Ahmadu) are circumcised, while

Senegalese Wolof women—including the illiterate and unschooled—are not. Notably, most African women do not think about circumcision in human rights terms or as a human rights violation. Women who endorse female circumcision argue that it is an important part of their cultural heritage or their religion, while women who do not endorse the practice typically argue that it is not permitted by their cultural heritage or their religion (see, for example, El Dareer 1983).

Moreover, among members of ethnic groups where female circumcision is part of their cultural heritage, approval ratings for the custom are generally high. According to the Sudan Demographic and Health Survey of 1989–1990 conducted in northern and central Sudan, of 3,805 women interviewed, 89 percent were circumcised. Of the women who were circumcised, 96 percent said they had or would circumcise their daughters. When asked whether they favored continuation of the practice, 90 percent of circumcised women said they favored its continuation (see Williams and Sobieszyzyk 1997, table 1).

In Sierra Leone, the picture is pretty much the same and the vast majority of women are sympathetic to the practice and appear to feel at home in their way of life. Even Olayinka Koso-Thomas, an anti-FGM activist, makes note of the high degree of support for genital operations, although she expresses herself with a rather patronizing voice and in imperial tones:

> Most African women still have not developed the sensitivity to feel deprived or to see in many cultural practices a violation of their human rights. The consequence of this is that, in the mid–80's, when most women in Africa have voting rights and can influence political decisions against practices harmful to their health, they continue to uphold the dictates and mores of the communities in which they live; they seem in fact to regard traditional beliefs as inviolate. (Koso-Thomas 1987, 2)

When it comes to maintaining their coming-of-age and gender-identity ceremonies, Koso-Thomas does not like the way many African women vote. While she thinks she is enlightened about human rights and health and that these women remain in the dark, Koso-Thomas indeed recognizes that most women in Sierra Leone endorse the practice of circumcision. (For recent evidence of high approval ratings among Mandinka women in the Gambia, see Morison et al. 2001.) Amy Kendoh, a member of the women's secret society in Sierra Leone, where more than 90 percent of adult women have been initiated, put it this way: "I have grown up to the age of fifty years, and this is the first time anyone has come forward to ask me why we do these ceremonies. It doesn't matter what other people think because we are happy with our customs. We will carry on with our lives" (French 1997, A4).

Further, although ethnic group affiliation is the best predictor of who circumcises and who does not, the timing and form of the operation are not uniform across groups. Thus, there is enormous variability in the age at which the surgery is normally performed (any time from birth to the late teenage years). There is also enormous variability in the traditional style and degree of surgery (from a cut in the prepuce covering the clitoris to the complete "smoothing out" of the genital area by removing all visible parts of the clitoris and all external labia). In some ethnic groups (for example, in Somalia and the Sudan) the smoothing out operation is concluded by stitching closed the vaginal opening with the aims of enhancing fertility, tightening the vaginal opening, and protecting the womb (see Boddy 1982, 1989, 1996; Gruenbaum 2001). The latter procedure, often referred to as *infibulation* or Pharaonic circumcision, is not typical in most circumcising ethnic groups, although it has received a good deal of attention in the anti-FGM literature. The procedure occurs in an estimated 15 percent of all African cases, although it is rare or nonexistent in many of the ethnic groups where some form of genital alteration for both males and females is culturally endorsed.

In places where the practice of female circumcision is popular, including Somalia and the Sudan, it is widely believed by women that these genital alterations improve their bodies and make them more beautiful, more feminine, more civilized, and more honorable.

More beautiful because the body is made smooth and a protrusion or "fleshy encumbrance" removed that is thought to be ugly and odious to both sight and touch (see, for example, Abusharaf 2001; Koso-Thomas 1987, 7; Lane and Rubinstein 1996, quoted herein, Meinardus 1967, 394; El Dareer 1982, 73). Here a cultural aesthetics is in play among circumcising ethnic groups—an ideal of the human sexual region as smooth, cleansed, and refined—that supports the view that the genitals of women and men are unsightly, misshapen, and unappealing if left in their natural state.

More feminine because unmodified genitals (in both males and females) are perceived as sexually ambiguous. From a female's perspective, the clitoris is viewed as an unwelcome vestige of the male organ, and its removal is positively associated with several desirable things: attainment of full female identity, induction into a social network and support group of powerful adult women, and ultimately, marriage and motherhood (Ahmadu 2000; Meinardus 1967, 389). Many women who uphold these traditions of female initiation seek to empower themselves by getting rid of what they view as an unbidden yet dispensable trace of unwanted male anatomy.

More civilized because a genital alteration is a symbolic action that says something about one's willingness to exercise restraint over feelings of lust, and self-control over the antisocial desire for sexual pleasure.

More honorable because the surgery announces one's commitment to perpetuate the lineage and value the womb as the source of social reproduction (see, for example, Boddy 1982, 1989, 1996).

As hard as it may be for "us" to believe, in places where female circumcision is commonplace, it is not only popular but fashionable. And as hard as it may be for us to believe (and I recognize that for some of us this is really hard to believe), many women in places such as Mali, Somalia, Egypt, Kenya, or Chad indeed are repulsed by the idea of unmodified female genitals, which they view as ugly, unrefined, undignified, uncivilized and hence, not fully human. They associate unmodified genitals with life outside or at the bottom of civilized society. They think to themselves, "Yuck, what kind of barbarians are these who don't circumcise their genitals?"

The "yuck" is, of course, mutual. Female genital alterations are not routine and normal for members of mainstream or majority populations in Europe, the United States, China, Japan, and other parts of the world, and it is not a common practice in the southern parts of Africa. For members of these cultures the very thought of female genital surgery produces an unpleasant visceral reaction; although it should be noted that for many of us the detailed visualization of any kind of surgery—a bypass operation, an abortion, a sex change, a breast implantation, a face lift, or even a decorative eyebrow or tongue piercing—produces an unpleasant visceral reaction. In other words, merely contemplating a surgery, especially on the face or the genitals, can be quite upsetting or revolting, even when the surgery seems fully justified from our own "native point of view."

In the United States and Europe, the practice of female genital surgery has been disparaged as "mutilation" (Hosken 1993; Rosenthal 1995). It has been associated with rape and torture and with the nightmare of some brutal patriarchal male (or perhaps a Victorian gynecologist) grabbing a young woman or girl, pulling her into the back room screaming and kicking, and using a knife or razor blade to deprive her of her sexuality. Various dramatic and disturbing claims have been made about the health hazards and harmful side effects of African genital operations, including the loss of a capacity to experience sexual pleasure.

Saying "yuck" to the practice has become a symbol of opposition to the oppression of women and of one's support for their emancipation around the world. Eliminating this practice thus has become a high priority for many Western feminists (and for some human rights activists in Africa, who very often, although not invariably, come from noncircumcising ethnic groups) and for some human rights organizations (for example, Amnesty International and Equality Now). Even some international organizations such as WHO and UNICEF have agreeably responded to the anti-FGM call to arms and have felt morally justified in expanding their mission statements to include the extermination of female circumcision as part of their own crusade. The technique for mission expansion is simple and direct. If their official aim is to rid the world of sickness, female circumcision gets classified as a health hazard or a disease. If their official aim is to protect political prisoners from torture, African parents get classified as "torturers" and African children defined as political prisoners held captive, coerced, and "mutilated" by their relatives.

Outside of Africa, especially in the United States and Europe, righteous opposition to female circumcision has become so commonplace and so politically correct that until very recently most anti-anti-FGM criticism has been defensive, superficial, or basically sympathetic. The sympathetic criticisms are mainly critiques of counter-productive "eradication" tactics. They provide advice on how to be more effective as an anti-FGM activist. For example, activists Susan Rich and Stephanie Joyce give this recommendation on how to gain the trust of African villagers in areas where circumcision is customary: bring them "malarial medicine, radios, and other gifts to 'smooth the path'" but wait until the sixth visit before you drop any hints about why you are really there (Rich and Joyce n.d., 4).

Under such circumstances, the potential for counterproductive activism is great. For example, Daniel Arap Moi, the president of Kenya, has twice tried to ban female (although not male) circumcision, and without great success. His second attempt was in 1989. In a top-down gesture of political authority (and perhaps with an eye toward the West), he denounced the custom, and the next day thousands of girls from ethnic groups with a tradition of circumcision stepped forward to be initiated, as a form of social, moral, and political protest.

There have also been occasional complaints that anti-FGM campaigns displace attention and take resources away from battles against social injustice in the United States and Europe (for example, Tamir 1996). And there have been expressions of concern about the anguished state of mind of African children living in the United States who are told by the media and by social service agencies that their own mother is "mutilated" and potentially dangerous to them too (Beyene 1999).

But these types of criticisms do not go very deep. In general, the purported facts about female circumcision go unquestioned, the moral implications of the case are thought to be obvious, and the mere query, "What about FGM?" is presumed to function in and of itself as a knockdown argument against both cultural pluralism and any inclination toward tolerance.[2]

## SO WHAT ABOUT FGM?

I shall treat this query as a real question deserving a detailed and considered response rather than as a rhetorical inquiry intended to shorten or terminate debate. For starters, the practice of genital alteration is a rather poor example of gender inequality or of society discriminating against women. Surveying the world, one finds few cultures, if any, where genital surgeries are performed exclusively on girls, although many cultures perform such surgeries only on boys or on both sexes. Male genital alterations often take place in adolescence and can involve major modifications (including subincision, in which the penis is split along the line of the urethra). Considering the prevalence, timing, and intensity of the relevant initiation rites and viewed on a worldwide scale, one is hard pressed to argue that this is an obvious instance of a gender inequity disfavoring girls. Quite the contrary; social recognition of the ritual transformation of both boys and girls into a more mature status as empowered men and women often is a major point of the ceremony. In other words, female circumcision, when and where it occurs in Africa, is much more a case of society treating boys and girls *equally* before the common law and inducting them into responsible adulthood in parallel ways.

The practice is also a poor example of patriarchal domination. Many patriarchal cultures in Europe and Asia do not engage in genital alterations at all, or (as in the case of Jews, many non-African Muslims, and many African ethnic groups) deliberately exclude girls from this highly valued practice and perform the surgery only on boys. Moreover, the African ethnic groups that circumcise both females and males are very different from one another in kinship, religion, economy, family life, ceremonial practice, and so forth. Some are Islamic, some are not. Some are patriarchal, some—such as the Kono, a matrilineal society—are not. Some have formal initiations into well-established women's organizations, some do not. (On the connection between circumcision and entrance into powerful women's secret societies in Sierra Leone see Ahmadu 2000.) Some care greatly about female purity, sexual restraint outside of marriage, and the social regulation of desire, but others (such as Kenyatta's [K]Gikuyu) are more relaxed about premarital sexual play and are not puritanical.

Indeed, in cases of female initiation and genital alterations, the practice almost always is controlled, performed, and most strongly upheld by women, although male kin often provide material and moral support. Typically, however, men have little to do with these female operations, may not know very much about them, and may feel it is not really their business to interfere to try to tell their wives, mothers, aunts, and grandmothers what to do. Rather, the women of the society are the cultural experts in this intimate feminine domain, and they are not particularly inclined to give up power or share their secrets.

In those cases of female genital alterations with which I am most familiar (having lived and taught in Kenya, where the practice is routine for some ethnic groups; see Kenyatta 1938; Kratz 1994; Thomas 2000; Walley 1997), adolescent girls who undergo the ritual initiation look forward to it. The ordeal can be painful (especially if done without anesthesia), but it is viewed as a test of courage. This is an event organized and controlled by women, who have their own view of the aesthetics of the body—a different view from ours about what is civilized, dignified, and beautiful. The girl's parents are not trying to be cruel to their daughter—African parents love their children too. No one is raped or tortured. Indeed, a celebration surrounds the event.

What about the devastating negative effects on health and sexuality so vividly portrayed in the anti-FGM literature? Relatively few methodologically sound studies exist on the consequences of female genital surgeries on sexuality and health. As Obermeyer (1999) discovered in her medical review, most of the published literature is "data-free" or else relies on sensational testimonials, second-hand reports, or inadequate samples. Judged against basic epidemiological research standards, much of the published empirical evidence—including some of the most widely cited publications in the anti-FGM advocacy literature (including the influential 1993 *Hosken Report*)—is fatally flawed (see Obermeyer 1999). Nevertheless, there is some science worth considering in thinking about female circumcision, which leads Obermeyer to conclude that the global discourse about the health and sexual consequences of female circumcision is not sufficiently supplied with credible evidence.

The anti-FGM advocacy literature typically features long lists of short- and long-term medical complications of circumcision, including blood loss, shock, acute infection, menstrual problems, child-bearing difficulties, incontinence, sterility, and death. These lists read like the warning pamphlets that accompany many prescription drugs, which enumerate every claimed negative side effect of the medicine that has ever been reported (no matter how infrequently). They are very scary to read, and they are very misleading. Stomach-churning, anxiety-provoking lists of possible medical complications aside, Obermeyer's comprehensive review of the literature on the actual frequency and risk of medical complications following genital surgery in Africa suggests that medical complications are the exception and not the rule, that African children do not die because they have been circumcised (rather, they die from malnutrition, war, and disease), and that the experience of sexual pleasure is compatible with the genital aesthetics and related practices of circumcising groups.

Obermeyer's conclusions converge with the findings of the very recent large-scale Medical Research Council study of the long-term reproductive health consequences of female circumcision (Morison et al. 2001). The study, conducted in the Gambia, compared circumcised women with those who were uncircumcised. In the Gambia the surgery most often involves a full clitoridectomy and either partial or complete excision of the labia minora. More than 1,100 women (ages fifteen to fifty-four) from three ethnic groups (Mandinka, Wolof, and Fula) were interviewed and also given gynecological examinations and laboratory tests. Very few differences were discovered in the reproductive health status of circumcised versus uncircumcised women. As noted in the research report, the supposed morbidities (such as infertility, painful sex, vulval tumors, menstrual problems, incontinence, and most endogenous infections) often cited by anti-FGM advocacy groups as common long-term problems of female circumcision did not distinguish between circumcised and uncircumcised women. The authors of the report caution anti-FGM activists against exaggerating the morbidity and mortality risks of the practice (see also Larsen and Yan 2000).

These findings are consistent with Edgerton's comments about female circumcision among the [K]Gikuyu in Kenya in the 1920s and 1930s, when Western missionaries first launched their own version of "FGM eradication programs." As Edgerton (1989, 40) remarks, the operation was performed without anesthesia and hence was very painful, "yet most girls bore it bravely and few suffered serious infection or injury as a result. Circumcised women did not lose their ability to enjoy sexual relations, nor was their child-bearing capacity diminished. Nevertheless the practice offended Christian sensibilities."

In other words, the standard alarmist claims in the anti-FGM advocacy literature that African traditions of circumcision have "maimed or killed untold numbers of women and girls" (Rich and Joyce n.d., 1) and deprived them of their sexuality may not be true. Given the most reliable (even if limited) scientific evidence at hand, these claims should be viewed with skepticism and not accepted as fact, no matter how many times they are uncritically recapitulated on the editorial pages of the *New York Times* or poignantly invoked on PBS.

If genital alteration in Africa really were a long-standing cultural practice in which parents, oblivious to intolerably high risks, disabled and murdered their pre-adolescent and adolescent children, there would be good reason to wish for its quick end. Carla Obermeyer's review suggests that this line of attack on the practice may be as fanciful as it is nightmarish, or, at the very least, dubious and misleading.

In their reactions to this African cultural practice, the anti-FGM advocacy groups behave much like yesterday's Christian missionaries. Given the importance of accurate information in public policy debates in liberal democracies, now would be a good time for them to either revise their factoids or else substantiate their claims with rigorously collected data. An organization such as Amnesty International (USA) discredits itself as a balanced and reliable source of information when it begins playing the "factoid game; they do this when they recycle pseudo-evidence, posting website bulletins such as, "In Egypt the practices of clitoridectomy and excision predominate and dozens of FGM-related deaths have been reported in the press." One hopes for a more critical assessment of the unsubstantiated claim that female circumcision is a serious threat to the lives of children. The real facts, I would suggest, are quite otherwise. With regard to the consequences of genital surgeries, the weight of the evidence suggests that the overwhelming majority of youthful female initiates in countries such as Mali, Kenya, and Sierra Leone believe they have been improved (physically, socially, and spiritually) by the ceremonial ordeal and symbolic process (including the pain) associated with initiation. Evidence indicates that most of these youthful initiates manage to be (in their own estimation) "improved" without disastrous or major negative consequences for their health (Larsen and Yan 2000; Morison et al 2001; Obermeyer 1999). This is not to say that we should not worry about the documented 4 percent to 16 percent urinary infection rate associated with these surgeries, or the 7 percent to 13 percent of cases in which there was excessive bleeding, or the 1 percent rate of septicemia (see Obermeyer 1999, 93). It would be instructive, however, to compare these rates with rates of infection and bleeding for other types of less controversial Third World surgeries. The reaction of many people to unsafe abortions, for example, is not to do away with abortions. Perhaps some pro-life advocates might be tempted by the argument that because some abortions are unsafe, there should be no abortions at all. However, a far more reasonable reaction to unsafe abortions is to make them safe. Why not the same reaction in the case of female genital alterations? Infections and other medical complications that arise from unsanitary surgical procedures or malpractice can be corrected without depriving "others" of rites and meanings central to their culture, personal identities, and their overall sense of well-being. What I do want to suggest, however, is that the current sense of shock, horror and righteous "Western" indignation directed against the mothers of Mali, Somalia, Egypt, Sierra Leone, Ethiopia, the Gambia, and the Sudan is misguided, and rather disturbingly misinformed.

## THE ENLIGHTENED FIRST WORLD AND THE DARK CONTINENT

Fifty years after the end of colonial rule, many First World intellectuals still think of Africa as the Dark Continent and imagine that genital surgery is a Dark Age

practice supported mainly by those who are unenlightened, uneducated, ignorant, and unsophisticated. Yet, contrary to such expectations, not only the uneducated, rural, or poor women of Africa promote the gender identity of their
children and grandchildren and celebrate their coming of age in this way. As
Jomo Kenyatta pointed out long ago, in many African ethnic groups, even high-
status, highly educated members of the community remain committed to these
ceremonies (see Ahmadu 2000). Meinardus (1967, 393) notes that in the eighteenth and nineteenth centuries, female circumcision was "universal in Egypt
and that it was adhered to by members of all social classes extending from
Lower Egypt to Aswan." From the viewpoint of education, urbanization, and
economic development, a good deal has changed in Egypt since the eighteenth
century. The prevalence rate of female (and male) circumcision, however, has
remained pretty much the same. Obermeyer (1999) points out that female genital
alterations are common even among the most educated groups of women in a
number of countries. She notes that one cannot assume that more schooling
necessarily will result in a dramatic reduction in the prevalence of genital surgery in a population for which it has been a customary practice. She indicates a
90 percent prevalence rate in Egypt for women with a secondary school education or beyond.

Dirie and Lindmark (1991, 70) make a similar point with regard to Somalia,
noting, "Early studies have revealed that education and economic status have no
influence on the practice of female circumcision, and the present study supports
these findings." It is probably a mistake to expect that in Mali, Sierra Leone, or
Egypt, women are going to give up a practice central to their sense of personal
dignity and cultural identity just because they have received a high school di-
ploma or even a Ph.D.

The following historical observation appears in a research report about circumcision in Nigeria (Olamijuto, Joiner, and Oyedeji 1983, 581).

> In December 1929, a British parliamentary committee, formed to study con-
> ditions of women and children in the crown colonies, strongly lobbied the
> British Government to take steps to, among other things, abolish circumci-
> sion of girls in Africa. In his contribution to the British effort, A. C. Burns,
> the then Deputy Governor of Nigeria, expressed optimism that the practice
> would disappear with advance in education.

The authors point out that the British deputy governor's prediction has not
come true, despite fifty years of top-down political concerns and a sharp rise in
literacy since free primary education was introduced in 1955. It is noteworthy
that in the face of "white man's burden" Christian missionary and colonial government efforts in Kenya and Nigeria in the 1920s, the customary practice of
female circumcision turned out to be highly resistant to either coaxed or forced
change. This was true even for sophisticated and educated members of society
(Kenyatta 1938; Ahmadu 2000; Thomas 2000).

Jewish circumcision practices have a similar profile. Throughout millennia,

Jews have continued to circumcise sons despite variations in the historical context of their lives. Jews continue to circumcise their male offspring despite imagined medical benefits or harms (the medical establishment has not been consistent) and regardless of dominant majority opinion, which at times viewed them as "mutilators" of babies and their practice as "barbaric" (see Gilman 1999; Gollaher 2000, ch. 1). Among Jews, when it comes to circumcision, it does not matter whether you are rich or poor, urban or rural, educated or uneducated, religious or secular. And it does not really matter what the medical establishment or Amnesty International or the Save the Children Fund happen to think. If you are Jewish, you circumcise your son. The practice has to do with a covenant between Jews and their God, and it has to do (as Kenyatta put it) with "the whole teaching of tribal law, religion and morality" (Kenyatta 1938, 133).

One should not expect less from other cultural traditions, especially those that are already equitable in their ritual treatment of the sexes—where girls too are promoted in this way into full membership in society. It is not ignorance that keeps the practice of female circumcision going, any more than it is ignorance that has kept male circumcision going for over three thousand years, even among highly educated Jews. Indeed, circumcision is an issue over which even the most highly educated and rational people can reasonably disagree.

## THE FIRST WORLD CURRICULUM ON NORMAL BODIES

When considering the connection between education and attitudes toward circumcision, it is useful to ask, "What precisely do we think these women in Sierra Leone (or in Mali or the Gambia or Somalia) don't know about normal human bodies?" And what might an enlightened curriculum incorporating the latest knowledge from our social, biological, and medical sciences offer that would change these women's minds about the importance and benefits of circumcision? Here I confess that I find it hard to imagine and to describe such a curriculum without sounding sardonic, or at least ironical, but I will try.

For example, perhaps we might teach them that we in the "First World" had a medicine man named Dr. Sigmund Freud, who taught us that women really want to be men and suffer from something called *penis envy*. On second thought, this is probably not a good idea, as Freud's thesis is a disempowering claim that circumcised African women may well have proved wrong.

Perhaps we might teach them that normal human beings don't engage in cosmetic surgery. Yet, could we say that with a straight face, when there are thousands of aesthetic surgeries licensed by the American Medical Association, including clitoridectomies for young women who don't like the way their genitals look or feel?

Or perhaps we might teach them that a genital alteration makes it impossible to enjoy sex—but where is the scientific evidence to support that claim? Obermeyer (1999) searched for it in vain. One suspects that the claim derives from our own ethno-anatomical folk beliefs rather than from any hard science. Most highly educated "First World" intellectuals are not biologists, and typically, most highly educated nonbiologists underestimate the true size and anatomical depth of the clitoris, much of the tissue structure of which (about 50 percent) is not external or visible to the human eye—thus much of it remains intact after any external modification of the genitals (Shell-Duncan and Hernlund 2000a, 26–27). Indeed, in spite of a lack of systematic investigations into this topic, circumcised African women have talked about their sexual experiences in ways that strongly suggest that they can and do enjoy sex (Ahmadu 2000; Edgerton 1989, 254; Lightfoot-Klein 1989; Gruenbaum 2001, 139–43).

Or perhaps we could teach these women that the medical risks of circumcision are too great to tolerate. Yet it seems likely that the risk of death associated with these operations compares quite favorably with the risks associated with many activities that are routine in our own lives, such as driving a car. Moreover, circumcised African women likely know that most initiates do not suffer medical complications from the surgery, as Obermeyer (1999) has shown (see also Morison et al. 2001). Malpractice does occur, of course, and these and other Third World operations certainly are not risk-free: Asma El Dareer (1982, iii) had a bad experience with circumcision, having developed an infection that was then treated with five injections of penicillin administered by the registered Sudanese nurse who performed the operation. Yet her experience is atypical. Most circumcised African women know that unsafe procedures can be made safer—without doing away with the practice.

Or we could teach African women that (without anesthesia) a circumcision ceremony is extremely painful and will leave them with scars—a customary point of the initiation ceremony of which they are fully aware, since the rite is a test of their courage and a proof of adulthood. This gives them an opportunity to prove to themselves and to others (including their parents) that they are tough enough to be adults.

Moreover, where female genital alterations are customary, the women don't view their scars as mutilations. With regard to West Africa, Koso-Thomas (1987, 55) writes,

> [The scar] may even be a stamp of identification for admission to other branches of the [women's secret] society, and, therefore, may be sought after. It is traditional for youths to mark and scar themselves as a sign of courage and endurance; women's initiation societies also include training in these qualities. Thus they see no disadvantage in being scarred.

Will higher schooling be designed to teach women that sexual behavior has nothing to do with honor or fertility? The anthropological literature on female circumcision contains some useful discussions of cultural variations in conceptions of the body and in the socially constructed ideals of sexual gratification associated with personal well-being (Parker 1995, 519–20; Boddy 1982, 1989, 1996; see also Lâm 1994). For women in many societies, the womb is thought to be the body part that is the biological essence of femininity and is treasured because of its association with fertility, fecundity, and the project of social reproduction. This is not true for all women, particularly in the United States and Europe. As a result of the women's liberation movement in the 1960s in the United States and Europe, a variation on the ethnoanatomy of femininity was constructed according to which the womb was devalued precisely because it was associated with "bad" things, such as big families, domesticity, and a sexual division of labor in which women stayed at home and were not paid for their work. A new body part—the clitoris—was valorized and reconceptualized as the biological essence of femininity and associated with "good" things, such things as autonomy, sexual freedom, orgasm, and even an independent capacity for pleasurable self-stimulation.

In effect, for a particular subculture of women in the West, the clitoris became the ultimate symbol of female emancipation from men, marriage, and the domestic life. During the 1960s, 1970s, and 1980s, this conception of femininity and its symbolic anatomy emerged and was embraced by many in the professional and white middle class in the United States and Europe. It was even embraced by women who in any other context would strongly oppose all forms of "essentialism" and "biological reductionism" and reject the idea that there is only one way to have normal sexual relations, or only one ideal body type for all women.

To avoid misunderstanding I wish to emphasize that I am not raising an objection to the aims of the women's liberation movement, or to the view that love and sex can be separated from marriage and pursued for their own sake. Nor is this meant to be a criticism of the doctrine of hedonism. I am simply reiterating a central message of many gender studies programs at colleges and universities in the United States. The point here is that definitions of femininity (or masculinity) and of normal sexual relations are essentially contestable. There is no single, essential, inherent or universally binding objective ideal for femininity or masculinity. Hence, it is hard to see why any one particular set of aims, views, and doctrines about sex, marriage, and femininity should be embraced by all rational human beings, regardless of cultural or religious background. Where and when norms are essentially contestable, education is not going to make difference go away.

Finally, to bring this travesty of education to an end, perhaps an enlightened school curriculum might teach African men and women that from an objective point of view uncircumcised genitals (male and female) are really beautiful. I am not even sure that most educated people in Europe and the United States really believe that, but let's assume they do. Is that attitude something you should learn in school? What we currently teach in our finest (and most liberal) colleges is that "beauty is in the eye of the beholder," and that Western eyes (or Christian missionary eyes or American feminist eyes) are not the only ones that count.

A good education certainly can correct erroneous beliefs. Some African men undoubtedly have fantastical views about what will happen to a woman's clitoris (its ultimate size) if she is not circumcised. There are also African men who share with many American men and women an incomplete picture of the anatomical structure of the clitoris and subscribe to the false belief that circumcised women do not enjoy sex. Perhaps also some women in Egypt, Somalia, or the Sudan choose infibulation as the preferred mode of genital surgery only because they subscribe to groundless views about the hazards of an unprotected or open vagina for reproduction and fertility. Challenging such beliefs is a good idea. Nevertheless, it will not bring an end to genital surgeries, because the main reasons for those surgeries and the initiation ceremonies in which they play their part have little to do with such mistaken beliefs.

Within ethnic groups that have a tradition of circumcision, prevalence rates are typically high; within groups that do not have this tradition, the rates approximate zero. For this reason, ethnic group membership (rather than education or literacy or socioeconomic status) is the best predictor of whether or not you circumcise. From the distribution of circumcision practices and beliefs both within and across societies in Africa and around the world, circumcision is one of those "path-dependent" phenomena that institutional economists talk about. Whichever way a social group happens to evolve (circumcise versus don't circumcise), the costs of going against the local current are very high and the benefits of being within the community's definition of "normal" are substantial.

This is not simply a matter of self-interested instrumental calculation—although deliberate cost-benefit analysis of the type described by Mackie (2000) likely plays a part in the perpetuation of the traditions of a social group. Within each of the two types of social groups described here—circumcising versus non-circumcising—is a developed set of attitudes, beliefs, and feelings about what is considered normal versus alien.

The psychological by-product of this type of divergent cultural evolution is a mutual "yuck" response between different ethnic groups. Majority populations in London and Paris feel repulsed or offended by (or at least out of sympathy with) the behavior of majority populations in Cairo or Timbuktu, and vice versa. The same is true within multicultural nation-states for the reactions of majority and minority groups to each other. Witness, for example, the adverse reaction of middle-class feminists in the United States to an American hospital proposal to allow Somali immigrant parents—with the informed consent and approval of their daughter—to safely and painlessly perform a minor and culturally meaningful genital surgery (see Coleman 1998). From a medical point of view, the proposed procedure (a small cut in the prepuce that covers the clitoris) was less severe than a typical American male circumcision. Nevertheless, the mainstream response to the unfamiliar practice was intensely negative, and the proposal, developed at Harborview Medical Center in Seattle, was discarded. The practice, however, is not unfamiliar for most in the Somali immigrant community, and many Somalis, male and female, living in the United States, deem a genital alteration to be practically and emotionally essential for their sense of dignity and well-being.

Perhaps that says something about the way communities are held together and perpetuate themselves through sex and marriage, which presupposes the sharing and coordination of very intimate judgments about what is beautiful or ugly, good or bad, honorable or dishonorable, and so forth.

The result, however, is that there are rational and morally decent people on both sides of this cultural divide. This may be the kind of case in which those who are rational, moral, and divided, but also wise, permit each other enough space to live and let live, and to disagree reasonably. Liberal free-thinking people in the United States need to debate openly the validity of that last suggestion— that a politically liberal, pluralistic society needs to accommodate both circumcising and noncircumcising ethnic groups and their associated cultural commitments and religious beliefs.

## IMPERIAL LIBERALISM AND ITS TOTALITARIAN IMPLICATIONS

In his book on the foundations of political liberalism, the philosopher John Rawls (1993, 61) cautions us, "it is unreasonable for us to use political power, should we possess it, or share it with others, to repress comprehensive doctrines [conceptions of the world elaborated from different standpoints] that are not unreasonable." Rawls contrasts *political liberalism* with *comprehensive liberalism*. Political liberalism means the minimum ground rules for social cooperation among free and equal citizens in a genuinely pluralistic democracy. Comprehensive liberalism is a particular and single-minded doctrine about the proper selection and ordering of values, and about ideals for a good life. I wish to invoke a further contrast between political liberalism (as Rawls defines it) and *imperial liberalism*.

Imperial liberalism is the general attitude that it is desirable for us to spread and enforce our liberal conceptions and ideals for the good life in all corners of society and throughout the world. More specifically, imperial liberalism is the doctrine that all social institutions and dimensions of social life (not just political but associational and family life as well) should be ruled by principles of autonomy, individualism, and equality—and by the particular ordering of values and ideals for gender identity, sexuality, work, reproduction, and family life embraced by liberal men and women in the United States today; and that those liberal principles and conceptions should be upheld using the coercive power of the state and, if possible, exported to foreign lands using the coercive powers of international institutions (such as the World Bank, the IMF, NATO, and the United Nations).

From such a stance of imperial liberalism, Susan Okin (1999, 14), for example, implies that virginity, domesticity, childbearing, and fidelity to marriage should not be selected as high ideals anywhere in the world. From the same imperial stance, Katha Pollitt (1999, 29–30) suggests that secular governments around the world should empower children to be autonomous and free of their parents' influence and religious beliefs. Pollitt especially would like to empower children against illiberal Muslim parents who subscribe to such notions as female modesty, family honor, and sexual restraint, and therefore want their daughters to wear a head scarf, or hijab, in school. This is the same stance, to cite a third example, that leads Olayinka Koso-Thomas (1987, 2) to discredit the women of

Sierra Leone for actually choosing to perpetuate the customs of their ethnic groups and to admonish them for not using their full voting rights and political power to liberate themselves from "tradition."

The imperial messages of this type of comprehensive liberalism are simple and powerful, and they appeal to many progressive secular individualists and cosmopolitan elites in the postmodern world. These messages may be summed up as follows.

- Acknowledging social distinctions is invidious and implies vicious discrimination.

- Where there are ethnic groups and social categories let there be individuals.

- Where there are individuals let them transcend their tradition-bound commitments and experience the quality of their lives solely in secular and ecumenical terms (for example, as measured by health or wealth or years of life).

Given that particular imperial liberal view of the world, Fuambai Ahmadu's self-empowering act of initiation into Kono womanhood, West African–style, can only seem retrograde, like a glimpse at some unwelcome and archaic past, when the marks of social, cultural, and gender identity ran deep into both body and soul.

Political liberals, I believe, ought to be concerned about the totalitarian implications of imperial liberalism. They should worry about the coercion that would be needed to enforce the imperial doctrine that our gender ideals are best, that our ideas about sexuality and reproduction are best, that our ideas about work and family are best, and moreover, good for everyone. They should be especially cautious with such an emotionally charged and poorly understood issue as circumcision (both male and female), where the temptation to demonize others and impose one's will is especially great and there is a general reluctance to recognize the particularity, even the peculiarity, of one's own point of view.

But to reasonably debate the issue, we need first to discount, or at least bracket, our own culturally shaped visceral reactions to the very thought of female genital alterations. If we don't, there will be no fair, informed, and even-handed engagement with the voices of the many African women who think that an "eradication program," or a threat to withdraw foreign aid, or a prison sentence, or some other means of compulsion, are not really appropriate responses to their valued way of life, and may be more a measure of our brutality and barbarism than theirs.

## SHOULD WE TOLERATE IT HERE?

Any public debate in the United States about female genital alterations must address the question: How much toleration of the practice ought to be reasonable in the context of the scientific, medical, legal, and moral traditions of a politically liberal, pluralistic democracy such as the United States?

On the scientific front, we have good reason to discount the horrifying representations in the anti-FGM advocacy literature. The most plausible account of the facts is that a real cultural divide exists in the world in moral, emotional, and aesthetic reactions to female (and male) genital alterations. What is thought to be virtuous, rational, beautiful, and normal by most members of some ethnic groups is seen as vicious, ignorant, ugly, and abnormal by most members of other ethnic groups. As a result of labor migration and the flow of political refugees, this cultural divide has reproduced itself within several European countries (for example, France and Norway) and in the United States, to the detriment of those minority groups who uphold the practice.

As discussed earlier, despite evidence that suggests circumcision is a source of esteem for men and women and that women are not typically injured or sexually incapacitated by the surgery, the practice of female circumcision continues to offend the sensibilities of majority populations in the "First World." If that evidence is reliable (and clearly we need more and better research on these issues), then every "political liberal" has a responsibility to ask whether an offense to one's own culturally shaped sensibilities alone is sufficient reason to eradicate someone else's way of life.

On the medical front, the issue is straightforward. Genital alterations for both girls and boys can be done safely, hygienically, and without major risks to physical health. Cosmetic genital surgeries for women are not customary in the United States, but cosmetic surgeons know how to do them, and they are safely done. Given the state of our medical sciences, unwanted pain can be controlled or eliminated. For some young women, however, enduring the pain may continue to be part of the point of the experience, just as it is for others who endure tests of courage and character, such as running a marathon.

Another relevant, less obvious scientific fact has to do with the justification of male circumcision and its bearing on claims about gender equity. One widely held folk belief in the United States is that surgical removal of the foreskin of the penis protects the health of men, but this is not strongly supported by evidence. During the 1990s, about 65 percent of male babies in the United States were circumcised, and the medical establishment did little to discourage the dubious claim that circumcision is salubrious for males. In fact, the medical case for male circumcision is so flimsy that in other English-speaking countries such as Canada, England, and Australia, medical doctors do not typically recommend the operation and only about 10 percent to 15 percent of infant boys are circumcised.

A relatively recent set of recommendations of the American Academy of Pediatrics (as of March 1, 1999) reads as follows: "The weight of the evidence would have to be significant for the academy to recommend an elective surgical procedure on every newborn male, and the evidence is not sufficient for us to make such a recommendation." The authors of the AAP recommendations recognize, however, that not all decisions about a normal or properly developed body can be reduced to medical or health criteria. They do not therefore recommend against the elective surgery for males, acknowledging that the decision really rests on religious and cultural grounds, not medical ones.

Thus, on the basis of our medical traditions the following two conclusions may be drawn, both of which will have a bearing on the question of tolerance for female genital alterations: genital surgeries for both males and females can be done safely; and if there are good reasons for the common American practice of male circumcision—as I believe there are—such reasons remain beyond the realm of modern medicine.

What about our legal and moral traditions? United States Supreme Court Justice William Brennan (*Michael H. v. Gerald D.*, 491 U.S. 110, 141 [1989], dissenting) has written, "We are not an assimilative, homogeneous society, but a facilitative, pluralistic one, in which we must be willing to abide someone else's unfamiliar and even repellent practice because the same tolerant impulse protects our own idiosyncrasies." Justice Brennan's pluralistic ideals may be theoretically appealing, but in the case of customary African genital alterations, the initial impulse in our society has been intolerant, single-minded, and assimilative in the extreme.

In September 1996, the Congress of the United States, without holding public hearings or seeking expert testimony and certainly without any attempt to understand the "native point of view," passed a statute targeted at the practice of female genital surgery among African immigrants. United States Representative Patricia Schroeder played a significant part formulating and lobbying for the legislation. The law, which went into effect in March 1997, criminalizes "female genital mutilation" and penalizes with fines or a prison sentence (up to five years) anyone who knowingly engages in surgery on any part of the genitals of a female under eighteen years of age. Exceptions are made for established medical practitioners engaging in already established surgical procedures thought to be necessary to the health of the person (for example, surgery on the genitals that might facilitate the delivery of a baby). The law explicitly states that in punishing offenders no account shall be taken of their belief that the surgery is required as a matter of custom or ritual.

In February 1999, a court in Paris went a step further and actually sentenced someone, Hawa Greou, a Malian immigrant who is a ritual circumciser, to eight years in prison. She is a woman whose services as an expert surgeon had been sought by other women in her ethnic group. The stiff prison sentence was imposed by the court despite the fact that neither Hawa Greou nor most other Malians believed she was morally culpable or had done any harm.

The *New York Times* journalist Celia Dugger writes that when passing "The Federal Prohibition of Female Genital Mutilation Act," the U.S. Congress also required "United States representatives to the World Bank and other international financial institutions that have lent billions of dollars to the 28 African countries where the practice exists to oppose loans to governments that have not carried out educational programs to prevent it" (Dugger 1996, A1). Further, in recent years the State Department's Annual Report on Human Rights has been publishing a list of African governments that have officially banned female genital alterations. Through the use of carrots and sticks, various First World international agencies and ambassadors who think that circumcision is a human rights violation have been actively trying to induce or force the political leaders of Africa to comply with our desire to eradicate their custom. Indeed, in response to pressure from international benefactors, some African governments (for example, Egypt, Senegal, Togo, Côte D'Ivoire) have agreed to prohibit female circumcision. The list of formally compliant African governments grows. Understandably, this gesture is not appreciated by a considerable number of women (and their male kinsmen) in these countries, which may explain why many African officials under pressure from the First World pass the required laws, take the money, then don't do anything. This is one way that tactical African leaders react to an unwelcome, unpopular, or difficult-to-implement yet unavoidable external demand in a situation of enormous material enticement or unequal bargaining power.

This rush to criminalize and penalize African female genital surgeries is distressing for several reasons. First, as we have seen, the decision is based on unsupported claims about the consequences of the genital surgery and highly dubious representations of African customs.

Second, the federal statute in the United States appears to be targeted at and causes selective injury to African immigrant and minority groups. The law treats their ritual life (and associated ideas about beauty, honor, femininity, marriage, and family life) with official contempt. The ban thereby causes distress to relatively powerless African immigrant families while allowing more highly placed citizens to make use of the coercive power of the state to further their particular single-minded vision of the good life.

Finally, by selectively criminalizing and penalizing female but not male genital surgeries, our lawmakers have overlooked several important normative issues that ought to guide any just consideration of this provocative and controversial case.

How might a fair consideration of the case proceed? To start such a discussion, it is useful to draw some distinctions between types of body alterations, in particular between: consensual versus nonconsensual alterations; major versus minor alterations; and reversible versus nonreversible alterations. With these distinctions in place, the following type of argument can be made in favor of limited toleration.

In order for the argument for limited toleration to succeed, one must first secure agreement on the following three principles.

Principle 1. *Certain types of genital alterations are permissible for boys.* Thus, for parents to surgically remove the foreskin of a male infant is permissible, even though the infant has not given consent, even though the procedure is irreversible, and even though no compelling medical justification exists for performing the operation. Circumcision is permissible in this case because the alteration is minor in two senses. From a medical viewpoint, the procedure is easy to perform and, aside from some short-term pain (in the absence of anesthesia), the operation is inconsequential with regard to its effects on basic biological functioning. The procedure also is minor from the viewpoint of social and psychological functioning, in the sense that circumcised males remain perfectly capable of attaining mental health and participating in a normal social life.

Male circumcision in infancy also is permissible because in our liberal pluralistic society we are willing to respect the cultural and religious traditions of the family, acknowledging and respecting, for example, the idea that circumcision is what Jewish people do to their sons because of their covenant with their God. Moreover, circumcision is permissible because we are willing to make room for family privacy and leave child care to parents rather than to the state, except under extreme circumstances. Indeed, in the case of infant male circumcision the procedure is so commonplace and tolerated that a sufficient reason for conducting the surgery is that the father does not want his son's genitals to look different from his own, or simply because he thinks it looks good.

This is not to suggest that this principle is incontestable or has never been contested. There are and have been anti–male circumcision advocates who view the removal of the foreskin as a mutilation. These advocates and other activists in the anti–male circumcision movement are prepared to be unmoved by claims of religious freedom, cultural rights, family privacy, or pluralism, and they seem prepared to disparage and castigate all religious and cultural traditions in which male circumcision is condoned. This is not a new phenomenon. Various historical and virulent attacks on Judaism (for example, the severe penalties imposed on mohels [one who is ordained to perform circumcisions] and mothers of circumcised infants by Antiochus Epiphanes, the ruler of Judea in the second century B.C.; and the English "Jew Bill" of 1753) have been associated with assaults on the practice of male circumcision (Gollaher 2000, 15, 28).

Moreover, it is quite possible for a surgical procedure to be minor in the two senses previously mentioned (biological and social functioning are not fundamentally impaired) yet still be substantial in its social implications. Imagine if Jews lived as a small minority group in a society where only Jews circumcised their sons. Imagine also that as a matter of cultural aesthetics and individual taste (judgments of beauty and ugliness, attraction and disgust), most non-Jewish women in this society were personally disinclined to marry a circumcised male and most Jewish women personally disinclined to marry an uncircumcised male. Then this minor medical procedure in effect would amount to a significant parental and cultural influence on the personal marriage choices of children and effectively would help perpetuate a sense of in-group identity and social distinction.

Sander Gilman (1999, 53), in a critique of some intellectual tempers that are much like the stance of imperial liberalism, quotes an Italian physician of the late nineteenth century who writes,

> I shout and shall continue to shout at the Hebrews, until my last breath: Cease mutilating yourselves: cease imprinting upon your flesh an odious brand to distinguish you from other men; until you do this you cannot pretend to be our equal. As it is, you, of your own accord, with the branding iron from the first days of your lives, proceed to proclaim yourselves a race apart, one that cannot, and does not care to, mix with ours.

Under such circumstances, in which the distinctive family life practices of different ethnic groups result in the development of divergent tastes that then function as personal inhibitions to marrying outside the group, would we want the government to step in to level the playing field? This could be done in either of two ways, mandating circumcision for all males in society or, alternatively, banning male circumcision for all. Under the banner of justice and equality in marriage choices, the law might require all American citizens to circumcise their sons or, alternatively, the government could just criminalize the ancient Jewish custom and start throwing Jewish circumcisers in prison along with Malian women, for up to five years. The latter alternative is the more likely, given that Jews are a small minority group. In either case, the government, in its wisdom, would be trying to ensure that men and women from different ethnic backgrounds find each other attractive so that patterns of preferential in-group marriage (like marrying like, on the basis of tastes and preferences acquired by virtue of ethnic background) would disappear from society. In either case, the state in effect would be promoting the cultural assimilation of Jews, and of any other minority group, bound together by selective marriage preferences related to its distinctive way of life. Perhaps even some imperial liberals might balk at that prospect.

Nevertheless, principle 1 as stated allows for minor genital alterations for boys, regardless of any social implications that may follow (unless the surgery makes it impossible for the person to have a meaningful and rewarding social life, in which case the social consequences of circumcision cannot be overlooked).

Principle 2. *Major body alterations are permissible if you know what you are doing and why such alterations are being done.* In other words, it is permissible for someone who has reached the appropriate age for autonomous decision making (or the age at which discretion is permitted, with parental consent) to alter his or her body in ways that are more substantial than would be allowed by principle 1 alone.

At some point in growing up we are granted rights of discretion over our own body. If a girl is old enough to get pregnant, we believe that she is old enough to have considerable discretion (either on her own or with parental backing) over any decision to abort the fetus. If she is old enough to experience her own body as ugly or hideous or distressing (or even just ordinary) and if she is mentally healthy and old enough to be cognizant of the costs and benefits of altering her body, we grant her considerable discretion to do so (either on her own or with parental permission) in major or irreversible ways.

If you have the support of your parents (and even in some cases if you don't), you do not have to wait until you are eighteen to have a breast implant or nose job, pierce your nipples, radically stretch your earlobes, or even engage in a sex-change operation. These more major body alterations are permitted because of *consent.* We believe that people who are old enough to care about themselves ought to be able to have the things they want that make them "happy," by their own lights. This holds true even if the things they want done don't make us happy, as long as the body alterations they bring upon themselves cause us no greater harm than offending our tastes or deviating from our idea of correct body politics.

Principle 3. *No major irreversible alterations of your body should be permitted without your consent.* In other words, we should have a strong presumption against non-consensual alterations of the body that have major consequences for either normal biological functioning or participation in a meaningful and fulfilling social life, and even more so if such alterations are irreversible. (There are some circumstances where even this strong presumption might be overturned—for example, in the case of someone who is unconscious and certain to die unless a leg is amputated.)

If we agree on those three principles, then the prevailing "First World" intolerance and repressive attitudes towards African genital alterations should be looked upon with suspicion. We should at least be willing to listen to the claims of those African immigrant mothers (see Coleman, 1998; Obiora, 1997) who believe that, in a tolerant pluralistic liberal democratic society such as the United States, there ought to be some room for their conceptions of femininity, family life ideals, and ideas of the good life.

For example, if genital alterations are permitted for boys on the grounds of family privacy, religious freedom, and the fact that they are not harmful to health or sexual functioning (principle 1), then to the extent that the same conditions hold, genital alterations should be permitted for girls as well. The determination of which types of procedures or styles of surgery should be allowed should rest entirely on scientific and medical evidence concerning the consequences of different procedures. There is no doubt that there are existing forms of female genital surgery which already are (or can be made to be) no more consequential for health and sexual functioning then the typical male operation as currently practiced in the United States.

Imagine an African mother who holds the following convictions. She believes that her daughters as well as her sons should be able to improve their looks and their marriage prospects, enter into a covenant with God, and be honored as adult members of the community via circumcision. Imagine that her proposed surgical procedure (for example, a cut in the prepuce that covers the clitoris) is no more substantial from a medical point of view than the customary American male operation. Why should we not extend that option to, for example, the Kono parents of daughters as well as to the Jewish parents of sons? This is basically what was proposed at the Harborview Medical Center in Seattle, Washington, until U.S. Representative Patricia Schroeder objected and raised the possibility of a violation of federal law (Coleman, 1998). Nevertheless, principles of gender equity, due process before the law, religious and cultural freedom, and family privacy would seem to support the option. The constitutional status of the federal prohibition remains untested.

And if body alterations such as breast implants or sex change operations are allowable with consent at an appropriate age (principle 2) then why not consensual genital alterations aimed at enhancing beauty and confirming appropriate gender identity (which, for some African immigrants, means getting rid of the male element in the female, and the female element in the male), as long as the procedure is done safely and is compatible with sexual and reproductive functioning? As Obermeyer's (1999) review of the medical evidence suggests, such procedures are not only feasible, they already exist.

Needless to say, there is plenty of room for argument about the appropriate age of discretion and the conditions for establishing informed consent. In ethnic groups with a heritage of both male and female circumcision, the psychological burden of being uncircumcised (of feeling ugly, sexually ambiguous, immature and unmarriageable) is likely to intensify as one begins to sexually mature, which might be a lower bound for an age of discretion (with permission from one's parents). But such issues are not unique to this case. One might start by considering the age at which young people are permitted (with parental consent) to have a breast implant or an abortion or a sex change operation.

There is also plenty of room for argument about what counts as a major body alteration and what counts as minor. There may be types of body alterations that are benign from the point of view of health and sexuality, yet nevertheless radically reduce a person's chances of having a meaningful and rewarding social and family life. Sane and rational parents do not do things to their child's body that they think will ruin the child's life or turn them into "freaks." The more uncertainty there is about whether this body alteration will ruin rather than enhance the child's life, the more the procedure should be viewed as major rather than minor, and the more the need for informed consent (principle 3). In the case of circumcision (for both males and females) the judgment about what is good for your child not only depends upon, but also affects, what is considered by relevant others beautiful or ugly, normal or monstrous. There is little risk that parents will circumcise their children in the absence of a community of relevant others who share the same tastes. Fortunately, there are many ways for men and women to live meaningful social lives without securing universal agreement about the aesthetics of the human body, especially when the body parts in question are private and not meant to be open to everyone's inspection. If happiness in life depended upon being physically attractive to all members of the opposite sex, happiness would be in short supply.

Under this scenario, all circumcisions would be either minor (and hence permissible at an early age) or would have to wait until some reasonable age of consent. Infibulations of young children would be out of the question, although that procedure might be freely chosen after the appropriate age of discretion. As infibulation is a relatively infrequent procedure even in Africa, it seems unlikely that in the United States it would emerge as a popular style of genital alteration. Of course, who would have predicted ear lobe plugs, tongue or nipple piercings or elaborate tattoos to become fashionable in the United States? If you grant to others various liberties or freedoms (of choice, association, expression, religion) and various protections (of bodily privacy), then what they do with and to themselves may offend your (Christian or feminist or bourgeois) sensibilities. It is the price you pay for freedom and equality in a politically liberal democratic society. Under such circumstances, it is the virtue of tolerance that makes it possible for people to be quite different from one another, yet socially cooperate with each other at the same time.

Imagine a sixteen-year-old female Somali teenager living in Seattle who believes that a genital alteration would be "something very great." She likes the look of her mother's body and her recently circumcised cousin's body far better than she likes the look of her own. She wants to be a mature and beautiful woman, Somali style. She wants to marry a Somali man, or at least a man who appreciates the intimate appearances of an initiated woman's body. She wants to show solidarity with other African women who express their sense of beauty, civility, and feminine dignity in this way, and she shares their sense of aesthetics and seemliness. She reviews the medical literature and discovers that the surgery can be done safely, hygienically and with no great effect on her capacity to enjoy sex. After consultation with her parents and the full support of other members of her community, she elects to carry on the tradition. What principle of justice demands that her cultural heritage should be "eradicated" and brought to an end?

## AFRICAN CUSTOMS AND POLITICAL PERSECUTION

In recent years in the United States, two political asylum requests related to female circumcision have been highly publicized, the 1996 case of Fauziya Kassindja, a refugee from Togo, and the 1999 case of Adelaide Abankwah, a refugee from Ghana. These cases are worth examining, in part, because of their peculiarities. (For a more comprehensive discussion of the circumstances surrounding both cases see Kratz, ch. 15 herein.)

The concept of political persecution as it has evolved in political asylum law has little relevance to the circumcision and initiation experiences of most African men and women. As we have seen, African men and women from ethnic groups with a heritage of circumcision generally endorse and identify with the practice and do not construe their own coming of-age ceremonies as forms of political terror—despite what anti-FGM activists have to say about it. Those activists might like to redefine the situation in that way—adding "political persecution" to their discourse about maiming, murder, torture, sexual dysfunction and mutilation—but in general one should beware of characterizing other peoples' valued customs from such an inaccurate, ideologically loaded and ethnocentric point of view. Nevertheless, it is not impossible to imagine extreme or unusual political situations in which either a fear of being forcibly circumcised or, alternatively, of persecution for performing a circumcision (the former Soviet Union penalized Jews for circumcising their sons) might be grounds for an asylum request. Whether that was the case in either of the two most celebrated recent cases is quite another matter.

Legitimate requests for political asylum are supposed to be based on "a well-founded fear of persecution [in one's native land] on account of race, religion, nationality, membership in a particular social group, or political opinion" (*Abankwah v. INS*, U.S. 2d Circuit Court of Appeals, No. 98–4304). The concept of persecution means that you are being unreasonably harmed and unfairly picked on owing simply to one of the aforementioned characteristics, and that no relief is possible short of migration. To consider a not-so-hypothetical case for example, a Chinese couple who is forced by their government to abort the pregnancy of their prospective child might have the basis for a political asylum request. Or, to consider an entirely hypothetical case, a man or woman in some African country who is forced by the government to have a genital alteration against his or her will, he or she might have the basis for a political asylum request as well.

The selective use of the coercive power of the state directed against particular ethnic groups in a country would be an obvious example of persecution. In addition, within any particular country, one might be vulnerable to persecution by organizations other than those of the state, especially if the state is in no position to protect an individual. In Kenya, male circumcision (customarily done in adolescence) is embraced and upheld by all ethnic groups, with the notable exception of the Luo. Imagine the following entirely hypothetical situation. The Kenyan government adopted a policy of forced circumcision of Luo males, rounding them up in adolescence and removing their foreskins so as to make sure that Luo males don't stand apart from any other males in Kenya. Perhaps they do this with the aim of promoting intermarriage between Luos and everyone else, or because health officials convince them that male circumcision reduces the risk of AIDS. Such an action might justify a request for political asylum in the United States.

The merits of the aforementioned types of political asylum cases are contestable. Is the coercive action truly unreasonable, or, for example, can the use of government force be justified in light of a population or health crisis? Is the coercive action arbitrary, discriminatory, or unfair to particular categories of persons, or is it applied to all members of society regardless of race, religion, nationality, or political opinion? Are remedies possible through normal political and legal institutions within the country of origin? Given that race, religion, and nationality are explicitly admissible grounds for establishing "a well-founded fear of persecution," should gender be included as admissible grounds as well? Is a person automatically a member of "a particular social group" simply by virtue of his or her sex? These are the types of tough-minded questions that need to be asked in such cases. Unlike the formal legal restrictions on male circumcision in the former Soviet Union or on childbirth in China, however, African coming-of-age and gender identity ceremonies and procedures are not matters of government policy. In African ethnic groups where both male and female circumcision is part of the cultural landscape, the surgery is customary of family life and social practice, and not a form of political persecution. It may occur so early in life that it never enters consciousness. Or it may occur in middle childhood, where it unfolds as a routine expectation in which parents entice, coax, or if necessary, insist that their child do what well-intended adults in Africa believe is in their child's best interest (just as we entice, coax, and if necessary, force our children to go to school, have their teeth drilled, or undergo a beneficial medical procedure, even when we know it may be painful). Or, as noted earlier, the operation may occur just before or during adolescence and unfold as a test of courage, a source of personal empowerment and an eagerly awaited step into mature adulthood (see Kratz 1994; Johnson 2000). It is not typically the case in Africa that an uncircumcised adult woman who does not want to be circumcised is forced into the operating theater or placed in an intolerably coercive situation where political asylum from her country of origin is the only remedy. Political asylum requests for uncircumcised African females are few and far between, and they tend to arise under strange and unusual (and in some instances, unbelievable) circumstances.

Adelaide Abankwah comes from an ethnic group in Ghana in which women are not circumcised, in a country where a majority of ethnic groups have no tradition of female circumcision, and the government does not endorse the practice. She claimed that she was going to be forcibly circumcised as punishment for not being a virgin, and that she could not receive protection anyplace in Ghana. Anti-FGM advocacy groups such as Equality Now were moved by her incredible and unique story (most of which was undocumented and almost all of which, including her name, turned out to be fraudulent; see Branigin and Farah 2000). Instead of first doing some basic fact-checking, these groups rallied to her side, enlisted celebrity, senatorial, and White House support, and she was granted asylum (see the case of *Adelaide Abankwah v. INS* and related news coverage; see also Kratz, ch. 15 herein).

Other cases seem more meritorious, but they appear to arise from unusual circumstances and reveal little about characteristic features of the local African scene. Fauziya Kassindja is a sympathetic figure from Togo. She asked for political asylum due to an unusual domestic situation in which one part of the family endorsed a tradition of female circumcision while her own parents did not. As a teenager, she grew up with no expectation or anticipation of being circumcised. Nevertheless, when her father died, her father's siblings arranged for her to be married into a family where female circumcision was part of the family tradition. She fled Togo and landed in Newark, New Jersey, where in 1994 Kassindja was arrested for trying to enter the United States illegally (see Kratz, ch. 15 herein). Two years later, just after she was granted political asylum and then heralded by anti-FGM advocacy groups as a feminist heroine who had been liberated from the "oppressive and barbaric" customs of Africa, Fauziya Kassindja was interviewed on Ted Koppel's television program "Night Line." In that interview, Kassindja surprised her host by announcing that most young women in Togo who come of age this way are happy to be circumcised and "think it is something very great." She spoke the truth, but her response did not compute within the terms of the global anti-FGM discourse. Since African genital alterations are torture and everyone must want to flee Togo—the basic assumption of the program—Koppel pressed on with his prepared story line (Walley 1997, 421). It remains to be seen whether other liberal, freethinking Americans—all of "us"—will be more able to "break frame," open our minds, uncover our ears, and listen.

## CONCLUSION: ON THE VIRTUES OF BEING SLOW TO JUDGE THE UNFAMILIAR AND HAVING A HARD SECOND LOOK

I can think of no better way to conclude than by quoting the legal scholar Lawrence Sager (ch. 8 herein), who writes,

> Epistemic concerns and the principle of equal liberty require that we be slow to judge the unfamiliar, and that we take a hard look at our own factual beliefs and normative judgments before we condemn culturally endorsed practices. They also require that extant legal categories of excuse and mitigation be open to the distinct experience of cultural minorities. Finally, they require that our robust tradition of constitutional liberty—including the rights of speech and belief, the right of parents to guide their children's development, and the right of people to be free from governmental intrusion into decisions that ought to be theirs alone—be available on full and fair terms to cultural minorities. (ch. 8, 173)

As a matter of epistemic concern, this chapter has tried to suggest that we should be skeptical of the anti-FGM advocacy literature and global discourse that portrays African mothers as mutilators, murderers, and torturers of their children. We should be dubious of representations that suggest African mothers are bad mothers, or that First World mothers have a better idea of what it means to be a good mother. We should be slow to judge the unfamiliar practice of female genital alterations, in part because the horrifying assertions by anti-FGM activists concerning the consequences of this practice (that is, claims about mortality, devastating health outcomes, and loss of a capacity to enjoy sex) are not well-supported with credible scientific evidence. That is reason enough to take a hard second look and hesitate before even using the epithet "FGM" ("female genital mutilation") to describe the coming-of-age and gender identity practices embraced by many millions of African women. African women too have rights to personal and family privacy, to guide the development of their children in light of their own ideals of the good life, and to be free of excessive and unreasonable government intrusion.

This chapter also has suggested that merely posing the question, "What about FGM?" is not an argument against cultural pluralism. With accurate scientific information and sufficient cultural understanding, it is possible to see the not unreasonable point of such practices for those for whom they are meaningful. The toleration begins with seeing the cultural point and getting the scientific facts straight. Our cherished ideals of tolerance (including the ideal of having a "choice") would not amount to very much if all they consisted of was our willingness to eat each other's foods and to grant each other permission to enter different houses of worship for a couple of hours on the weekend. Tolerance means setting aside readily aroused and powerfully negative feelings about the practices of immigrant minority groups long enough to get the facts straight and engage the "other" in a serious moral dialogue. It should take far more than overheated rhetoric and offended sensibilities to justify a cultural eradication campaign. Needless to say, the question of toleration versus eradication of other people's valued way of life is not just a women's issue.

The controversy over female circumcision in Africa is not an open-and-shut case. Given the high stakes involved, cultural pluralists—both men and women—who are knowledgeable about African circumcision practices have a responsibility to step forward, speak out, and educate the public about this practice. Many African women, out of a sense of modesty, privacy, loyalty, or a well-founded fear of political persecution, may hesitate to speak for themselves. Everyone has a responsibility—anti-FGM activists and cultural pluralists alike—to insist on evenhandedness and the highest standards of reason and evidence in any public policy debate on this topic—or at least to insist that there is a public policy debate, with all sides and voices fully represented.

---

Many friends, colleagues, and experts on African initiation ceremonies have generously (and tolerantly) discussed this topic with me or critiqued an earlier version of the chapter. Without in any way holding them responsible for my perspective on this controversial issue, I wish to express my deepest gratitude to Fuambai Ahmadu, Margaret Beck, Janice Boddy, David Chambers, Jane Cohen, Elizabeth Dunn, Robert Edgerton, Arthur Eisenberg, Ylva Hernlund, Albrecht Hofheinz, Sudhir Kakar, Jane Kaplan, Frank Kessel, Corinne Kratz, Dennis Krieger, Maivân Lâm, Heather Lindkvist, Saba Mahmood, Hazel Markus, Martha Minow, Carla Obermeyer, Anni Peller, Jane Rabe, Lawrence Sager, Lauren Shweder, Gerd Spittler, and Leti Volpp. This chapter was prepared while I was a Fellow at the Wissenschaftskolleg Zu Berlin (The Institute for Advanced Study in Berlin). A much shorter version of this chapter appeared in the Fall 2000 issue of *Daedalus: Journal of the American Academy of Arts and Sciences* 129(4).

## NOTES

1. Fuambai Ahmadu is a Kono woman from Sierra Leone. She grew up in the United States and is a Ph.D. candidate in anthropology at the London School of Economics and Political Science. At age twenty-two she returned to Sierra Leone to be initiated into the women's secret society and to be circumcised according to the customs of her ethnic group.

2. Things are starting to change. Essays that are more incisive, ethnographically informed, nondefensive, or profoundly skeptical of the current anti-FGM global discourse are beginning to appear. See, for example, Abusharaf 2001; Ahmadu 2000; Boddy 1996; Coleman 1998; Gilman 1999; Gosselin 2000, Gruenbaum 2001; Johnson 2000, Kratz 1994, 1999; Larsen and Yan 2000; Morison et al. 2001; Obermeyer 1999, Obiora 1997; Parker 1995; Thomas 2000. For a sample of views and representations

concerning female initiation and circumcision also see Abusharaf 2000; Boddy 1989; Cooper 1999, El Dareer 1982; Gruenbaum 1988; Gunning 1991–1992; Hernlund 2000; Horowitz and Jackson 1997; Kenyatta 1938; Lane and Rubinstein 1996, Meinardus 1967; Slack 1988; Walley 1997; Williams and Sobieszyzyk 1997.

## REFERENCES

Abusharaf, Rogaia Mustafa. 2000. "Rethinking Feminist Discourses on Infibulation: Responses from Sudanese Feminists." In *Female "Circumcision" in Africa: Culture, Controversy and Change*, edited by Bettina Shell-Duncan and Ylva Hernlund. Boulder, Colo.: Lynne Rienner.

————. 2001. "Virtuous Cuts: Female Genital Circumcision in an African Ontology." *differences: A Journal of Feminist Cultural Studies* 12: 112–39.

Ahmadu, Fuambai. 2000. "Rites and Wrongs: An Insider/Outsider Reflects on Power and Excision." In *Female "Circumcision" in Africa: Culture, Controversy and Change*, edited by B. Shell-Duncan and Y. Hernlund. Boulder, Colo.: Lynne Rienner. Also presented in the Panel on Female Genital Cutting: Local Dynamics of a Global Debate, November 18, 1999, 98th Annual Meeting of the American Anthropological Association, Chicago, Illinois.

Beyene, Yewoubdar. 1999. "Body Politics and Moral Advocacy: The Impact on African Families in the U.S." Oral presentation in the panel on "Revisiting Female Circumcision: Beyond Feminism and Current Discourse. 98th Annual Meeting of the American Anthropological Association, 20 November, Chicago.

Boddy, Janice. 1982. "Womb as Oasis: The Symbolic Context of Pharaonic Circumcision in Rural Northern Sudan." *American Ethnologist* 9: 682–98.

————. 1989. *Wombs and Alien Spirits: Women, Men and the Zar Cult in Northern Sudan.* Madison: University of Wisconsin Press.

————. 1996. "Violence Embodied? Circumcision, Gender Politics, and Cultural Aesthetics." In *Rethinking Violence Against Women*, edited by R. E. Dobash and R. P. Dobash. Thousand Oaks, Calif.: Sage.

Branigin, William, and Douglas Farah. 2000. "Asylum Seeker Is Imposter, INS Says." *Washington Post*, December 20, 2000: A1.

Coleman, Doriane L. 1998. "The Seattle Compromise: Multicultural Sensitivity and Americanization." *Duke Law Review* 47: 717–83.

Cooper, Mary H. 1999. "Women and Human Rights." *Congressional Quarterly Researcher* 9: 353–76.

Dirie, M. A., and G. Lindmark. 1991. "Female Circumcision in Somalia and Women's Motives." *Acta Obstetricia Gynecologica Scandanavia* 70: 581–85.

Dugger, Celia W. 1996. "New Law Bans Genital Cutting in United States." *New York Times*, November 12, 1996: A1.

Edgerton, Robert B. 1989. *Mau Mau: An African Crucible.* New York: The Free Press.

Egan, Timothy. 1994. "An Ancient Ritual and a Mother's Asylum Plea." *New York Times*, March 4, 1994: A25.

El Dareer, Asma. 1982. *Women, Why Do You Weep? Circumcision and Its Consequences.* London: Zed Books.

————. 1983. "Epidemiology of Female Circumcision in the Sudan." *Tropical Doctor* 13: 43.

French, H. F. 1997. "Grafton Journal: The Ritual—Disfiguring, Hurtful, Wildly Festive." *New York Times*, January 31: A4.

Gilman, Sander L. 1999. "'Barbaric' Rituals." In *Is Multiculturalism Bad for Women?* edited by Susan M. Okin. Princeton, N.J.: Princeton University Press.

Gollaher, David L. 2000. *Circumcision: A History of the World's Most Controversial Surgery.* New York: Basic Books.

Gosselin, Claudie. 2000. "Handing Over the Knife: Numu Women and the Campaign Against Excision in Mali." In *Female "Circumcision" in Africa: Culture, Controversy and Change,* edited by B. Shell-Duncan and Y. Hernlund. Boulder, Colo.: Lynne Rienner.

Gruenbaum, Ellen. 1988 "Reproductive Ritual and Social Reproduction: Female Circumcision and the Subordination of Women in Sudan." In *Economy and Class in Sudan,* edited by Normal O'Neill and Jay O'Brian. Brookfield, Vt.: Avebury.

———. 1996. "The Cultural Debate over Female Circumcision: The Sudanese Are Arguing This One Out for Themselves." *Medical Anthropology Quarterly* 10: 455–75.

———. 2001. *The Female Circumcision Controversy: An Anthropological Perspective.* Philadelphia: University of Pennsylvania Press.

Gunning, Isabelle R. 1991–1992. "Arrogant Perception, World-Travelling and Multicultural Feminism: The Case of Female Genital Surgeries." *Columbia Human Rights Law Review* 23: 189–248.

Hernlund, Ylva. 2000. "Cutting Without Ritual and Ritual Without Cutting." In *Female "Circumcision" in Africa: Culture, Controversy and Change,* edited by B. Shell-Duncan and Y. Hernlund. Boulder, Colo.: Lynne Rienner.

Horowitz, Carol R., and Carey Jackson. 1997. "Female 'Circumcision': African Women Confront American Medicine." *Journal of General Internal Medicine* 12: 491–99.

Hosken, Fran P. 1993. *The Hosken Report: Genital and Sexual Mutilation of Females.* Lexington, Mass.: Women's International Network News.

Johnson, Michelle. 2000. "Becoming a Muslim, Becoming a Person: Female 'Circumcision,' Religious Identity, and Personhood in Guinea-Bissau." In *Female "Circumcision" in Africa: Culture, Controversy and Change,* edited by B. Shell-Duncan and Y. Hernlund. Boulder, Colo.: Lynne Rienner.

Kenyatta, Jomo. 1938. *Facing Mount Kenya: The Tribal Life of the Gikuyu.* London: Secker and Warburg.

Koso-Thomas, Olayinka. 1987. *The Circumcision of Women: A Strategy for Eradication.* London: Zed Books.

Kratz, Corinne A. 1994. *Affecting Performance: Meaning, Movement and Experience in Okiek Women's Initiation.* Washington, D.C.: Smithsonian Institution Press.

———. 1999. "Contexts, Controversies, Dilemmas: Teaching Circumcision." In *Teaching Africa: African Studies in the New Millennium,* edited by Misty Bastian and Jane Parpart. Boulder, Colo.: Lynne Rienner.

Lâm, Maivân. 1994. "Feeling Foreign in Feminism." *Signs: Journal of Women in Culture and Society* 19: 865–93.

Lane, Sandra D., and Robert A. Rubinstein. 1996. "Judging the Other: Responding to Traditional Female Genital Surgeries." *Hastings Center Report* 26: 31–40.

Larsen, Ulla, and Sharon Yan. 2000. "Does Female Circumcision Affect Infertility and Fertility? A Study of the Central African Republic, Côte d'Ivoire, and Tanzania." *Demography* 37: 313–21.

Leonard, Lori. 2000. "Adopting Female 'Circumcision' in Southern Chad." In *Female "Circumcision" in Africa: Culture, Controversy and Change,* edited by B. Shell-Duncan and Y. Hernlund. Boulder, Colo.: Lynne Rienner.

Lightfoot-Klein, Hany. 1989. "The Sexual and Marital Adjustment of Genitally Circumcised and Infibulated Females in the Sudan." *Journal of Sex Research* 26: 375–92.

Mackie, Gerrie. 2000. "Female Genital Cutting: The Beginning of the End." In *Female "Circumcision" in Africa: Culture, Controversy and Change*, edited by B. Shell-Duncan and Y. Hernlund. Boulder, Colo.: Lynne Rienner.

Meinardus, Otto. 1967. "Mythological, Historical and Sociological Aspects of the Practice of Female Circumcision Among the Egyptians." *Acta Ethnographica: Academiae Scientiarum Hungaricae* 16: 387–97.

Morison, Linda, Caroline Scherf, Gloria Ekpo, Katie Pain, Beryl West, Rosalind Coleman, and Gijs Walraven. 2001. "The Long-Term Reproductive Health Consequences of Female Genital Cutting in Rural Gambia: A Community-Based Survey. *Tropical Medicine and International Health* 6: 643–53.

Obermeyer, Carla M. 1999. "Female Genital Surgeries: The Known, the Unknown, and the Unknowable." *Medical Anthropology Quarterly* 13: 79–106.

Obiora, L. Amede. 1997. "Rethinking Polemics and Intransigence in the Campaign Against Female Circumcision." *Case Western Reserve Law Review* 47: 275–378.

Okin, Susan Moller. 1999. "Is Multiculturalism Bad for Women?" In *Is Multiculturalism Bad for Women?* edited by Susan M. Okin. Princeton, N.J.: Princeton University Press.

Olamijuto, S. K., K. T. Joiner, and G. A. Oyedeji. 1983. "Female Child Circumcision in Ilesha, Nigeria." *Clinical Pediatrics* 22: 580–81.

Parker, Melissa. 1995. "Rethinking Female Circumcision." *Africa* 65: 506–24.

Pollitt, Katha. 1999. "Whose Culture?" In *Is Multiculturalism Bad for Women?* edited by Susan M. Okin. Princeton, N.J.: Princeton University Press.

Rawls, John. 1993. *Political Liberalism*. New York: Columbia University Press.

Rich, Susan, and Stephanie Joyce. N.d. "Eradicating Female Genital Mutilation: Lessons for Donors." Available at Wallace Global Fund for a Sustainable Future, 1990 M Street, NW, Suite 250, Washington, D.C. 20036.

Rosenthal, Abraham M. 1995. "The Possible Dream." *New York Times*, June 13: A25.

Shell-Duncan, Bettina, and Ylva Hernlund. 2000a. *Female "Circumcision" in Africa: Culture, Controversy and Change*. Boulder, Colo.: Lynne Rienner.

———. 2000b. "Female 'Circumcision' in Africa: Dimensions of the Problem and the Debates." In *Female "Circumcision" in Africa: Culture, Controversy and Change*, edited by B. Shell-Duncan and Y. Hernlund. Boulder, Colo.: Lynne Rienner.

Slack, Alison T. 1988. "Female Circumcision: A Critical Appraisal." *Human Rights Quarterly* 10: 437–86.

Tamir, Yael. 1996. "Hands Off Clitoridectomy." *Boston Review* (October/November).

Thomas, Lynn. 2000. "Ngaitana (I Will Circumcise Myself): Lessons from Colonial Campaigns to Ban Excision in Meru, Kenya." In *Female "Circumcision" in Africa: Culture, Controversy and Change*, edited by B. Shell-Duncan and Y. Hernlund. Boulder, Colo.: Lynne Rienner.

Walley, Christine J. 1997. "Searching for 'Voices': Feminism, Anthropology, and the Global Debate over Female Genital Operations." *Cultural Anthropology* 12: 405–38.

Williams, Linda, and Teresa Sobieszyzyk. 1997. "Attitudes Surrounding the Continuation of Female Circumcision in the Sudan: Passing the Tradition to the Next Generation." *Journal of Marriage and the Family* 59: 966–81.

# Chapter 12

## About Women, About Culture: About Them, About Us

### Martha Minow

Why do so many public and scholarly discussions of cultural conflict and cultural defenses focus on women? Consider the intense debates over how much a particular industrialized society should accommodate minority members who participate in cultural practices at odds with the majority. Common examples are female genital cutting, capturing young women to force compliance with arranged marriages, cultural defenses after the murder of a wife or daughter, traditional membership and property rules that disadvantage women, and the veil or scarf worn under religious compulsion by females (Okin 1999a; Resnik 1989, 671; Shachar 2000). These are also the frequent examples in debates over whether international human rights law affords universal rights or imposes Western practices (Higgins 1996, 89; Charlesworth 1993, 1, 9).[1] The concerns certainly extend to female children—and sometimes to all children—but the examples that recur involve the bodies and social roles of women and girls. While the central focus in fact should be children, why do women instead seem so central?

Whether risks to women figure most in clashes between democratic states' law and minority cultural practices, or human rights norms and traditional societies, is for others to debate. Important, however, is the inextricable connection between so-called women's issues and men's behavior—as polygamous husbands, those who demand genital cutting, or those whose conduct shames their wives (Piccalo 2000; "Legal Loophole Results in Forced Marriages in Britain" 1999). Yet cultural clashes predominately arise as women's issues in the minds of academics, reporters, and advocates.

### WHY WOMEN?

Recent patterns of globalization and industrialization expose to view practices that formerly were less visible because they were local and private. Globalized news media, hungry to fill their twenty-four-hour habits, scour places previously remote from urban and Western eyes. Migration patterns bring into contact foreign or "traditional" people with Westerners surprised or disturbed by what they see as different. Why do the activities of women and how men treat them surface so often in the resulting coverage and debates?

One reason may be that men seem more ready, at least superficially, to assimilate to globalized work structures and practices. In something as simple as clothing, men are more likely to converge in Western-style suits (or pants and shirts), while women's garb is much more varied; and women from other societies hang on to their traditional clothing much longer. This observation may simply restate the question: Why do men more readily than women, at least superficially, assimilate?

The answer could lie in gender roles and gender divisions in the home societies of immigrants or in the receiving culture of the host nation. Cultural practices separating men and women—and assigning women to a private sphere and men to a public sphere—can be carried over even as people migrate to a society with little or no resistance to including women in the public sphere and paid work world. If only immigrant men participate in the work world and public settings, they (but not the women in their families) would face pressures and expectations for assimilation in the city or nation to which they migrate. If women stay at home (or in some other sense are expected to preserve the distinction between home and work, private and public), their bodies mark the distinction by the very location of their selves and by the clothing and markings they use. They may continue to dress according to their home tradition even if they join the workforce or shop in public places (McCoy 1999). Or subtle distinctions between home and work, private and public, may greet the arriving immigrants and sort women into the role of preserving traditions and men into the role of assimilating.

Perhaps at work here is a convergence in the hierarchies of power across social groups, within and between societies, that preserves the power among men and the relative subordination of women. Immigrants' countries of origin and receiving nations both may arrange relatively greater power for men and more restrictions placed on women, however different in form and degree. In this congruence, women's status and bodies become the focus for expressions of control and demarcation.

Earlier waves of industrialization—during the nineteenth and early to mid-twentieth centuries—often led men to migrate to new places ahead of women and children. Established in the new setting before the others—and cut free from the domestic sphere, where traditions are preserved and reinforced—men often seemed, at least in public iconography, to assimilate sooner (Silver 1975; Jones 1992).[2] Participating in workplaces, labor activities, and public recreation and social scenes, men then and now would have more occasions to mix with diverse others, to see dominant customs at close hand, and to try them on. In an increasingly globalized economy, even residents of Third World nations who do

but also violate the law of Pakistan (Bamber 2000; Bel 2000). Yes, culture is too often used to excuse cruelty and violence, but before condemning the culture, people with concern should interrogate the claim that "my culture made me do it" (Honig 1999, 36).

More basically, however, culture defenders challenge the individual as the proper and sole unit of analysis, and individual choice as the ultimate good. (In a particularly deft effort to embrace individual rights and embedded social life, Martha Nussbaum [1999b] suggests that when offered effectively, universalist values also afford women solidarity and affiliation—often with other women. See Honig 1999, 49.)

Culture defenders also suggest that what is seen as choice in any setting may be better understood as a reflection of socialization (Al-Hibri 1999, 45). Preferences, desires, and therefore choices are formed—or deformed—within social experience; preferences and desires are not simply natural or internal to an individual. Culture defenders emphasize that as a result, what liberals view as free choices are themselves framed by social experiences and pressures. So a Muslim woman who claims that she wants to wear the hajib (veil) is no more misguided or impaired in her choice making than a woman who wants breast augmentation plastic surgery; to the culture defender, both women can be viewed as capitulating to social norms and pressures, or instead as expressing and negotiating their own desires within the inevitable specificity of their own cultural environment.

A liberal may reply, for example, that being socialized into a world that values individual choice makes the identification and expression of choices different than when socialization lacks this commitment. Indeed, one socialized to value choice is likely to be more alert to interferences with it. Or the liberal may emphasize that social practices and structures that deform choice must be changed—especially practices and laws "concerning marital rape, domestic violence, and women's legal rights over children" (Nussbaum 1999b, 13), and structures assigning women to second-class status and daily fears (Nussbaum 1999b, 151).[8]

Dueling accusations of false consciousness can escalate with no end. Indeed, here is a risk of infinite regression. You say that women in my culture have false consciousness, but you say this because of your own false consciousness—or I think this because of my own false consciousness, and so forth. These kinds of exchanges essentially are incorrigible. No facts of the matter then can prove or disprove false consciousness without a prior agreement about what one ought to want.

Moreover, to anyone committed to the advancement of women, questioning a woman's ability to make choices is itself a disturbing reminder of the rationales for denying women choices. These rationales, historically, pointed to women's vulnerabilities, lack of education, inadequate rationality, overweening emotionality, or other impairments. To question the choices of women who wear scarves, defend and engage in genital cutting, or undergo arranged or polygamous marriages, is to echo those arguments for denying women's choices. Demonstrating how women—or members of any oppressed group—adapt to cur-tailed choices can demolish claims of inherent inferiority or impairment, but even this risks reinforcing images of their vulnerability (Sen 1995).

However problematic, exchanges over false consciousness and choice pro-duce intriguing twists. Liberals can claim that internal hierarchies prevent women from exercising control over the shape of traditional practices. Culture defenders counter that liberal interventions neglect larger colonial and anti-colonial struggles or other ongoing intergroup conflicts. In these contexts, immi-grant and minority group women may well rather align with the men in their group than be "rescued" by outsiders (Sassen 1999, 76–78; Bhaba 1999, 79, 83–84).[9]

In a very different context, one observer comments that the Hindu right in India, using the languages of secularism and civil law, "has attempted to posi-tion itself as the guardians of the rights of women from minority religious com-munities as part of its more general project of undermining the very legitimacy of these communities" (Kapur 1999, 143, 148). Liberals who oppose cultural de-fenses may not have such an explicit project, but to members of minority cul-tural groups or Third World cultures resisting universal human rights, it may seem as though they do. Especially when immigrants embrace a traditional cul-tural practice as a form of resistance to oppression by the dominant culture, the dominant group's challenges to that culture can seem like an extension of that oppression (Sassen 1999, 77). The Western liberal speaks with authority and con-fidence in the name of universally applicable principles and against special ex-emptions. Many on the other side ask why they show so little humility, give so little acknowledgment of the contingency of each person's claim of truth, and manifest so little respect for the resources internal to each culture to rectify its own oppressions (Al-Hibri 1999, 46; Parekh 1999, 74).

In fact, both liberals and culture defenders recognize the multiplicity and di-versity within any group—and the shifts in group practices and beliefs over time. Yet rather than a point of commonality, this recognition generates grist for each side's arguments. For liberals, the presence of different subgroups and viewpoints within a culture provides yet another reason to ensure individual choice rather than confine any individual to one set of cultural practices (Tamir 1999, 52). For culture defenders, such mutability and variety within any culture give reason for humility. They infer that divergence within the group and shifts over time caution against any claims about what everyone wants or needs (Gilman 1999, 53, 55). Outsiders therefore should refrain from imposing individ-ual rights as the only method for internal group change. Finding the play in the joints in even the most coherent cultural world should generate greater respect for the individuals who can and do wend their own ways through complex cultural worlds. Indeed, to the extent that minority group practices are them-selves oppressive, culture defenders maintain that group members can and do engage in their own internal group struggles, which allow them to preserve their group while redressing the offensive group practices (Bhabha 1999, 82–84; Nussbaum 1999a, 105, 108).[10]

The liberal thus reacts; then the mutability of cultures should remind us never to use law to freeze (with minority rights or exemptions from universal human rights) cultural practices that otherwise could change, under pressure or natural evolution (Tamir 1999, 51–52; Okin 1999b, 118). Granting any kinds of group-based protections may even strengthen dying practices that are revived as gestures against external powers or last-ditch efforts by internally powerful figures to hang on to their positions (Pollitt 1999, 29; Tamir 1999, 49–51). The fate of an inevitably shifting set of practices should be left to group members, but only if those members each have rights to participate fully in such self-determination (Tamir 1999, 50–51).

Yet, the culture defender responds, this very mutability should remind us that Western liberal rights grew from and in response to particular circumstances; therefore, that familiar political and civil liberties are suited to checking oppression in very alien settings is not at all clear (Parekh 1999, 73–74; Post 1999, 68). Moreover, the fluidity and contestation within cultures count against outsiders who attribute an objectionable practice to the entire culture and who wrongly trust external interference more than internal processes of dissent and reform (Bhabha 1999, 82–84).

Perhaps, a mediating voice replies, the mutability of culture should encourage us to reform the oppressive qualities of our own—and to preserve the chance for others to reform the oppressive qualities of theirs, rather than to condemn them wholesale (Raz 1999).[11] Yet liberals claim that the particular culture in which women find themselves is an accident. Women do not choose its norms nor choose to endorse them unless they have other genuine and attractive options (Nussbaum 1999a, 54).

Table 12.1 summarizes the debate (additional rejoinders appear in brackets).

## THE UNDERLYING PREOCCUPATION WITH CHOICE AND PREFERENCE

The debates circle round and round a preoccupation with choices and preferences. Who can know his or her own wants—and under what conditions? Who can speak for anyone about his or her desires? The academic debate is usually just that—a debate among academics, for even those who speak as culture defenders are themselves members of the Western liberal academic tradition, whatever their culture of origin. They may call for listening to the voices of women genuinely immersed in groups whose practices come under challenge—but they then will clash over who best speaks for those who still cannot be heard (Okin 1999b, 122–23; Al-Hibri 1999, 41, 42).

Choice—and its complex determinants—surface in a more subtle way. Any journalist or scholar addressing culture clashes chooses what ought to be of concern for others, but why do they choose as they do? This question returns us to the opening query. Why the focus on women, in discussions about cultural

TABLE 12.1 / Arguments About Gender, Human Rights, and Culture

| Liberal | Culture Defender |
| --- | --- |
| Cultural defenses hurt women. | Liberals neglect gender domination in their own societies. |
| Cultural defenses only help those already in power. | Cultural defenses preserve settings for human flourishing. |
| Cultural defenses reflect condescension or guilt about the Third World. | Liberal rights risk abandoning girls, while liberal theorists offer nothing to sustain the girls' identity and dignity in return. |
| Traditional women, when given a choice, like what liberalism offers: women can find community even as they explore and seize liberal rights; [socialization of individual choice itself is different from socialization without it]; recognizing the social dimension of desire should not lead to abandoning the priority of individual choice, but rather should enable reforms of moral education and laws and institutions constraining women. | Horror stories violate indigenous norms too; but choice is problematic because it is too individualistic and neglects the group in which meanings are made; why should the individual and individual choice be paramount when it undermines or undervalues the group?; everyone is socialized more than individually capable of choice. |
| Internal group hierarchies prevent women from shaping social practices, so why should women be stuck with those practices? | Internal group hierarchies pale before hierarchies between Western and Third World nations, and between majorities within Western countries and their minority groups; minority group members understandably and rightly choose group solidarity against larger domination. |
| Group practices and beliefs change, so law should not be used to freeze minority practices or exempt them from universal human rights. | Group practices and beliefs change, so outsiders should refrain from using individual rights to alter traditional groups. |
| [Contests can always occur within a culture about what its practices are, so to use law (through cultural defenses or exemptions from human rights) to prefer one version over others in any way that interferes with individual rights is wrong.] | [Contests can always occur within a culture about what its practices are, so to use law to arm some—through individual rights—against others is wrong.] |

*(Table continues on p. 260.)*

TABLE 12.1  /  *Continued*

| Liberal | Culture Defender |
|---|---|
| [Western rights evolved over time, so to point out how needed they are elsewhere is no insult.] | Western rights evolved over time in specific circumstances, so there is no reason to believe that their current particular form is well-suited to respond to oppressions in alien societies and cultures. |
| | The mutability of culture should remind Western and other dominant groups to reform their own—and leave reform of others to their respective members. |
| Women neither choose their culture nor necessarily endorse its norms unless they have genuine choices—meaning attractive alternatives and the capacity to choose among them. | [This yet again elevates the individual and individual choice over all other goods, including the texture of a culture and interdependence of a group.] |
| | [In addition, genuine concerns about enhancing women's capacities for choice would support internal reform movements and also address the material and social contexts in which they live rather than use the superimposing individual rights and constraining cultural practices.] |

*Source*: Author's compilation.

clashes and accommodations? Those who emphasize concerns for women reflect their own priorities, stemming from their own experiences and cultural contexts.

If debaters consulted members of immigrant communities or residents in Third World countries—even small groups of the women in these settings—and asked them about their priorities, would these individuals choose the circumstances of women above all others? Would they pick the means of individual rights above all others? What if, instead, they pick as their priority economic equity for their entire group when compared with other groups? (Bhabha 1999, 81; Sassen 1999, 77–78; An-Na'im 1999, 59, 62; Halley 1999, 100, 103–4).[12] Or what if they do focus on a women's issue, such as domestic violence, but prefer to draw on village tradition over liberal rights, so as not to exit or destroy their group in order to address the problem? (Sadasivan 2000, 6–9). To assume that these kinds of choices would be mistaken—indeed, to bypass such choices and simply assert an outsider's preference—is to engage in the kind of imposition that the rhetoric of choice should render problematic. This will only seem unproblematic to those whose power is sufficiently great that they do not even see the coincidence between their interests and the way decisions are debated and made.

What an irony: precisely in the moment of claiming concern for others, we risk neglecting how our own self-interest and worldview frames what we claim on their behalf. This is reminiscent of voting rights reforms in the United States, intended to enable the election of minority group members even in majority-dominated districts, but operated to allow the white majority to select the minority candidate that they—not the minority community's own majority—reportedly preferred (Guinier 1994).

Choices and preferences are of course central to the liberal conception to freedom, to individual rights, and to the struggle against inherited and assigned status and constraints. Three linked difficulties arise, though, when women and choice come together in debates over cultural clash and accommodation. The first is that the very effort to respect choice can stymie advocates for women's rights if they find women disagreeing with what the advocates think they should want. They do have to find them and consult them, though, for this to happen. Beside logistical difficulties, the risk of discovering disagreement could be a powerful reason not to try.

The second difficulty is that ensuring the conditions under which women's preferences and choices would seem trustworthy will often entail changing their circumstances rather dramatically, so that they have genuinely attractive options, education, and safety. Undertaking economic development projects, promoting literacy and self-improvement for women, extending medical services, and subsidizing local reform efforts require enormous commitments of time and resources. Making such efforts work demands consistent efforts to earn trust. Working in this way—in Third World countries or impoverished parts of developed nations—would show how arid it is to discuss choice remote from conditions that enable it, even while revealing that no assistance can work unless the supposed beneficiaries choose for it to do so.

The third difficulty is that such shifts actually require altering the immediate contexts of socialization: the family, the school, and the community affecting children's development. Not only is this an enormous and challenging undertaking, it is at the heart of what cultural groups understandably view as most important of all: passing on their ways to the next generation (Okin 1999b, 130–31).[13]

Honest consideration of the centrality of choice should make it clear that children, not women, lie at the heart of questions of cultural clash and accommodation (Halley 1999, 100, 103–4).[14] Indeed, children are the prime targets of socialization, and children, even in liberal societies, are not viewed as yet capable of choice. Any genuine effort to enable choices must focus on children. Yet any such effort then collides forcibly at the heart of culture, at the center of immigrant communities, at the core of Third World societies, even at the most fundamental freedoms—to reproduce and raise children—ensured by law to individuals in Western, democratic societies. No comfort can be found by asserting that children themselves choose efforts that constrain or interfere with their parents' and communities' own child-rearing and socializing practices. Reconciling what it takes to equip children as choosers with what it takes to respect parents and communities as child rearers is as hard as any task gets.

## CHILDREN, THE PROBLEM THAT HAS NEVER BEEN SOLVED

Questions about children, child rearing, and socialization are especially difficult because Western liberals are perplexed about how to handle cultural disputes in this terrain, even among themselves.[15] Critical, high-profile disputes over state power and individual rights often stem from intergroup conflicts. The U.S. Supreme Court announced parental rights over children's education after one state, due to anti-immigrant sentiment, tried to prevent instruction in German and another tried to restrict Catholic education (see *Meyer v. Nebraska*, 262 U.S. 390 [1923]; *Pierce v. Society of Sisters*, 268 U.S. 510 [1925]). As even these cases suggest, children often become simply pawns in conflicts among adults (Minow 1987).

No doubt this helps to explain why, in the United States, a patchwork quilt of rules and court decisions recognize rights for children in some circumstances but not in others. This pattern also reveals ongoing ambivalence about whether to empower the state to act for children or instead strengthen parental prerogatives. When children are threatened directly by the state, they are more likely to be recognized as rights bearers; when the state disagrees with parental practices, the state may intervene or may instead acknowledge parents as primarily responsible for and relatively empowered over their children.

Thus, the U.S. Supreme Court has ruled that minors have the right to counsel, due process, and against self-incrimination when facing state juvenile justice or criminal charges (see *In re Gault*, 387 U.S. 1 [1967]). A parent (or guardian) may not make a martyr of his child—and may not on religious grounds gain an exemption from otherwise justifiable child labor restrictions (see *Prince v. Massachusetts*, 321 U.S. 158 [1944]). Yet Amish parents won the power to keep their children out of high school and the Court did not even require consultation with the children (see *Wisconsin v. Yoder*, 406 U.S. 205 [1972]). Otherwise, the Court acknowledged, the Amish community would not only face constraints on their religious freedoms, they would risk losing their way of life. Each state, under its own laws, requires children to obtain schooling. Yet each is constrained, under the Constitution, to permit parents to opt out of the common public schools and to satisfy this requirement in line with their own religious and personal commitments.[16] Parental autonomy, along with religious free exercise, is the chief instrument of cultural pluralism in this country. Any greater state incursions on parental control over children's education and development will be viewed as assaults on parental prerogatives and family privacy. Children thus remain under parental control except under limited circumstances, and then state supervision takes the form of protections even more than assurances of individual rights.[17]

I would be the first to acknowledge—indeed, I have argued extensively elsewhere—that relationships, not freedoms, are what children need (Minow 1990, 267–311; 1986, 1; 1995, 1573). Children need environments where they can learn what is just, what it means to have their needs met, and what it means to have and fulfill obligations to others. Sensibly, democratic legal systems expect parents and immediate communities to be the frontline providers for children while offering backup and support, chiefly through education opportunity and agencies charged to guard against child abuse and neglect. This acknowledges that nurture is a face-to-face task and that parents are the ones most likely—though not universally—able and motivated to do what is best for their children. This also establishes a framework of pluralism and avoids state standardization of children; and it privatizes most decisions about children. Primary responsibility and power to parents conceal much that affects children from public view. Such responsibility avoids both public controversies and public responsibility about everything from what constitutes appropriate moral instruction to what for children are decent standards of living, medical services, and time with loving adults.

Here then is the problem for those who would address the place of children in cultural clashes. Moving children from private to public concern puts front and center debates over what is a good life, what values should guide children's development, and how much children's needs should be met by people other than their immediate family. Any answers involve more state control than we have had. What state control can be adopted, compatible with constitutional commitments to parental prerogatives and religious freedom, to equip children as choosers? What methods can be adopted, compatible with respecting all individuals, to address minority or immigrant cultural practices that trouble the majority?

Any special state protections for immigrant children against the practices of their parents risks charges of—if not actual—invidious discrimination as well as occasions for heightened disputes about what is or should be viewed as unacceptable practices. State prohibition of female genital cutting leads then to claims that male circumcision also should be disallowed (Povenmire 1998, 87). Once a marker of minority religions, later a widely accepted practice, male circumcision now has reemerged as a contested issue within Western societies. Should it then no longer be a parental prerogative—and if so, what special claims should be available for Jews and Muslims who still conscientiously believe in the practice?

Greater state involvement in the lives of families and children, most basically, exposes to view the deep debates over raising children that run throughout Western industrialized societies well apart from conflicts over the practices of recent immigrants. State supervision of the child disciplinary practices of immigrant parents would, if fairly done, also lead to supervision of the disciplinary practices of all parents. This not only would be enormously expensive and invasive, but also would expose to view the deep split in the nation over corporal punishment (Yip 1999).[18] The division may run even inside families, even inside the heads of parents: in a recent American poll, 55 percent of parents believed that corporal punishment was "sometimes necessary," while 94 percent of those with children had spanked their children within the year (Yip 1999; Garavelli 2000; Gardner 1998). If you think the fight over women's status is intense, wait until you see the fight over children—and with children, the option of trying to consult those most affected seems even more remote and less reliable.

Perhaps, nonetheless, we can learn from the predictable moves in the debate over women and cultural accommodation. Perhaps we can acknowledge that all of our preferences are shaped, willy-nilly, by cultural practices and options and try to enhance those options with sufficient humility to respect the people whose lives we mean to assist. Along the way, we will have to acknowledge that debates over cultural conflict and assimilation are not just about women, and not just about immigrants, minority groups, or Third World nations; they are about all of us.

## NOTES

1. Additional concerns address whether international norms and institutions should extend into the domestic sphere—and whether failure to do so reflects gender bias in the very construction of international law (Romany 1996).

2. African American men also migrated without their families to wherever they could find jobs—but assimilation typically was not offered as an option.

3. Reporting Amartya Sen's finding that 100 million women are "missing" in Africa and Asia, killed by female infanticide, unequal food and medical care, forced childbearing, and domestic violence (Landsberg 1992).

4. Any such names are at risk of reflecting one rather than another side; perhaps these names appear to come from the liberal perspective and associate culture only with those who defend traditional cultures when one of their basic arguments is that every person has and reflects a culture. Yet *liberal*, however pleasing the name may be to adherents, has the negative associations of imperial myopia when named by opposing circles. So consider these names crudely descriptive, from both perspectives.

5. Nussbaum (1999b, 36) criticizes those who oppose universalism only to leave in place "religious taboos, the luxury of the pampered husband, educational deprivation, unequal health care, and premature death."

6. "We do not reject our culture when we find it replete with oppression and the violation of rights; we try to reform it. We should not assume the right to reject or condemn wholesale the cultures of groups within ours in similar circumstances" (Raz 1999, 95, 97).

7. Okin (1999b, 122) quotes a Malaysian Muslim woman who asserted against culture defenders that " 'No woman likes polygamy!' "

8. Nussbaum (1999b) citing work of Amartya Sen on adaptive preferences.

9. Both Sassen and Bhabha would be better described as hybrid watchers than culture defenders; both argue that it is nigh impossible to separate cultural groups in terms of values, rights, and arguments given long-standing cross-cultural contact and hybridization.

10. Raz (1999, 97–98) writes,

    So if we can think of taking steps to put an end to the existence of distinct cultural groups in our midst it is only because we are outsiders to these groups. Members can disown their group and try to assimilate to the majority group—

and we should certainly enable them to do so. Or they can strive to change their group. But they cannot responsibly wish for its extinction. Outsiders can, and members can when they see themselves as outsiders. But, particularly horrendous groups excepted, we should not do so precisely because we are outsiders.

11. Another mediating position urges state intervention that both enables cultural diversity and empowers at-risk individuals within cultural groups that disempower them (Shachar 2000; 1998, 295–305).

12. Okin's critics point to poverty, caste, colonialism, and mistreatment of children as serious issues that compete with and also intersect with the treatment of women in the fight over priorities for reform.

13. Okin (1999, 130–31) is explicit on this subject, couched in the specific context of religions: "Given that it is central to most religions that their members try to pass on their beliefs to their children, it would strike an intolerable blow at religion not to allow this to take place." She recommends that liberal states nonetheless expose all children to information about all religions and secular beliefs and thereby prevent any parent from preventing their children from learning enough about the existence and content of alternatives to never be able to choose their beliefs for themselves.

14. Halley (1999, 100, 103) writes, "cultural survival policies often focus not on women but on children. And this is no accident: raising a child in a culture—any culture— implants not only the child in the culture but the culture in the child." Halley argues that adult superordination over children is the locus of illiberalism, but that there will inevitably be some form of constraint in any acts of child rearing.

15. Justice Thurgood Marshall asked me what I wanted to do after clerking for him; I told him work for children's rights. He replied, "That's the problem that's never been solved."

16. See *Pierce v. Society of Sisters*, 268 U.S. 510, 534–35 (1925). Even the parental right to opt out of public education has limits, however, "if it appears that parental decisions will jeopardize the health or safety of the child, or have a potential for significant social burdens." *Wisconsin v. Yoder*, 406 U.S. 205, 234 (1972).

17. See also *Parham v. J.R.*, 442 U.S. 584 (1979): parents may commit their children to state mental institutions subject to neutral review by the admitting physician.

18. Yip (1999) describes widely disparate practices and views of a state agency decision that a minister committed child abuse when he used a belt to smack his son.

# REFERENCES

Al-Hibri, Azizah Y. 1999. "Is Western Patriarchal Feminism Good for Third World/Minority Women?" In *Is Multiculturalism Bad for Women?* edited by Susan Moller Okin. Princeton, N.J.: Princeton University Press.

An-Na'im, Abdullahi. 1999. "Promises We Should All Keep in Common Cause." In *Is Multiculturalism Bad for Women?* edited by Susan Moller Okin. Princeton, N.J.: Princeton University Press.

Bamber, David. 2000. "Asian Practice of Forced Marriage to Be Outlawed." *Sunday Telegraph* (London), June 18: 13.

Bel, Gavin. 2000. "Indecent Proposals." *Scotsman*, April 8: 1.

Bhabha, Homi. 1999. "Liberalism's Sacred Cow." In *Is Multiculturalism Bad for Women?* edited by Susan Moller Okin. Princeton, N.J.: Princeton University Press.

Charlesworth, Hilary. 1993. "Alienating Oscar? Feminist Analysis of International Law." In *Reconceiving Reality: Women and International Law*, edited by Dorinda G. Dallmeyer. Studies in Transnational Legal Policy no. 25. Washington, D.C.: American Society of International Law.

Garavelli, Dana. 2000. "Smacking: Should We Be Cruel to Be Kind?" *Scotsman*, February 13: 12.

Gardner, Michael. 1998. "No, Beating Children Is Not 'Reasonable.'" *Times* (London), June 23.

Gilman, Sander. 1999. "'Barbaric' Rituals?" In *Is Multiculturalism Bad for Women?* edited by Susan Moller Okin. Princeton, N.J.: Princeton University Press.

Guinier, Lani. 1994. *The Tyranny of the Majority: Fundamental Fairness in Representative Democracy*. New York: The Free Press.

Halley, Janet. 1999. "Culture Constrains." In *Is Multiculturalism Bad for Women?* edited by Susan Moller Okin. Princeton, N.J.: Princeton University Press.

Higgins, Tracy E. 1996. "Anti-Essentialism, Relativism, and Human Rights." *Harvard Women's Law Journal* 19: 89.

Honig, Bonnie. 1999. "My Culture Made Me Do It." In *Is Multiculturalism Bad for Women?* edited by Susan Moller Okin. Princeton, N.J.: Princeton University Press.

Jones, Jacqueline. 1992. *The Dispossessed: America's Underclasses from the Civil War to the Present*. New York: Basic Books.

Kapur, Ratna. 1999. "The Two Faces of Secularism and Women's Rights in India." In *Religious Fundamentalisms and the Human Rights of Women*, edited by Courtney W. Howland. New York: St. Martin's Press.

Landsberg, Michele. 1992. "Human Rights Must Include Women's Right to Escape Abuse." *Toronto Star*, September 12.

"Legal Loophole Results in Forced Marriages in Britain." 1999. *The Hindu*, August 6.

McCoy, John. 1999. "Muslim Says Mall Expelled Her Over Veil; Guards Misunderstood Rule on Hidden Faces, Official Says." *Dallas Morning News*, May 12, 1999: 27A.

Minow, Martha. 1986. "Rights for the Next Generation: A Feminist Approach to Children's Rights." *Harvard Women's Law Journal* 9: 1.

———. 1987. "We the Family." *Journal of American History* 74(3): 959–83.

———. 1990. *Making All the Difference: Inclusion, Exclusion, and American Law*. Ithaca, N.Y.: Cornell University Press.

———. 1995. "Children's Rights: Where We've Been and Where We're Going." *Temple Law Review* 68: 1573.

Nussbaum, Martha C. 1999a. "A Plea for Difficulty." In *Is Multiculturalism Bad for Women?* edited by Susan Moller Okin. Princeton, N.J.: Princeton University Press.

———. 1999b. *Sex and Social Justice*. New York: Oxford University Press.

Okin, Susan Moller. 1999a. *Is Multiculturalism Bad for Women?* Princeton, N.J.: Princeton University Press.

———. 1999b. "Reply." In *Is Multiculturalism Bad for Women?* edited by Susan Moller Okin. Princeton, N.J.: Princeton University Press.

Parekh, Bhiktu. 1999. "A Varied Moral World." In *Is Multiculturalism Bad for Women?* edited by Susan Moller Okin. Princeton, N.J.: Princeton University Press.

Piccalo, Gina. 2000. "Attorneys to Cite Similar Incident in Drowning Case Defense; Courts: Saying Cultural Values Caused Woman to Try to Kill Her Children." *Los Angeles Times*, February 17: B11.

Pollitt, Katha. 1999. "Whose Culture." In *Is Multiculturalism Bad for Women?* edited by Susan Moller Okin. Princeton, N.J.: Princeton University Press.

Post, Robert. 1999. "Between Norms and Choices." In *Is Multiculturalism Bad for Women?* edited by Susan Moller Okin. Princeton, N.J.: Princeton University Press.

Povenmire, Ross. 1998. "Do Parents Have the Legal Authority to Consent to Surgical Amputation of Normal Healthy Tissue from Their Infant Children?: The Practice of Circumcision in the United States." *American University Journal of Gender, Social Policy and the Law* 7(1): 87.

Raz, Joseph. 1999. "How Perfect Should One Be? And Whose Culture Is?" In *Is Multiculturalism Bad for Women?* edited by Susan Moller Okin. Princeton, N.J.: Princeton University Press.

Resnik, Judith. 1989. "Dependent Sovereigns: Indian Tribes, States, and the Federal Courts." *University of Chicago Law Review* 56: 671.

Romany, Celina. 1996. "Black Women and Gender in a New South Africa: Human Rights Law and the Intersection of Race and Gender." *Brookings Journal of International Law* 21: 857.

Sadasivan, Bharati. 2000. *Community Justice: West Bengal's Women Draw on Village Tradition to Stop Domestic Violence.* Ford Foundation Report, New York.

Sassen, Saskia. 1999. "Culture Beyond Gender." In *Is Multiculturalism Bad for Women?* edited by Susan Moller Okin. Princeton, N.J.: Princeton University Press.

Sen, Amartya. 1995. "Gender Inequality and Theories of Justice." In *Women, Culture, and Development: A Study of Human Capabilities,* edited by Martha Nussbaum and J. Glover. Oxford: Clarendon Press.

Shachar, Ayelet. 1998. "Group Identity and Women's Rights in Family Law: The Perils of Multicultural Accommodation." *Journal of Political Philosophy* 6(3): 295–305.

———. 2000. "On Citizenship and Multicultural Vulnerability." *Political Theory* 28: 64.

Silver, Joan Micklin. 1975. *Hester Street.* Film.

Tamir, Yael. 1999. "Siding with the Underdogs." In *Is Multiculturalism Bad for Women?* edited by Susan Moller Okin. Princeton, N.J.: Princeton University Press.

Yip, Yvonne. 1999. "The Case of a Father's Refusal to Spare the Rod." *Christian Science Monitor,* September 15: 1.

# Part III

## The Universal Human Rights Debate: Mobilization and Resistance

# Chapter 13

# Between Nationalism and Feminism: Indigenous Women, Community, and State

## Maivân Clech Lâm

The over-all scenario is that in such a deprived and oppressed culture it would seem ludicrous to suggest that either sex could be a victor.
—Jackie Huggins, "Aboriginal Women and the Women's
Liberation Movement of Australia" (1990)

I'm always emphatic that while we are recognized as a
women's organization, we're more than that. We represent
our families and we represent our communities and we represent our Nations. . . . We still know amongst ourselves
that we have a responsibility to put them [the men] back on
track regardless of the system of the nation that we come
from.
—Marilyn Kane, Native Women's Association of Canada
(Turpel 1990)

It is also said that when a girl is born the mountain laughs
and the birds cry, because her future activities are not connected to logging the forest in order to sow, and her work
will not feed the birds. In the case of boys the opposite is
said, that the mountain sheds tears and the birds laugh, because the men destroy part of the mountain in order to cultivate it and, at the same time, the food they grow will also
serve to feed the birds. Through these metaphors the difference is defined culturally . . . but not a superiority or inferiority between the functions.
—Leonor Zalabata Torres, "Keeping Traditions Alive"
(1998)

Feminist theories of the West rose out of a European male
dominance of European women that could only perceive
women and children as property or chattels. This is not our
history. Maori society recognised *Wahine Rangatira* (Maori

> women chiefs), *Tohunga* (experts, wise women) and *Ariki*
> (high priests or paramount chiefs) who made binding deci-
> sions for her people.
> —Moana Sinclair, "Pakeha Land Legislation in
> Aotearoa" (1998)

The Fourth World Conference on Women was held in Beijing from September 4 to 15, 1995. The host of the conference, the government of the People's Republic of China, segregated the deliberations of official state delegations to the conference from those of representatives of nongovernmental organizations (NGOs). The latter consequently met, not in Beijing, but in the nearby location of Huairou, from August 30 through September 8, 1995. Some 110 indigenous women, representing almost as many indigenous organizations based in 26 different countries, participated in the NGO Forum section of the conference. Dissatisfied with the joint Draft Platform for Action that was drawn up at the conclusion of the Beijing and Huairou proceedings, these women issued a parallel statement of their own, entitled the 1995 Beijing Declaration of Indigenous Women (International Work Group for Indigenous Affairs 1998, 316–26). The document records its authors' views of the distinctive circumstances, needs, and aspirations of indigenous women in local, state, and global society; it also underlines their differences with the majority Draft Platform for Action.

This chapter proposes that the Beijing Declaration, when read in the context of the last three decades' campaign of indigenous peoples for the recognition and protection of the rights of their communities at the United Nations, locates indigenous women in a discursive space that might be called multicultural feminism and that lies somewhere between the past century's powerful discourses of nationalism and liberal feminism. The chapter further suggests that indigenous women's negotiation of that space holds considerable relevance for the debate that has emerged in the increasingly multicultural states of Western Europe, North America, Australia, and New Zealand–Aotearoa on the place of multiculturalism in the liberal state and, correlatively, the relationship of individual choice to cultural group constraint. That such a debate now exercises these societies is due to the unprecedented transnational movement of peoples unleashed in the last decades by the global economy's profound disruption of prior social, political, and geographical spaces. The disruption in turn has engendered the most radical interrogation of the nation-state—its assumptions, function, and relevance—heard since the French Revolution first synthesized that institution in 1789 (Anderson 1991; Chatterjee 1986; Gellner 1983; Greenfeld 1992; Hobsbawm 1992; Smith 1983; Young 1976). In the process, it has become evident that the ideology of the nation-state—that is, nationalism—while clearly liberatory of the Third World as a whole at midcentury, at the same time imposed significant constraints on a number of groups within it. Foremost among these were women and indigenous or tribal peoples (Chatterjee 1993; Lâm 2000).

The constraints were prompted by the anticolonial movement's need to unify peoples and glorify histories as it sought to generate and amass the political energy required to evict colonizers and build independent modern states. The task of unification, nationalism taught, demanded the suppression of ethnic difference; and so it was that Ibo and Yoruba had to become Nigerian, just as Breton and Auvergnat had had to become French two centuries earlier. The task of glorifying the past, in contrast, entailed a certain exaggeration of gender distinctions. As Partha Chatterjee has observed in the case of India, the more colonialism—and later, independence—drew men out of their traditional milieu into the ambivalent workplace of an imposed and later borrowed modernity, the more it fell to women to assure the reproduction of what passed, in an already irreversibly transformed society, for the authenticating and reassuring domain of tradition (Chatterjee 1986).

In reality, of course, things were not so clear-cut. Political unification and historical glorification did not touch ethnic communities and social classes equally. Groups at the center of the political vortex generally underwent a greater transformation than those existing at its margins. The parties affected, in addition, were not necessarily recalcitrant. Independence and tradition did figure as weighty values, worthy of pursuit and sacrifice, to many if not most in the Third World after World War Two. Today, however, as the grip of nationalism loosens in parts of Asia and Africa, and the intrusion of global capital deepens in all parts of the world, ethnic communities as well as organizations of women are emerging who question the costs of their assigned roles under the lingering order of the nation-state.

Indigenous women stand at the confluence of these two groups, a fact that those who met in Beijing made clear. As such, indigenous women throw in their lot with—but not under—their communities, or so the statements of those who speak in public fora on their behalf indicate. The dual task in which indigenous women are engaged—protecting and restoring their communities inside states, and negotiating their own rights and obligations within those communities—thus speaks to the question now facing many states, and indeed figures as the subject of this chapter: Can individual, group, and state rights coexist?

## THE 1995 BEIJING DECLARATION OF INDIGENOUS WOMEN

The Beijing Declaration consists of three parts. The first asserts a number of fundamental propositions that its authors espouse, the leading one being "The Earth is our Mother." The Declaration next states that indigenous women have come together "to collectively decide what we can do to bring about a world which we would like our children and our children's children to live in." The section then asserts its kinship with existing international instruments that advance the rights of indigenous peoples and of women respectively, such as the 1994 United Nations Draft Declaration on the Rights of Indigenous Peoples and the 1979 Convention on the Elimination of All Forms of Discrimination Against Women (CEDAW) (United Nations Document E/CN.4 1995). The section goes on to emphasize indigenous women's insistence on their communities' rights to self-determination and territory. Next, the triple nature of indigenous women's oppression—as indigenous, female, and poor—at the hands of colonial and neo-colonial states is emphasized. The section identifies rich industrialized states, transnational corporations (TNCs), and financial institutions as the forces whose policies on globalization and trade liberalization rain abuse on indigenous lands and communities. It also decries the World Trade Organization (WTO) for privatizing and appropriating indigenous communities' intellectual legacies via the creation of a regime of trade-related intellectual property rights (TRIPS). Finally, the Human Genome Diversity Project is condemned.

The second part of the Beijing Declaration faults the Beijing Draft Platform for Action for certain commissions as well as omissions. The offending commissions consist of the platform's support for trade liberalization and open markets, and its advocacy of equal power, status, and pay for women in the face of its silence over the inequality between nations, races, and classes. Omissions include the platform's failure to: critique the New World Order; provide a coherent analysis of women's poverty; challenge the underlying premise of structural adjustment programs; question the Western orientation of education and health programs; and link the violence to and trafficking of indigenous women to the engulfing phenomena of globalization, militarization, and tourism. The section concludes, "The Platform's overemphasis on gender discrimination and gender equality depoliticizes the issues confronting indigenous women."

The third and final part of the Beijing Declaration sets out a number of demands. The first asks states and international organizations to recognize indigenous peoples' right to self-determination and to provide for their historical, political, social, cultural, economic, and religious rights in appropriate constitutional and legal instruments. Accordingly, states are asked to ratify the U.N. Draft Declaration, which advances these rights. The remaining sets of demands are for territory; intercultural, bilingual, nonracist and nonsexist education; affordable health services, promotion of the reproductive health of indigenous women, respect for indigenous healers and a healthy environment; protection against ethnocide, genocide, forced sterilization and other antifertility programs, media debasement of indigenous women, domestic and state violence; the investigation and prosecution of rapes and sexual enslavement of indigenous women by state agents; promotion of customary laws that support women victims of violence and eradication of customary laws that discriminate against women; the return and rehabilitation of displaced indigenous persons; respect for indigenous peoples' intellectual and cultural legacies; equal participation of indigenous women in community, state, and international fora, governmental as well as NGO.

Overall, the Beijing Declaration reflects the dual consciousness of its authors both as members of communities that are under siege from outside forces, and as members of a gendered class of persons who experience violence directed at it primarily from outside, but also from within. The women behind the Beijing Declaration thus point to changes needed in their own societies, but also clearly identify the global economy and its agents as the primary source of the damage being visited on them, their health, culture, lands, and communities. Consequently, the women demand greater empowerment on all external fronts, from enclosing states, intergovernmental institutions, and NGOs.

## THE INDIGENOUS PEOPLES' CAMPAIGN AT THE UNITED NATIONS

Beginning in a concerted fashion in the 1970s, members of indigenous communities, ably assisted by a number of academic and NGO allies, asked the United Nations to investigate and arrest the deteriorating situation—amounting in some cases to ethnocide and genocide—of indigenous and tribal peoples around the world that, they pleaded, resulted from states' disregard of and discrimination against their communities. Responding to this request, the United Nations in 1983 formed a Working Group on Indigenous Populations (see Lâm 2000). Composed, in U.N. parlance, of five independent experts who are appointed by states but act in their individual capacities, the Working Group has met annually in Geneva since its inception to receive information on the situation of indigenous peoples around the world, and to propose standards for state-indigenous relations. The latter effort culminated in a 1994 U.N. Draft Declaration on the Rights of Indigenous Peoples that is currently being reviewed in a higher forum of the United Nations—the Human Rights Commission, a body made up exclusively of state representatives. In time, the Commission likely will forward the Declaration to the Economic and Social Council of the General Assembly, which in turn is expected to submit it to the full General Assembly for debate and adoption. Should the latter adopt the document, its terms then become standards that states are expected, but not obliged, to meet in their relations with indigenous peoples. A subsequent process for generating a convention then would have to be launched and completed before the standards at issue become binding rules of international treaty law. Alternatively, the same standards become binding rules of customary international law to the extent that states and international organizations generally invoke and observe them, as some have begun to do.

The Working Group deliberately refrained from supplying a definition of indigenous peoples in its 1994 U.N. Draft Declaration; at such an incipient stage of the U.N. lawmaking process, it judged that a definition would be both premature and divisive. As a result, U.N. fora concerned with indigenous peoples continue to operate on the basis of a working description advanced in 1971 by the author of the first U.N.-commissioned study on indigenous peoples, José R. Martínez Cobo. The Cobo formula is understood to cover both tribal and indigenous peoples.

> Indigenous communities, peoples and nations are those which, having a historical continuity with pre-invasion and pre-colonial societies that devel-

oped on their territories, consider themselves distinct from other sectors of the societies now prevailing in those territories, or parts of them. They form at present non-dominant sectors of society and are determined to preserve, develop and transmit to future generations *their ancestral territories*, and their ethnic identity, as the basis of their continued existence as peoples, in accordance with their own cultural patterns, social institutions, and legal systems. (United Nations 1987, emphasis added)

As the 1994 U.N. Draft Declaration now stands, its most controversial item—one that indigenous peoples vehemently assert and states almost as vehemently resist—is Article 3 (United Nations Document E/CN.4 1995, 2), which states, "Indigenous peoples have the right of self-determination. By virtue of that right they freely determine their political status and freely pursue their economic, social and cultural development." An identical provision (United Nations Document A/4684 1961)—with the exception of the opening phrase "All peoples" instead of "Indigenous peoples"—first appeared in the 1960 General Assembly Declaration on the Granting of Independence to Colonial Countries and Peoples, a document that stands as the decolonization instrument par excellence of the U.N. system.

While the right of self-determination in international law is understood to confer on its holder the legal ability to choose a political status ranging anywhere from incorporation with an existing state to free and reversible association with it to total independence, virtually all colonial territories in the latter half of the twentieth century invoked the right to create their own independent states. Owing to this history, U.N. member-states today associate any substate entity's invocation of this right with the specter of secession. They apparently forget that the right of self-determination also encompasses other options, such as the status of free association that, for example, currently binds (for finite but renewable increments of years) the sovereign state of the Federated States of Micronesia to the United States. Instead of exploring further variants of this flexible status of free association for state-indigenous relations, a number of states—among which the United States figures prominently—categorically oppose recognizing the right of self-determination in indigenous peoples.

This is the case, notwithstanding that the overwhelming majority of representatives of indigenous peoples at the United Nations consistently affirm that they expect to apply the right, not to claim independence, but to negotiate modes of free association with their enclosing states that would ensure the survival and welfare of their communities. That is, indigenous peoples seek something that looks like autonomy on the ground but that unlike autonomy (which is a state's voluntary and hence reversible devolution of its power onto a substate entity) would be anchored in the international legal right of self-determination—which no state may transgress at will.

While the debate on whether or not indigenous peoples have a right to self-determination simmers on in the Human Rights Commission, it should be noted that, to date, most U.N. member-states in Geneva appear surprisingly open to the remaining provisions of the U.N. Draft Declaration, which taken as a whole already enshrine a broad range of self-governing powers for indigenous communities in their traditional territories. The question that the recognition of substate group rights here raises is twofold: How is self-government of indigenous communities to be reconciled with the sovereignty of their enclosing states, and how are individual human rights of members of such communities to be guaranteed against infringement by their own societies? The first issue calls into question the very notion of the nation-state; the second implicates among other things the status of women within indigenous communities.

## SELF-DETERMINATION VERSUS NATIONALISM

If self-government for substate ethnic entities sounds anomalous today, no doubt this is because the homogenizing and totalizing idea of the nation-state, consolidated in France as recently as 1789, went on to seize the imagination of much of the rest of the world over the next two centuries. For most of human history, however, the notion that the unitary polity of the state must be matched by its cultural unity did not exist. Instead, where premodern centralized polities arose, these generally assumed the form of loosely knit empires or tributary networks whose culturally diverse constituent entities the central authority recognized and accommodated in varying degrees. Even in the case of the Ottoman Empire, which lasted well into the twentieth century, accommodation rather than assimilation remained the order of the day with the result, among others, that several parallel legal systems with special jurisdiction over corresponding ethnic and religious groups that the empire enclosed coexisted within a single state. Given that states today fit less and less well the imagined profile of the nation-state, the time has come to probe former polities such as the Ottoman Empire for perspectives and approaches that might again prove useful, or at least suggestive, in the present globalizing moment.

Nationalism, admittedly, retains its spell, as recurrent attempts in various parts of the world (most recently, Eastern Europe and Indonesia) to fashion new ethnically congruent states out of old multicultural ones demonstrate. At first glance, the ongoing compulsion of some ethnic groups to mutate into new nation-states at a time when globalization is rendering the institution of the state itself increasingly impotent appears incomprehensible. On closer inspection, however, a certain logic emerges that suggests that globalization itself is driving the engine of nationalism. To begin with, since transnational institutions increasingly make the economic decisions that affect national as well as local communities, the latter understandably seek direct access to such institutions so as to influence them, in the same way that they previously sought direct access to the state in order to influence it. To date, there is but one way of accessing the WTO, the IMF, and the World Bank—and that is to be or become a state.

Further, while states have yielded much of their economic sovereignty to transnational institutions such as the WTO, most continue to assert a staunch sovereignty in human rights matters. To put it differently, the traditionally ambiguous role of the state as simultaneous coercer and succorer of the citizenry is breaking now as states increasingly defend their ability to oppress even as they plead an inability to protect, at least in the economic realm (Diamond 1974, 254–80). No wonder then that as states offer less and less even as they permit the taking of more and more by global economic forces, the minority ethnic groups that the states enclose seek out ways of going it alone. Nationalism is one such way.

Finally, there is the matter of meaning, understood in its conceptual as well as affective sense. The global economy currently advances, with the abetment of states, within an associated complex of political, legal, and cultural practices variously called structural adjustment, law reform, the marketplace of ideas, and so on. For many, this complex is experienced as deeply intrusive and destructive of their preexisting systems of power, order, and meaning. When aroused by gifted and unscrupulous leaders, some consequently reach for the ideology of a narrow nationalism or communalism in the hope that it restores to them a sense of intactness, meaning, and power.

The statements of indigenous peoples' representatives at international fora, however, interestingly suggest that they are searching for a rather different response to globalization, one that departs in fundamental respects from the earlier nationalistic reaction to colonialism. For one thing, few indigenous spokespersons intone the absolutist language of nationalism or actively pursue separate statehood. Their reasons probably include their recognition of the typically small size (demographic as well as territorial) of their communities, which makes the grand narrative of nationalism sound implausible. Perhaps as important, the indigenous world—which many now call the Fourth World—unlike the classical colonies in the Third World became an organized international force in the postmodern present when grand narratives in general (excepting that of the market) are losing much of their mystical aura. Additionally, from the start of their campaign at the United Nations, indigenous organizations have been intimately associated with an array of NGOs whose characteristically internationalist (as opposed to nationalist) bent apparently rubbed off. Finally, and perhaps most importantly, indigenous peoples simply are enacting their own history, not reenacting that of the Third World. In today's overly homogenizing world, what they concretely seek is the preservation and reconstitution of their historically shaped and territorially based cultural communities, and not the creation of idealized new nation-states.

The 1994 U.N. Draft Declaration, which by and large encodes the aspirations that indigenous peoples made known to the Working Group for over more than a decade, thus contemplates a plausible mix of closure and exposure for their communities vis-à-vis their enclosing states. Attentive to indigenous peoples' expressed wish to retain the rights and obligations of citizenship in the multicultural states in which they live even as they reclaim control over their traditional territories contained therein, the Declaration in effect advances a model for delinking ethnicity and citizenship. Whether and how the model will work—or even get a chance to work—remains to be seen; at best, it constitutes a conceptualization of a work in progress, to be tested through trial and error as states and indigenous peoples execute its provisions.

In any event, the very crafting of the Declaration in the highly visible public forum of the United Nations over the course of the last decade already has released palpable new energy in that body. Many U.N. member-states now readily acknowledge that their societies are multicultural ones. Furthermore, most seem prepared to accept a substantial measure of self-government for the indigenous communities that they enclose. Indigenous peoples, for their part, are enunciating something like a concentric conception of political space that they wish to inhabit. As such, their scheme departs markedly from the simpler conceptual worlds of both liberalism and nationalism. At the core of their scheme lie their territorially based communities over which they demand maximal political authority. The adjoining circle is the enclosing state, in which most indigenous peoples continue to assert personal civic rights and accept personal civic responsibilities. The outermost circle represents international society, in which indigenous peoples now insist on playing a formal, regularized role.

## LIBERAL VERSUS MULTICULTURAL FEMINISM

The dominant feminist discourse in the world today is properly termed Western and liberal because, like the general human rights matrix that surrounds it, liberal feminism has roots in and is marked by the European Enlightenment, an intellectual enterprise that above all consecrated individual liberty. Liberal feminism, like nationalism, has proved both helpful and harmful to women in the Third and Fourth Worlds. The good that the liberal feminist movement has brought to women there and in the West in the last decades lies primarily in the extraordinary global attention that the movement has managed to focus in a relatively short period of time on a range of injustices, old and new, that women suffer. Scanning legal developments on the international front alone, a recent publication of the Center for the Study of Human Rights at Columbia University (1996) lists forty-five "basic" documents of human rights law that in either general or specific terms address the situation and needs of women. Most of the documents, in addition, were drawn up in the last two decades, which attests to an intensification of the international focus on women's issues. This remarkable (if incomplete and occasionally miscast) turnaround of consciousness in the world regarding gender issues of course is not limited to the field of international law but also influences, generally to the benefit of women, national and international policies and practices in the areas of education, employment, health, and development. Given the lack of resources in the countries of the South, together with the surplus of state authoritarianism typically expended there on behalf of the status quo, that an impact of this magnitude in this short a time would have resulted from a feminist movement that had originated in the South rather than the North is highly unlikely.

At the same time, the strong imprint of Western history and culture on liberal feminism is now causing many women (and also men) mainly from the South but also from the North to challenge some of its key premises and advance alternative ones under an approach that is loosely termed *multicultural feminism*. The critique that multicultural feminists offer of liberal feminism, in a nutshell, is that the individualistic and imperialistic constraints of its milieu of origin blind it to the realities of the lives of most women in the world today (Okin 1999). Among other things, the individualistic constraint drives liberal feminists to see virtually all gender differences in all cultures as intolerable injustices that must be fixed on behalf of the injured individual regardless of the severity of the disparity, its cause, or her society's readiness for such intervention. Thus, while nationalism typically subordinates the concrete needs of women in the Third World to the allegedly higher imperatives of the fanciful nation-state, liberal feminism too often devalues, in the name of a chimerical global sisterhood, the ties to their sociocultural communities that most women in the world continue to prize and nurture. The imperialistic legacy of the West for its part habituates Westerners to a status of hegemony—including a hegemony of truth—vis-à-vis persons in the South. This unexamined habit of power, as much as ingrained habits of thought, impels Western feminists to brandish their particular understanding of the subordination of women as the universal understanding.

While individualistic and imperialistic constraints hem in liberal feminism, they by no means invalidate its entire discourse, elements of which often have served women well. Likewise, the tradition-derived and nationalism-reinforced emphasis on social obligation that generally dominates discourse in the South conditions, but does not vitiate, its emerging discourse of multicultural feminism. At the same time, to say that both North and South are simply equally constrained on the subject of feminism advances nothing. Power by and large resides with the North, not the South: the power to name, direct action, ignore, and be free from self-doubt. Therein lies all the difference. Indeed, this very difference—and all that it betokens for an authentically empowering feminist movement that is reflective of and responsive to the particular experiences of women—is what multicultural feminism now wants recognized. Abdullahi An-Na'im (1987, 491–516) puts it this way:

> Our commitment should not be to the right of women in the abstract, or as contained in high-sounding international instruments signed by official delegations. It should be a commitment to the rights of women in practice; the rights of rural and nomadic African and Asian women to live in very "traditional" or tribal communities and practice Islam, or other religious beliefs, out of genuine conviction. These women cannot and should not be invited to subscribe to a supposedly "international" feminist vision without enabling them, at the same time, to live in harmony with their immediate environment.

The multicultural critique of liberal feminism thus does not so much challenge its analysis of the situation of women in the North (where the circumstances of certain classes of women lend themselves well to a liberal feminist analysis) as it decries the latter's often unsophisticated, reductionist, and finally dismissive construction of gender roles in the South. Chandra Mohanty (1988, 70), who has written extensively on this problematic construction, observes,

> Thus all women, regardless of class and cultural differences, are seen as being similarly affected by this system. Not only are *all* Arab and Muslim women seen to constitute a homogeneous oppressed group, but there is no discussion of the more specific *practices* within the family which constitute women as mothers, wives, sisters, etc. Arabs and Muslims, it appears, don't change at all. Their patriarchal family is carried over from the times of the Prophet Muhammad. They exist, as it were, outside history.

The essentializing of an entire sex in an entire religious world as oppressed reinforces and is reinforced by liberal feminism's tendency to give a univalent reading to unfamiliar cultural symbols and practices that it encounters in the south: all veiling, all instances of purdah, all forms of female genital modification mean one thing and one thing only—the subordination of women (Mohanty 1988). In the process, liberal feminism dismisses both the complexity of culture and the agency of the women of the South.

While misperception and reductionism typically characterize all cultural groups' construction of the Other, the power to affect the life of the Other through such distortions is not detained equally by all groups. To the extent that women in the North hold greater power than women in the South, the former's errors in its construction of the lives of the latter are not merely regrettable but sometimes downright dangerous. Azizah al-Hibri (1994) illustrates this in the context of international human rights conferences. She relates that, much to the dismay of women from the Third World, First World women exploited their vaster resources at the 1981 U.N. Mid-Decade for Women conference in Copenhagen, the 1993 World Conference on Human Rights in Vienna, and the 1994 International Conference on Population and Development in Cairo to control their proceedings and to speak in the name of all women. In Copenhagen, First World women announced that the gravest concerns of Third World women were veiling and clitoridectomy; in Cairo, they said that these were contraception and abortion. When Third World women finally spoke on their own behalf in Cairo, they asserted instead that their highest priorities were peace and development. Their voices, however, were drowned out by those of First Worlders keen on pushing the Cairo conference to focus, as al-Hibri (1994, 9) puts it, on "reducing the number of Third World babies in order to preserve the earth's resources, despite (or is it 'because of') the fact that the First World consumes much of these resources."

The First World's single-minded reproductive agenda in Cairo, which many in the developing countries saw as racist, seriously tainted some Third World women who participated in that conference in their own countries. In addition, because First Worlders in Cairo "forced the issue of abortion on everyone," thereby provoking a conservative backlash in Muslim countries, women there have since found it more difficult to obtain an abortion. According to al-Hibri, "This presents a retrenchment, since, for hundreds of years, Muslim jurists have had quite a liberal analysis of abortion, and, unlike the situation that used to exist in the United States, safe abortions were widely available in many Muslim countries" (1994, 9).

Al-Hibri (1994, 11) concludes from these experiences that Third World feminists now must forge their own paths.

> They will recruit supportive First World feminists to help them in their efforts, but they will specify the kind of support needed, and they will lead their own battles. They will not seek to achieve their liberation by denigrating their religion or culture or by forcing upon their communities inappropriate priorities and demands.

An-Na'im, Mohanty, al-Hibri, indigenous women quoted at the beginning of this chapter, and those who expressed themselves in the Beijing Declaration all share this in common: a high appreciation of the importance of the ties that bind women to their communities. Nevertheless, the question remains: What legal protection, if any, should an individual have against abuse from her own cultural community?

## INDIGENOUS RIGHTS: INDIVIDUAL AND COLLECTIVE

This question in essence was raised twenty years ago in two cases brought by indigenous women against a tribal government in the United States and the Canadian government, respectively. In the first, Julia Martinez and other female members of the Santa Clara Pueblo challenged in federal court a 1939 tribal ordinance that denied tribal membership—and its attached entitlements—to the children of female members who married outside the tribe, but not to children of male members who did likewise. This disparate treatment of children based on the sex of their parents, the women charged, violated the equal protection guarantee of the 1968 Indian Civil Rights Act, which Congress had enacted and imposed on tribes. In a 1978 decision, the U.S. Supreme Court held that the Act, which was silent on the matter, did not confer on Indians the right to bring a private cause of action in federal court against their tribes, and so ruled against Martinez (*Santa Clara Pueblo v. Martinez*, 436 U.S. 49 [1978]). The Court noted that the Act balanced two goals: the advancement of the rights of individual Indians, and the preservation of tribal government. Under the circumstances, the Court found, Congress did not intend to subject tribes to suits brought in federal court by their own members; it merely intended that the Act become the substantive law applied by tribal courts, which alone could hear a private suit brought under it against a tribe.

At about the same time that the U.S. Supreme Court decided *Martinez*, the *Case of Sandra Lovelace*, with quite similar facts, reached the U.N. Human Rights Committee in Geneva (United Nations Document A/36/40 1981). Lovelace, a Maliseet Indian woman, married a non-Indian in 1970, thereby running afoul of Canada's federal 1869 Indian Act. The latter not only defined Indian status patrilineally throughout Canada regardless of particular tribes' own systems of descent, it also specified that an Indian woman who marries a non-Indian loses her Indian status and associated privileges vis-à-vis government programs, but an Indian man who marries out is not similarly divested (Bayefsky 1982). Lovelace charged that Canada's federal law violated the 1966 International Covenant on Civil and Political Rights, which forbids discrimination on the basis of sex. The U.N. Human Rights Committee agreed and ordered Canada to amend its law, which it did in 1985 following prolonged consultations with tribes.

The two cases thus highlighted the question of the rightful legal relationships between an individual, her tribe, the state, and in the case of *Lovelace*, international society. Liberal feminists generally decried the *Martinez* outcome, and applauded that in *Lovelace*. Native American legal commentators in the United States, however—male and female—generally praised the *Martinez* outcome for its defense of Indian tribal self-government. Gloria Valencia-Weber and Christine Zuni (1995, 91–92) write,

> For Indian feminists, every women's issue is framed in the larger context of Native American people. . . . Tribes insist that treaty-based sovereignty supersedes any other federal mandate. . . . The return to tradition, retraditionalization, coupled with the evolution of gender roles in American Indian society continue the complementary and mutual roles enjoyed by women and men.

The writers point out that the ordinance at issue in *Martinez* did not reflect a general situation of disadvantage for women in tribal societies, as other tribes (such as the Navaho and the Onondaga) allot residence and other privileges matrilineally. In addition, internal changes produced by the tribes' own reinterpretation of their traditions already have elevated several women to the position of tribal head. The writers note that the United States, by comparison, has still to elect its first woman president. While arguing that change, where needed, best comes through the internal reinterpretation of tradition, Valencia-Weber and Zuni (1995) nevertheless recognize that indigenous women need an avenue of recourse when abuses go unchecked in their own communities. Given the sorry history of U.S.-tribal relations, however, the writers clearly prefer that such recourse be to an international, rather than state or federal, body. In any event, Valencia-Weber and Zuni believe that the mechanism for delimiting tribal membership belongs with tribes. The *Lovelace* decision does not run counter to this view, because the U.N. Human Rights Committee there overturned Canada's definition of Indian status, and not that of a tribe.

International recourse does not now exist for indigenous individuals with complaints against their communities, for the simple reason that the latter do not enjoy under international law legal personality that for the moment is reserved to states, international organizations, and exceptional entities such as the Vatican and the P.L.O. As a result, indigenous communities have neither specific rights nor obligations under international law. However, provisions in the U.N. Draft Declaration, if converted into law, would offer them a form of international legal personality. At that point, it stands to reason, they would have to accept commensurate international obligations relative to human rights. The jurisdiction of the Human Rights Committee in theory could be enlarged at that time to reach their actions, along with those of states. In addition, as Valencia-Weber and Zuni note, the U.N. Draft Declaration could, but did not, include provisions offering protection for indigenous individuals relative to their communities. That omission remains remediable.

In the absence of such international recourse, indigenous women who feel aggrieved in their own communities now must turn to formal institutions of the enclosing state, as in the *Martinez* case, with results that may either disappoint the women or injure their communities. The *Martinez* trap, however, in theory could be avoided if civil, rather than governmental, institutions of the enclosing state become sites of recourse and redress. In the United States and Canada, for example, where tribes share a history of joint action vis-à-vis their enclosing states, the appropriate institution might be, as some scholars have proposed, a pan-tribal council with powers of moral suasion if not enforcement. Alternatively, a council of independent experts, such as currently staff the U.N. Human Rights Committee, could be jointly constituted by tribes and the enclosing state to review complaints of a certain gravity that indigenous individuals lodge against their communities. What works will differ according to context.

The balancing of individual liberty with cultural group rights within the context of the contemporary liberal state thus remains very much a work in progress, if indeed the work has begun at all. As such, rigid allocations of legal rights and responsibilities are premature, if not altogether inappropriate. Instead, broad constitutive principles that recognize the inviolability of core individual liberties, as well as the essential value of cultural traditions to their holders, need to be enshrined, along with creative processes for resolving conflicts between these two principles when they arise. In addition, where mechanisms within states prove unsatisfactory, regional and international ones must be provided. As the dialogue on the dialectics of individual liberty and collective culture proceeds on all these levels—local, state, and international—cultural communities, ever-changing, likely will themselves find a satisfactory method for mediating the dialectic.

Indigenous women active in their communities today express a strong but reflective solidarity with their men. This reflexivity springs from, among other things, ideas that the women have culled from the liberal feminist discourse to which they have been exposed in state and international fora, but which they have reprocessed (as the Beijing Declaration shows) through the lens of their own keen commitment to the interdependencies that weave their lives. This commitment has motivated indigenous peoples worldwide to sustain a three-decade-long campaign at the United Nations to have their right to self-determination and territory recognized. In the process, indigenous women—much more so than their counterparts in the Third World at decolonization—also voiced their gender's specific needs. They were able to do so because indigenous men (unlike those of the Third World) are not particularly distanced from indigenous women; the pull of modernity by definition largely bypassed both genders. Moreover, indigenous peoples' relatively modest project of preserving or reconstituting their small-scale societies generates no grand myth that calls for the suppression of women. Where suppression exists it issues rather from poverty, negative acculturation, and the desperation that these circumstances breed, as the Beijing Declaration makes clear.

At the same time, even though the state directly or indirectly has impoverished indigenous communities in modern times, the latter can now rarely function without some material assistance from the former. Yet indigenous communities cannot survive at all (in the cultural if not physical sense) if they do not soon succeed in limiting the intrusion of the state and transnational capital in their territories. For this reason, the U.N. Draft Declaration proposes a stance of simultaneous closure and exposure for indigenous peoples vis-à-vis enclosing states. The territorially bounded self-government indigenous peoples seek, while seemingly drastic, nevertheless is probably easier for the liberal state to envisage than a system of nonterritorially based group rights. For this reason, the accommodation being worked out at the United Nations for indigenous peoples may not translate easily to other groups. However, an important principle does.

An individual, undistorted by nationalist ideology or by an acute political crisis, does not love family, ethnic community, and state with equal intensity. While only totalitarian regimes demand that the most intense of loves be lavished on the state, all nationalisms in fact veer in the same direction. How the reversal of this dangerous trend is to happen remains to be seen. The U.N. Draft Declaration represents an early experiment.

Women will not become automatic victims in such an experiment. While a substate cultural group can certainly mete out discrimination and violence, it normally cannot match the coercive power of the state to do the same. In addition, a cultural community is not organized around limited interests but persists only if it reconciles the diverse needs of individuals and collectivities that compose its unity. A culture's tenets, values, and practices are thus binary, as Levi-Strauss first noted, if not multivalent. Women are both subordinate and dominant within it. Furthermore, cultures change from internal pressure as well as external stimuli. Finally, the discourse of human rights is now fairly ubiquitous, and effective where mechanisms for enforcing core individual liberties exist.

Yet the human rights movement will not grow if it holds out Western values as universal ones. Michael Ignatieff (1999, 54) reminds us that even the 1948 Universal Declaration of Human Rights was not about advancing Western values; instead it was about eternally banning some of them, such as sexism, racism, and anti-Semitism. Ignatieff (1999, 41) further writes, "Human rights is universal not as a vernacular of cultural prescription but as a language of moral empowerment. Its role is not in defining the content of culture but trying to enfranchise all agents so that they can freely shape that content."

At the same time, because human existence is fundamentally dialogical (see, for example, the work of Charles Taylor), these free agents also will engage in conceptual exchanges, in their cultural communities and, increasingly, across them (Gutman 1994)—a dialogue, hopefully, not of universalists, but of beings open to intersubjectivity.

---

The author gratefully acknowledges Martha Thomas's invaluable role in the genesis of this chapter.

# REFERENCES

Al-Hibri, Azizah. 1994. "Who Defines Women's Rights? A Third World Woman's Response." *Human Rights Brief* 2(1): 9, 11.

Anderson, Benedict. 1991. *Imagined Communities: Reflections on the Origin and Spread of Nationalism.* London: Verso.

An-Na'im, Abdullahi. 1987. "The Rights of Women and International Law in the Muslim Context." *Whittier Law Review* 9: 491–516.

Bayefsky, Anne F. 1982. "The Human Rights Committee and the Case of Sandra Lovelace." *Canada Yearbook of International Law* 20: 244–65.

Center for Human Rights. 1996. *Women and Human Rights: The Basic Documents.* New York: Columbia University Press.

Chatterjee, Partha. 1986. *Nationalist Thought and the Colonial World: A Derivative Discourse.* London: Zed Books.

———. 1993. *The Nation and Its Fragments.* Princeton, N.J.: Princeton University Press.

Diamond, Stanley. 1974. *In Search of the Primitive.* New Brunswick: Transaction Books.

Gellner, Ernest. 1983. *Nations and Nationalism.* Ithaca, N.Y.: Cornell University Press.

Greenfeld, Liah. 1992. *Nationalism: Five Roads to Modernity.* Cambridge, Mass.: Harvard University Press.

Gutman, Amy. 1994. "The Politics of Recognition." In *Multiculturalism*, edited by Amy Gutman. Princeton, N.J.: Princeton University Press.

Hobsbawm, E. J. 1992. *Nations and Nationalism Since 1780.* 2d ed. Cambridge: Cambridge University Press.

Huggins, Jackie. 1990. "Aboriginal Women and the Women's Liberation Movement of Australia." In *Indigenous Women on the Move*, edited by The International Work Group for Indigenous Affairs. Copenhagen: International Secretariat of IWGIA.

Ignatieff, Michael. 1999. *Whose Universal Rights? The Crisis in Human Rights.* The Hague: Praemium Erasmianum Foundation.

International Work Group for Indigenous Affairs, eds. 1998. *Indigenous Women: The Right to a Voice*. Copenhagen: International Secretariat of IWGIA.

Lâm, Maivân Clech. 2000. *At the Edge of the State: Indigenous Peoples and Self-Determination*. Ardsley, N.Y.: Transnational.

Mohanty, Chandra. 1988. "Under Western Eyes: Feminist Scholarship and Colonial Discourses." *Feminist Review* 30: 70.

Okin, Susan Moller. 1999. *Is Multiculturalism Bad for Women?* edited by Susan Miller Okin. Princeton, N.J.: Princeton University Press.

Sinclair, Moana. 1998. "Pakeha Land Legislation in Aotearoa: The Continuous Resistance by Maori Women." In *Indigenous Women: The Right to a Voice*, edited by The International Work Group for Indigenous Affairs. Copenhagen: International Secretariat of IWGIA.

Smith, A. D. 1983. *State and Nation in the Third World: The Western State and African Nationalism*. Brighton, U.K.: Wheatsheaf Books.

Torres, Leonor Zalabata. 1998. "Keeping Traditions Alive." In *Indigenous Women: The Right to a Voice*, edited by The International Work Group for Indigenous Affairs. Copenhagen: International Secretariat of IWGIA.

Turpel, Mary Ellen. 1990. "The Women of Many Nations in Canada." In *Indigenous Women on the Move*, edited by The International Work Group for Indigenous Affairs. Copenhagen: International Secretariat of IWGIA.

United Nations. 1987. *Study of the Problem of Discrimination Against Indigenous Populations*. Vol. 5. *Conclusions, Proposals and Recommendations*. New York: United Nations.

Valencia-Weber, Gloria, and Christine P. Zuni. 1995. "Domestic Violence and Tribal Protection of Indigenous Women in the United States." *St. John's Law Review* 69: 91–2.

Young, Crawford. 1976. *The Politics of Cultural Pluralism*. Madison: University of Wisconsin Press.

# Chapter 14

# Neither Victim Nor Rebel: Feminism and the Morality of Gender and Family Life in a Hindu Temple Town

## Usha Menon

This chapter attempts to answer a question that appears to puzzle and trouble many feminist activists working in India today. Why, feminists ask, have they been relatively ineffective so far in mobilizing Hindu women both to protest gender injustices and directly fight them? Moreover (and this is a bitter pill to swallow), why has "politicized religion" (Jeffrey and Basu 1998) been so much more successful in motivating Hindu women to take to the streets in defense of a variety of religious causes?[1] As the feminist scholar Patricia Jeffrey (1998, 221) acknowledges, "Feminists can surely derive little satisfaction, for instance, from the BJP's [Bharatiya Janata Party] ability to mobilize women in defense of Ram's [an incarnation of the Hindu god Vishnu] birthplace, often in far greater numbers than feminist organizations have managed to mobilize women to protest dowry murder."

While this chapter does not attempt to address the latter question directly, with respect to the former I suggest that the reason why feminist groups working in India find themselves out of touch with ordinary Hindu women is because they offer these women little in terms of message and meanings that resonates with their lives. I submit that feminism is so particular a product of Western social and intellectual history and its moral order constructed so explicitly in terms of equality, individual rights, and personal choice that it appears completely alien to Hindu women, who live within another, equally elaborated moral order that cherishes self-control, self-improvement, duty to the extended family, and service to others.[2]

Hindu women here refers to upper-caste, predominantly Brahman women, who adhere to a fairly rigid code of conduct that revolves around self-control and service to others. These women, living in temple towns (that is, centuries-old traditional urban centers) and rural areas, hardly cosmopolitan in their outlook, are part of the traditional, ritual elite in Hindu India, even today. Women belonging to the lower castes (whether rural or urban), are not expected to and indeed do not follow Brahmanical practice and custom. Such practice remains the cultural ideal, however, and when a lower caste claims higher ritual status, it does so on the grounds that its customs and practices are becoming progressively more Brahmanical—the process termed *Sanskritization* by the Indian anthropologist M. N. Srinivas, the first to describe it.

Without overstating the distinctions between individualistic and group-oriented cultures (see, for example, Dumont 1980; Shweder and Bourne 1984; Markus and Kitayama 1991), the ideology of individualism that inspires feminism certainly can be identified as the primary reason for its failure to mobilize large numbers of Hindu women. Feminism, by focusing on the rights of women as individuals, attempts to challenge and dismantle family structures. Feminism targets such structures because it views them as constraining and restrictive of individual freedom—perhaps a basic distinction between feminist and Hindu thinking. In Hindu thought, an individual completes him- or herself as a human being through deepening and elaborating his or her relationships and interconnections with others: social and familial structures enable rather than impede such maturation. One finds oneself not through detaching or separating oneself from society but rather in and through one's relationships with others (Marriott 1976; Parish 1994). Thus, for upper-caste Hindu women living predominantly in temple towns and rural areas, the family roles they occupy when they mature and age provide them with the deepest sense of who they are. By discounting the importance of the family in these Hindu women's lives, feminist activists in India—whose avowed goal is to improve the life circumstances of these women—betray a lack of appreciation and a fundamental misunderstanding of their lived experiences.

The various feminisms, despite their many differences, share this ideology of individualism—even Carol Gilligan's relational feminism. Gilligan's (1993) version, which distinguishes itself from other varieties by stressing the importance of relationships in the lives of women, would be unacceptable to most upper-caste Hindu women. Gilligan (1993, 149) sees women as achieving maturity as moral beings when they are able "to consider it moral to care not only for others but for themselves"; she questions the morality of selflessness and suggests that an understanding of the concept of rights enables women to see "that the interests of the self can be considered legitimate." Thus, although Gilligan emphasizes the ethics of caring and importance of relationships to women, the primacy of the individual is never in question. This emphasis on the self would puzzle most upper-caste Hindus, men and women. They would see it as narcissistic, in some ways deeply immoral, and ultimately futile, because they believe that the experiencing self does not exist apart from one's connections with others.

## THE HINDU WOMAN UNDER THE FEMINIST GAZE

For many decades, the lives and experiences of Hindu women have proven a fertile ground for observation and academic scholarship. What follows is an overview of general trends rather than a full account of this impressive body of scholarship. In the early years, the predominant tendency was to emphasize the utter passivity of these women and sometimes their active complicity in their own subordination (a sample of such works includes Jeffrey 1979; Dhruvarajan 1989; Kondos 1989; Roy 1975; Allen 1976). While scholarly expositions on the Hindu woman as victim (see Balakrishnan 1994; Das 1995; Mani 1989; Rajan 1993) continue to appear with remarkable regularity, another trend has emerged: to emphasize the "agency" and "activism" these women supposedly display. Here, inspired by Scott's (1985) work on peasants in the Malaysian village of Sedaka, many feminist scholars have suggested that Hindu women only apparently acquiesce to male domination (Appadorai, Korom, and Mills 1991; Banerjee 1989; Jeffrey and Jeffrey 1996; Karlekar 1991; O'Hanlon 1991; Oldenberg 1991; Raheja and Gold 1994; Wadley 1994).[3] Using Scott's terms of reference, these scholars point to the "everyday forms of resistance" that Hindu women supposedly perform: "In various low-profile ways, women critique their subordination and resist the controls over them—in personal reminiscences or songs, in sabotage and cheating. The husband treated like a lord or deity to his face may be derided behind his back or given excessively salty meals" (Jeffrey 1998, 222). In a similar vein, while speaking of the expressive traditions of north Indian women, Raheja and Gold (1994, 26) suggest that "the active rebellion that may at one moment be impractical or impossible may at another moment become plausible precisely because the idea of social transformation has been nourished in proverbs, folk songs, jokes, rituals, legends, and languages."

Homegrown Indian feminists, stung by criticisms that they "are out of touch with local realities and are the only malcontents," apparently are drawing solace from such evidence of rural women's discontentment—it makes them feel less isolated and "deculturated" (Raheja and Gold 1994, 231–232). They are beginning to take heart because the "one vital message in the voices of unlettered village women, unaware of feminism as conventionally understood, is that they do critique their situations" (Jeffrey 1998, 232). The assumption, of course, that women's discontent with their particular life circumstances immediately and unproblematically translates into a desire to join the fight for women's rights appears naive. Feminists seemingly are unaware that all people, including Hindu women, are capable of reflecting on their situations and expressing dissatisfaction without necessarily seeing themselves as the victims of insidious, systemic exploitation, who need to rebel against inequitable social arrangements.

This is precisely the point that suggests an explanation for the failure of feminist organizations to muster the kind of substantial grassroots support they have been working toward since the 1970s. Feminist activists fail to appreciate that the large majority of Hindu women indeed do not perceive themselves as victims of systemic gender inequities. They may readily acknowledge that some women sometimes face difficulties during different phases of their lives, but they believe such situations are ameliorated through the actions of individual women and their family members, and do not require any kind of substantial and genderwide mobilization.

The question then arises: Why do Hindu women tend not to believe that they are the victims of systemic gender inequities? The answer lies primarily in the meanings that Hindu women derive from participating in the lives of their extended families. The following section represents the lives and experiences of Oriya Hindu women, within the context of the extended family, to show the ways in which, through participating wholeheartedly in their family life practices, they gain "meaning, purpose and a sense of power" (Menon and Shweder 1998, 140) in their lives. I use material gathered through observation and conversation over several years of fieldwork done in the temple town of Bhubaneswar in eastern India, during which I came to know many of the women who speak on these pages intimately.

## CUSTOMARY PRACTICE AND THINKING IN THE TEMPLE TOWN

The temple town of Bhubaneswar in Orissa, eastern India, has been described (for example, Seymour 1983, 1999; Mahapatra 1981; Shweder 1991; Menon and Shweder 1998) as centered around a medieval temple (tenth to eleventh century) dedicated to the Hindu god Siva, worshiped here in his form as Lord of the Phallus (Lingaraj). Most residents of the temple town belong to families that have hereditary connections with the temple, and they tend to follow customary Hindu thinking and practice in most aspects of their lives, even today.

Thus, like Hindus elsewhere (see Marriott 1990; Lamb 1993), Oriya Hindus here believe in the materiality, in the substantiality, of all phenomena; nothing is nonmaterial, not even space and time, and the only distinctions that can be drawn between different substances is in terms of subtlety and grossness. They also conceive of the body as open, fluid, and relatively unbounded, which, all through life, is partially shared and exchanged with others, through events such as birth and marriage and acts such as sharing food and living together (Inden and Nicholas 1977; Daniel 1984). Similarly, Hindus do not think of the person as indivisible and bounded—as an individual. Rather, the Hindu person is "dividual and divisible" (Marriott 1976, 111), continually changing and being reconstituted by the givings and receivings he or she engages in.

While believing that exchanges between people are inherent and inevitable, Hindus also use this theory of the relative permeability of the human body to deliberately manipulate and transform their physical substances to refine themselves. Throughout the life course, therefore, through daily practices (nityakarma) and rituals of refinement (samskara), Hindus regulate, manipulate, and transform themselves, the final such ritual of refinement (antim samskara) being the funeral rites performed after death.

All human bodies are permeable, but those of women are far more so. This greater permeability—and therefore, the greater potential for transformation of women—results from the fact that women menstruate and reproduce. The cultural emphasis on self-refinement requires them to be more concerned than their menfolk with regulating the exchanges in which they are involved. This they do by secluding themselves within family compounds, interacting predominantly with familiar persons and relatives, and meticulously observing prescribed daily practices.

## THE ORIYA HINDU WOMAN'S LIFE WITHIN
## THE EXTENDED HOUSEHOLD

The Oriya Hindu women of the temple town who shared their lives and experiences with me are predominantly upper-caste women who belong to families of hereditary priests. Therefore, their views and their moral sense are inevitably upper caste. Literate in the local language, Oriya, but not necessarily formally schooled, most of these women have had arranged marriages and have spent their entire lives within the compounds of their natal and conjugal households, having only minimal contact with the world outside.

### Life in an Extended Household

While nuclear living arrangements do occur in families of the temple town, extended-family households are most certainly regarded as the ideal, and a tendency always exists to maintain or move toward such living arrangements rather than the reverse. Such households, most commonly three-generational and numbering at least ten to fifteen who share a single cooking hearth, break up when either the oldest male or female member dies. The adult sons may set up separate nuclear households, but with the marriages of their resident sons and births of their grandchildren, their households again become extended.

No woman claims that living in one's husband's extended household, adjusting to it, and assimilating into it is easy: the women all see their entry into and life within their conjugal families as a challenge. From their perspective, their husbands' extended families present opportunities to excel and to fail. Success means integrating so well with one's conjugal family that ultimately every member in it comes to depend on the mature, senior woman. Elaborating on this definition of success and explaining why she finds it hard to go visiting in the neighborhood, Biraja, an older woman and the fulcrum of her extended household, says, "All these people—sons, daughters, nephews, nieces, sons' wives, husbands' younger brothers, grandsons—all will come looking for me. They want me to do this or that; they want to ask me about this or that. That's how it is."

Indispensable to the smooth running of the household, in control of household finances and deciding its expenses, life within the conjugal family affords these women opportunities to exercise their skills and expertise as knowledgeable, professional managers.[4] Chhanjarani, a still-married mother-in-law, clearly derives a special sense of pride in her accomplishments. As she told me,

> When one is able to take five or twenty-five people along with one, then one gets satisfaction. When a husband and wife live together by themselves, what is there in that? There is no special happiness in that. But, if you live within a family with husband's mother, husband's sister, hus-

band's younger brother, husband's elder brother, then there is a special quality to your happiness—there is something special in doing that.

None of the women with whom I spoke understood their virilocal residential system as patrilineal or patriarchal, but rather spoke of it as women-dominated. None bemoaned their transfer to their husbands' mothers' households as particularly hard to endure. Unlike the northern Indian women, who describe the practice of women leaving their natal households at marriage to join those of their husbands' mothers' as "this custom of degenerate times" (Raheja and Gold 1994, 187), Oriya Hindu women say succinctly, "When we are born as women, it is to live in our sasus' [husbands' mothers] households."

Even more to the point, they identify as their birthplace not their fathers' households but rather the conjugal households into which they were reborn through the rituals of marriage (bibaho) as new wives. This is a remarkable assertion, radically different from Raheja and Gold's (1994, 104) report about the women of Pahansu who say, "You know, we never call our sasural [household of one's husband's mother] one's own house (apna ghar). We only call our pihar [natal village of a married woman] 'one's own house.'" When I suggested to the women of the temple town that their birthplaces could not possibly be these conjugal households, they protested, saying, "How can you say that this is not our birthplace? When we came here we were reborn as bous [sons' wives] and we will die here. This is where our atman [soul] will give up [tyaag] our bodies—this is our home."

These women remember their childhoods in their father's homes with great nostalgia, an idyllic phase of their lives when they were completely irresponsible, but, as they say, their life's business is bound up in the affairs of their conjugal families. Indeed, their sense of being reborn through marriage as bous (sons' wives) is critical in this identification with their conjugal households. Thus, when talking of the frequency with which they visit their natal household, many women say,

Nowadays, I go maybe once a year. In the early days, I used to go much more frequently—three or four times a year but now what is there for me, there? Nothing. Now my life is in this house, with these people, they need my attention and care—the children, husband's mother, husband's father.

## Complementarity Between Males and Females

Another noteworthy perception common in this neighborhood has to do with the complementarity of male and female in the process of creation. Manu says, "Some wise men value the seed, others the field, and still others both the seed and the field" (10.70).[5] Oriya Hindus belong to the last group because they explicitly maintain that male and female are equally the cause and source of what is created. Even the origin story that is commonly told in the temple town illustrates this predisposition to see the male and female as playing an equal role in creation.[6] Unlike the Kannada creation myth quoted by Ramanujan (1993) that it resembles, this story gives unusual prominence to the Goddess, the female. In Ramanujan's story, the female is "destroyed, divided, and domesticated," while in the temple town version the Goddess precedes the male gods, and is so potent that only Siva can absorb her (Ramanujan 1993, 120). Yet—and here is where the element of complementarity creeps in—this story emphasizes that Devi cannot create parthogenetically: she needs to unite with a male (purusa) in order to give birth to new life.

Interestingly enough, the yoni-lingam (the phallus within the vagina) is a ubiquitous icon found in many roadside shrines, decorated with flowers, among them the hibiscus, Siva's favorite. For Oriya Hindus, the yoni-lingam symbolizes unequivocally the complementarity between the male and female principles, whose union results in all of creation.

Oriya Hindus therefore regard both mother and father as contributing equally to the formation of new life. The formal way of referring to mother and father is as birthgivers—janani and janaka (or janamdata)—reflecting the indigenous belief that a child is created when a man's bija (seed) and the woman's raja (female seed or secretions) mix. They argue that a woman is more than just the field (kshetra) in which the seed is sown; she is more than just the bearer of the fetus in the womb (garbhadharani). In defense of their position, Oriya Hindus provide as evidence the story about the sage Kasyapa and his two wives, Aditi and Diti.[7] They ask, "How could a single father sire both gods, Adityas (the sons of Aditi) and anti-gods, Daityas (the sons of Diti)?" This could only happen, they suggest, because the mother contributes more than just the womb to grow in; she also provides the female seed. A mother then is as much a birthgiver as is a father.

## The Centrality of Women in Their Conjugal Households

Like Hindus elsewhere, Oriya Hindus of the temple town also believe that the primary task of any community is to reproduce itself. They believe that only through perpetuating themselves do human societies transcend the depredations of time; and for them, the family represents the most appropriate site for such social reproduction. Therefore, both men and women regard the domestic domain—the home and family—as perhaps the most important sphere of human action. Significantly, within the family compounds of the temple town, senior women control and manage all household affairs.

These women are very conscious of the influence they exercise within families, and both they and their menfolk recognize that women ultimately hold families together. Women see themselves as embodying the energy-power of Devi, the Great Goddess of Hinduism, and they are not shy about claiming that a family's material prosperity depends not on what men earn and bring home but on how the women manage the household and its members. Thus, Mamata, a forty-two-year-old mother of four and the seniormost woman in her household, says,

> If a man was to earn a lakh [100,000] of rupees today and bring it home, and if a woman was not to run the household as she should, then despite the money, the household would never prosper. . . . Those Puranas, the Bhagwata [a particular Purana], those ancient texts that we read, in those we have seen that a woman's energy-power [stri sakti] is the greatest there is. If that energy-power is not properly used, then a man can do nothing.

From this perspective, a family's prosperity and its perpetuation depend less on the men who are born into it and more on the women who, born into other families, marry into it. Women clearly recognize the irony of the situation: they are the in-marrying strangers who literally provide lifeblood to the extended family, who embody the auspiciousness of the family, and who hold the material and spiritual prosperity of the family within the palms of their hands (paribarore sukho-shanti, taar unnoti, amor hathore ochi). More important, the women see their contribution to the future continuation of the extended family as significant and transformative: because the womb is more than a space to nourish the unborn child, and because a child is created through the mixing of the man's semen and the woman's female seed, children share in their mother's nature as much as they do in their father's.

A related point, and one that has great significance for how women relate to their husbands and their conjugal families, has to do with how marriage is viewed by Oriya Hindus. Marriage is seen as perhaps the most significant ritual of refinement that upper-caste men and women experience. For men, marriage completes them, making them mature adults, reproductive heads of households, and the performers of household rituals (kartta). For upper-caste women, marriage confers on them the high ritual rank of the twice born (dvija): women are reborn as bous. This understanding of the significance of marriage for women echoes Manu's when he says, "the ritual of marriage is traditionally known as the Vedic transformative ritual for women" (2.67).

Furthermore, marriage transforms women into embodiments of auspiciousness. Feminist scholars, somewhat obsessed with elaborating on the misogyny that they see exemplified in Hinduism, focus almost exclusively on the terrible stigmas attached to being a Hindu widow, ignoring the potent auspiciousness that suffuses a married woman. Widowhood is dreaded precisely because its contrary condition—marriage—is so highly valued and celebrated. The auspiciousness that all married women embody is marked by particular signs of auspiciousness (subha lakhana) that every married woman wears on her person—glass and shell bangles, silver toerings, the vermilion in her part as well as on her forehead, black beads around her neck, and brightly colored saris with broad borders. Through wearing these signs, a married Oriya Hindu woman creates a magical aura of protection that maintains her husband's health and long life.

These women truly believe that they are the custodians of their husbands' lives and well-being and of their families too. I do not know a single Oriya Hindu woman in the temple town, however unhappily married she may be, who deliberately has removed any of these signs of auspiciousness. Of the many women who became my friends in the temple town, two have separated from their husbands and have returned to their fathers' households. Childless and rejected, their lives are sad and empty, their situations precarious, but both still think of themselves as married. Neither has removed any of these signs of auspiciousness—actions that, according to indigenous thinking, would be tantamount to murdering their husbands.

## Cultivating Self-Control, Being Chaste

In the temple town, a married woman is thought to embody her conjugal family's fund of auspiciousness and therefore to hold within the palms of her hands its future. If she is careless and irresponsible in her management of the family's resources, the family does not prosper materially; if she is promiscuous, the family disintegrates. Spendthrift habits and sexual promiscuity attract repeated misfortunes and guarantee a family's final destruction.

Yet (and here Oriya Hindus are careful to make the distinction) such control over one's appetites—whether greed or lust—must come from within a person. Unlike the upper-caste Hindu men from Banaras who spoke to Derne (1994), Oriya Hindus, men and women, believe that family structures and external forces are relatively ineffective in controlling human behavior. For such control to be truly effective and enduring, the impulse must come from within—and culturally defined means are available that enable everyone to cultivate and nurture this impulse.

These culturally defined means to refine oneself revolve around two notions: the surrender of one's sense of self (atma samarpana) and service to others (sewa). Surrendering one's sense of self requires enormous self-control, because one learns to discipline one's urges and desires through deferring their gratification. Proper service is no less demanding, because it requires satisfying the needs and desires of others to the best of one's abilities, something that, as Vatuk (1990, 72) reminds us, has both a physical and "mental component" to it. Merely taking care of the physical needs of others in the family is not enough; their peace of mind also must be ensured, which requires sincere and thoughtful service.

No Oriya Hindu woman would suggest that these are easy things to do, but many of the explicitly recognized duties of married women are encompassed by these notions of "surrendering one's sense of self" and service. Thus, cooking, serving food, fasting, eating last, eating leftovers, and taking care of the physical and emotional needs of the members of the extended family selflessly—all are expected of married women and all are thought to help them achieve self-control.

Perhaps the most significant virtue that married Hindu women strive for is chastity (satitva)—in this case, being sexually active only with one's spouse. Many would echo Mamata when she says,

> We have a saying, "Let there be a thousand qualities to a woman, but her character is her bulwark" [hazaro guna roho pochare, striro charitro hou tar osare]. If a woman's character is right, then with the strength of this right character she can do a great deal, even that which is undoable she can accomplish. . . . For a woman to control herself is not such an easy matter, but only she can do it.

A woman is responsible for her own chastity. She is chaste not because she lives in an extended family and others exercise a watchful eye over her (compare with Derne 1994), but because she disciplines herself for the continuing welfare of her husband and his family and, ultimately, for her own happiness.

## FAMILY DYNAMICS IN THE TEMPLE TOWN

Clearly, Oriya Hindu men and women believe that men have a very limited role to play in ensuring a family's survival and its material and spiritual well-being—such matters are determined by the conduct of its womenfolk. More important, within these households, as senior women grow powerful, their husbands become mere figureheads to whom formal deference is paid, but little else of substance. To the limited extent that men exercise power within the household, they do so as young fathers—the phase during which their mother's powers are waxing. Indeed, any discussion of who is in control must be made in terms of the sequence of life phases, the more senior controlling the activities of the more junior.

In most Oriya families, senior members decide the occupations their sons and daughters will follow as well as whom they will marry. While men can move and interact with others quite freely, women value restricted contact and limited movement for itself. To shun contact, to maintain exclusivity, confers a mark of distinction and refinement on the person who shuns. Some older married women proudly acknowledge their aversion to intimate contact with others by saying that they do not fondle or kiss (gelo koriba) their own infant grandchildren; and they will point to the distaste a child displays when fondled as a sign of his or her innate refinement (sanskriti).

Indeed, even younger Oriya Hindu women do not desire the freedom to move and interact with people indiscriminately, and they value positively their lack of geographical mobility and limited interaction with the outside world as signs of their superiority, of their independence of the outside world. Many women pitied my having to do fieldwork, a predicament that necessitated my "wandering." I remember asking Netramani, a middle-aged widow, whether she would be sending her seventeen-year-old daughter to college, and she responded good-humoredly, "Why? So that she will become like you, going from door to door talking to everyone?"

When younger women complain about restrictions on contact and movement, they have in mind restrictions (in the early years of marriage) on visiting their natal households, on meeting people who live in their father's neighborhood, on standing in the front doorway and seeing the world go by. They are not thinking of a lack of restrictions on one's movements—to go see a movie alone, for example, or go shopping on one's own or walk out of the house unaccompanied whenever one feels like it. Oriya Hindu women find such activities pleasurable only to the extent that they share them with others. They would not regard such independence from others as freedom; on the contrary, they would interpret it as rejection, as lack of interest and concern on the part of others in the family. Many old widows, at liberty to move freely around the neighborhood or even further afield, hardly value this privilege. Just like the Bengali widows whom Lamb (1993) describes, all of them bemoan this freedom as a measure of their lack of centrality within the household.

## Gynarchy Rules

Within the compounds of the extended households in the temple town, men are peripheral; women, particularly senior women, control the flow of life. The responsibility for enculturating the next generation rests almost exclusively in their hands, making them influential social actors. More important, the senior women monitor and regulate the activities of junior women; in terms of who does what, how, and when, senior women dominate and control events.

So do junior women of the household resist the control exercised by senior women? Do they view it as oppressive? Do they, through "everyday acts of resistance," challenge the control of senior women? Are they like the rural women in Haryana and Rajasthan, who are "not radical enough to envision a world without marriage and family" (Raheja and Gold 1994, 123) but are sufficiently subversive to question, in verse and song, the demands made by patrilineal kinship structures? I think not.

Many junior wives in the temple town admit that during the early years of marriage, life is difficult and stressful. Yet they are unanimous in ascribing their difficulties to their incomplete assimilation into the family. Sharing Hindu understandings of the person as a fluid and relatively unbounded entity, these women know that assimilation requires that they open themselves up to the family and allow themselves to be remade in terms of the substances of the family into which they have married.[8]

Although it is appropriate for a woman to display modesty and reticence (lajja) at most times and in most places (Menon and Shweder 1994), the early years of marriage is the one life phase during which a woman is supposed to try to avoid experiencing this particular emotion (bhabo)—at least not with her husband's mother and his sisters—and if she cannot help experiencing it, she should at least avoid displaying it. According to local thinking, a son's wife should open herself completely to her husband's mother, keep nothing hidden, and be as candid as she would be with her own mother, for only such behavior guarantees complete assimilation with the family into which she has married. As Oriya Hindus say,

> If the son's wife thinks, "Why should I speak of this? I feel too modest [lajjit] to tell anyone about this, I will keep it in my own stomach." Then she is only doing herself a disservice. It all depends on the son's wife—if she continues to see herself as separate [poro] from the house, then the others in the house will also treat her as separate, but if she treats her husband's mother as she would her own mother, if she opens her mind-heart completely and tells her everything frankly, if she empties herself of all old feelings and thoughts, then the husband's mother too will look on her as a daughter and not as a son's wife.

Furthermore, every woman understands that even the juniormost wife can begin to use her most clearly understood duty—that of cooking and serving family members—to achieve the kind of power needed first to make decisions for herself and later to make decisions for the family. As many women said,

> It is appropriate for us, it is right for us to do our duty—service [sewa] to our husbands, service to our husband's mother-father [sasu-sasur]. A son's wife, when she comes as son's wife to her husband's mother, how can she not do service? When she has left her own people and come, she has to merge with us and live—otherwise, how will she merge? How will she become one with the family?

When a junior woman cooks, serves, and takes care of others in the extended family, she is building relationships and exerting influence in various substantial ways.[9] She (or at any rate her essences and qualities) pervades the food she touches and cooks. By eating the food she prepares, people within the family are transforming themselves in her direction in subtle ways. Through every act of cooking, serving, and feeding, she is giving of herself to others within the family, making herself a vital channel within the family body, and bringing others within the ambit of her influence.[10]

## Everyday Acts of Resistance or Acts of Dominance?

Women do sometimes express discontent with life within the conjugal family. Yet senior rather than junior women express such discontentment. Complaining loudly is a powerful tool senior women employ to make their feelings known.

disappears. God is taken care of nowadays by the bous [sons' wives]. Now that they do all that, what is there left for me to do? Nothing.

Sarala reminisces nostalgically about the old days when she exercised great power within the family; at the same time, she recognizes the futility of her longings. "If I can go back to the way I used to live, then I will have peace of mind. I think this inside my mind's mind, but I sit quiet. I don't tell anyone. Who could I tell? Who could give me back that life?"

Other old women appear to have managed the transition from being at the center of the household to the margins more smoothly. For instance, Phuladevi, a seventy-two-year-old widow, recognizing perhaps that such transitions are part of the nature of things, has relinquished her responsibilities to her sons' wives with little regret. As she says, "Now that I am old, I eat a fistful of rice that they give me and I sit. What else is left for me in life? Why should I try and keep the nuisance and trouble of running the household in my head?"

This shift in power from one generation to the next is taken for granted by those who live here—mothers of married sons know that sooner or later they will have to relinquish the supervision and management of household activities to their sons' wives. Such relinquishment allows the senior women to begin their process of disengagement from the household and prepare for their final disengagement from the world. During this phase of their lives, senior women become geographically more mobile. They worship daily at the temple, they bathe in the public tank that adjoins the temple, they go with their husbands on pilgrimages, to Puri, Brindaban, Ayodhya, Rishikesh, staying away from home for months at a time.

Everyone here shares this future-oriented perspective, viewing life as perpetually flowing forward. They look on family life as an incomplete process, one that is continuously shifting and changing. Sandhyarani, a junior wife of only two years standing, already is looking ahead to the day when her husband's younger brothers will marry and their wives will enter the household. At present, she is the juniormost woman in the household: her husband's widowed mother and her husband's elder brother's wife are above her. When asked of her present and future responsibilities within the household, she replies,

Can I say what's in my heart now? When I am the sana ja [junior son's wife]? The youngest? I've just been married. Now elder sister tells me what to do, she decides everything. But, when the younger brothers get married, then I will become senior, and then I will have the responsibility of telling the junior wives what should be done, how things should be done in this household. Not now, but after some years.

Clearly, junior wives maintain the structures of household authority today because they see themselves dominating and controlling those structures in the future. They see no advantage in rebelling against positions of power that they fully expect to occupy.

# FEMINISM AND THE ORIYA HINDU WOMAN

The Hindu women in the temple town of Bhubaneswar—a patrilineal, patrilocal community where women, unlike men, do not inherit property and do change their residence at marriage—contrive to lead fairly fulfilling, contented lives. The reasons they do so are several.

First, their identification with Devi, the Great Goddess of Hinduism, is a source of substantial self-worth. Like her, they see themselves embodying the energy-power of the universe (see Shweder and Menon forthcoming). The fairly strong sakta tradition in coastal Orissa, where the temple town is located, guides these self-perceptions. For instance, the fifteenth century Oriya poet, Sarala Dasa, popular even today, articulates this female oriented sakta perspective. His version of the Hindu epic, the *Bilanka Ramayana*, diverges from the north Indian one by portraying Sita as transforming herself into Devi, the Great Goddess, blindingly radiant, who decapitates the thousand headed anti-god Ravana while her husband, Rama, stands cowering in the shadows.

Second, these women are universally regarded as being central to the perpetuation, material prosperity, and spiritual welfare of their conjugal families. Most would echo Mamata's words, "for the man, for the children, for everyone, for the family, only a woman's contribution is really crucial." Through feeding family members and through producing its future members, they see themselves, in a very concrete sense, as the maintainers and sustainers of the life of their conjugal families.

Third, these in-marrying women identify themselves unreservedly with their conjugal families within a few years of marriage. They would agree unhesitatingly with the Hindu Newaris of Nepal who say, "Interdependency is where you find yourself. In relationships, you discover what and who you are, where you are going, and what you need to do" (Parish 1994, 129).

Furthermore, after the first year of marriage, hardly any gifts come from a junior wife's natal household—strikingly different from the practice reported for the villages of Haryana and Rajasthan (Raheja and Gold 1994). And very soon, an Oriya Hindu woman ceases to have any sense of entitlement with respect to her father's home. Her position within her conjugal family rests, not on the stream of gifts that flow from her natal household, but on the appreciation she actively earns through working hard at achieving successful assimilation. As Ranjana, a young woman on the eve of her marriage and departure from her natal household observes dispassionately,

> Our parents haven't given us our karma, they have given us only birth [janma]. They have given me birth, and they have also given me learning [sikhya] and competence [jogyata]—that is my good fortune [bhagya]. Now with that, if I decide to do good work in their household, then it will arouse their appreciation [prashansa jagrato hebo]. But if I don't do good work, they will criticize me [ninda koribe] and that I will have to endure.

But it is all in my hands. If I want to do good and gain appreciation, it is in my hands.

When feminists therefore challenge family structures, identifying them as sites where gender discrimination is perpetuated, and work to dismantle them, Hindu women see such efforts as directly threatening their sense of identity and personhood. They cannot conceive of themselves as distinct and detached from their families. To ask them to define themselves as separate entities violates their deepest sense of who they are. Feminists who require them to do so are ignoring an important feature of Hindu cultural reality: one does not find one's self through isolating or removing oneself, but rather through embedding oneself in "webs of relatedness" (Parish 1994, 125–87).

Feminist scholars and activists acknowledge their relative lack of success in influencing the ideas and behaviors of Hindu women. Yet few are willing to say bluntly that this is because Hindu women are victims of false consciousness, complicit in their own subordination. They emphasize instead the supposed "resistance" and ignore the possible complicity. By doing so, as Kurtz (1996, 80) points out, "the analytic imposition of Western values on Hindu culture is driven underground, where it is less susceptible to exposure and critique."

This chapter presents ethnographic evidence demonstrating that Oriya Hindu women are not victims of false consciousness, and to that limited extent I agree with feminist scholars. Yet neither are these women incipient rebels; rather, they are mature adults who inhabit a moral universe very different from that familiar to most feminists. In this moral universe, the cherished values worth pursuing are not freedom of choice or equality for all or achievement of personal satisfaction but instead self-control, self-improvement, and the service of others. Thus feminists have tended to misunderstand the reasons for their failure in mobilizing Hindu women.

In India's struggle for independence, huge numbers of people forgot their differences and came together to achieve freedom from colonial rule. In sharp contrast, the hegemonic idea feminists are trying to impose on Hindu women seeks to divide and separate them from their male kin, categorizing the latter as oppressors. Feminists argue that women's interests are best served when they resist and finally rebel against patrilineal kinship structures—but this does not resonate with the way most Hindu women see life.

Feminists are also incorrect when they bemoan the success that "politicized religion" apparently has enjoyed in mobilizing large numbers of Hindu women (Jeffrey and Basu 1998). On the contrary, political entrepreneurs such as the Hindu nationalists have succeeded in mobilizing entire families, not just women, by activating provocative images—that of the Hindu patrilineage under threat from Muslims, for instance, or from the West or from the state. Any perceived threat to the survival of their patrilineages or the future of their children mobilizes both men and women, and it is as groups—as family units—that these Hindus become politically active and take to the streets.

Yet feminists try to mobilize women against their families and do not succeed, because many married Hindu women, like the Oriya women of the temple town, identify themselves wholeheartedly with their conjugal families. Feminists seek to mobilize Indian women by doing nothing more than emphasizing the shared experience of being female—but being female is only one element in an Indian woman's self-definition, and this is not sufficient in and of itself. In India, caste, class, region, language, and religion are important crosscutting categories used by women (and men) to construct their sense of who they are. In trying to create a broad-based women's movement in India, feminism therefore is doubly burdened: its ideology of individualism goes against the grain of Hindu thinking, and its lack of icons or images that transcend the differences between Indian women make it impotent to rally them to its call. That feminists have been less than successful in inspiring Indian women to fight for a radical reordering of social arrangements is hardly surprising.

## NOTES

1. By feminist activists and scholars I mean a group of Western or Westernized activists and scholars, predominantly though not entirely women, who target Hindu cultural traditions as the root cause of gender injustices and gender exploitation on the South Asian subcontinent today. Their goal is "absolute and complete equality as far as is humanly possible in any given situation, at any given time" (Narayanan 1999, 26). If one had to identify the sites of feminism in India today, one would locate them in metropolises such as Bombay, New Delhi, and Bangalore, among a small, leftist-oriented, and highly privileged elite, educated either in the West or in Westernized institutions in India. In postindependence India, such groups flourished under the aegis of the Nehruvian state, having jobs in state-supported academic institutions or in state-funded organizations engaged in various kinds of research.

    Such feminist activists are not the only group working to improve the lot of Indian women. Others exist, but—and this is a crucial difference—these other groups are working not for gender equality but for female empowerment. These activists, men and women, while working toward social justice and freedom, explicitly distance themselves from Western feminism—the most famous example being Madhu Kishwar, the editor of *Manushi*, a journal about women and society in India (see Kishwar 1990). These groups believe that feminism, as an intellectual perspective and a movement, is located in a particular historic and sociocultural context and therefore has little relevance to contemporary India. These activists are characterized by their belief that the potential for radical social transformation in India can be found within indigenous cultural traditions—one does not need to look for inspiration to the West.

2. As those familiar with Hindu India are quick to point out, the term *Hindu* is itself problematic. Hindu is not an indigenous term, but rather one that Arab traders and settlers used centuries ago to refer to those who lived beyond the river Sindhu, or Indus, as it is better known. In India today, the legal understanding of Hindu is as a residual category: anyone who is not a Muslim, Christian, Parsi, or Jew is regarded as a Hindu. When Hindu is used herein to classify ideas, customs, and practices, this primarily refers to Brahmanical traditions, those followed by the highest Hindu caste, the Brahmans, who constitute roughly 3 percent of India's population.

3. Scott (1985) argues, in his fascinating ethnography on the village of Sedaka, that the peasants there cannot be seen as victims of false consciousness because they recognize the full extent of their exploitation at the hands of the landlords. They clearly are aware of the structures of oppression that operate to their disadvantage, and they demonstrate this awareness by continually engaging in acts of resistance, small and relatively risk-free though they may be, such as foot-dragging, noncooperation, non-communication.

4. Men earn, but almost without exception they hand over their earnings to the senior women of the family.

5. Manu refers to the Laws of Manu, *Manudharmasastra*, a pivotal Sanskrit text composed in the early centuries of the Common Era, consisting of over 2,600 verses that deal with the social, moral, and ritual obligations of the different castes and of people at various stages of life.

6. Temple town residents claim that the textual source for this story is the *Siva Purana*, one of the eighteen *Puranas*. These texts are collections of myths and ritual lore generally thought to date back to the medieval period.

7. Kinsley (1988) describes Aditi and Diti as part of a group of ten inauspicious or fierce female spirits who devour and afflict young pregnant women or children up to the age of sixteen, after which they become more benign. Oriya Hindus of the temple town, however, describe Aditi and Diti as daughters of Dakhsa, twin sisters, primordial mothers, the wives of Kasyapa.

8. This process of remaking the substance of the woman is begun explicitly during the rituals of marriage and is symbolized, at least in upper-caste Oriya Hindu households, by the new name given her at the time of marriage.

9. With reference to cooking, a junior wife controls the process; she decides the ingredients as well as the mode of preparing particular foods, although the senior wife usually decides what will be cooked.

10. Here is employed the body image familiar to most Hindus. In the indigenous medical tradition known as Ayurveda, the human body is visualized as a collection of channels through which fluids run smoothly in and out and sometimes collect (Kakar 1982; Zimmermann 1979).

11. The Oriya language does not distinguish between male and female pronouns. The Oriya third-person pronoun *se* is rendered as "he," but it refers to both men and women.

# REFERENCES

Allen, Michael R. 1976. "Kumari or 'Virgin' Worship in Kathmandu Valley." *Contributions to Indian Sociology* 10: 293–315.

Appadorai, Arjun, Frank J. Korom, and Margaret A. Mills. 1991. *Gender, Genre and Power in South Asian Expressive Traditions*. Philadelphia: University of Pennsylvania Press.

Balakrishnan, Radhika. 1994. "The Social Context of Sex Selection and the Politics of Abortion in India." In *Power and Decision: The Social Control of Reproduction*, edited by G.

Sen and R. Snow. Cambridge, Mass.: Harvard School of Public Health and Harvard University Press.

Banerjee, Sumanta. 1989. "Marginalization of Women's Popular Culture in Nineteenth Century Bengal." In *Recasting Women: Essays in Colonial History*, edited by K. Sangari and S. Vaid. New Delhi: Kali for Women.

Bennett, Lynn. 1983. *Dangerous Wives and Sacred Sisters: Social and Symbolic Roles of High-Caste Women in Nepal*. New York: Columbia University Press.

Daniel, E. Valentine. 1984. *Fluid Signs: Being a Person the Tamil Way*. Berkeley: University of California Press.

Das, Veena. 1995. *Critical Events: An Anthropological Perspective on Contemporary India*. New Delhi: Oxford University Press.

Derne, Steve. 1994. "Hindu Men Talk About Controlling Women: Cultural Ideas as a Tool of the Powerful." *Sociological Perspectives* 37: 203–27.

Dhruvarajan, Vannaja. 1989. *Hindu Women and the Power of Ideology*. Granby: Bergin and Garvey.

Doniger, Wendy, and Brian W. Smith. 1991. *The Laws of Manu*. Middlesex, England: Penguin Books.

Dumont, Louis. 1980. *Homo Hierarchicus*. Complete Revised English Edition. Chicago: University of Chicago Press.

Gilligan, Carol. 1993. *In a Different Voice*. Cambridge, Mass.: Harvard University Press.

Inden, Ronald B., and Ralph A. Nicholas. 1977. *Kinship in Bengali Culture*. Chicago: University of Chicago Press.

Jeffrey, Patricia. 1979. *Frogs in a Well: Indian Women in Purdah*. London: Zed Books.

———. 1998. "Agency, Activism and Agendas." In *Appropriating Gender*, edited by P. Jeffrey and A. Basu. New York: Routledge.

Jeffrey, Patricia, and Amrita Basu. 1998. *Appropriating Gender*. New York: Routledge.

Jeffrey, Patricia, and Roger Jeffrey. 1996. *Don't Marry Me to a Plowman: Women's Everyday Lives in Rural North India*. Boulder, Colo.: Westview Press.

Kakar, Sudhir. 1982. *Shamans, Mystics and Doctors*. New York: Knopf.

Karlekar, Malakiva. 1991. *Voices from Within: Early Personal Narratives of Bengali Women*. New Delhi: Oxford University Press.

Kinsley, David. 1988. *Hindu Goddesses*. Berkeley: University of California Press.

Kishwar, Madhu. 1990. "Why I Do Not Call Myself a Feminist." *Manushi* 61 (Nov.–Dec.): 5.

Kondos, Vivienne. 1989. "Subjection and Domicile: Some Problematic Issues Relating to High Caste Nepalese Women." In *Society from the Inside Out*, edited by J. N. Gray and D. J. Mearns. New Delhi: Sage.

Kurtz, Stanley. 1996. "Who Is Kali?" Paper presented at the Conference on the Goddess Kali, Barnard College, New York (September 19–22).

Lamb, Sarah. 1993. *Growing in the Net of Maya*. Unpublished Ph.D. diss., University of Chicago.

Mahapatra, Manmohan. 1981. *Traditional Structure and Change in an Orissa Temple*. Calcutta: Punthi Pustak.

Mani, Lata. 1989. "Contentious Traditions: The Debate on Sati in Colonial India." In *Recasting Women: Essays in Colonial History*, edited by K. Sangari and S. Vaid. New Delhi: Kali for Women.

Markus, Hazel, and Shinobu Kitayama. 1991. "Culture and the Self: Implications for Cognition, Emotion and Motivation." *Psychological Review* 98: 224–253.

Marriott, McKim. 1976. "Hindu Transactions: Diversity Without Dualism." In *Transaction and Meaning: Directions in the Anthropology of Exchange and Symbolic Behavior*, edited by B. Kapferer. Philadelphia: Insitute for the Study of Human Issues.

————. 1990. *India Through Hindu Categories*. New Delhi: Sage.

Menon, Usha, and Richard A. Shweder. 1994. "Kali's Tongue: Cultural Psychology and the Power of 'Shame' in Orissa, India." In *Emotion and Culture*, edited by S. Kitayama and H. Markus. Washington, D.C.: American Psychological Association.

————. 1998. "The Return of 'White Man's Burden': The Moral Discourse of Anthropology and the Domestic Life of Hindu Women." In *Welcome to Middle Age!* edited by R. A. Shweder. Chicago: University of Chicago Press.

Narayanan, Vasudha. 1999. "Women of Power in the Hindu Tradition." In *Feminism and World Religions*, edited by A. Sharma and K. Young. Albany: SUNY Press.

O'Hanlon, Rosalind. 1991. "Issues of Widowhood: Gender and Resistance in Colonial Western India." In *Contesting Power: Resistance and Everyday Social Relations in South Asia*, edited by D. Haynes and G. Prakash. New Delhi: Oxford University Press.

Oldenberg, Veena. 1991. "Lifestyle as Resistance: The Case of the Courtesans of Lucknow." In *Contesting Power: Resistance and Everyday Social Relations in South Asia*, edited by D. Haynes and G. Prakash. New Delhi: Oxford University Press.

Parish, Steven. 1994. *Moral Knowing in a Hindu Sacred City*. New York: Columbia University Press.

Raheja, Gloria, and Ann Gold. 1994. *Listen to the Heron's Words*. Berkeley: University of California Press.

Rajan, Rajeshwari. 1993. *Real and Imagined Women: Gender, Culture and Postcolonialism*. London: Routledge.

Ramanujan, A. K. 1993. "On Folk Mythologies and Folk Puranas." In *Purana Perennis*, edited by W. Doniger. Albany: SUNY Press.

Roy, Manisha. 1975. *Bengali Women*. Chicago: University of Chicago Press.

Sarkar, Tanika, and Urvashi Butalia. 1995. *Women and Right-Wing Movements*. London: Zed Books.

Scott, James. 1985. *Weapons of the Weak*. New Haven: Yale University Press.

Seymour, Susan. 1983. "Household Structure and Status and Expressions of Affect." *India Ethos* 11: 263–77.

————. 1999. *Women, Family and Childcare in India: A World in Transition*. Cambridge: Cambridge University Press.

Shweder, Richard A. 1991. *Thinking Through Cultures*. Cambridge, Mass.: Harvard University Press.

Shweder, Richard A., and Edward J. Bourne. 1984. "Does the Concept of the Person Vary Cross-Culturally?" In *Culture Theory*, edited by R. A. Shweder and R. A. LeVine. Cambridge: Cambridge University Press.

Shweder, Richard A., and Usha Menon. Forthcoming. "Dominating Kali: Hindu Family Values and Tantric Power." In *Encountering Kali: Cultural Understanding at the Extremes*, edited by R. McDermott and J. Kripal. Berkeley: University of California Press.

Vatuk, Sylvia. 1990. "To Be a Burden on Others." In *Divine Passions: The Social Construction of Emotions in India*, edited by O. M. Lynch. Berkeley: University of California Press.

Wadley, Susan. 1994. *Struggling with Destiny in Karimpur, 1925–1984*. Berkeley: University of Berkeley Press.

Zimmermann, Francis. 1979. "Remarks on the Body in Ayurvedic Medicine." *South Asian Digest of Regional Writing* 18: 10–26.

# Chapter 15

# Circumcision Debates and Asylum Cases: Intersecting Arenas, Contested Values, and Tangled Webs

Corinne A. Kratz

Cultural pluralism often entails situations where interests and values conflict, raising questions and debates about the judgments inevitably made about the practices, people, and communities that clothe abstract values in daily experience. When such disputes land in the courts, decisions must define new issues in terms of existing legal principles and precedents, though they might also set other precedents that limit pluralism and tolerance. Case studies provide critical ways to understand conflicting values and norms from the diverse perspectives of those involved, tracing social processes over time to determine how and when such contradictions arise.

This chapter focuses on debates and cases that have swirled around practices of genital modification, called *female circumcision, female genital cutting* (FGC), and *female genital modification* (FGM), also known as *female genital mutilation* among activists opposing the practice.[1] International debates about these practices have continued for decades, since early last century. Yet international campaigns against female genital modification reached new prominence in the past twenty-five years, bolstered by extensive media attention in the 1990s and the formation of new advocacy groups. The late 1980s and 1990s also saw prominent legal cases about female genital operations in Europe and North America, as growing immigrant communities brought traditional customs to new locales. Defendants were charged with assault in France, but most legal cases in the United States have been framed in terms of immigration, refugee, and asylum law.[2]

For participants, such cases can be extremely unsettling: understandings are topsy-turvy, familiar assumptions and ways of reasoning are fundamentally contested. Yet what hangs in the balance is highly consequential for some participants. International debates about circumcising practices contain similar disjunctions. In the courts, however, the collisions between different values, social organizations, religious and aesthetic convictions undergo further translations into specialized legal language and procedures. In considering such disputed practices and contentious circumstances, to separate their different dimensions and divergent perspectives and identify the basic grounds of dispute and moral and ethical principles at issue is important (Kratz 1999a). This underlines "just how complicated inter-cultural dialogue on rights questions actually becomes *when all cultures enter the dialogue on grounds of moral and intellectual equality*" (Ignatieff 1999, 34, emphasis added). Such equality rarely is part of the international debates, however, and this worrisome inequality in representation and power is exacerbated by lobbying efforts and media blitzes aimed at the courts. Two legal cases considered herein illustrate the shape, scope, and effects of these efforts.

I consider both international debates and legal cases because these represent different aspects of the long, far-reaching social processes through which issues related to female genital modification have been defined. The debates typically are formulated through a broad division between "Western" and "traditional" cultures; anticircumcision campaigns usually ignore differences among circumcising practices and differences among and within the many societies that practice them (Kratz 1994, 1999b). Court cases may still rely on these simplified, polarizing characterizations, though the very situations presented demonstrate their fallacies. Societies that practice female genital modification are not uniform, homogeneous, or unchanging, and these debates occur in multiple settings—local, regional, national, international, and global, with alliances across settings. Indeed, divisions, alliances, and changes in societies and settings where genital modifications are practiced and debated already have shaped the representation of a case when it reaches court.

## A RANGE OF PERSPECTIVES ON GENITAL MODIFICATION

The following quotes illustrate these diverse perspectives and situations by showing how a range of people describe genital modifications, raising critical questions for legal cases. How are different actors portrayed and represented in court? Which gain a hearing, and how? How should parents' rights, children's rights, and community rights be weighed against one another? How do universal rights apply to the judicial process itself? How do such cases modify definitions of these rights and cultural pluralism? How should the multiple locales and understandings shaping participants' situations be taken into account?

I was circumcised at eleven with my cousin. We were lucky to get anaesthetics. . . . Everybody in the family was very happy—my mom, my dad. [What about you?] I was happy. Everyone would call you names, saying that you are not a grown woman. The ones who were circumcised had more honor. So you feel alone and ashamed if you're not circumcised. (Young Somali woman, in Mire 1994)

In the U.S., when you tell your new friends that you have been circumcised, they seem to avoid you and they feel uneasy with you, thinking that something's wrong with you. It's difficult to make them understand. (Young Somali woman, in Mire 1994)

It is important . . . that we not be looked at as . . . victims. . . . There's a wide spectrum of opinion among women—Somali men and Somali women—on this, but I think I can safely say, as for who perpetuates the actual tradition, that's firmly in the hands of women. It's in the hands of our grand-mothers and our mothers who very much believe that in order to ensure their daughter's livelihood, their marriage, their virtue, their honor, this has to be done to them. And so what you, I guess, need to take yourselves to is this leap of faith that there's an incredible amount of love that's involved in this experience. (Young Somali woman, in Mire 1994)

Circumcision is one of the more unfortunate of Somali customs. Hopefully in the near future we hope our people will give it up. (Young Somali man, in Mire 1994)

My friends state that [infibulation] is performed on young girls in order to make them clean (*nazeef*), smooth (*na'im*), and pure (*tahir*). . . . Circumcision prepares her body for womanhood, whereas marriage provides her with the opportunity to advance her position through giving birth, especially to sons. (Women in "Hofriyat," Sudan, paraphrased in Boddy 1982, 687)

All my friends were getting circumcised. I felt that if I was left out I would become the laughing stock. So I ran away from home and went to stay with grand mum who gave me the greenlight to become a woman. (Mary Nyamboki, Kenyan woman who ran away at age fifteen because her mother refused to allow her to be circumcised, in Wachira 1995)

In a male dominated society, female circumcision is one way of subjugating women. (Jennifer Mwikabi, lawyer in Nairobi, Kenya, in Wachira 1995)

[Female genital mutilation is] the most widespread existing violation of human rights in the world. (Rosenthal 1993)

Female circumcision is the popular but medically incorrect term most frequently used in Africa and the Middle East for a variety of genital mutilations of female children and young girls. . . . The real purpose is to reduce or extinguish sexual pleasure and keep women under male sexual control. (Hoskens n.d.)

No evil intent should be read into excision. They do it because they love their children. Parents think they're doing the right thing. (Hélène Liehnard, technical adviser to the Department of Population and Migration,

Interior Ministry, France, during 1991 trial of Sory and Sémité Coulibaly and Aramata Keita from Mali, in Peyrot 1991)

The procedure is carried out for the noblest of reasons, the best of intentions and in good faith. . . . In Africa, the rationales for genital surgery are as diverse as the continent itself. However one overriding perspective is that it is conceptualized as a process that applies to both men and women. Hence a framework that differentiates it according to gender is not a useful tool of analysis. Be that as it may, here are some of the posited reasons for carrying out the procedure on women. For some cultures it is a component of a rite of passage to socially acceptable adulthood. For others it is a nuptial necessity. For yet others, it is a mark of courage. . . . For some it is a reproductive aid, increasing fertility. For others it enhances sexuality. (Iweriebor 1996)

Frankly, I don't give a damn if opposing this is a violation of someone's culture. To me, female genital mutilation is a violation of the physical and spiritual integrity of a person. (Mr. Hasche, lawyer for Nigerian Lydia Oluloro's immigration case in Oregon, in Egan 1994)

A judge's role is to maintain public order, but by combating excision, he would disturb public order. (Mr. Fofana, Justice Ministry, Côte d'Ivoire, in Dugger 1996c, A5)

The various local, national, and international spheres of practice and debate have long been joined in larger, shared fields of social action (compare with Gluckman 1958 [1940]). Their connections are complex, for the larger social fields are composed of semiautonomous arenas (Moore 1978), interacting yet structured and defined differently.[3] This means, for example, that actions by U.S. organizations might influence the way African national policies or local disputes play out. Yet despite Ignatieff's (1999) ideal, neither debates nor cases involve even and equal playing fields. Participants are characterized by differences of knowledge, influence, and resources as well as different cultural outlooks and values. To consider, then, from a variety of social positions the moral, ethical, and aesthetic values in conflict—and indeed, the social processes that constitute debates and cases about circumcising practices—is critical.

The two American asylum cases discussed herein involve three broad interacting arenas: home countries, Euro-American countries, and international campaigns (Kratz 1999a). This framework helps define the crosscutting contexts and multiple perspectives involved.

*Home countries* are countries in Africa, the Middle East, and Southeast Asia, where circumcising practices have traditional standing. Various traditions and practices may exist within home countries, and different positions within communities. Actors might include national government and politicians, local nongovernmental organizations (NGOs) and action groups, international action groups, churches, and members of ethnic and religious communities with their own differences of age, gender, education, religion, wealth, and so on. Debates about genital modification also have long histories in some countries, for example, Kenya and Sudan (Murray 1974, 1976; Thomas 1996, 1998; Abusharaf 1999).

*Euro-American countries* also have a history of genital operations for both girls and boys—histories related to changing understandings of health, class, ethnicity, gender, and sexuality. Clitoridectomy was a recognized medical treatment in many Euro-American countries through the 1950s, used to treat insomnia, sterility, and masturbation (Morgan and Steinem 1980, 293–96; Pederson 1991, 672). Contemporary concern about female genital operations within these countries is related particularly to immigrants from the home countries just discussed. The operations are subject to recent laws in Sweden, the United Kingdom, Switzerland, the United States, and other Euro-American countries; actors include national and state governments and courts, agencies dealing with immigrants (for example, INS and Health and Human Services), immigrants from home countries with different histories and circumcising practices, various host communities in Europe or the United States, immigrant community organizations, national action groups and organizations concerned with women and children, and international action groups. Differences of gender and generation within immigrant families and communities may be exacerbated through differential engagement with education systems, job opportunities, and other features of host countries.

*International campaigns* are related to the two other arenas, yet constituted by their international reach and involvement in several domains of debate at once. Key actors include international action groups based in different countries, international agencies such as the United Nations and the World Health Organization, as well as some religious officials, journalists, and others.

Such multisided disputes and decisions about genital modification point to serious questions about who speaks for whom in the debates and cases, which perspectives and interests are recognized, and how different actors are involved. Shifts in circumcising practices and debates in home countries show increasing interconnection among home-country settings and among home countries and the other two arenas.[4] Ritual practice always has been historically and socially adaptable—even if practitioners claim unchanging tradition. Yet this wide wave of change is notable, if variable in direction and type. Further, a common shift is discernable in the discussion about genital modification in many home countries: local practitioners and communities increasingly discuss practices in ways that separate the ritual into different segments, debating which is more important—genital modification *or* the other ritual events in which it is embedded. Such discussion underlines that many individuals and families everywhere are making difficult decisions about their circumcising practices.

The courts also are making difficult decisions, but how do the complex social and political processes and interconnections of the debates enter court cases, and how much of this flux in practice registers there? While international debates about female genital modification encompass and cross the three arenas, particular areas of national law define horizons for most court cases. This affects and limits legal strategies. Though influential, the broader contexts and debates might be unknown to lawyers or judges, or not seem germane or admissible in a narrower legal sense. Comparing the asylum cases of Fauziya Kassindja and Adelaide Abankwah illustrates just how elusive are the "grounds of moral and intellectual equality."

## TWO CASES FOR ASYLUM: FAUZIYA KASSINDJA AND ADELAIDE ABANKWAH

The *Kassindja* and *Abankwah* cases are not the only immigration cases concerning female genital modification heard in the United States, but they certainly have been the mostly widely discussed.[5] Conducted from 1994 to 1996 and 1997 to 1999, both set precedents. Kassindja's was the first case where the Board of Immigration Appeals (highest tribunal of the Immigration and Naturalization Service) recognized fear of genital operations as a valid basis for an asylum claim, changing guidelines for all immigration judges. Abankwah's case was the first time a federal court supported an asylum petition based on this fear. For the two young women, the cases were part of life-changing experiences that included stressful departures from their homelands, years of detention in the United States, and eventually, lives in a new country.[6] My concern here is how they figure in the production and circulation of knowledge and social values, for this shapes contexts for free exercise of cultural practices.[7]

Before the cases began, public attention and familiarity with debates about female genital modification increased dramatically in the United States in the 1990s. In 1992 and 1993, the practices were hotly debated in editorial pages of the *New York Times*; *Warrior Marks* (the book and film by Alice Walker and Pratibha Parmar) appeared; and *Time* magazine ran a story on the heightened American debates (Kaplan, Lewis, and Hammer 1993).[8] In 1994, the case of Lydia Omowunmi Oluloro made national news—again including *Time*, the *New York Times* and television profiles.

A Yoruba woman from southern Nigeria, Oluloro moved to Portland, Oregon, in 1986 to join her husband, who had permanent resident status. They divorced in 1993, with two daughters born in the United States, and deportation proceedings were begun against Oluloro because her residency papers had not been filed. She requested suspension of deportation on the grounds that her daughters, American citizens, would be forcibly circumcised if returned to Nigeria with her. Oluloro was circumcised as a girl and supported the practice but said materials from anticircumcision campaigns changed her mind.[9] Her husband claimed that "her change of heart had coincided with the Government's move to deport her," but she "won support from feminists and human rights advocates across the United States" (Egan 1994). Her deportation was suspended in March 1994, a decision "controversial among many Africans, who said that Oluloro was from the Ijebu branch of the Yoruba in southern Nigeria, where FGM is not practiced" (Fokkena 1994). Such distinctions, relevant to African realities, did not enter American legal arenas, though they may well have been pertinent.

The *Time* article on Oluloro quotes Colorado Congresswoman Pat Schroeder, who in 1993 introduced federal legislation prohibiting and criminalizing female genital modification. Similar bills were introduced in the Senate (1995) and several state legislatures soon thereafter. The congressional bill passed in late September 1996 and took effect six months later. Schroeder and others also involved themselves in the fall 1996 controversy over proposals by Harborview Medical Center in Seattle. Harborview sought to work with the local Somali immigrant community to devise a simple, largely symbolic procedure that addressed their need and wish to "circumcise" their daughters without harming them (Coleman 1998). When their efforts were publicized, the ensuing furor foreclosed the solution.

When seventeen-year-old Fauziya Kassindja arrived in Newark, New Jersey, in mid-December 1994, this was the context for her case. Celia Dugger wrote of the 1996 legislation, "Support for these measures—included in an end-of-session spending bill—mounted this year as the case of Fauziya Kassindja, a young woman who fled Togo to avoid having her genitals cut off and sought asylum here, gained attention in the American news media, Government officials said" (1996d; Dugger probably refers to excision, but such descriptions make it hard to tell). Kassindja's case continued until June 1996, when she was granted asylum. Adelaide Abankwah's immigration case began soon after, when she arrived in March 1997, and continued until she received asylum in August 1999. Kassindja herself became a figure in Abankwah's case, visiting her with Gloria Steinem while in detention.

The *Kassindja* and *Abankwah* cases are complex tales involving many people, places, and organizations. The following sketches reconstruct events, though the interconnections and timing of events are not always clear from the material available. Tables 15.1 through 15.3 show timelines for the cases and for 1990s media and legal developments in the U.S.

## The *Kassindja* Case

Fauziya Kassindja was the youngest daughter of a well-to-do family of the Tchamba-Koussountou people living in Kpalimé, a town in northern Togo.[10] Her father had long-standing disputes with his brother and sister over his marriage to her mother, the education of his daughters, and circumcision of the family's daughters. Kassindja was caught in these disputes after her father died in January 1993. Her father's siblings gradually took over his affairs, sent her mother away after the prescribed mourning period, removed Kassindja from her secondary school in Ghana, and arranged for her to marry and be circumcised in October 1994. With the help of her older sister and money from her mother, Kassindja fled as her marriage and preparations for circumcision were being finalized. Her sister arranged for her to be taken illegally into Germany; two

TABLE 15.1   /   Timeline of Media and Legal Developments in the United States

| | |
|---|---|
| 1992 to 1993 | Debates in U.S. news (Rosenthal, Walker, Mekuria, Dawit, et al.) |
| 1993 | *Warrior Marks* book & film (after *Possessing the Secret of Joy* in 1992) |
| 1993 | Congresswoman Schroeder and Senator Reid propose federal legislation prohibiting and criminalizing FGM |
| March 1994 | Oluloro case |
| December 1994 | Kassindja arrives in United States and is detained |
| 1995 to 1996 | Kassindja campaign |
| June 1996 | Kassindja granted asylum |
| September 1996 | Congress passes law (takes effect six months later) |
| Fall 1996 | Harborview controversy |
| March 1997 | Abankwah arrives in United States and is detained |
| Spring 1998 to 1999 | Abankwah campaign |
| August 1999 | Abankwah granted asylum |

*Source:* Author's compilation.

months later, she bought a fake passport and continued to the United States, hoping to be given political asylum and contact an uncle in New Jersey.

On arrival in December, she asked for political asylum and was sent to a detention center. Her first hearing was in Philadelphia in late August 1995, argued by Layli Miller Bashir, then a law student at American University who had worked on the case for some months as a clerk for the lawyer Kassindja's cousin had retained. Asylum was denied—Kassindja's account was found inconsistent and not credible. Miller Bashir sought help with the appeal from Surita Sandosham of Equality Now, an organization dedicated to action for women, human rights, and refugees, and from Karen Musalo, acting head of the International Human Rights Clinic at American University. Sandosham "agreed to work her media and political contacts to bring attention to the case" (Dugger 1996b, B6) and Musalo agreed to handle the appeal pro bono.

A request for parole in mid-October was denied a month later; an appeal brief and accompanying affadavits were submitted in early December. The case was mentioned briefly in a *New York Times* article around the same time. Equality Now had Kassindja write notes to key reporters, and coverage began to increase in 1996. They also organized letters from Congress to the attorney general and a

TABLE 15.2  /  Timeline of *Fauziya Kassindja* Case

| | |
|---|---|
| January 1993 | Kassindja's father dies |
| October 1994 | Kassindja flees home during wedding period; leaves Togo for Germany |
| December 17, 1994 | Arrives in the U.S.; on illegal entry, sent to NJ detention center |
| August 1995 | First hearing in Philadelphia, represented by Miller Bashir; asylum denied |
| Fall 1995 | Miller Bashir seeks help from Sandosham of Equality Now and Musalo of American University's International Human Rights Clinic. Musalo takes on appeal; Equality Now agrees to help |
| October 1995 | Request for release on parole |
| November 1995 | Request for release on parole denied |
| Fall 1995 to Spring 1996 | Equality Now mounts letter writing campaign to U.S. Justice Department and contacts members of Congress and media (including Mann of *Washington Post* and Dugger of *New York Times*) |
| December 1995 | Appeal brief and affadavits filed; first brief mention of case in *New York Times:* Equality Now has Kassindja write notes to reporters |
| March 1996 | Writ of habeas corpus filed; *Washington Post* article, then other coverage |
| April 1996 | In the United States: |
| April 5 | Justice Department brief filed defending continued detention (risk for flight) |
| Mid-April | *New York Times* stories by Rosenthal and Dugger add to attention and pressure to release |
| April 24 | Kassindja released from detention pending resolution of appeal; soon after, Kassindja appears on Nightline, CNN, CBS; Gloria Steinem and others meet and champion Kassindja |
| April 1996 | Meanwhile in Togo: US Embassy in Lomé a) sends staff to interview Kassindja family; b) sends Justice Department a study on inci- |

*(Table continues on p. 318.)*

TABLE 15.2  /  *Continued*

| | dence in Togo; c) contacts Suzanne Aho, director of Togo's Office for Protection and Promotion of the Family, who talks to Kassindja's father's brother |
|---|---|
| May 2 | Appeal heard |
| June 13 | Political asylum granted |

*Source:* Author's compilation.

public letter-writing campaign. The first full news article on the case appeared in the *Washington Post* in mid-March, just after Kassindja's lawyers filed a writ of habeas corpus trying to get her released. In April, the Justice Department defended continued detention. That same month, the U.S. embassy in Togo sent staff to interview Kassindja's family in Kpalimé; contacted Suzanne Aho, director of Togo's Office for Protection and Promotion of the Family (part of the Ministry for the Promotion of Women and for Social Services), who also spoke with Kassindja's uncle; and sent the Justice Department a new report on the incidence of "female genital cutting" in Togo (Dugger 1996b).

Further media attention came in the wake of the *Post* article, including a column by A. M. Rosenthal in the 12 April *New York Times*. *The Times* reporter Celia Dugger visited Kassindja in mid-April 1996 and published the first of several front-page stories on 15 April, catapulting the case into full media scrutiny. Kassindja was released from detention nine days later, "because she has developed in recent months strong ties to religious and human rights groups who have promised to support her and insure she shows up for legal hearings," and because "an April 15 article in the *New York Times* detailing the case and the conditions of her detention led to a public outcry, a barrage of news accounts, and the promise of continuing protests by an array of advocacy groups" (Dugger 1996a). Coverage continued, with television appearances for Kassindja on Nightline, CNN, and CBS, and support from such public figures as Gloria Steinem.

Kassindja's appeal was heard in early May; the decision granting her asylum was issued in mid June. Dugger did an extensive follow-up in the *Times* in September (1996b), after visiting Togo and interviewing Kassindja's relatives and government officials. Among developments and repercussions in Togo: Kassindja's mother asks forgiveness from her husband's brother; he holds a contentious meeting of the extended family about abandoning female genital modification, since the attention is "spoiling the family reputation"; and Fauziya receives a substantial book contract. Dugger also learns that in recent years, girls in Koussountou are being circumcised between the ages of four and seven instead of in their teens due to opposition to the practice. Dugger continued to write about "female genital cutting" until the end of 1996, focusing on Côte d'Ivoire, the new congressional law, and finally, on African immigrants in the United States.

TABLE 15.3  /  Timeline of *Adelaide Abankwah Case*

| | |
|---|---|
| July 1996 | Abankwah's mother dies |
| Later in 1996 | Abankwah moves to Accra |
| Starting five weeks later | Dispute over money with employers, who contact people in Abankwah's village; fearing people from village will come, she leaves |
| March 29, 1997 | Arrives in the U.S.; on illegal entry, sent to NY detention center |
| June 1997 | Narymsky, attorney for Hebrew Immigrant Aid Society, takes case |
| September to October 1997 | Immigration hearings, Otumfuor testimony and affadavits submitted, pleas for asylum and withholding of deportation denied |
| Spring 1998 | Women's Commission for Refugee Women and Children, celebrities, and media draw attention to the case and begin campaign (*Marie Claire* article in May) |
| July 1998 | Board of Immigration Appeals (BIA) denies appeal |
| August 1998 | Appeal filed with Second Circuit Court of Appeals |
| Spring 1999 | Campaign by Equality Now; Jonathan Rauchway, new lawyer for appeal, recruited by Women's Commission for Refugee Women and Children; internet and letter campaigns; protests by immigrant rights groups and NY legislators; media coverage; joint visit to detention center by Kassindja and Steinem; press conferences held by NOW-NYC; NY legislators write to Attorney General and hold press conference |
| May 3, 1999 | Second Circuit Court case argued |
| July 9, 1999 | Second Circuit Court decision reverses appeal (sending it back to BIA) |
| August 1999 | Asylum granted by BIA |
| December 2000 | Further INS investigation finds "Abankwah" to be false identity and her claims to be fraudulent |

*Source:* Author's compilation.

## The *Abankwah* Case

Adelaide Abankwah arrived in the United States in late March 1997; she was twenty-seven years old. After passing through immigration, an inspector called her back to recheck her documents (Sikes 1998, 56). Arrested for traveling under a false passport, she asked for asylum and explained why she left Ghana. Newspaper reports repeatedly describe her as sobbing and speaking in "broken English" during her account (English is a national language in Ghana, but Abankwah only finished primary school; see Waldman 1999).

Abankwah said she belonged to a small (six hundred–member) tribe in central Ghana called Nkumssa; her mother had been the queen mother. When her mother died in 1996, Abankwah's grandmother told her she would assume office, though no elders approached her about it. Becoming queen mother was said to involve a virginity test, and later, marriage to a man the elders would select. Abankwah had had sexual relations with her boyfriend and so would fail the test; she reported that circumcision would be her punishment.[11] To avoid this, she went to Accra, the capital, stayed with a friend's family and found employment. After five weeks, her employers accused her of stealing money, reported her to the Nkumssa, and members of the tribe came to Accra to find her. At this point, about eight months after her mother's death, she purchased a fake passport, visa, and a plane ticket and fled to the United States. No available court decisions or newspaper stories provide names for anyone mentioned in the account or for Abankwah's home in central Ghana. The INS hearing transcript, however, notes that her village is called Briwa (*Abankwah v. INS*, 2d Cir. Matter of Abankwah, transcript, File A 74 881 776 [1999], 55).

Abankwah had eight short immigration hearings between April and July 1997 and was given a list of legal aid groups; the case was postponed each time, since she had not yet found representation. After two short court appearances in July 1997 with both a lawyer and an interpreter, her hearing was postponed at the request of Olga Narymsky, an attorney with the Hebrew Immigrant Aid Society who had just taken the case and needed time to prepare. The case was heard in September 1997, with a Fanti interpreter. Two Ghanaians gave supporting evidence in October: Victoria Otumfuor, a Pentecostal minister living in the Bronx, and her son, Kwabena Danso Otumfuor, who had met Abankwah in Accra.[12] The request for asylum and withholding of deportation was denied, as was Abankwah's initial appeal heard nine months later in July 1998 by the Board of Immigration Appeals. An appeal was filed with the Second Circuit Court of Appeals a month later.

In spring 1998, *Marie Claire* magazine featured Abankwah's case in a story on women refugees, noting that the Women's Commission for Refugee Women and Children was trying to bring attention to it and that celebrities (such as Vanessa Redgrave) were becoming involved. The *Marie Claire* photography editor Nancy Weisman, "who visited Abankwah when the magazine ran [the] story . . . inadvertently became an activist on Abankwah's behalf. 'I sent out press packets, color photocopies of stories, facts on the case, legal documents, pleas to people'" (McCarthy 1999, 22). Jonathan Rauchway, recruited by the Commission from "a prestigious law firm" in New York, also agreed to argue Abankwah's appeal in federal court (Thompson 1999a; McCarthy 1999).

By spring 1999, Equality Now had joined the campaign and a range of supporters "made her case a cause célèbre" (Waldman 1999). NOW-NYC held press conferences, as did Senator Charles Schumer and Representative Carolyn Maloney, surrounded by a dozen people wearing "Free Adelaide Now" T-shirts, to announce their letter to the attorney general about Abankwah's release (Thompson 1999b). Fauziya Kassindja and Gloria Steinem visited Abankwah together; Rosalyn Carter and Julia Roberts also lent their names to the effort. Between April and August 1999, the *New York Times* ran seven articles on the case by several reporters, but placed them in the Metro section, not on the front page, like earlier stories about Kassindja. Media coverage was extensive—but Abankwah did not find a Celia Dugger who followed her case closely, writing prominently and sympathetically about characters and places involved.

Abankwah's appeal was argued before the Second Circuit Court in May and granted in July 1999. The judge agreed that Abankwah's fear was subjectively grounded but overturned the earlier ruling of insufficient objective grounds. The earlier ruling found no credible evidence that genital operations were used as claimed to punish lack of virginity or that they were common practice in Abankwah's home area, noted that the practice was outlawed in Ghana in 1994, and found that Abankwah had not established membership in a particular, cognizable social group subject to persecution, as required for asylum. (The group membership claimed was "women of the Nkumssa tribe who did not remain virgins until marriage.") The circuit court judge determined that Abankwah's own testimony could be the basis not only for the subjective component of "well-founded fear" but also could establish the necessary objective basis of the fear, supported by Otumfuor's testimony. Otumfuor gave general evidence about "FGM," but admitted she had no specific knowledge of Abankwah's ethnic group or area.

The circuit court decision sent Abankwah's case back to the Board of Immigration Appeals for consideration. She remained in detention ten days while supporters demanded her release; Senator Schumer's staff was "relentlessly pressing the agency [INS] to grant Ms. Abankwah's release" (Jacobs 1999). Released on parole, Abankwah was granted asylum the following month. Soon after, she appeared with supporters at a news conference at *Marie Claire* magazine (Hu 1999) and went to stay with Otumfuor.

## INTERSECTING ARENAS, ETHNOGRAPHICA, AND THROUGH-THE-LOOKING-GLASS MOMENTS

As seen from the United States and portrayed in American media, the *Kassindja* and *Abankwah* cases were dramatic, clear-cut examples of how young women could be threatened and oppressed by "tribal customs." Extended detention in the United States—Kassindja's, under harsh conditions—heightened their plights. The two cases also created narratives and trajectories of involvement stretching from West Africa to the United States. Their similarities and differences can help us consider the international debates and court cases about genital modification and different perspectives on the cases. In analyzing the cases, I map actors and arenas involved, then consider the ethnographica—that is, fragments of cultural and historical information—about Togo and Ghana invoked in producing knowledge, narratives, and social values in each case. This also involves Through-the-Looking-Glass moments, where common understandings and assumptions seem upside down, incompatible, or irrelevant.[13] When actors, arenas, representations, and values are compared in these cases, patterns and trends in the social and political processes linking debates and cases also are considered.

Tables 15.4 and 15.5 summarize the actors involved in the *Kassindja* and *Abankwah* cases. In both, actors come from all three arenas discussed earlier, though international campaigns seem involved primarily as sources of literature submitted in court.[14] Though situations begin in Kassindja's and Abankwah's home countries, American organizations and actors have the major involvement in their court cases; U.S. law defines the horizon of relevance once they arrive there. Only in Kassindja's case is assistance and information sought in her home country *during* the case, crossing arenas through the Lomé embassy. Information on Kassindja's situation in Togo is specific and detailed in media reports and court materials (for example, relatives and locations are named and described). Information on Abankwah is vague and general; that Adelaide Abankwah is the real name of the woman in court is not even clear at times.

Some U.S. organizations and public figures were involved in both cases. For instance, Equality Now heightened attention to both, but joined Abankwah's case when other organizations already were seeking public notice and high-caliber legal assistance. Kassindja herself joins celebrities visiting Abankwah. Similarly, Karen Musalo is an expert commentator in media coverage of *Abankwah*. Now directing the Center for Gender and Refugee Studies, Musalo's representation of Kassindja is not noted when she is quoted in the later case (Thompson 1999a; Sachs 1999; McCarthy 1999).

Comparing the two cases, however, suggests both repetition and escalation. The precedent the *Kassindja* case created was not only legal, it also demonstrated how a media–political action campaign could gain attention and apply pressure in other cases of genital modification (*Abankwah* most immediately) and elsewhere (Kaplan 1999). The Abankwah campaign followed a similar pattern but involved more organizations and celebrities, even as the Justice Department seemed to put less effort into examining her specific home-country situation.[15] Taken with the 1994 *Oluloro* case, the three cases suggest a trend of increasing media coverage and involvement by rights organizations. This parallels the trend noted earlier within home countries toward increasing contact and interaction across settings and arenas in the same period.

TABLE 15.4 / Actors and Arenas in the *Kassindja* Case

Home Countries (In Togo)

Locations:
Kpalimé (and Koussountou in later developments)—towns in northern Togo
Lomé, capital of Togo

Family and communities:
Tchamba-Koussountou people
Kassindja family (father, mother, father's brother, father's sister, sister all
named or interviewed)
Husband-to-be (named)

National government, NGOs, and organizations:
No law in Togo against female genital operations
Officials report no request for aid in such a case yet, though constitutional
provision ensuring physical integrity could be applied (Dugger 1996b)

Media:
Little coverage in Togo (Dugger 1996b)

Euro-American Countries (In Germany)

Kassindja spent several months in Germany, befriended by German woman,
and bought passport there

Euro-American Countries (In the United States)

National government, NGOs and Organizations:
Immigration and Naturalization Service (including Board of Immigration
Appeals)
Initial law firm where Miller Bashir got involved in the case
Equality Now (letter campaign, contacts with politicians and media)
International Human Rights Clinic (of American University)
Congressional representatives (Pat Schroeder and others)
Attorney general (letters addressed to)

Media:
Newspapers: *Washington Post*, *New York Times*, *Los Angeles Times* and others

Television:
Nightline, CNN International

Public figures and celebrities:
Gloria Steinem (see also congressional representatives)

Crossing Togo–United States

Family:
Cousin in United States hires first lawyer

*(Table continues on p. 324.)*

TABLE 15.4 / *Continued*

National governments and NGOs:

 U.S. Embassy in Togo—interviews family & groom; sends recent study
 showing highest incidence of genital cutting in Kassindja's ethnic group

 Office for Protection and Promotion of the Family (in Ministry for the
 Promotion of Women and for Social Services)—talked with Kassindja's
 father's brother at embassy's request

Media:

 *New York Times* reporter Dugger travels to Togo for follow-up story

International campaigns

 Exhibits include material produced by international campaigns (for example,
 Toubia, published by Rainbo, distributed by Women Ink)

*Source:* Author's compilation.

Media coverage of *Oluloro*, *Kassindja*, and *Abankwah* also shows decreasing representation of the cases and circumcising practices as contested and debated. Stories about *Oluloro* in the *New York Times* and *Time* mention both larger debates about genital operations and disagreements specific to the case. Coverage of Kassindja's case makes clear that family disagreements existed; Dugger's (1996b) follow-up quotes several people who believe the practice is right and important. In *Abankwah*'s coverage, however, the contested nature is largely absent or muted. This might be related to Abankwah's description of genital cutting as punishment. This also might indicate a shift in U.S. public understanding that has come with increasing coverage and familiarity with the debates, especially the well-advertised standpoint of campaigns against genital modification. The starting point for *Abankwah* coverage, then, seemed not to be the debates and disagreements—ongoing in home countries and immigrant communities overseas—but a certain position in those debates.

This shift in the extent to which genital modification is portrayed as contested had parallels in court hearings as well. The *Kassindja* case included an exchange on reasons for female circumcision that mirrors one impasse between conflicting cultural values and outlooks prominent in the larger debates, but here Immigration and Naturalization Service (INS) general counsel was in the position of explaining cultural and moral beliefs he did not hold when asked by the Board of Immigration Appeals (BIA), "Does the Government have a view as to why FGM is imposed?" (*In Re: Kasinga* 1996a, 17–18).

 INS: Well, no. I mean, it is part of a cultural practice there. It's not necessarily for us to try to justify. We are trying to submit—

 BIA: Well, I'm not asking you to justify it. I'm asking you does the Government have a position as to why this cultural practice is imposed?

TABLE 15.5  /  Actors and Arenas in the *Abankwah* Case

Home countries (in Ghana)

Locations:
  Village in central Ghana (usually unspecified; named as Briwa in INS
    transcript)
  Accra, capital of Ghana

Family and communities:
  Nkumssa people

  Abankwah's family (mother, grandmother [Mother's Mother? Father's Mother?],
    elders—no specific names or backgrounds)

  Family of a friend in Accra (unspecified name and circumstances)
  Employer in Accra (unspecified name)

National government, NGOs, and organizations:
  Law passed in Ghana in 1994 against female genital cutting

Media:
  Newspapers: The *Ghanaian Chronicle* (other articles reported)

Euro-American countries (in the United States)

National government, NGOs, and organizations:
  Immigration and Naturalization Service (including Board of Immigration
    Appeals)

  Second Circuit Court of Appeals
  Hebrew Immigrant Aid Society (lawyer for first hearings)

  Women's Commision for Refugee Women and Children (recruited lawyer for
    federal appeal and sought initial media attention)

  Orrick, Herrington, and Sutcliffe—"prestigious law firm" in New York
    (lawyer for federal appeal)

  Equality Now
  NOW-NYC
  Congressional representatives (Charles Schumer, Carolyn Maloney, and
    others)

  Attorney general (letters addressed to)

Media:
  Newspapers and magazines: *Marie Claire, New York Times, Washington Post,
    Newsday, Village Voice, Ms.*

  Television: *WWORTV*

Public figures and celebrities:
  Gloria Steinem, Vanessa Redgrave, Julia Roberts, Rosalyn Carter (see also
    congressional representatives)

(*Table continues on p. 326.*)

TABLE 15.5  /  *Continued*

Crossing Ghana and United States

Ghanaians living in United States:
  Victoria Otumfuor and Kwabena Danso Otumfuor (befriend and testify for
    Abankwah as expert witnesses)

International campaigns

  Exhibits include material from Ranbo (Research, Action, and Information
    Network for the Bodily Integrity of Women) and country-specific reports
    from State Department

*Source:* Author's compilation.

> INS: No, we—we do not. But we—we are at a loss to come up with a reason that would be regarded as legitimate and—and that's another reason why this particular circumstance—the practice should be regarded as meeting the threshold of—of shocking the conscience.

> BIA: Well, some of the background evidence in front of the Immigration Judge, for example, characterize FGM as a form of sexual oppression based on manipulation of women's sexuality in order to assure male dominance and exploitation. Does the Government disagree with that?

> INS: Well, we indicated in our brief that—that there are important sociological insights and descriptions of that kind. We do not think that it's necessary for us to take a position on that one way or another. We suggest in particular that we are not—that the Board is not required to analyze the practice in those particular terms. Certainly, there's an element of that—of exactly what that description is—and again, it's our position that there is no particular reason that our society is prepared to regard as legitimate— that entails it even as a practice.

In rebuttal, Kassindja's lawyer stated her position emphatically: "there is much evidence in the record to explain the reason why FGM is inflicted . . . the practice of FGM is purely for the purpose of gender subjugation and the perpetuation of social injustice" (*In Re: Kasinga* 1996a, 23).[16]

The contested nature of genital modification was indicated, but the real question in court was not whether it was deplorable but whether this case fit the framework of asylum law: Could Kassindja be defined as a member of a social group suffering persecution? A new "shocks the conscience" test was INS counsel's effort to grapple with questions of intentionality—a point of cultural contention and misunderstanding in broader debates and central to objections to the term *female genital mutilation*.

> The advantages seen by the Service [INS] of this test evidently include: 1) the ability to define FGM as "persecution" notwithstanding any lack of

intent to "punish" FGM victims on the part of the victims' parents or tribe members who may well "believe that they are simply performing an important cultural rite that bonds the individual to the society." (*In Re: Kasinga* 1996a, 21)

The *Abankwah* case did not deal even tangentially with the contested nature of reasons and intentions related to the practices. When Abankwah described the Nkumssa practice as punishment, it came closer to standard understandings of persecution. As argued in Kassindja's case, "Persecution usually means deliberate infliction of suffering or harm. It's often equated with punishment" (*In Re: Kasinga* 1996a, 17). Abankwah's case instead focused on the objective basis of her claims, whether or not genital modification was practiced in her area, and in ways recounted (as will be seen).

Contested cases transform in meaning and implication as they move through different arenas; presentation and evidence come to fit the arena at hand. As narratives are told and retold in communicative interaction during the asylum process, the salience of particular actors, situations, and notions of responsibility might shift (Kratz 1991, 2001). Both Kassindja's and Abankwah's accounts were questioned, particularly in early forms. The first immigration judge found Kassindja's account inconsistent because he did not understand premises relevant to her situation in Togo.[17] Abankwah's "broken English" and tears made her initial account difficult to understand. Further, when her first asylum claim as a member of the social group "candidates for the queen mother position who are unable or unwilling to accept that position" was found too narrow and cast her situation as "'an individual predicament' or 'personal problem,'" the social group was redefined on appeal as "women of the Nkumssa tribe who did not remain virgins until marriage" (*In Re: Abankwah* 1998, 2–3). As Piot (1999, 8) notes, a situation that might best be seen as a family dispute in the original context must be recast into defined social groups for a viable asylum claim. In a judicial setting and particular national arena, certain aspects are defined as important and legitimate while others are devalued and rendered irrelevant. These criteria and judgments feed back into other arenas and discussions.

Mapping actors and arenas in these two cases reveals a complicated web of social and political relations and transformations. Involvements and influences interconnect both within and across arenas: the Kassindja family meets in Togo to reconsider genital modification because U.S. publicity is spoiling their name; basic information submitted into evidence comes from international organizations campaigning against genital modification; advocacy organizations "work media and political contacts" and politicians "relentlessly press" government agencies in order to influence and draw attention to court cases; judicial and legislative decisions reverberate with one another. Tracing the web of social connections and relations in these cases shows that the different arenas cannot be seen as separate, and that differential access to key social connections in each arena can significantly influence attention to and treatment of a case.

Such interconnections are part of the workings of society and the very processes through which cultural understandings and expectations are redefined. Yet how particular social webs are woven and by whom can have real implications for the so-called free exercise of culture. Other immigrant residents' preferences, practices, and possibilities are caught in that same web, though their influence in shaping social circumstances is far less. The question of how judicial standards are applied in the context of increased lobbying and media pressure is particularly important. The answer should lead us to carefully consider the role of the judicial system in the production of knowledge and values and how it is caught up with larger debates concerning genital modification as well as other issues.[18]

The full web of connections results from many actions and decisions over time that are not fully coordinated or planned. Well-meaning efforts toward worthy goals can have unintended consequences. Consider how particular narratives, forms of knowledge, and values were produced in the *Kassindja* and *Abankwah* cases: for instance, how stereotypes of Africa and Africans fed into the cases, not only being recreated and reinforced but perhaps influencing standards of evidence and critical evaluation as well. Indeed, Piot (1999, 6) noted of the *Kassindja* case,

> There is no discussion whatsoever of Tchamba and what they are like, no testimony by anyone familiar with present day Togo, no inkling that two decades of discussion by Africanist scholars has established as orthodoxy that homogeneous "social groups" don't exist and that group identity is often fluid and shifting, and no reference to any anthropological literature on genital cutting. Moreover, these silences were filled by the crudest, most essentializing images and stereotypes. Thus, Kasinga was assumed by all in attendance to be a member of a "patriarchal tribe" with "immutable cultural norms" that practices "forced polygamy" and "mutilates" its women.[19]

Here I simply compare the ethnographica and expert witnesses used in the two cases, keeping in sight the effects over time of this increasingly interconnected web. I also consider several Through-the-Looking-Glass moments that bring material in Abankwah's case into conversation with opinions and perspectives from other arenas, foregrounding questions of evidence and critical judgment. I call the cultural and historical information invoked in the cases "ethnographica" because it often seems, to an anthropologist, to be a collection of fragments and factoids, not pieced together in ways that provide coherent or comprehensive understanding of circumstances under question. Indeed, the absence of basic information is astonishing at times, but those joined in legal contest have limited time for argument and investigation, and their goal is not to demonstrate the changing complexities and nuances of cultural practice. But that is why they have recourse to expert witnesses.

In such cases, expert witnesses include people who themselves cross arenas, with experience and knowledge of both home country and the United States. Kassindja's counsel submitted affidavits from two experts, Charles Piot and Merrick Posnansky. Piot, an anthropologist who did research in northern Togo in the 1980s, first reviewed the literature on the Tchamba people (Piot 1999, 1; *In Re: Abankwah* 1998, 6). His affidavit became part of the record early in the case. Posnansky, an archaeologist who worked at universities in Uganda and Ghana for years, with extensive research and administrative experience in Togo, submitted his affidavit with the appeal brief to help counter the initial ruling about Kassindja's credibility. Kassindja's counsel calls him an expert on Togo (*In Re: Kasinga* 1996a, 4) who "analyzed her case on the basis of her affidavit . . . [and] was meticulous in explaining the facts and reasoning underlying each of his conclusions" (*In Re: Kasinga* 1996b, 7).[20]

Abankwah's expert witnesses were Victoria Otumfuor and Kwabena Danso Otumfuor, who sent an affidavit from Ghana. National origin seems to have been the basis of their expertise, though Ghana is home to dozens of cultural groups and languages. Kwabena Danso Otumfuor's expertise was dismissed in the BIA decision as "based only on what the applicant told him" with "no indication that he is . . . an expert in the traditions of the applicant's tribe" (*In Re: Abankwah* 1998, 3–4); the later decision did not challenge this assessment. Victoria Otumfuor's affidavit and testimony were discounted in the BIA decision as not material to Abankwah's situation. She "specifically stated that she did 'not know a great deal about [the applicant's] tribe.' Moreover, when asked if she knew that the applicant's tribe practiced FGM as punishment, she replied, 'No, really, I can't say I know it specifically'" and indicated that punishment for premarital sex in her own village would be banishment, not FGM (*In Re: Abankwah* 1998, 4). Indeed, the hearing transcript shows that the word *expert* was expunged from her affidavit (*Abankwah v. INS* 1999, 61). Yet the Second Circuit Court decision found that specific knowledge was not necessary and accepted Otumfuor's expertise because she visited home biannually during her twenty years living in the United States. Though no background information submitted indicated that genital modification was used as punishment anywhere in the world, the court took as sufficient corroboration her explanation that "'Ghana is a country of many ethnic groups. We speak ten languages and forty dialects, and every village has a little practice. . . . [I]t's not all the practices that are being put to the government. . . . It would take time. There are some up in the limelight, and some are still in the distant'" (*Abankwah v. INS* 1999, 7).

Many scholars of Ghanaian culture and history would disagree, but they were not called as expert witnesses. The historian Jean Allman sent the *Ghanaian Chronicle* a copy of her letter to *Marie Claire* magazine shortly after Abankwah was granted asylum.[21] Former head of the Ghana Studies Council, Allman has been doing research in Ghana for several decades and was there when Abankwah's case was most highly publicized in the United States. Her letter began, "Surely a magazine of your stature employs investigative reporters capable of fleshing out the facts of a story," and continued,

I am disgusted that your magazine has made Adelaide into a cause celèbre when there is every indication that her story is contrived. Female genital mutilation is not only NOT practised in the area of Ghana from which Adelaide claims to come, but NEVER has been. . . . Nowhere in Ghana and, in fact, nowhere on the African continent, is FMG [*sic*] used as a punishment against those who have lost their virginity. Her claims are preposterous and any glance at any relevant literature or a conversation with any one of the Ghanaian immigrants in NYC, or the Ghanaian Consulate, would have made this clear, [it] is a felony offence in Ghana. ("U.S. Professor Exposes Deceit on Ghana" 1999)

Yet Otumfuor indeed was one of those Ghanaian immigrants in the New York City area; what kinds of facts and fact-checking were part of these cases?

Kassindja's circumstances were described in considerable detail; people and places were named and characterized. The various ethnographica—customs regarding widows (hence Kassindja's mother), excision in the midteens, details of marriage ceremonies—were well attested for the Tchamba people and area from which she came. The account was specific enough for representatives of both the United States and Togolese governments to corroborate it and speak with some of the principals in Togo. In comparison, Abankwah's account (as told in court decisions and media) was vague; no particular places or people were identified or described in detail. Despite the ambiguity, apparently no inquiries were made by American or Ghanaian officials in Ghana, or by Ghanaian officials in the United States. As the Ghanaian press noted, "Adelaide also failed to tell the US authorities and the rest of the world exactly which village in the Central Region she ran away from, a very important detail that would have required just a phone call from the Ghana Embassy in Washington to cross check" (Anokye 1999).[22] The ethnographica of Abankwah's case also were peculiar compared to other information and research on Ghanaian society, culture, and history.

When I first heard of the *Abankwah* case, I was struck by three aspects of the Nkumssa tradition of genital modification that were described. These features were unusual, perhaps unique, and as far as I could tell, unattested in the ethnographic record: limiting the practice to a small group of women within an ethnic group, using genital modification as punishment, and circumcising an adult woman of Abankwah's age (twenty-seven years old).[23] These features also made me doubt the reported story. Initial searches for information on Nkumssa (with various spellings) turned up nothing in major library collections on African studies, anthropology journal indexes, general reference books on Africa, or the Ethnologue index of world languages. I turned next to literature on Ghana and to colleagues (Ghanaian and American) who study Ghanaian culture and history, from which I learned the following. On closer look, much of Abankwah's other ethnographica also seemed strange.[24]

- The office of queen mother is part of the institution of chieftancy among Akan-speaking peoples in southern Ghana. When a new chief or queen mother is installed, usually several candidates are available. If one is unwilling, that person would not be forced to serve; another candidate would take the position.

- A virginity test for queen mother is documented nowhere else in Ghana, though a candidate might be expected to have demonstrated her fertility by having children.

- There are many queen mothers and chiefs, each associated with a particular community and organized into larger hierarchical systems or networks within Akan groups. Thus, for Nkumssa and their queen mother (said to be Abankwah's mother) not to be known more widely, even if Nkumssa are a small group, would be unusual.

- The bragoro puberty rite for girls is rare now, but still practiced in certain Akan-speaking areas. Girls were presented to the queen mother, but it did not involve circumcision. Young women were prohibited from becoming pregnant before bragoro, but not from losing virginity. Punishment for early pregnancy was banishment, as Otumfuor noted (*Abankwah v. INS* 1999, 111).

- My first inquiry to colleagues was about the name *Nkumssa*, because searches were fruitless. Was there such an ethnic group, or was it the name of Abankwah's village or clan? No one knew of a Nkumssa ethnic group, community, or clan in Ghana. Further, Abankwah's name and claimed home area clearly identified her as Akan. A Ghanaian linguist offered further analysis, breaking the word down to translate: "The word Nkumsaa subjected to Akan morphological analysis will be N (negative particle) + kum (kill) + me (me) + saa (that way), meaning 'Don't kill me this/that way.' Nkumsaa is thus a well-made Akan word to fit the story" (personal communication). Fauziya Kassindja did not correct misspelling of her name as *Kasinga* by the first immigration officers she encountered, a mistake carried through her case. I wondered if the so-called tribal name Nkumssa reflected misunderstanding of Abankwah's tearful account in "broken English," similarly perpetuated? This seemed unlikely, however, once I read the hearing transcript, because Abankwah states and spells the name through the Fanti interpreter.

- The hearing transcript raised still more questions about Abankwah and her identity. She said she usually used the name Kukwa Norman; Abankwah came from her father's father, Adelaide was used occasionally at school. The birthdate given in testimony differs from the one on the fake passport, made through photo substitution. Questions to Abankwah and Otumfuor in the hearing sought to determine whether the name Adelaide Abankwah simply had been adopted since it was on the passport she received (*Abankwah v. INS* 1999, 54, 63–64, 86–89, 100).

With all these peculiarities, Abankwah's account presented another world as far as Ghanaians and scholars of Ghana were concerned, with elements of familiar practices and customs twisted and combined in bizarre ways (later to be disproved). Ghanaians did not find it amusing, but rather "a national embarrassment" where "the country's name and integrity are compromised" (Anokye

1999). A colleague in Ghana at the time said, "people were quite upset at the slander of their cultural reputation" (personal communication). For Americans to recognize these peculiarities, however, they needed more than ethnographic fragments and had to look beyond popular American images of Africa (see Kratz 2002, 104–11).[25]

Stereotypes were evident both in American newspaper reports and in details of other accounts of the case. When Abankwah was accused of stealing money from her employers in Accra, for instance, it was said they "reported it to her tribe" so they could come after her.[26] My guess at the situation behind this description is that Abankwah found employment through people she knew at home or at school. When she got in trouble, they tried to resolve it through these same networks rather than go to the police—which would either create more serious trouble or simply be ineffective. The notion of "reporting someone to their tribe" makes little sense without explanation of the social and political relations involved.[27]

Abankwah's appeal lawyer, Jonathan Rauchway, also made very clear the framework of stereotypes through which Abankwah's case was interpreted in his comment to the *New York Times* (Thompson 1999a, 41).

> In places like Ghana, Mr. Rauchway said, people do not have basic identification papers like birth certificates or driver's licenses. Ms. Abankwah's identification is a tattoo on her forearm that reads "Marmenorman Briwa." The first word, she said, translates loosely as "older sister." The second is the name of her village. "If I am dead somewhere," she said, showing the tattoo, "they can look at this and they will know where I come from."

Ghanaians would not recognize their country in these remarks. They present another Through-the-Looking-Glass moment for citizens of the first African country to regain independence from colonialism (in 1957), home of Kwame Nkrumah, Kofi Annan, and four universities, where adult citizens in even the most rural parts of the country hold identity cards and vote in national elections. Anokye's (1999) comment in *The Ghanaian Chronicle* is an apt rejoinder.

> With Adelaide's case all doubts I had before about the ignorance of many Americans about Ghanaian and other African societies have evaporated. It requires a lot of education to correct the jaundiced view of many on the other side of the ocean. I hope it will not be too much to ask of the people who can believe Adelaide's story right away, without checking her story, that they should know that people this side of heaven also live in skyscrapers, drive cars, wear Calvin Klein and Gucci and watch television. Indeed, I wish to have all know that it is possible to e-mail the White House from Adelaide's village or, for that matter, from mine deep in the forest of the great Asante Kingdom of the Ashanti Region of Ghana.

Yet Victoria Otumfuor gave sworn testimony supporting Abankwah. Could these other knowledgeable people be mistaken? Abankwah's account was so vague that all were extrapolating to some extent—how else to explain Otum-fuor's deposition? While Abankwah's lawyers argued her membership in a social group that would support her asylum claim, other social group memberships might have encouraged or shaped supporting testimony. Ghanaian colleagues raised this possibility, introducing yet another Through-the-Looking-Glass moment, one that turns upside down certain American assumptions about the legal process.

Legal systems differ in many ways, and understandings of what it means to be a witness and give testimony are not universal. The American legal system defines allegiance to "fair and impartial justice" as an overriding concern for witnesses, with serious sanctions for perjury. Exceptions are made for close relationships that might create conflicts of allegiance (for example, spouses need not testify against one another). Those experienced in the legal system, however, find that ideals of impartiality and fairness must be pursued vigilantly, and organizations working for international social justice and democracy regularly protest corrupt or biased legal systems in other countries. Similarly, other forms of allegiance might influence witnesses and their testimonies.

In Abankwah's case, a colleague advised, "Learn from these two Akan proverbs: (a) If you can tell lies which resemble the truth, you always have an escape route; (b) She who is fighting to bring home property should not be prohibited but should be helped. . . . Remember what constitutes a crime in one society may not be a crime or an insult in another." The second proverb suggests that Ghanaians—especially Akan (assuming Abankwah to be from an Akan group)—who testified publicly against Abankwah might be seen as hindering a fellow Ghanaian, not helping them prosper. Historically, colonial courts in Ghana and elsewhere also provide cases where people agreed to a story that helped someone needing aid. Kwabena Danso Otumfuor's testimony was deemed to repeat what Abankwah told him, with no other expertise or independent knowledge. Victoria Otumfuor's expertise eventually was accepted, but what understandings of court, testimony, allegiances, and social groups informed her testimony? Were American and Ghanaian understandings somehow combined?

As different assessments of the Otumfuors' testimonies suggest, notions and standards of evidence also are debated in American courts, and decisions about evidentiary standards were important in the *Kassindja* and *Abankwah* cases. Kassindja's appeal lawyers remarked on her extensive objective evidence, "more corroboration than most asylum applicants" can provide (*In Re: Kasinga* 1996a, 3).[28] As noted earlier, the appeal decision overturned a previous judgment that applied assumptions based on American life to find Kassindja's account unbelievable. If interpretation of evidence became more reasonable and responsive to case circumstances in successive *Kassindja* rulings, however, *Abankwah* case rulings seemed to take a reverse trajectory. Her BIA appeal judge seemed to have read case material closely, pointed out disjunctions with Abankwah's claims, and raised questions about expert witnesses. The decision made several of the aforementioned points raised by Ghanaians and scholars of Ghanaian culture and history. Yet the Second Circuit Court felt "the BIA was too exacting both in the quantity and quality of evidence that it required . . . it must be acknowl-edged that a genuine refugee does not flee her native country with affidavits, expert witnesses, and extensive documentation" (*Abankwah v. INS* 1999, 6, 7). Applying a much more forgiving evidentiary standard, this decision found Abankwah's own testimony sufficient objective evidence for her account, backed by Otumfuor, as well as subjective evidence of her fear. From the perspective of some Ghanaians and scholars, this standard suspended critical evaluation and judgment and took little account of contemporary Ghanaian realities.

Those who found Abankwah's account puzzling or implausible (including me) often supported broadly tolerant decisions about immigration and asylum. Yet each case has to be taken seriously and stand up to fair, knowledgeable, but critical evaluation. Abankwah's vagueness turned her case into both a Rasho-mon tale and a Rorschach test for American ideas about Africa and genital mod-ification. Why was no apparent effort made to clarify or verify such an account? The high level of media and advocacy attention seemed to bring greater clarity and detail to Kassindja's case, but not to Abankwah's. While hard to predict, the influence of intensified media scrutiny and lobbying can certainly make a differ-ence to rulings.

When the clamor subsided after Abankwah's release, the district INS officer began looking into her background. Within months, agency investigators had interviewed people in Ghana, located relevant records, and assembled "what one called 'overwhelming evidence' of fraud" (Branigin and Farah 2000). When the news came out, the *Washington Post* sent a reporter to Ghana. The woman claiming to be Adelaide Abankwah was really Regina Norman Danson, a former hotel worker from the town of Biriwa (eighty miles from the capital, Accra). She was never a candidate for queen mother (not being from a royal family), her mother was still living, and she had married in 1996. The local chief, Nana Kwa Bonko V, confirmed that "female circumcision plays no role in his tribe's tradi-tion and that there is no punishment for rejecting nomination as a queen mother" (Branigin and Farah 2000). As Danson's former employer in Biriwa summarized, "Her whole story is a complete lie . . . she left because she wanted to go to the United States."

Investigators recommended in late 1999 that Danson be prosecuted for fraud, but the "Justice Department has been reluctant to proceed for fear of embarrass-ing politicians and top administration officials who weighed in on Danson's be-half" (Branigin and Farah 2000; Murphy 2000). In December 2000, Danson was selling French beauty products in New York, studying for her high school equiv-alency certificate, and sticking to her story.[29] Though the ultimate outcome of the Abankwah-Danson saga is not yet clear, the belated INS inquiry resolved ques-tions her story raised—yet it also raises other, more troubling questions. As a Ghanaian colleague asked, "if they could investigate afterwards, why not be-fore?" Did political lobbying and media outrage short-circuit judicious reason-ing? Do different standards of evidence and expertise apply for Africa?

The *Kassindja* and *Abankwah* cases set legal precedents that will be used in other asylum decisions, but they created other precedents as well. If *Kassindja* showed how political advocacy groups can combine with relatively responsible journalism to make a sometimes flawed legal system more accountable, *Abankwah* showed how misplaced support by the same alliance might help subvert careful examination and due process. How will the *Abankwah* legal precedent be applied now that the objective basis of her case has been undermined?

One aspect now common to both cases, however, should become a standard for future practice. When the Abankwah-Danson story finally was investigated, what made the difference was trying to ascertain and understand the Ghanaian circumstances from which she had come. Kassindja's story was confirmed through similar efforts, with support from undisputed experts. Asylum cases inevitably cross international arenas, but home-country contexts cannot be ignored when they involve unfamiliar customs and circumstances. To act responsibly, legal investigations, journalists, and advocacy groups alike must take account of the multiple groundings and social relations involved, and not rely on fragmented ethnographica or projected stereotypes.

## DEFINING CIRCUMSTANCES AND DISPLACED DEBATES

These two cases show how debates and cases about genital modification intersect and interact within and across arenas, linked moments in the sociopolitical processes through which these practices are defined and redefined in various settings. Though focused in the United States, such cases and actions in the Euro-American arena reverberate both within that arena and elsewhere. The analysis has implications beyond circumcising practices as well: it suggests how possibilities for the free exercise of cultural practices are shaped, narrowed, or broadened. Separately, these cases offer instructive comparisons and contrasts, but to see them as different points in a larger social process is equally important.

The long-standing debates about genital modification are difficult to resolve and do not stand still. As stances, stakes, and participants change, defined in particular situations, issues and debates also might be displaced. Understanding why people practice genital modification, for instance, presents a fundamental intercultural impasse in international debates. When raised at Kassindja's appeal hearing, interlocutors did not understand or believe the stance of practitioners in home countries. The original stakes and stances were much attenuated in this new setting; the perplexed INS counsel was at a loss to explain practitioners' social and moral convictions and values. Through-the-Looking-Glass moments also transform in different settings: in *Abankwah*, they encompassed a wide range of cultural practice for Ghanaians and scholars but had little to do with issues fundamental to ongoing debates about genital modification.

Comparing the *Kassindja* and *Abankwah* cases suggested what a difference thorough, grounded knowledge can make when it goes beyond fragmented ethnographica whose vague contours are easily filled in with stereotypes. Such debates are full of obfuscating representations and assertions that are unsubstantiated though repeated incessantly (Obermeyer 1999; Parker 1995; Obiora 1997; Mugo 1997; Kratz 1994, 1999a). If the images and rhetoric of anticircumcision campaigns now have circulated so relentlessly that "counterdiscourse about the meaning of genital cutting is today for most Westerners utterly unthinkable" (Piot 1999, 6), what does that mean for "facing up to a demanding inter-cultural dialogue in which all parties come to the table under common expectations of being treated as moral equals" (Ignatieff 1999, 40)? Female genital modification often is taken as an extreme case that tests the limits of pluralism and tolerance for Euro-Americans (Shweder, ch. 11 herein), but shouldn't that mean extra care is taken with arguments, evidence, and enabling dialogue?

Exploring questions at the limits can throw into relief problems, processes, and assumptions that may be harder to recognize in other circumstances. This discussion of debates and cases about female genital modification shows how tangled the webs of interconnection can become and how important it is to consider these complex social dimensions when looking at contested cultural practices and at the debates and cases themselves. The changing nature of social relations, cultural understandings, and circumstances involved means that questions about cultural pluralism may be impossible to answer in the abstract—but situationally defined guidelines should recognize that the playing field is never even, and take careful account of its contours and shifts.

---

Discussions with Ivan Karp helped me formulate and clarify arguments presented here; I thank him for our ongoing conversation and for reading drafts. Peter Brown, Arthur Eisenberg, Anni Peller, Charles Piot, Rick Shweder, and Beverly Stoeltje commented helpfully on an earlier version. Jean Allman, Anthony Appiah, Gracia Clark, Christine and Ross Kreamer, Samuel Obeng, and Beverly Stoeltje offered guidance on Ghanaian customs, history, and politics. Discussion of the Abankwah case with Arthur Eisenberg, Larry Sager, and others in the SSRC–Russell Sage working group was a great help. Thanks to Charles Piot and Beverly Stoeltje for helpful sources, and the Center for Gender and Refugee Studies for the *Abankwah* hearing transcript and other material.

## NOTES

1. Never neutral, the choice of terms always implies a stance toward the debates. See Kratz (1994, 1999a) on their history and rhetorical and political implications. I use the term *female circumcision* to refer to specific community traditions where practitioners view male and female circumcision as parallel practices (and often translate their own term into English as *circumcision*). Otherwise, the terms *genital modification, genital operations*, and *circumcising practices* are used for the broader array of practices grouped together in international debates. Occasionally, I use *genital cutting* or FGC, but this is not as neutral as it is intended to be. The journalist Celia Dugger helped popularize

that term, yet combined it with lurid descriptions of women having "their genitals cut off." Quotes are used when following terminology in citations.

2. See Winter (1994) for an overview of French cases, which began in 1983, and Simons (1993) for an American news account.

3. Anthropologists have long used notions such as semiautonomous fields (Moore 1978) to understand the structure and processes involved in complex, large-scale social and political interactions. These concepts could be combined in profitable and illuminating ways with recent, more structurally amorphous formulations of global phenomena in terms of "flows" and "scapes" (Appadurai 1990).

4. Looking across different home countries, shifts in practice go in all imaginable directions: from adoption of genital modification by noncircumcising communities (Leonard 1999) to modification of long-standing rituals toward what I call "circumcision by pronouncement" or "performative circumcision" (substituting a verbal formula for actual cutting; see Abusharaf 1999, 7; Hernlund 1999) to modification through medicalization (Obiora 1997; Shell-Duncan 2001) to recontextualizing ceremonies with genital modification within refugee camp settings. Many other social, political, and economic transformations in home countries have coincided with increasing pressure from anticircumcision campaigns; these often have been more significant than campaign pressure in producing shifts.

5. Twenty are listed on the Center for Gender and Refugee Studies web site at *www.uchastings.edu/cgrs/summaries/persecute.html*.

6. For Kassindja, this included sudden financial success. She received more than half of a $600,000 contract for a book coauthored with the law student who first presented her case (Dugger 1996b; Kassindja and Miller Bashir 1998).

7. I base this discussion on material readily available about the cases, mainly U.S. media coverage and copies of court decisions. I could not visit libraries with Ghanaian or Togolese newspapers before writing this chapter; on-line archives are very limited. While I made final revisions, news broke that further INS investigation showed Abankwah's claims to be fraudulent (Branigin and Farah 2000; Murphy 2000).

8. Efua Dorkenoo, who works with the Minority Rights Group in London, was a consultant for the film. In 1983, she coauthored their report *Female Circumcision, Excision, and Infibulation: The Facts and Proposal for Change*, revised and reissued in 1992 as *Female Genital Mutilation: Proposals for Change*—a title revision that indicates shifts that occurred as debates heightened during the intervening decade.

9. Yoruba boys and girls are circumcised when small. Circumcision and excision are not connected with initiation for the Yoruba people but are related to moral concepts associated with shame and fertility.

10. Tchamba-Koussountou combines the two areas where the extended Kassindja family live. In her book, Kassindja also mentions relief at speaking Éwé with another woman from Togo who arrives at the detention center. None of the media or case material identifies the language(s) she speaks, but a search of Ethnologue (an extensive database on world languages) shows that: Tchamba is the name for a language also known as Akaselem, with Tchamba as its main center; Koussountou is the name for a language also known as Bago, with main centers in areas bearing those names; and Éwé is spoken in both Ghana and Togo (by 20 percent of Togo's population), is widely

known as a second language, and has a main center at Kpalimé, where Kassindja's family lives.

11. What kind of operation this was supposed to be is hard to know. Abankwah spoke Fanti (an Akan language) in court proceedings, and said that people from her village traded in Kumasi, a major Asante town. Knudsen (1994, 54–56) notes that very few Akan groups—who make up the population of southern and central Ghana—practice female genital modification: those who do either practice sunna circumcision (taking off "the hood of the clitoris—or the prepuce—with precision") or else make four scarification marks "on the clitoris without cutting the hood or the prepuce off."

12. Only the hearing transcript specifies the relation between these two; they figure little in news coverage. The final *Times* story (Hu 1999) refers to Victoria as Otumfuor-Neequaye and notes that she left Ghana twenty-two years ago. Victoria testified that her son introduced her to Abankwah at a funeral in Accra in early 1997 and then called her when he knew Abankwah was in detention (*Abankwah v. INS*, 2d Cir. Matter of Abankwah, transcript, File A 74 881 776 [1999], 115–17). This portion of the testimony also sought to determine whether she was using the name Adelaide Abankwah in Accra (see following discussion).

13. This sort of experience is described in Lewis Carroll's classic books, *Alice's Adventures in Wonderland* and *Through the Looking-Glass*.

14. Given the problematic representations of circumcising practices in some campaign literature, this has implications for how the debates and practices were understood. Note that *mutilation* was the term used throughout Abankwah's hearings.

15. These two trends are not necessarily linked, except coincidentally. I do not know if the Justice Department and the U.S. embassy in Accra communicated during the case, as with the embassy in Lomé. Nonetheless, the belated investigation that disproved "Abankwah's" story shows that this could have made a difference (Branigin and Farah 2000). The number of organizations devoted to women's rights and refugees also increased in the past decade as problems both increased and received greater attention. The Women's Commission was founded in 1989, and Equality Now in 1992.

16. Piot (1999, 5) also comments on this exchange. Note, however, that the practice is described by all here as "imposed" or "inflicted" and that *FGM* is taken as standard, uncontested terminology.

17. For instance, the judge found it incredible that Kassindja did not know where her mother was, not understanding that her father's family could properly send the widow away after a reasonable mourning period and that this happened while Kassindja was away at school. Her lawyer argued, "Togo is not the United States and the Judge's reliance upon U.S. cultural norms to judge Ms. Kasinga's credibility regarding the whereabouts of her mother was totally improper" (*In Re: Kasinga* 1996a, 4).

18. The 2000 presidential election showed that even the highest U.S. court can be embroiled in partisan advocacy. Mikva (2000) discusses other threats to judicial integrity.

19. Abankwah may be from a matrilineal society, like most Akan in southern and central Ghana; discussions of the queen mother position showed no recognition of this. In fact, there is little sense that history is relevant to "traditional" customs. "Traditional" is often assumed to mean unchanging, rather than seen as ascribing value to certain domains of practice (Hobsbawm and Ranger 1983; Kratz 1993).

20. Posnansky's affidavit notes that he visited Togo sixteen times and had been to Kpalimé on several occasions (1998, 419).

21. *Marie Claire* did not publish or respond to the letter (Jean Allman, personal communication).

22. The hearing transcript has more information, including the village name (Briwa) and nearby place where Abankwah attended school (District Konso), but hearing participants did not have the background or experience to relate these details or Abankwah's account to regional, social, cultural, and historical patterns in Ghana.

23. Societies that practice female genital modification typically prescribe it for all women, though some don't participate because of church membership, opposition, or other reasons. As Allman's letter underlined, a century of research has failed to identify any society in Africa that defines genital operations as punishment. Circumcising practices usually are understood in terms of initiation into adulthood, fertility, and sexuality. Usual age varies across different societies, but puberty and late teens are the top of the range. In isolated cases, older adult women decide to be circumcised when they marry into a circumcising society (Gosselin 1999, 7). Knudsen (1994, 50) notes examples in Ghana, with observations of particular relevance to Abankwah's claims. "In such marriages the Akan woman has other problems. *In some cases, the Akan woman's children may become chiefs or queen mothers one day among her own people. Therefore, they must not have any scarification on their faces, bodies or on the outer genitalia*" (emphasis added). These are individual exceptions and actions taken by the women concerned, not accepted customs prescribing genital modification for older women.

24. See Stoeltje (1997) on the Asante queen mother institution; Yankah (1995) on Akan chiefs and royal language; Dakubu (1988) on Ghanaian languages; Nukunya (1992) for an overview; and Ardayfio-Schandorf and Kwafo-Akoto (1990) for an extensive bibliography on women in Ghana.

25. See Kratz (2002, 104–111) on these images and how stereotypes are recreated and circulated.

26. The BIA decision (*In Re: Abankwah* 1998, 2) describes this differently, more neutrally.

> The applicant also apparently fled because of a problem she had in Accra regarding lost money. She claimed that she was assisting the individuals with whom she was staying in Accra, and when some money was lost, she was accused of losing or taking it. She then fled from Accra. These individuals then went to her village to look for her and it was in this way that the villagers learned she was in Accra (Tr. at 72–73). The applicant acknowledged that no one from her village came to look for her until after they had been visited by the individuals who claimed she took or lost their money (Tr. at 82–83).

This episode, which relates Abankwah's flight to other circumstances, is not mentioned in most news accounts or in the Second Circuit Court decision.

27. Appiah (1992, 168–69) discusses how people adjusted to the decline of the Ghanaian state in the 1970s, providing relevant social and historical context for interpreting the notion of "being reported to the tribe."

> Life went on. Not only did people not "get away with murder," even though the police would usually not have been in a position to do anything about it, but

people made deals, bought and sold goods, owned houses, married, raised families. If anything could be said about the role of state officials (including the army and the police), it was that by and large their intervention was as likely to get in the way of these arrangements as to aid them, as likely to be feared and resented as welcomed. . . . Disputes in urban as well as in rural areas were likely to end up in arbitration, between heads of families, or in the courts of "traditional" chiefs and queen mothers, in procedures that people felt they could understand and, at least to some extent, manage: once the lawyers and magistrates and the judges of the colonial (and, now, with little change, the postcolonial) legal system came into play, most people knew that what happened was likely to pass beyond their comprehension and control.

Much has changed and improved since the 1970s. Ghana now is seen as having one of the most efficient and reputable electoral systems in Africa and having made "considerable progress . . . [from] a near 'failed state' in the late 1970s toward becoming a stable, integrated, constitutional, and democratic polity" (Joseph forthcoming).

28. Kassindja's evidence included letters, an unsigned marriage certificate, and photographs as well as background material on female genital modification in Togo.

29. The real Adelaide Abankwah is a former college student whose passport was stolen in Accra in 1996 (Branigin and Farah 2000).

# REFERENCES

Abusharaf, Rogaia Mustafa. 1999. "Beyond 'The External Messiah Syndrome': What Are Sudanese People Doing to End Ritualized Genital Surgeries?" Paper presented at the Annual Meetings of the American Anthropological Association, session on Female Genital Cutting: Local Dynamics of a Global Debate. November 18, Chicago, Illinois.

Anokye, Frank. 1999. "Genital Mutilation Made in America." *Ghanaian Chronicle*, May 24–25: 10.

Apena, Adeline. 1996. "Female Circumcision in Africa and the Problem of Cross-Cultural Perspectives." *Africa Update* 3(2): 7–8.

Appadurai, Arjun. 1990. "Disjuncture and Difference in the Global Cultural Economy." *Theory, Culture and Society* 7: 295–310.

Appiah, Kwame Anthony. 1992. *In My Father's House: Africa in the Philosophy of Culture*. New York: Oxford University Press.

Ardayfio-Schandorf, Elizabeth, and Kate Kwafo-Akoto. 1990. *Women in Ghana: An Annotated Bibliography*. Accra: Woeli Publication Services.

Boddy, Janice. 1982. "Womb as Oasis: The Symbolic Context of Pharaonic Circumcision in Rural Northern Sudan." *American Ethnologist* 9: 682–98.

Branigin, William, and Douglas Farah. 2000. "Asylum Seeker Is Impostor, INS Says." *Washington Post*, December 20: A1.

Breitung, Barrett. 1996. "Interpretation and Eradication: National and International Responses to Female Circumcision." *Emory International Law Review* 10(2). Available at: *www.law.emory.edu/EILR/volumes/win96/breitung.html*.

Coleman, Doriane. 1998. "The Seattle Compromise: Multicultural Sensitivity and Americanization." *Duke Law Journal* 47(4): 717–84.

Dakubu, Mary Esther, ed. 1988. *The Languages of Ghana*. London: Kegan Paul International for the International African Institute.

Dugger, Celia W. 1996a. "U.S. Frees African Fleeing Ritual Mutilation." *New York Times*, April 25: A1.

———. 1996b. "A Refugee's Body Is Intact but Her Family Is Torn." *New York Times*, September 11: A1.

———. 1996c. "African Ritual Pain: Genital Cutting." *New York Times*, October 5, 1996: A1.

———. 1996d. "New Law Bans Genital Cutting in United States." *New York Times*, October 12: A1.

Egan, Timothy. 1994. "An Ancient Ritual and a Mother's Asylum Plea." *New York Times*, March 4: B12.

Fokkena, Laura. 1994. "Female Genital Mutilation: The Circumcising of Women Stirs Up World-Wide Debate." *Acculturation*. Available at: *www.avalon.net/~laurafo.fgm.html*.

Gluckman, Max. 1958 [1940]. *Analysis of a Social Situation in Modern Zululand*. Rhodes-Livingstone Paper No. 28. Reprint, Manchester, U.K.: Manchester University Press.

Gosselin, Claudie. 1999. "'Light Like Fire': Excision and Women's Sexuality in Urban Mali." Paper presented at the Annual Meetings of the American Anthropological Association, session on Female Genital Cutting: Local Dynamics of a Global Debate, November 18, Chicago, Illinois.

Hernlund, Ylva. 1999. "Ritual Negotiations and Cultural Compromise: An Alternative Initiation in the Gambia." Paper presented at the Annual Meetings of the American Anthropological Association, session on Female Genital Cutting: Local Dynamics of a Global Debate, November 18, Chicago, Illinois.

Hobsbawm, Eric, and Terence Ranger, eds. 1983. *The Invention of Tradition*. Cambridge: Cambridge University Press.

Hoskens, Fran. n.d. "Genital and Sexual Mutilation of Females." WIN News summary distributed at U.N. Decade for Women conference, Nairobi, 1985.

Hu, Winnie. 1999. "Woman Fearing Mutilation Savors Freedom." *New York Times*, August 20: A21.

Ignatieff, Michael. 1999. *Whose Universal Values? The Crisis in Human Rights*. The Hague: Praemium Erasmianum Foundation.

*In Re: Abankwah*. 1998. A74 881 776 (Board of Immigration Appeals).

*In Re: Kasinga*. 1996a. A73 A76 695 (Board of Immigration Appeals) Transcript of hearing. Available at: *www.courttv.com/library/rights/mutilation.html*.

*In Re: Kasinga*. 1996b. A73 A76 695 (Board of Immigration Appeals) Reply Brief for Respondent.

Iweriebor, Ifeyinwa. 1996. "Brief Reflections on Clitoridectomy." *Africa Update* 3(2): 2.

Jacobs, Andrew. 1999. "U.S. Frees African Woman Who Fled Genital Cutting." *New York Times*, April 15: A1.

Joseph, Richard. Forthcoming. "War, State Making, and Democracy in Africa." In *Beyond State Crisis: Africa and Post-Soviet Eurasia in Comparative Perspective*, edited by Mark Beissinger and Crawford Young. Washington, D.C.: Woodrow Wilson Center Press.

Kaplan, Caren. 1999. "Resisting Biomedicine: Intersex Activism and Transnational FGM Discourse." Paper presented at the Annual Meetings of the American Anthropological Association, session on Female Genital Cutting: Local Dynamics of a Global Debate, November 18, Chicago, Illinois.

Kaplan, David, Shawn Lewis, and Joshua Hammer. 1993. "Is It Torture or Tradition?" *Newsweek*, December 20: 124.

Kassindja, Fauziya, and Layli Miller Bashir. 1998. *Do They Hear You When You Cry*. New York: Delacourt Press.

Knudsen, Christiana Oware. 1994. *The Falling Dawadawa Tree: Female Circumcision in Developing Ghana*. Højbjerg, Denmark: Intervention Press.

Kratz, Corinne. 1991. "Amusement and Absolution: Transforming Narratives during Confession of Social Debts." *American Anthropologist* 93(4): 826–51.

———. 1993. "We've Always Done It Like This . . . Except for a Few Details: 'Tradition' and 'Innovation' in Okiek Ceremonies." *Comparative Studies in Society and History* 35(1): 30–65.

———. 1994. "Appendix A: Initiation and Cirumcision." In *Affecting Performance: Meaning, Movement, and Experience in Okiek Women's Initiation*. Washington, D.C.: Smithsonian Institution Press.

———. 1999a. "Contexts, Controversies, Dilemmas: Teaching Circumcision." In *Great Ideas for Teaching About Africa*, edited by Misty Bastian and Jane Parpart. Boulder, Colo.: Lynne Rienner.

———. 1999b. "Female Circumcision in Africa." In *Encarta Africana*, edited by Kwame Anthony Appiah and Henry Louis Gates, Jr. Redmond, Wash.: Microsoft.

———. 2001. "Conversations and Lives." In *African Words, African Voices*, edited by David William Cohen, Stephan Miescher, and Luise White. Bloomington: Indiana University Press.

———. 2002. *"The Ones That Are Wanted": Communication and the Politics of Representation in a Photographic Exhibition*. Berkeley: University of California Press.

Leonard, Lori. 1999. " 'We Did It for Pleasure Only': Hearing Alternative Tales of Female Circumcision." Paper presented at the Annual Meetings of the American Anthropological Association, session on Female Genital Cutting: Local Dynamics of a Global Debate, November 18, Chicago, Illinois.

McCarthy, Sheryl. 1999. "No Activism, No Asylum." *Ms.* October-November: 21–22.

Mikva, Abner. 2000. "The Wooing of Our Judges." *New York Times*, August 28: editorial page.

Mire, Soraya. 1994. *Fire Eyes*. New York: Filmmakers Library.

Moore, Sally Falk. 1978. "Law and Social Change: The Semi-Autonomous Social Field as an Appropriate Object of Study." In *Law as Process*. London: Routledge & Kegan Paul.

Morgan, Robin, and Gloria Steinem. 1980. "The International Crime of Genital Mutilation." *Ms.* March: 65–7.

Mugo, Micere. 1997. "Elitist Anti-Circumcision Discourse as Mutilating and Anti-Feminist." *Case Western Reserve Law Review* 47(2): 461–80.

Murphy, Dean E. 2000. "I.N.S. Says African Woman Used Fraud to Gain Asylum." *New York Times*, December 21, 2000: C21.

Murray, Jocelyn. 1974. "The Kikuyu Female Circumcision Controversy, with Special Reference to the Church Missionary Society's 'Sphere of Influence.' " Ph.D. diss., University of California, Los Angeles.

———. 1976. "The Church Missionary Society and the 'Female Circumcision' Issue in Kenya, 1929–1932." *Journal of Religion in Africa* 8(2): 92–104.

Nukunya, G. K. 1992. *Tradition and Change in Ghana*. Accra: Ghana Universities Press.

Obermeyer, Carla Makhlouf. 1999. "Female Genital Surgeries: The Known, the Unknown, and the Unknowable." *Medical Anthropology Quarterly* 13(1): 79–106.

Obiora, L. Amede. 1997. "Bridges and Barricades: Rethinking Polemics and Intransigence in the Campaign Against Female Circumcision." *Case Western Reserve Law Review* 47(2): 275–378.

Parker, Melissa. 1995. "Rethinking Female Circumcision." *Africa* 65(4): 506–24.

Pederson, Susan. 1991. "National Bodies, Unspeakable Acts: The Sexual Politics of Colonial Policy-making." *Journal of Modern History* 63: 647–80.

Peyrot, Maurice. 1991. "Tribal Practices Pose Dilemma for Western Society." *Le Monde*, March 8, 9, 10, 11, 1991. Translation in *Guardian Weekly*, March 24, 1991. Reprinted in *Passages* 3(1992).

Piot, Charles. 1999. "Representing Africa in the Kasinga Asylum Case." Paper presented at the Annual Meetings of the American Anthropological Association, session on Female Genital Cutting: Local Dynamics of a Global Debate, November 18, Chicago, Illinois.

Posnansky, Merrick. 1998. "Affadavit of Professor Merrick Posnansky." *Review of Law and Women's Studies* 7(373): 418–28.

Rosenthal, A. M. 1993. "Female Genital Torture." *New York Times*, November 12: A33.

Sachs, Susan. 1999. "Fears of Rape and Violence: Women Newly Seeking Asylum." *New York Times*, August 1: Week in Review.

Shell-Duncan, Bettina. 2001. "The Medicalization of Female 'Circumcision': Harm Reduction or Promotion of a Dangerous Practice?" *Social Science and Medicine* 52: 1013–28.

Sikes, Gini. 1998. "Why Are Women Who Escape Genital Mutilation Being Jailed in America? Marie Claire Campaign." *Marie Claire*, May: 52–56.

Simons, Marlise. 1993. "Mutilation of Girls' Genitals: Ethnic Gulf in French Court." *New York Times*, November 23: A13.

Stoeltje, Beverly J. 1997. "Asante Queen Mothers: A Study in Female Authority." In *Queens, Queen Mothers, Priestesses, and Power: Case Studies in African Gender*, edited by Flora Kaplan. New York: Annals of the New York Academy of Sciences.

Thomas, Lynn. 1996. "'Ngaitana (I will circumcise myself)': The Gender and Generational Politics of the 1956 Ban on Clitoridectomy in Meru, Kenya." *Gender and History* 8(3): 338–63.

———. 1998. "Imperial Concerns and 'Women's Affairs': State Efforts to Regulate Clitoridectomy and Eradicate Abortion in Meru, Kenya, c. 1920–1950." *Journal of African History* 39(1): 121–45.

Thompson, Ginger. 1999a. "No Asylum for a Woman Threatened with Genital Cutting." *New York Times*, April 25, 1997: A35.

———. 1999b. "Lawmakers Want an Asylum Rule for Sex-Based Persecution." *New York Times*, April 26: B8.

"U.S. Professor Exposes Deceit on Ghana." 1999. *The Ghanaian Chronicle*, October 4.

Wachira, Charles. 1995. "Kenya Custom: Dilemma of Female Circumcision." Newsgroup: *Soc.culture.african*. January 24.

Waldman, Amy. 1999. "Woman Who Feared Genital Cutting Adapts to New Freedom." *New York Times*, July 21: B2.

Winter, Bronwyn. 1994. "Women, the Law, and Cultural Relativism in France: The Case of Excision." *Signs* 19(4): 939–74.

Yankah, Kwesi. 1995. *Speaking for the Chief: Okyeame and the Politics of Akan Royal Oratory*. Bloomington: Indiana University Press.

# Chapter 16

# From Skepticism to Embrace: Human Rights and the American Anthropological Association from 1947 to 1999

## Karen Engle

In 1947, the executive board of the American Anthropological Association (AAA) submitted its Statement on Human Rights to the United Nations. Anthropologists have been embarrassed ever since. In the late 1940s, anthropologists saw the Statement as limiting tolerance. In recent years, embarrassment has come from a sense that the document refused to place a limit on tolerance.

Anthropologists have recently returned to the Statement in recent years as part of a resurgence in interest in minority rights, and a debate over the extent to which such rights might conflict with universal human rights. This debate has taken place in many different disciplinary and practical terrains. Political theorists such as William Kymlicka (1995; 1999, 31) and Susan Moller Okin (1999), philosophers such as Richard Rorty (1991; Robbins 1997, 209) and Martha Nussbaum (1999, 105), and literary critics such as Pheng Cheah (1997, 233) and Bruce Robbins (1997) all have participated in debates within their disciplines over the relationship between human rights and culture. In the debate, culture and human rights largely have been seen as oppositional. To be for human rights would be to oppose the acceptance of cultural practices that might conflict with one's interpretations of human rights norms. To support an acceptance of conflicting cultural practices would be to oppose human rights.

This debate also has captivated public international human rights legal discourse. Yet the question about the role of culture in an international human rights regime, while having resurfaced lately, has a long history in the development of international human rights law. In particular, issues about rights and culture surfaced in debates around the drafting of the Universal Declaration on Human Rights. Indeed, the AAA's own 1947 Statement was offered in response to an invitation by the United Nations Educational, Scientific and Cultural Organization (UNESCO) to draft a statement on human rights to aid in the formulation of the Universal Declaration (UNESCO 1949, 251).[1] Hence, when some contemporary anthropologists turn to human rights and argue against the skepticism of human rights that they believe has prevailed in anthropology, that they turn to the 1947 Statement is not surprising. They often attempt to apologize for the Statement because it has been read primarily as arguing for culture and against rights, having warned the United Nations against adopting a universal bill of rights that did not attend to cultural particularities.

In June 1999, the membership of the AAA adopted by official ballot a Declaration on Anthropology and Human Rights. Its primary proponent, a newly organized Committee for Human Rights within the association, considers the 1999 Declaration to be a "complete turnaround" from the 1947 position. This chapter questions the characterization of the 1999 Declaration as a complete turnaround by studying the role that the 1947 Statement has played in the development of anthropological views on human rights. In examining the AAA human rights committee's discourse and the recent Declaration adopted by the AAA, I do not assume that these positions represent the state of American anthropology in the 1990s. Indeed, one of the striking aspects of prorights anthropology is that it asserts a human right to culture, often failing to attend to conflicts within cultures, despite the tendency in much of anthropology over the past fifteen years to complicate or even abandon the notion of culture.

## THE 1947 STATEMENT

In response to UNESCO's invitation, the executive board of the American Anthropological Association submitted its now infamous Statement, primarily authored by Melville Herskovits, a student of Franz Boas.[2] Boas is known largely for his turn-of-the-twentieth century critique of cultural evolution. His critique implied "the relativistic notion that the pride of Western society in its own accomplishments is misplaced" (Hatch 1983, 42). In rejecting the notion of cultural evolution, "Boasians identified a very different pattern in history, and in doing so they expressed a very different (and relativistic) viewpoint about the evaluation of other peoples." Boasians stressed random cultural diffusion, arguing that "[t]he history of a culture is one of contact with others and a slow but continuous borrowing of traits. . . . The borrowing of traits is dependent on such fortuitous matters as whom one has as neighbors, how long the association lasts, and the quality of the relationship." This identification of diffusion ultimately led to what Hatch terms "skepticism in ethics" or "Boasian ethical relativism," which he describes as "the view that nothing is really either right or wrong, or that there are no moral principles with a reasonable claim to legitimacy." Hence, one should express tolerance of other cultures and societies. Herskovits was one of the principle proponents of Boasian ethical relativism, and the 1947 Statement is seen as a prototypical statement of American cultural relativism (Hatch 1983, 42, 64, 65, 45–50).

Although the Statement has been the topic of much discussion in anthropology over the years, it is rarely given a detailed reading. While the Statement calls for tolerance of difference—or cultural relativism—it is more nuanced than that description suggests. The Statement also argues for biological sameness—that is, while cultures might be different (but also are similar in many ways), and individuals develop their identities within their cultures, human beings are biologically the same. The argument for sameness is important for supporting the call for tolerance. Written in a time when colonialism was still commonplace and largely justified by a belief that colonized peoples were biologically inferior, the Statement was antiracist and anticolonialist. Finally, the 1947 Statement acknowledged at some level that conflicts might exist within cultures, and that the dominant position should not necessarily succeed.

## Tolerance of Difference

The 1947 Statement tends to be known as a call for tolerance, and much of the text supports this interpretation. The Statement begins by stating that equally important to respect for the individual is "respect for the cultures of differing human groups" (American Anthropological Association 1947, 539). It further suggests that this position is not controversial in most of the world.

> In the main, people are willing to live and let live, exhibiting a tolerance for behavior of another group different from their own. In the history of Western Europe and America, however, economic expansion, control of armaments, and an evangelical religious tradition have translated the recognition of cultural differences into a summons to action. (American Anthropological Association 1947, 540–43)

Hence, the Statement considers the West aberrational in its response to cultural difference; tolerance is the norm.

This call for tolerance is reflected in much of the rest of the document. The Statement sets forth three propositions that it sees as dictated by the "study of human psychology and culture . . . in terms of existing knowledge" (American Anthropological Association 1947, 541). Each of these propositions taken on its own could be seen as supporting tolerance for difference:

- The individual realizes his personality through his culture, hence respect for individual differences entails a respect for cultural differences.

- Respect for differences between cultures is validated by the scientific fact that no technique of qualitatively evaluating cultures has been discovered.

- Standards and values are relative to the culture from which they derive so that any attempt to formulate postulates that grow out of the beliefs or moral codes of one culture must to that extent detract from the applicability of any Declaration of Human Rights to mankind as a whole.

The last sentence of the document supports the three propositions: "Only when a statement of the right of men to live in terms of their own traditions is incorporated into the proposed Declaration, then, can the next step of defining the rights and duties of human groups as regards each other be set upon the firm foundation of the present-day scientific knowledge of Man" (American Anthropological Association 1947, 539–42).

As this last sentence underscores, the 1947 Statement does not argue against the idea of a declaration on human rights. Rather, it suggests that any declaration must attend to differences among cultures. A declaration based on only one culture (Western culture), the third postulate suggests, would not be universal and would be inapplicable to "mankind as a whole."

## Preference for Collective over Individual Rights

The call for tolerance of difference, combined with the possibility of a declaration on human rights that would be applicable to "mankind as a whole," suggests that such a declaration might protect collective or group rights. Indeed, the Statement never argues that individual rights should not be protected, only that any declaration should "also take into full account the individual as a member of the social group of which he is a part, whose sanctioned modes of life shape his behavior, and with whose fate his own is thus inextricably bound" (American Anthropological Association 1947, 542). This same position can be found in the first proposition that "respect for individual differences entails a respect for cultural differences," and in the discussion of that proposition: "There can be no individual freedom, that is, when the group with which the individual identifies himself is not free" (American Anthropological Association 1947, 542). In other words, the Statement calls for Western liberal tolerance regarding individuals to be extended to groups outside the West. This position is essentially a call for collective rights, or the right to cultural protection.

## Attention to Cultural and Biological Similarities

Although the main theme of the 1947 Statement might be respect for difference, a strong undercurrent asserts biological similarities. In the discussion of the history of Western European and American expansionism, the Statement argues that "[d]efinitions of freedom, concepts of the nature of human rights, and the like, have . . . been narrowly drawn." Through Western control of non-European peoples, the Statement continues, "[t]he hard core of *similarities* between cultures has consistently been overlooked" (American Anthropological Association 1947, 540).

The Statement also asserts biological sameness. As part of its discussion of the first proposition, the Statement declares, "Man, biologically, is one. *Homo sapiens* is a single species, no matter how individuals may differ in their aptitudes, their abilities, their interests" (American Anthropological Association 1947, 540). Through this assertion, the Statement suggests that, to the extent that cultural differences exist, such differences are unrelated to biology. Indeed, "[t]hat cultures differ in degree of complexity, of richness of content is due to historic forces, not biological ones." For the Statement, culture in fact is so indeterminate that "any normal individual can learn any part of any culture other than his own, provide only he is afforded the opportunity to do so" (American Anthropological Association 1947, 548, 541–42).

## Awareness of Conflicts Within Cultures

Although the 1947 Statement recognizes that culture is not naturally determined, it does leave the impression that culture is something that can be located. Whether it be the culture of Western Europe and America or the culture of "the Indonesian, the African, the Indian, the Chinese" (American Anthropological Association 1947, 543), the Statement suggests that each has a definable culture that can be discovered. That conflicts might exist about the substance of culture within those groups is not a focus of the Statement.

Toward the end of the Statement, however, one paragraph belies the aforementioned understanding of culture. This paragraph received a lot of attention by anthropologists in the late 1940s (American Anthropological Association 1947, 543).

> Even where political systems exist that deny citizens the right of participation in their government, or seek to conquer weaker peoples, underlying cultural values may be called on to bring the peoples of such states to a realization of the consequences of the acts of their governments, and thus enforce a brake upon discrimination and conquest. For the political system of a people is only a small part of their total culture.

This paragraph generally is acknowledged as the Nazi Germany paragraph; it provided a way for the AAA to call for tolerance without seeming to condone Nazi Germany. Although (as will be discussed) this paragraph was read largely as undermining the call for tolerance, it may also be read as an acknowledgment that cultures should not be accepted at face value. Competing claims well might exist about what comprises the culture of a particular state. "Underlying cultural values" could be deployed to combat the claim asserted by the government.

This paragraph created a lot of stir in its time; it also represents an ongoing struggle between relativistic and universalistic impulses in human rights discourses, including within the AAA's Committee for Human Rights. That the Statement acknowledged the conflict, and even proposed some approach to mediating it, generally is overlooked in today's discussion of the Statement.

# EMBARRASSMENT

For the past fifty years, the 1947 Statement has caused the AAA great shame. Indeed, the term *embarrassment* continually is used in reference to the Statement. The Statement embarrasses contemporary anthropologists who consider themselves human rights advocates, but it also embarrassed anthropologists who considered themselves scientists in the 1940s. If the Nazi Germany paragraph was the source of much of the embarrassment in the 1940s, it might have provided a means of redeeming the Statement in the 1990s. Instead, the paragraph largely has been ignored.

In 1948, *American Anthropologist* published two "Brief Communications" on the Statement, one by Julian Steward (1948, 351) and the other by H. G. Barnett (1948, 352). Both critiqued the Statement for its lack of scientific rigor. Barnett argued that the Statement "places the Association on record in a way that embarrasses its position as a scientific organization" (Barnett 1948, 352). For him, the entire enterprise taken on by the AAA was flawed because it flew in the face of the anthropological aspiration of objective cultural study (Barnett 1948, 353). Anthropologists are merely to study and record the value systems of people they study, and therefore "[i]t is an inescapable fact that we cannot at the same time be moralists (or policy makers) and scientists." To the extent that the AAA should take political positions (and Barnett believed it sometimes should), "let us admit, either tacitly or explicitly that we have an axe to grind and dispense with the camouflage." To do otherwise, "to advocate predilections disguised as universals," would be to "jeopardize what little scientific repute we have" (Barnett 1948, 353–55).

Steward expressed similar concerns. He considered that "the Statement is a value judgment any way it is taken," and was therefore outside the realm of science. Steward seemed to disagree with Barnett's notion that the AAA should ever take political or moral positions. Rather, individuals might make value judgments, but "[a]s a scientific organization, the Association has no business dealing with the rights of man" (Steward 1948, 351, 352).

While both Steward and Barnett were critical of the sheer attempt of the AAA to formulate a statement on human rights, they also critiqued the substance of the document. For Barnett, the document was ethnocentric in that it represented American values. In particular, a basic premise of the 1947 Statement, "that 'man is free only when he lives as his society defines freedom'" was "a value or a standard that is relative to American tradition. There are a great many people in the world to whom it is not self-evident fact; and it certainly is not a discovery of science." The irony of the Statement setting forth a universal position against universals did not escape Barnett. "Thus, the Statement unwittingly sets up what it aims to attack, namely an absolute in the carnival of values" (Barnett 1948, 354).

Additionally, Barnett and Steward shared a concern over the paragraph that seemed to create an exception for Nazi Germany. That paragraph, by suggesting a limit to tolerance, would seem to undermine the rest of the document. For would-be scientists, the contradiction was unbearable. As Steward agonized, "This may have been a loophole to exclude Germany from the advocated tolerance, but it looks to me like the fatal breach in the dyke. Either we tolerate everything, and keep hands off, or we fight intolerance and conquest—political and economic, as well as military—in all their forms. Where shall the line be drawn?" And later, "[t]he conclusion seems inescapable that we have gotten out of our scientific role and are struggling with contradictions" (Steward 1948, 352). For Barnett, the paragraph represented the "weakness that is inherent in all evaluative approaches to social problems," and he seemed dismayed that the AAA could have included it "apparently without embarrassment." While important, the dilemma raised by the paragraph ("the ultimate dilemma of democracy") did not justify anthropologists "throw[ing] themselves on its horn with a 'scientific' solution" (Barnett 1948, 354–55). In mourning the decline of the scientism of the profession, Barnett (1948, 355) put some of the blame on contradictions engendered by the desire to take political positions while at the same time professing tolerance.

> To date our performance in the field of cultural anthropology has not been very promising. We can do an excellent job of reporting and analyzing, but beyond that we are, as a group, badly confused. . . . And as long as we cannot ourselves divorce our opinions from our facts we cannot expect others to take us at face value as scientists.

The Statement's call for tolerance in the tradition of Boas was largely impervious to Barnett's critique that its call for tolerance was ethnocentric, or "relative to American tradition." Although Boasian ethnographic method rigorously opposed moral judgments of the cultures it studied, it equally rigorously promoted antiracism. Boas himself called for the "equality of treatment for even the most 'primitive' or 'savage' society" (Purcell 1973, 68). For Boasian anthropology then, the argument for tolerance was merely an extension of the scientific method of objective study of cultures. As Edward Purcell (1973, 71) explains, "anthropologists throughout the interwar years saw their work as not only scientific, but also didactic and moral." Indeed, "[a]fter the turn of the century anthropology was one of the strongest and earliest forces in attacking racism in all its forms."

Yet Boasian anthropology was far from impervious to Steward's and Barnett's critique of the Nazi Germany paragraph in the 1947 Statement. This paragraph was seen as problematic by anthropologists desperately trying to keep a grasp on the scientific reputation of the profession. The paragraph did indeed contradict the themes set forth in the rest of the document, fueling the speculation that Herskovits did not even author the paragraph (Washburn 1987, 939). But more was at stake.

According to Purcell (1973), the popularization of anthropology in the 1920s and 1930s was a major effect of the rise of an ethics derived from the attack on Euclidean geometry. That is, "[I]f non-Euclidean geometry proved that there were alternate but logically unassailable systems of geometry based on axioms fundamentally different from those of Euclid, then it appeared obvious that deductive reasoning, by assuming contradictory postulates, could produce systems of ethics radically different from that of traditional Christianity." Once this approach was applied to other forms of deductive reasoning, it "robbed every rational system of any claim to be in any sense true, except insofar as it could be proved empirically to describe what actually existed." The rise of Nazism in the 1930s called into question non-Euclidean ethics by making it "an immediate and frightening reality. *Mein Kampf* had outlined a crude but extremely dangerous system on non-Euclidean ethics." Although in the mid-1930s, some anthropologists began to acknowledge the "double-edged" nature of non-Euclideanism, it was already fully entrenched. For Purcell, "[s]ocial scientists were thus forced to accept the moral precepts of all cultures as nondebatable postulates. . . . As scientific naturalism had denied the possibility of validating ethical judgments by inductive methods, non-Euclideanism denied it to deductive ones" (Purcell 1973, 53, 65, 72).

Thus, in its historical context, the Nazi Germany paragraph is both completely understandable and an offense to the non-Euclidean method that drove the Statement. Preventing future atrocities such as those committed by Germany during the Second World War was, after all, the primary impetus behind the Universal Declaration. For the AAA—an association comprised of anthropologists deeply committed to antiracist principles—to draft a Statement that altogether denied that context would have been difficult. Even without the paragraph, the Statement could be seen as having played an important role in pointing to and attempting to prevent the atrocities of colonialism. Such a position might have seemed disingenuous, however, without what turned out to be the offending paragraph.

If the Nazi Germany paragraph was offensive to the non-Euclidean method and to aspiring scientists of the time, it largely has been ignored by contemporary anthropologists. The Statement, along with the relativist principles that the document has come to represent, continues to cause embarrassment. In a recent Harvard Law School roundtable, David Maybury-Lewis (1999) applauded the fact that anthropology "has outgrown its ethical impotence," and dated anthropology's reputation for "extreme relativism" to the 1947 Statement. He began his explanation of the Statement: "At that time, I'm embarrassed to say, the executive board of the Anthropological Association sent a memorandum to the United Nations criticizing the draft Declaration by saying that it was much too western" (Maybury-Lewis 1999, 25). His very next sentence was, "It probably was." He then discussed some of the language from the document, but never explained the source of his embarrassment. He also never mentioned the Nazi Germany paragraph, which would seem to temper the Statement's relativism. Maybury-Lewis is not alone in considering relativism an embarrassment to the profession. Elvin Hatch (1983, 104) has noted that "World War II was a moral embarrassment to ethical relativism." For Wilcomb Washburn (1987, 940), anthropology moved in the twenty years after the Statement "from optimism to pessimism, and from a naive faith in cultural relativism to an embarrassed and skeptical unease concerning the doctrine."

This postwar attack on relativism was just the beginning. By the time Clifford Geertz (1984, 263) published "Anti Anti-Relativism" in 1984, it would seem that no anthropologist, including Geertz, would call him- or herself a relativist. Relativism had come into disrepute, and no one was willing to defend it. Pointing to what he considered antirelativist hysteria, Geertz discussed how relativism was considered "responsible for the whole modern disaster—Lenin and Hitler, Amin, Bokasso, Sukarno, Mao, Nasser, and Hammarskjold, Structuralism, the New Deal, the Holocaust, both world wars, 1968, inflation, Shinto militarism, OPEC, and the independence of India" (Geertz 1984, 267; Johnson 1983). If relativism was not responsible for all that, it was at least seen as nihilistic (Jarvie 1983, 44).

Thus, even in 1984, anthropology continued to be haunted by a critique of its relativist past. According to Hatch (1983, 103), by the 1970s, relativism "was almost universally rejected by the discipline." Boasian anthropology's non-Euclidean theory was seen as incapable of condemning fascism; the Nazi Germany paragraph in the 1947 Statement remained unconvincing. If Geertz's description is even partly accurate, the antirelativist rhetoric during the 1980s rivaled that during and immediately following the war. Perhaps poststructuralist and postmodernist thought was conjuring up the fear of nihilism, which immediately tied it back to an era where non-Euclidean thinking had failed to respond to the atrocities of the war.

## THE 1990S: A DECLARATION FOR RIGHTS AND CULTURE

Given the apparent death of—even strong antagonism toward—relativism, the way would seem to be paved for anthropologists to take up human rights issues. If the Statement and the views it embodied were an embarrassment to the profession, the profession had tried to remake itself. In the 1940s and 1950s, a number of anthropologists analyzed ethnographic data to attempt to locate common if not universal values (Hatch 1983, 106–8), and in the 1970s, many anthropologists turned to serving the needs of the Third World (Hatch 1983, 126–32). The AAA took activist positions in the 1960s and 1970s, against racism and against United States intervention in Vietnam. Despite these years of nonrelativist method and activism, when the Committee for Human Rights formed in the 1990s, the 1947 Statement continued to present an obstacle.

For many contemporary anthropologists, the Statement has hampered the ability of anthropologists to participate in human rights debates. In an article exploring reasons why anthropologists rarely are involved in human rights advocacy, Ellen Messer (1993, 221, 224) cites "the 'burden' of cultural relativism," explaining that the Statement "rejected the notion of universal human rights." The 1995 *Annual Report* of the AAA Commission for Human Rights (the precursor to the current Committee for Human Rights), echoes this sentiment, declaring that "cultural relativism is a major factor which has severely retarded anthropological involvement in human rights since the Executive Board's 1947 [S]tatement." Consequently, the commission makes clear that its work on human rights is a "complete turn around from the 1947 stance" (Sponsel 1995).

In light of the pervasive antirelativist sentiments after the war and again in the 1980s, this move away from the 1947 Statement is not surprising. Yet the embarrassment over the Statement, and over cultural relativism generally, is more tempered than it might at first seem. At the same time those anthropologists who argue for human rights feel the need to distance themselves from the Statement, they also emphasize many of the substantive positions behind the Statement. Indeed, in many ways their positions vary little from that expressed by the Statement fifty years ago.

Prorights anthropologists have tempered their embarrassment over the Statement in a variety of ways. Far from abandoning relativism for universalism, even the staunchest proponents of human rights among anthropologists find some support for their view in Boasian relativism. Over time, a number of strategies have developed to attempt to mediate the tension between rights and relativism, three of which are discussed here: reclaiming Boasian relativism for its antiracism and anticolonialism; arguing for the human right to the cultural protection of groups, particularly of indigenous peoples; and calling for a relativism that places limits on tolerance. I contend that the seeds for all three of these attempts at limiting tolerance can be found in the 1947 Statement. Although each of these strategies mediates the conflict in some way, none adequately addresses the very concern that seemed to be raised by the Nazi Germany paragraph. That is, what happens when people within cultures disagree about the meaning of the culture? While lip service is paid to this difficulty within most of the work, none addresses it head-on.

## Reclaiming Boasian Antiracism and Anticolonialism

At the same time that some blame anthropologists' lack of involvement in human rights issues on Boasian relativism, others use Boasian anthropology to show that interest in human rights is natural for anthropologists. In doing so, they tend to focus on the ways that Boas and his followers were antiracist (including antifascist) and anticolonial.

In her opening address to the AAA's 1994 meeting, the theme of which was human rights, AAA's president, Johnetta Cole, pointed to the discipline's "long tradition of concern about human rights," attributing it directly to Boas (Cole 1994, 445). At one point, she noted the association's public stands against racism, and traced them back to the anti-Nazi work of Boas and the anthropologist Ruth Benedict. As for Boas,

> In American anthropology, there is a particularly strong tradition of taking public positions against racist ideas and ideologies. Perhaps you are aware

that in our American Anthropological Association we have passed four resolutions against racism: in 1968, 1969, 1971, and 1972. . . . We can trace this kind of activism back to Franz Boas. In response to the Nazi notion of Aryan racial superiority, Boas spoke out in newspapers and articles about the dangers of this ideology. He also spoke out against the myth of black inferiority, and was among the first anthropologists to caution us about differences among the concepts of race, culture, and language. (Cole 1994, 445)

The reference to anti-Nazi work is not accidental. Even if anthropology was ambivalent about or even antagonistic toward human rights, anthropologists have a lot at stake in resurrecting their anti-Nazi past. Yet perhaps because of the Statement or how relativism is seen by some to require tolerance of everything (therefore making the Nazi Germany paragraph a contradiction), the antiracist agenda of Boasian anthropology continually needs to be reasserted.

Hatch (1983) has made a similar point about Boasian anthropology with regard to its anticolonial stance, noting that the "call for tolerance was an appeal to the liberal philosophy regarding human rights and self-determination." Putting the doctrine in its historical context, Hatch (1983) explains,

The call for tolerance (or for the freedom of foreign peoples to live as they choose) was a matter of immediate, practical importance in light of the pattern of Western expansion. As Western Europeans established colonies and assumed power over more and more of the globe, they typically wanted both to Christianize and civilize the indigenous peoples. . . . The treatment of non-Western societies by the expanding nations of the West is a very large blot on our history, and had the Boasian call for tolerance— and for the freedom of others to define "civilization" for themselves—been heard two or three centuries earlier, this blot might not loom so large today.

Although Hatch (1983, 85–101) ultimately argues that ethical relativism "goes too far by giving indiscriminate approval to every foreign institution," he defends its general anticolonialist bent. Alison Renteln (1990, 63) similarly has argued that "[c]ultural relativism was introduced in part to combat . . . racist, Eurocentric notions of progress."

For contemporary anthropologists, apparently, Boasian relativism is embarrassing to the extent that it is tied to inaction or lack of moral condemnation. When relativism is connected to antiracist or anticolonial views, it would seem to be redeemed. The challenge for prorights anthropologists therefore is to separate the two strands of relativism.

## Asserting a Right to Culture

If Boasian relativism provides a basis for antiracist and anticolonialist thought, it is also invoked by some prorights anthropologists as a basis for the rights of indigenous peoples. After discussing the "burden" of cultural relativism in making anthropologists seem uninterested in human rights, Messer (1993, 224) argues that the lack of interest is belied by the extent to which "anthropologists have tended to advocate rights of collectivities, especially indigenous peoples." Similarly, Carole Nagengast and Terence Turner (1997, 270) have connected indigenous advocacy to Boasian relativity, observing, "Cultural relativity has been a part of anthropological consciousness for at least half a century, having been developed by Boas, Benedict, Mead, and others as an attempt to instill respect for variability and especially to defend indigenous peoples from ethnocide and genocide."

Prorights anthropologists call for such support for indigenous peoples to be translated into a right to culture. Since indigenous rights have become "legitimate demands within the international legal framework" over the past forty-five years, Messer (1993, 236) argues that "the acceptance and advocacy of the human rights legal framework by anthropologists [is] an important means of protecting indigenous cultures and interests." Here Messer highlights the main source of the new interest in human rights by anthropologists. Rather than constituting a potential obstacle to indigenous protection as the 1947 Statement feared, human rights law and discourse now seem to provide promising vehicles for promoting indigenous peoples' rights.

The work of the Committee for Human Rights bears out this instrumental use of human rights in two ways: in its choice of cases to pursue and in the wording of its Declaration. The committee has decided to limit its interventions to two types of cases: "One is where anthropologists or their associates are themselves threatened because their professional work reveals an officially embarrassing instance of human rights abuse. A second is where a specific ethnic and minority group is subjected to human rights abuse, or threat thereof, targeted as a result of its cultural distinctiveness" (American Anthropological Association 1997, 4). Although the first type involves the protection of an individual right, it is presumably emphasized to protect the second right. In other words, because individual anthropologists will be required to report abuses of the second type, they must be protected in doing so. The work of the committee demonstrates that their interventions in fact follow these guidelines. In 1997, for example, the committee investigated two instances of threats against anthropologists for revealing human rights violations, and eight cases involving the human rights of cultural minorities (American Anthropological Association 1997). In 1998, the committee pursued cases regarding the displacement of the Peheunche of southern Chile by a dam project financed in part by the World Bank, the killing of a native hunter in Zambia, the massacre of Mayan villagers in Chiapas, the expulsion and harassment of a Brazilian anthropologist accused of fomenting native opposition to gold mining, and the assassination of a Guatemalan priest who reported human rights abuses against indigenous peoples in Guatemala (American Anthropological Association 1998, 6–8).

The AAA's focus on group rights is specifically meant to counter the traditional focus on individual rights. As the committee's *Guidelines* state, "[m]any existing human rights NGOs focus on individual rights, and they treat violations of civil and political rights to the exclusion of economic, social, and cultural rights and indigenous and environmental rights" (American Anthropological Association 1995, 2). In other words, while the committee is taking advantage of an increasing acceptance of indigenous rights in international law, it also sees itself as pushing the envelope. The preamble to the 1999 Declaration states that the committee's interventions require "expanding the definition of human rights to include areas not necessarily addressed by international law. These areas include collective as well as individual rights, cultural, social, and economic development, and a clean and safe environment" (American Anthropological Association 1999).

In pursuing this expanded notion of human rights, the committee in many ways expresses the concerns of the 1947 Statement. The 1999 Declaration, for example, emphasizes difference.

> As a professional organization of anthropologists, the AAA has long been, and should continue to be concerned whenever human difference is made the basis for a denial of basic human rights, where "human" is understood in its full range of cultural, social, linguistic, psychological, and biological senses.
>
> Thus the AAA founds its approach on anthropological principles of respect for concrete human differences, both collective and individual, rather than the abstract legal uniformity of Western tradition.

Terence Turner (1997, 273, 286) has expanded on similar language in an earlier statement by the AAA Commission on Human Rights by noting that "while difference is explicitly cited in this statement only as an invalid basis for denying rights, rather than a positive principle of right in itself, the implication is that the right to difference may constitute a positive, transcultural basis of human rights." As with the 1947 Statement, the 1999 Declaration thus emphasizes respect for cultural difference.

## Limiting Tolerance

The prorights anthropologists of the 1990s continue to struggle with the same question that the Nazi Germany paragraph addressed: What are the limits of tolerance? A way to mediate tension between relativism and rights, or observation and action, would be to put some limit on what relativism will tolerate, to demarcate a moment when the observer must act. Beginning with Hatch's work in the 1980s, to distinguish types of relativism for this purpose has become almost commonplace.

In this vein, Hatch and Renteln both attempt to take the tolerance out of ethical relativism. Both are concerned to find a way to make moral judgments that would lead to action. Hatch (1997, 394), for example, "disagree[s] with Benedict and Herskovits to the extent that they held that warrantable judgments across cultural boundaries can never be made, if only because the failure to act is itself an action that may have unacceptable consequences for other people—consequences which are unacceptable to us." Still, he does not want to abandon tolerance altogether. "[W]hen we do not find good reason to make judgments about the actions or ways of life of other people, we ought to show tolerance toward them, and we should do so on the basis of the moral principles that people ought to be free to live as they choose" (Hatch 1997, 394). Recognizing that his own theory incorporates ethical relativism, Hatch (1997, 394) complains that the difficulty is that there is no moral theory to replace relativism, to allow one to take a moral stand. In the end, then, he is loathe to reject any part of relativism other than its inability to make moral judgments.

While this critique has long been aimed at relativism, it also has been undermined by the fact that Boas, Benedict, and Herskovits all took positions on racism and colonialism, as well as by the Nazi Germany paragraph in the 1947 Statement. Indeed, we could imagine the drafter(s) of that paragraph going through the same modes of analysis as Hatch. As such, that anyone ever took seriously the view that relativism required inaction would be hard to claim. As Geertz (1984, 265) puts it,

> The image of vast numbers of anthropology readers running around in so cosmopolitan a frame of mind as to have no views as to what is and isn't true, or good, or beautiful, seems to me largely a fantasy. There may be some genuine nihilists out there, along Rodeo Drive or around Times Square, but I doubt very many have become such as a result of an excessive sensitivity to the claims of other cultures; and at least most of the people I meet, read, and read about, and indeed I myself, are all-too-committed to something or other, usually parochial. "'Tis the eye of childhood that fears a painted devil": anti-relativism has largely concocted the anxiety it lives from.

In the end, Hatch (1983, 144) wants merely to "excise[ ] what is unacceptable" from relativism and replace it with moral judgment that he seems incapable of justifying. If Geertz is right, no excision may be necessary.

Renteln tackles the same problem, but argues against seeing tolerance as central to ethical relativism. For her, the main tenet of Boasian relativism is enculturation—"the idea that people unconsciously acquire the categories and standards of their culture"—not tolerance (Renteln 1990, 74). This focus on enculturation can be found in the 1947 Statement's notion of biological sameness, in which anyone can learn another's culture. Renteln further argues that enculturation leads to ethnocentrism, because individuals tend to see their own society's values as superior to any others, and concludes that "[t]here is nothing inherent in the theory of relativism which prevents relativists from criticizing activities and beliefs in other cultures. But relativists will acknowledge that the criticism is based on their own ethnocentric standards and realize also that the condemnation may be a form of cultural imperialism" (Renteln 1990, 75). Consequently, Renteln attempts to avoid the dilemma posed by Hatch. She simply erases the conflict by denying any contradiction between arguing for tolerance and making moral judgments.

Related to attempts by Hatch and Renteln to excise or separate tolerance from relativism, other anthropologists have seen relativism as a method, not a theory. In this understanding, relativism is "a commitment to suspending moral judgment until an attempt can be made to understand another culture's beliefs and practices in their full cultural, material, and historical contexts" (Turner 1997, 274).

All these attempts to redeem some form of relativism rely on the separation of relativism from tolerance. Yet how this separation adds to (or detracts from) the theory in any way that differs significantly from the Nazi Germany paragraph is not clear. Although the focus of that paragraph might have been to draw a distinction between the culture of a people and its government, it stood for much more than that; it suggested a limit to tolerance.

Despite all the critiques leveled at the tolerance associated with Boasian anthropology, the 1999 Declaration does little to disavow tolerance. Indeed, the limits it proposes are as buried (or at least as nuanced) as that found in the 1947 Statement. The Declaration reads, "People and groups have a generic right to realize their capacity for culture, and to produce, reproduce and change the conditions and forms of their physical, personal and social existence, so long as such activities do not diminish the same capacities of others" (American Anthropological Association 1999). Perhaps the idea here is twofold: that cultures are not static or monolithic, and that the limit of tolerance is intolerance. While the latter is a classical liberal idea (and dilemma), the former would seem to open up the possibility of conflict within cultures. If so, such a possibility is presented no more clearly than in the 1947 Statement. Just as the Nazi Germany paragraph could be seen as in conflict with the rest of the Statement in 1947, this Declaration too can be seen as embodying an internal contradiction—it calls for a right to difference, then places limits on it.

## CONTINUING CONFLICTS

In many ways, contemporary prorights anthropologists have merely reproduced the struggles apparent in the 1947 Statement. In addition to seeking ways to mediate the tension between rights and relativism by finding justifications for action, they also claim to act on a new generation of concerns. Nagengast and Turner (1997, 270), for example, identify a difficulty with the argument for culture, claiming that it has "definite repercussions for the acceptance of the universality of some human rights, especially those that pertain to women, 'minorities,' and indigenous peoples, and especially when violations of rights are perpetuated in the name of 'tradition' in the so-called private space of the household as well as in the community." In his critique of Iris Young, Turner (1997, 289) claims that "she overlooks the far more repressive forms of gender, class, and ethnic inequality that have historically been based on essentialized 'logics of difference.'" In contrast, "[i]t is precisely against such abuses of human difference that the statement of the AAA Committee for Human Rights is directed" (Nagengast and Turner 1997, 270).

By lumping together "gender, class and ethnicity" or "women, 'minorities,' and indigenous peoples," Turner and Nagengast fail to recognize the potential conflicts among these groups. Moreover, how the Declaration or the committee attends to potential conflicts within culture any more than the 1947 Statement is not clear. The activities of the Committee for Human Rights, for example, focus on the protection of indigenous groups, but with an assumption that what is best for the group—in accordance with its culture—can be known. While the 1999 Declaration specifically states that "[h]uman rights is not a static concept," it does not say the same about culture.

Although the notion of culture in much of anthropology has undergone radical transformation since 1947, its meaning within human rights discourse, even among prorights anthropologists, has remained surprisingly constant. Indeed, the more that some anthropologists have complicated the meaning of any stable cultural identity or practice, the more others seem to argue for a relatively unproblematic protection of cultural identity. If part of anthropology's resistance to human rights in 1947 was to avoid the imposition of outside values on indigenous peoples, the AAA's 1999 Declaration largely reflects the same aim.

Ann-Belinda Preis (1996, 286, 297) has argued that the types of mediating techniques described herein

offer no real solution to the methodological and theoretical questions pertaining to human rights and culture; at best, [they reproduce] them at a different, perhaps more sophisticated, level. Because there now seems to be wide agreement among various scholars, politicians, and practitioners that in the years to come some of the most crucial intellectual, moral, and ideological battles about human rights issues are likely to turn on their cross-cultural intelligibility and justifiability, a radically new and far more dynamic approach to culture is needed.

Preis asserts that contemporary anthropology provides just such a dynamic approach, in that over the past ten to fifteen years, globalization has led anthropologists to rethink not just relativism but "its underlying assumption of 'culture' as a homogeneous, integral, coherent unity." Referring to the work of Appadurai, Barth, and Clifford, she notes a paradox: "during precisely the same period as cultural relativism has been an active component of human rights research and debates (from which anthropologists have been excluded to some extent), the theory has gradually, but effectively, lost its import within anthropology itself" (Preis 1996, 288).

Preis's article adds an important piece to the history of anthropology. Yet, if the AAA or the debate over human rights within the association is any indication of the state of the discipline (which it may not be), Preis surely overestimates the extent to which the relativism debate has "lost its import."

Although this chapter has focused on debates about relativism and rights within anthropology, these debates are not unique to anthropology. Indeed, the anthropological debates have both anticipated and mirrored those in other disciplines—including international law—about the relationship between culture and rights and when one limits the other. In this sense, there are few disciplines in which relativism has "lost its import."

Anticolonial and antiracist commitments of anthropology have changed little over the past fifty years. Yet the AAA clearly has moved from being skeptical of human rights law and discourse to embracing them. Just as skepticism offered hope, embrace is filled with doubts. The 1947 Statement imagined that there could be a document with worldwide applicability, while the 1999 Declaration fails to address the potential of conflicts among rights.

Comparing the AAA of the 1940s with that of the 1990s, at least with regard to human rights issues, demonstrates how anthropology, like other disciplines, has been and continues to be captured by a dichotomy between rights and culture. Yet the question is not now—nor was it ever—whether to be for or against human rights. Rather, the debate always has been over the definition and limits of these rights.

The techniques of today's prorights anthropologists are representative of attempts to define human rights within a framework that assumes that rights and culture are antithetical. Collective rights, along with the other mediating techniques, might provide new justifications for the AAA to act, but they do not determine *how* it should act. When anthropologists and others attempt to justify their desire to act, it is worth remembering that it was not Herskovits, but the scientific critics Steward and Barnett, who believed that the association should refrain from making moral judgments.

## NOTES

1. Somewhat ironically, given all the attention the Statement has received within anthropology, it was not among the responses that UNESCO chose to publish in its 1949 volume. The Statement presumably was among the responses to the questionnaire that UNESCO forwarded in a report to the Commission on Human Rights. According to Johannes Morsink, the commission "did not pay much attention to the UNESCO report and was even a bit miffed at what had been done"; indeed, the commission did not distribute the report to all member states (Morsink 1999, 301). In short, although it has plagued anthropologists for the past fifty years, the AAA's Statement seems to have had little or no impact on either UNESCO or the Human Rights Commission.

2. Although the 1947 Statement only lists the AAA Executive Board as the author, Herskovits generally is considered the author.

# REFERENCES

American Anthropological Association. 1999. *Declaration on Anthropology and Human Rights*. Arlington, Va.: American Anthropology Association.

American Anthropological Association, Committee for Human Rights. 1995. *Guidelines*. Arlington, Va.: American Anthropology Association.

———. 1997. *1997 Annual Report*. Arlington, Va.: American Anthropology Association.

———. 1998. *1998 Annual Report*. Arlington, Va.: American Anthropology Association.

American Anthropological Association, Executive Board. 1947. "Statement on Human Rights." *American Anthropologist* 49: 539.

Barnett, H. G. 1948. "On Science and Human Rights." *American Anthropologist* 50(8): 352–55.

Cheah, Pheng. 1997. "Posit(ion)ing Human Rights in the Current Global Conjecture." *Public Culture* 9(2): 233–65.

Cole, Johnetta. 1994. "Human Rights and the Rights of Anthropologists." *American Anthropologist* 97(3): 445–47.

Geertz, Clifford. 1984. "Distinguished Lecture: Anti-Anti-Relativism." *American Anthropologist* 86(2): 263–78.

Hatch, Elvin. 1983. *Culture and Morality: The Relativity of Values in Anthropology*. New York: Columbia University Press.

———. 1997. "The Good Side of Relativism." *Journal of Anthropological Research* 53(3): 371–81.

Jarvie, I. C. 1983. "Rationalism and Relativism." *British Journal of Sociology* 34: 44–60.

Johnson, Paul. 1983. *Modern Times: The World from the Twenties to the Eighties*. New York: Harper & Row.

Kymlicka, William. 1995. *Multicultural Citizenship: A Liberal Theory of Minority Rights*. Oxford: Clarendon Press.

———. 1999. "Liberal Complacencies." In *Is Multiculturalism Bad for Women?* edited by Susan Moller Okin. Princeton, N.J.: Princeton University Press.

Maybury-Lewis, David. 1999. "Anthropologists, Anthropology and the Relativist Challenge." In *Interdisciplinary Faculty Perspectives on the Human Rights Movement*, edited by the University Committee on Human Rights Study. Cambridge, Mass.: Harvard University Press.

Mead, Margaret. 1935. *Sex and Temperament in Three Primitive Societies*. New York: W. Morrow.

Messer, Ellen. 1993. "Anthropology and Human Rights." *Annual Review of Anthropology* 22: 221–49.

Morsink, Johannes. 1999. *The Universal Declaration of Human Rights: Origins, Drafting & Intent*. Philadelphia: University of Pennsylvania Press.

Nagengast, Carole, and Terence Turner. 1997. "Introduction: Universal Human Rights Versus Cultural Relativism." *Journal of Anthropological Research* 53(3): 269–72.

Nussbaum, Martha C. 1999. "A Plea for Difficulty." In *Is Multiculturalism Bad for Women?* edited by Susan Moller Okin. Princeton, N.J.: Princeton University Press.

Okin, Susan Moller. 1999. "Is Multiculturalism Bad for Women?" In *Is Multiculturalism Bad for Women?* edited by Susan Moller Okin. Princeton, N.J.: Princeton University Press.

Preis, Ann-Belinda S. 1996. "Human Rights as Cultural Practice: An Anthropological Critique." *Human Rights Quarterly* 18(2): 286–315.

Purcell, Jr., Edward A. 1973. *The Crisis of Democratic Theory: Scientific Naturalism & The Problem of Value*. Lexington: University Press of Kentucky.

Renteln, Alison. 1990. *International Human Rights: Universalism Versus Relativism*. Newbury Park: Sage.

Robbins, Bruce. 1997. "Sad Stories in the International Public Sphere: Richard Rorty on Culture and Human Rights." *Public Culture* 9(2): 209–32.

Rorty, Richard. 1991. "Intellectuals in Politics." *Dissent* 38: 483–90.

Sponsel, Leslie E. 1995. "1995 Annual Report Commission for Human Rights." Available at: *www.aanet.org.committees/cfhr/ar95.htm*.

Steward, Julian H. 1948. "Comments on the Statement on Human Rights." *American Anthropologist* 50(2): 351–52.

Turner, Terence. 1997. "Human Rights, Human Difference: Anthropology's Contribution to an Emancipatory Cultural Politics." *Journal of Anthropological Research* 53(3): 273–92.

UNESCO. 1949. "Memorandum and Questionnaire Circulated by UNESCO on the Theoretical Bases of the Rights of Man." In *Human Rights: Comments and Interpretations: A Symposium Edited by UNESCO*. New York: Columbia University Press.

Washburn, Wilcomb B. 1987. "Cultural Relativism, Human Rights, and the AAA." *American Anthropologist* 89(4): 939–43.

# Part IV

## Conceptions of Difference and the Differences They Make

# Chapter 17

# Cultural Models of Diversity in America: The Psychology of Difference and Inclusion

Victoria C. Plaut

How are Americans thinking about the growing diversity of their workplaces? How are they grappling with issues of difference and inclusion in an increasingly diverse society? To find some answers to these questions, a series of interviews was conducted at the world headquarters of a large American commercial bank.[1] Of interest was the nature of intergroup relations among employees at this highly demographically diverse organization. The first interviews came from the international client services department, composed of about one hundred employees who represented twenty-five countries and who together spoke approximately forty languages. Dan—a white, middle-aged male—was the manager of this division.[2] In response to questions about diversity in his department, he quickly pointed out, "I agree that conflict may be a problem in some workplaces, but I have to tell you, we don't have any conflict here." Dan then proceeded to explain that the lack of tension was due to his own upbringing. "As a matter of fact, I was brought up in a very open-minded Italian American household in Brooklyn, and so I believe that people are all the same. After all, at the end of the day we all want the same thing." He added, "People are people . . . we're different but similar. I don't see a person as being from this culture or that culture, instead I see them for who they really are."

These words are strikingly familiar—the idea that people should be seen for who they are "deep down" and not for some group characteristic. Dan's view of diversity seemed designed to counter any concern that he was prejudiced or made judgments about people based on their cultural or racial affiliation. The differences Dan did see were differences of language and food. His employees were able to speak different languages to carry out transactions with the bank's diverse clients, and their diverse ethnic backgrounds ensured a variety of ethnic foods at social events. Dan believed the "solution" to the problems of diversity was "exposure to different people" and because diversity was relatively superficial, contact with other cultures was a sufficient condition for effective intergroup relations.

Notably, Dan's subordinates—employees who had immigrated from Venezuela, the West Indies, and Taiwan—offered descriptions of intergroup relations in their workplace that diverged considerably from the picture painted by their manager. Oscar, a midlevel manager from Venezuela, reported positive impressions of upper management's diversity—they were, he believed, becoming more diverse, although they still had a "lack of Asians." Moreover, Oscar asserted that because of the global nature of the business, the national and ethnic diversity reflected in the upper ranks "strengthens the organization." Early in the interview, he also declared, "It is the kind of organization I want to be in." Yet shortly into the discussion about diversity, Oscar admitted that because he was "Latin," he felt that he did not have certain characteristics, particularly "brashness and boldness," that were valued and viewed as reflecting leadership potential. Oscar thought this would keep him from advancing in the organization and that if he were more European (that is, Argentine or Chilean), he might be viewed as having more "promotion potential." Oscar's biggest complaint about his job, however, was the lack of connection fostered by the organization: "I want to be more connected with the people I work with . . . the workplace needs to be more meaningful and fulfilling." Oscar expressed his wish that his "Latin group" be permitted to play salsa music on the radio while they worked, and that there be more corporate social events to reflect cultural differences and bring people together. His interview reflected an interplay of independent and interdependent ideas and values. On one hand, Oscar recognized the necessity to be assertive and wished that he had more of those traits; on the other hand, he wished that the firm would take more of an interest in the interpersonal needs of employees. In addition, Oscar asserted that he valued respecting others and being respected.

Ann, an employee from Taiwan, argued that management should have different policies for different employees, suggesting, for example, that employees with a strong work ethic and self-direction should be "left alone," while others, such as the "complaining Americans," needed more rules. In addition, Ann recognized that some of her Asian colleagues were having problems they could not discuss with management, because they were used to a sharp distinction between management and subordinates and thus were fearful about expressing opinions and making suggestions. Ann felt that her manager should realize that different employees have different interactional styles and may require different management styles or relationships.

Carol, an employee from Jamaica who had worked for the bank for thirty years, was at first very reluctant to engage questions about diversity, and her responses for the most part were in sharp contrast with Ann's and Oscar's. Carol told us that she mostly wanted respect in her job and apart from that, she mostly "stayed away from hassles." She also revealed that her life outside of work revolved around her family, and she had tried to instill the same values in her children. "I go to work, do my job, I do a good job, and I go home." Any mention of race or culture was strikingly absent from the first part of the conversation with Carol. Later in the interview, however, Carol began to comment on her impressions of who got promoted within the department; she said she had noticed that "certain people get helped or moved along." According to Carol, it was no accident that "proactive" and "aggressive" white males were the ones who got promoted to management positions.

Other interviews were conducted with people who had some say in creating, instituting, and overseeing policies surrounding diversity. This particular bank had a large human resources department, which housed an active diversity group charged with the duties of instituting and monitoring the bank's diversity programs and policies worldwide. Within this group we found, yet again, very different understandings of diversity and a wide array of opinions on which ideas and practices about diversity should be instituted. Christina, a Hispanic human resource officer in charge of diversity training (but a lower-ranking employee in her group), vehemently attested, "people are different and these differences can teach us something. . . . [Diversity] can be a strength because we don't necessarily know best. . . . Differences should be valued and utilized." Tori, an African American human resource officer and internal consultant who did employee advocacy and training, asserted, "Just have tolerance for difference . . . be able to handle my disagreement with you. Then what my physical image looks like becomes irrelevant, because all I have to do is be different. Be able to agree to disagree." She added, "because, at the end of the day we are a bank, so it is revenue production that matters most." With respect to formal diversity practices within the bank, Tori advocated the implementation of a set of organizationwide values that her group had developed and begun to disseminate. These values influenced every aspect of an employee's work life—from sick days to dress code to how he or she should interact with other employees. The purpose of this worldwide implementation was to foster a common set of values, norms, and goals in which employees across cultures could identify how to "be" an employee of that bank.

Elizabeth, an African American vice-president of human resources in diversity staffing and development, worked closely with upper management on issues such as the promotion and retention of high-level minority managers. Elizabeth saw her most important job within the company as persuading upper management to view diversity as a valuable resource—one that could have a direct impact on the profitability of their business. With this aim in mind, she had created four "business roundtables," or working groups, each consisting of middle- or senior-level managers and representing one minority population— women, African Americans, Asians, or Hispanics. Each group met once per month to develop their group project, which had been specifically designed to reflect the commonly held view of the strength of that particular minority group. The women's group worked on a work-life balance–dual career couples program; the African American group worked on marketing to the growing African American market segment; the Asian group worked on a technology program, and the Hispanic group worked on a mentorship program. This system had been instituted in order to show upper management how diversity in the workforce, particularly diversity at the top levels, can contribute to the bottom line.

These different ideas about diversity and practices surrounding diversity, and the fact that they seemed to be related in some way to the social and cultural positioning of the informant, suggested that a number of models of diversity are currently being simultaneously entertained by Americans. What Americans make of the differences in their communities is currently under collective construction. While the notion that people are essentially all the same resonated with Dan (a white male manager), Oscar (his Hispanic subordinate) took comfort in a model that engaged and celebrated the notion of cultural difference. Whereas Ann (a Taiwanese woman) wanted her cultural background to be taken into account in her interactions with her boss, Carol (a West Indian woman) preferred to see race as irrelevant to her and her work life.

Each of these views reflects the employee's specific experience and positioning within the bank context. Dan's model of diversity, for instance, most likely has been shaped by his experience as a male majority group member in a high-status position within his company. Tori and Elizabeth's models of diversity likely have been contoured by their experiences as African American women engaging with European American mainstream culture, from fairly high policy-making positions within the organization. Christina, whose position allows her to institute programs but not organizationwide policies, engages a model of diversity that probably has been influenced by her position as well as her interaction with both Hispanic and European American cultures.

The accounts of diversity drawn out in these interviews present strikingly divergent perspectives on how people should think about, pay attention to, and incorporate difference in their work practices. While some employees' anxieties were raised by the suggestion that people are "different," others were disappointed by a system that failed to attend to cultural differences—in communication styles, work habits, and needs for connection. While some company policy makers touted incorporating difference in organizational practices, they diverged in their conceptions of the correct and effective way of doing so—and yet another policy maker avowed that differences should be tolerated but played down and replaced with an overarching value system. As America becomes increasingly diverse, there is, simultaneoulsy, a growing diversity in how to think about difference and inclusion. Based on this set of interviews, subsequent studies (Plaut and Markus 2002), and a survey of the most influential psychological literature on intergroup relations, this chapter will document four models of diversity that currently appear to permeate both popular discourse and social science thinking. These models will be termed *Sameness*, *Common Identity Creation*, *Value-added*, and *Mutual Accommodation*.

Models of diversity can be defined as shared understandings and practices of how groups come together or should come together, relate to one another, and include and accommodate one another in light of the differences associated with group identity. These notions about diversity, which can take highly implicit or transparent forms, can be thought of as cultural models. Cultural models (see Shore 1996), which give form to individuals' engagement with the world and allow people to communicate with one another, are themselves shaped by individuals as they interact with the world and with each other and as they construct meaning. Different cultural models are likely to evolve and influence individual thought and action depending on the sociocultural context with which the individual has engaged and is currently engaging. As the interviews herein suggest, people likely will engage different models based on their status or position, and they may engage different models in different situations. Drawing on a combination of interviews, surveys, a media content analysis, and a review of the intergroup relations literature, this chapter will explore the prevalence of different models and how their distribution might vary depending on social status and cultural context.

The models presented are not meant to be inclusive of all possible models of diversity. Fredrickson (1999), for example, describes two other models that also could be considered models of diversity. One is ethnic hierarchy, in which one powerful group—even a small group—controls the distribution of resources, and the other is group separatism, where groups have little or no interaction with each other. Under a related model, people may form voluntary associations with people of their "own kind" without interfering with each other, practicing a live-and-let-live philosophy. Further, the models depicted are not necessarily mutually exclusive, and sometimes the distinctions between models may be blurred. Yet for the most part these models represent four fairly cohesive sets of ideas and practices grounded in certain shared understandings of difference and inclusion. These models provide the foundation for the discourse of diversity in America, and they increasingly will be implicated in debates over how to combine diversity and democracy. The story of intergroup relations in America has been dominated by one model of diversity—the Sameness model—but there are other ways of thinking about groups getting together. The nondominant models (often, but not always, affiliated with the minority perspective) need to be attended to, because the most common model (reflecting the majority perspective) actually can work against incorporating difference.

An additional aim of this chapter is to fill a gap in the social psychological literature on intergroup relations. Social psychology has produced many powerful insights on stereotyping and prejudice, but it has not investigated the ideologies that frame attitudes about groups and practices of relations between groups. This chapter attempts to make explicit the cultural models that ground theories of intergroup relations. Given the ongoing dynamic between culture and science (Farr 1993; Kuhn 1962; Moscovici 1984), the review interweaves aspects of how models are represented by the public and by social psychology. Indeed, many of the psychological theories described herein have been used in legal cases (for example, Social Science Statement; see Allport et al. 1953) and to inform government policies (for example, Berry's work on multiculturalism) and organizational policies (see Thomas and Ely 1996).

There are many possible dimensions of difference: age, gender, sexual orientation, culture, race and ethnicity, nationality, social class, status, and so on. *Diversity* here refers to any way in which people differ because of their different positioning in the world. This chapter focuses on notions of cultural, racial, ethnic, and social status differences, because that is how diversity is most commonly interpreted by Americans (Plaut and Markus 2002) and in the social psychological literature.

# MEANING MAKING: CULTURAL MODELS AND SOCIAL REPRESENTATIONS

Ideas and practices about diversity are developed by individuals in interaction with specific sociocultural and sociohistorical contexts. Models of diversity bundle a large set of culturally bound assumptions about the world and can operate implicitly, outside of conscious awareness. The literature on cultural models and social representations provides important insights into how thinking necessarily is linked with the social environment and how socially constructed knowledge can be deceptively invisible.

## Cultural Models: Culture Inside and Outside the Mind

The notion of culture as a necessary aspect of mind and mental functioning is reflected in the tradition of cultural models developed in cultural and cognitive anthropology and in cultural psychology (for example, D'Andrade 1990; Fiske et al. 1998; Quinn and Holland 1987; Shore 1996; Shweder 1990). Underscoring the notion of shared meaning, for instance, D'Andrade (1990, 809) describes a cultural model as "a cognitive schema that is intersubjectively shared by a cultural group." Quinn and Holland (1987, 4) argue that cultural schemas are "presupposed, taken for granted models of the world that are widely shared (though not to the exclusion of other alternative models) by the members of a society and that play an enormous role in their understanding of the world and their behavior in it."

But cultural models not only reside in the minds of people in a particular cultural context, they also inhabit the world itself. Shore (1996, 44) elaborates the definition of cultural model or schema by making it clear that models can exist "both as public artifacts 'in the world' and as cognitive constructs 'in the mind' of members of a community." In other words, models are externalized as shared, discernable institutions as well as internalized by individuals (see Berger and Luckmann 1966). The existence of these models is "contingent, negotiated through endless social exchanges" (Shore 1996, 47). Models constitute a community's conventional resources for meaning making—they constrain attention and guide what is perceived as salient through social norms and feedback.

In addition, because social institutions play a large role in meaning making, they necessarily shape cultural models (Shore 1996). People occupy and are very much materially involved with their place in the world, which includes cultural participation in the local economy, the legal system, schools, politics, and other institutions. Values and information depend heavily on particular practices and institutions that are grounded in and make up material culture (Bourdieu 1977; Giddens 1990; Harris 1979). For example, cultural models of diversity are given form by the institutional life of a particular sociocultural context, and will be reflected by the people who interact with and make up those institutions.

## Social Representations: From Individual to Social

The theory of social representations has paralleled the cultural models tradition in its trajectory and contribution to our understanding of the socially constructed nature of human thought. Whereas the cultural models concept comes mostly from the tradition of cognitive anthropology, the notion of social representations comes from social psychology and is rooted in sociology (see, for example, Durkheim 1974 [1898]).

A social representation is, according to Moscovici (1973, xiii),

a system of values, ideas and practices with a twofold function; first, to establish an order which will enable individuals to orientate themselves in their material and social world and to master it; and secondly to enable communication to take place among the members of a community by providing them with a code for social exchange and a code for naming and classifying unambiguously the various aspects of their world and their individual and group history.

Thus, the purpose of social representations is first to make the strange familiar and second to make communication relatively nonproblematic (Moscovici 1984, 1998). Social representations are formed through implicit negotiations in the course of conversations in which people are oriented toward particular symbolic models, images, and shared values. This process allows people to acquire a common repertoire of interpretations and explanations, rules, and procedures that they can apply to everyday life (Moscovici 1984). In many ways, social representations constitute a psychology of common sense or social sense. For example, social representations of diversity constitute what makes sense to people about how to perceive and label differences among people and how to act in light of these differences.

Social representations are transmitted and spread, and they change in the process of spreading (Sperber 1985). They also can be met with resistance. Individuals may resist or fail to incorporate public and mutually constructed ideas into their meaning-making systems (Oyserman and Markus 1998). In addition, social representations can be affected by life transitions as well as living in multiple cultural contexts, which can make competing claims on a person (Oyserman and Markus 1998).

Because of their similarity of function, *cultural models* and *social representations* will be used fairly interchangeably. Several important points may be gleaned from these various theoretical traditions. People behave and think within a semiotic—or meaning—space that is determined by their social and cultural positioning, or social vantage point. Within this space they socially construct models or representations, or cultural values, ideas, and practices, and they may institutionalize some of the models created in that space. This creative and dynamic meaning-making process ultimately serves to orient people with respect to one another, makes communication possible, and gives form to the relations between individuals and groups of people. Models, or representations, can be implicit or explicit and are both individually and collectively held and resisted.

Ideas about diversity that are permeating and guiding popular and social scientific thought can be better understood when viewed through the lens of cultural models or social representations. Accordingly, four models of diversity are portrayed in terms of their theoretical foundations as well as their prevalence in popular thought, with some attention to the problems or potential of the model for successful diversity. The description of the theoretical foundations of each model focuses mostly on social psychological approaches to intergroup relations as well as some important cultural ideals, both of which give some insight into and reflect the prevalent cultural models of diversity in a particular historical period. These approaches have also directly and indirectly shaped how people think about diversity, how they differ, and how those differences should be ignored, suppressed, or accommodated, and they have helped to create important policies that have been instituted in many domains of American life.

## THE SAMENESS MODEL: PEOPLE ARE PEOPLE

The Sameness model, epitomized by Dan's belief that "people are people," is characterized by the notion that differences among people are superficial and mostly irrelevant. This model is widely manifest in advertising campaigns and other public representations (Shweder 1991). For instance, a recent Merrill Lynch advertisement states, "the color of your skin is less important than the color of your imagination . . . you are larger, in the knowledge that the only race that really matters is the human one." And, when Supreme Court Justice Scalia declares, "In the eyes of government, we are just one race here. It is American," the Sameness model is instantiated in the legal system (*Adarand Contractors v. Pena*, 515 U.S. 200, 239 [1995]).

As suggested by Dan's response, America has an ideological struggle with the notion of difference. On one hand, America is a culture that prizes difference, uniqueness, and nonconformity. On the other hand, America is a culture that believes in individualism and equality, which necessitates treating everyone the same; it is a society that touts (even if it does not effectively practice) color blindness. Americans participate in a powerful legal and political culture that holds that "all men are created equal" and that one should treat people "as free and equal beings." Further, policy makers, social scientists, managers, and teachers work within a system that encourages people to believe that marking racial or ethnic difference is bad—a system that reflects the following sentiment in Supreme Court Justice O'Connor's opinion in *Shaw v. Reno* (509 U.S. 630, 657 [1993]): "Racial classifications of any sort pose the risk of lasting harm to much of our society. They reinforce the belief, held by too many for too much of our history that individuals should be judged by the color of their skin." To mark racial difference therefore is to court charges of racism. The solution has been to adopt an ideology of sameness with regard to diversity, championing such beliefs as "essentially we're all the same" and "at the end of the day we all want the same thing." According to this model, equality is understood as "similarity" (Shweder 1991), diversity is seen as just a matter of superficial differences, and many develop the presumption that once people are given "access" and treated with "respect and dignity" the rest is easy (see Thomas and Ely 1996, Fairness and Discrimination paradigm). In the past few decades, this model has become widespread in America's economic, educational, and legal institutions.

## Contact, Equality, and Individualism

Social psychologists have been not only descriptive in their theoretical investigation of intergroup relations but also prescriptive, and they have turned their attention to strategies for decreasing intergroup bias. Thirty-two social scientists, for instance, supplied evidence of the harmful effects of segregation (Allport et al. 1953) in the historic 1954 case *Brown v. Board of Education of Topeka*, in which the Supreme Court overturned the 1896 decision of *Plessy v. Ferguson*, which permitted states to mandate "separate but equal facilities for blacks and whites." The *Brown* Court maintained that segregation generated feelings of inferiority among blacks and violated the equal protection clause of the U.S. Constitution. Many social psychologists were optimistic that increased contact between blacks and whites would improve race relations. The "contact hypothesis," which holds that under certain conditions (for example, equal status, common goals, and egalitarian norms) direct contact between members of conflicting groups will reduce prejudice, was proffered as a means to achieve harmonious intergroup relations (Allport 1954; Amir 1969; Cook 1978). In this early theory and subsequent additions, we see the development of the Sameness model of diversity, one that is entrenched in a perceived need for color blindness based on equality.

This principle is itself intertwined with America's cultural ideal of individualism, where value is placed on independence, individual rights, and the tendency of people to see themselves as individuals rather than as members of a group (Hofstede 1980; Triandis 1995). This worldview is prevalent in North American and European societies—particularly among white middle-class people—and emphasizes the natural rights of the individual and personal achievement, which reinforce one another within the American cultural frame. The social representation of individualism in American society has been molded by the history of a war for independence and the belief in the right to individual freedom, epitomized in the Declaration of Independence and the Bill of Rights, as well as by mainstream Protestant values such as hard work, self-reliance, achievement, and discipline (Weber 1958 [1904]). These values of independence and achievement together have given force to the "American Dream," the mentality that claims that it is possible to get to the top and achieve almost anything if one works hard enough and with direction and perseverance (Spindler and Spindler 1990; Hochschild 1995). As a result, the American individualist stance highlights and rewards personal merit and success and promotes the judgment of others on the basis of personal success (Augoustinos 1998; Fiske 1991).

This cultural emphasis on achievement and locating its causes within the individual has played a large role in shaping American cultural models of diversity. According to Augoustinos (1998), liberal individualism, which abstracts and separates the individual from society and sees the individual as possessing inalienable rights, continues to "exercise ideological constraints on the way people think, live, and behave." Augoustinos (1998, 162–63) claims, "Individualism has been described as the most pervasive ethos characterizing liberal democracies because it has the ability to make sense of the social conditions of a capitalist society." The American economic system rests on a view of fair and equitable relations so that competition, the cornerstone of capitalism, can take place effectively and efficiently. This economic system then serves to legitimize and encourage views of the self that are grounded in equality and individualism. The Sameness model, which rests on these same principles, therefore can be seen as deriving from the free individual in the marketplace (Carr 1997).

In addition, in America, group life is seen largely as a matter of choice, and therefore, belonging to a group is not seen as natural; what is basic and natural is the individual. The United States is a nation of individuals seemingly bound together by a commitment to the protection of individual rights—not group rights. The 1954 decision to end segregation and the Civil Rights Acts of 1964 and 1968 fueled the process of dismantling differential treatment of groups. In essence, though, these legal decisions were meant to protect equal opportunity among individuals. Since group treatment heretofore had been associated with negative outcomes—and because the focus was on individual as opposed to group rights—a new ideology vaulted into America's racial discourse: color blindness. Liberals learned that they should not treat people based on their group membership or the color of their skin, but rather on the basis of sameness.

## Decategorization

Within the social sciences, elements of the Sameness model were developed further by proponents of decategorization. Insights from anthropology and social identity theory lured researchers toward a theory that attended specifically to the notion of group membership and categorization.[3] The anthropologists LeVine and Campbell (1972) suggested that the "crossing" of group memberships may help control the incidence of intergroup conflict by encouraging loyalties to more than one group. The social psychologists Deschamps and Doise (1978) found that "criss-cross" categorizations or multiple cross-cutting category distinctions led to a decrease in intergroup discrimination. Worchel and colleagues (1978) suggested that cooperation would increase intergroup liking to the extent that it reduces the salience of the group boundaries or distinctions. These claims were based on the finding that in-group–out-group categorization was sufficient to lead to intergroup bias (Brewer 1979).

In light of these findings and in an effort to build on the conditions necessary for contact to have a positive influence on intergroup relations, Brewer and Miller (1984) developed the "decategorization" approach. This approach draws on the idea that with respect to category-based intergroup contact, categories can be based on differences in ethnicity, social class—even on single arbitrary distinctions (see Brewer 1979)—and that maintenance of category-based distinctions can undermine positive intergroup attitudes (Brewer 1988). According to Brewer and Miller (1984, 287), "an emphasis on intergroup distinctions introduces dysfunctional social competition and out-group rejection that interferes with collective action and interpersonal acceptance." The authors posit that intergroup interaction should be designed so as to eliminate the salience of social categories. Yet they argue that reduction of categorical responding does not "necessitate that real differences or perceived distinctions between groups be eliminated" (Brewer and Miller 1984, 289). Although Brewer and Miller argue that this is compatible with an integration approach, decategorization does not offer any indication of how differential group experience should be included, incorporated, or valued. In this sense, the decategorization approach is patterned by the tenets of the Sameness model in that it encourages people to decrease their perception of social categories, even if it does not suggest tuning them out altogether.

## Prevalence of the Sameness Model

Evidence from the diversity interviews, subsequent studies, and other practices shows that the first model of diversity is the most prevalent, at least among the European American majority. This "color-blind" perspective—characterized by Rist (1974) as a viewpoint that sees racial and ethnic group membership as irrelevant to how individuals are treated—is widely applied in education policy and pervasively instantiated in schooling practices. Schofield (1986a, 1986b) has studied the presence and effects of the color-blindness perspective in desegregated schools. She argues that this perspective is widespread in American schools, as part of official policy or as an informal but powerful social norm. Although the color-blind perspective is appealing because it coheres with American individualism, however, "it easily leads to a misrepresentation of reality in ways which allow, and sometimes even encourage discrimination against minority group members" (Schofield 1986b, 233). The idea that people should be judged by their behavior as individuals and not as members of particular social categories encourages institutions to try to ignore race completely. Yet the evidence that clues about race influence and guide people's perceptions and behavior, even as they deny the influence of race, is voluminous. Schofield finds that although teachers claim not to notice race, it remains a factor in their perception and treatment of students, and racial categories still are salient to the students and continue to structure student interaction patterns (for example, with whom they sit during the lunch period).

The Sameness model is inherently tied to the concept of aversive racism, which focuses on the fact that although many whites are committed to a nonprejudiced self-image, they may have some degree of negative feelings toward minority groups such as blacks (Gaertner and Dovidio 1981, 1986, 1997). Aversive racism is a form of prejudice that surfaces in subtle ways—not as hostility or hate but rather as discomfort, uneasiness, or fear that motivates avoidance of race rather than intentionally destructive behaviors. This form of bias can lead to a failure in acknowledging one's negative racial sentiment, and it can be easily rationalized by principles such as fairness and equality. The availability of non-race-related rationales for behavior can help perpetuate negative outcomes for minority students (Schofield 1986b). To the extent that the color-blind perspective and its corollaries "help to remove awareness of race from conscious consideration, they make other explanations for one's behavior relatively more salient. Thus, they free the aversive racist to act in a discriminatory fashion" (Schofield 1986b, 247). Likewise, institutional racism (see Jones 1997 [1972]) is equally pernicious, because even though individual attitudes about race may have changed (through sets of policies, practices, and procedures), institutions continue to discriminate. Outcomes of aversive and institutional racism include discrimination by individuals who believe themselves to be unprejudiced when they can explain their behavior in ways that do not challenge their liberal self-concept when nonracial rationales are available to justify the action. Indeed, Schofield's (1986a, 92) findings suggest "to the extent individuals or institutions imagine that they are color-blind, they may well ignore social processes that perpetuate differential outcomes for members of majority and minority groups."

Another challenge posed by the Sameness model is how to come to terms with the fact that racial, ethnic, or cultural groups—who occupy a different position within the societal matrix—can have very different models of diversity. The assimilationist approach that results from the Sameness model starkly contrasts the pluralist approach advocated by members of minority groups: that is, to recognize cultural diversity and acknowledge the validity of "subcultural values" and "communal identities" (Schofield 1986a). For the European American majority, the Sameness model of diversity makes sense; it may even seem to work. Yet for others from different cultural contexts, and for those who operate from the vantage point of a different social position, people don't look the same. Nor do they necessarily aspire to be the same. Nor is "sameness based on fairness" really adequate.

According to our own studies, people who engage primarily in European American cultural contexts tend to hold the view that diversity among people is relatively superficial. In contrast, people who come from or who currently engage in some non–European American cultural contexts, or who occupy a lower social position in a mainstream context, are more likely to be aware of significant differences between themselves and others. In one study (Plaut and Markus 2002), a questionnaire of attitudes toward and representations of diversity was administered to undergraduate students from different racial, ethnic, and cultural backgrounds that were associated with different social positioning on campus. Minority undergraduate students endorsed the following statements more strongly than did white students: I feel comfortable around others from different cultural and ethnic backgrounds; it's important to have multiple perspectives on campus; diversity is the fair thing to do; there is something special about diverse groups; differences among people from different cultural and ethnic backgrounds are substantial. In contrast, white students endorsed the following statements more strongly: people are all the same; people are similar to me; too much diversity is harmful so we should emphasize the ways we are similar; diversity is irrelevant to me. These findings reflect an underlying tension between white and minority groups' responses. White students tend to focus on similarity and sameness, whereas minority students see differences between cultural and ethnic groups. Those who have been constituted as different or have learned through personal experience that color blindness does not really exist are more likely to endorse items supporting diversity and notice that people have different values and ways of thinking.

To document some current public understandings of diversity, we also are analyzing representations of diversity in a wide variety of magazines (Plaut and Markus 2002). This study looks at the prevalence of representations of diversity and draws on the fact that the media publishes advertisements with representations of diversity that advertisers think will resonate with the public. We have found the Sameness model widely represented in advertisements in a variety of publications. These advertisements explicitly tout a color-blind model and mention the lack of significance of group boundaries (such as the "color of your skin"). In advertising these messages and images, the media thus influences the public's conceptualizations of diversity.

## THE COMMON IDENTITY CREATION MODEL: FROM DECATEGORIZATION TO RECATEGORIZATION

The Common Identity Creation model holds that perceived differences among people and groups are substantial and should be minimized, and that a common, overarching identity should be created. This model is reflected in Tori's (the human resources consultant) efforts to implement an overarching, organizationwide set of values, norms, and goals that would reinforce employees' identification with the bank across cultural boundaries. One magazine advertisement (see figure 17.1) aptly characterizes the Common Identity Creation model: the ad proclaims, "This is our idea of teamwork." The caption then continues, "Zebras never wonder if they're white with black stripes. Or black with white stripes. They work together so they won't be lunch for a lion." Notice here that it does

FIGURE 17.1 / Ersnt & Young Advertisement

not matter if you are black or white—successful teamwork depends on the subordination of differences to a group identity or goal.

## Cooperation, Common Goals, and Similarity

One of the cornerstones of the contact hypothesis is the condition of cooperation between racial groups. Social scientists incorporated and developed this idea in later research on effective intergroup relations. For example, Sherif and his colleagues (Sherif 1966; Sherif et al. 1961) found that a series of "superordinate goals" are necessary for the reduction of intergroup hostility between two groups of boys in a summer camp. The "jigsaw" classroom technique developed by Aronson and colleagues (Aronson et al. 1978) also focuses on cooperative learning behavior. In this technique, each component of a lesson is mastered by one person in an interracial group of students, and cooperation with each person is necessary for the group to learn the lesson. Aronson's technique, developed in newly desegregated schools in Texas, focuses on equalizing student participation to enhance cooperation and on demonstrating a common purpose or goal.

The idea of demonstrating a shared purpose within an interracial group resonated with other social scientists as well. Some researchers (for example, Pettigrew 1969) argued that Allport's (1954) conditions reduce prejudice because they maximize the probability that shared values and beliefs will be demonstrated and perceived and therefore would provide the basis for interpersonal attraction between in-group and out-group members. This hope was reflected in the evolution of the "similarity-attraction model"—that people like others who are similar more than those who are dissimilar (Newcomb 1961; Byrne 1969, 1971). Byrne purported that a focus on similarity between groups rather than their differences may capitalize on this association between similarity and liking. In a series of studies, Byrne found that people who filled out an attitude survey and then were presented with the responses of other supposed participants liked this other person more when they perceive him or her to have similar attitudes. More recently, Grant (1993) found that perceived similarity led male and female groups to be more positive toward each other than did perceived dissimilarity.

## Common In-Group Identity Model

Some social psychological theories of intergroup bias and strategies for reducing it have recognized that people do not normally operate under a color-blind model. For instance, the social categorization perspective highlights the notion that people constantly perceive group boundaries. Turner (1981, 99), a proponent of this perspective, argues that the most effective way of resolving intergroup conflict is "through the creation of common or superordinate identifications." Gaertner and colleagues' common in-group identity model, firmly grounded in these theoretical insights, reflects the principles of the Common Identity Creation model. Whereas Brewer and Miller (1984) stressed the importance of decategorization (the minimization of category-based interaction), Gaertner and colleagues (1993) have proposed that recategorization is necessary for the reduction of intergroup bias. They argue that intergroup bias can be reduced by changing categorization, or group boundaries, from *us* and *them* to *we*. In their study of a multicultural high school, for instance, reductions in bias were predicted by stronger common in-group representations and ethnic-racial identities that included a superordinate American identity (Gaertner et al. 1994). The common in-group identity model is based on principles of the social categorization perspective (Brewer 1979; Tajfel and Turner 1979; Turner 1987)—that is, the idea that categorization of a person as an in-group member produces more positive evaluations (Brewer 1979; Tajfel 1969) and perceptions of greater belief similarity (Brown and Abrams 1986; Byrne 1969). Gaertner and colleagues have claimed that common in-group identity is essential to group functioning (Gaertner et al. 1996).

## Prevalence of the Common Identity Creation Model

This perspective focuses on creating a single salient, inclusive category or identity with which many different people from different backgrounds, who would otherwise draw on different categories for self-categorization, can identify. The Common Identity Creation model bears some resemblance to the Sameness model; the idea of making people similar is linked to the idea of perceiving people as the same. However, while the Sameness model focuses on a broader identity (seeing people as "people," or as "all the same race"), the Common Identity Creation model works in a more confined way. This model does not require people to assume sameness on a large number of features or deny that differences exist. Just one group identity, at a level closer to the individual identity rather than as broad as all humanity, is sufficient. The Common Identity Creation model—the idea that if you make a diverse group of people focus on a common purpose, in some respects they can work together and like each other—is very appealing. This idea has come to life in many aspects of American culture, such as the military, which heralds the creation of one shared identity and institutes this model in such practices as dress and the perception of a common goal and enemy. The notion that "we are all playing on the same team" also is manifest in sports, where subgroup boundaries, such as race or ethnicity, often are minimized and replaced by a superordinate team identity. This model has appeared frequently in the social psychological literature as well, and although not one of the most prevalent themes in our media analysis, is not entirely absent from media representations of diversity.

Although an appealing conception of diversity, the model of creating a common identity has come under attack from a multiculturalist perspective. For instance, recent social psychological studies by Hornsey and Hogg (2000b) demonstrate that emphasizing a superordinate category actually could increase bias, while bias was lowest when subgroup categories were made salient.

# THE VALUE-ADDED MODEL: RECOGNITION AND INTEGRATION OF DIFFERENCES

According to the Value-added model, differences among people and groups are substantial, and some should be utilized because they add value. Christina (the human resources diversity manager) suggests that important differences exist among people from different groups, and these differences should be valued by the organization. This model also is promulgated in the following, from a Morgan Stanley Dean Witter advertisement:

> Diversity: It's not an obligation—it's an opportunity. To make a difference, a company must keep its eyes open to different ways of thinking. That's why we take diversity seriously in all aspects of our business, including the way we select the companies that supply us with the goods and services that enable us to do business.

The Sameness model and the Common Identity Creation model are particularly attractive in a culture in which any mention of difference among people can inspire fear that one is alluding to genetic differences or essential differences in personality, motivations, goals, or values. Social psychology tells us, however, that while race and ethnicity do not create essential differences, people do differ owing to their different experiences and different positioning in society—because they are not treated the same. Indeed, the main contributions of social psychology have revolved around the lesson that people's psychological functioning (such as how they think, feel, act, and perceive themselves and others) varies because it is so profoundly influenced by different contexts and situations (see Ross and Nisbett 1991). Likewise, cultural psychology has deepened that tradition and has shown how psychological tendencies are shaped by people's engagement with the ideas, practices, and institutions that inhabit their cultural contexts and that guide and give meaning to their lives (see Fiske et al. 1998).

The Value-added model is rooted in this tradition of research that elaborates the dimensions along which people across cultures can be expected to differ. The Value-added model views differences among people as contributing value. Yet because notions about the values of particular differences are not highly elaborated or analyzed in the literature or popular discourse, the Value-added model encompasses a wide variety of perspectives on the incorporation of difference.

## Pluralism, Integration, and Multiculturalism

Pluralism refers to the "maintenance or development of separate cultures or distinctive ethnic identities in a given society" (Hewstone and Brown 1986, 21). While the conventional definition of pluralism calls to mind the notion of different cultures simply living side by side within a society, pluralist approaches can differ from group to group. According to Pettigrew (1988), for instance, the image of the melting pot has long been a part of our national imagery, and reflects the Anglo-American concern with unity in the face of an enormously heterogeneous population. But the 1960s civil rights movement and demand for black inclusion caused an ideological shift, and the melting pot metaphor came under attack for obscuring "the cultural distinctiveness and contributions of ethnic groups" (Pettigrew 1988, 21). As a result, some groups have espoused a concept of pluralist integration that involves the maintenance of the "cultural integrity" of the group as well as the movement by the group to become an integral part of the larger societal framework (for example, the "mosaic" as opposed to the "melting pot"; Berry 1984). While pluralism had been based mostly on assimilation and seemed to reflect the needs of white minority groups (such as Catholics and Jews), a notion of pluralism tied to integration took ground that referred to the inclusion processes for a racial group (blacks, for instance) that had a "unique history of rigorous exclusion" (Pettigrew 1988, 20; see also Berry 1984 and Ogbu 1994 for a description of voluntary versus nonvoluntary minorities). Some scholars have argued, however, that integration was actually an idea about how blacks would become psychologically white (Triandis 1988; see Taylor 1974). Triandis and others propose a multiculturalist approach opposing current attempts at integration that disregard cultural differences. Multiculturalism, the way it has been referred to by cross-cultural psychologists in particular, grapples somewhat more directly with the notion of how differences should be recognized and included. According to Berry (1984), for a society to be multicultural requires the presence of both pluralism and a positive multicultural ideology in public attitudes and policy (that is, one that sees diversity as a resource rather than a problem). Most recently, Jones and his colleagues (2000) have proposed that positive consequences of diversity will occur if participation is reasonably representational and cultural identity is valued.

## Categorization Revisited

The multiculturalist perspective and the Value-added model also have been influenced by the social categorization tradition in social psychology. Hornsey and Hogg (2000a) dub social identity theory an "analogue to multiculturalism." Some researchers have suggested, however, that the conditions outlined by Brewer and Miller's (1984) formulation for positive intergroup contact (which also grew out of the social categorization approach and emphasizes decategorization) may not always lead to decreased bias. Hewstone and Brown (1986) suggest that contact should be "intergroup," not "interpersonal." In other words, individuals should be distinguished by the experience and expertise they bring to the situation. Their approach is aimed at the recognition and appreciation of both similarities and differences. Recent research by Wolsko and his colleagues (2000) also questions the assumption that social categories must be deemphasized for positive intergroup contact.

## Prevalence of the Value-Added Model

These perspectives all argue that differences between people are substantial and should be valued (or at least recognized), and the Value-added model is starting to seep into the diversity discourse. One of the most salient categories to emerge from the media analysis, for instance, has been the importance of different ideas, ways of thinking, and perspectives. We also have found many advertisements that represent a group of racially, ethnically, or culturally diverse people or simply present the term *diversity*. Yet the idea that differences in ways of thinking might in some meaningful way be tied to different group identities is absent from such advertisements, as is any concrete suggestion for what these different ways of thinking are or how they should be utilized. Moreover, in many organizational settings, even if different perspectives are recognized, they are not often integrated into the organization's practices.

Likewise absent from "diverse people" ads is any mention of how their differences are acknowledged or utilized. Indeed, notions about what kind of value people from diverse backgrounds bring are not highly elaborated or analyzed. Some organizations may emphasize cultural differences (for example, to gain access into different market segments) and place people in positions on the basis on culturally related characteristics, but fail to analyze how such differences function and are used within the organization (Thomas and Ely 1996). The Value-added model in practice therefore risks pigeonholing people into niches according to identity group membership. This practice is reflected in the interview of Elizabeth, whose business roundtable program assigned each minority group to a project based on its group identity and skills perceived to go with that identity. In her case, this strategy indeed is being used to legitimize the hiring and promotion of minorities explicitly based on their group-specific abilities. Closely linked to this approach to diversity is the widespread recognition of superficial group differences—that is, the practice of making sense of difference primarily in terms of ethnic "food and festivals." People are trying to celebrate and have some appreciation for some aspect of diversity—such as Dan, who reminded us of the importance of different backgrounds because of their link to various ethnic foods. Yet the question remains, how do we continue the intercultural conversation once we want to move past the international buffet?

## THE MUTUAL ACCOMMODATION MODEL

Ann's (the Taiwanese employee) desire to have her culturally based concerns heard and incorporated into management and work practices reflects a desire for mutual accommodation. Similarly, Oscar and Carol's concern that "certain" people get promoted points to their questioning of the inclusiveness of their workplace. These concerns reflect the Mutual Accommodation model, which focuses on the notion that differences among people and groups are substantial and must be accommodated whether or not they are perceived to add value. This model calls for differences between groups to be perceived as contributive and nonlimiting. The Mutual Accommodation model does not deny that "people are people." Yet unlike the Sameness model, which implies that "we are all the same," mutual accommodation stresses the idea that seeing "people as people" requires recognizing that people have engaged with different sociocultural contexts and therefore have legitimately different perspectives and beliefs. Despite limited evidence for the Mutual Accommodation model in the interviews and in some recent social psychological research, it has not been represented—at least in a clearly elaborated way—in American society. It is missing, for example, in our magazine advertisements focusing on diversity.

To date, few social psychologists have adopted the premises of the Mutual Accommodation model directly, but this model can be gleaned from recent research. Investigators have begun to suggest that ethnicity should be taken into account, for example, in the process of organizational socialization (Brewer, von Hippel, and Gooden 1999), but apparently this research nevertheless advocates that organizational, or superordinate, identities should take priority over other social identities. Thus, accommodation seems for the most part to be a step on the way to common identity creation instead of a goal in itself. The Mutual Accommodation model also bears some resemblance to the Value-added model in that it recognizes the value of group differences in lived experience, but it goes further to argue for meaningful change in policies or institutions to accommodate such differences. The integration and multiculturalist perspectives described herein do not necessarily lead to accommodation and mostly take the viewpoint of the high-status group (the European American majority). In contrast, Mutual Accommodation in essence is a power-sharing model that calls for the expectation of change.

The Mutual Accommodation model begins with the assumption that individuals need to feel safe, valued, and respected in order to contribute to their full potential. Recall from the bank interviews that all of Dan's nonwhite subordinates asserted their desire for respect in the workplace, and at least two of these informants gave some indication of not feeling valued because of their lack of certain traits. Some recent research has begun to grapple with the complex task of creating environments and instituting practices that both acknowledge difference and allow differences to be respected and valued. The "Identity safety" approach, for instance, while recognizing group differences, accepts them as nonlimiting and contributive and attempts to reduce the threat that can be attached to a group's identity in critical settings (Markus, Steele, and Steele, ch. 21 herein). According to Markus and her colleagues, in this way the cross-group trust necessary for inclusion to occur can be built. Sending a message of identity safety, as opposed to one of color blindness, has been found to increase performance and trust and decrease stereotype activation among black college students (Purdie, Steele, and Crosby 2000).

The Mutual Accommodation model also involves a set of practices that require an institution to accept, adjust to, and incorporate group differences. According to Schofield (1986a), schools should recognize the special values and behavior patterns of minority students and deal with them fairly, which emphasizes the responsibility of the school to adjust to its students rather than students' need to adjust to the school. Practices that involve only the one-way assimilation of minority groups ignore cultural differences that influence the way students operate in school and ignore the importance of using learning materials that reflect the interests and life experiences and identity of minority students (Schofield 1986b). This model is difficult to implement, however, in a system so firmly entrenched in a Sameness model, which demands one-way assimilation.

## Prevalence of the Mutual Accommodation Model

This tension between one-way assimilation and an accommodation approach is reflected in our own surveys of Stanford and San Jose State University students. As reported in the foregoing, variation was found between white and minority students on their perceptions of the amount and importance of difference as opposed to that of sameness or similarity. Minority undergraduate students also endorsed the following statements more strongly than did white students: to incorporate diverse perspectives, the university should change; government policy should ensure that organizations reflect the diversity of the population; immigrants should maintain and share their culture. In contrast, white students endorsed the following statements more strongly: people from minority groups must assimilate; having multiple perspectives does more harm than good; multicultural policy will cause conflict. So in addition to reflecting a discrepancy in the emphasis on similarity, these findings reflect another underlying tension between white and minority groups' responses. While white students support an "assimilation" model of diversity (where minorities should make adjustments to fit the majority culture), minority students seem to support the "accommodation" model of diversity (where the majority culture should change to accommodate minority perspectives). In an open-ended questionnaire, minority and white students also were distinguished by their reports of positive experiences with diversity. Minority students' responses were the only ones that contained any mention of learning, changing, or dispelling stereotypes. One African American female reported, for example, "You never know how sheltered you really are until you experience and learn from those different from you," and an African American male wrote, "Living in the Native American theme house last year I had to change my views of the stereotypical 'Indian' that I had."

Although espoused by several social scientists, the Mutual Accommodation model is relatively absent from mainstream discourse. The Mutual Accommodation model rests on the capacity to recognize group-based differences while ensuring that the salience of group categories does not intensify social competition and discrimination between groups (see Brewer and Miller 1984; Brewer, von Hippel, and Gooden 1999; Deschamps and Doise 1978; Turner 1981). Despite the positive social science findings of adopting such an approach to diversity, our media analysis has found very little evidence of the Mutual Accommodation model and the message that diversity of experiences and perspectives can be recognized in a safe environment that respects and values difference.

One possible reason for the absence of the Mutual Accommodation model is that the pervasiveness of the Sameness model has introduced a sometimes seemingly insurmountable challenge to people's ability to grasp and practice mutual accommodation. The Sameness model is so deeply entrenched that institutions have come to see the necessity (legal, moral, economic) of "treating everyone the same." Indeed, one of the few advertisements to address the Mutual Accommodation model reflects this struggle between the Sameness and Value-added or Mutual Accommodation models. In a Dun and Bradstreet advertisement (see figure 17.2), a somewhat inconsistent or contradictory message unfolds as it grapples with how to hold both sameness and value-added or mutual accommodation notions at the same time. The advertisement starts with a clear color-blind message: it shows shadows of graduates (masking their group identities) and asks "Does it matter . . . ?" but then draws from a Value-added model when it states, "people's differences are our strengths." Finally, the message shifts to a Mutual Accommodation model, reflected in the phrase, "a company where people feel included and valued." So within one advertisement, three models of diversity are engaged, spanning the representational space from not dealing with difference (or the source of difference) to claiming the assets represented by different backgrounds, and finally to being concerned with valuing difference and being inclusive.

## TOWARD A MORE MULTIFACETED INDIVIDUALISM

After reviewing the concerns that arise in each of the four models, it seems that a sustainable model of diversity must be capable of valuing difference while: assuring that differences will be seen as contributive and nonlimiting, protecting the minority group against pigeonholing and negative views of difference, and assuaging the European American majority's fear of non-color-blind policies and practices. Given the problems posed by group membership, one may wonder why we cannot see people simply as individuals, as suggested by Brewer and Miller's (1984) model, which calls for purely "interpersonal" interaction in intergroup situations. Yet one of the main lessons of social and cultural psychology is that one cannot be a self by oneself. People cannot extract themselves from their historical, sociocultural, and situational grounding. A life without these three props is a life without meaning or basic orientation. The self is formed and reified by the cultural meanings and practices made available through group life. To think about oneself or others simply as individuals therefore is impossible. The opposite view—that people should be seen only as group members—is equally untenable. This approach certainly can lead to some of the concerns

FIGURE 17.2  /  Dun & Bradstreet Corporation Advertisement

presented by Brewer and Miller (1984) or expressed by Justice O'Connor (*Shaw v. Reno* 1993).

The question of individual versus group is not really a question of either-or but rather how. People can be viewed as individuals but risk misrepresenting, misunderstanding, or limiting others if they ignore the affordances of *multiple group memberships, roles,* and other socially meaningful associations. In other words, seeing people as individuals may require recognizing *multiple affiliations and identifications* (Hermans and Kempen 1998). Thus a possible solution that can be enacted within the framework of Mutual Accommodation is a *tacking back and forth between individual and group-based perspectives.* This approach requires seeing people as individuals within the context of a culturally and structurally patterned world.

As we intend to show in future research, the effectiveness of this practice rests on at least four conditions. First, people must recognize that culture and structure are not deterministic—racial categories or groups (and even group relations) are not fixed essences, but rather are very much social and cultural constructions that can change with time and use. A sense of the potential malleability of social categories could decrease concern with being seen as determined by one's culture or of making deterministic classifications of others, which in turn could decrease fear of difference. In addition, institutional practices should set up a norm of expecting differences, of assuming that these differences do not reflect "essential" differences, and of accepting that to notice them is okay. Second, people should recognize that they construct the world as much as it constructs them. Being labeled as a member of a group also is an opportunity to define what it means to be a member of that group. In a culture in which autonomy is such an important feature of our collective consciousness, this notion of agency in world construction could be crucial to the effectiveness of relations between groups. Third, flexibility, or having different sensibilities (which has been understudied and underappreciated), also should be recognized as a valuable skill. As cultural psychology has shown, people are different in meaningful ways and they inhabit and construct different worlds (Kim and Markus, ch. 20 herein; Shweder, ch. 11 herein); therefore they must learn to navigate in these different worlds and not take for granted that one's own way is always the right or only way. Lastly, the success of this model in practice rests on its acceptance by the dominant, majority group, which must recognize the importance of changing to accommodate different perspectives. Owing to its dual emphasis on the individual and that person's multiple group affiliations, the engagement of a Mutual Accommodation model used in this way could lead to the creation of settings in which individuals' anxiety about being negatively judged on the basis of group identities are minimized.

This chapter has aimed to document and make explicit a variety of models of diversity, characterized by different ideas and practices surrounding the notion of difference. The Sameness model, characterized by the idea that the differences among people are superficial and mostly irrelevant, is by far most prevalent.

This model is given force by American principles of equality and individualism. However, because of the Sameness model's explicit disavowal of differential treatment based on group identity, it paradoxically can lead to ignoring pervasive patterns of injustice and inequality. The Common Identity Creation model, somewhat prevalent in public discourse and organizational life, is based on the notion that groups will get along best if they can identify with a salient, overarching purpose and feel that they belong to the same "group" or "team." Some recent studies have shown, however, that such a strategy actually can lead to increases in intergroup bias. The Value-added model, which attempts to recognize and engage the increasingly diverse aspect of society, is slowly becoming more widespread. However, within this model, notions of difference are not well elaborated and organizations operating under this model may risk the negative consequence of pigeonholing people into niches that do not allow for the full development of their potential. In contrast, the Mutual Accommodation model, while recognizing differences, does not base its inclusion of difference on the perception of whether or not particular group-based differences add value. Rather, it seizes on the notion that different ways of being should be incorporated in an effort to create environments where people can feel respected and valued and also have some significant stake in important resources, decisions, and policies. This model is not at all prevalent, although of all the models considered here, it may have the most potential for appeasing the concerns of both minority and majority groups. For these reasons, while the other three models are not without merit and may even be preferable in certain situations, Mutual Accommodation may be the most sustainable model of diversity and the one with the most promise for building a successful diverse society.

Moscovici (1984, 33) claims that social psychologists have focused too much on the analytic operation of classification involving specific features (such as skin color) and on the judgments of similarity or difference according to one feature or another.

> If my observations are correct, then all our "prejudices," whether national, racial, or generational or what have you, can only be overcome by altering our social representations of culture, of "human nature" and so on. If on the other hand, it is the prevailing view that is correct, then all we need to do is persuade antagonistic groups or individuals that they have a great many features in common, that they are, in fact, amazingly similar, and we will have done away with hard and fast classifications and mutual stereotypes. However, the very limited success of this project to date might suggest that the other is worth trying.

Models of diversity in essence are representations of culture and humanity—specifically, the important aspects of being human and the dimensions along which people differ, and how to come to terms with those differences. Although social psychology has given us many tools for dismantling intergroup bias, it has not looked carefully at the ideological assumptions that undergird its theories and applications, and it has not taken stock of the heterogeneity of representations of diversity that can be engaged by different individuals and different groups in different contexts and situations. Perhaps it is time to heed Moscovici's advice and step back from the categorization and similarity perspective to gain a deeper appreciation of how people think human nature operates.

Although many Americans tend to believe in psychic unity—that deep down in the mind, we're really all the same—in reality, significant and fundamental differences exist in people's understandings of themselves and their social worlds (Shweder 1990, 1991; Markus, Mullally, and Kitayama 1997). The different life experiences of people from different cultures and social positioning necessarily produce important psychological diversity among them (Markus and Kitayama 1991; Markus, Kitayama, and Heiman 1986; Shweder 1990). As this chapter has aimed to illustrate, people who have experienced different sociocultural positioning bring with them basic differences in beliefs and practices that reflect their understanding of what difference means, how to relate to people from different cultural and ethnic backgrounds, and how difference should be included. Future studies will examine more systematically how status and power scaffold models of diversity as well as how to develop individual and institutional practices that foster the inclusion and accommodation of difference.

These different models can have powerful and often subtle and unintended effects on the experiences of groups and on relations between groups. While once dominated by the melting pot ideology, as the interviews and studies suggest, American understandings of diversity are starting to reflect a variety of thinking about difference, what it means, and how it should be included. What form the ideological landscape of diversity will take remains to be seen, and working toward a more effective and inclusive diverse society will require careful attention to the content and functioning of cultural models.

## NOTES

1. These interviews were conducted with Hazel Markus as part of an ongoing project on models of diversity and inclusion in American life.

2. Names have been changed to preserve anonymity.

3. Social identity theory concerns the cognitive and motivational processes that underlie identity formation and lead to in-group bias, and is based on the notion of social categorization—that people categorize individuals into social groups (Tajfel 1969, 1982; Tajfel and Turner 1979). Tajfel, Billig, Bundy, and Flament (1971) found that the mere fact of social categorization of self and others was enough to trigger in-group favoritism. To explain this finding, social identity theory was proposed. First, people categorize, then they compare (characterize on the basis of similarity or difference from self, and exaggerate in-group differences and in-group similarities), and finally, because they are motivated to enhance self-esteem, they confer positive distinctiveness on the in-group, which reflects well on the self. Self-categorization theory (Turner 1987) is a

more recent, exclusively cognitive extension of social identity theory, which focuses not on motivation but rather on the psychological basis of group formation and the process of self-categorization.

# REFERENCES

Allport, Floyd H. et al. 1953. "The Effects of Segregation and the Consequences of Desegregation: A Social Science Statement." *Minnesota Law Review* 37: 427–39.

Allport, Gordon W. 1954. *The Nature of Prejudice*. Cambridge, Mass.: Addison-Wesley.

Amir, Yehuda. 1969. "Contact Hypothesis in Ethnic Relations." *Psychological Bulletin* 71: 319–41.

Aronson, Elliott, Cookie W. Stephan, J. Neville Sikes, Nancy T. Blaney, and Matthew Snapp. 1978. *The Jigsaw Classroom*. Beverly Hills, Calif.: Sage.

Asch, Solomon. 1952. *Social Psychology*. Englewood Cliffs, N.J.: Prentice-Hall.

Augoustinos, Martha. 1998. "Social Representations and Ideology: Toward the Study of Ideological Representations." In *The Psychology of the Social*, edited by Uwe Flick. Cambridge: Cambridge University Press.

Berger, Peter L., and Thomas Luckmann. 1966. *The Social Construction of Reality*. Garden City, N.Y.: Doubleday.

Berry, John W. 1984. "Cultural Relations in Plural Societies." In *Groups in Contact: The Psychology of Desegregation*, edited by Norman Miller and Marilynn B. Brewer. Orlando, Fla.: Academic Press.

Bourdieu, Pierre. 1977. *Outline of a Theory of Practice*, translated by R. Nice. Cambridge: Cambridge University Press.

Brewer, Marilynn B. 1979. "Ingroup Bias in the Minimal Intergroup Situation: A Cognitive-Motivational Analysis." *Psychological Bulletin* 86: 307–34.

———. 1988. "A Dual Process Model of Impression Formation." In *Advances in Social Cognition*, edited by Thomas K. Srull and Robert S. Wyer. Hillsdale, N.J.: Erlbaum.

Brewer, Marilynn B., and Norman Miller. 1984. "Beyond the Contact Hypothesis: Theoretical Perspectives on Desegregation." In *Groups in Contact: The Psychology of Desegregation*, edited by Norman Miller and Marilynn B. Brewer. Orlando, Fla.: Academic Press.

Brewer, Marilynn B., William von Hippel, and Martin P. Gooden. 1999. "Diversity and Organizational Identity: The Problem of Entrée After Entry." In *Cultural Divides: Understanding and Overcoming Group Conflict*, edited by Deborah A. Prentice and Dale T. Miller. New York: Russell Sage Foundation.

Brown, Rupert, and Dominic Abrams. 1986. "The Effects of Intergroup Similarity and Goal Interdependence on Intergroup Attitudes and Task Performance." *Journal of Experimental Social Psychology* 2: 78–92.

Byrne, Donn. 1969. "Attitudes and Attraction." In *Advances in Social Psychology*, edited by Leonard Berkowitz. Vol. 4. New York: Academic Press.

———. 1971. *The Attraction Paradigm*. New York: Academic Press.

Carr, Leslie G. 1997. *"Color-blind" Racism*. London: Sage.

Cook, Stewart W. 1978. "Interpersonal and Attitudinal Outcomes in Cooperating Interracial Groups." *Journal of Research and Development in Education* 12: 97–113.

D'Andrade, Roy. 1990. "Cultural Cognition." In *Foundations of Cognitive Science*, edited by Michael I. Posner. Cambridge, Mass.: MIT Press.

Deschamps, Jean-Claude, and Willem Doise. 1978. "Crossed Category Memberships in Intergroup Relations." In *Differentiation Between Social Groups*, edited by Henri Tajfel. London: Academic Press.

Durkheim, Emile. 1974 [1898]. *Individual and Collective Representations: Sociology and Philosophy*. New York: Free Press.

Farr, Robert M. 1993. "Common Sense, Science and Social Representation." *Public Understanding of Science* 7: 189–204.

Fiske, Alan P. 1991. *Making Up Society: The Four Basic Relational Studies*. New York: Free Press.

Fiske, Alan P., Shinobu Kitayama, Hazel R. Markus, and Richard E. Nisbett. 1998. "The Cultural Matrix of Social Psychology." In *Handbook of Social Psychology*, edited by Daniel T. Gilbert, Susan T. Fiske, and Gardner Lindzey. New York: McGraw-Hill.

Fredrickson, George M. 1999. "Models of American Ethnic Relations: A Historical Perspective." In *Cultural Divides: Understanding and Overcoming Group Conflict*, edited by Deborah A. Prentice and Dale T. Miller. New York: Russell Sage Foundation.

Gaertner, Samuel L., and John F. Dovidio. 1981. "Racism Among the Well-intentioned." In *Pluralism, Racism, and Public Policy: The Search for Equality*, edited by Edwin G. Clausen and Jack Bermingham. Boston: G. K. Hall.

———. 1986. "The Aversive Form of Racism." In *Prejudice, Discrimination, and Racism: Theory and Research*, edited by John F. Dovidio and Samuel L. Gaertner. Orlando, Fla.: Academic Press.

———. 1997. "On the Nature of Contemporary Prejudice: The Causes, Consequences, and Challenges of Aversive Racism." In *Racism: The Problem and the Response*, edited by Jennifer L. Eberhardt and Susan T. Fiske. Thousand Oaks, Calif.: Sage.

Gaertner, Samuel L., John F. Dovidio, Phyllis A. Anastasio, Betty A. Bachman, and Mary C. Rust. 1993. "The Common Ingroup Identity Model: Recategorization and the Reduction of Intergroup Bias." In *European Review of Social Psychology*, edited by Wolfgang Stroebe and Miles Hewstone. Chichester, U.K.: Wiley.

Gaertner, Samuel L., Mary C. Rust, John F. Dovidio, Betty A. Bachman, and Phyllis A. Anastasio. 1994. "The Contact Hypothesis: The Role of a Common Ingroup Identity on Reducing Intergroup Bias." *Small Group Research* 25(2): 224–49.

———. 1996. "The Contact Hypothesis: The Role of a Common Ingroup Identity on Reducing Intergroup Bias Among Majority and Minority Group Members." In *What's Social About Social Cognition? Research on Socially Shared Cognition in Small Groups*, edited by Judith L. Nye and Aaron M. Brower. Thousand Oaks, Calif.: Sage.

Giddens, Anthony. 1990. *The Consequences of Modernity*. Stanford: Stanford University Press.

Grant, Peter R. 1993. "Reactions to Intergroup Similarity: Examination of the Similarity-Differentiation and the Similarity-Attraction Hypotheses." *Canadian Journal of Behavioural Science* 25: 28–44.

Harris, Marvin. 1979. *Cultural Materialism: The Struggle for a Science of Culture*. New York: Random House.

Hermans, Hubert J., and Harry J. Kempen. 1998. "Moving Cultures: The Perilous Problems of Cultural Dichotomies in a Globalizing Society." *American Psychologist* 52: 1111–20.

Hewstone, Miles, and Rupert Brown. 1986. "Contact Is Not Enough: An Intergroup Perspective." In *Contact and Conflict in Intergroup Encounters*, edited by Miles Hewstone and Rupert Brown. Oxford: Blackwell.

Hochschild, Jennifer L. 1995. *Facing Up to the American Dream: Race, Class, and the Soul of the Nation.* Princeton, N.J.: Princeton University Press.

Hofstede, Geert. 1980. *Culture's Consequences.* Beverly Hills, Calif.: Sage.

Hornsey, Matthew J., and Michael A. Hogg. 2000a. "Intergroup Similarity and Subgroup Relations: Some Implications for Assimilation." *Personality and Social Psychology Bulletin* 26(8): 948–58.

———. 2000b. "Subgroup Relations: A Comparison of Mutual Intergroup Differentiation and Common Ingroup Identity Models of Prejudice Reduction." *Personality and Social Psychology Bulletin* 26(2): 242–56.

Jones, James M. 1997 [1972]. *Prejudice and Racism.* Reprint, Reading, Mass.: Addison-Wesley.

Jones, James M., Patrick D. Lynch, Amanda A. Teglund, and Samuel L. Gaertner. 2000. "Toward a Diversity Hypothesis: Multidimensional Effects of Intergroup Contact." *Applied & Preventive Psychology* 9: 53–62.

Kuhn, Thomas S. 1962. *The Structure of Scientific Revolutions.* Chicago: University of Chicago Press.

LeVine, Robert A., and Donald T. Campbell. 1972. *Ethnocentrism: Theories of Conflict, Ethnic Attitudes and Group Behaviour.* New York: John Wiley.

Markus, Hazel R., and Shinobu Kitayama. 1991. "Culture and the Self: Implications for Cognition, Emotion, and Motivation." *Psychological Review* 98: 224–53.

Markus, Hazel R., Shinobu Kitayama, and Rachel Heiman. 1986. "Culture and Basic Psychological Principles." In *Social Psychology: Handbook of Basic Principles*, edited by E. Tory Higgins and Arie W. Kruglanski. New York: Guilford Press.

Markus, Hazel R., Patricia R. Mullally, and Shinobu Kitayama. 1997. "Selfways: Diversity in Modes of Cultural Participation." In *The Conceptual Self in Context*, edited by Ulric Neisser and David A. Jopling. New York: Cambridge University Press.

Miller, Norman, and Marilynn Brewer. 1986. "Categorization Effects on Ingroup and Outgroup Perception." In *Prejudice, Discrimination, and Racism: Theory and Research*, edited by John F. Dovidio and Samuel L. Gaertner. Orlando, Fla.: Academic Press.

Moscovici, Serge. 1973. Preface. In *Health and Illness: A Social Psychological Analysis*, by C. Herzlich. London: Academic Press.

———. 1984. "The Phenomenon of Social Representations." In *Social Representations*, edited by Robert M. Farr and Serge Moscovici. Cambridge: Cambridge University Press.

———. 1998. "The History and Actuality of Social Representations." In *The Psychology of the Social*, edited by Uwe Flick. Cambridge: Cambridge University Press.

Newcomb, Theodore M. 1961. *The Acquaintance Process.* New York: Holt, Rhinehart and Winston.

Ogbu, John U. 1994. "Racial Stratification and Education in the United States: Why Inequality Persists." *Teachers College Record* 96(2): 265–98.

Oyserman, Daphna, and Hazel R. Markus. 1998. "Self as Social Representation." In *The Psychology of the Social*, edited by Uwe Flick. Cambridge: Cambridge University Press.

Pettigrew, Thomas F. 1969. "Racially Separate or Together?" *Journal of Social Issues* 25(1): 43–69.

———. 1988. "Integration and Pluralism." In *Eliminating Racism: Profiles in Controversy*, edited by Phyllis A. Katz and Dalmas A. Taylor. New York: Plenum Press.

Plaut, Victoria C., and Hazel R. Markus. 2002. "'Essentially We're All the Same': Ideological Challenges to Diversity in America." Unpublished paper. Stanford University.

Purdie, Valerie, Claude M. Steele, and Jennifer R. Crosby. 2000. "Implications of Models of

Difference for African American College Students." Unpublished paper. Stanford University.

Quinn, Naomi, and Dorothy Holland. 1987. "Culture and Cognition." In *Cultural Models in Language and Thought*, edited by Dorothy Holland and Naomi Quinn. Cambridge: Cambridge University Press.

Rist, Ray C. 1974. "Race, Policy, and Schooling." *Society* 12(1): 59–63.

Ross, Lee, and Richard E. Nisbett. 1991. *The Person and the Situation: Perspectives of Social Psychology*. New York: McGraw-Hill.

Schofield, Janet W. 1986a. "Black-White Contact in Desegregated Schools." In *Contact and Conflict in Intergroup Encounters*, edited by Miles Hewstone and Rupert Brown. Oxford: Blackwell.

———. 1986b. "Causes and Consequences of the Colorblind Perspective." In *Prejudice, Discrimination, and Racism*, edited by John F. Dovidio and Samuel L. Gaertner. New York: Academic Press.

Sherif, Muzafer. 1966. *In Common Predicament: Social Psychology of Group Conflict and Cooperation*. Boston: Houghton Mifflin.

Sherif, Muzafer, O. J. Harvey, B. Jack White, William R. Hood, and Carolyn W. Sherif. 1961. *Intergroup Conflict and Cooperation: The Robbers' Cave Experiment*. Norman: Oklahoma Book Exchange.

Shore, Bradd. 1996. Culture in mind: Cognition, culture, and the problem of meaning. New York: Oxford University Press.

Shweder, Richard A. 1990. "Cultural Psychology: What Is It?" In *Cultural Psychology: Essays on Comparative Human Development*, edited by James W. Stigler, Richard A. Shweder, and Gilbert Herdt. Cambridge: Cambridge University Press.

———. 1991. *Thinking Through Cultures: Expeditions in Cultural Psychology*. Cambridge, Mass.: Harvard University Press.

Sperber, Dan. 1985. "Anthropology and Psychology: Towards an Epidemiology of Representations." *Man* 20: 73–89.

Spindler, George D., and Louise S. Spindler. 1990. *The American Cultural Dialogue and Its Transmission*. New York: Falmer Press.

Tajfel, Henri. 1969. "Cognitive Aspects of Prejudice." *Journal of Social Issues* 25(4): 79–97.

———. 1982. *Social Identity and Intergroup Relations*. London: Cambridge University Press.

Tajfel, Henri, Michael G. Billig, R. P. Bundy, and Claude Flament. 1971. "Social Categorization and Intergroup Behaviour." *European Journal of Social Psychology* 1(2): 149–78.

Tajfel, Henri, and John C. Turner. 1979. "An Integrative Theory of Intergroup Conflict." In *The Social Psychology of Intergroup Relations*, edited by William G. Austin and Stephen Worchel. Monterey, Calif.: Brooks-Cole.

Taylor, Dalmas A. 1974. "Should We Integrate Organizations?" In *Integrating the Organization*, edited by Howard L. Fromkin and John J. Sherwood. New York: Free Press.

Thomas, David A., and Robin J. Ely. 1996. "Making Differences Matter: A New Paradigm for Managing Diversity." *Harvard Business Review* 74: 79–90.

Triandis, Harry C. 1988. "The Future of Pluralism Revisited." In *Eliminating Racism: Profiles in Controversy*, edited by Phyllis A. Katz and Dalmas A. Taylor. New York: Plenum Press.

———. 1995. *Individualism and Collectivism*. Boulder, Colo.: Westview Press.

Turner, John C. 1981. "The Experimental Social Psychology of Intergroup Behavior." In *Intergroup Behavior*, edited by John C. Turner and Howard Giles. Oxford: Blackwell.

———. 1987. *Rediscovering the Social Group: A Self-Categorization Theory*. Oxford: Blackwell.

Weber, Max. 1958 [1904]. *The Protestant Ethic and the Spirit of Capitalism*, translated by T. Parsons. New York: Scribner.

Wolsko, Christopher, Bernadette Park, Charles M. Judd, and B. Wittenbrink. 2000. "Framing Interethnic Ideology: Effects of Multicultural and Color-Blind Perspectives on Judgements of Groups and Individuals." *Journal of Personality and Social Psychology* 78(4): 635–54.

Worchel, Stephen, D. Axsom, F. Ferris, G. Samaha, and S. Schweizer. 1978. "Determinants of the Effect of Intergroup Co-operation on Intergroup Attraction." *Journal of Conflict Resolution* 22: 429–39.

# Chapter 18

# The Micropolitics of Identity-Difference: Recognition and Accommodation in Everyday Life

Austin Sarat

> [P]rovidence has been pleased to give this one connected country to one united people—a people descended from the same ancestors, speaking the same language, professing the same religion, attached to the same principles of government, very similar in their manners and customs.
> —John Jay, *Federalist Papers* (1964 [1787])

> We are not an assimilative, homogeneous society, but a facilitative, pluralistic one, in which we must be willing to abide by someone else's unfamiliar or even repellant practice because the same tolerant impulse protects our own idiosyncrasies."
> —Justice Brennan, *Michael H. v. Gerald D.* (1989)

In its January 20, 1992, issue, *People* ran a story entitled "Die, My Daughter, Die!" that described the murder of Tina Isa, sixteen-year-old daughter of Palestinian emigrés Zein and Maria Isa who, with their seven children, came to the United States from the West Bank in 1985. While the other Isa children consistently adhered to the strict, traditional values of their Palestinian parents, Tina quickly began to assimilate to the anything but traditional values of American adolescence. Tina as well as her brothers and sisters all had been forbidden to go on school trips, to concerts, to visit friends on weekends, or to date. Unlike her siblings, however, Tina refused to abide by these prohibitions. Defying her parents, Tina took a job as a counter girl at Wendy's fast-food restaurant and dated an African American schoolmate. In so doing, she violated long-standing Arab understandings concerning appropriate behavior for young women and, in the eyes of her parents, brought shame and dishonor on the family name.

Opposite a half-page photo of her father in a blood-stained sweater, the *People* article detailed how Tina's father had hoped to arrange a marriage for her, as he had done for her three older sisters (*People* 1992). Zein wanted Tina to return to his native village and marry a relative of one of his sons-in-law. To do this required that she be a virgin.

Tina resented and resisted her father's plans concerning her marriage. As a result, they had frequent fights during which her father warned her about her offensive behavior (for example, allowing herself to be seen in public with her boyfriend) and threatened to vindicate the family's damaged honor. On the night of Tina's death, Zein again confronted her and accused her of shaming the family by virtue of her allegedly promiscuous behavior and, while Maria (Tina's mother) held her down, he stabbed her to death with a seven-inch knife. *People* quotes an anthropologist—born and raised in Jerusalem—who said that "the way Tina lived offended her father's sense of honor." He continued, "'Everyone growing up [as Tina had] in the Middle East knows being killed is a possible consequence of dishonoring the family'" (*People* 1992, 71; see also Abu Odeh 1984).

Charged with first-degree murder, the Isas sought to raise the so-called cultural defense (see "Cultural Defense in Criminal Law" 1986; "Cultural Defense" 1987; "The "Availability of the 'Cultural Defense'" 1986; Renteln 1987–1988). They claimed that they could not justifiably be found guilty, since what they did to Tina would not have been treated as a crime in their homeland. This defense failed, as it generally does (see, for example, *People v. Helen Wu* 1991; *Trujillo-Garcia v. Rowland* 1992; *State v. Aires Correia* 1991; *People v. Kimura* 1985; *People v. Kong Moua* 1985), and the Isas each were convicted of first-degree murder and sentenced to death.

One response to the tragic story of Tina Isa's death is to worry about the us versus them dynamic that stories such as the *People* portrait of the Isas conjure up. "We," *People* suggests, would never do the kind of thing that Zein and Maria did; "they" do such things (Connolly 1991).[1] Another response is to use stories such as Tina's to call into question how difference is constituted and given meaning in popular culture and most especially in the institutional practices of American law.

The story of Tina Isa provides a vivid image of the drama and dilemma of cultural difference in a nation of many peoples. Cultural differences provide building blocks for as well as barriers to the achievement of a system of values and way of life that is recognizably American. The honor code invoked by Tina's parents is an example of the kind of meaningful cultural commitments frequently romanticized by those who seek to retrieve what they perceive to be the lost ideals of community and solidarity.

To be an American is to live an ambivalent relationship to difference (Gordon 1981, 454; Post 1988, 297): it is to be a neighbor to difference and at the same time harbor suspicions that difference may be our national undoing, that differences can never be bridged, and that without assimilation, disorder lurks just below the surface of our national life (Schlesinger 1992). Yet beyond the dramatic appeal of such an understanding and such cases as Tina's, difference is an integral part of American culture; America is a hybrid nation. Difference, and the daily life it generates, has been a part of the cultural life of Americans since the nation's founding (Tocqueville 1876 [1835]).[2]

To whatever extent the many races, ethnicities, and identities that compose America have or have not amalgamated, the perception and fear that America would be a nation of many peoples who would not "amalgamate" has prompted a strong desire for sameness and community. Evidenced in such disparate sources as John Jay's celebration of our unity and in the aspirations of contemporary civic republicans, this desire creates what Michael Kammen (1972, 128) calls "A dialectic of pluralism and conformity"; that dialectic, Kammen argues, lies "at the core of American life." While embracing freedom and diversity, Americans value connection; we strive to remain individuals but also wish to be a people. This dialectic of pluralism and conformity lies at the core of what here is referred to as the everyday life of identity-difference, especially as it is played out in the routine practices of communities and institutions.

Tina Isa's death is only one type of identity-difference story. Hers is an example of difference turned violent, and of a cultural claim made for exemption from the reach of otherwise valid laws. It is a story of what elsewhere I have called *disorderly difference*—that which threatens the allegedly fragile harmony and stability of this nation of immigrants (Sarat and Berkowitz 1994, 285).

When acted on, disorderly differences violently and brutally impose themselves on others. Disorderly differences, like the familial honor code that justified Tina's murder, forcefully raise the question of when and how differences can (and should) be recognized and accommodated (Minow 1990; 1991). They require us to ask whether we can or should justify or excuse conduct that, while it may seem reprehensible to us, reflects a deeply felt cultural or religious conviction. Yet could they be the wrong kinds of stories from which to understand the politics of identity-difference and claims for the free exercise of culture in the United States?

If all we had were stories such as that of Tina Isa, we might conclude rightly that the identity-difference issues confronted in this society were just another variation of the unresolved universalism versus relativism debates among philosophers and academics. Indeed, we might conclude that the more difference is recognized, the more vexing the effort to accommodate difference in our institutional lives and practices becomes (Minow 1990). As the *People* story suggests, difference frequently appears to be the fearsome presence within rather than the enlivening wellspring of democratic politics. Difference is a source of dread, a fear of the unknown, an "apprehension of a future heavy with the possibility of danger" (Craft 1992, 521).

Stories like that of Tina Isa regularly make national news, riveting our attention to the seemingly threatening presence of cultural difference and the seemingly irreconcilable demands of justice on one hand, and cultural recognition on the other. Yet they constitute only one end of a continuum in which claims to the free exercise of culture are asserted. Some of these claims, like the Isas' cultural defense, are disruptive and dramatic; others are barely visible and cause little stir. In between are a variety of ways of asserting and responding to these claims. This chapter examines the way institutions and practices in the United

States are being altered to accommodate difference, such that the politics of recognition can, with some confidence, be said to be alive and well in what I call the everyday life of identity-difference.

## THE IDEA OF THE EVERYDAY

While the idea of the everyday appears episodically and variously in a range of research and theory, from the phenomenology of Alfred Schutz (1967) to the critical Marxism of Henri Lefebvre (1991), it is not an ordinary and familiar concept in social and legal analysis (Douglas 1970). In contemporary social theory, feminism now often carries the banner of the everyday—that being the world most often inhabited by women (MacKinnon 1987). While in feminist scholarship the everyday is called the "private," elsewhere it is variously styled the "life world," "the realm of the ordinary," and "the domain of the banal."

No matter what it is called, claims made about the everyday as a category of analysis and grounds for theory sometimes are quite extravagant. As one example, Lefebvre (1991) argues, "In so far as the science of man exists, it finds its material in the 'trivial', the everyday." Precisely because the trivial is not trivial, the everyday in Lefebrve's view might become the basis for a science of man.

Where such grand claims are not made, the everyday nonetheless often is used as a trope of authenticity and a standard of critique. The everyday is the domain of unalienated experience, the "life world" that is contrasted to what Habermas (1984, 337) calls the world of "communicative action," of discursive rationality, instrumental action, choice, design, and project. Praising the former while understanding the inexorable pull of the latter is one way of giving dignity to ordinary persons and the ordinary in all persons. The everyday is the domain of situated, bounded, local place and time; it is the domain of the human against the technological superhumanness of the modern, and it reminds us of the alienation and dangers of our era (Habermas 1975; Simmel 1978; Gabel 1980, 28–29). As Lefebvre (1991, 127) asks,

> Is it not in everyday life that man should fulfill his life as a man? The theory of superhuman moments is inhuman. Is it not in day-to-day life . . . that the truth in a body and a soul must be grasped? If a higher life, the life of the "spirit", was to be attained in "another life" . . . it would be the end of mankind, the proof and proclamation of his failure. Man must be everyday, or he will not be at all.

Thus Lefebrve and others see the defense and rehabilitation of everyday life as an essential political gesture that begins in critique and ends in social transformation (Heller 1984). The everyday becomes the uncriticized critique, the here and now, the un(self)conscious present, juxtaposed to the abstraction and artifice of the artistic, the bureaucratic, the technological, the dramatic. The everyday is the immediate and the familiar juxtaposed to the distant, strange, and cosmopolitan (Lefebvre 1991).[3] The everyday is origin and home, point of departure, and place of return.

In the work of Schutz (Schutz and Luckmann 1973) and Habermas (1984) among others, the so-called life world is pretheoretical and prescientific: it is the background for the projects of reason and science (Zizek 1989), the world of the taken for granted, and

> the reality which seems self evident to men. . . . This reality is the everyday life-world. It is the province of reality in which men continuously participate in ways which are inevitable and patterned. . . . The world of everyday life is consequently man's fundamental and paramount reality. . . . It is the unexamined ground of everything given in my experience . . . the taken-for-granted frame in which all the problems which I must overcome are placed. (Schutz and Luckman 1973, 3–4)

Since it is self-evident and taken for granted, the everyday always sits just beyond the grasp of those who live in and with it; it always contains the dim perception of a horizon, never reached. The everyday contains its own compression of time and space, being at once an assurance and a suggestion, a present and an unknowable future. Thus the everyday is that which goes without saying, because it cannot be said; it is the word on the tip of the tongue that never completely issues forth. As Maurice Blanchot (1987, 14–15) puts it,

> Whatever its other aspects, the everyday has this essential trait: it allows no hold. It escapes. . . . This makes its strangeness—the familiar showing itself . . . in the guise of the astonishing. It is unperceived, first in the sense that one has always looked past it . . . the everyday is always unrealized in its very actualization. . . . Nothing happens, that is the everyday.

Blanchot helps plot a way of thinking about the everyday that frees it from its status as the always solid, always reliable other to modernity's alienating movement. The everyday, as Blanchot understands it, need be neither an object of nostalgia nor a remnant of the tranquil, quiet, locally contained life of some bygone, Andy-of-Mayberry place and time. The everyday is and has always been a premonition of the modern experience, and it always partakes in the elusive known, but unknowable, quality of that experience.[4]

Seen in this way, the everyday is a domain of action as well as events, and of production as well as of an imperceptible taken-for-grantedness. Since it is a scene of action and production, we can turn to the everyday to see the way dramatic problems and complex practices are reenacted and remade far from the well-recognized, well-marked sites of their most well-publicized occurrences (Geertz 1983). This is as true in the domain of the politics of identity-difference as in other areas of our social and cultural lives.

The Micropolitics of Identity-Difference

## THE EVERYDAY LIFE OF IDENTITY-DIFFERENCE: EXAMPLES FROM CLOSE TO HOME

In the everyday world of identity-difference in the contemporary United States, recognition and accommodation—including important alterations in the practices of hospitals, welfare bureaucracies, and schools—are much more pervasive than scenes of dramatic conflict. Sometimes such alterations come about through visible struggles, sometimes through seemingly routine efforts to reform or alter outmoded ways of doing business, sometimes in response to the overt articulation of demands, sometimes as a result of quiet, behind-the-scenes negotiation. Moreover, as we will see, recognition and accommodation often come as an after-the-fact acknowledgment of changes that make difference simply a fact of everyday life. As Alexander and Smelser (1999, 17) put it, "Faced with the pressures of growing institutional complexity and cultural diversity, new forms of democratic integration have developed. Those working at the grass roots of American society have created new, normatively sanctioned institutional arrangements and new ways to negotiate conflicts."

Scholars interested in the politics of recognition need to pay attention to cases all across the continuum on which claims of difference occur. We must attend as much to the grass roots, to micropolitics of difference, and to the everyday practices of recognition and accommodation as we do to dramatic, attention-grabbing cases such as that of Tina Isa. If and when we do, we will be able to chart the terms on which such accommodations are made and the various ways in which cultural difference and multiculturalism are transforming, often in barely visible ways, the fabric of American life.

In the rest of this chapter I discuss two examples of what I call the everyday life of identity-differences taken from the town in which I live. I offer them not because I think either that this town or the examples which I describe are representative of the situation in the entire nation or indeed that they are the best examples of the everyday world in which identity-difference is recognized and accommodated, but because they may suggest a pattern that is worth investigating or attending to elsewhere.

A headline in my local newspaper, "Parents Object to 'West Side Story' Production," announced the controversy about the politics of the recognition and accommodation of identity-difference in Amherst, Massachusetts (*Amherst Bulletin*, November 5, 1999).[5] The choice of the annual spring musical at the Amherst Regional High School became newsworthy when members of the town's Puerto Rican community objected to *West Side Story*.

"It is a very racist play," said Elizabeth Capifali, a native New Yorker of Puerto Rican descent. Capifali, who started the protest, claimed that the play is filled with racial stereotypes. "It portrays Puerto Ricans in a negative light, hanging out on street corners, participating in gang violence." Hers was a generational protest, carried out in the name of a new generation against the taken-for-granted representational practices of an earlier generation. In an effort to stop the musical, Capifali wrote a letter to the play's directors saying that "The play is replete with racial discrimination, creating negative images of Puerto Ricans and poor European immigrants. . . . How do you think this addresses the goals of Becoming a Multicultural School System?" she asked, calling attention to the school district's program that aims to adjust curriculum and programs to recognize and accommodate cultural difference in the community.

That Amherst has the explicit goal of Becoming a Multicultural School System (BAMSS) is perhaps one mark of the town's unrepresentativeness. Nonetheless, this goal has played a large role in reorienting the politics of identity-difference in the schools. As the superintendent of schools explained,

> When I was hired as superintendent, which was over ten years ago now, the School Committee identified for me dealing with issues of cultural diversity in our community as one of the large challenges the new superintendent would face. What I discovered was that there were a lot of activities in the schools that had begun ten or twenty years before I got here that were directed toward multicultural education and affirmative action, toward making this an environment in which students and teachers had a great deal of respect for one another and that everyone was appreciated. What was lacking was any real commitment or leadership from administrators and the School Committee. Beginning in 1991 I pulled together a group to talk about what it meant to be a diverse school district and what kind of goals we had to set for ourselves. A year later we brought a mission statement and goals to the School Committee which they approved. . . . More recently we have reconstituted and reinvigorated the BAMSS steering committee to examine implementation and monitor progress in achieving the BAMSS goals.

According to the BAMSS mission statement, the Amherst schools seek "to provide all students with a high quality education that enables them to be contributing members of a multiethnic, multicultural, pluralistic society. We seek to create an environment that achieves equity for all students and ensures that each student is a successful learner, is fully respected, and learns to respect others." To achieve this mission, BAMSS focuses on five areas: curriculum and instruction, affirmative action, professional development, student achievement, and institutional practices. In each area, goals are identified to make the Amherst schools more accommodating to identity-difference concerns. In the area of institutional practices, the superintendent explained, BAMSS "really gets into the issue of how people in the schools . . . respond to differences in the community. . . . What kinds of accommodations do the schools have to make in order to invite all peoples into the school on some sort of equal basis." This was the area toward which the complaint about *West Side Story* was addressed.

Others joined Mrs. Capifali in protesting the choice of musical, including a Puerto Rican member of the school board who said that "as a Puerto Rican I feel totally offended." Promising to raise the issue with the committee, he announced, "I will boycott the play if it is produced." Predictably, these claims of cultural insensitivity initially were resisted. The teacher responsible for directing the production, while acknowledging that "The depiction of students in gangs and the absence of positive depiction of Latinos . . . has concerned us," argued that the message of the story is not racism but rather that of children leading adults to confront cultural difference. She said that while she thought the production should go on, it should be accompanied by a panel discussion and discussions in middle- and high-school classes focusing on issues raised by the Puerto Rican community.

Following the initial complaints were a series of meetings among leaders of the Puerto Rican community, which was itself divided over the appropriateness of staging the musical, and of concerned parents, teachers, and school administrators. Everyone seemed to agree that the controversy surrounding *West Side Story* should be used to advance the BAMSS goals.

For a while, it looked like no accommodation could or would be reached. The school superintendent issued public statements opposing what he called "censorship." "No group," he said, "neither in the majority nor in the minority, should have the ability to censor the decisions of our community's educators make about what to teach, what to read, or what to produce on the stage." Discussion occurred at a meeting of the School Committee, but no resolution was reached. Petitions were circulated and signed, with coalitions forming across cultural lines and divisions deepening in the Puerto Rican community.[6]

Negotiations continued behind the scenes, which exposed the fact that racial, cultural, or identity groups often do not confront issues of recognition and accommodation in a unified fashion, and that demands for recognition and accommodation—put forward by some as the minimum condition for genuine inclusion in a community—may be seen by others as a form of blackmail masquerading as victimization. Eventually, an accommodation was reached. *West Side Story* was canceled, and the issues it had sparked would be worked into classes at the middle school and high school. At first, all sides declared victory, claiming that the real beneficiaries would be students of all heritages who would have an opportunity together to take steps on the path of multicultural progress.

Yet the debate about the musical and its relation to the town's effort to accommodate difference quickly escalated as a result of the decision to cancel the production. Video stores reported a sudden surge in rentals of *West Side Story*. Echoing the school superintendent's concerns about censorship, some parents and citizens organized demonstrations to protest the cancellation and to pressure the high school principal to do something other than to let the cancellation of the play slip quietly into Amherst's history. They urged that the production's cancellation become a subject of discussion in the school and in town, some even calling for a community staging of the musical (*Amherst Bulletin* 1999). Further, in what some residents saw as an ironic twist, what had been a local effort to accommodate identity-difference took on the dimensions of a *People* magazine event. Cancellation of the production moved this case toward the divisive and dramatic end of the identity-difference continuum, in which accommodation of difference appears to some to threaten cherished values. National media picked up the story, and national groups (in this instance, the People for the American Way, a First Amendment protection group) threatened to stage its own production in Amherst and to recruit Rita Moreno, who won a 1961 Academy Award for her portrayal in the film, to speak to the townspeople (*Amherst Bulletin* 1999). What had seemed to be an instance of the daily life of the recognition and accommodation of identity-difference quickly was turned into a skirmish in a culture war.

Almost four years earlier, another headline in the local newspaper seemed to proclaim that a skirmish in culture wars would be played out in Amherst. In this instance, however, the schools' own efforts to recognize and accommodate identity-difference sparked the controversy. The headline proclaimed, "Exhibit Proposal Brings Controversy: Gay Family Photos May Be Shown in Elementary Schools" (*Amherst Bulletin*, January 19, 1996).

That exhibit, "Love Makes a Family: Living in Lesbian and Gay Families," containing twenty photos and captions, was created by a trio of local residents who without incident had presented a similar exhibit on multiracial families in the schools several years earlier. The photographer and writers of "Love Makes a Family," with the support of the Amherst Gay, Lesbian, and Bisexual Parent Network and the High School Gay Lesbian Alliance, first presented a proposal to the school superintendent to show the exhibit in the high school, middle school, and the four elementary schools in the district. The superintendent told them that due to other commitments in the elementary schools he was not prepared to host the exhibit there, but that they should bring it to the high school, where it was shown without incident in October 1995.

When the producers of the exhibit subsequently contacted him about mounting the show in the elementary schools, the superintendent said he would leave the determination of the appropriateness of presenting "Love Makes a Family" in elementary schools to the principals of each school, subject to the proviso that they consult with their respective school councils, which include teachers and parents, before determining whether the exhibit would be shown.

During January 1996, as that process of consultation got under way, opposition mounted. Initially, it was led by teachers who made arguments that seem quite familiar in the ongoing debate about identity-difference in the United States. Some teachers said that they were concerned about being required to talk to children about an issue that parents might prefer to address. Others worried that "schools could take on so many social issues that teachers won't have time to deal with the regular curriculum." Still others suggested that showing an exhibit of gay and lesbian families would promote division in the schools. "It would be better," one teacher said, "if the pictures were part of a larger exhibit on all kinds of families and fit in with the curriculum unit on families." Finally, a former leader of the local teachers union came out against the exhibit on the grounds that the schools should not be selective in their embrace of and respect for difference. "Would there be an exhibit of little Catholic girls making Holy Communion or of men with guns and dead deer? I'm not sure the school system would validate the children of hunters."

In spite of this opposition, each of the principals seemed disposed to host the exhibit, following the protocol that was used for the exhibit on multiracial families, namely, placing the photos in the foyer or the main hallway of the school so that every student would see it. One principal said he believed that "the exhibit would build understanding among the entire community and help any student whose parent is gay or lesbian feel safer and more welcome in the school. It will prepare students to live in a pluralist society. Some may wish," he continued, "that they lived in a world populated by people just like themselves, but that is pure fantasy. It is the job of the public schools to prepare students to live in the world as it is."

Another principal said that the exhibit was a response to certain "facts":

If you come from a family with two moms or two dads, you are likely to be the object of teasing and name-calling. What is different is, especially for young children, threatening, so they react by trying to distance themselves from it. I would like to see that end. We need to inform kids of the importance of accepting difference and to try to ward off bias and prejudice that kids pick up at an early age.

A third principal explained his support for the exhibit this way:

We no longer live in a "Father Knows Best" world in which everyone is white, heterosexual, well off, and under the domination of a man. We can act like we do, and try to keep the schools from recognizing the worlds from which our students come, but that would be a deep disservice to them and to the community at large. Do we imagine that the children of Amherst, Massachusetts do not see gay and lesbian families on the streets, in the supermarkets, at the movies? Schools have to deal with facts on the ground. That should be the guiding value as we think about cultural difference. If there are kids from gay and lesbian families in schools, and there are, we have several choices. We can ignore that fact or act as if that difference makes no difference. Or we can try to come to terms with it, recognizing the student population for what it is, helping everyone come to terms with the way the world really is.

This refrain, dealing with "the way the world really is" or dealing "with facts on the ground," was crucial to the micropolitics of identity-difference as it played out around the gay and lesbian families exhibit. Those in favor of recognition and accommodation presented their position as if they were merely reacting, coping, coming to terms with changes that already had taken place. While the emerging default rule in Amherst seems to be recognition and accommodation, at least in regard to "Love Makes a Family," the schools were ready to practice only what might be called *defensive* or *reactive* accommodation.

Yet even this reactive or defensive posture did not appease critics who, as the principals came out in favor of the exhibit, moved their fight to the School Committee. They hoped that in a more openly political environment, their concerns would receive a more receptive response. In meetings with the School Committee, parents opposing the exhibit claimed that it could not be shown in a purely neutral, informational manner. They argued that the exhibit constituted advocacy of a particular way of living, and that such advocacy was inappropriate for schools that should be serving all members of the community—including those for whom gay and lesbian lifestyles were abhorrent.

Eventually, the committee decided not to take a stand on the question of whether to allow the exhibit to be shown in the elementary schools, at the same time reminding principals of the need to follow the school system's so-called controversial issues policy, which states,

> The School Committee believes that controversy is an essential part of the democratic process and that an important goal of public education is to help students to develop the capacity to respectfully, critically and positively participate in the discussion and analysis of controversial issues. . . . Discussion and analysis of controversial issues has a legitimate place in our schools and should enable all participants to learn from one another. All staff and students have a right to express their opinions and a right to a respectful hearing. . . . Teachers will offer students and parents who might be offended by a presentation because of their religious or personal beliefs the opportunity not to participate in a presentation.

Immediately after the committee's refusal to intervene, one principal announced in the school newsletter that the school would host the exhibit. As she explained her decision, she noted,

> I would like to make it clear that we are not advocating anything but a commitment to having a school where children are free from the harm of oppressive language, harassment and put-downs. That is the driving force behind our decision to host the exhibit. It will provide an impetus for discussion. It is a vehicle for making visible a segment of our families who have, for a variety of reasons, been "invisible" members of our community. It can help us reinforce the belief that all families deserve respectful treatment within our community. . . . At the direction of the Amherst School Committee we will treat discussions of the exhibit in accordance with the committee's Policy on Controversial Issues. This means that before holding class discussions specifically related to the exhibit, parents/guardians will be given the opportunity to have their children exempted.

Still another principal announced his decision in a letter sent to all families.

> I have decided that we will host the exhibit. . . . We will put it in the context of a broader "celebration of families." Many people said that they would support the exhibit if it included a wide range of families. No such

exhibit has been offered to us so we will create one by inviting every student and staff member to display a photo or drawing of their family at the same time the photo-text exhibit is on display. . . . Both the display by the artists and our "homemade" display will be exhibited in the hallways for everyone to see. This will accomplish several important purposes. . . . It will provide all students with an opportunity to share and acknowledge their families proudly, affirming that everyone matters and is included. It will provide us with a special opportunity to teach that mistreatment of anyone is wrong. . . . However, the school will not endorse, and teachers will be directed not to endorse, any lifestyle.

Neither the School Committee's action nor these responses quelled the controversy. Several gay and lesbian parents were troubled with the opt-out possibility, saying that it allowed those most in need of confronting and accepting the facts about their families to avoid doing so. Here one form of accommodation seemed to conflict with what some took to be central to the goals of another form. Thus gay and lesbian parents argued that all students should be required to see and discuss the exhibit, as had been the case during the showing of photographs of biracial families, and that anything less would suggest something shameful about their families. Others argued that embedding the photographs of gay and lesbian families in an exhibit about all families missed the point. As one lesbian mother put it, "This is the worst perversion of tolerance and inclusion. We are yet again rendered invisible, or barely visible, made yet again into an oddity among all the smiling heterosexual families. The heterosexual family hardly needs to be acknowledged proudly. Why can't people stand to look into our faces and the faces of our families, without hiding those faces among hundreds of others?"

For fundamentalist opponents of the exhibit, neither the opt-out solution nor the proposal to include "Love Makes a Family" in an exhibit with photographs of other families went far enough. As a result, several families retained a lawyer and threatened suit. In a letter to the superintendent, the School Committee, and the elementary school principals announcing this intention, their lawyer stated,

I represent a large and growing group of Amherst parents who oppose the decision to bring a photography exhibit entitled "Living in Gay and Lesbian Families" to the several Amherst Elementary schools. . . . The parents want me to be clear that they fiercely resent your proposal to teach their children things that conflict with their deeply held religious and moral beliefs and that contradict their example and home training. The text accompanying the exhibit advocates a radical re-definition of marriage, patronizes widely held moral views of sexuality, and promotes acceptance of a lifestyle which many find morally and legally objectionable. It is advocacy, not diversity and tolerance education. . . . Many parents of all faiths the world over have deeply held religious convictions about the definition of marriage and the sanctity of monogamous sexuality, which they have tried to teach their children by precept, by example, and by exposure to religious training. Your exhibit teaches the children that their parental and religious training is of no importance, by saying that what they have been taught as wrong is actually right.

The lawyer further alleged that showing the exhibit would violate the School Committee's controversial issues policy requiring the presentation of differing viewpoints. "A truly even-handed alternative," he claimed, "would be a presentation of diverse religious viewpoints on homosexuality." The lawyer said that at the very least, the exhibit must be "isolated, with viewing by parental permission, and only after informed consent." Otherwise, he claimed, the exhibit would violate the constitutionally protected liberty of parents to raise their children as they see fit. Finally, he contended, the exhibit was both inappropriate for the age group in elementary schools and inconsistent with the Massachusetts sodomy statute.

In response to these allegations, the superintendent defended the propriety and legality of the exhibit and at the same time offered a compromise. "Nothing," he wrote,

> would be more inappropriate, it seems to me, than not to be tolerant of the views of those who do not want their children to see the exhibit, when the exhibit's main point is to contribute to understanding, acceptance, and tolerance of one group of families in the community. . . . Although one teacher plans to do so, I do not think it is necessary to present exhibits of other kinds of families because students have ample exposure through their homes, their friends and the media to images of a variety of families. . . . Moreover, no one will be discussing views on sodomy or same sex marriage or advocating homosexual lifestyles. . . . Accordingly, the principals and I have agreed that the photo exhibit will be displayed in school libraries where access by children can be controlled. . . . Parents will have the opportunity to exempt their children from participation in the exhibit or discussions about it.

The lawyer representing the objecting parents replied to the proposed compromise by saying, "You have taken a step in the right direction, in the face of a lot of political pressure," but he noted that his clients "will not back down one bit. They are emphatically not ready for the show to go on." In a further exchange of correspondence with the superintendent, he proposed that each child in each school bring in a picture of his or her family and that only these photos be displayed. This, he said, would not "set one type of family above another and allows all families to be considered equal. It celebrates the diversity of the school community, and teaches children about that diversity, without preaching or shoving particular views down anyone's throat."

Several days later the superintendent rejected this counterproposal.

Having seen the exhibit previously, I would not agree with you that it advocates same-sex marriage and sodomy. If anything, the show only advocates for schools (and communities) to be sensitive to the needs of children who grow up in gay/lesbian families. Since there are a growing number of such children in our schools, and since there is ample evidence that these children experience prejudice in our community, the exhibit is timely. The only question is an educational rather than legal one. Can we discuss this issue with young children? . . . The great majority of our teachers believe we can and are willing to prepare themselves to do so. Similarly, the great majority of the parents in our community have indicated that they would like their children to see the exhibit.

After unsuccessful efforts to obtain a restraining order to stop the exhibit, it went forward in each of the town's elementary schools in accordance with the superintendent's compromise.

Yet in the end, the way in which this example of accommodation and recognition was achieved left some very unsatisfied. Some gay and lesbian parents believed that the schools had "caved in" to the opposition. "We have tolerated nothing but heterosexual images in schools forever," one observed. "How they can call us intolerant because we won't let them stop showing portraits of our families in schools is beyond me." Another parent said that she found the superintendent's defense of the exhibit troubling. "It seemed like grudging acceptance. We've got all these queer kids in schools, and we don't want them harassed. Well, okay, that's fine, but it seems to focus more on the school's needs to maintain order than our need for something more than tolerance." As this parent explained it, "something more than tolerance" means that the exhibit should have been used to help students see gay and lesbian families as more than tolerable. As she put it, "We want the community to see and embrace the value of the lives we lead."

A member of the School Committee, speaking about the final resolution of the dispute over the exhibit, expressed a similar concern.

I don't think it is a wonderful solution, but I think a lot of what happens in schools is compromise to try to avoid confrontation, you know, making accommodations so that people don't have to deal with the harder issues. They don't have to say "I think it is so important for your child to see that it is alright for people to actually be gay or lesbian that I'm not going to allow anyone to opt out."

One employee in the schools suggested,

Gus presented all this as if the real point was to show that there are no differences, other than the most obvious and superficial ones, between gay and lesbian and heterosexual families. The exhibit should have been an occasion to note the real, substantial differences that exist in this town and this society and to affirm them.

Several others in the school system worried that the superintendent had acted as if difference could be accommodated only if a majority of the community supported it. This means "that what we do is held hostage to the prejudices of the many. Where will the fault line be? Where will recognizing difference run up against the community's prejudice, and what will we do then?"

Others, however, defended the way in which the dispute over the exhibit was worked out. As one teacher put it, "It helped establish our schools as taking steps to honor multiculturalism. It recognized that what exists in our community must be a part of what we do in schools. A small step, sure, but one like many others that we make every day in ways that no one notices." In his own defense, the superintendent noted,

> Look, not everyone got exactly what they wanted, but I think we made an important point. There are different ways of living in our community, schools welcome difference, and if we are going to have that diversity we have to respect things we may not agree with. It isn't everything, but it is a pretty good lesson which the rest of the society would be better off if it learned.

When asked to explain how he could reconcile canceling *West Side Story* and holding the "Love Makes a Family" exhibit, one school official explained,

> We canceled the play when it became clear that what we initially thought was a neutral gesture could reasonably be taken as being inhospitable to a culture which we seek to recognize and make welcome in schools which for far too long have been self-consciously and proudly Eurocentric. We held the exhibit to seek to do the same thing for another group which might rightly claim we have been less welcoming to its members than we should have been.

Finally, another school official summarized what she saw as the relationship between these two decisions.

> Every day in our classrooms, our gyms and recreational areas, our cafeterias, we are building what I call a tapestry of humanity. We bring people together who have different ways of being in the world in ways that help recognize those differences at the same time we build new communities by recognizing that there is much in common. Sometimes we won't do things that we would thirty years ago have done without thinking. Sometimes we will do new things that thirty years ago we would never have considered doing. Society changes, schools change. We are building a new community in which differences exist in ways that bring us together rather than driving us apart. In this way, by honoring difference we also are heading toward unity.

## CONCLUSIONS

How far is it from the case of Tina Isa to the gay and lesbian family photograph exhibit in Amherst, Massachusetts? In one sense it is very far, but in another perhaps less so. While the Isas claimed an exemption from valid law for a practice that was both violent and patriarchal (Okin 1999), the photography exhibit was well within what the law allowed, and it was an indication of one of the fissures in the armor of patriarchy. In one case, the difference that presented itself easily could be branded as unacceptable in a society committed to equality; in the other, equality demanded recognition and accommodation.

Throughout the United States, the recognition and accommodation of identity-difference is going on every day, sometimes in small and barely visible ways, sometimes under the glare of at least local, if not national, media attention. Sometimes it is accomplished with barely a ripple, sometimes it comes only after intense conflict. For every instance such as the Isas, in which the claims of difference are rejected, are dozens such as the decision to cancel *West Side Story* or to host "Love Makes a Family." As Alexander and Smelser (1999, 15) note, "polarized cultural rhetoric has obscured emergent processes of normative mediation . . . American society has continually incorporated out groups through a complex interplay between affirming traditional values and expanding and hyphenating them." Even more important, in the lives of schools all over the country, fights over *West Side Story* and photo exhibits are themselves extraordinary events.

That these cases involved contests over representations, over who should control the content and presentation of images of identity-difference, is hardly coincidental. These contests are as much a part of the micropolitics of difference as are more instrumental issues of inclusion-exclusion. Yet what their impact is on the views of culture and cultural difference of those who actively participate in them, or of students and staff who provide one audience for these contests, remains to be seen. People need to recognize that the real, everyday recognition and accommodation of difference is to be found in encounters in the lunchroom, class discussions, and play on athletic fields.

Yet one still might reasonably ask about the terms of inclusion exemplified in the cases described herein and whether they move us very far toward the free exercise of culture. In response, several things should be noted. First, in the daily accommodation of identity-difference, Kammen's (1972, 128) "dialectic of pluralism and conformity" seems alive and well. Difference is recognized and accommodated in ways that are thought to unify, to articulate not only what we do not share but what is shared across cultures.

For schools of even liberal communities such as Amherst, the terms of inclusion apparently require a denial or at least a diminution of difference, the reassuring acknowledgment that what seems different is only superficially so—that they are a lot like us. This is because all discussions of difference are haunted by the specter of cases such as the Isas, where difference is imagined rhetorically as an invitation to disorder. Only those differences that can be folded into a narrative of our underlying unity—that is, only those differences that have been sufficiently domesticated to fit within prevailing cultural assumptions and institutional routines—are recognized and accommodated.

Moreover, much of the everyday recognition and accommodation of identity-difference may be (as it seems to be in Amherst) reactive, emerging almost naturally from changes in the "facts on the ground." Recognition and accommodation thus will proceed at different rates in different places, as distinct identity or cultural groups establish their presence. Officials and citizens alike may be overly attentive to the possibility that each claim for recognition will invite others, in a multiplying and unlimitable progression, as if within every demand for recognition and accommodation is the question, If this, then what? (Renteln 1987–1988, 26). While such questions and statements sometimes are an indication of bad faith (Schlesinger 1992), they also reflect reasonable beliefs that the proliferating recognition of difference may itself generate an accelerating and realignment of institutional practices.[7]

Tendencies to reject such calls for a realignment of institutional practices by equating difference with disorder can be condemned as naive or backward or simply the repressive response of an intolerant culture fearful of losing expected privileges. Though such condemnations sometimes may be called for, they do little to advance the claims of difference or to advance the chance for a politically progressive response and accommodation of difference. Those who would champion difference and make it an energizing presence in democratic politics must learn to constitute difference in such a way as to recognize the multiple and contradictory affiliations and identities that give our lives meaning and at the same time to tame the specter of disorder. As a result, as in the disputes about *West Side Story* and "Love Makes a Family," accommodations may be framed only in the language of tolerance rather than affirmation.

Tolerance is, as any vocabulary for recognizing and accommodating difference must be, a relativist theory of difference. Relativization, or perspectivism, acknowledges that people can be different from oneself and yet not be inferior (Todorov 1985, 189–91; 1993, 32–90). Without perspectivism, those who do not speak your language or worship your gods are barbarians. As a concept that in theory allows others to live according to their own truths, tolerance is a relativist doctrine that seeks coexistence and moderation instead of the imposition of one universalizing idea of virtue.[8]

Perhaps recognition and accommodation of identity-difference that expresses itself as a hope for unity in reactive and defensive terms and in the language of tolerance always will appear inadequate. Some may find that the kind of everyday recognition and accommodation described herein falls far short of engaging what William Connolly (1991, 43) calls "the enigma of otherness," or that Todorov (1985, 247) is right when he says,

> [T]he other remains to be discovered. . . . [H]uman Life is confined between . . . two extremes, one where the I invades the world, and one where

the world ultimately absorbs the I. . . . And just as the discovery of the other knows several degrees, from the other-as-object, identified with the surrounding world, to the other-as-subject, equal to the I but different from it . . . we can indeed live our lives without ever achieving a full discovery of the other.

Yet the daily practices of American institutions make it increasingly difficult to imagine that identity-difference does not exist and to escape engagement with it. Canceling theatrical productions and putting up photo exhibits are hardly the stuff of great moral controversy, but such events are part of the everyday world of cultural difference. As one school official put it, reflecting on the controversies in Amherst surrounding *West Side Story* and "Love Makes a Family," "Behind the headlines great progress has been made with little or no fanfare, no publicity, few raised voices. The Amherst schools are being changed from the bottom up, day by day. That is the real story." Whether he is right about the extent of the progress or depth of change that it represents, and while full discovery of otherness without doubt has yet to be achieved, perhaps just beyond our gaze, in the taken-for-grantedness of the everyday world, identity-difference increasingly is finding its place.

## NOTES

1. Connolly (1991, 64) writes, "the maintenance of one identity . . . involves the conversion of some differences into otherness, into evil, or one of its numerous surrogates. Identity requires difference in order to be, and it converts difference into otherness in order to secure its own self-certainty."

2. As Tocqueville (1876 [1835], 65) observed at the start of the nineteenth century,

   The human beings who are scattered over this space do not form, as in Europe, so many branches of the same stock. Three races, naturally distinct, and, I might almost say, hostile to each other are discoverable amongst them at the first glance. Almost insurmountable barriers had been raised between them by education and law, as well as by their origin and outward characteristics; but fortune has brought them together on the same soil, where, although they are mixed, they do not amalgamate.

3. As Lefebvre (1991, 251) puts it,

   The programme we have sketched for a critique of everyday life can be summed up as follows: (a) It will involve a methodological confrontation of so called "modern" life on the one hand, with the past, and on the other—and above all— with the *possible*. . . . (b) Studied from this point of view, human reality appears as an opposition and "contrast" between a certain number of terms: everyday life and festival—mass moments and exceptional moments—triviality and splendour. . . . The critique of everyday life involves an investigation of the exact relations between these terms. It implies criticism of the trivial by the exceptional—*but at the same time* criticism of the exceptional by the trivial.

4. As Blanchot (1987, 17) puts it,

> The everyday, where one lives as though outside the true and the false, is a level of life where what reigns is the refusal to be different, a yet undetermined stir: without responsibility and without authority, without direction and without decision, a storehouse of anarchy, since casting aside all beginning and dismissing all end. This is the everyday.

Here Nietzsche (1968 [1901], 126) might be thought of as a great (though seldom recognized) theorist of the everyday.

> And do you know what "the world" is to me? Shall I show it to you in my mirror? This world: a monster of energy, without beginning, without end; . . . enclosed by "nothingness" as by a boundary; not something blurry or wasted, not something endlessly extended, but set in a definite space as a definite force, and not a space that might be "empty" here or there, but rather as force throughout . . . ; a sea of forces flowing and rushing together, eternally changing, eternally flooding back . . . ; out of the simplest forms striving toward the most complex, out of the stillest, most rigid, coldest forms toward the hottest, most turbulent, most self-contradictory, and then again returning home to the simple out of this abundance, out of the play of contradictions back to the joy of concord, still affirming itself in this uniformity of its courses and years, blessing itself as that which must return eternally, as a becoming that knows no satiety, no disgust, no weariness.

5. Amherst, a racially and ethnically diverse college town of about 35,000 residents, is situated at the foothills of the Berkshire Mountains about 100 miles west of Boston. As described in a recent article in the *Boston Globe* (Daley 1999), "on the multiculturalism meter [it] is close to overheating. The UN flag flies on the common, and officials regularly pass international resolutions."

6. Almost at the same moment, in what some saw as a bitter irony, the town celebrated Puerto Rico Day on November 19. As part of this annual event, designed to honor the town's Puerto Rican residents and their heritage, the Puerto Rican flag is flown over Town Hall.

7. For Schlesinger (1992, 138, 128), the "great unifying Western ideas of individual freedom, political democracy, and human rights" define a unique American nationality and are opposed to the "cultures based on despotism, superstition, tribalism, and fanaticism" that exist in the non-European (African) civilization. For an interesting critique of Schlesinger's book see Fish 1992.

8. Some point out what they see as the defining inadequacies of tolerance. For critics, though it appears relativistic, tolerance also is hierarchical. Tolerance is "permission granted by authority" and an "allowance, with or without limitations, by the ruling power," and the allowing of "that which is not actually approved; forbearance; sufferance" (*Oxford English Dictionary* cited in McClure 1990, 362). Tolerance presupposes a hierarchical relationship between someone who requests tolerance and an authority that tolerates only if and when it wishes. Tolerance presupposes one power—namely, the liberal state—that can decide whether or not to tolerate the activities of other less powerful actors. The alleged complicity between tolerance and power has led some to question its desirability as a vocabulary for organizing difference. Despite its rhetorical

association with respect for difference, liberal tolerance, say its critics, itself has become a guarantor of order. Herbert Marcuse (1965), for example, argues that tolerance stifles nonconformist attitudes and protects the authority of those who get to choose which differences are tolerated. In addition, Audre Lorde (1984, 111) eloquently writes of how "[a]dvocating the mere tolerance of difference between women is the grossest reformism." Tzyetan Todorov (1985) further suggests that tolerance often is nothing more than a forbearance of a despised or hated people whom one hopes to assimilate.

# REFERENCES

Abu-Odeh, Lamma. 1984. "Honor Crimes and the Construction of Gender in the Arab World." Typescript.

Alexander, Jeffrey, and Neil Smelser. 1999. "Introduction: The Ideological Discourse of Cultural Discontent: Paradoxes, Realities, and Alternative Ways of Thinking." In *Diversity and Its Discontents: Cultural Conflict and Common Ground in Contemporary Society*, edited by Neil Smelser and Jeffrey Alexander. Princeton, N.J.: Princeton University Press.

*Amherst Bulletin*. 1999. "National Speech Advocates Enter the Fray." December 3.

"The Availability of the 'Cultural Defense' as an Excuse for Criminal Behavior." 1986. *Georgia Journal of International and Comparative Law* 16: 335–54.

Blanchot, Maurice. 1987. "Everyday Speech." *Yale French Studies* 76: 12–25.

Connolly, William. 1991. *Identity/Difference: Democratic Negotiations of Political Paradox*. Ithaca: Cornell University Press.

Craft, Gretchen. 1992. "The Persistence of Dread in Law and Literature." *Yale Law Journal* 102: 521–46.

"The Cultural Defense in Criminal Law." 1986. *Harvard Law Review* 99: 1293–1311.

"Cultural Defense: One Person's Culture Is Another's Crime." 1987. *Loyola Los Angeles International and Comparative Law Journal* 9: 751–83.

Daley, Beth. 1999. "A Community Divided: Amherst Reflects." *Boston Globe*, December 2.

Douglas, Jack. 1970. *Understanding Everyday Life*. Chicago: Aldine.

Fish, Stanley. 1992. "Bad Company." *Transition* 56: 60–7.

Gabel, Peter. 1980. "Reification in Legal Reasoning." *Research in Law and Sociology* 3: 25–51.

Geertz, Clifford. 1983. *Local Knowledge: Further Essays in Interpretive Anthropology*. New York: Basic Books.

Gordon, Milton. 1981. "Models of Pluralism: The New American Dilemma." *The Annals*: 178–88.

Habermas, Jürgen. 1975. *Legitimation Crisis*. Boston: Beacon Press.

———. 1984. *The Theory of Communicative Action*. Vol. 1: *Reason and Rationalization in Society*. Boston: Beacon Press.

Heller, Agnes. 1984. *Everyday Life*. London: Routledge.

Humphrey, Michael. 1994. "Community Disputes, Violence and Dispute Processing in a Lebanese Muslim Immigrant Community." *Journal of Legal Pluralism* 22.

Jardine, Alice. 1980. "Prelude: The Future of Difference." In *The Future of Difference*, edited by Hester Eisenstein and Alice Jardine. Boston: G. K. Hall.

Jay, John. 1964 [1787]. *Federalist Papers*. New York: Washington Square Press.

Kammen, Michael. 1972. *People of Paradox: An Inquiry Concerning the Origins of American Civilization*. New York: Knopf.

Lefebvre, Henri. 1991. *Critique of Everyday Life*. London: Verso.

Lorde, Audre. 1984. "The Master's Tools Will Never Dismantle the Master's House." In *Sister Outsider*. Freedom, Calif.: The Crossing Press.

MacKinnon, Catherine. 1987. *Feminism Unmodified: Discourses on Law and Life*. Cambridge, Mass.: Harvard University Press.

Marcuse, Herbert. 1965. "A Critique of Pure Tolerance." In *A Critique of Pure Tolerance*, edited by Robert Paul Wolff. Boston: Beacon Press.

McClure, Kristie. 1990. "The Limits of Toleration." *Political Theory* 18: 361–91.

Minow, Martha. 1990. *Making All the Difference: Inclusion, Exclusion, and American Law*. Ithaca, N.Y.: Cornell University Press.

———. Minow, Martha. 1991. "Partial Justice: Law and Minorities." In *The Fate of Law*, edited by Austin Sarat and Thomas R. Kearns. Ann Arbor: University of Michigan Press.

Nietzsche, Friedrich. 1968 [1901]. *The Will to Power*. New York: Vintage Books.

Okin, Susan Moller. 1999. *Is Multiculturalism Bad for Women?* edited by Susan Moller Okin. Princeton, N.J.: Princeton University Press.

*People v. Helen Wu*. 1991. 235 California App. 3d 614.

*People v. Kimura*. 1985. No. A–091133. Los Angeles City Superior Court.

*People v. Moua*. 1985. No. 315972–0. Fresno County Superior Court.

*People Magazine*. 1992. "Die, My Daughter, Die!" January 20: 71.

Post, Robert. 1988. "Cultural Heterogeneity and the Law: Pornography, Blasphemy and the First Amendment." *California Law Review* 76: 297–335.

Renteln, Alison Dundes. 1987–88. "Culture and Culpability: A Study of Contrasts." *Beverly Hills Bar Association Journal* 22: 17–27.

Sarat, Austin, and Roger Berkowitz. 1994. "Disorderly Differences: Recognition, Accommodation, and American Law." *Yale Journal of Law & the Humanities* 6: 285–316.

Schlesinger, Jr., Arthur M. 1992. *The Disuniting of America: Reflections on a Multicultural Society*. New York: W. W. Norton.

Schutz, Alfred. 1967. *The Phenomenology of the Social World*. Evanston, Ill.: Northwestern University Press.

Schutz, Alfred, and Thomas Luckmann. 1973. *The Structures of the Life World*. 1973. Evanston, Ill.: Northwestern University Press.

Simmel, George. 1978. *The Philosophy of Money*. London: Routledge.

*State v. Aires Correia*. 1991. 600 A2d 279.

Tocqueville, Alexis de. 1876 [1835]. *Democracy in America*. Boston: John Allyn.

Todorov, Tzyetan. 1985. *The Conquest of America: The Question of the Other*. New York: Harper & Row.

———. 1993. *On Human Diversity: Nationalism, Racism, and Exoticism in French Thought*. Cambridge, Mass.: Harvard University Press.

*Trujillo-Garcia v. Rowland*. 1992. U.S. Dist. LEXIS 6199.

Zizek, Slavoj. 1989. *The Sublime Object of Ideology*. Oxford: Verso.

# Chapter 19

# Plural Society and Interethnic Relations in Guinea-Bissau

## Joanna Davidson

I n June 1999, several weeks after the popular military victory over João Bernardo "Nino" Vieira's nineteen-year presidential career in Guinea-Bissau, young soldiers supposedly representing the Muslim-led junta military, now occupying the capital city of Bissau, raided the central market and rounded up youth wearing trendy or immodest clothing, such as miniskirts, tight shirts, platform shoes, and hip-hop garb. Once identified, these youth were publicly intimidated and castigated (some physically) by their peers in the military. The point seemed clear: in the newly established moral order, such promiscuous habits would have to go. Miniskirts were out, the new representatives of state authority asserted with their batons, and a Muslim sense of modesty was in.

This was exactly the situation I had expected. Indeed, I had come to war-torn Guinea-Bissau to conduct preliminary ethnographic research on norm conflict—that is, clashes among conflicting cultural mores and practices. Muslims in Guinea-Bissau—made up largely of the Fula and Mandinga ethnic groups—comprise about 35 percent of the population. Muslims have had a largely marginal postindependence political history, as Fulas were perceived to have sided with the Portuguese during the eleven-year Independence War and thus were denied major political roles or influence in the African Party for the Independence of Guinea and Cape Verde (PAIGC), the ruling party of Guinea-Bissau since independence in 1974 (Forrest 1992). Now that a Muslim-led military campaign had successfully overthrown the PAIGC establishment, I assumed they would be quick to establish leadership on many fronts, and the market raid on immodestly dressed youth certainly seemed a step in that direction.

When I arrived in Guinea-Bissau in June 1999—less than two months after the last day of the war and just a few weeks after the market raid—I expected to witness a fair amount of change and was prepared to observe a struggle over cultural norms that would define the newly reliberated Guinea-Bissau. Yet after a few days (and increasingly confirmed during the course of my stay and by news reports since I left), I came to realize just how wrong my initial set of assumptions were. No one set of cultural and religious norms would be imposed easily on this ethnically and religiously diverse population, even if driven by military might. Pluralism was alive and well, protected vigilantly on both micro and macro levels.

Take, for instance, the immediate aftermath of the market raid. The public outcry was instantaneous, and objections to the attempt to scold trendy youth were voiced not only by urban young people themselves but by a multigenerational, multiethnic, and multireligious vox populi. Within two days of the raid, the junta leadership publicly apologized on the radio, insisting that the soldiers were acting on their own accord, and that such actions did not represent the views or intentions of the junta. Whether or not people believed them was for the most part irrelevant; pluralism had been preserved for the moment, and attempts to dictate a dress code have not happened since.

This event—and more importantly, the reaction to it and discourse that surrounded it—encapsulates many of the issues involving diversity, pluralism, and cultural norm conflict that I hoped to explore. I found increasingly a deep-seated and effective resistance to a nationally based hegemonic order, and—especially compared to other countries in the region and the continent as a whole—a relative lack of interethnic animosity. This is not to say that all is harmonious in Guinea-Bissau; quite the contrary. I am well aware of the irony of emphasizing the absence of conflict in a region currently engulfed by violent conflicts. The 1998 military uprising and subsequent political instability attest to the very real presence of manifold tensions and conflicts in the country. Yet the relative and historical lack of *norm*-based conflict—especially expressed along ethnic lines— opens up questions about pluralism and collective identity formation. What factors help to explain this phenomenon? And how does the case of Guinea-Bissau shed light on—or challenge—conventional understandings of norm conflict?

## "BLACK BABEL": TROPES OF HETEROGENEOUS GUINEA-BISSAU

Reflections on the "remarkable diversity" of ethnic groups in Guinea-Bissau resonate throughout much of the ethnographic, historical, and travel literature on the region. As Pattee (1973, 58–59) remarks,

> The records of the early [Portuguese] visitors reveal their astonishment at the variety of ethnic groups and the mosaic-like character of this piece of the West African coast. . . . There are to be found in Guinea representatives of almost every ethnic group scattered throughout West Africa from Sierra Leone northward.

Fifteenth-century writers also observed the diversity of its inhabitants: Guinea-Bissau (or what was then Portuguese Guinea) was described as an "'ethnographical museum,' a 'Black Babel,' and a medley of tribes and tongues" (Biggs-Davidson 1966, 14). Pattee (1973, 58) frames the issue thus:

When one considers . . . the variety of tribal groups in the total population
. . . it is clear that within the territorial limits of Portuguese Guinea there is
a synthesis of West Africa, a veritable laboratory on a small scale of race
relations, degrees of economic development, social differentiation, and potential tribal conflict.

Approximately thirty-three ethnic groups reside in this small nation-state,
with a current population of just over one million. Most of these groups are
related to others in the Senegambian area, and spill over current national borders. The five major ethnic groups that constitute present-day Guinea-Bissau
include the Balanta, Fula, Mandinga, Manjaco, and Papel.

Population movements, especially among the coastal groups, are the result of
successive waves of conquest and migrations, particularly during the thirteenth-
century expansion of the Malian Empire and the Fulani invasions between the
fifteenth and nineteenth centuries. During the late colonial era, increased internal migration contributed to the complex ethnic demography of Portuguese
Guinea. This dislocation was further exacerbated by the independence struggle
during the 1960s and early 1970s.

What stands out in the scant ethnographic and historical literature on the
country is the perplexing realization that, given the ethnic heterogeneity of
Guinea-Bissau, relatively little interethnic conflict exists. Some writers, to be
sure, point out particular ethnic-based fault lines and struggles in specific historic and economic circumstances.[1] Attention to these ethnic-based rivalries,
however, is far outweighed by the recurring trope of Guinea-Bissau as a successful plural society. How then is this relatively peaceful coexistence among such
diverse groups explained?

One readily apparent factor often pointed out by Guineans themselves is the
unifying element of a common language—Crioulo—which is a mixture of Portuguese and Mande languages. Crioulo originally developed as a trade language
on the Cape Verde Islands, and its use spread to Guinea-Bissau in the late fifteenth century. Its use as a vernacular dramatically increased during the Independence War, when communication among various ethnic groups fighting the
Portuguese was crucial. Unlike common languages in other parts of West Africa,
such as French and English, Crioulo is a noncolonial common language, and
Guineans take pride in the homegrown aspect of their lingua franca. Within the
past two generations, many Guineans have learned to speak Crioulo as a first
language (Scantamburlo 1999).

## THE PORTUGUESE LEGACY

Another possible explanation for the state of interethnic relations in Guinea-
Bissau lies in the distinctive legacy of Portuguese colonialism. Portuguese navi-
gators first landed on the Upper Guinea Coast in 1446. From 1446 to 1878, the

Portuguese were less concerned with colonizing these territories than with establishing trading networks along the coast; their presence in the region was defined largely in terms of trade, and especially the slave trade (Hawthorne 1998). Most of the European commerce on the Upper Guinea Coast was carried out through white settlers known as lançados, some of whom were Portuguese Jews escaping the Inquisition. The lançados dispersed along the coastal region, and most adopted local religions and customs.

> They lived in huts, "married" African women, and, as privileged guests, were partially integrated into riverain communities. . . . More acculturated to the African surroundings than their counterparts in Angola and Mozambique, the wives and "Luso-African" offspring of *lançados* in Guinea served as interpreters and culture-brokers and were invaluable in extending trade into the interior. (Crowley 1990, 99)

Their counterparts were grumetes—Africans who facilitated coastal trade working mainly as ship hands, were either salaried or enslaved, and who partially adopted Portuguese conventions such as names, clothing, and Christianity. During the early colonial period, Portugal had "extremely superficial control" of this territory, and "African rulers only tolerated the colonial presence. . . . [T]he relationship was one of African hosts and Portuguese guests" (Crowley 1990, 107).

Guinea-Bissau's colonial history is inextricably intertwined with the Cape Verde Islands. Portuguese activities in this region were headquartered in Cape Verde, an important slave depot and port for ships involved in the Atlantic trade. The Portuguese established their administrative base on Cape Verde; from 1446 until 1879, "Guinea-Bissau was a dependency of the Cape Verde Islands and seemed to be more of a colony of Cape Verde than of Portugal" (Crowley 1990, 97). Such an infrastructure helps explain the limited control and influence the Portuguese exerted in Guinea-Bissau during this period, especially since "communications between Cape Verde and its dependency were infrequent. During the entire period of colonial rule only six governors posted in Cape Verde ever visited Guinea" (Crowley 1990, 103–4).

Only with the decline of the slave trade did Portuguese Guinea become an autonomous overseas colony (in 1871), administered separately from Cape Verde for the first time, after almost four hundred years of Portuguese presence. Yet the turning point in Portuguese colonial administration of Guinea-Bissau did not come until 1912 to 1915, which marked the beginning of effective Portuguese domination and occupation through a series of so-called pacification campaigns. This period of colonial occupation ran roughly from 1915 to 1960.

The War of Liberation, spearheaded by Amílcar Cabral and the African Party for the Independence of Guinea and Cape Verde, began in 1963, after a rapid political mobilization of the rural population. The independence struggle lasted for eleven and a half years, culminating in official independence in September 1974, shortly after the breakdown of Portugal's fascist government.

## Lusophone Africa: A Meaningful Category?

Some scholars argue that "Lusophone Africa" or "Portuguese Africa" no longer is a tenable scholarly category. They insist on a more Africa-centered perspective that situates scholarship on these countries in a subregional or continental context, rather than only in relation to each other's colonial past. Alpers (1995, 96–97, 101–2) asserts, for example,

> The concept of what we are . . . calling lusophone Africa is entirely a colonial construct and owes nothing at all to any African historical reality that is not rooted in the late nineteenth and early twentieth century conquests of Angola, Guiné-Bissau, and Mozambique. . . . The concept of lusophone Africa is not sufficient by itself to provide meaningful contexts for understanding the African experience of Portuguese colonial domination. . . . Is there anything deeply rooted in any of these societies that would identify them from an Africa-centered perspective primarily as lusophone? I doubt it very much. . . . The concept of Portuguese Africa . . . does not make sense any longer for students of Africa, historical or contemporary. . . . It's time to let go.

While I sympathize with Alpers's call for an Africa-centered perspective, to simply "let go" of Lusophone Africa as a relevant construct is equally damaging to any analysis of this region. To be sure, scholarship on Guinea-Bissau should be situated in particular subregional, thematic, economic, or other contexts through which it can be analyzed. Yet much is to be gained from an analysis of Guinea-Bissau taking full consideration of its identity as a former Portuguese colony. The very fact of Portuguese presence in this wedge of West Africa for more than five hundred years has undoubtedly shaped its trajectory in ways that are different from former French and British colonies in the region. Moreover, Guinea-Bissau's relation to other Portuguese-speaking colonies both during and after colonial rule plays a significant part in its political and cultural history and in fashioning its identity in relation to Portugal. Although other factors might play a more central role in certain circumstances, distinguishable and important hallmarks of Portuguese colonialism branded these countries in particular ways.

One obvious distinguishing feature of Portuguese presence in this region of Africa is simply its longevity.[2] In a 1966 report on Portuguese Guinea to the British Survey, John Biggs-Davidson (1966, 13) observes, "The old fortress of São Jose de Bissau . . . reminds the British visitor how recent, compared with the Portuguese, is our own Africa experience. They were Guinea-bound when England was torn by the Wars of the Roses."

Another particular feature of Portuguese colonialism is its rhetoric of multiracial unity as part of the colonial endeavor. Portugal perceived its colonizing mission as a way to unite people in a grand Lusotropical culture regardless of geography, race, or ethnicity. This discourse intensified as independence movements in other African countries started forcing Portugal to justify its ongoing presence in the region. In a 1961 address given by Portugal's Overseas Minister, Adriano Moreira, Portugal's "policy of integration" was reiterated, targeted largely for the international community whose sympathy for colonialism was waning. Moreira (1961, 10–11) began by stating, "we wish to underline before the community of nations Portugal's decision to continue its policy of multi-racial integration, without which there will be neither peace nor civilization in black Africa: a multi-racial integration . . . inspired as always in the past by the belief in the equal dignity of all men, regardless of their color." In an increasingly futile attempt to legitimize Portuguese rule in Guinea-Bissau, Moreira (1961, 8, 31–2) asserted,

> [T]he Portuguese overseas, in the exercise of public or private activities, always had a clear notion that they were the instruments of a great and civilizing mission. Without it, the vast territories and the millions of individuals to whom we gave the benefits of our nationality might not have been brought into contact with the main current of history . . . Africa gained when we implanted there the ideas of State and of Nation which were alien to its peoples. . . . It is our opinion in short that the Portuguese formula is the most beneficial for Africa south of the Sahara.

In the Portuguese colonial mind, Guinea-Bissau and other territories were all districts of one Lusophone nation. As Biggs-Davidson (1966, 15) explained in his report, "In Portuguese theory, Guinea is not a colony but a province, as is Algarve—or Angola." Unlike France or Britain, Portugal refused to relinquish its colonies in Africa until its own revolution in 1974. Trying to render intelligible the Portuguese reluctance to let go, Biggs-Davidson (1966, 20) pointed out one of the guiding principles in Portuguese colonial ideology: "The Portuguese are paying dear for the defence of this part of the last group of African territories under the Government of a NATO power but they will not give Guinea up. To abandon it would betray their ideal of one multi-racial, Luso-tropical nation."

Moreira (1961, 9) elucidated this mentality by calling for "an increase [of] the settlement of our Africa by European Portuguese who will make their home there and encounter in Africa a true continuation of their country." Biggs-Davidson was evidently convinced by this oratory. His report to the British Survey echoes Portuguese colonial propaganda. "Guinea is colour-blind. Culture is the criterion for advancement. In Cathedral, club or cinema, school or swimming pool, race is no barrier" (Biggs-Davidson 1966, 20).[3]

Moreira's official stance was backed up by other apologists for Portuguese colonial rule in Guinea-Bissau, even as late as 1973. On the eve of Guinea-Bissau's imminent independence, Richard Pattee advocated for continued Portuguese rule in Guinea-Bissau by heralding its altruistic intentions and its role in preventing interethnic violence. Pattee (1973, 63) asserted that "the great common denominator of Portuguese sovereignty was the most certain guarantee against a revival of inter-tribal conflict or the imposition of the more numerous group or groups over the others. . . . Peace and harmony depend on the super-structure of Portuguese sovereignty."[4]

Much recent scholarship has focused on the links between colonial classification schema and recent assignation of ethnic labels to colonized groups (Amselle 1990; Appadurai 1996; Bravman 1998; Comaroff and Comaroff 1993; Dirks 1992; Mark 1999; Spear and Waller 1993; Stoler 1995). These studies have revealed that many contemporary ethnic classifications emerged from colonial officials' often confused attempts to make order out of seeming chaos, demonstrating the colonial origins of ethnic categories assumed to be "natural," or at least to have had longer histories. While beyond the scope of this chapter, it would be instructive to extend this line of inquiry into Portuguese colonialism in the Upper Guinea Coast and compare how different brands of European colonialism in the region might have differently impacted ethnic classification and ensuing interethnic relations. In particular, one might investigate how Portuguese integrationist and colorblind colonial rhetoric worked itself out on the ground, and whether (as has been argued in the case of French and British colonialism in the region) Portuguese presence actually helped foster enmity or at least harden distinctions between previously porous ethnic boundaries.

## DECENTRALIZED RELIGIOUS AND POLITICAL STRUCTURES

Another important facet of Guinea-Bissau's distinctive cultural history is the religious composition of its population. Unlike its largely Islamic neighbors to the north (Senegal, Mali, Mauritania) or a number of Catholic- or Protestant-dominated West African nations to the south, no single religious group possesses special political or social power. Although Muslim conversion is increasing, Christianity has remained a largely urban phenomenon, and only accounts for approximately 5 percent of the total population (Crowley 1988). The majority of the population (60 percent to 65 percent) is spiritist (Lobban and Forrest 1988).[5]

Ethnographic work by Eve Crowley suggests that the prevalence of spiritism is critical for understanding the multiethnic political context of Guinea-Bissau. Crowley's investigation focuses on the multiethnic and cross-regional appeal of particular spirit shrines. She suggests that spiritism's wide-ranging participation is due to "the diffuse structure of spiritism, its simple rules of consultation, and the basic functions it fulfills" (Crowley 1988, 31). Crowley goes on to argue that "some indigenous African religions may . . . acquire important regional aspects that cut across major political and ethnic boundaries" (1988, 29). This helps to elucidate why ethnic-based conflicts might be mitigated through common spiritist practices. Crowley explains that regional spirit shrines function as local bases of dispute resolution, "delimiting community relations as sites of initiation rituals, establishing and modifying laws, and many other important social events" (1988, 31).

In addition to this "diffuse structure" of spiritism, much of the indigenous political and social organization—as well as the postindependence state organi-

zation—can be characterized by a generally decentralized ethos. This is epitomized by the Balanta—the majority ethnic group in contemporary Guinea-
Bissau—whose acephalous political structure has consistently helped them defy
subjugation (first by the expanding Mandinga Empire, and later by Portuguese
colonial officials).[6] Regarding the postindependence period, Joshua Forrest discusses the failure of the postcolonial central state to penetrate rural power (Forrest 1988). Ironically, the village-level political substructure is a by-product of the
anticolonial struggle, during which the PAIGC formed village committees comprised of members elected by villagers. The intended postindependence role of
these committees was to act as local bases through which the central state government could exert its authority. Yet the state has never been able to achieve
this level of coordination. As Forrest (1988, 3–4) explains,

> It is the local authorities or individual peasant families—rather than state
> officials—who wield power at the village level. . . . On the whole, then,
> village committees have not served as institutional linkages between state
> and peasant allowing for government penetration of the rural political
> arena, but rather as village-level bulwarks against state penetration, en-
> abling local leaders to preserve their hold on micro-level power structures.

While Forrest is principally attentive to the political and economic implications
of this arrangement in terms of the role of the postcolonial state, his analysis also
can be read in terms of the ramifications of such a situation for mitigating norm
conflict, especially in the form of hegemonic state power. The continuation of
dispersed, decentralized, localized power structures—and the inability of the
state to either capture this power base or pit ethnic groups against one another
on the basis of unequal access to state resources—probably has contributed to
the relative lack of norm-based conflict.

Perhaps this helps explain the ineffectiveness of norm impositions such as the
June 1999 attempt in Bissau's central market. There is a long and solid history of
independent decision making, and submission to centralized authority—whether
in the form of the Mandinga Empire, Portuguese colonial officials, or the postindependence nation-state—is simply not done, or at least, not done simply.

In sum, a common noncolonial language, the particular legacy of Portuguese
colonialism, the nature and role of spiritism, a broadly defined decentralized
character, and the lack of effective and centralized state control combine to provide a compelling array of reasons for the relative absence of norm-based conflict in Guinea-Bissau.[7]

## BLURRY BOUNDARIES

Debates about norm conflict in the United States are predicated on the encounter—and sometimes clash—between cultural groups whose customs are strange
to one another. In West Africa (and Africa more widely), such encounters among

stranger groups has long been a defining feature of social formation. From early migrations across the continent to the genesis of new polities on the internal frontier to trans-Saharan trade routes connecting North and West African peoples through establishment of precolonial states to relatively more recent encounters through the Atlantic slave trade, colonialism, urban migration, and nation-state formation, African history is in many ways a history of such encounters. Igor Kopytoff's frontier thesis implies that the very formation of most African societies we recognize today has been a process of encountering, incorporating, or excluding strangers (Kopytoff 1987). Richard Werbner (1989, 226) notes that West African societies in particular "have had strangers living in their midst . . . for centuries, well before modern colonialism. The crossing of strangers between communities and states, from one culture to another, is an ancient problem. . . . Unlike a modern novelty, it must be studied in the light of historic continuity with the past."

On the Upper Guinea Coast, Peter Mark recently addressed the dynamics of one such encounter—between Portuguese and Africans in the fifteenth century—and the ensuing implications for identity formation in the region. Mark (1999, 173) explores how the descendants of Portuguese and West African unions—who were called Luso-Africans and who called themselves Portuguese—"developed a culture that was itself a synthesis of African and European elements." According to Mark (1999), the self-ascription of "Portuguese" identity for Luso-Africans was based not on physical characteristics but on cultural and socioeconomic criteria, such as occupation, language, Catholic identity, and material culture. Mark (1999, 180) argues that these processes of creolization and hybridity reflect tendencies toward assimilation and inclusivity as principles of Luso-African groups.

> The movement of individuals back and forth between the physical spaces . . . and, more significantly, between the cultural spaces of African, *lançado* and Cape Verdean societies suggests a crucially important characteristic of mainland Luso-African society: it was not firmly bounded, nor was it exclusionary of those of African origin. Rather, Luso-African culture was open to individual assimilation at the margins.

Mark (1999, 182) takes his conclusions one step further by asserting that these principles of fluidity across cultural lines were not just emblematic of the Luso-African syncretic groups that arose in the late fifteenth and sixteenth centuries but were consistent with a precolonial, "indigenous" coastal African sense of ethnic identity.

> The boundaries were fluid rather than fixed indicators of the "otherness" of opposed populations. . . . In this respect, Luso-Africans represent a model of identity formation quite rare in the modern world. . . . One is led, if not to deny that coastal Luso-Africans conceptualized "otherness" in the construction of their own sense of being "Portuguese," at least to suggest

that this sense of the "other" played a relatively circumscribed role in creating their image of who they were. This model of identity formation—flexible, malleable, and based on cultural and socio-economic factors—was characteristic of societies along the Upper Guinea Coast and derived from a local identity paradigm.

Mark thus uses this case to challenge Frederik Barth's (1969) notion of bipolar model of identity formation, which "presumes a later, essentially Western approach to identity, one that is not appropriate for the sixteenth and early seventeenth century Upper Guinea Coast" (Mark 1999, 183). Mark accuses Barth of "overschematizing" distinctions between self and other in his focus on boundaries between groups. Mark's Luso-African example is meant to demonstrate that, contrary to Barth's formulation, "Not all boundaries are alike, and some are more permeable than others" (Mark 1999, 182–83).

In addressing the changes in Luso-African identity in subsequent centuries, Mark (1999) points to the ultimate dominance of the seventeenth-century European formulation of identity being largely based on skin color, and the reclassification of coastal Luso-Africans accordingly. Interestingly, " 'Portuguese' [Luso-Africans] bore the brunt of the pre-colonial European discourse on identity . . . [because their] very existence was testimony to the cultural and physical assimilation between Africans and Europeans, [and thus] posed an ontological challenge to European identities which, by the time of the Enlightenment, were based on the premise of a non-white, non-European 'other' " (Mark 1999, 188). In other words, Luso-Africans were not "other" enough to uphold now-reigning bipolar European distinctions, and thus were denied self-definition as an ethnic category. Their existence as a liminal and ambiguous group—the fact that they did not fit neatly into any single social box—threatened the very basis of an Enlightenment classificatory schema.

While Mark overstates his case opposing Barth, he provides an informative and illuminating analysis of a culturally and historically different mode of identity formation and social categorization. Other scholars also have noted the "traditional" fluidity of African cultural identities and the general tendency toward incorporating "others"; incorporation processes typically emphasized cultural dimensions—fictive kinship and adoption of language, mode of dress, type of livelihood, and religious practices—over political and legal status (see especially Shack and Skinner 1979). The obvious question is why. Why would West African "indigenous" models of identity and social groupings be based on principles of fluidity, inclusivity, and cultural factors while European models favor principles of opposition, exclusion, physical characteristics, and politico-jural formulations of personhood? What factors would lead to the emergence of such different schema for organizing human difference?

Kopytoff's now classic discussion of ethnogenesis on the African frontier provides a partial explanation. African frontiersmen as social and political entrepreneurs had to attract and retain adherents to their emerging polities, which occurred through absorption of strangers as kinsmen and subjects. Kinship provided the most typical model and idiom for incorporating new members into these societies, which was usually accomplished through ritual means to establish "blood" affinity within the host group (Kopytoff 1987). Sometimes, if a polity grew, it moved from a kin-group model to one based on rulers and subjects in which subjects were absorbed by either annexing and incorporating nearby groups or "taking over" existing groups by establishing a new social order and hence politically, socially, and ritually redefining a previously occupied territory (Kopytoff 1987).[8]

The extent to which incorporation processes effectively erased differences between strangers and hosts differed across societies. Scholars have typically discussed this variation along a stateless versus centralized axis. In their early landmark volume, *African Political Systems*, Fortes and Evans-Pritchard (1969) posit that the incorporation of strangers into stateless societies tends to be both quick and relatively complete. Kramer (1993) makes the same claim, emphasizing that acephalous societies are distinct in their insistence on cultural assimilation of foreigners, whereas centralized societies tend to be concerned with political and juridical status based on descent or contract.[9]

Furthermore, despite Mark's criticism, Barth's seminal work on ethnic groups and boundaries provides some important insights in this realm. Barth is recognized most often for shifting the anthropological gaze from cultural aspects that define an ethnic group to boundaries—often shifting and renegotiated—between groups. Barth has room in his theory for conceptualizing various modes of identity formation and classification schema. He insists, for example, that polyethnic societies are structured differently in terms of domains of interaction and domains of segregation among ethnic groups (Barth 1969). Such a perspective becomes especially important when considering the interactions among ethnic groups in so-called plural societies. According to Barth, not only do ethnic groups draw boundaries based on various configurations of cultural content, but also the interaction among ethnic groups is structured in various ways reflective of the groups themselves and the larger social system. Lumping polyethnic societies together "under the increasingly vague label 'plural' society'" obfuscates how polyethnic societies work differently (Barth 1969, 17).

Understanding how diverse polyethnic contexts work in terms of the "systematic set of rules governing inter-ethnic encounters" enables us to plug ethnic identity into a larger structure of social organization (Barth 1969, 34). Such dynamics provide not only more relevant information for the working of particular ethnic boundary-making processes, but expand the field of inquiry to include the interdigitation of various identities (for example, national, religious, gender, and class) within a given system. Indeed, this set of intersections is itself a rich site for analysis, otherwise obscured by a unidimensional concept of plurality. Investigations into the various modes and processes of differentiation among ethnic groups in polyethnic societies can shed light on a range of complex social dynamics and enable us to ask: Under what conditions is horizontality among ethnic groups possible? And when is hierarchy integral to the organization of ethnic distinction?

Such questions bring us back to Mark's identification of alternative classification schema—that is, culturally specific ways of organizing difference. A sense of cultural distinction that stems in part from Aristotelian logic of noncontradiction, in which *A* often is defined in opposition to (and sometimes elimination of) *B*, is locked inextricably into a system of inevitable norm conflict. The ethnographic and historical case of Guinea-Bissau opens up opportunities for inquiry into social boundary-making processes that might challenge deeply ingrained Western notions of identity formation and offer insights into nonconflictual processes of negotiating cultural difference.

Perhaps non-contradiction is not a universal operating principle across space and time. Pluralism no doubt means different things in different places, and comparative analysis might help us better understand how the coexistence of different norms in the same society is thought about, talked about, and acted upon in a variety of ways that might not inevitably involve conflict.

While I have painted (somewhat for heuristic purposes) a largely positive picture of Guinea-Bissau's successful cultural pluralism, this chapter concludes with a somewhat less optimistic outlook. In addition to the aforementioned factors, Guinea-Bissau's historic lack of ethnic- or norm-based conflict perhaps is due to a matter of priorities. Guinea-Bissau has been consumed by war—first against the Portuguese, then against political corruption—for a large part of its recent history as an emerging nation-state. These wars, while devastating in so many ways, have served to unite the population across many divides to conquer a common enemy. Yet, as is the case in so many neighboring countries, once this common enemy is defeated, other differences begin to percolate to the surface. The 1999 election campaigns in Guinea-Bissau show that this tendency is a preoccupation—not just among politicians but among the electorate. In the only face-to-face debate between the runoff candidates, the issue of ethnic rivalry loomed large, and each candidate accused the other of potentially turning Guinea-Bissau into a Liberia, Sierra Leone, or even Rwanda. Furthermore, in his inauguration address in February 2000, newly elected president Kumba Yala pledged above all else to "try to overcome the differences among the people of Guinea-Bissau" (Gidley-Kitchin 2000).

While the reaction to the market raid on suggestively dressed youth described in the beginning of this chapter demonstrates popular concern for plurality, the very fact that the raid occurred is cause for concern. The future of interethnic relations and norm conflict in Guinea-Bissau, subsequent to the 1998 armed conflict and ensuing overhaul in political leadership, remains unclear.

---

This chapter is based, in addition to library research, on preliminary ethnographic research conducted in Guinea-Bissau in June through July 1999 and July through August 2000. As of September 2001, the author will be conducting extended field-work (two years) in the region. This chapter thus represents an initial assessment, based on as yet limited research, of issues pertaining to norm conflict and interethnic relations in Guinea-Bissau. Funding for research was generously provided by the Social Science Research Council working group on Ethnic Customs, Assimilation and American Law, the National Science Foundation predoctoral fellowship, the Institute of African Studies at Emory University, and the Department of Anthropology at Emory University.

## NOTES

1. In the late nineteenth century, for example, rubber-tapping opportunities attracted primarily Manjaco workers, who profited considerably compared to the rice-cultivating Balanta and Djola. In addition to this economic disparity, "the fact that Manjaco reportedly attacked Djola women and pilfered their livestock provoked violence between Manjaco and neighboring populations" (Crowley 1990, 148–49).

2. The long presence of the Portuguese in this region does not necessarily translate into effective colonial control. As noted earlier, the Portuguese did not have much control at all in Guinea until the early twentieth century.

3. This was precisely the brand of colonial rhetoric that Amílcar Cabral was so effective at exposing and challenging. Cabral asserted,

   The fascist colonialism of Portugal also took care to suppress all means of nonofficial information about its "overseas provinces." A powerful propaganda machine was put to work at convincing international opinion that our peoples lived in the best of all possible worlds, depicted happy Portuguese "of colour" whose only pain was the yearning for their white mother-country. (See Davidson 1969, 1.)

4. Pattee strangely contradicts himself, though, when he first insists, "There has been no destruction of indigenous life; no policy of forced conversion or even assimilation during all these centuries" (1973, 59), then later admits, "It is true that the Portuguese professed a doctrine of 'assimilation,' that is the ultimate aim of making the peoples of Guinea part and parcel of the one common Portuguese nation. . . . Assimilation was and is the ultimate goal" (1973, 62). The Portuguese were actually quite up-front about their doctrine of assimilation. Until independence, Africans in Portuguese Guinea officially were classified as either *indigenous* or *civilized*, and were subjected to different rules accordingly. The indigenous were recognized as being under the rule of a chief and were subject to African customary law. The objective of such a division among the overall population was to gradually guide the indigenous into assimilated status, which, once obtained, provided access to education, civil service jobs, and valuable commodities by European standards.

5. Following Crowley, the term *spiritist* here refers to the diverse array of African indigenous religions (often called *animist* or *pagan*) that are based on "the belief that a wide range of supernatural entities serve to varying degrees as intermediaries between people and God and, by virtue of this position, as agents for influencing the natural, social, and supernatural worlds" (Crowley 1988, 27).

6. For a useful discussion of Balanta history, particularly in terms of the maintenance of acephalous political and social systems throughout the period described herein, see Hawthorne 1998.

7. Another important factor beyond the scope of this chapter is the influence of Amílcar Cabral's vision of a postindependence Guinea-Bissau. Cabral crafted an ideologically based independence struggle that actively worked to transcend ethnic boundaries, and he often is credited by both Africanist scholars and Guineans themselves for mitigating ethnic-based divisiveness (see Cabral 1973, 1979).

8. Strangers, of course, were not always incorporated into their host societies. Alongside processes of incorporation exist a series of exclusionary mechanisms meant to maintain the bounds of existing social units and perhaps even exacerbate differences among stranger groups. One notable example is Cohen's (1969) analysis of Hausa immigrants in Yoruba towns. Contrary to the detribalization described in much of the early Manchester School urban studies, Cohen asserts that Hausa migrants to Yoruba urban centers actually retribalized, accentuating their Hausa identity even more stridently than in their "homeland."

9. Although much ethnographic and historical literature emphasizes the fluidity of African social boundaries and the tendency toward incorporation over exclusion, some changes in this realm are important to note. Relatively recent macro-level political and economic transformations—such as colonialism, independence, and democratization—no doubt have had a profound impact on micro-level incorporation practices. Shack and Skinner (1979, 5) provide a somewhat undernuanced assessment of these transformations:

> In the main, both before the imposition of colonial rule in Africa and during the dependency period, indigenous African and non-African strangers were left virtually free to move from one traditional African polity and temporarily resettle in another. They were true strangers in the sense that Simmel meant—immigrants, but not aliens. In the contemporary era of self-government, newly independent African nation-states have increasingly treated *jus in personam* and *jus in rem* as rights to be defined and enforced by the state within its legal and political boundaries. But exercising this privilege of sovereignty has reversed, as it were, the "normal" process of change in the status of strangers.

Such changes, combined with the vulnerability of strangers and foreigners as visible scapegoats in moments of political and social upheaval, have contributed to several unfortunate events in Africa's recent history (such as the immediate postindependence propensity to expel "foreigners," Uganda being the most infamous example).

## REFERENCES

Alpers, Edward A. 1995. "Studying Lusophone Africa: Retrospect and Prospect." *Ufahama* 23(3): 94–109.

Amselle, Jean-Loup. 1990. *Mestizo Logics*. Stanford: Stanford University Press.

Appadurai, Arjun. 1996. *Modernity at Large: Cultural Dimensions of Globalization*. Minneapolis: University of Minnesota Press.

Barth, Frederik, ed. 1969. *Ethnic Groups and Boundaries*. Prospect Heights, Ill.: Waveland Press.

Biggs-Davidson, John. 1966. "Portuguese Guinea." *British Survey* 28(207): 12–21.

Bravman, Bill. 1998. *Making Ethnic Ways: Communities and Their Transformations in Taita, Kenya, 1800–1950*. Portsmouth, N.H.: Heinemann Educational Books.

Cabral, Amílcar. 1973. *Return to the Source: Selected Speeches by Amílcar Cabral*. New York: Monthly Review Press.

———. 1979. *Unity and Struggle: Speeches and Writing*, translated by Michael Wolfers. New York: Monthly Review Press.

Cohen, Abner. 1969. *Custom & Politics in Urban Africa: A Study of Hausa Migrants in Yoruba Towns*. Berkeley: University of California Press.

Comaroff, Jean, and John L. Comaroff. 1993. *Modernity and Its Malcontents: Ritual and Power in Postcolonial Africa*. Chicago: University of Chicago Press.

Crowley, Eve. 1988. "Regional Shrines and Ethnic Relations in Guinea-Bissau." *Africana Journal* 17: 27–39.

———. 1990. "Contracts with the Spirits: Religion, Asylum, and Ethnic Identity in the Cacheu Region of Guinea-Bissau." Ph.D. diss., Yale University.

Davidson, Basil. 1969. *No Fist Is Big Enough to Hide the Sky: The Liberation of Guiné and Cape Verde, Aspects of an African Revolution*. London: Zed Books.

Dirks, Nicholas B. 1992. *Colonialism and Culture*. Ann Arbor: University of Michigan Press.

Forrest, Joshua B. 1988. "State Peasantry in Contemporary Africa: The Case of Guinea-Bissau." *Africana Journal* 17: 1–26.

———. 1992. *Guinea-Bissau: Power, Conflict, and Renewal in a West African Nation*. Boulder, Colo.: Westview Press.

Fortes, Meyer, and E. E. Evans-Pritchard. 1969. *African Political Systems*. London and New York: Published for the International African Institute by Oxford University Press.

Gidley-Kitchin, Virginia. 2000. "Democracy Returns to Guinea-Bissau." British Broadcasting Company Report, February 17, 2000.

Hawthorne, Walter. 1998. "The Interior Past of an Acephalous Society: Institutional Change Among the Balanta of Guinea-Bissau, c. 1400–c. 1950." Ph.D. diss., Stanford University.

Kopytoff, Igor, ed. 1987. *The African Frontier: The Reproduction of Traditional African Societies*. Bloomington and Indianapolis: Indiana University Press.

Kramer, Fritz. 1993. *The Red Fez: Art and Spirit Possession in Africa*. London and New York: Verso.

Lobban, Richard, and Joshua Forrest. 1988. *Historical Dictionary of the Republic of Guinea-Bissau*. Metuchen and London: Scarecrow Press.

Mark, Peter. 1999. "The Evolution of 'Portuguese' Identity: Luso-Africans on the Upper Guinea Coast from the Sixteenth to the Early Nineteenth Century." *Journal of African History* 40: 173–91.

Moreira, Adriano. 1961. "A Policy of Integration, an Address Given by the Minister for Overseas." Oporto Commercial Association.

Pattee, Richard. 1973. "Portuguese Guinea: A Microcosm of Plural Society on Africa." *Plural Societies* 4(4): 57–64.

Scantamburlo, Luigi. 1999. *Dicionário do Guineense*. Vol. 1. Lisbon: FASPEBI.

Shack, William A., and Elliott P. Skinner, eds. 1979. *Strangers in African Societies*. Berkeley: University of California Press.

Spear, Tom, and Richard Waller, eds. 1993. *Being Masai: Ethnicity and Identity in East Africa*. Athens: Ohio University Press.

Stoler, Ann Laura. 1995. *Race and the Education of Desire: Foucault's History of Sexuality and the Colonial Order of Things*. Durham, N.C.: Duke University Press.

Werbner, Richard P. 1989. *Ritual Passage, Sacred Journey: The Process and Organization of Religious Movement*. Washington, D.C., and Manchester: Smithsonian Institution Press/Manchester University Press.

# Chapter 20

# Freedom of Speech and Freedom of Silence: An Analysis of Talking as a Cultural Practice

## Heejung S. Kim and Hazel Rose Markus

> Be a craftsman in speech that thou mayest be strong, for the strength of one is the tongue, and speech is mightier than all fighting.
>
> —Maxims of Ptahhotep, 3400 B.C.E.

> Speech is civilization itself. The word, even the most contradictory word, preserves contact—it is silence which isolates.
>
> —Thomas Mann, *The Magic Mountain*

> He who knows does not speak.
> He who speaks does not know.
>
> —Lao Tzu, *The Way of Lao Tzu*

> Misfortune stems from the mouth.
>
> —Chinese proverb

A long article (Lubman 1998) appearing recently in the *San Jose Mercury News* described a problem that California educators are struggling to solve. According to the report, colleges and universities with large numbers of East Asian and East Asian American students are concerned that although many of these students earn very high grades, they do not participate actively in the academic community. The problem, in the eyes of some faculty and administrators, is that East Asian students often do not talk in class and this is a pressing concern because students "need to express themselves" to become "independent thinkers." The article focuses on a variety of interventions to increase the talking of East Asian students in the hope of making them "better" thinkers.

The problem here is one of difference—in this case, a difference among students in their willingness and ability to talk in classes and seminars. A careful analysis of the "talking problem" is useful in its own right, but it also is significant because America's diverse and multicultural communities are increasingly likely to encounter issues and debates that have a structure very similar to this one. These problems will result from a clash in cultural practices, and those involved often may assume that their own practices are natural while those of others in their schools and workplaces are somehow unnatural. Or they may believe that their practices are good, proper, moral, or advanced, while the other practices are bad, deficient, immoral, or backward. What typically will be obscured in these clashes is that the so-called deficient or unsophisticated practices in question often are aspects of complex cultural systems that have their own histories, philosophies, institutions, and ways of life. Moreover, at first sight what will be even less visible is that one's own practices are not natural or inevitable but are in fact the particular results of cultural commitments and ways of life that are not universally held and practiced. For the California educators, silence connotes passivity, slowness, confusion, mental inactivity, or perhaps a type of social loafing, while talking is the very signature of engagement and mental life or power. From some non-Western perspectives, however, silence can connote truthfulness, attentiveness, and sincerity, while talking can connote a lack of respect or lack of thoughtfulness.

Speech, verbal expression, and debate occupy vitally important places in much of Western and particularly European American education as valued practices in themselves and also as tools to enhance thinking. The widely observed silence of many East Asian students—including many who have grown up in America—is a problem for educators who want to teach their students what they believe to be the right things in the right way and would like students to gain the most from their classroom experiences. With nothing but good intentions, American teachers actively urge these students to participate more, to contribute more, and to talk more. Yet is talking always good, and does it necessarily promote better thinking? Is the fact that many East Asian students are quiet in the classroom setting a problem that needs to be fixed?

Humans talk. Being able to use language distinguishes humans from other living creatures, and the ability to talk is the unique and universal nature of human animals. Talking is undeniably one of the most important forms of communication, one of the best avenues to thinking, and one of the most common forms of expression. Yet talking is not an automatic response to the sound of another voice or to the internal pressure of an unexpressed thought. Talking, like many seemingly mundane social acts, is a culturally saturated activity. The ways in which people talk are socially shaped and shared and entail the incorporation of culture-specific models (Bruner 1996; D'Andrade 1990, 1995; Fiske et al. 1998; Quinn and Holland 1987; Shore 1996; Shweder 1991). These cultural models are bundles of ideas and practices, many of them tacit, about why to talk, how to talk, when to talk, to whom to talk, and toward what end. Striking variation in these cultural models among Americans—associated with socially significant categories such as ethnic group, region of the country, class, and gender—poses further challenges to the effective functioning of diverse groups in schools and workplaces. Moreover, the example of cultural diversity in the meanings and practices of talking can illuminate how much of the cultural specificity of every-day action—including the most simple and seemingly straightforward of ac-tions—goes unseen, and how acknowledgment of this diversity can be an im-portant step in mutual engaging and accommodating cultural differences.

## TALK—CHEAP OR DEAR, PLAIN OR FANCY, NECESSARY OR RISKY?

Cultural contexts vary in their prevalent models of talking and silence and how they are woven into the practice of everyday life. How people make sense of each other's habits of talking depends on these models, which include the rea-sons for speaking and the value of speaking. As Austin (1962) has established, utterances have various functions besides conveying information, and these functions depend on the context. Talking in some cultural contexts has a gener-ally positive meaning and is thought to be a sign of power and control (as in the chapter epigraphs) and an art that requires skill and practice. In other contexts, not talking or silence carries positive connotations and is regarded as a sign of respect and attentiveness or as a way of controlling what goes on (Giles, Coup-land, and Wiemann 1992; Marsella 1993). Even a cursory review of the literature on the practices of talking and not talking reveals a surprising diversity of views and underscores the necessity of understanding the meanings of talking and silence that are common in a given sociocultural context. A given act of talking or remaining silent can be constructed and responded to in any number of ways.

In many American contexts, speaking one's mind often is synonymous with being a person. One of the most obvious roots of this understanding is the Car-tesian notion of the person, which emphasizes thinking as the very core of hu-man existence. As Descartes (1993 [1637]) declared, "I am a substance the whole nature or essence of which is to think." Thinking with regard to talking has been a Western preoccupation at least since the time of the ancient Greeks. Homer repeatedly emphasizes debate as a necessary skill (Nakamura 1964–85; Nisbett et al. 2001). Not everyone communicates their thoughts easily, and how much Americans talk varies tremendously among individuals, groups, and regions. Yet along with the freedom to choose one's government and religion, in America the right to speak one's mind, should one so desire, is protected as an absolute birthright. Speech is part and parcel of America's democratic traditions, and speakers have a responsibility to exercise their rights to communicate what is on their mind. Moreover, owing to the importance of speech in representing and mediating personhood and the world, speech often is assumed to be a reflection of true knowledge and true underlying meanings, thoughts, feelings, and inten-tions. Thus, in many American contexts, the assumption is that words can be taken at face value, and that lying, or saying something other than what one means, is widely regarded as hypocritical or immoral. Further, those who do not speak their minds are at fault if they are misunderstood or ignored. In American contexts, talking becomes interwoven with speaking the truth, with the meanings and practices of freedom, with individual rights, and with expression and personhood; it becomes cemented as a foundational and uncontested good.

The act of talking also can have significant artistic, social, and entertainment functions. Carroll (1988), for example, contends that for many French speakers, talking, especially in conversation with another, is taken very seriously. The ideal conversation, she writes, would "resemble a perfect spider's web: delicate, elegant, brilliant, of harmonious proportions, a work of art" (Carroll 1988, 25). Talking also is an important aspect of personhood in many Arab contexts and is said to require mubalaqha, which Almaney and Ahwan (cited in Smith and Bond 1999) translate as "exaggeration." According to this practice, if statements are not made in an exaggerated form, they will not be believed, and listening may even infer the opposite. Smith and Bond (1999) note that misunderstanding the role of exaggeration in impression management figures prominently in conflicts between America and countries of the Middle East. Still other analyses reveal that a great emphasis is placed on the spoken word in some African and African American contexts as well. According to the African concept of nommo, for example, the word is the life force, and once something is put into words it is believed to be binding and to have a creative power. Smitherman (1994, 8) contends that in many African American contexts, highly verbal talkers are respected and valued, as is the "skillful use of rappin', lyin', signifyin', testifyin', playin', and dozens of other verbal rituals."

While talking is essential and natural in some contexts and situations, in others talking is tied to a different repertoire of cultural models in which verbal reserve and silence are virtuous and good. Smith and Bond (1999) report that in Finland, for example, silence is the valued skill. Silence conveys attentiveness and encouragement to the speaker and is a highly valued response. In Japanese communication practices, instead of assuming that the speaker has the responsibility to speak directly and convey what is on his or her mind, the major responsibility is placed on the listener, who should be as empathic as possible, precisely so that the speaker does not have to communicate ideas and opinions too explicitly. Being a person in many Japanese contexts is tied more to cultivating omoiyari, or sympathy, than to speaking one's mind. Listening and not talking are highly valued as ways of demonstrating sympathy and trying to understand what others are feeling. When these types of ideas about talking prevail, words are less likely to be taken at face value and meaning is to be inferred rather than conveyed. While straight talking is a good way to convey one's meanings in many Western contexts, indirectness is a powerful theme of Japanese life, and silence facilitates this indirectness.

When silence is appreciated and valued with this perspective on talking, other forms of communication become important. The Japanese term ishin denshin, for example, marks the culturally significant idea of "an immediate communication between two minds which does not need words" (Morsbach 1987, 202). Indeed, the closer individuals are assumed to be, the more they are thought to rely on nonverbal communication that relies on inferences from cues of gesture and tone (Azuma 1986; Clancy 1986). Yan (1987), in characterizing

Chinese communication, says that communication is viewed as a process in which people first try to understand others, then try in turn to be understood by them. Gao, Ting-Toomey, and Gudykunst (1996) claim that in China, only a privileged few are believed to be skillful in talking and that as a consequence talking is not a primary path to self-identity or achieving individual needs and goals.

While the source, nature, and distribution of these differences in approaches to talking is a fascinating set of problems currently being addressed and investigated by linguists and anthropologists, here we are interested in the wide-ranging psychological implications of these differences. Talking is a perfect example of a human action that is full of meaning and cannot be understood without regard to particular and intertwined sets of local cultural, historical, and institutional representations and practices. In the course of tracing the meaning of talking in a given cultural context, one finds an intricate knot of meanings and practices, all of which recruit and implicate each other. In one cultural tradition, talking is powerfully associated with notions of individuality, freedom, equality, democracy, reason, intelligence, and honesty. In yet other cultural traditions, the act of talking is intricately bound with notions of relationship, hierarchy, status, face, empathy, and with conceptions of immaturity and carelessness as well. As will become apparent, for nontalkers to become talkers as the sole solution to what is perceived to be a problem is not always a simple matter.

## CULTURAL MEANINGS OF TALKING

Talking serves various functions. Two of the most commonly discussed functions of talking are the expression of thoughts and ideas and communication with others. As talking makes up an important part of people's social lives, however, its functions are more than just expression and communication, and its meaning expands because talking always implicates the self and the other. The meaning of talking should be affected by the concept of the self, because the act of talking involves projecting one's thoughts and ideas into the world. The meaning of talking also should be affected by the concept of the relationship, because talking functions as a tool of connecting and maintaining connectedness among people. Thus, to the extent that the concepts of self and relationship vary from one society to another, what the act of talking means also should differ across cultures.

### Models of Self and Relationship

A cultural analysis takes into account the core cultural ideas, social representations, and background understandings relevant to talking, as well as those practices and institutions—from the official and formal to the local and everyday—within which talking takes place. One of the most important tacit understandings within this net of ideas and practices is what it means to be a "good" or "proper" person (Markus and Kitayama 1991; Markus, Mullally, and Kitayama 1997). In many cultural contexts of the United States, the individual is understood and practiced as a separate or distinct entity whose behavior is determined by some amalgam of internal attributes. The cultural model of the independent person is one of the most prevalent models in North America, reflected in the rational actor of game theory, the reasonable person of the legal system, and the authentic self of most psychological theorizing. This model of a person holds that: the person is a stable, autonomous, "free" entity; he or she possesses a set of characteristic, identifying, and self-defining attributes—preferences, motives, goals, attitudes, beliefs, and abilities—that are the primary forces that enable, guide, or constrain behavior; individuals take action oriented toward the expression of their opinions and beliefs, realization of their rights, and achievement of their goals; and finally, that the individual often regards relationships as competing with personal needs and considers the expectations of others and obligations to others as interfering with personal goals (for full discussion of these and other cultural commitments of individualism see Fiske et al. 1998). Talking clearly is important in cultural contexts where this model of the person prevails. Talking is an act that defines and affirms the American self because it is one way in which internal thoughts and feelings can be most directly and clearly expressed.

In many cultural contexts, however, the person commonly is understood not as an independent entity but primarily a relational entity. In models of the self that are prevalent in many East Asian contexts, including China, Japan, Korea, and South Asia, the relationship has a type of moral primacy and the person is viewed as connected with others (Triandis 1989; Markus and Kitayama 1991; Shweder and Bourne 1984). These cultural models of the person place greater stress than individualist models on social and relational concepts such as empathy, reciprocity, belonging, kinship, hierarchy, loyalty, honor, respect, politeness, and social obligation. Typically in these contexts, social relationships, roles, norms, and group solidarity are more fundamental to social behavior than self-expression. This model holds that a person is a flexible, connected entity who is bound to others; participates in a set of relationships, groups, and institutions that are the primary forces that enable, guide, and constrain actions; conforms to relational norms and responds to group goals by seeking consensus and compromise; often regards personal beliefs and needs as secondary to norms and relationships (Fiske et al. 1998). Interdependent theories of the person and interdependent constructions and models of the world associated with them have powerful consequences for the analysis and practice of talking and silence. When others and relations with others are focal, words perhaps are more easily constructed as weapons and their potentially harmful consequences more evident. The expressive function of talking will be more salient in places and situations where the self is viewed primarily as independent. In cultural contexts where it is important to construct the self as interdependent, the communicative or relational function of talking will be emphasized.

In an initial explanation of these hypothesized differences in the cultural meanings of talking, a survey that included the open-ended question, "Why do you think the ability to speak is important/unimportant?" was administered to comparable college student samples from a Korean cultural context (where the self is represented to be more interdependent), and to an American cultural context (where the self is represented to be more independent).

Participants overall generated a fairly similar list of responses in that the majority of both groups thought the ability to speak is important because it "allows us to communicate" and "allows us to express." Yet the survey showed large cross-cultural differences in which of these two responses were emphasized, and even larger differences in how participants focused on subtle aspects of these responses.

Fifty-two percent of Korean participants and 62 percent of American participants thought that the ability to speak is important because of communication. Similarly, 48 percent of Korean participants and 42 percent of American participants thought that the ability to speak is important because of expression. Yet these groups differed a great deal in what they thought was the content of expression or communication. The majority of Korean participants (61 percent) indicated that to speak because of expression or communication with *others* is important (for example, "to communicate in order to maintain and improve relationships with other people"; "communications to influence and convince other people"; "to let my thoughts be communicated to others and to learn about other people's thoughts"), whereas only 25 percent of American participants mentioned *others* in their responses. Moreover, Korean participants also listed more relational responses more often than their American counterparts. Korean participants thought it was important to speak because it helps us "to understand other people" (21 percent vs. 4 percent), "to ease relationships" (14 percent vs. 0 percent), or "to cooperate with others" (7 percent vs. 0 percent).

In contrast, the majority of American participants (51 percent) thought the communication or expression functions are important because they convey personal ideas, thoughts, and feelings (for example, "language serves to give us signifiers for our abstract ideas. It is a tool, and can be used by nearly anybody to express thoughts, ideas, and values"; "a medium of thought. It is a way to express ideas and feelings within the mind"; and "we can express our innermost ideas and desires in a way that is unique to our species"), whereas only 21 percent of Korean participants mentioned such themes. In addition, American participants (8 percent) also mentioned "help learning" significantly more than did Korean participants (0 percent). American participants (19 percent) tend to mention "to express oneself" somewhat more than Korean participants (9 percent), although this cultural difference was not statistically significant.

These results support the idea that people engaged in cultural contexts or situations where the focus primarily is on the individual may invoke different models of talking. People may view the purpose of talking as the expression of one's ideas and thoughts. Yet people engaging in cultural contexts or situations where the emphasis is more on the person as relational or interdependent may tend to see the purpose of talking as connecting the self with others.

When people are relatively more concerned about the recipients of talking and cast talking as a relational activity, they may be relatively more aware of the impact talking can have on others. Talking has many more negative connotations in East Asian cultural contexts than in American cultural contexts (Kim 2000b). A popular Korean proverb echoing Lao Tzu's maxim (quoted in the chapter epigraph) and referring to people who are big talkers says, "The empty carriage makes a lot of noise." The act of talking thus is associated with a lack of wisdom and immaturity and not with intelligence and better thinking, as it is in American cultural contexts (Kim 2000b; Markus, Kitayama, and Heiman 1996).

Some historians argue that America has its roots in ideas and in documents that reflect these ideas and can be viewed predominantly as a culture of ideas and the expression of these ideas (Angell 1999). Talking occupies a special position among other human actions in these cultural contexts because talking defines a person and is a culturally resonant and significant action. Freedom of speech is the first and foremost right a person should be able to enjoy in the American cultural context. Forty-seven different talk shows currently are on television, and talking—expressing one's ideas and opinions—perhaps has become the predominant American cultural activity.

In contrast, individuals from cultural contexts where interdependent models of the self are more prevalent will tend to define themselves with their social positions and roles (Ip and Bond 1995; Markus and Kitayama 1991; Markus, Mullally, and Kitayama 1997). According to Confucian thinking (fostered in many Chinese policies, practices, and institutions), one's actions should be guided by the person's place in social order. Since people need to position themselves in a hierarchy and perform their roles, talking thus is determined by the nature of one's relationship and position in the hierarchy. In public conversation or in conversation with those outside one's family and friends, the expression of one's own ideas, opinions, and feelings is expected to attend to these status differences and reveal a concern with protecting the face of the conversation partner (Bond and Lee 1981; Gao, Ting-Toomey, and Gudykunst 1996). By remaining silent, one refrains from imposing one's thoughts and feelings on others and thereby constraining the nature of the relationship.

Not everyone is allowed to talk in many East Asian settings; people need to be recognized to voice their opinions. Typically, recognition is a consequence of experience, education, or power position. According to Gao, Ting-Toomey, and Gudykunst (1996), a "spoken" voice is synonymous with seniority, authority, experience, knowledge, and expertise. Given that one of the functions of talking is the expression of an individual's thoughts and ideas, this act of distinguishing and asserting one's own ideas can be seen as an act of independence and self-promotion. By talking, the talker claims power and demands the right to be heard. Thus, the right to talk means the person is in a social position in which the person can demand the right. Historically, in many cultures, the right or standing to talk has been given to people who are higher up on the hierarchy through age, class, or merit. A king could initiate talking, but his subject could not unless the right to talk is given by the king. A master had the standing to talk, but not an apprentice who had not yet acquired the wisdom to share.

Thus, talking represents individuals' power, and equal opportunity to talk in a group represents the egalitarian nature of the group dynamic. Talking also is an act that can attenuate hierarchy. When and where this type of egalitarian ideology is shared and valued, talking and the right to talk, regardless of any potential differences in hierarchy, will be cherished. In American cultural contexts where the core ideology includes social equality, for example, the right to talk is highly valued: it is simultaneously a manifestation and an instrument of freedom. Where the ideology of social equality is not such a dominant cultural theme, or is emphasized to a lesser degree, freedom of expression will not be a particularly significant activity. Indeed, in many East Asian cultural contexts, talking is merely one of many social actions and different types of communication and may not occupy any special place in practical and intellectual tradition.

Some analyses of East Asian communication processes argue that because of the central importance of maintaining harmonious relations and honoring hierarchy, the processes of face saving and face negotiating are recognized in some situations to be more important than honest or truthful negotiation (for example, Gao, Ting-Toomey, and Gudykunst 1996). Being open, straightforward, or assertive in public East Asian situations rarely have any of the positive connotations of honesty, power, confidence, or competence they have in many American contexts. Instead, actions of this type can threaten the cohesion of relationships and even signal the bad character of the individuals involved (Tseng 1973). What appears as passivity or critical lack of assertiveness from an American viewpoint carries with it in many East Asian contexts a whole palette of highly positive associations, including intelligence, flexibility, managing face, cooperativeness, caring, and maturity.

## Talking and Intelligence

Is talking a sign of intelligence or a sign of ignorance? The answer depends on how one defines intelligent thinking. As with the meanings of talking, the models of intelligent thinking also vary across cultures. In Western cultural traditions, for example, intelligent thinking often is defined as a linear and analytical reasoning relying on formal logic and explicit rules (Lebra 1993; Markus, Kitayama, and Heiman 1996; Nisbett et al. 2001). In East Asian cultural traditions, intelligent thinking often involves holistic thinking attending to relations among objects as well as relational thinking, in which listening to and talking on another's viewpoint are emphasized (Azuma 1994).

Different models of intelligent thinking implicate difference in the degree of importance of talking in thought processes. Psychological research has shown that the nature of the effect of verbalization largely depends on the type of task (see Ericsson and Simon 1993; Wilson 1994). Thought processes involved with linear and analytical reasoning are found to be easy to verbalize (Ericsson and Simon 1993; Schooler, Ohlsson, and Brooks 1993), and talking while thinking indeed can help to clarify the thought process (Hafner 1957; Ericsson and Simon

1993; Loftus and Bell 1975). In other words, talking is quite compatible with analytical reasoning. Yet thought processes involved with insight (Schooler, Ohlsson, and Brooks 1993) or holistic thinking (Penney 1975) are found to be difficult to verbalize, and talking while thinking can hinder the thought processes (Schooler, Ohlsson, and Brooks 1993; Kim 2000a).

Another cultural difference with regard to intelligence is what different people may infer about someone from both the content and context of his or her speech. How well a person can reason in speech often gives good clues about how intelligent the speaker is. At the same time, how thoughtful and sensitive the speaker is regarding social surroundings and context also gives good hints about how intelligent he or she is. Sometimes, clues about the speaker gathered from both sources are compatible, but other times, these different sources may provide incompatible information about the speaker. When such incompatibility occurs, cross-cultural differences arise in which source is taken as more important in making inferences about the speaker's intelligence.

According to the classification proposed by Hall (1976) regarding language use, some cultures—such as American cultural contexts—tend to focus more on the content of a speech (called *low-context* culture). Other cultures—such as East Asian cultural contexts—tend to focus more on the context of a speech, such as who the speaker is and the particular setting of the speech (called *high-context* culture). In other words, a person probably should talk more and better in low-context cultures, but a person should talk more cautiously, paying attention to oneself and others, in high-context cultures to appear intelligent.

## CULTURAL PRACTICES OF TALKING

Cultural meanings and collective representations about talking are embodied in common social practices through which collective beliefs implicitly are transmitted to people in the cultural contexts where the beliefs commonly are shared (Bruner 1990; Farr 1998). In social interactions and institutions, such as parenting and education practices, and interactions in workplaces, are core beliefs that guide which behaviors should be encouraged and which behaviors should be discouraged in order to maintain the integrity of the society. These principal beliefs and sentiments are products of collective consciousness (Moscovici 1993). Moreover, to the extent that differences in beliefs will occur from one community to another, differences in the social practices that implicate these beliefs also will occur. Thus, divergent cultural beliefs about talking also should be reflected in divergent social practices and interactions where talking is either encouraged or discouraged.

### Talking in Parenting and Education

The purpose of parental and formal education is to cultivate beliefs, skills, and feelings to support particular cultural ways of understanding the world (Bruner

Many Americans complain that doing business with their East Asian counterparts is difficult because their intentions and goals are not expressed directly. Yet in the workplace, many Asians consider talk to be less important than other forms of communication. In one study of Chinese managers, for example, oral communication skills were seen as least important for prospective employees (Hildenbrandt 1988). Compared to American settings, feedback, challenging, questioning, and interrupting others are reduced or absent in managerial meetings (Lindsay and Dempsey 1985). Being assertive and outgoing are considered to be among the most positive and essential features to be a leader or to succeed in American business contexts (Peters 1987). In many work settings, being vocal is a trait necessary to leadership, and thus is an important factor in both hiring and promotion decisions. Expressing one's ideas is listed in many American business books as one of the key traits.

Thus, even titles of many American business advice books, such as *Talk Your Way to Success* (Wilder 1986), *Talk Your Way to the Top* (Flaherty 1999), *Everything You Need to Know to Talk Your Way to Success* (Kaplan 1995), or *I Wish I'd Said That: How to Talk Your Way Out of Trouble and into Success* (McCallister 1994), emphasize the importance of talking in business success. One book suggests, "Don't be afraid of the sound of your own voice, show off your expertise, offer your insight" (White 1995, 156).

This public advice is indeed taken in actual business practices. For example, in an incident that happened to an acquaintance of one of the authors, an applicant for a fashion designer job was not hired after an interview with the potential employer, and the explanation given by the interviewer was that the applicant appeared to be too shy. While the applicant, who is a Korean American, thought she was being appropriate and respectful in the situation, the interviewer thought her shy and passive, and hence, the cultural misunderstanding of the meaning of talking cost the applicant a job.

Another striking aspect of the incident was that even for those jobs for which verbal skill is not an essential ability, employers still want people who are outgoing and assertive. Being able to express one's thoughts is a matter not only of ability but also personality, as an outgoing person is a "good" and likable person in American cultural contexts (Kim 2000b). As a consequence, individuals who do not share the tendency to express themselves are disadvantaged in decisions of hiring and promotion that make a difference in occupational success.

One of the most common complaints from Asian Americans is that they are notably absent at the higher levels of administration and managerial occupations, and that despite their relatively high education, there is a clear glass ceiling. Statistics regarding the numbers of Asian Americans in leadership indeed support this perception. One of the reasons for the glass-ceiling phenomenon seems to be that Asian Americans often are seen as passive and reserved, and hence lacking leadership (Takaki 1990). The perceived problem is that Asian Americans do not talk enough to make themselves stand out and show that they can lead—an effort that goes against their cultural ideals of thoughtful silence.

## TALKING AND THINKING

The collectively represented meanings of talking shape social practices in a given cultural context, and through these practices also influence the psychology of individuals who participate in the cultural context. The cultural practices reinforce and foster certain psychological tendencies over others (Bruner 1996; Shweder 1991), and thus to develop those tendencies that are culturally reinforced is likely. If talking is important in a cultural context and encouraged in practices, talking is more likely to play an important role in the psychology of people. If talking is unimportant, and is not particularly encouraged or even discouraged, talking will play a less significant role in people's psychology.

Thinking often has been studied in relation to talking in psychology, as thinking and language are considered to be closely connected with each other (for example, Ericsson and Simon 1993; Wierzbicka 1992). Yet the assumption behind studies that automatically bind talking and thinking as related aspects of psychology may be reflecting Western cultural assumptions regarding talking, rather than reflecting a universal psychological reality. Cultural differences in the meanings of the act of talking should lead to differences in how people think and how talking and thinking interact with each other. These differences also should be reflected in how much people rely on language when they are thinking, and the effect of talking should differ for people from different cultural contexts.

Talking has been closely related to thinking in Western cultural contexts (Whorf 1956; Wierzbicka 1992). Thought is believed to be internalized speech (Plato as shown in Miller 1981; Watson 1920). Since Ancient Greek civilization, as exemplified by the Socratic method, eloquence has been highly regarded, and the skill of debate was considered one of the most important skills for a man to have (Nisbett et al. 2001).

The connection between thinking and talking is weaker in many East Asian cultural traditions. Since ancient Chinese civilization, East Asians have believed that talking impairs higher-level thinking. Using the metaphor of water for mind, East Asians believe that only in its very serene state, or contemplative state, can mind clearly reflect the truth. In these contexts, talking is considered to be a disturbance that hinders people from understanding the truth (Markus, Kitayama, and Heiman 1996; Nakamura 1964–85; Needham 1962).

To examine the influence of cultural beliefs about talking and the actual effect of talking on thinking, the cultural variation of the effect of talking on thinking was examined (Kim 2000a). The research utilized the think-aloud method often used to gain access to people's thought processes in psychology. In the procedure of thinking aloud, people are instructed to vocalize their internal thinking process as they occur. For example, as a person is working on a problem, $2 \times 5 = ?$, the procedure of thinking aloud would have the person say, "two times five equals ten" out loud concurrently as these thoughts enter his or her mind.

Obviously, this methodology is founded on the assumption that internal thinking processes are conscious, accessible, and easy to verbalize. Questioning the universality of this assumption, the research examined the effect of talking (that is, thinking aloud) on thinking, focusing on whether talking enhances, impairs, or does not affect cognitive problem solving. In the studies, East Asian American and European American participants were asked to think aloud as they were working on a standardized reasoning test, and their performance was measured as an indication of how talking affected their thinking.

The first study examined the basic question of whether or not cultural differences in beliefs about the effect of talking on thinking in East Asian and American cultural contexts are reflected in actual difference in cognitive performance of people from the respective cultural contexts. The results showed that while the overall performance did not differ between the two groups of participants, the impact of talking on each group's performance differed greatly. Verbalization of the thought process significantly impaired the performance of East Asian Americans, whereas the same verbalization did not affect the performance of European Americans. These results demonstrated that psychological tendencies in how talking affects thinking indeed are consistent with the cultural assumptions about how talking and thinking are related.

The second study was conducted to understand the reasons for this cultural difference in the effect of talking on thinking. The study suggested and tested a possibility that the cultural difference in the effect of talking on thinking partly can be explained by the difference in the relative reliance on language in thinking for people from different cultural contexts. That is, different cultures could differ in their relative use of verbal versus nonverbal thinking. Verbal thinking is easier to talk aloud than nonverbal thinking because verbalization of thought requires only simple vocalization of the process that is already verbal. Yet with nonverbal thinking, talking aloud is a lot more taxing because verbalization of thought requires conversion of the thought into a verbal form before vocalization is possible. Building on this point, it was predicted that talking would hinder the thinking of East Asians because they are more likely to engage in nonverbal thinking, but that talking would not affect the thinking of European Americans because they are more likely to engage in verbal thinking. The second study tested this possibility by examining the effect of an articulatory suppression task—designed to suppress internal speech—in combination with the effect of thinking aloud on the thinking of people from different cultural contexts. The results showed that the degree to which people from the different cultural contexts use verbal thinking differs: European Americans were more likely to use verbal thinking, whereas East Asian Americans were less likely to use verbal thinking. In other words, talking was less likely to affect European Americans' performance as much because they tended to use more verbal thinking that is easier to verbalize, but talking was more likely to impair East Asian Americans' performance because they tended to use more nonverbal thinking that is more difficult to verbalize.

The findings from the studies illustrate two points that we would like to underscore. First, cultural beliefs regarding the relationship between talking and thinking reflect the cultural realities in East Asian and European American contexts. The cultural beliefs are not only abstract beliefs, but also a reflection of the cultural realities. How people process information is not free or independent from the social and cultural contexts in which the processes take place, and therefore, can have quite divergent behavioral and social consequences. The results from this research support the idea of the social construction of even *basic* psychological processes. Second, a notable aspect of the findings is that the performance outcome of both verbal and nonverbal modes of thinking did not differ, showing that one mode of thinking is not necessarily superior to the other. Yet the effect of talking on thinking differed, countering the common American assumption that talking is good for thinking, and that encouraging someone to talk will make the person engage in better thinking. Even an identical act that is thought to lead to the same experience for everyone in fact may not be experienced as the same act by different actors. The act can have different meanings and effects on individuals depending on whether or not they are from cultural contexts where the cultural assumptions behind the act are represented and practiced.

The assumptions of how talking is related to thinking is culturally specific. The task of thinking aloud feels natural for people from cultural contexts where assumptions are shared, but feels unnatural and debilitating for people from cultural contexts where assumptions are not shared. Without recognizing the important and fundamental influence of cultural experiences on shaping people's psychology, one may easily overlook the deeper implications of the expectation of behavioral assimilation—such as that of active verbal participation in class—that sometimes can lead to negative and unforeseen consequences.

## THE PSYCHOLOGY OF DIVERSITY

### Talking as a Cultural Practice

As much as talking is a tool universally used for communication and expression in every culture, and language is one of the most distinctive aspects of human nature, the act of talking is a social and cultural act, and the meanings and practices of talking are as culturally diverse as any human acts. Psychological phenomena, such as the effect of talking on psychology, often are reflections of cultural values and beliefs, and hence, psychology cannot be separated meaningfully from practices or beliefs. Once society recognizes this interdependence between culture and psychology, to understand how closely related the issue of assimilation of psychology is to the issue of assimilation of cultural creed becomes easier. The act of talking is a practice replete with cultural meanings. Not unlike many other cultural practices, the practice of talking is intricately integrated with relevant cultural systems. Isolating talking from its appropriate cultural context limits a full appreciation of what talking means to people and how talking affects the minds of these individuals.

The cultural misunderstanding that talking is positive, desirable, and useful for everyone comes from the assumption of psychic unity (Bruner 1990; Shweder 1995) that considers talking as a universal and uniform phenomenon of humans, independent of sociality. By assuming the universality of the meaning and psychological effect of talking that might be only true in a particular cultural context, one also assumes the rightness of the particular meaning and the truthfulness of the effect, and hence the wrongness of other meanings and effects that deviate from such meaning. This assumption of psychic unity could lead not only to a theoretically limited understanding of psychology, but also to unfortunate practical implications in a multicultural world.

## Psychology in a Multicultural World

The issue of talking and Asian American students dramatizes a crucial point concerning diversity in the growing multicultural world, especially in higher education settings. Without fully recognizing the cultural meanings of the act of talking, educators may problematize a tendency of students who do not hold the common cultural model, thereby creating and perpetuating the stereotype that Asian students are passive and uncreative thinkers. This example highlights the fact that developing a truly diverse university may involve incorporating diversity even with respect to pedagogical assumptions, such as the link between talking and thinking.

Even very common and basic acts and tasks imply culturally specific beliefs and assumptions. This idea leads to challenging questions about acculturation and one-way assimilation. Should East Asian students be encouraged to take debate or theater classes so as to become more comfortable with standing out and expressing oneself, or should mainstream educational principles be encouraged to reflect diversity in styles and conditions of thinking?

By assuming one way as the only way, society can privilege one meaning system against people who do not share the same meanings. The implications of this should be extended beyond the case of East Asian Americans and the issue of talking. We suggest that before the merit of a person is discussed, the first question to ask is how merit is judged. To what extent do the so-called objective criteria that constitute merit reflect culturally specific values and assumptions, and to what degree do the criteria systematically favor groups who share the dominant values and assumptions of the particular cultural context?

A society needs unifying assumptions and values to function as a unit, and to enforce a particular set of assumptions and values over others to some extent is necessary. If the enforcement of assumptions creates systematic privileging of certain groups over others, however, a multicultural society that values individual rights should raise the difficult question of whether individuals should assimilate to the existing assumptions, or whether the assumptions need to be questioned and modified to reflect the diverse needs and realities of individuals. If educators in California are concerned that East Asian and East Asian American students do not actively participate in the academic community, they should begin to question whether talking in class is necessarily beneficial for these students, and whether the students should be encouraged to talk more or be allowed the freedom to pursue learning in alternative ways.

One answer to this question might be that America is a place where the positive meaning of talking is assumed, and students who are learning in America should learn the American way of doing things, because this is ultimately beneficial for anyone who wants to excel in America. Another answer might be that whereas the lesson of talking is important, the lesson of silence and listening also is valuable, and hence, American educators should emphasize the positives from both sets of cultural beliefs and revise the unifying set of educational assumptions and values. Yet another answer might be that American educators should provide enough freedom for students to speak up and think and to stay silent and think as they see fit, and this value of freedom should be the unifying assumption of America.

This is a difficult question, and we are yet to figure out which answer is right or best. One thing to bear in mind is that considering these answers requires one to understand that the act of talking is a cultural practice, and that freedom of speech should not be pressure to speak. Freedom of silence might be no less fundamental a cultural right.

## REFERENCES

Angell, Jerome. 1999. *Words That Make America Great*. New York: Random House.

Austin, John L. 1962. *How to Think with Words*. Oxford: Oxford University Press.

Azuma, Hiroshi. 1986. "Why Study Child Development in Japan?" In *Child Development and Education in Japan*, edited by Harold Stevenson, Hiroshi Azuma, and Kenji Hakuta. New York: Freeman.

———. 1994. *Japanese Discipline and Education*. Tokyo: Tokyo University Press.

Backlund, Phil. 1990. "Oral Activities in the English Classroom." In *Perspectives on Talk and Learning*, edited by Susan Hynds and Donald Rubin. Urbana, Ill.: National Council of Teachers of English.

Bond, Michael H., and P. W. H. Lee. 1981. "Face-saving in Chinese Culture: A Discussion and Experimental Study of Hong Kong Students." In *Social Life and Development in Hong Kong*, edited by A. Y. C. King and R. P. L. Lee. Hong Kong: Chinese University Press.

Bruner, Jerome S. 1990. *Acts of Meaning*. Cambridge, Mass.: Harvard University Press.

———. 1996. *The Culture of Education*. Cambridge, Mass.: Harvard University Press.

Carroll, R. 1988. *Conversation*, translated by Carol Volk. Chicago: University of Chicago Press.

Caudhill, William, and Helen Weinstein, 1969. "Maternal Care and Infant Behavior in Japan and America." *Psychiatry* 32: 12–43.

Clancy, Patricia M. 1986. "The Acquisition of Communicative Styles in Japanese." In *Language Socialization Across Cultures*, edited by Bambi B. Schieffelin and Elinor Ochs. Cambridge: Cambridge University Press.

D'Andrade, Roy. 1990. "Some Propositions About the Relations Between Culture and Human Cognition." In *Cultural Psychology: Essays on Comparative Human Development*, edited by J. W. Stigler, R. A. Shweder, and G. Herdt. New York: Cambridge University Press.

———. 1995. *The Development of Cognitive Anthropology*. New York: Cambridge University Press.

Descartes, René. 1993 [1637]. *Discourse on Method*. Indianapolis: Hackett.

Ericsson, K. Anders, and Herbert. A. Simon. 1993. *Protocol Analysis: Verbal Reports as Data*. Cambridge, Mass.: MIT Press.

Farr, Robert M. 1998. "From Collective to Social Representations: Aller et Retour." *Culture and Psychology* 4(3): 275–96.

Fiske, Alan, Shinobu Kitayama, Hazel Rose Markus, and Richard E. Nisbett. 1998. "The Cultural Matrix of Social Psychology." In *Handbook of Social Psychology*, edited by Daniel T. Gilbert, Susan T. Fiske, and Gardner Lindzey. New York: McGraw-Hill.

Flaherty, Tina S. 1999. *Talk Your Way to the Top*. New York: G. P. Putnam.

Gao, Ge, Stella Ting-Toomey, and William B. Gudykunst. 1996. "Chinese Communication Processes." In *Handbook of Chinese Psychology*, edited by Michael H. Bond. Hong Kong: Oxford University Press.

Giles, Howard, Nikolas Coupland, and John M. Wiemann. 1992. "'Talk Is Cheap . . . but My Word Is My Bond': Beliefs About Talk." In *Sociolinguistics Today: Eastern and Western Perspectives*, edited by Kingsley Bolton and Helen Kwok. London: Routledge.

Hafner, A. J. 1957. "Influence of Verbalization on Problem Solving." *Psychological Reports* 3: 360.

Hall, Edward T. 1976. *Beyond Culture*. New York: Doubleday.

Hildenbrandt, H. W. 1988. "A Chinese Managerial View of Business Communication." *Management Communication Quarterly* 2: 217–34.

Ip, G. W. M. and Michael H. Bond. 1995. "Culture, Values, and the Spontaneous Self-Concept." *Asian Journal of Psychology* 1(1): 29–35.

Kagan, Jerome, Richard B. Kearsley, and Philip R. Zelazo. 1977. "The Effects of Infant Day Care on Psychological Development." *Evaluation Quarterly* 1(1): 109–42.

Kaplan, Burton. 1995. *Everything You Need to Know to Talk Your Way to Success*. New York: Prentice Hall Trade.

Kim, Heejung S. 2000a. "We Talk, Therefore We Think? A Cultural Analysis of the Effect of Talking on Thinking." Unpublished paper. Stanford: Stanford University.

———. 2000b. Collective representation of talking. Unpublished data. Stanford: Stanford University.

Lebra, Takie S. 1993. "Culture, Self, and Communication in Japan and the United States." In *Communication in Japan and the United States*, edited by William B. Gudykunst. Albany: State University of New York Press.

Lindsay, Cindy P., and Bobby L. Dempsey. 1985. "Experiences in Training Chinese Business People to Use U.S. Management Techniques." *Journal of Applied Behavioral Science* 21(1): 65–78.

Loftus, Geoffrey R., and Susan M. Bell. 1975. "Two Types of Information in Picture Memory." *Journal of Experimental Psychology: Human Learning and Memory* 1(2): 103–13.

Lubman, Sarah. 1998. "Some Students Must Learn to Question." *San Jose Mercury News*, Feburuary 23: 1A, 12A.

Markus, Hazel Rose, and Shinobu Kitayama. 1991. "Culture and the Self: Implications for Cognition, Emotion, and Motivation." *Psychological Review* 98(2): 224–53.

Markus, Hazel Rose, Shinobu Kitayama, and Rachael J. Heiman. 1996. "Culture and 'Basic' Psychological Principles." In *Social Psychology: Handbook of Basic Principles*, edited by E. Tory Higgins and Arie W. Kruglanski. New York: Guilford.

Markus, Hazel Rose, Patricia R. Mullally, and Shinobu Kitayama. 1997. "Selfways: Diversity in Modes of Cultural Participation." In *Conceptual Self in Context: Culture, Experience, Self-Understanding*, edited by Ulric Neisser and David Jopling. Cambridge: Cambridge University Press.

Marsella, Anthony J. 1993. "Counseling and Psychotherapy with Japanese Americans: Cross-Cultural Considerations." *American Journal of Orthopsychiatry* 63(2): 200–8.

McCabe, Allyssa. 1998. "At Nicky's House: Developing Imagination to Deal with Reality. *Cahiers de Psychologie Cognitive* [Current Psychology of Cognition] 17(2): 229–44.

McCallister, Linda. 1994. *I Wish I'd Said That: How to Talk Your Way Out of Trouble and into Success*. Chichester, N.Y.: John Wiley & Sons.

Miller, George A. 1981. *Language and Speech*. San Francisco: W. H. Freeman.

Minami, Masahiko. 1994. "English and Japanese: A Cross-Cultural Comparison of Parental Styles of Narrative Elicitation." *Issues in Applied Linguistics* 5: 383–407.

Minami, Masahiko, and Allyssa McCabe. 1995. "Rice Balls and Bear Hunts: Japanese and North American Family Narrative Patterns." *Journal of Child Language* 22(2): 423–45.

Mindell, Phyllis. 1995. *A Woman's Guide to the Language of Success: Communicating with Confidence and Power*. Englewood Cliffs, N.J.: Prentice Hall.

Morsbach, Helmut. 1987. "The Importance of Silence and Stillness in Japanese Nonverbal Communication: A Cross-Cultural Approach." In *Cross-Cultural Perspectives in Nonverbal Communication*, edited by Fernando Poyatos. New York: Goettingen, Hogrefe & Huber.

Moscovici, Serge. 1993. *The Invention of Society*, translated by W. D. Halls. Cambridge, Mass.: Blackwell.

Nakamura, Hajima. 1964–85. *Ways of Thinking of Eastern Peoples*. Honolulu: University of Hawaii Press.

Needham, Joseph. 1962. *Science and Civilization in China, Physics and Physical Technology*. Cambridge: Cambridge University Press.

Nisbett, Richard E., Kaiping Peng, Incheol Choi, and Ara Norenzayan. 2001. "Culture and Systems of Thought: Holistic vs. Analytic Cognition." *Psychological Review* 108(2): 291–310.

Pear, T. H. 1936. "The Desirability of Teaching School Children the Technique of Discussion." *British Journal of Educational Psychology* 6: 9–22.

Penney, Catherine G. 1975. "Modality Effects in Short-Term Verbal Memory." *Psychological Bulletin* 82(1): 68–84.

Peters, Roger. 1987. *Practical Intelligence: Working Smarter in Business and Everyday Life*. New York: Harper & Row.

Quinn, Naomi, and Dorothy C. Holland. 1987. "Introduction." In *Language and Thought*, edited by Dorothy C. Holland and Naomi Quinn. New York: Cambridge University Press.

Rhee, Eun, James Uleman, Hoon Lee, and Robert Roman. 1995. "Spontaneous Self-Descriptions and Ethnic Identities in Individualistic and Collectivistic Cultures." *Journal of Personality and Social Psychology* 69(1): 142–52.

Schooler, Jonathan W., Stella Ohlsson, and Kevin Brooks. 1993. "Thoughts Beyond Words: When Language Overshadows Insight." *Journal of Experimental Psychology: General* 122(2): 166–83.

Shore, Bradd. 1996. *Culture in Mind*. New York: Oxford University Press.

Shweder, Richard A. 1991. *Thinking Through Cultures: Expeditions in Cultural Psychology*. Cambridge, Mass.: Harvard University Press.

———. 1995. "Cultural Psychology: What Is It?" In *Cultural and Psychology Reader*, edited by Nancy R. Goldberger and Jody B. Veroff. New York: New York University Press.

Shweder, Richard A., and Edmund J. Bourne. 1984. "Does the Concept of Person Vary Cross-Culturally?" In *Culture Theory: Essays on Mind, Self, and Emotion*, edited by Richard A. Shweder and Robert A. LeVine. Cambridge: Cambridge University Press.

Smith, Peter B., and Michael H. Bond. 1999. *Social Psychology Across Cultures*. Needham Heights, Mass.: Allyn and Bacon.

Smitherman, Geneva. 1994. *Black Talk: Words and Phrases from the Hood to the Amen Corner*. Boston: Houghton Mifflin.

Takaki, Ronald. 1990. *Strangers from a Different Shore: A History of Asian Americans*. New York: Penguin Books.

Thonssen, Lester, and Howard Gilkinson. 1955. "Speech." *Review of Educational Research* 25: 139–53.

Tobin, Joseph J., David Y. H. Wu, and Dana H. Davidson. 1989. *Preschool in Three Cultures: Japan, China and the United States*. New Haven: Yale University Press.

Triandis, Harry C. 1989. "The Self and Social Behavior in Differing Cultural Contexts." *Psychological Review* 96(3): 506–20.

Tseng, Wen-Shing. 1973. "The Concept of Personality in Confucian Thought." *Psychiatry: Journal for the Study of Interpersonal Processes* 36(2): 191–202.

Watson, J. B. 1920. "Is Thinking Merely the Action of Language Mechanisms?" *British Journal of Psychology* 11(11): 87–104.

White, Kate. 1995. *Why Good Girls Don't Get Ahead, but Gutsy Girls Do*. New York: Warner Books.

Whorf, Benjamin L. 1956. *Language, Thought, and Reality: Selected Writings*. Cambridge, Mass.: MIT Press.

Wierzbicka, Anna. 1992. "Talking About Emotions: Semantics, Culture, and Cognition." *Cognition & Emotion* 6(3–4): 285–319.

Wilder, Lilyan. 1986. *Talk Your Way to Success: Wilder Method for Effective Business Communication*. New York: Simon & Schuster.

Wilson, Timothy D. 1994. "The Proper Protocol: Validity and Completeness of Verbal Reports." *Psychological Science* 5(5): 249–52.

Yan, J. J. 1987. "On Establishing the Field of Chinese Communication [in Chinese]." *Xing Wen Xue Kan* 10: 50–53.

# Chapter 21

# Color Blindness as a Barrier to Inclusion: Assimilation and Nonimmigrant Minorities

## Hazel Rose Markus, Claude M. Steele, and Dorothy M. Steele

The successful assimilation of millions of immigrants from strikingly different worlds into one society is a compelling American story. In the shadow of this story is another story: the struggle to include millions of nonimmigrant minorities—African Americans, American Indians, Latinos—within the mainstream of society. The first story is a celebration of difference that reveals America as a haven for religious, cultural, and political difference. The second story tells of an ongoing struggle with difference—in this case, a difference not of religion or cultural values but in social, racial, and ethnic status. This story turns on how to bring the powerful American ideal of equality and equal opportunity together with reality of difference in psychological and social experience that derives from the differential status in society.

In trying to understand this struggle over inclusion, our analysis begins with a known but perhaps underappreciated fact: the societal settings that are central to a group's movement into mainstream American life, such as school and the workplace, may be experienced differently by America's nonimmigrant minorities than by majority group members. These groups share similarities of experience in these settings; but tied to group identity, important differences arise. Minority group members know, for example, that their group has long experienced discrimination in the setting. They worry that negative stereotypes about their group influence how they are treated and evaluated in the setting. In reaction to these concerns, they feel unwelcome and alienated in the setting. Such group differences in how these public settings are experienced, we suggest, may play an underappreciated role in the shadow story of America's struggle with inclusion.

Yet underappreciation does not mean that as a society we do not acknowledge historical and ongoing inequalities between these minorities and the American mainstream in access to education, wealth, even freedom of movement. We are a society with a great capacity for self-examination. Yet for some reason, we have been reluctant to see that these group differences in lived experience and perspective might be relevant to the goal of achieving inclusion in important public settings such as school and the workplace. Here, where our understanding of group differences in lived experience should inform our efforts to achieve inclusion, there is a disconnect. Why?

We will argue that an irony is at play, that one of the chief causes of this disconnect is less the prejudices of American society than one of our society's best products: the desire to remedy group prejudice by not seeing group difference, an essentially progressive norm of the post–civil rights era in American life. The core of this idea, given legal force by the Fourteenth Amendment, is that people are equal, that differences between people in race and ethnicity should not affect opportunity in society, that to be color-blind is desirable, and that despite some variation in life circumstance, people can succeed in this society roughly in proportion to their efforts and talents. This can be thought of as the race-neutral or color-blind model of how to form a community of people with diverse backgrounds. This model does recognize that the life circumstances of all groups are not actually equal, that our local worlds still are substantially organized by race and ethnicity, and that resources, standing, and respect are powerfully associated with these factors. Yet this model rests on the faith that not seeing difference is the surest route to reducing these inequalities and improving inclusion. In recent years, however, both in public discussion and social science research, there is a growing sense that this model has important limits (Berry 1984; Brewer and Brown 1998; Hornsey and Hogg 2000a, 2000b; Schofield 1986a, 1986b; Wolsko et al. 2000). Indeed, the color-blind model may make it difficult for our public institutions to see group differences in lived experience and appreciate their role in inclusion; it may constitute a cultural injunction not to see group difference.

We propose that alternative models of inclusion may preserve the American commitment to equality of opportunity, but in the effort to achieve it, acknowledge group differences in status and lived experience. These other models strive to reduce the threat that can be attached to a group's identity in critical public settings such as school and the workplace, and thus achieve what we call *identity safety*. The goal is to acknowledge differences attached to group identity and create a setting that is accepting of differences as nonlimiting and as a basis of respect. Following Thomas (1992), we use the term *downward social constitution* to refer to the experience of being in a setting where, based on a given group identity, one is exposed to a concert of representations, historical narratives, possible judgments, treatments, interactions, expectations, affective reactions, and so on, that can limit and devalue one (Thomas 1992). Identity safety refers to the effort to rid a setting of this potential for group-linked downward constitution. We assume that identity safety is a prerequisite of full inclusion. In this sense, then, people's difference—the identity on which this downward constitution is based—must be addressed. Otherwise, one's sense of being threatened in the setting will linger, becoming its own barrier to full inclusion.

An identity cannot be achieved or maintained by one's self alone. Identity is a social product and social process that is interdependent with one's ongoing interactions. Through engagement with and recognition by others, an individual becomes a person and identities are conferred. Settings characterized by broad patterns of ethnic, racial, or cultural downward social constitution will interfere with a person's ability to develop an effective identity as a student, as an employee, as a citizen.

## COLOR BLINDNESS IN THE CLASSROOM: MAINSTREAM AND MINORITY PERSPECTIVES

To illuminate some of the tacit social psychological barriers to inclusion, we offer the following fictional episode between a white teacher and black parents in a parent-teacher conference about the couple's third-grade son, Bennett Wilson. After discussing Bennett's performance, the parents raise concerns with the teacher, Mrs. Dalton, about the overall racial climate of the classroom and the school.

TEACHER: I appreciate your concerns, Mr. and Mrs. Wilson, but the guiding ethic of this school and of my classroom is one of color blindness. We believe that all of our children are equal; we strive every day to treat them the same.

MRS. WILSON: I accept your intentions and your personal concern. But we noticed that there are no black children in the top third-grade reading group.

TEACHER: That's true, and I am concerned. But I just don't have any black students who read at the pace of that group. They are a very bright group. To be fair, and to hold to the same standards for all students, the reading group assignments have worked out this way at this point.

MR. WILSON: Bennett has another worry. He's afraid he will be sent to the principal's office, like a lot of the black kids. He also says that the white kids come from a different part of town and that it's harder to be friends with them and do things together.

TEACHER: Even if these things are true, they don't have anything to do with race. I try to treat everyone the same, regardless of their race or background. And the principal of this school holds the same value. I hope you don't think this school is racist.

MR. WILSON: I don't know. It's just that the black kids seem to be seen as troublemakers. They get disciplined an awful lot, and they get harsher punishments. They never get into the gifted and advanced classes. This is hard to ignore.

TEACHER: Please don't be oversensitive. We work really hard not to discriminate on race. We don't see differences based on skin color. We work to make this a place where race does not matter.

MRS. WILSON: But Bennett seems to feel like black kids don't get the benefit of the doubt; like race does matter here.

Here are people trying to bridge the American racial divide to form an effective schoolroom community that meets the needs of both the individuals involved and the larger society. The challenge they face is that although they are all talking about the same classroom and school, minority students may experience this setting quite differently than do those in the majority. The pictures on the wall are the same for the two groups, as are the teachers, students, many of the goals, rules, class plans, and so on. Yet this single school setting can be a very different life context for members of different ethnic groups.

## The Mainstream Perspective of the Teacher

The teacher, and those students who share her racial and social class background, are part of a social category of people whose sense of belonging in the classroom is taken for granted. As members of the dominant group, their belonging in the central institutions of society, such as the school, is implicit—not likely to rise to the level of a conscious idea. They are relatively free to engage the manifest goals of the classroom without worry that their group identity will cause them to be devalued there. Thus for the teacher, the functions and goals of the classroom can be taken more or less at face value.

Moreover, in responding to the social diversity in her classroom, the teacher can draw on the broad American value that stresses the equality of all Americans, and be comforted by the principle that to treat people from all groups the same way is important. This is a cultural ideal that the teacher tries to achieve. Indeed, the mere existence of diversity in her classroom may lead the teacher to adhere to it even more. Thus, because her own experience is not likely to alert her to group differences in the experience of society's settings, and because she is committed to the cultural ideal of treating all people the same way, the teacher may not readily see that Bennett and his family are likely to experience this same classroom in different ways.

## The Minority Perspective of the Wilson Family

For Bennett and other minority students, the experience of the teacher's classroom might be quite different than it is for majority students. Learning goals, future ambitions, and recognition of the importance of education to progress in society are shared, but there are often differences that have implications for achievement in the setting. For black students, the classroom is among other things a site of contact with the American mainstream. Reflecting the long history of their group's experience in American society as well as the ongoing nature of that experience, black students can feel at risk of devaluation in this setting. For them, this classroom is a setting that contains an element of what we call an *identity threat*.

## Identity Threat

This sense of threat has multiple sources tied to the history and structure of American society. That considerable racial and group discrimination continues, and the fact that race and ethnicity organize society in ways that sustain group inequalities, makes it difficult for members of nonimmigrant minority groups to dismiss the threat of devaluation based on group identity. Next is the one-way nature of the assimilation in America. Members of the minority group, such as Bennett and his parents, must assimilate to the culture, standards, and styles of the societal or classroom mainstream, while the latter—the teacher and majority students—are not required to take an interest in or value any of the distinguishing characteristics of the minority groups. Also, the styles, histories, and appearances that are projected as markers of success in mainstream settings are predominantly those of the majority group and culture. Functioning together, these features of the school and classroom offer Bennett and his family conditional terms of inclusion: you can succeed here, but you will have do so in the face of the possibility of discrimination, a value scheme that disadvantages the characteristics of your group relative to those of the majority group, and a group-based social organization that can insulate you from mainstream opportunities. In short, the Wilsons are likely to come into this school situation with a default concern: that the school will not provide Bennett with the same opportunity structure it provides to majority students.

## Different Experiences, Different Psychologies

Accordingly, this classroom is likely to afford the Wilsons and minority students more generally a different psychology than it affords majority students and the teacher. This classroom alerts them to their group identity, making it a relevant lens through which to see and judge their experience in the setting; it makes an easy trust of the setting difficult. Having a sense of trust in what schooling has to offer minority students is difficult when discrepancies exist between how the diversity goals are represented and how they seem to be implemented. These students cannot reasonably ignore the possibility that owing to their group identity, whether theirs is an identity chosen and affirmed or ascribed to them by others, they may be devalued in the setting, treated stereotypically, or have their prospects neglected. As a consequence, the Wilsons may feel that in this setting they need to be concerned about their group identity—which places them under threat—and to assert its positive features and defend its claims to equal treatment. If Bennett were an American Indian or a Latino, the details of the situation would vary, but many similar concerns about identity safety also would be present.

## The Need for Identity Safety

The Wilsons' situation has a clear implication: for this classroom to provide truly equal opportunity for both majority and minority students, the teacher and school must model the school experience so that it assures identity safety to minority students such as Bennett. The school setting must foster a clear commitment to the principle that one's group identity will not be a source of one's downward constitution, at least not in the classroom setting. Moreover, since a sense of identity threat is likely to be a default assumption of minority families entering the situation, the school should take a proactive approach toward building this understanding.

Some teachers might be disinclined at first to accept the legitimacy of minority students' sense of identity threat and mistrust. In many cases, these teachers can rightfully feel that they have done little to provoke it. They can note their efforts to implement the American ideal of equal treatment for everybody—and following on this idea, they can believe that the problem of mistrust stems from the minority students' oversensitivity.

A genuine racial divide can ensue.

## MODELS OF COMMUNITY AS CULTURAL MODELS

As Mrs. Dalton interacts with Bennett, a number of interrelated associations, ideas, images, attitudes, expectations, schemas, and response tendencies tied to his ethnic group identity are likely to be chronically accessible to this teacher. These representations are a function of her participation in a color-stratified world. The question is how these elements will lend meaning to her situation. Invoking the widely held notion that race is a difference that should not matter, the teacher is attempting to be color-blind. She is striving to be fair and to display her commitment to fairness in her actions with the claim that race is irrelevant in her classroom and in her school. Indeed, this teacher may well be a very accepting person who would score as non-prejudiced on measures of individual racism and prejudice. Yet her commitment to a model of community that says difference does not matter works against the recognition of difference in experience that accompanies minority group status—and however inadvertently, this teacher works against trust and inclusion.

The teacher could use a different model to make sense of the representations and actions that accompany her interactions with Bennett. She could try to organize the situation according to a model of community in which the teacher actively resists the tendency to stereotype, limit, and downwardly constitute Bennett on the basis of his ethnic group identity.

## Defining Models

Models of community, like the color-blind model, are overarching cultural models that, during a given historical period, organize how Americans form community from peoples of diverse backgrounds. In developing our idea of models of community, we are building on the concepts of social representations and cultural models (Markus, Mullally, and Kitayama 1997; Moscovici 1988, 1998; Shore 1996; Sperber 1990). A cultural model is a collection of understandings and practices. According to Shore (2000, 8), these models do several significant kinds of work: "Models make possible our orientation to the world and to each other. Models allow conceptualization, making it possible for us to remember, to think and even to feel. Models enable communication of these thoughts, memories, and feelings to others." In this sense, we think of models of community as collectively held, elaborated, communicated, and diffused interpretive frameworks that are at once forms of knowledge and social practices (Moscovici 1988). These cultural models are powerful precisely because they typically are taken for granted, transparent. When some life context is organized according to a cultural model—such as the specifics of Bennett Wilson's third-grade classroom—it often appears as natural, necessary, and inevitable.

## ONE-WAY ASSIMILATION: AMERICA'S FUNDAMENTAL MODEL OF COMMUNITY

In America, the color-blind–one-way assimilation model described to the Wilson family succinctly by Bennett's teacher is what might be called the fundamental model of community. This is the model that currently seems the best fit to the American philosophical and ideological foundation and is the one incorporated and fostered by the legal system; it is the model that, at least as an ideal, is now proudly extended to all Americans. We suggest, however, that the ideological and legal stance of color blindness, because it denies socially constituted differences associated with race—increasingly well supported by social science research—can work to perpetuate and institutionalize the very racial and ethnic divisions among people that it seeks to overcome.

In the time since the 1964 Civil Rights Act, the seams of this fundamental model have begun to show. Although the model, with its stress on equality and justice, has become the reigning cultural ideal, few social scientists would argue that it has become a reality. America, for example, is still a substantially segregated society (Massey and Denton 1993). While the full consequences of this growing diversity remain to be seen, some outcomes already are dramatically apparent. As indicated by socioeconomic status, health, housing, and education, nonimmigrant minority groups are not thriving. The poverty rate of Latinos and African and Native Americans remains critically higher than that for non-

Hispanic whites (Lamison-White 1997). The mean net worth of whites, for example, is $95,667, almost four times the $23,818 mean net worth of African Americans (Oliver and Shapiro 1997). Moreover, rates of infant mortality, of living in substandard housing, and of crime and victimization all are much higher among African and Native Americans and Latinos than among whites (National Center for Health Statistics 1998; U.S. Department of Housing and Urban Development and U.S. Bureau of Census 1997; Bureau of Justice 1997).

Further, the assumptions of the fundamental model about the nature of difference and inclusion have come under considerable contest. Alternative models of community are not color-blind and not assimilationist—several forms of multiculturalism, for example, even separatism, have sprung to the foreground of public discourse. In some quarters, certainly universities, public schools, and even work organizations, model wars have ensued. At the center of these wars are questions about how to understand group difference and how to develop community that, as Prentice and Miller (1999, 19) put it, can "recognize and appreciate ethnic and cultural differences without reifying divisive group boundaries."

## History and Terms of the Model

As it emerged in the 1950s with the 1954 *Brown v. Board of Education* desegregation decision of the Supreme Court, the great advantage of the one-way assimilation–color-blind model was that it sought to overcome segregation and separate-but-equal laws that dominated American race relations from the beginning of the century; it was not a new model. Assimilation was always the official model of inclusion in relation to America's European immigrant groups. Yet in the 1950s, and again bolstered by the 1964 Civil Rights Act, assimilation was extended to include African Americans and other disenfranchised groups, thus becoming, at least as a governing ideal, America's fundamental model of community.

In the color-blind model, group differences are seen to be largely superficial, certainly not substantial enough to warrant a claim on public policy or organization. After all, this was a model in counterpoint to the separate-but-equal law that had reified racial difference to the point of apartheid. Moreover, this model, at least at the official level, offers straightforward terms of inclusion: if individuals assimilate to the cultural mainstream, they will be included in the American community regardless of color and will be moved along; if individuals do not assimilate, all bets are off. In this deal, incorporation into American society is conceptualized for the most part as a one-way process.

Currently within the United States, most educational and workplace settings are engaging and promoting this color-blind–one-way assimilation model of community. Certainly, differences are to be observed among people, yet the assumption holds that these differences are the result of other factors such as talent and merit, but not race or ethnicity. To acknowledge differences among people that may be associated with their group identity is understood to be the same as stereotyping or homogenizing them; it denies them their individuality. At the same time, the need to appreciate and understand group difference is a persistent concern.

## A Pervasive and Contradictory View

The broad incorporation of the color-blind model of community was documented recently in a study of current American thought about difference and diversity. Plaut and Markus (2002) sampled the cultural environment, conducting what Thurstone (1931) referred to as a "trawl of public opinion." They conducted focus groups, surveys, and content analyses of media and found that the most frequently expressed response to differences and diversity in schools and workplaces is that differences among people associated with race and ethnicity are superficial and mostly irrelevant.

When probed, this common understanding reveals itself to be complex and self-contradictory: it holds that ethnic and racial variety is pleasing and important, both to the various groups themselves and to society as a whole. Indeed, diversity is so important that it can and should be celebrated. This idea, however, typically is coupled with the notion that despite the important diversity to be found in ethnic foods, costumes, customs, and festivals, in the most important respects, "people are really all the same." The view is that differences found among people typically coded by race and ethnicity—although potentially significant and worthy of appreciation—do not and should not affect how society functions.

The paradoxical pairing of the idea that society should celebrate difference with the idea that this difference doesn't really matter is not accidental. This perspective on difference is an all-American effort to reconcile diversity with equality. As Shweder (1991) observes, the implication is that since people are equal, they must be similar. Any diversity claimed is just a matter of superficial difference that can and should be ignored. The notion that at the end of the day, people are people is a pleasant and comforting thought; when supported by such general propositions as "everyone likes to be treated with respect," it is hard to resist.

Built into the foundation of the one-way assimilation–color-blind model is a thoroughly modern assumption—one that is still at the core of many perspectives on race, ethnicity, and culture in the social sciences. This assumption holds that race, ethnicity, and cultures are relatively superficial features of personhood overlaid on the "basic" person, and that to ignore them in the quest for a general and universal personhood is possible. As one of Plaut and Markus's (2002) respondents, a white manager of a very large diverse group of employees in a bank avowed, "I see people for who they really are. When you shed the superficial stuff like color, you can get at the real person."

Plaut and Markus (2002) also examined the content of current magazine ad-

these particular structural realities. For example, to the extent that Bennett experiences being left out or picked on, he may withdraw and not raise his hand to read. The teacher may thus receive "behavioral confirmation" (Snyder and Swann 1978) of her view that Bennett does not read well enough or show enough motivation to be in the top group. If the teacher were to try to encourage Bennett, despite his lack of "appropriate" or "enthusiastic" behavior, she might begin to afford a different social and psychological experience for Bennett, one in which he could feel valued and included. This type of effort to cross a structural divide could change Bennett's interpretation of what the teacher thinks about him and eventually provide a different psychological experience for Bennett, one in which he might identify with and succeed in school.

The ways in which social locations, situations, and practices regulate, express, and transform the human psyche and shape psychological experience is the subject matter of social and cultural psychology. Research in these areas is progressively revealing that despite the ideology of individualism and the manifold political and legal practices that privilege the individual, people are not just autonomous individuals solely under their own production and orchestration. They also are centers of dynamic interpersonal relationships that are significant in determining who they are, who they try to be, and how they behave. Although popular discourse and research in the social sciences and humanities often cast identity as an individual choice (Waters 1990), it is increasingly evident that identity is indeed a group project. Identity depends to some large degree on how others see you and identify you. We are, as Mead (1934) recognized, caught in, made possible by, and held together by each other's nets of meanings, interpretations, and actions. If the nets involve a preponderance of representations, beliefs, expectations, and actions relevant to one's ethnic group that are negative, marginalizing, essentializing, or limiting, they will be impossible to ignore or reject.

Ironically, to the extent that these nets are positive, supportive, and foster culturally valued abilities, skills, and potentials—as they do for many people in majority groups—they are likely to be unnoticed. As a result, learning, growth, and advancement are most often seen and experienced as the result of individual effort. The ways in which individual behavior and development are scaffolded by a vast network of positive representations and supportive interpersonal relationships are usually invisible.

## The Social Nature of Learning

In the exchange between the Wilson family and the teacher, the Wilsons know that the group with which they are most likely to be identified stands in a subordinate relationship to the teacher's group. Regardless of the teacher's claims, what the Wilson family knows is that her views, her understandings, and her expectations cannot be easily separated from those that are broadly communicated and institutionalized within society toward their ethnic group, despite her intentions toward fairness and color blindness. This is not a failing of the teacher to reason independently or free herself from the shackles of custom and social pressure, but a straightforward reflection of the fact that thoughts, feelings, and actions are given structure and form by those meanings, schemas, scripts, and practices that are chronically available and widely distributed in the community at large. Thought and action outside these interpretive frameworks require the development and dissemination of alternative systems of meanings and practices with respect to downwardly constituted ethnic groups.

Thus, Bennett and others like him find themselves in a school where they are being constituted by relationships, classroom practices, and learning opportunities that do not reflect them as valued members of the class. The experience of being a young student in a situation in which he is being downwardly constituted by those entrusted with his development as a person and student has a powerful influence on Bennett's ability to identify with and freely approach the task of learning. He is in the process described by Mead as "attending to and incorporating the views of others." When these views are limiting, this can be a substantial barrier to learning.

Specific dramatic evidence for the powerful consequences of the views of others on individual performance is accumulating rapidly and recently has been reviewed in a number of places (Crocker, Major, and Steele 1998; Steele, Spencer, and Aronson forthcoming; Jones 1997). In one compelling example, Steele and Aronson (1995) designed a series of experiments to test whether the stereotype threat that black students might experience when taking a difficult standardized test could significantly depress their performance on the test. They asked highly qualified black and white college students at an elite university to take a test made up of items from the advanced Graduate Record Examination in literature. Most of the students were college sophomores, which meant that the test was challenging for their abilities; Steele and Aronson reasoned that this feature would make the testing situation a different experience for black participants and for white participants. For black students, difficulty with the test could make the stereotype of their group relevant to the interpretation of their performance. They know they are especially likely to be seen as having limited ability due to the prevailing representation of their ethnic group. Groups not stereotyped in this way will not experience this intimidation. This extra worry on the part of African American students is that their performance might cause them to be seen stereotypically, or might inadvertently confirm the stereotype that they do not belong to the walks of life, in the jobs and careers, in which they have been heavily invested.

In a series of studies, Steele and Aronson (1995) found that when the threat of being stereotyped as less intellectually able than white students was present— that is, when the test was represented as diagnostic of ability, so that frustration with it could be taken as confirming the racial stereotype—black students did much worse than white students even when skill differences between the two groups were controlled. Yet when the threat of being stereotyped was removed by representing the test as a lab measure of problem solving that was *not* diagnostic of individual differences in ability, black students performed just as well as qualified white students—on the same test. Simply giving the students the instruction before the test that it was not a measure of their general intellectual ability removed the possibility of invoking the stereotype of lower intellectual ability for the black students. These studies demonstrate that something other than ability is involved in producing gaps in performance. Clearly, small changes in the environment can change the meaning of the situation in a way that benefits learning and achievement.

## CULTURAL CHANGE IN THE CLASSROOM: CREATING IDENTITY SAFETY

The perspective of social constitution suggests that cultural change involves the specific actions and interpretations of individuals who create and maintain, but who also can modify, sociocultural realities. Accordingly, to improve intergroup relations and individual outcomes, it should be possible within a given niche (say a school) to change some subset of the prevailing meanings and practices and thereby change the prevailing model of community to improve intergroup relations and individual outcomes. The key is to recognize that race and ethnicity are undeniable social realities that are constitutive of the person and that create differences among people. These differences are by no means essential or immutable; they change as the nature of the social situation changes. They matter, however, because people themselves live their lives in these terms and require recognition of them, and because people respond to one another through the meanings associated with race and ethnicity. This means that a color-blind model may not always be the best model for every situation. Through a concerted action in a given niche, it is possible for educators and parents and students to move away from an exclusive focus on a color-blind model of community and to develop and institute models of community that focus on achieving identity safety. These models are likely to include practices that strive for some mutual accommodation whenever possible, and that acknowledge the real differences in experience that low status and marginality in American society has imposed historically on the nonimmigrant minorities and increasingly on new immigrants (Suárez-Orozco, ch. 1 herein).

To bridge this divide between mainstream experiences and minority group experiences and to more closely approach the ideal of equal opportunity, we argue that school and classroom settings should not always endeavor to be color-blind. Instead, they should strive for a climate in which group difference—the difference in the local worlds experienced by minority and nonminority students in the setting—commonly is recognized by all in the setting and used in achieving a respectful understanding and valuing of all students. Such practices convey to minority students that their group identity will not be used to downwardly constitute them—see them as problematic members of the setting—but instead will be used to incorporate them and their perspectives into the setting, and to foster their achievement there. These interventions will mostly be sensitive to group identity and its consequences yet also attend to the details of individual social circumstances.

At this point, one might ask, Why not just affirm the minority students' talents and their valued membership in the class without recognizing their group identity? Our answer is that this might work well in the short run, on single occasions. Over time, however, when the minority students' group identity is not addressed, in the midst of a larger society that makes a great deal of it, these students may doubt whether they are really safe from identity threat. They may wonder at what point their belonging to their group might make them vulnerable to devaluation.

Other strategies exist for dealing with diversity in the classroom that at first glance would seem to help create identity safety but in fact work against this goal. Were the teacher in our example to read our arguments, she might be tempted to "celebrate diversity" by displaying in her classroom positive particulars of minority culture such as pictures of minority heroes, festivals, artwork and the like. Her intentions here would be good, but the effectiveness of this strategy has everything to do with implementation. Unless these particulars are represented as being of central value for all students, and unless these celebrative displays are embedded in a general classroom climate in which the intellectual potential of minority students is taken seriously, such celebrations may be mistrusted by minority students and simply ignored by majority students. Indeed, if these celebrative displays are not coupled with other practices that assure identity safety (for example, challenging work designed to move students to high levels of achievement), they may backfire, deepening minority students' sense of identity threat and leading majority students to underappreciate the contributions made by those from the minority culture.

Another important challenge to forming community from diversity in the classroom is how to handle the need for skill remediation. Our teacher, for example, believed that she had no minority students who could read at the level of the top reading group. In any third-grade class, children's levels of reading skills will vary, especially at the beginning of the school year. In some communities, skills will vary even more, and this variation may be linked to students' race or social status. In these communities, minority students may enter the classroom with weaker skills than majority students, reflecting a variety of prior educational inequities.

What should our third grade teacher do? First, perhaps, examine this diagnosis: it fits so closely with prevailing stereotypes that one might constructively hold it under suspicion enough to reexamine it carefully. Before placing students in stratified reading groups, for example, the teacher first would need to use multiple sources of assessment to determine her students' current level of achievement in reading. Still, the teacher may find differences in achievement between black and white students. Then what?

The guiding principle is that the effort to remediate skills in the setting must not suggest, even indirectly, that the distribution of skills between the groups somehow reflects a limiting group difference. This is the risk of group remediation strategies that allow a confounding of group identity with skill remediation, especially for groups whose abilities already are negatively stereotyped in the larger society. Ability tracking in elementary and secondary schools often has the feature of minority students being disproportionately placed in lower tracks—presumably suited to more limited abilities. Some minority programs at the college level also have the feature of targeting remediation efforts almost exclusively at the minority student population. Such practices likely make the negative group stereotype highly salient in the broader school setting, greatly exacerbating the sense of identity and stereotype threat that minority students experience.

## Practices That Promote Identity Safety

To promote identity safety, the school and our teacher must take a group difference that is often negatively represented in the larger society and model it in the local world of the school as a nonlimiting difference that is a basis for respect, rather than a basis for downwardly constituting a person as less smart, less deserving, less culturally appropriate, and less valuable to the school community. This idea perhaps can be best illustrated by describing some practices that our teacher might have used in her classroom. Had these practices been in place, they might have preempted the Wilsons' concerns.

In the context of showing that she recognizes the positive features of minority students' group identity (for example, by representing it in classroom displays, books, music, and other curriculum areas), the teacher can express through her actions and words the highest expectations for all students' learning—expressly for minority students. She can focus on the idea that every student comes to school to learn, and that with work—regardless of their current level of skills and understanding—all students can steadily progress to the highest levels. This practice seeds the local environment with the idea that the minority group identity is no barrier to learning. Challenging work, coupled with access to academic help, promotes learning in students from any social group. This challenging work conveys the idea that they are capable, and with work and practice, will catch up. The opportunity to do hard work in the context of high expectations for success may also go a long way toward achieving a sense of identity safety among minority students.

The teacher can mainstream positive features of the minority group culture and identity. That is, in presenting this material—in classroom displays, curriculum materials, and learning tasks—she can stress its value to all students, not just to those of the relevant minority group. Conveying the general value of the many cultures represented in the classroom helps to construct the group identity of the minority students in this local environment in positive terms that diminish their sense of identity threat.

The teacher can avoid groupings that confound group identity with skills levels. Having advanced reading groups with no minority students in them certainly is not a good idea from the standpoint of minority student identity safety and is not the only way to foster progress among good readers. If such a grouping seems unavoidable, however, efforts should be made to ensure the groupings are only temporary. Countervailing groupings should be created in the classroom around other intellectual activities that do not confound minority status with academic skills. When students work in groups cooperatively on challenging tasks, they will be exposed to various perspectives and intellectual contributions. By focusing on cooperative learning instead of competition, students will develop their trust and respect of one another.

Finally, respect and caring for each of the students should be evident in every interaction between the teacher and students. Moreover, teachers should help students treat one another with respect and fairness. When students are in conflict, for example, teachers can approach the situation as a learning opportunity. They can avoid blaming, avoid acting as judge and jury, and avoid accidentally targeting minority students for punishment. Instead, the teacher, in her respectful and caring relationship with each student, can convey the worth of all students and help them learn to get along.

## DIFFERENCE, TOLERANCE, AND INCLUSION

We have argued here that the failure to successfully include millions of non-immigrant minorities in the mainstream of society stems in some large part from a pervasive downward social constitution of these groups by the majority culture, not by individual racism. This tacit and very often unintended set of processes results in many African Americans, American Indians and Latinos being persistently devalued and having their prospects and opportunities limited or neglected. This general devaluation and continuing threat to identity occurs at both the collective level in terms of public representations and institutionalized policies and practices, and at the individual level in terms of attitudes, expectations, relationships, and actions. The ideological-legal stance of color blindness functions as a barrier to assimilation and integration because it argues for ignoring differences in race and ethnicity, working against the recognition of these powerful societal dynamics and the real differences in psychological experience such dynamics afford.

Accordingly, we argue that the color blind model that is broadly affirmed in American society might be replaced in some significant contexts with models that value race and identity and that work to promote identity safety. Others' views and evaluations of an individual are powerful and world-shaping, even if these views are ignored or contested by the individual. Central to breaking the cycle of downward social constitution produced by minority status are practices that promote inclusion and a sense that one's group identity will not be a source of devaluation. This approach to assimilation requires mutual accommodation by the mainstream and minority cultures. Proactive efforts to work against ex-

Shweder, Richard A. 1990. "Cultural Psychology: What Is It?" In *Cultural Psychology: Essays on Comparative Human Development*, edited by James W. Stigler, Richard A. Shweder, and Gilbert H. Herdt. Cambridge: Cambridge University Press.

———. 1991. *Thinking Through Cultures: Expeditions in Cultural Psychology*. Cambridge, Mass.: Harvard University Press.

Shweder, Richard A., and Maria A. Sullivan. 1990. "The Semiotic Subject of Cultural Psychology." In *Handbook of Personality: Theory and Research*, edited by Lawrence A. Pervin. New York: Guilford Press.

Snyder, Mark, and William Swann. 1978. "Behavioral Confirmation in Social Interaction: From Social Perception to Social Reality." *Journal of Experimental Social Psychology* 14: 148–62.

Sperber, Dan. 1985. "Anthropology and Psychology: Towards an Epidemiology of Representations." *Man* 20: 73–89.

———. 1990. "The Epidemiology of Beliefs." In *The Social Psychological Study of Widespread Beliefs*, edited by Colin Fraser and George Gaskell. Oxford: Clarendon Press.

Steele, Claude M., and Joshua Aronson. 1995. "Stereotype Threat and the Intellectual Test Performance of African Americans." *Journal of Personality and Social Psychology* 69: 797–811.

Steele, Claude M., Steve Spencer, and Joshua Aronson. Forthcoming. "Contending with Group Image: The Psychology of Stereotype and Social Identity Threat." In *Advances in Experimental Social Psychology*, edited by Mark Zanna. San Diego: Prentice-Hall.

Taylor, Charles C. 1989. *Sources of the Self: The Making of Modern Identities*. Cambridge, Mass.: Harvard University Press.

Thomas, Laurence. 1992. "Moral Deference." *Philosophical Forum* 24: 238.

Thurstone, Louis Leon. 1931. "The Measurement of Social Attitudes." *Journal of Abnormal and Social Psychology* 26: 249–69.

U.S. Department of Housing and Urban Development and U.S. Bureau of Census. 1997. *The American Housing Survey*. Unpublished tabulations.

Waters, Mary C. 1990. *Ethnic Options: Choosing Identities in America*. Berkeley: University of California Press.

Wolsko, Christopher, Bernadette Park, Charles M. Judd, and Bernd Wittenbrink. 2000. "Framing Interethnic Ideology: Effects of Multicultural and Color-Blind Perspectives on Judgments of Groups and Individuals." *Journal of Personality and Social Psychology* 78: 635–54.

# Index

Numbers in **boldface** refer to figures or tables.